Computational Solutions for Knowledge, Art, and Entertainment:

Information Exchange Beyond Text

Anna Ursyn
University of Northern Colorado, USA

A volume in the Advances in Multimedia
and Interactive Technologies (AMIT) Book
Series

An Imprint of IGI Global

Managing Director:	Lindsay Johnston
Production Manager:	Jennifer Yoder
Publishing Systems Analyst:	Adrienne Freeland
Development Editor:	Allyson Gard
Acquisitions Editor:	Kayla Wolfe
Typesetter:	John Crodian
Cover Design:	Jason Mull

Published in the United States of America by
Information Science Reference (an imprint of IGI Global)
701 E. Chocolate Avenue
Hershey PA 17033
Tel: 717-533-8845
Fax: 717-533-8661
E-mail: cust@igi-global.com
Web site: http://www.igi-global.com

Artwork within the cover image © 2014, by Anna Ursyn. Used with permission

Library of Congress Cataloging-in-Publication Data

Ursyn, Anna, 1955-
  Computational solutions for knowledge, art, and entertainment : information exchange beyond text / by Anna Ursyn.
    pages cm
  Includes bibliographical references and index.
  Summary: "This book focuses on the methods of depicting knowledge-based concepts in order to assert power beyond a visual explanation of scientific and computational notions"-- Provided by publisher.
  ISBN 978-1-4666-4627-8 (hardcover) -- ISBN 978-1-4666-4628-5 (ebook) -- ISBN 978-1-4666-4629-2 (print & perpetual access) 1. Knowledge management. 2. Knowledge economy. 3. Visual communication--Data processing. 4. Entertainment computing. 5. Art--Data processing. I. Title.
  HD30.2.U77 2014
  001--dc23
                                    2013025027

This book is published in the IGI Global book series Advances in Multimedia and Interactive Technologies (AMIT) (ISSN: 2327-929X; eISSN: 2327-9303)

British Cataloguing in Publication Data
A Cataloguing in Publication record for this book is available from the British Library.

For electronic access to this publication, please contact: eresources@igi-global.com.

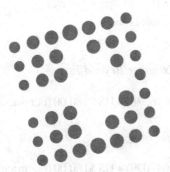

Advances in Multimedia and Interactive Technologies (AMIT) Book Series

ISSN: 2327-929X
EISSN: 2327-9303

MISSION

Traditional forms of media communications are continuously being challenged. The emergence of user-friendly web-based applications such as social media and Web 2.0 has expanded into everyday society, providing an interactive structure to media content such as images, audio, video, and text.

The **Advances in Multimedia and Interactive Technologies (AMIT) Book Series** investigates the relationship between multimedia technology and the usability of web applications. This series aims to highlight evolving research on interactive communication systems, tools, applications, and techniques to provide researchers, practitioners, and students of information technology, communication science, media studies, and many more with a comprehensive examination of these multimedia technology trends.

COVERAGE

- Audio Signals
- Digital Games
- Digital Technology
- Digital Watermarking
- Gaming Media
- Internet Technologies
- Mobile Learning
- Multimedia Services
- Social Networking
- Web Technologies

IGI Global is currently accepting manuscripts for publication within this series. To submit a proposal for a volume in this series, please contact our Acquisition Editors at Acquisitions@igi-global.com or visit: http://www.igi-global.com/publish/.

Titles in this Series

For a list of additional titles in this series, please visit: www.igi-global.com

Computational Solutions for Knowledge, Art, and Entertainment Information Exchange Beyond Text
Anna Ursyn (University of Northern Colorado, USA)
Information Science Reference • copyright 2014 • 457pp • H/C (ISBN: 9781466646278) • US $180.00 (our price)

Perceptions of Knowledge Visualization Explaining Concepts through Meaningful Images
Anna Ursyn (University of Northern Colorado, USA)
Information Science Reference • copyright 2014 • 457pp • H/C (ISBN: 9781466647039) • US $180.00 (our price)

Exploring Multimodal Composition and Digital Writing
Richard E. Ferdig (Research Center for Educational Technology - Kent State University, USA) and Kristine E. Pytash (Kent State University, USA)
Information Science Reference • copyright 2014 • 352pp • H/C (ISBN: 9781466643451) • US $175.00 (our price)

Multimedia Information Hiding Technologies and Methodologies for Controlling Data
Kazuhiro Kondo (Yamagata University, Japan)
Information Science Reference • copyright 2013 • 497pp • H/C (ISBN: 9781466622173) • US $190.00 (our price)

Media in the Ubiquitous Era Ambient, Social and Gaming Media
Artur Lugmayr (Tampere University of Technology, Finland) Helja Franssila (University of Tampere, Finland) Pertti Näränen (TAMK University of Applied Sciences, Finland) Olli Sotamaa (University of Tampere, Finland) Jukka Vanhala (Tampere University of Technology, Finland) and Zhiwen Yu (Northwestern Polytechnical University, China)
Information Science Reference • copyright 2012 • 312pp • H/C (ISBN: 9781609607746) • US $195.00 (our price)

Multimedia Services and Streaming for Mobile Devices Challenges and Innovations
Alvaro Suarez Sarmiento (Universidad de las Palmas de Gran Canaria, Spain) and Elsa Macias Lopez (Universidad de las Palmas de Gran Canaria, Spain)
Information Science Reference • copyright 2012 • 350pp • H/C (ISBN: 9781613501443) • US $190.00 (our price)

Online Multimedia Advertising Techniques and Technologies
Xian-Sheng Hua (Microsoft Research Asia, China) Tao Mei (Microsoft Research Asia) and Alan Hanjalic (Delft University of Technology, Netherlands)
Information Science Reference • copyright 2011 • 352pp • H/C (ISBN: 9781609601898) • US $180.00 (our price)

Streaming Media Architectures, Techniques, and Applications Recent Advances
Ce Zhu (Nanyang Technological University, Singapore) Yuenan Li (Harbin Institute of Technology, China) and Xiamu Niu (Harbin Institute of Technology, China)

www.igi-global.com

701 E. Chocolate Ave., Hershey, PA 17033
Order online at www.igi-global.com or call 717-533-8845 x100
To place a standing order for titles released in this series, contact: cust@igi-global.com
Mon-Fri 8:00 am - 5:00 pm (est) or fax 24 hours a day 717-533-8661

Table of Contents

Section 1
Making a Visual Statement

Section 3
Computing Solutions for Entertainment

Foreword

Computing technology has evolved dramatically in recent years. Computers transitioned from machines designed to perform calculations to tools helping us to communicate. The modes of communications that modern computers enable have also evolved enormously. The smart phone that I carry in my pocket today is able to capture images, video, and sound in real time. It can send and receive such content effortlessly over the Internet via wireless connections. It also has ten times more computational power than the world's fastest supercomputer did at the time I was working on my graduate studies 30 years ago and enables direct on-screen manipulation of complex 3D scenes in real time.

The changes in capabilities are accompanied with vast changes in what people actually do with computers. These changes started occurring with the adoption of the World Wide Web in the mid 1990s. At that time, we observed users starting to use the computer not only as a work related tool but also as a tool for information consumption as more and more services were added to the World Wide Web. This tendency increased as personal computers became more ubiquitous.

Along with the introduction of Web technologies, we observed a marked increase in data communications. When you look at the volume of data that is transmitted via the Internet every year, there is a clear point of acceleration that occurs coincident with the introduction of the first Web browser. Since that time, the yearly increase in the volume of data transmission over the Internet has consistently been greater than 40% every year. The most remarkable increase is in mobile data transmission. Since 2005, that number has more than doubled every single year. This suggests that Internet users are using their devices as a means for accessing larger and larger amounts of content. Not only are they accessing content but they are also increasingly posting content for consumption by others. One statistic released recently by YouTube is that over 72 hours of videos are uploaded to YouTube every minute. Users are not only consuming content created by large media outlets, they are more and more using social networks to post their own creations to be consumed by other.

These technological changes, along with the implications of having access to the Internet at all times, especially via mobile devices, vastly enlarge the number of modes of communications that are available to us. Whereas we would have had to schedule the use of dedicated rooms equipped with specialized hardware capabilities in order to simply be able to set up a point to point video conference just ten years ago, today we can use our mobile devices to set up a group video conference on the fly with multiple attendees participating from all over the globe at a moment's notice. We can share screens and even collaboratively navigate virtual environments in 3D using the tools that are available to us.

The changes in the computing environment are not only limited to the machines we now use and their capabilities. The pervasive nature of the Internet itself also comes into play. In particular, the rise of services that were not available 10 years ago changes the way we communicate. Social networks like

Facebook, Google Plus, or Twitter, video sharing services like YouTube, virtual reality environments like Second Life are all relatively new. They present us with new opportunities for communication that have never existed before.

The challenge that we face, given the variety of tools that are now available to us, is how to select the most appropriate vectors of communications for the information that we wish to communicate. Given the variety of tools at our disposal, whether they be device capabilities directly available on the machine that we are using or services offered via the Internet, what are the advantages and disadvantages of each? To be able to answer such questions, we need to reflect on what it means to exchange information in an environment that is always connected while enabling multiple modes of representation and delivery of the content that we wish to communicate.

That is what Anna Ursyn addresses in this book. To do so, she first takes us through an exploration of the mechanics of human creation. In order to communicate, we need to understand how we perceive the world around us. She moves on to address how we create, focusing specifically on the visual modes. She covers topics such as art, thinking with pictures, and collage. She then dedicates a full chapter to art resulting from computing, where she presents the reader with various aspects of art using computers and what that implies. Next, she discusses aesthetics in the context of new media art. How does aesthetics change with these new media and how do we adapt this new aesthetics into more mainstream art world? The final chapter in this section addresses issues of criticism.

The second section of this book looks to science to see what lessons we can learn from it. First, she discusses many real world examples ranging from astronomy to nano-worlds. She then transitions to a discussion of the human response to nature through computer art using several examples as the basis for the discussion. Finally, the last chapter in this section deals with the educational implications including discussions of the implications of virtual presence in education.

The final section of this book covers the subject of computing solutions in entertainment. In the first chapter, she delves into the various forms of entertainment that directly involve elements of computing. Topics covered in this chapter include computer animation, virtual and augmented reality, games, live entertainment, and social media. The next chapter deals with changes in game design, covering subjects such as games for learning and games for healing, as well as addressing the pros and cons of gaming. The next chapter deals with visual and verbal storytelling. In it, she addresses storytelling in general as well as storytelling in multimedia. The following chapter addresses the notions of metaphorical portraits, describing various approaches and their implications. The final chapter covers visual music with multiple examples.

This book is addressed to everybody interested in integrating science, technology, engineering, art, and mathematics. It covers ideas behind interdisciplinary education, visualization of scientific concepts, picturing processes and products, as well as the role of computing in advancing integrative visual education and visual literacy skills.

One of the most striking elements of this book is its focus on a highly visual approach. The visual approach to knowledge learning, retaining, and understanding grows in importance because of its pervasive use in network-based, shared, multisensory strategies applied in modern communication.

Alain Chesnais
TrendSpottr, Canada

Alain Chesnais is the immediate past President of the Association for Computing Machinery (ACM), having served in that position in 2010-2012. Prior to his election as ACM president, Chesnais was vice president, as well as secretary/treasurer. He also served as president of ACM SIGGRAPH (Association for Computing Machinery's Special Interest Group on Computer Graphics and Interactive Techniques) and a SIG Governing Board Chair. Chesnais founded TrendSpottr, which develops web services to identify real time trends in social media such as Twitter and Facebook. Chesnais earned a Maîtrise de Mathématiques, de Structure Mathématique de l'Informatique, and a Diplôme d'Etudes Approfondies in Computer Science at l'Ecole Normale Supérieure de l'Enseignement Technique and l'Université de Paris.

Preface

A SUMMARY

This book examines and acknowledges the power existing beyond visual explanation and presentation of scientific and computational problems. An array of concepts, data, and information belonging to a number of disciplines has been discussed as possible resources useful for visual presentation, visualization, and finding visual solutions of science- and technology-related concepts. On the other hand, these resources may support our computational solutions for many of the cognition-, art-, and entertainment-related problems. For these reasons, this book may be of interest for those people who make a focus of their attention the integration of science, technology, computing, art, and mathematics.

This book discusses projects involving the readers' cooperation. Text and images are of service to assist the readers in enhancing their solutions with explanatory visuals, and maybe finding joy in these tasks. With regard to teaching and learning, the visual approach to knowledge understanding, learning, and retaining grows in importance because of its pervasive use in network-based, shared, multisensory strategies applied in communication. The book offers discussion of issues related to interdisciplinary education, picturing processes and products, as well as the role of computing in advancing integrative visual education.

The topics introduced below are spread between the two books titled *Perceptions of Knowledge Visualization: Explaining Concepts through Meaningful Images* and *Computational Solutions for Knowledge, Art, and Entertainment: Information Exchange Beyond Text*.

NEEDS AND ISSUES THAT AMOUNTED TO SHAPE THIS BOOK

Visual Presentation of Knowledge

The aim of the book is to give support in presenting abstract concepts and data in a visual way. As information becomes more visual every day, many highly specialized individuals find themselves in need of not only understanding visual aspect of communication, but also they want to get rid of their inhibitions, patterns, and preconceptions related to art and design as a whole. In an increasing rate, visual literacy and feeling at ease with visuals becomes a crucial faculty; for this reason a workbook for investigating personal artistic and/or technological aspirations might become the most sought, compelling aid, useful in enhancing visual literacy of the science- and technology-oriented specialists.

This book explores connections and relationships between diverse disciplines, occurrences, processes, laws, products, and transformations. The author's intent is in offering the reader both denotations and connotations of scientific concepts and terms. Denotations would provide their distinct meanings, while connotations would be closely tied to their heuristic, phenomenological, aesthetic, and intuitive sense, so the reader would connect and react to multi-faced perception of scientific themes. The aim of the book is to shift that attitude and give support in presenting data in a visual yet abstract way.

Interactive Way of Reading this Book

The mini-topics, presented as visual solutions of the reader, serve as a link between theory and the reader's own practice, so the data would reveal a visual aspect of a discipline under discussion. Throwing light on the selected multi-subject topics, along with a collection of related data and author's views on those trends, aims at the linking and connecting the conceptual with the depicted, and including the reader in an active, visual style of processing and outputting information. Projects offered in the text combine topics related to science, art, and computing; they encourage the reader to explain concepts in a visual way. Rather than following a textbook-like style, this book offers information about basic concepts and facts as inspiration for visual solutions coming from examples of both current and ancient visual applications of knowledge, as well as trends resulting from the developments in technologies.

Many figures in this book have the QR codes (quick response codes) for the URL of the author's Website containing color pictures in order to bridge the offline text with online presentation of art by enabling the reader to access the Webpage and look at the color art works. A structure of QR code matrices is designed to be detected as a 2-dimensional digital image by a semiconductor image sensor and then digitally analyzed by a programmed processor. A QR code is a matrix barcode consisting of black modules (square dots) arranged in a square pattern on a white background that record information about an item.

Combining Disciplines in Particular Topics

This book is an array of concepts, data, and information, all belonging to a number of disciplines. This is caused by the fact that recent advances in knowledge result from cooperation of specialists in seemingly unrelated domains. What's more, the progress often moves forward through networking, chatting, using Skype, or simply updating the school-based knowledge. Fields of research become interdisciplinary, interactive, and often integrated. One cannot discuss the cosmos without bringing up concepts derived from physics (often quantum physics), mechanics, mathematics, and philosophy; one cannot talk about living systems without touching biochemistry, physics, and electromagnetic phenomena. For this reason, many themes belonging to this book's profile have been annotated with explanatory notes, some of them being obvious for readers focused on the issues under discussion, and many appearing to be unrelated for those concentrated on quite other fields of interest.

A question arises about the ways the teaching about art and design could be combined with programming and computing. Both are aimed at enhancing higher-level thinking skills, abstract thinking, creativity, and novelty. Many artists apply programming to create art works or visualizations, and many computing scientists and programmers do the same. The content of these programs becomes a question belonging to the art domain, while inquiries what can be done to make these programs aesthetic become the problems belonging to the usability territory. After pursuing a study of the arts, a programmer may gain a viewpoint about the purposes for programming the individual projects and making sense of it in further phases, and thus achieve more ontological attitude relative to the essence of being.

While constantly immersed in the mind puzzling natural phenomena, objects, and processes explored by sciences, we gain knowledge and experience, a good deal of it ensuing from our school education. However, educational assessment involves multiple-choice tests as a typical form of testing. In order to prepare ourselves to tests, we have often memorized particular facts, laws, and formulas, each and every one with the test questions in mind. This kind of knowledge interweaves with a whole landscape of knowledge we acquire later. Our knowledge constantly changes along with the developments in technology. At the same time, the school tests are the same for all students, disregarding the diversity of the intelligence types described by Howard Gardner (1983, 2006, 2007): visual/spatial intelligence, verbal/linguistic, logical/mathematical, bodily/kinesthetic, musical/rhythmic, interpersonal, intrapersonal, naturalistic, and existential intelligence. We may feel our own visual or verbal preferences in dealing with our tasks. The projects presented in this book are designed to inspect selected themes from a totally different perspective.

A Place for the Arts in the Multimedia-Oriented Social Environment

One may say art is an interpretation of human perception saved accordingly. This book focuses on visual approach to natural events rather than on their detailed analyses. It encourages the readers to perform some mental activities in a visual way. Many agree that our ways of communication are drifting toward visual media; our efficiency in sharing knowledge and emotions may depend on our adaptability and ability to convey them in an up-to-date way. It may have something in common with a Barbara Smaller's wish that was pictured in the June 4, 2012 issue of *The New Yorker* (p. 114): "I'm looking for a career that won't be obsolete before my student loan is paid off." This book attempts to respond to the changing role of art and promotes including the learning of art into the technology-oriented world.

Viewers used to appreciate art they considered beautiful, which often was meant as the lifelike art works that resembled real-life objects. At the present time, due to the pervasive presence of social networking sites, groups of interconnected people exchange information and cooperate applying computing. Their creative activities involve higher-level thinking processes aimed at approaching multisensory, interactive actions. We may notice art-related schools, which were traditionally named the Art and Design departments, now introduce themselves as the Art and Media or the Art and Technology schools, with computing and programming described as a requisite both for the studies and future work.

This Book as a Form of Entertainment

Many agree that mental exercises make the best entertainment. Japanese prize-winning writer, Haruki Murakami (2011, p. 175), assumes that what may be called intellectual curiosity, a desire to obtain knowledge at the universal level, is a natural urge in people. Jean-Baptiste Dubos (1670-1742) wrote that man does nothing but what fulfills his needs; one of them is a need for keeping his own mind busy; otherwise, he becomes bored and unhappy:

The soul hath its wants no less than the body; and one of the greatest wants of man is to have his mind incessantly occupied. The heaviness which quickly attends the inactivity of the mind, is a situation so very disagreeable to man, that he frequently chuses to expose himself to the most painful exercises, rather than be troubled with it. (Dubos, 1717)

With Facebook becoming the most popular social networking site involving about a billion active users, Google being probably the Internet's most visited Website, console gaming becoming a widely used instructional tool, and cinematic effects in motion pictures and games valued as motivational tools, we often consider play as a tool for learning, sharing, and entertainment. Within this template, learning can provide entertainment and amusement.

Dean Simonton (2003, 2004) points out that creativity of scientists is a constrained, stochastic, randomly determined behavior, as the new theories in all sciences are. When we realize that the results of our research are characterized by conjecture and accidental or unpredictable events (Simonton, 2004, p. 41), our curiosity may be enhanced. We cannot predict the results we can only know after computing them. Simonton reminds us of the Albert Einstein's remark:

It is, in fact, nothing short of a miracle that the modern methods of instruction have not yet entirely strangled the holy curiosity of inquiry; for this delicate little plant, aside from stimulation, stands mostly in the need of freedom; without this it goes to wreck and ruin without fall. (Schlipp, 1951, p. 17)

Many would agree our thinking often depends on the tools we use; more areas are available for thought experiments by reason of the developments in technology. Tools may enhance our imagination. Thought activities are often shared, and thus become more entertaining, because almost everything we examine can be visualized. This allows creating technology-based entertainment such as films based on scientific books, worlds populated by avatars and beings existing in the past, the future, or in fictitious environments. Charles Jencks, an architect and writer questioning postulates expressed by the Modern architecture and describing its successors – the Late, Neo, and Post-Modern architecture, wrote:

Whatever the reasons, contemporary science has not yet transformed the cultural landscape not led to a renaissance in thought. … In any case, I believe that the ideas of contemporary science do provide the basis for a cultural reawakening and that a new iconography must be made more tangible through art if it is to be assimilated. (Jencks, 2003, p. 20)

Nathan Yau (Lima, 2011, p. 248) describes the citizen science that is based on social data collection, "Although not everyone who 'analyzes' this data will have a background in the proper techniques, a certain level of data literacy must be developed. Visualization will be essential in making the data more accessible." Yau (2011) emphasizes the engaging quality of interactive, flying data that he finds not only explanatory but also compelling and entertaining. Non-professionals become involved in visualization and analysis when they take on microblogging and engage with social applications like Twitter and Facebook. The task is to add structure and tools that take advantage of these open applications, to see the undiscovered relationships, and to interact with our surrounding.

Figure 1. The Golden Record. Image in the public domain.

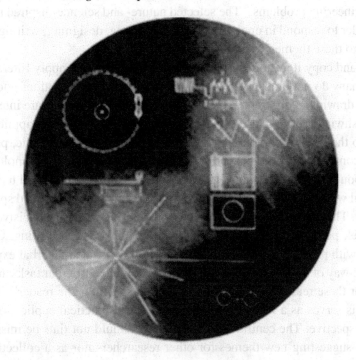

The Power of Visualization and Visualizing Thoughts

According to the pioneer in the field of data visualization Edward Tufte (1983/2001), vision is the only universal language. Gyorgy Kepes (1906-2001), who published an influential book about design and design education *Language of Vision* (1944/1995, p. 13) wrote, "Visual communication is universal and international; it knows no limits of tongue, vocabulary, or grammar, and it can be perceived by the illiterate as well as by the literate."

The Voyager, which is conveying the data about the heliosphere and the interstellar space, had sent into the deep space a gold-plated copper disk containing visual descriptions as a record of our civilization (Figure 1). A committee chaired by Carl Sagan of Cornell University selected the content of the record for NASA. The spacecraft may approach another planetary system in at least 40,000 years (NASA Jet Propulsion Laboratory, 2012).

Available at http://www.jpl.nasa.gov/images/voyager/gold_record-browse.jpg

Projects for the Reader

Themes for particular chapters in this book have been selected with several objectives in mind. First of all, descriptions of natural and technological processes are focused on visual ways of explanation. Second, the readers are invited to look at the underlying physical and natural laws and actively react to the nature- and science-derived facts and processes. Translation into the art and visualization oriented frames of thinking supports current methods of communication going through networked, linked, and shared media. Developments in science, technology, and art created with the use of a computer come in a great part from biology-inspired sources. As Gérard Battail (2009, p. 323) wrote, "Life is an outstanding expert in solving engineering problems." The selected nature- and science-inspired themes are intended to encourage the reader to respond in one's own way, by creating, designing, writing, and programming individual reactions to these themes.

Many of us scan and copy items or use Internet resources, and then apply filters to transform them into line drawings; many do not draw at all. We can see this trend in animations and feature films. Perhaps the meaning of drawing is different in electronic media, where images are interactive, linked, and open-ended. Paul Fishwick (2008, p. 4) defines aesthetic computing as "the application of the theory and practice of art to the field of computing." For him, it is the study of artistic, personalized, formal model structures in computing that go beyond representation and events in technology.

The book tells about a number of nature-inspired projects, applications, and technologies, selected with a focus on visual way of communicating solutions. Readers will find framed spaces for their visual and verbal responses. The spaces left for reader's thought and action are the decisive parts of this book; it is a place for novel, personal interaction in the form of drawing and writing. Combining selected fields of knowledge with practical applications in terms of the visual and verbal expression serves as a tool used to show the way of applying one's visual way of solving particular tasks and to work on one's ability to do this. For these reasons, I see the tables with a space for the reader's input as an inherent part of the book. This serves as a link between theoretical and practical application of visual literacy seen from a new perspective. The central aim of this book should not thus be misunderstood, neither as a research source suggesting new themes for other researchers nor as a collection of exercises for particular groups of people.

The goal of art therapists lies in helping people with problems at the cognitive, motor, emotional, and psychomotor levels, to name just a few. It is not necessary that "patients" fully comprehend this material, with its scope spanning from science, engineering, and computing to art concepts. This book is meant for those thinking at the higher, abstract thinking level, who grew to the point of opening themselves to current venues and experiences. Thus, the main thesis of the book is in proclaiming a need for shifting the readers' thinking and acting towards creating visual explanations and solutions based on a selected knowledge base. Filling out by the reader each framed space adheres to the book's intention.

Projects suggested in this book are meant to support visual way of thinking and developing visual communication with the use of visual semiotics by constructing signs, symbols, icons, iconic objects, analogies, and metaphoric connotations, thus conveying some meaning in a visual way. The text is interlaced with projects to be solved by the reader within the boxes designated to their visual/verbal answer to the project. The empty boxes in the text are for sketches; the reader can sketch or can choose to continue working further on the computer. Projects are open-ended in nature and integrative. The sources for inspiration are contained within the background information provided, rather than in a description of an expected outcome. The reader may go any direction one would choose, look for answers on the Internet, or try to create something totally new. My students' solutions accompany the text, along with the author's visual solutions, which are printed black-and-white here.

Each project challenges you to react to a theme under discussion, add your input or modify the content, visualize the concept, and then complete your visual/verbal answer. Each empty space is a place intended for your planned idea for a project. First, you may want to describe it, to sketch, draw, design a concept map, or draw some key frames. Then you may feel ready for writing a program, designing a software application or an app for mobile devices, use graphic software, and create a picture or a sculpture (for example from wooden blocks or the found objects). Finally, you may want to make a photo or a short video of your project, post it online, thus adding your active, creative, independent solution or interpretation and explaining it to others. Your projects may take form of an artwork, a verse, a story, a concept map, animation, comics or manga, or a smart phone app.

The purpose behind these activities lies in their explanative and motivational power to enhance one's visual, graphical, and visualization literacy (both of the readers and of those who would look at their projects). Our environment and its changes influence our thinking and our acting, which we do mostly with the use of computing. For this reason, the following text tells about the connectivity between our daily life, knowledge, art, and entertainment. In a quest for things that last longer, people work on making materials indestructible and designing intelligent applications. This connectivity becomes even stronger because of the changes we experience when our knowledge about the world we live in becomes bio-inspired, nano-oriented, and progressively shared because:

1. The impact of biology-inspired knowledge, technology, and art is growing
2. The focus on nanotechnology drives the advances in many domains and brings changes in materials, technologies, and applications, influencing each other
3. The Web-based networking results in changing the way we now solve our problems (with the immediate help coming from often unidentified sources), entertain (we can enjoy gaming with people from far away), and develop in social media, new media art, or networked art (existing in real time and/or in virtual spaces)
4. Programming became accessible and easier due to the visual way of instruction such as processing, with free online instruction (such as HTML, free courses, Apple Developers' kits, SDK – Software Development Kits, etc.), so the art creating often fuses with the manufacture, while the designing of games becomes an art medium.

In a quest for objects that would last longer, people work on making materials indestructible and designing intelligent applications. Projects interweaving the text are intended to associate knowledge with practical applications, facilitate the integration of particular facets of science that have been routinely segregated into special fields, and to follow the current advances in various areas. Our thinking may probably change not only with the technical progress but also with the experienced reality changing along with the advancements in technology and everyday life. Projects are aimed to hopefully engage the readers in practicing visual communication and visual organization of data and knowledge, with a focus on the meaning, not exclusively on data or numbers. When working on these projects, you may hesitate to look at or copy the ready examples, because copying may influence a person who copies and may have an impact on one's personal visual statement. As a summary, the projects offered in this book will most likely prompt inspiration to find progressive solutions based on the informed way of thinking.

As a conclusive remark, with the advent of pervasive computing, with computer-mediated way of thinking and living at many fronts, one might ponder about a need for a talent search and support for all talents that could further advance our ways of living. Three issues come to mind:

1. A need for a free access to the Internet for everyone, disregarding all differences and levels, so every idea-driven and motivated individual could explore, learn, produce, and share knowledge and achievements. This issue seems to face similar obstacles as a free access to water.
2. A need for solving the image- and video-related copyright problems, so every author could freely illustrate one's writings with visual examples, rather than provide complex, lengthy, and often

Figure 2. Anna Ursyn, "Visualize Knowledge in Kindergarten" (© 2013, A. Ursyn. Used with permission).

short-living links. For that, an international agreement would be needed to address profit-based issues.

3. In regard to mining and supporting talents, training and education of children should be focused on recognizing and supporting the innate abilities of children. This would allow starting a holistic training of young minds by providing knowledge visualization early, that means from kindergarten (Figure 2). Knowledge visualization has a power to introduce an outline of major ideas and connections between science, mathematics, and programming.

Figure 2 conveys an opinion that before a child learns typical attitudes, misconceptions, and classifications, we can introduce a big picture as inspiration to finding their own interest, focus, and future path. Ongoing developments in computer graphics and visualization techniques may make us to reconsider the needs of education. With a shortage of programmers combined with usual fear of mathematics, programming, and science, one may consider knowledge visualization as a tool for showing the world at the time when attitudes are open and children' brains are curious.

With the use of visualization techniques, themes related to science, nature, math, art, and how they mutually influence each other might be presented to young children as a big holistic spectrum of knowledge. We may instill abstract thinking in young children by supporting an understanding of the surrounding world, which would allow making connections. On the basis of openness to a wider picture, they may have a chance to shape their own, individual focus on what stirs their curiosity, in relation to other levels of knowledge. To enhance instruction with knowledge visualization component, early childhood specialists and departments would need to welcome knowledge visualization specialists on the board.

CONTENT

Section 1: Making a Visual Statement

Chapter 1: "Looking and Seeing: Communication through Art: Creating, Conveying, and Responding to Art"

Projects described in this chapter are aimed at enhancing our thinking with pictures. After examining the artistic process, the text encourages the readers to engage in visual projects. The following text comprises a comparative inquiry about the ways of designing, conveying, and receiving images. Three basic processes in communication in the arts appear to be decisive for both the traditional and digital artwork: articulation of a visual message through creation of an electronic picture and its transitions, communication with a viewer, and reception of the artwork by a viewer. Thus, the three levels in a creative process comprise an artist as a sender of a message (an idea), media of art (a process), and the viewer as the receiver (rethinking of an idea, interactive response by reshaping a work, new interpretation, or a new idea). Many hold that the artistic process requires a cognitive, psychological, and emotional involvement from the artist that remains similar in whichever medium one actually creates – computing, paint, or chisel. In this study, language of an artwork as the expression of a message is discussed both in the traditional and electronic media framework of art.

Chapter 2: "Thinking with Pictures: Art as an Instrument of Acquiring Knowledge"

Visual presentation through art is considered an effective instrument for acquiring knowledge. Projects aimed at developing visual literacy and skills include: 1) timed sketching of one's own shoe – intended to enhance self-confidence about one's ability to depict things, and build a feeling of being prepared to make quick drawings on a board or a tablet. This project will encourage the reader to make sketches that strengthen one's own argumentation, show what one wants to be seen, and convey one's own solution in a visual way. 2) Creating a composition with a crowd – drawing a manikin and then a group of people by applying visual reasoning and showing background scenery that has an explanatory power, which serves as first exercise toward information visualization related thinking. 3) Collage – one may say without exaggeration that in the digital times most artists apply the form of a collage in their work. The Internet is flooded with ready images, clipart, art and design samples, and intriguing specimens. More importantly, ideas cannot be copyrighted. Further text discusses how, before the advent of computers, artists applied techniques of cutting and pasting readymade material, thus making collages (two dimensional) and assemblages (three dimensional) of different forms.

Chapter 3: "Art Resulting from Computing"

This chapter examines many types of new media art that are being created with computing. One may point to a parallel between theories about art production and scientific theories and technologies. Displaying art becomes a tool for exchanging information and ideas that also creates channels for the viewers' input through digital art interactive events. Biology-inspired computing applied for artistic tasks has a mutual relationship with scientific research involving evolutionary computing. Net art, along with other electronic art media, may be seen as closely related to the semantic networks and social networking media. Many times these media provide computational solutions for entertainment.

Chapter 4: "Aesthetics in the Context of New Media Art and Knowledge Visualization"

This chapter discusses aesthetic values in mathematics, science, and computing, including aesthetic computing and aesthetic issues related to digital environment. A study of aesthetics has always been related to the arts, philosophy of art, and our judgments about sensory or emotional values of specific art works; they are in the focus of neuroaesthetics. The objectives of aesthetic studies have been changing following the developments in computing technology, shifting the stress on usability and efficiency of projects and visualizations. Challenges and demands in aesthetics and art are then discussed, starting from an essential question what is an artwork and what is not an artwork, art definitions, art manifestos, opinions on the role of art, beauty, and aesthetic perception of art. Aesthetic education and ways of looking at art complete the chapter.

Chapter 5: "Criticism versus Objectives and Assessment for the New Media Art and Design"

This chapter examines some of the changes in views about art, criticism of art works, and art-related teaching objectives, as they evolve with the developments in the new media art, works created through the Web, social networking, art created on portable devices, as well as the information technologies. First, this chapter examines the changing meaning of the aesthetics notion in mathematics, science, information art, and information technology, as well as changes in the views about instruction in art criticism. Examination of these approaches is then contrasted with the models adopted in education. The four-part model used in instructional design, based on audience, outcome, environment, and usability, is adapted to suit the needs of art criticism. Materials based on a literature review provide the rationale for a four-part model to facilitate art critique. The next part is about the changing dimensions of criticism in the new media art and product design in respect to the product semantics analysis.

Section 2: Lessons from Science

Chapter 6: "The Journey to the Center of the Earth"

In the "Journey to the Center of the Earth" project, pictorial and verbal presentations are integrated with the physical geology-related concepts, events, and processes. Inspiration for this project comes from the theme of the interior of the Earth and some literary connotations. It is mental investigation about the interior of the Earth intended to encourage the reader to conduct an experiment in thinking and communicating with the use of visual language: an imaginary trip in a transparent, pressure, and temperature resistant elevator descending to the center of the Earth, visualizing its core, and making the visual and verbal notes from the trip. In this project graphic activities are integrated with physical geology-related concepts, events, and processes, language arts, and connotations pertaining to cellular biology. It is also about our awareness of the dynamics, forcefulness, and fragility of the matter under the ground we are living on.

Chapter 7: "Taking Inspiration from Astronomy for Visual and Verbal Projects"

The chapter comprises projects about some basic concepts related to astrophysics in a visual, verbal, or both ways, for example in the form of a comics medium: comic books, comic strips, or cartoons. The reader is encouraged to envision particular events, processes, and products and then transform the concepts into another level of understanding. Projects involve visualizing or describing the relationship between frequency, wavelength, and energy, and the energy of light as the electromagnetic wave. Themes for projects include the solar system, the Kepler's explanation of the forces acting at the solar system's motion and planetary movement, creating frames for animation about the expansion of the universe, a travel to the sun's center to explore nuclear fusion, examination of light and electromagnetic spectrum, elementary particles and quantum mechanics, and visualizing and designing one's own household goods with related devices, furniture, objects, and appliances, along with their arrangement and decoration.

Chapter 8: "Imaging and Picturing Volcanism"

This part of the book invites the reader to look closer at plate tectonics and volcanism and then draw inspiration from geological events, processes, and products for creating visual and/or verbal projects. The next part is about earthquakes, tsunami, explosive eruptions of volcanoes such as Mt. St. Helens, Yellowstone, and Mount Vesuvius, about the Japan 2011 earthquake, and the impact of volcanism on human fates. The chapter examines how the events such as the destruction of Pompeii and Herculaneum buried by an eruption of the Mount Vesuvius, which provide a new access to a frozen slice of life in an ancient civilization, change the way we view past events from the art historical, anthropological, and archeological point of view.

Chapter 9: "Picturing Minerals and Rocks"

In this chapter, we draw inspiration from the study of Earth structures and materials, as well as processes and forces that change these structures, which is the core of the domain of physical geology. We examine minerals, main types of rocks, gems, and other more mundane earth baubles, the rock cycle, and processes that change the structure of the minerals. Projects are aimed at linking these physical and chemical processes and events with our ambient surroundings and personal perceptions of our own experiences.

Chapter 10: "Energy and Environment"

The theme of this chapter is energy (such as kinetic, potential, mechanical, electrical, chemical, light, radiant, nuclear, and heat energy), energy conversion, and rules that must be obeyed when we perceive a need for its conservation. It also tells about the environmental concerns related to energy production and use. Visual and verbal solutions provide analogies and comparisons of some energy related processes and events to our everyday experiences.

Chapter 11: "Nano World"

This part of the book provides information and projects for the readers about the omnipresence of nanoscale objects – soft matter, colloids, liquid crystals, carbon nanotubes, nanoshells, and the developments in nanoscale and molecular-scale technologies involving these small structures. Nanotechnology concerns structures measuring between 1 and 100 nanometers and allows manipulating individual atoms and molecules. Since Norio Taniguchi of Tokyo Science University first used the term nanotechnology in 1974, the governments, corporations, and venture capitalists invest every year billions of dollars in nanotechnology and more than a half of advanced technologies incorporate nanotechnology products in different ways.

Chapter 12: "Acceleration"

This part of the book provides an occasion to combine visual presentation of concepts related to speed, velocity, and acceleration with the real-life circumstances (such as car or horse races) and at the same time with artistic connotations about motion and artistic responses to it. The goal of this project is to show acceleration, speed, and velocity by producing an image that would look very dynamic. For example, dynamic changes of motion can be presented as a scene with racecars or horses. Connotations related to art may enhance both our knowledge about acceleration and a message it evokes.

Chapter 13: "Carbon: A Gem, a Molecule, and a Heart of Nanotechnology"

"Carbon: A Gem, a Molecule, and a Heart of Nanotechnology" is about related habitats and technologies seen from the scientific, artistic, and educational points of view. It explores carbon as mineral: coal, carbon as a molecule, carbon as soft matter, and biologically inspired models for computing. Art inspired by carbon and enhanced by digital technologies are a means to understand and interpret nature- and science-related concepts.

Chapter 14: "Mathematics-Related Visual Events"

A mathematical way of thinking may often involve the visual processes while the beauty of forms derived from mathematical formulas may become an inspiration and a source for creating art works. This text examines organic/geometric forms present in nature, mathematics, and art, symmetry, fractals, artists' responses, and computational solutions in the form of visual presentations. This is followed by some aesthetical and critical notions about mathematics-derived art.

Chapter 15: "Poem Illustration for the *Spoon River Anthology* by Edgar Lee Masters"

This project makes connection between visual arts and literary analysis of the masterpiece collection of poems, *Spoon River Anthology*, by Edgar Lee Masters, as well as his work and his times. Masters created imaginary stories about people whose names he found on gravestones. The aim of this project is to create one's own artistic expression of our understanding of Edgar Lee Masters's work as a personal response to the spirit and the meaning of the verse, as well as to the author's comments on the philosophical, social, and historical issues. In addition, the reader is asked to visually interpret Masters's literary descriptions of imaginary events in the lives of the deceased people.

Chapter 16: "Four Trapped in an Elevator"

In this physics/psychology related integrative project, gravitation acting on the elevator riders is discussed in psychological terms. It may be interesting to portray some characters and convey their emotional states and actions in this unusual situation. Science-based themes that serve as inspiration for this project refer to the physical concepts of gravitation as a natural force causing objects with mass to attract one another, acceleration due to gravity, and the potential energy of the stuck elevator. This project is also about an artistic interpretation of psychological and social aspects of the unusual and stressful circumstances.

Chapter 17: "The History of Love"

This text provides insight about love, seen as a power that lets people survive in spite of all overwhelming forces. It helps us to understand, preserve the natural world, and protect values; love as a force gives us strength and motivation to perform both heroic and everyday deeds, develop knowledge at the macro, micro, and nano levels, produce medicine drugs and vaccines, initiate social changes, and enhance communication networks to share and exchange information.

Chapter 18: "Architecture and Media"

This part of the book explores how architects and urban developers apply computational solutions and create a fusion of architecture and media. The use of new technologies for communication, sustainability, functionality, and economy of resources is discussed next. Issues that are relevant to computational methods in design, urban aesthetics, ambient computing, sustainable habitats, novel materials, biology-inspired projects, and many others all pertain to innovative solutions that we can observe in architecture. Themes related to some of the tools and technologies, models of architectural structures, intelligent buildings, and sustainable and green architecture complete this chapter.

Chapter 19: "Educational Implications"

An integrative art-science approach to teaching is described, involving imaging concepts about science, with three approaches to integration of art and science: 1) visual presentation of scientific concepts, 2) creating art by finding inspiration in a science-based topic, 3) learning visually for other courses taken concurrently by arranging data into a structured whole. The next part of the chapter is about several dimensions that seem important in blended and online learning regarding social networking and the collaborative virtual environments. Virtual education in a first life and a Second Life classroom environment is discussed next.

Section 3: Computing Solutions for Entertainment

Chapter 20: "Ways to Entertain with the Use of Computing Technologies"

Entertainment has gained some new values, and our participation in amusement has become more active along with the developments in social communication technologies. Examples that discuss the meaning of computational solutions for entertainment include intelligent environments, augmented and virtual reality, computer animation, games, live entertainment, and social media. This text examines the enhanced role of the participant's self-consciousness while engaging in social networking, and the role of the biologically active substances such as oxytocin and dopamine in shaping the ways of entertaining with the use of computing technologies.

Chapter 21: "Challenges in Game Design"

Electronic games and gaming can serve as the tools for visual solutions. It depends on the methods through which the games are delivered and the ways people think about electronic games. First, traditional and electronic gaming is described, and then, various goal-oriented game applications are discussed. Game features acting in favor of or against gaming complete this part of the book.

Chapter 22: "Visual-and-Verbal Storytelling"

This part of the book tells about combining pictorial and verbal solutions. Visual and verbal expression is gaining additional communication possibilities by the developments in data organization techniques, such as search engines on the Internet, cognitive and semantic structuring of information, concept mapping, social networking, and cloud computing. Electronic art, Web design, and communication media support creation of electronic media languages in visual representation and design. This chapter is focused on text visualization and on storytelling delivered in various literary styles.

Chapter 23: "Metaphorical Portraits"

Telling stories verbally and visually involves structuring the data toward different metaphorical representations of a person. Creating metaphors for a set of factors that make up a profile or a portrait will allow showing individual features of a portrayed person. This text encourages the readers to apply their visual literacy and exercise their cognitive processes related to imaging.

Chapter 24: "Visual Music"

Visual music projects involve visuals combined with music in various configurations. They may refer to the use of images, light, and sound, such as music and voice, including songs, and also haptic experiences, touch, and gesture. This chapter examines this century-old form of entertainment in terms of the technology options available in the successive decades.

Anna Ursyn
University of Northern Colorado, USA

REFERENCES

Battail, G. (2009). Living versus inanimate: The information border. *Biosemiotics, 2*, 321–341. DOI 10.1007/s12304-009-9059-z. Retrieved October 19, 2012, from http://www.springerlink.com/content/r376x87u5mk68732/fulltext.pdf

Dubos, J. B. (1748). *Critical reflections on poetry, painting, and music*. Retrieved October 19, 2012, from http://archive.org/details/criticalreflecti01dubouoft

Fishwick, P. A. (2008). *Aesthetic computing*. The MIT Press.

Jencks, C. (2003). *The garden of cosmic speculations*. Frances Lincoln.

Kepes, G. (1995). *Language of vision*. Dover Publications.

Lima, M. (2011). *Visual complexity: Mapping patterns of information*. New York: Princeton Architectural Press.

Murakami, H. (2011). *1Q84*. New York: Knopf.

NASA Jet Propulsion Laboratory. (2012). Retrieved October 19, 2012, from http://voyager.jpl.nasa.gov/spacecraft/goldenrec.html

P. A. Schlipp (Ed.). (1959). *Albert Einstein: Philosopher-scientist*. New York: Harper & Row. (Original work published 1951).

Simonton, D. K. (2003). Scientific activity as constrained stochastic behavior: The integration of product, process, and person perspectives. *Psychological Bulletin, 129*, 475–494. doi:10.1037/0033-2909.129.4.475 PMID:12848217.

Simonton, D. K. (2004). *Creativity in science: Chance, logic, genius, and zeitgeist*. Cambridge, UK: Cambridge University Press. doi:10.1017/CBO9781139165358.

Tufte, E. R. (1983/2001). *The visual display of quantitative information*. Cheshire, CT: Graphics Press.

Yau, N. (2011). *Visualize this: The flowing data guide to design visualization and statistics*. New York: Wiley.

APPENDIX: SELECTED WEBSITES WITH ART WORKS SUPPORTING THE TEXT

Listed are some art related Web addresses that may support the text. While links become perishable, there are still Google Images available.

Figures in color and time-based works can be viewed at http://ursyn.com/student%20gallery/index.html; color figures have the QR codes (quick response codes) for the URL of the author's Website.

- **Art History Resources on the Web:** http://arthistoryresources.net/ARTHLinks.html
- **Contemporary Art:** http://arthistoryresources.net/ARTHcontemporary.html
- **WEB Museum:** (Nicolas Pioch) http://www.ibiblio.org/wm/
- **Guggenheim Museum:** New York, Venice, Bilbao, Berlin, Abu Dabi, International Exhibitions: http://www.guggenheim.org
- **SFMOMA ArtScope:** Established for exploring the Museum collection, http://www.sfmoma.org/projects/artscope/index.html#artwork=48370&r=73&zoom=4 shows art works from the San Francisco Museum of Modern Art; artwork images and descriptions pop-up
- **Whitney Museum:** http://www.whitney.org/
- **Whitney Artport:** http://artport.whitney.org - Artport is the Whitney Museum's portal to net art and digital arts, and an online gallery space for commissioned net art projects.
- **Emerging Artistic Practices:** http://www.rhizome.org
- **National Gallery of Art, Washington D.C.:** http://www.nga.gov/copyright/toc.htm
- **New Museum, New York:** www.newmuseum.org/
- **Book Sources:** http://en.wikipedia.org/wiki/Special:BookSources/9780520204782. This page allows users to search for multiple sources for a book given the 10- or 13-digit ISBN number. Spaces and dashes in the ISBN number do not matter. In Wikipedia, numbers preceded by "ISBN" link directly to this page.
- **Published Reproductions of Art:**
  - *The Art Book.* Phaidon Press. ISBN 0714864676. Available in a big format or a pocketsize edition (4.8 x 1.1 x 6.4 inches) for $ 9.34, ISBN 071484487X / 9780714844879.
  - *The American Art Book.* Phaidon Press. ISBN 9780714838454.
  - *The 20th Century Art Book.* Phaidon Press. ISBN 0714847984. Works of selected artists are presented in alphabetical order with short descriptions; a glossary of artistic movements complements the collection.
- **Photoshop Resources:** http://sixrevisions.com/photoshop/70-excellent-photoshop-resources/

Acknowledgment

First, I would like to thank the members of the IGI Global publishing team: Erika Carter, Lindsay Johnston, Jan Travers, Monica Speca, and Allyson Gard, as well as all team members for their cheerful and personal assistance with this project.

My thanks go to Alain Chesnais for writing a Foreword to this book.

I would like to thank my students, who contributed to this book by providing images and texts illustrating their projects.

Many thanks go to the reviewers who diligently carried out a double blind review of this book, provided supportive suggestions and critiques, and thus helped to make each part of the book better.

My warmest thanks to my family, friends, and colleagues.

Anna Ursyn
University of Northern Colorado, USA

Section 1
Making a Visual Statement

Chapter 1
Looking and Seeing:
Communication through Art: Creating, Conveying, and Responding to Art

ABSTRACT

This chapter examines the artistic process and then encourages the readers to engage in visual and verbal projects. It contains a comparative inquiry about the ways of designing, conveying, and receiving images. The chapter comprises a comparative inquiry and a discussion about creating, conveying, and receiving art as three basic processes in communication in the arts: articulation of a visual message through creation of an electronic picture and its transitions; communication with a viewer; and reception of the artwork by a viewer. They appear to be decisive for both the traditional and digital artwork. Thus, the three levels in a creative process comprise an artist as a sender of a message (an idea), media of art (a process), and the viewer as the receiver (rethinking of an idea, interactive response by reshaping a work, new interpretation or a new idea).

INTRODUCTION

It might be worth a while to consider what would we gain and if we would loose anything due to the advance of new media arts involving web based, interactive, and virtual multidimensional forms. Many years ago Timothy Binkley (1990) described computer imagery as both abstract and concrete; one can produce different kinds of art forms defined by a collection of numbers in a program, each of them being an original. Artists using electronic media may discern a distinction between a natural form in physical sense and a

DOI: 10.4018/978-1-4666-4627-8.ch001

form in aesthetical sense, i.e., creation of mind. Human-made creations have been seen as art when they displayed traits common to all art works and restricted only to art works. Inquiries about defining the nature and properties of art works expanded into areas of new media art, real-time, interactive, and virtual installations, visualization, and simulation of process/product relations. An artistic event depends often on the viewer's real-time interaction with the computer program. Art does not always intentionally communicate a message to the viewers; it may be created without such intent but there is always a possibility of finding the message by the audience. To employ the full potential of the computer for art creation, both artists and viewers merge their scientific inventiveness with the demands for artistic quality of the product; it's a well established opinion among computer scientists that computing helps connect the talents of artists with those of scientists. Hence we may ask several questions about how visual communication has been changing in digital environment; how the transfer of an artwork through the web, e-mail, compressed video, or an augmented reality environment changes the meaning of an original work; and what happens to the artist, the message conveyed, and the viewer if the net art, electronic writing, generative imaging, animation, virtual environment, or streaming performance is sent to another continent the same moment it is being created, so manipulation with a message of the image becomes possible for both its sender and the recipients.

CREATING AN ARTWORK

Artwork as Expression of a Message

One can say art saves human perception accordingly. A semiotician and philosopher Umberto Eco (1990, p. 166) writes, "Art is created by imagination, which organizes its own vision, giving to life a harmonious whole. If there exist any rules or preexisting structures (because of tradition, language, culture in general), imagination destroys them and rebuilds them with a kind of nonanalyzable impulse. The creation has a new, original, harmonious form like that of a living being." Phases of visual problem solving may go through looking, seeing, imaging, and conveying our solution. In similar terms we can see nonverbal communication through art as creating a picture, conveying a message, and receiving the message by viewers, which involves articulation and exchanging codes along with social interactions. In further text we will examine the three phases of such creative process.

An artist may choose to create an artwork by looking from a distance at a wall-size image projection from a computer, tablet, or a smart phone, having electronic tools placed conveniently by the hand or using a touch screen visual display that can detect the presence and location of artist's finger or hand within the display area. Thus, there is enough distance for a good examination of the artwork and the effects of applying particular changes in a program. Artists can just see brilliant colors from a distance when they create electronic art. New media take on a growing number of varied forms, mostly digital, often interactive, networked, linked, open-ended and just open to reorganization by its users. For example, there is 2D digital and analog art, 3D digital art and design, time-based art, sound art, animation from traditional frame by frame animation to 3D computer animation, bio-inspired art, the virtual reality art, art using location-based technologies such as augmented reality, GPS-based and mobile applications, alternate reality games, and games as an art form.

The same may apply to the web-based art, visualization, and simulation. The net art combines elements of programming, electronic writing, digital imaging, animation, virtual environments, streaming performances, and it creates a shared social networking space. It has happened once at an art exhibition that a personal e-mail checked by someone on a computer used for a web-based art project accidentally replaced the projection on the ceiling so all viewers could examine it. Thus, for a short moment it became a piece of art.

Saving Good Decisions within the Artwork

The making of a painting or a digital work consists of a round of changes made on traditional materials, computer screen, a touch screen of a tablet computer such as iPad, or a smart phone, leading to the personal, thus the unique expression. Within the digital mode of creating, computer memory gives us the option of preserving brilliant decisions. The spirit of the artwork, determined at the very beginning, can be saved and expressed in spite of changes made, because the artist unconsciously preserves the original premises. It takes time to evaluate one's own decisions and decide whether each change is in accordance with the dominant character of the artwork. For this reason, the creation of the artwork is contemplative and takes place not only in front of the easel or a screen, but often at the most surprising moments. The perceiver may usually see the final effect of actions, often forgotten by the artist, that make up a whole of the artwork.

The particular way the artist starts to create an artwork may determine its progress, even if the lighting or other features of the object were changed. The setting expressed by a color scheme, line, composition, or artist's motivation is decisive to the final result of the artist's work. We may find in the history of art a great variety of versions created under the same title. The "Mount St. Victoire" paintings by Paul Cezanne (2002, URL provided in References), and Claude Monet's (no date, URL provided in References) series of cathedrals or water lilies may serve as examples of such attempts. Also in electronic art we may find many examples telling how many possible solutions may exist as a series of different versions (for example, Maeda, 2001). This process certainly affects the emotional content of the artwork and thus influences its appraisal by the viewers. Saving subsequent stages of the work done on a computer may create an interesting material telling about preserving the best moments of the creative process. Moreover, one may rework saved images by selecting a fragment, blowing it up, refinishing it, and then adjusting the final composition as the brilliant decisions and "good points" that were previously given up for the sake of a whole composition. Thus the perfect picture would be a collage consisting of lucky solutions, if only composition made up of recreated fragments could be arranged harmoniously. When working with traditional media one

may take successive images with a digital or Polaroid camera or scan the progress of the work. It would however come to no good because the colors, textures, a scale of the artwork, and even the lights and darks of the picture would change due to the process. Such observations relate to what is said further on the dissimilar reception of the painting and its reproduction. Such fragments containing lucky solutions could then become a starting point for a dazzling animation. In order to create an animation of visual quality, one often starts with a figure (which then can be often seen as a still image in a catalog), and changes the communication path through transformations or through inducing interactivity.

Levels of Visual Representation

Creating an artwork may go at three sequential levels of visual representation:

- The first step is an observation of a subject of the artwork. Imagery as a source for art creation depends on whether the artist glances at the physical object, draws from memory (especially when being endowed with the eidetic memory), makes use of sketches, proceeds from a visual source such as photographs and scans, or applies the computer memory and the www resources (with permissions). On the other hand, impressionist and expressionist painters, contrary to the realists, keep themselves from narrating and enhancing the details, even when they possess the photographic memory. This way they develop further levels of seeing. In the electronic media art we may associate rhythmic patterns in nature with the perfection of algorithms.
- The second level in the creative process seems to involve creation of the image, because cognitive nature of the design comprises the generative process following ob-

servation. An image evoked by the artist's perception of the object and emotion revived by memory is now represented on a screen or a canvas. Images preserved in the artist's memory and translated into pictures can be later deconstructed, interpreted, and even interactively changed by the viewers.

- The third level involves transformation of the artwork. Working inside the structure of the artwork on its transformation may include for example, working on mathematical formula (such as fractals) and color relations. The artist is in contact with the artwork, but not with its starting point, like the model or a set of data. In fact, what the viewer would see is free from the source: the model is gone, the data translated, and objects used for a still life already rotten and trashed. However, even with the starting point being detached, the artwork would stir the viewer's feelings because the artist's original emotions may be preserved in the artwork even when they are not depicted in a narrative way. In a similar way, emotions caused by past events can be preserved, then used and reworked without recreating the events causing those emotions. In the case of computer-based work, ready representation of the data or the object, rather than a drawing from observation serves often as a starting point for creating an artwork. Some hold that using this shortcut may divest the artist of the phenomenological experience of drawing, whether with traditional drawing media such as charcoal, graphite and paper (Harty, 2012) or an Apple iPad with Brushes and Sketchbook Pro apps (Hockney, 2012).

Having the image algorithmically defined or saved, one may search for further formal transformations or employ some random choices and spontaneous expressions. It is possible to save the stages of the artwork, and then rework the copies in different ways. For example, algorithms that are built into painting packages support transforming images in three dimensions. In order to rework the image, one may include color, shade, or fill it with patterns, cut, copy, rotate and paste it into other images, zoom and visualize its different sides. What is important, exploration and experimentation in the course of creating an artwork on the screen may be done without destructing its consecutive stages, while the layers of paint would hide previous attempts. It could be considered helpful for the representation of metaphorical thinking, in the same way as the scanned forms or symbols may often work as icons when put inside a structure of the whole work.

Imagination and Sources for Art Creation

Whether the artist looks at the object, draws from the eidetic memory resources, or re-activates previous emotion, imagination is crucial for all levels of seeing. A Polish/American specialist in aesthetic education Harry Broudy (1987; 1991) referred imagination to the image-making function of the mind. Imagery constructed this way truly or falsely claims to be images of reality that viewers can further interpret. Concepts, images, and memories available to provide meaning for the viewer have been called by Broudy the allusionary base. American painter Stuart Davis and the French writer Emil Zola both described a piece of art as a part of nature seen through the artist's temperament. Davis meant art as an understanding and interpretation of nature in various media. If one would a group of people to render realistically a portrait of a person sitting in a studio, certainly all the works would differ one from another, even when created in the same place and in the same light.

Wooden forms that remain after we have picked the parts of an intended art form and constructed a model of an animal or a vehicle retain the features defining the project, its pattern and design. We can see them as forms without the content. We may think in terms of imprinting, about human memory where time and other people take off the remembrance of single facts but the general intellectual formation remains intact. We can fill the empty spaces with new data such as our present knowledge about software, marketing, architecture, and also art (images).

The essential questions in making artwork are: what and how, or in another way, a theme and a formal solution. It is not always clear what becomes more important for the artist; sometimes the theme is a starting point and then goes a form. Some hold that people can derive their creative potential exclusively from the sources of nature, due to physiological reasons or from a need for visual perception. A French abstract painter Georges Mathieu determined the creative process as a sequence of actions aiming to pass on from what is conceptual to what is real, then from real to abstract, and from abstract to possible. With the electronic media, one can begin with a picture and then conceptually manipulate the space and analyze its dimensions. One may search for the unity of an artwork, and build the space of the work by regrouping on the screen its recurrent elements and contrasting ordered and chaotic relations between lines. For example, one may convey the order and regularity of natural forms by digitally rendering graphic patterns in nature or shading and coloring surfaces of objects in a still life painting. With any theme, one may develop a series of associations that would generate formal solutions. The intentions of the artist are often changed into a series of random actions. For an American realist painter Edward Hopper, elements not related to the most thrilling vision were always annoying, as those elements inevitably dissolved this vision and collided with the progress of the work. Activation of neuronal system responsible for perception of an object results in the viewer's personal idea of this object. For this reason, the artist departing from naturalistic imaging may

cause that each perceiver would build individual and varying reception of the artwork.

Inspiration for next actions may be triggered by external circumstances that may strongly affect one's feelings, such as criticism of one's own work or exposure to other kinds of art (e.g., music). Strong aesthetic experience elicited by someone's art may result in a sensation of one's increased artistic potential and a need for doing one's own artwork. Both relaxation and stress may stimulate the artist to work. A Polish philosopher Wladyslaw Tatarkiewicz (1976) indicated a distinction specific for some languages, between the act of creation from nothing (by the Creator, as described in the Bible) and the act of creation from something (by an artist). If a painting is a product of imagination, one may ask whether human imagery can create something non-existing in nature or an artist draws exclusively from natural sources. Inquiries about art became even more difficult because they expanded into areas of visualization (both in a micro and macro scale) and simulation of process/product relations. Structures of what is not visible, for example, molecules, atoms, and nano forms of carbon such as fullerenes can often evoke awe. Biological or physical forms, whether seen in a nano, micro or macro scale, are the most used points of departure in art. It's not easy to find purely fantastic forms having no relation to nature or mathematics. It is nature and mathematics that rouse admiration and delight, thus inspiring art. Correctness of an algorithm, a formula, or natural order evokes an aesthetic experience while creating or appreciating abstract art, whether the work is an abstract expressionism, geometric abstraction, or electronically created graphics. Forms of engineering may be also accounted to natural patterns, for example, airplane wings, or ergonomically designed machines. In a similar way, bringing synthetic polymers and plastics into artistic practice may be inspired by natural polymers and resins of a volcanic origin. The design of objects made from synthetic materials is often made to resemble those made of wood, metal or crystal glass. What is even more surprising, images obtained through the transformation of mathematical formula, such as fractals, bear so strong resemblance to natural forms, that they may be easily related to their homological forms in the natural fractal environments such as patterns of branches in a tree, fern leaves, viruses' shells or rocky formations. Computer-graphics and animation artists utilize such transformations in their work. In his books on computer art, Clifford A. Pickover (2001) explored visualizations, simulations, and imaginative curiosities derived from natural sources.

It depends on the artist whether imagined fragments will combine to a good composition of the artwork, distribution of color values, the order of colors (any third color may change the two Albers, 1963/2010), the relative importance given to color patches in space, and the amount of space in the work. Color relations have often been discussed in many artists' notebooks. A color chosen to express the brilliance of an illuminated object would determine colors of other objects in the artwork. Thus, seeing means choosing because one chooses an expression of what was so impressive within the particular subject.

Expression Coming from the Cerebral Hemispheres

In fact, everyone feels a need to create art and a want to find a substitute for speech in order to let the right hemisphere express itself. Artistic activity allows for synthetic, analogous expression typical of the right hemisphere (in contrast to analytic and logical statements produced by the left hemisphere). Thus the right hemisphere activity may be expressed through painting, drawing, computer art or another artistic action. Broudy (1991, p. 7) stated, "Sensory images can often convey meaning directly with a clarity that formal analysis and reasoning cannot rival." This approach may help the artist to reprocess the data different way it was presented, to look at the world

from a different vantage point, to get outside, and feel more comfortable. Depending on one's right- or left-brain preference, one may be inclined to create visually appealing imaginary art, or may prefer to construct a cloud computing diagram, a concept map for organizing knowledge, or visualization that communicates ideas. In terms of philology, one may venture an analogy between expression made with the use of speech or art, and expression with the use of the English or Japanese language. Typical features of English language are seen as a digital mode of description, logical approach, linear structures, quantitative measure, and easy scientific description, while the Japanese language is characterized by the analogous mode of description, emotional approach, qualitative evaluation, and easy poetic expression. Artists will often write, finding this type of creative activity supplemental to their visual work. This is more and more true within social networks where one can not only share a story but also determine the events and the outcomes of the experience in interactive way, discuss basic approaches to designing an artwork with all related freedom/ precision compromises, and explore connections between the analogue and digital mode (ACM SIGGRAPH's Digital Arts Community, 2012). The web of data and sign systems can be processed directly and indirectly by machines (Berners-Lee, 2012). Semantic Web, a collaborative movement led by the World Wide Web Consortium oversees the Web's development and converts the existing Web into "a common framework that allows data to be shared and reused across application, enterprise, and community boundaries" (W3C, 2012). Tim Berners-Lee, the inventor of the World Wide Web is the director of W3C.

Figure 1, "Action Steps" is an abstract counterpart of our decision-making processes aimed at selecting a course of action to meet our needs, interact with our surroundings, and act in a logical way according to the accepted plan. Our goals and objectives may work better when our actions are interrupted by the interactive nature of our plan.

Figure 1. Anna Ursyn, Action Steps (© 2010, A. Ursyn. Used with permission)

This is even truer within social networks where we may share our actions, experiences, and decisions in interactive way.

VISUAL COMMUNICATION WITH A VIEWER

A message coming from the artist and the way it is conveyed to the viewer make up the essence of visual communication. One may say the act of creating an artwork is neither a cause nor a purpose of artist's work. However, it occurred many times that effective communication with viewers and critics, as well as recognition of the artwork came along a long time after its creation, as it happened with the paintings of Vermeer

about 200 years after their creation. The content to be conveyed may refer to a subject matter, the image itself, and also to other issues resulting from the choices made by the viewer engaged in a responsive behavior in examining the complete art environment, especially an interactive art installation. The viewers' interaction with the artwork and their contribution to the presentation environment makes a strong asset of designing interactive art as a distinct category at exhibitions. Interactive installations, multimedia presentations, and virtual reality events create artifacts and interactions between the artist, the viewer and the artwork, where audience can actively participate in an artistic event by changing the state of the computer, and thus manipulate the object, and control the image and its movement.

Artist's choices may be seen in all types of art, both digital and traditional. In conventional art forms, such as a still life, a portrait, or a landscape painting, the choice of a landscape as the subject matter of the picture is usually made for rendering the color and light relations. An artist selects a few color surfaces from the examined scenery, to direct the viewer's eye towards the preferred regions, to limit possible influences, or suggest them to the viewer. Further choices include the fixing of a source of light and setting the rhythmic order of accentuated planes and masses in a picture. Free of details, the synthetic expression of the landscape may draw the viewer's attention to qualities that have earlier inspired the artist, such as rhythm, color, and light. In effect of such sequential choices, the work may then be qualified as an abstract art.

Visual and Symbolic Signs

Transmission of meaning may be considered visual communication between the artist who is the sender of the message and the viewer who is its receiver. The type of information conveyed in the message may depend on signals. An art creation as a vehicle of meaning comprises symbols, signs, and signifiers. Signals used in visual communication through art are both the visual stimuli, e.g., colors, and the symbols of those stimuli – the signs. Visual signs may be arbitrary, showing a resemblance of a stimulus to its symbol, or conventional, unrelated. As an art theorist Rudolf Arnheim (1954/2004) put it, the creation of art may be considered a form of reasoning in which perceiving and thinking are indivisibly intertwined. According to Arnheim (1969/2004), productive thinking is perceptual thinking, as visual perception lays the groundwork of concept formation. Word and picture cannot be split up into parts that have any meaning separately (Arnheim, 1990). Visual mathematics uses visually appealing computer graphics for constructing models and as a guide for intuition. It serves an educational resource promoting students' interest and motivation, as it connects the talents of artists with those of scientists. Algorithmic images of a cube created from 1970s by Manfred Mohr (2012) may serve as an example of work of art that can be rationally understood, and yet there is room for associations and imagination. As it was stated by Manfred Mohr (Keiner, Kurz, Nadin, 1994, p. 154), "My art is not a mathematical art, but an expression of my artistic experiences. I don't want to show cold mathematics but a vital philosophy." Helaman Ferguson (1994) is considering mathematics both an art form and a science, when he transfers thought forms, formulated in terms of topological mathematics, to physical materials using a method of telecarving, where geometric forms drawn on a computer screen are translated into instructions on direct carving the stone.

Figure 2, "Altitude, Latitude, Longitude, Solitude" tells how a cell phone and a laptop can alleviate a feeling of the solitude in a crowd when traveling.

Open and Closed Messages, Open and Closed Forms

While designing an artwork, a mathematician is careful to avoid ambiguity, so everybody can see the exact and precisely defined formula representation. On the contrary, visual communication in fine arts is often based on metaphors. Everyone may receive different, unique, and individual messages from the same artwork. While looking at a sculpture one may say a closed form, with no inside or an exclusive inside seeks perfection in its smallest possible surface; if it would be a living creature it would help it survive. An open form, ready to cover and shield, can transform itself, adapt and evolve, thus preventing killing. A semiotician and writer Umberto Eco (1979, 1989, 1990) differentiated between the closed texts with one interpretation and the open texts that might have possibilities of multiple interpretations made by the readers. In semiotics, when someone sends

Figure 2. Anna Ursyn, Altitude, Latitude, Longitude, Solitude. (© 2010, A. Ursyn. Used with permission)

a message, someone else in the audience (an addressee) decodes the message according to one's own cognitive framework and the semantic and syntactic rules related to particular social and cultural codes. But cultural codes are changing fast; fat could be previously perceived an equivalent of wealth but became a threat in prosperous societies. One may think about the meaning of body fat while looking at art works created by Peter Paul Rubens (1577-1640), Giovanni Giacometti (1868-1933), Amadeo Modigliani (1884-1920), Fernando Botero (born 1932), and also Joseph Beuys (1921-1986) in terms of the meaning of fat in his art works. Thus, a message invokes denotations about its primary, immediate meaning and connotations built by a person in addition to its intended meaning, for example understood as

symbols. It may cause that the receiver decodes and interprets message differently from what the sender intended to send. Many sentences may thus easily become the open ones. One may ponder whether poetry, especially the haiku form (a Japanese verse consisting of three lines with five, seven, and five syllables that evoke connotations related to natural world) may be seen as an open message. We may also ponder whether the use of a metaphor offers us a closed or open tool for communication, when it simplifies, focuses our attention, and makes a notion more precise.

Decoding of the message is possible on a basis of a code shared by both the artist and the viewer. However the code of the addressee is often different from this of the sender. It could be such a case were an American painter Arthur Pinkham

Ryder evaluated as a seascape painter only, and a Swiss symbolist painter Arnold Böcklin exclusively as an illustrator of mythology. There are also deliberately open messages using periphrases, symbols, or synesthetic signs that could be freely interpreted and also generated cooperatively by the viewer. "How to produce texts by reading them" asks Umberto Eco (1979, p. 2).

We may think about communication through sending and decoding messages in broader contexts of nature, the animal, human, and machine languages, and art; we may thus look for common patterns in communication. One may find many ways of sending and receiving information in nature, whose two-dimensional shapes and three-dimensional forms are loaded with meaning. Many times it is a spherical form (such as spherical celestial bodies or river stones) that seem to be closed, that is the most effective, and demanding minimal operations. We may say a flower communicates with an insect of the particular species with the use of color, a degree of opening its corolla, or the chemical substances sent by its stigma or stamens. Open or closed, a flower seems to convey a closed message. Animals send their calls openly or make them decipherable only for their future mates. In human cultures, maybe we may consider a canon being a closed message by which things and deeds are judged. We may think a documentary film is a closed message, while blogging and tweeting are open. Human art such as cave painting remains open because we are not able to decode its real meaning or a purpose. In painting, abstract art seems more open to interpretations than traditional representations. One may ask whether there is a relationship between the sending of open messages and creating interactive art, for example the street sculptures, which bystanders can modify producing synchronicity and coincidence of the resulting products. The idea of an open form implies that every viewer understands the message in one's own way, while the idea of an interactive art suggests that every visitor co-creates the work in a different way.

The Openness of the Visual Message

We may think about the open and closed forms in a similar way as we think about the open and closed messages. We may assume that a closed form in art has an exterior only, while many open forms in art, whether it is a sculpture, architecture, or interactive installation, may display interplay, interrelationship, dependency, and communication between their exterior and interior parts.

Painting is as old as the humankind is, because of the need for artistic expression of feelings, emotions, attitudes, and experiences. For this reason one may presume that the essential kinds of painting: a human figure (also nude), a portrait, a landscape, and a still life will always exist as a form of expression in art. Traditional kinds of painting are therefore resumed by artists not just for cultivation of the tradition but as a means of expression. The open aesthetic statement allows for various interpretations, so both an artist and a viewer may relate their internalized models to the most probable states of objects. So, we may identify a table or a mountain when created by the French post-impressionist painter Paul Cezanne (1839-1906), even if it is painted in his own unconventional perspective. A plate, when foreshortened, should be rather painted as an ellipse while a Cezanne's plate, painted as a circle, may be seen as a sign of dominance of artist's knowledge over his observation.

The impact of computing that moved the feelings about art has also produced changes in thinking about computer programs where meaning is formalized as the definite program structures and models. Logical operations may be closed, leaving no space for interpretations, or open where there are many possible computational solutions of a single problem (there are many ways to prove a Pythagorean theorem $a^2 + b^2 = c^2$) and many programs making these solutions applicable to reality. Is a golden section a closed message/solution/form? Artists are pushing the progress of technology in a creative way, utilizing the changes of meaning resulting from the changes of forms. Interactive art with the viewer's involvement in the artwork creates possibilities for open communication. A work of art is composed so that due to the viewer's sensitive and intelligent reaction to an arrangement of forms, each perceiver can recreate the original idea conceived in artist's imagination. At the same time, the aesthetic value of the artwork may elicit an emotional climate and a flow of associations. This response to the artwork is exclusive for each viewer and causes an emotional need to form own ideas and associations by the viewers, and their varied reception of the artwork. Due to artist's choices and transformation of own experiences, the aesthetic quality attained in the artwork results in deformation, distance, and openness of the work. This is conducive to the formation of own ideas and associations by the viewers, and their varied reception of the artwork. A subject of a landscape painting is a theme recalling an idea of natural scenery, while a landscape painting itself is the product of imagination, and then a process of reworking the picture. Natural scenery is not necessarily depicted as a landscape; hence there is a gap, a deformation, and a room for an open message of the artwork. At the same time, the viewer may judge the method of evoking the ideas received from the work. However, the openness of the image may become chaotic, for example, a board used by many artists for pinning a cardboard in order to draw or paint on it is often smudged with many colors, as the tool goes often beyond the surface of a paper. Could this be acclaimed an artwork when taken out of the studio? This board shown as an artwork may demonstrate the artist's individual style due to specific color scheme, color smudge characteristics, and the way they are repeated.

Levels of a Message in Communication

The same way as it may happen with the levels of perception, there is diversity of issues in com-

munication through the artwork: a subject of an artwork (for example, a set of data, landscape as natural scenery), a theme for an artwork (for example, social network activity, a landscape painting as an artist's view of this scenery), and the aesthetic, associational, or other hidden issues resulting from the artist's choices, and hence the artist's view. Thus visual communication may go on many levels, for example, as a narrative about the qualities of objects present in an artwork and their relationship; as an anecdotic account of motion, occurrence, action of models; as an aesthetic message about the two-dimensional space with some references to the third dimension; as a multidimensional work of art; as an interaction with the viewer; or in any imaginable way. According to Tony Robbin (1992), by accepting the cultivated experience, i.e., a culture of seeing the fourth dimension as multiplicity of spaces and points of view, we can learn to see the fourth dimension as real. Jean Nouvel (De Bure, 1992, p. 15) explained the interactive approach to the computerized architecture as a form of art as "a synergy between the different ideas, the possible solutions – an interaction, a connection, depth, complexity. This process shows how best to utilize the specific conditions of the program, the moment, the people." Human computer interaction can be attained in other means, for example, by interactive art, with a possibility of finding different eyeball positions of one object and creating its image by real-time interaction.

Communication through the Image Design

Unlike black-and-white graphics, the making of color graphics may be discussed as the developing of the space of an artwork by contrasting colors of different values instead of drawing lines. For this reason, with well-selected colors, a picture's value (and space) is retained even when inspected with a low brightness of the screen, or when the printout is seen under dim illumination. This is possible due to the activation of rod shaped cells in the retina (as cones require more intense light for proper operation). When constructing the space of a picture with the use of the color value, the narrative or anecdotic way of communication with the viewer is not decisive for reception of a painting. Many times the viewers notice painterly solutions such as space, color, texture, value, and motion within a picture and its dynamics, so they feel aesthetically impressed without analyzing the narrative and anecdotic contents. One may look that way at the human shapes painted by a Dutch/American abstract expressionist Willem de Kooning, dynamic motion contained in American painter's belonging to the New York School Robert Motherwell paintings, or landscape paintings done by the postimpressionist painters. A shift from a factual and narrative level to a painterly level of communication may happen without the artist's intention. The use of the pure painterly solutions may involve the viewer into active reception of the artwork. Activation of neuronal structures responsible for visual perception of objects results in creation of individual images of those objects. For this reason, an artist who gives up naturalistic rendering will possibly gain an individual reception in everyone looking at the artwork. Sometimes artists take advantage of optical illusions resulting from afterimage or ambiguous pictures to influence viewers' reception.

The Role of the Artist's Statement

It may be discussed in terms of phonology, whether linguistic denotation system is based on an onomatopoeic, symbolic, or conventional principle. In the visual arts, acceptation of one or another system of signs may conceivably determine the genre of artworks one creates: whether they are figurative, realistic (such as French Academy paintings), symbolic (such as Orthodox Eastern Church icons), or conventionalized (such as paintings from the Far East). Yet communication by art cannot be considered explicit. An art historian

Edwin Panofsky (1972; 1997) detailed three strata of subject matter or meaning. First, the primary or natural subject matter is natural, pre-iconographic, based on simple identification of objects. The secondary or conventional meaning is iconographic, derived from the understanding of abstract notions in the theme. Finally, there is an intrinsic, inner symbolic meaning of principles rather than individual motifs; it may reveal their essence and symbolic value. Depending on a system of signs accepted in an artwork, the same work may be apprehended in different ways. For this reason, curators of exhibitions often supply information about works, such as paintings from the Baroque period or objects of oriental art, and explain a content of each picture providing a translation of images into their symbolic meaning. Besides an opportunity of indulging an aesthetic experience, the viewers are given an already forgotten code for the symbolic meaning, and thus they can take a secondary message that was hidden for them.

The Role of the Title of the Artwork

A title may provide a link between visual and verbal communication. Perception of an artwork may often depend on knowledge of the title. When a non-figural artwork is provided with a title, viewer's attitude to the work may be guided by the title. For example, Jackson Pollock entitled his non-figurative painting "Night Mist" (1944), while a feature of the Mark Rothko's painting has been enhanced by its descriptive title "Light Red over Black" (1957). That way, one may successfully apply a title that would guide the reception of an artwork. The Stanislaw Fijalkowski's painting (from the collection of the Museum of Contemporary Art in Lodz, Poland) has a title: 'Step back seven steps.' Due to the artist's imperative, the viewers are drawn into the space laid out between them and the surface of the painting. Reception of the painting may be thus improved due to involuntary reaction of the viewers. In generative art, a distance between the artist's eye and the computer screen is rather small. In many computer art graphics, the title and/or the artistic statement became an integral part of the artwork and sometimes necessary for its understanding.

The Role of Naming Image Content

A creative process takes place in a visual domain. In respect of language visual differentiation is much better than verbal one. It is possible to discriminate 7,500,000 color tints. Computer languages describe colors as a bitmap grayscale, 256, thousands, or millions of colors. Yet, only about 4,000 colors can be officially named in English. Thus the image of the world is impoverished by verbal description. While it is difficult to accept the Wittgenstein's (1973/2009) opinion that human mind cannot go beyond limits of language, one must agree that modern art is entangled in verbal self-consciousness. Viewers became used to verbalize, so they often translate images into words and reject its untranslatable elements. On the other hand, the language of art is considered autonomous and hardly translatable into speech.

An artistic problem may be sometimes solved faster by ascribing it a verbal form, even the form of inner monologue. The artistic expression may possibly be influenced by language in its way of representation. This linguistic determinant can be recognized (the Crayola's color-naming contests play a role here) and names of colors, e.g., orange or lemon, influence the child's decisions about coloring pictures of those fruits. According to linguists, every pictorial code may possibly be translated into words, but not the other way round; however this position seems to be questionable to most of painters. In any language, there is a specific system for coding tints, hues and shades of colors; visual representation of colors may be determined by mental characteristic and imagery of people speaking this language. In psychiatric practice, mental patients express their attitudes in form of pictures or put them into words; this activity may be sometimes effective in therapeu-

tic correction of attitudes. In education, verbal methods of instruction and pictorial codes are used equally often.

About the Artist's and the Viewer's Knowledge About the Object

Artists create visual references of concepts derived from mathematics, computing, or science, and discover the power of their visual forms. The computer may be considered a unique medium that allows for the fast, inspiring and efficient interaction between science concepts and their visual references. By choosing science-related themes, one may create an artwork that is not only a recording of reality but also the effect of conscientious participation in nature and the reality resulting from this participation. One may believe that a success in cooperation between scientists and artists depends on both technological and visual (artistic) literacy possessed by both cooperating parties. While there is a still a growing number of computer scientists who become apprentices in art (as well as artists who learn programming), many think there is no need for a digital artist to possess the drawing ability because so many resources are available for making image collages, manipulation, and interaction with graphic software. Having ready tools (stronger than had been available for many established artists) and solutions for designing a picture, everybody can feel confident to design digital artwork through the ready image application, without the artist's intervention. Many feel disheartened from setting to hand drawing, because "recent advances in software have allowed the artist to create a level of geometric complexity that one would normally not have the patience to create." (Huff, 1999, 19). Moreover, one may often encounter an opinion from the part of computer scientists that "Engineers' art background is not important because there may be cooperation with artists." While collaborating with the "Experiments in Art an Technology " (E.A.T.) group that was founded in the sixties by the artist Robert Rauschenberg and the engineer Billy Klüver, an artist Lilian Schwartz (1985; Schwartz & Schwartz, 1992) "discovered that scientists often want to be considered artists." She was ready to agree with A. Michael Noll, "The most creative engineers and scientists have their own artistic ideas and aesthetic sensitivities which match those of a particular artist with probability zero" (Noll, 1970, p. 12). An open aesthetic statement allows various interpretations. Viewers internalize models that correspond with the most probable states of objects. It may also apply to the artist's view. Additionally, subjective states of the viewer have a bearing upon reception of the painting.

The Role of Emotion

It is generally known from the experimental psychology that the stronger are emotion and motivation, which accompany the perception of the artwork, the stronger is reaction to the stimulus. Therefore, the kind and degree of the response to the image depend on the quality of visual and emotional environment for perceiving art. Circumstances and emotions that accompany an inspection of an artwork might influence dynamics, as well as a kind, character, and intensity of viewer's reaction. For example, quite different message is taken when somebody inspects an artwork while suffering a toothache in a glaringly illuminated dentist's office, or in a stressful atmosphere of suspense and subordination. When going to a museum in order to look at art, or during a friendly meeting, one may react quite differently to the same painting placed in good lighting. A conditioned reaction to an artwork may be reinforced by the next contact; the artwork may recall a situation of the first contact with it, thus providing a certain emotional attitude. Commercials are often designed in a way to promote developing an emotional response from the viewer. Lions and tigers shown in the background may convince the

viewers of their good feeling about themselves while driving an advertised model of a car.

Interactive Ways of Communication

Artists may seek information about the viewers for whom they create creating (if not just for the art's sake), and how they may utilize media technologies in service of formulation and transmission of ideas. In the times of the Middle Ages the mainstream art had been developed under an influence of the ecclesiastical or secular patron. However, while performing their duty, artists created in their own style, sometimes even developing their own schools. The task of a viewer was to experience a state of religious ecstasy evoked by visual representation of some sacred events. Intensity of viewers' ecstasy induced by perception of an artwork was considered a measure of its quality. The role of the viewer gains in importance, as the notion of interaction in art could only be developed when the viewer becomes an addressee, and a kind of a model for an artist: a standard of behavior to be included into the artwork. This idea began to crystallize in the seventies and the eighties with the happenings and installations where viewers became important and active, and interactive communication was no more unidirectional. Co-operative creations on the web illustrate this approach, where task of an artist is not only to satisfy the viewer's demand for exquisite art, but also to make the viewers interact with the artwork, and make them the integral part of it.

With the use of software and apps, people who were disheartened from commencing any artistic activities because they were afraid to spoil a sheet of paper may program or design projects and feel artistic through application, manipulation, and interaction with computer graphic software offerings. As it may be discovered by studying art show catalogs, a considerable part of new media art accepted to international competitions and exhibitions of electronic art have been originated for the needs of advertisement firms or commissioned by big corporations for professional marketing. As a consequence of the readiness for creative activities from the part of computer scientists, computer graphic magazines are presenting art graphics created under inspiration with electronic technology. Fine artists are not necessary engaged to make an artwork: it may be done by the commissioners themselves or their R&D departments. For this reason, the perceivers to whom the artwork was addressed are potential consumers of the subject of an artwork, not necessary recipients of art itself. The weak involvement, interest, and appreciation of electronic art from the mainstream art-world critics and members of the established art-world institutions may result from accepting those approaches and criteria for creating, both by artists creating art works and curators selecting art works to exhibitions and galleries.

Synesthetic Language of Computer Graphics

Electronic artwork messages in the form of images, sounds or animations can be analyzed as metaphors and seen as important sign systems working beyond the literary culture. Synesthetic ways of expression, widely applied in electronic art, performance arts, data presentation, technical implementations, design, advertisement, visualizations and simulations for scientific and educational purposes address and interact with the varied audience. However, modes of knowledge based on the culture of the image differ from those based on the culture of the text. With diminishing distinctions made between sending messages with words, images, sounds and things, synesthetic modes of cognition seem to operate outside the language-based structures of thinking. Messages conveyed in the non-verbal mode of visual communication media are often being more abstract and more interactive with the viewer. By crossing senses, viewers construct in their own art-historical and cultural contexts their perception of the reality communicated by an artist. Strong aesthetic

experience elicited by synesthetic art may result in a sensation of increased artistic potential and a need for doing one's own artwork.

RECEPTION OF THE ARTWORK

Levels of Reception of the Artwork

One may say, the observer or critic is recreating art created by the artist. In a qualitative, then quantitative study of the artist-perceiver relation, Mihaly Csikszentmihalyi and Rick E. Robinson (1991) described the conceptual model of flow and optimal aesthetic experience in four dimensions: perceptual dimension which concentrated on elements such as balance, form, and harmony; an emotional response, an intellectual response, and communicative response defining the transcendence of actuality. Thus the concomitance of several strata of psyche may possibly influence viewer's reception of an artwork. The psycholinguistic theory of linguistic universals, and universal grammar, which is now a matter of considerable controversy (Pesetsky, 2009) presumed that all languages have certain phonetic, syntactic, and semantic features in common due to human genetic predispositions, hence they are marked by general similarities and universal generalities. It was noted by anthropologists that basic aesthetic experiences result from recognition of forms with a quality of the archetypes, and they gain a general acceptance as the aesthetic objects. A joy and excitement experienced by an eight-month old infant when recognizing a picture of familiar face, may serve as an example that is well known in a developmental psychology. At first, the baby without any emotion perceives two circles that later on will stand for the eyes. The circles gain the meaning of the eyes, as the semicircle is put below those circles and is recognized by the infant as a smiling mouth.

An artwork is a form of an aesthetic statement; reception of a work does not mean the recognition and contemplation of the mere theme of the artwork. A pictorial scheme used by an artist may imply some meanings to be conveyed to a viewer. Due to an artificial setting of the subject and an openness of a message, the artist may lead a viewer to some associations of ideas, far from the direct recognition of the objects shown in the graphics. The act of perception may result in shaping a model, and such model may serve to make further perceptions, actions, and in interactive behavior. Former knowledge of viewers may add up to their expectations concerning the aesthetic message. For this reason, reception of works of art that lack the predetermined pictorial models is most difficult; non-representational works are unlike anything, so many times they do not evoke much of aesthetic experience. For someone studying signs and symbols, an artwork is aesthetically valuable because it is open, not fully explicit, and thus draws viewer's attention. Exploration of possible meanings contained in particular works of art led Jacques Derrida (1991) to creating "The Truth in Painting" – a study of idiom in painting, where possible meanings, translations, examples, etymologies, and supplementary parergas were composed into a piece of literary art.

Forms of Display: The Original Artwork Versus its Reproduction

One may see many reasons why it is much better to appreciate an original work of art rather than to be acquainted with it indirectly. The mere insufficiency of illumination makes a content of a painting becoming more important than its form and color values. Moreover, each artwork has a scale of its own, which has to be observed in the reproducing process; for the purpose of making reproductions, one is often forced to change the size. The reception of an original artwork known till now by the downscaled copies only may be affected by our own idea of the regular scale of it. It may also apply to value, texture, and space of the painting, mostly lost for a viewer who is

acquainting with the painting by its reproduction. This should be kept in mind while discussing advantages and drawbacks coming from exposition of art on the web: one may visit virtually any current exhibition in a leading museum in a far away city, but the scaling and copying options offered by computer technology may be insufficient for full appreciation of the artwork.

On the contrary, even direct aesthetic experience may be enhanced when the viewer is familiar with the appearance of the artwork in its reproductions online, in art books, slides, videos, and movies. The imaginary content of a museum without walls, a collection of viewer's previous experiences, visual references and notions called by André Malraux (1958/1974) a museum of imagination, is being developed in the minds of viewers and may transform and enrich their reception of any specific artwork, connotations and ideas which are evoked or previously learned, and the artist – viewer communication.

We go even further with all the web links available, so we may access any exhibition, thus feeding our memory and imagination on a different level.

The Role of Information about the Artwork

An awareness of a common recognition of the particular artwork may influence our response to it, while trends developed by a society or a generally accepted opinion may hinder the viewers in shaping their personal disposition toward an artwork, especially in new media. Aesthetic experience coming from their reception of an artwork may depend on the value ascribed to it, so the awareness of the value of the artwork may stimulate the sensation of its beauty. The viewer may ascribe to the work some previously learned qualities. Knowledge about a content of the artwork, the way it was done, technique used, and history of the artwork's ups and downs, all enrich one's connotations. Due to their mutual interaction, all those meanings are received on many levels. Viewers may derive pleasure from their own ability to recognize the artist on the ground of the artwork's style (Alleyne, 2011); they may want to spot some influence over the artist or identify the periods of artistic production. Ample information on the artwork, its originator, and a period may be conducive to the reception of messages present in the painting.

A level of viewer's aesthetic sensitivity may be modified by emotional attitude toward the artwork; it may be directed toward the works of a particular artist, specific style in art, historical context of the favorite artwork, or because of its price. It may be also influenced by the location of an artwork at the exhibition, good quality of a museum's cafeteria, or an inclination to be in possession of chosen works. In a way, reception of a painting may be altered out of sheer snobbery or on account of viewer's bonds within the artistic society. Computer-savvy viewers may be apt to praise the features of the works resulting from technology and pertaining to their own mastery.

An unprepared viewer, while encountering the artwork taken out of its context, may feel lost and doubtful about one's own evaluation of the artwork; it is often also caused by misapprehension of the artist. The importance of this factor has been confirmed in the poll conducted by Komar and Melamid (1997), where 24% of 476 respondents state they go to art museums less than once a year or don't go there at all (another 24% of respondents), as "they don't feel comfortable in art museums because they don't know a lot about art" (Komar and Melamid, 1997, p.26, and a "Cross Tabulation of the American Poll," question 88). For this reason, chairs of the art shows are keen on defining the scope of the show according to a leading theme, the way it is done every year by the SIGGRAPH Art Shows or by the Documenta (http://d13.documenta.de), an international art show in Kassel, Germany that is organized every five years and lasts for 100 days and exhibits recent art works in a wide variety of new contexts, concepts, and media. The

scope of images and mental associations evoked by reception of a painting may vary according to the art chair's intentions: whether the works are hanged in order to optimally expose their quality, or they are organized along with the art chair's general concept of the show. Some exhibition themes: "Geometry and Emotion" or "Color in Painting" may serve as examples of general ideas for exhibitions.

Another way of communication with the viewer may be achieved by arranging a one-artwork exhibition, where a separate artwork, unrelated to any big collection is presented to the viewer. An artwork is shown together with discussion of philosophies, a set of media, objects, and articles used as accessories for the artwork. Moreover, such exhibition may be supplemented by a documentary videos and sets of photographs showing the lifestyle of the epoch and the history of the artwork. For example, the London National Gallery used to present series entitled "The Focus" comprising one-masterpiece exhibitions from the museum's own collection, which is often supplemented by a documentary set of photographs showing the life style of the epoch, the artist's technique and tricks, the replicas of items used as accessories for it, the history of the artwork, and the story of its renovations.

The Role of the Environment of the Electronic Artwork

With 2,405,518,376 people using the Internet on June 30, 2012 (out of 7,071 billion on March 2013, according to the United States Census Bureau), world total population on December 31, 2011), we can stress the importance of the artwork environment in the context of web galleries and virtual art exhibitions (Internet usage statistics, 2012). Web-based communities are considered a new type of media, with the main groups of users being the users of message boards, chat groups, and weblogs (Bishop, 2007; 2009). Since the dawn of the millennium online communities of this type

Figure 3. Anna Ursyn, Breakfast Club. (© 2007, A. Ursyn. Used with permission)

gather the Internet users that post messages and add content to the message boards, newsrooms, chatrooms, file sharing sites, and social networking sites. However, most of online community members are lurkers – those who do not participate actively, just reading discussions on the online community sites and listening to people in the voice-over Internet protocols such as Skype and Ventrilo or other interactive systems.

Figure 3, "Breakfast Club" portrays direct encounters. Some come alone, some group together for a direct contact, rather than the mobile phone or Internet exchange. Such contacts tend to be vanishing now and in many individuals evoke sentimental, nostalgic memories.

Artwork selected for a web site is often transformed, put on an aggressive background, organized according to a preprogrammed page design and separated by colorfully framed text panels or

animated commercials. However, by escalating aesthetical standards for developing web sites, accomplished leaders in web design contribute to bringing into full development a superior level of mastery in creating the web environment for artwork. Both in an electronic installation setting and in a traditional gallery, the esthetic experience may go through several stages: passive or active, intellectual or emotional, spontaneous or cognizant, and may be altered by changes in the surrounding. The virtual environment of a masterpiece may enhance its emotional, non-verbal expression, thus evoking creative co-operation of the viewer, the same way as an actor may change an initial passive stand of the viewer into an active participation within the performance. The viewer may be induced to some degree of enchantment by breaking barriers of a self-consent for sending himself into uncontrollable emotions one can indulge at the moment. Therefore, much attention is being given to the arrangement of electronic works in gallery interior and the selection of works forming a compound picture perceived at the very first moment while entering the room. On approaching a particular artwork, a viewer may notice a relationship, which exists among adjacent works. Thus the meaning of an artwork may be changed depending on an impact of aggressive neighboring pictures, or the equipment of a museum room. The way a work is presented influences viewers' capacity to perceive the quality of a picture, even when a dark picture is adjacent to a colorful work easily attracting attention. The impact of walls on the perception can be realized when, as it sometimes happens before a show, the artists miss to identify their own works when they are leaning against a wall among others. A plate with an artist's name, title of the artwork, and a statement, fixed next to a picture, may possibly be informative and instructive, but it may also shift viewer's attention from an aesthetic experience to an anecdotic matter. A frame may locate a picture and link it with a surrounding space, the same way as a window may frame a landscape seen outside the walls. A thickness, width, color, and an embellishment of a frame may change the meaning of the artwork itself, and add some ambience. Sometimes, a color scheme dominant for the work is applied, to obtain an unobtrusive framing, or the content of the work expands on a surface of the frame.

Possible Ways to Improve the Reception of Electronic Art

Art education is probably the most important factor in improving interest and understanding of electronic art, with computer art production by students being decisive for developing their interest and motivation. Reception of electronic art may be strongly improved by the online and the school instruction in everyday use of the web, the CD-ROMs and other optical storage technolo-gies interactive with the computer. Familiarizing teachers and students with electronic artists and their work depends on promoting technology in schools, to enable the CD ROM presentations and instruction in computer art production through the web-delivered courses. Software packages for imaging, professional magazines, book and software reviews provided for students may be crucial for this purpose. Artwork and books on electronic art supplemented with art contests are still rare in public libraries, mobile art exhibitions, film and video shows, and educational programs for young and adult museum visitors.

Several organizations and programs support arts education, for example, ArtsEdge (2012) provides through the web numerous teaching resources, lessons and activities, and other materials. Electronic art promotion delivered by the SIGGRAPH Educational Committee consists from inviting the students to participate in the juried shows SPACE – Student Poster and Animation Competition & Exhibition, production of student slide sets, and publication of students' art in Educational Committee Brochures which tell about student successes. D-Art Gallery and the IV – Information Visualization Conference programs are aimed to encourage cooperation of scientists and artists, so do Prix Ars Electronica and Eurographics policies. Even with all these doings, when looking at the newest works of art, numerous viewers can hardly cope with their perception of the artwork, due to the insufficient comprehension and communication.

Educational Implications

According to David Perkins (1994), works of art demand various kinds of cognition, so careful looking at art requires thinking and thus cultivates our disposition to use reflective intelligence. Looking at art may be done for the intrinsic pleasure and for the extrinsic benefits. Perkins described how teaching of art has been changing. In late 19th century verbal analysis was taught, of black-and-white or sepia reproductions. Also, moral messages of art would inculcate morality into students. Then, the teaching of art was based on the concept of creativity. If children learned to be creative with paste and paper and crayons in school, their creativity would transfer to help them become creative as adults. Research done by Perkins and others on transfer of learning discredited such naive views. Perkins recommended fostering transfer of learning through applying the learned skills in varied contexts, and making connections between skills and contexts of knowledge. A thoughtful looking is a way to make thinking better, and art makes a supportive context because it provides sensory anchoring, personal engagement, and wide-spectrum cognition. As stated by Perkins, we see meanings, such as shapes, solids, backs, proportions, positions, materials, styles, economics, functions and weight, as intelligent eye makes sense of what lies before it. Knowledge of art is important for understanding images and contexts and answering questions. The eye can easily be wrong, as optical illusions show; so intuitive conclusions depend on our experiential intelligence, the contribution of intuitively applied prior experience to intelligent functioning. Critics and experts in art history show what hides in an artwork, but as Wordsworth wrote, we murder to dissect. However, it is good to know what a group of artists thought they were up to, and then try to avoid hasty, narrow, fuzzy and sprawling thinking for richer experience and better cognition with the use of reflective intelligence.

In the process of learning, visual computing may help to recognize configurations and relationships described by formulas. The impact of visuals on learning as a cognitive activity gains attention because of a facilitating effect of visual materials in the process of communication. It seems, the same way as we may list three basic elements of communication in the arts: the artist as a sender of a message, art media, and a viewer as the receiver, we may translate these elements in educational terms: the teacher as a sender, vi-

sual educational materials, and the student as the receiver. In terms of pedagogical constructivism, learning is an interpretive process leading to the construction of the individual's subjective reality, not identical with the knowledge of the teacher. The value of computing for the arts used as of visual educational materials might be in their emotional impact that might bridge the distance between the object and the viewer. Thus cognitive and expressive meanings conveyed through the shared media art containing signs, symbols, and metaphors may improve the capacity for learning. Using visual thinking and learning with relation to semiotic practices seems rare. The creation of illustrated and annotated web resources would provide materials for visual learning. In educational terms, by supplying an access through the new media art to the images and artists' approaches to their work, it is possible to develop new curricula for teaching contemporary art with the core based on semiotic analysis of the art content and the technological thought, not just historical chronology. When students learn to apply visual signs, symbols, and meanings in relation to any subject matter under study, they can extract more information from data they collected. Instruction in computer art graphics and new media art serves a tool to facilitate students' learning in other disciplines and their growth in artistic creation. Through art inspired by science-related concepts it is possible to visually present these concepts and discover the power of their visual forms. By designing art assignments that are based on scientific concepts, I have developed an integrative program for instruction in computer graphics where students can grow both in terms of their artistic inspiration and of their enhancement in learning.

A problem is, to what degree has electronic art defined its own specific language of design, which could be recognized and appraised by the mainstream art criticism seeking for technically innovative yet visually attractive artistic solutions. The selection of entries for art shows is usually gained through a consensus among jurors coming from a variety of art related fields of specialization, some of the jurors representing the mainstream art environment. However, the mainstream art criticism is not giving enough attention for this art form. The presence of quality works at the art shows seems to indicate that their acceptance to the exhibitions has not been only limited by a strict demand for interactivity or innovative use of recent advances in computer technology.

CONCLUSION: INTENTIONS AND CONCERNS

Each artist can choose to create an artwork by looking from a distance at a wall-size image: a monitor or a projection from a computer screen and using a hardware, a keyboard and a mouse placed conveniently by the hand. Thus, there is enough distance to examine the artwork, and the effects of applying particular brushstrokes or other tools, with no more scrolling the image on a monitor, nor walking back and forth from the surface of the canvas to the spot that allows for a good examination of the artwork. A possibility of creating brilliant colors and seeing them from a distance provides excellent conditions for creating a good quality electronic art, whether the 2-D, 3-D, interactive, time-based, or virtual 3-D forms.

Whatever would be a medium or a meaning of the work of an artist, there is still an ongoing discussion on the importance of the quality of the artwork. With all the variety of the media and technical tools and a trade-off between pressure of knowledge and a need for a discipline in the creative process, an exposure to electronic artwork may evoke in the viewers a need for the reconsideration of a question, whether artists use the computer to its fullest artistic potential and respond to technical developments with quality artwork. Also, whether they attain a composition free from unnecessary technical sophistication resulting from a desire to employ all possibilities

provided by the deceitfully attractive hardware and software. According to some jurors' statements, the quantity of the types of software used and the trickery of their application does not account for the visual quality of the images sought for by the jurors.

REFERENCES

ACM SIGGRAPH. (2012). *Digital arts community*. Retrieved February 11, 2012, from http://siggrapharts.ning.com/

Albers, J. (1963/2010). Interaction of color: Revised and expanded ed. Yale University Press. ISBN 03001146930

Alleyne, R. (2011, May 8). Viewing art gives same pleasure as being in love. *The Telegraph*. Retrieved December 12, 2011, from http://www.telegraph.co.uk/culture/art/8501024/Viewing-art-gives-same-pleasure-as-being-in-love.html

Arnheim, R. (1954/2004). *Art and visual perception: A psychology of the creative eye, fiftieth anniversary printing*. Berkeley, CA: University of California Press.

Arnheim, R. (1969/2004). *Visual thinking, thirty-fifth anniversary printing*. Berkeley, CA: University of California Press.

Arnheim, R. (1990). Language and the early cinema. *Leonardo, Digital Image*, 3-4.

ArtsEdge. (2012). Retrieved February 11, 2012, from http://artsedge.kennedy-center.org/educators.aspx

Berners-Lee, T. (2012). *Official site at W3C*. Retrieved February 11, 2012, from http://en.wikipedia.org/wiki/Tim_Berners-Lee

Binkley, T. (1990). Digital dilemmas. *Leonardo, Digital Image*, 13-20.

Bishop, J. (2007). Increasing participation in on-line communities: A framework for human–computer interaction. *Computers in Human Behavior, 23*, 1881–1893. doi:10.1016/j.chb.2005.11.004.

Bishop, J. (2009). Enhancing the understanding of genres of web-based communities: The role of the ecological cognition framework. *International Journal of Web Based Communities, 5*(1), 4–17. doi:10.1504/IJWBC.2009.021558.

Broudy, H. S. (1987). *The role of imagery in learning*. Occasional Paper 1. Malibu, CA: The Getty Center for Education in the Arts.

Broudy, H. S. (1991). Reflections on a decision. *Journal of Aesthetic Education, 25*(4), 31–34. doi:10.2307/3332900.

Cezanne, P. (2002). *The Mount St. Victoire series of paintings*. Retrieved February 28, 2013, from http://www.ibiblio.org/wm/paint/auth/cezanne/st-victoire/

Csikszentmihalyi, M., & Robinson, R. E. (1991). *The art of seeing: An interpretation of the aesthetic encounter*. Malibu, CA: J.Paul Getty Museum.

de Bure, G. (1992). *Jean Nouvel, Emmanuel Cattani, and associates: Four projects*. Zurich: Artemis.

Derrida, J. (1991). *The truth in painting*. Chicago: The University of Chicago Press.

Eco, U. (1979). *The role of the reader, explorations in the semiotics of texts: Advances in semiotics*. London: Indiana University Press.

Eco, U. (1989). *The open work* (A. Cancogni, Trans.). Cambridge, MA: Harvard University Press.

Eco, U. (1990). *The limits of interpretation*. Indianapolis, IN: Indiana University Press.

Eco, U. (2004). *History of beauty* (A. McEwen, Trans.). Rizzoli.

Eco, U. (2007). *On ugliness* (A. McEwen, Trans.). Rizzoli.

Ferguson, C. (1994). *Mathematics in stone and bronze*. Erie, PA: Meridian Creative Group.

Harty, D. (2012). Drawing//digital//data: A phenomenological approach to the experience of water. In A. Ursyn (Ed.), *Biologically-inspired computing for the arts: Scientific data through graphics*. Hershey, PA: IGI Global. doi:10.4018/978-1-4666-0942-6.ch019.

Hockney, D. (2012). *Personal webpage*. Retrieved February 9, 2012, from http://www.hockneypictures.com/home.php

Huff, K. A. (1999). *Electronic art and animation catalog*. Paper presented at SI99RAPH. New York, NY.

Internet Usage Statistics. (2012). Retrieved March 9, 2013, from http://www.internetworldstats.com/stats.htm

Keiner, M., Kurz, T., & Nadin, M. (1994). *Manfred Mohr*. Weiningen-Zürich: Viviane Ehri.

Lebwohl, B. (2011, July 25). Semir Zeki: Beauty is in the brain of the beholder. *EarthSky*. Retrieved December 12, 2011, from http://earthsky.org/human-world/semir-zeki-beauty-is-in-the-brain-of-the-beholder

Maeda, J. (2001). *Maeda@Media*. Universe.

Malraux, A. (1958/1974). *La métamorphose des dieux*. Paris: Gallimard.

Mohr, M. (2012). *Personal website*. Retrieved February 8, 2012, from http://www.emohr.com/

Monet, C. (n.d.a). *A series of cathedrals*. Retrieved February 28, 2013, from (http://en.wikipedia.org/wiki/File:Claude_Monet_-_Rouen_Cathedral,_Facade_(Sunset).JPG

Monet, C. (n.d.b). *A series of water lilies*. Retrieved February 28, 2013, from http://en.wikipedia.org/wiki/File:Claude_Monet_-_Water_Lilies.JPG

Noll, A. M. (1970). Art ex machina. *IEEE Student Journal, 8*(4).

Panofsky, E. (1972). *Studies in Iconology: Humanistic themes in the art of the renaissance*. Westview Press.

Panofsky, E. (1997). *Perspective as symbolic form by Erwin Panofsky* (C. S. Wood, Trans.). Zone Books.

Perkins, D. N. (1994). *The intelligent eye: Learning to think by looking at art*. Occasional Paper. Getty Center for Education in the Arts.

Pesetsky, D. (2009). Linguistic universals and universal grammar. In R. A. Wilson & F. C. Keil (Eds.), *The MIT encyclopedia of the cognitive sciences*. Cambridge, MA: MIT Press. Retrieved February 8, 2012, from http://web.mit.edu/linguistics/people/faculty/pesetsky/Pesetsky_MITECS_Universals_UG.pdf

Pickover, C. A. (2001). *Computers, pattern, chaos and beauty*. Dover Publications.

Robbin, T. (1992). Fourfield: Computers, art & the 4th dimension. Boston: A Bulfinch Press Book. Little, Brown and Company. ISBN 082121909X

Schwartz, L. F. (1985). The computer and creativity. *Transactions of the American Philosophical Society, 75*, 30–49. doi:10.2307/20486639.

Schwartz, L. F., & Schwartz, L. R. (1992). *The computer artist's handbook: Concepts, techniques, and applications*. New York: W. W. Norton & Company.

Tatarkiewicz, W. (1976). *Dzieje szesciu pojec*. Warsaw, Poland: PWN.

W3C Semantic Web Activity World Wide Web Consortium (W3C). (n.d.). Retrieved February 11, 2012, from http://www.w3.org/2001/sw/

Wittgenstein, L. (1973/2009). Philosophical investigations. Wiley-Blackwell. ISBN 1405159286

J. Wypijewski (Ed.). (1997). *Komar and Melamid's scientific guide to art: Painting by numbers*. New York: Farrar Straus Giroux.

Chapter 2
Thinking with Pictures:
Art as an Instrument of Acquiring Knowledge

ABSTRACT

Projects described in this chapter are aimed at enhancing our thinking with pictures. "Thinking with Pictures" encourages the reader to use visual thinking as an instrument of acquiring knowledge, and introduces two projects aimed at developing visual literacy and applying various ways of visual expression. "Collage" introduces collage technique as a tool for visual communication. Two projects provided in this chapter are aimed at enhancing visual literacy and skills. "Sketching a shoe" is intended to amplify one's confidence about one's ability to depict things, and build a feeling of being prepared to make quick drawings on a board or on iPad. This project will encourage the reader to make sketches that strengthen one's own argumentation, show what one wants to be seen, and help to convey one's own solution in a visual way. "Creating a Composition with a Crowd" encourages the reader to draw a group of people and apply visual reasoning by showing background scenery that has an explanatory power. The next part of the chapter tells about collage because one may say without exaggeration that in the digital times most artists apply the form of a collage in their work. The Internet is flooded with ready images, clipart, art, and design samples, intriguing specimens. More importantly, ideas are not copyrighted. Before the advent of computers many artists applied techniques of cutting and pasting readymade material, thus making collages (two dimensional) and assemblages (three dimensional) of different forms.

INTRODUCTION

Workshops, books, and handouts designed to assist non-artists in developing visual literacy contain usually exercises pertaining to the reader's perception (such as: where does your eye go first and where it goes after that), art appreciation (where is the light coming from and how light affects the mood of the image), and ways to communicate about the artwork (e.g., information about the details and people shown in the image, and the creator's possible perspective on the subject). Rhetoric involves effective and persuasive communication through speech or

DOI: 10.4018/978-1-4666-4627-8.ch002

writing. Traditionally, rhetoric involves grammatical purity, clearness, force, and elegance of composition (Hill, 1878/2007). The creation of meaning with the use of visual language is a part of visual rhetoric. Visual rhetoric involves communication with the use of rhetorical figures including metaphors focused on the data, which are aimed at enhancing understanding for the user by inserting figures of connection, comparison for similarity or opposition, and figures of combination – a pictorial simile (Lengler & Vande Moere, 2009). The authors postulate that designers should be educated in principles of rhetoric to become effective in communication in a particular knowledge domain, solve the problems of aesthetics, and achieve visual inference.

According to Semir Zeki (1999, 2001) a neurobiologist at the University College London, the visual brain searches for gaining knowledge about the world. He defines a general function of art as an extension of the major function of the visual brain in a search for the constant, essential features of objects, surfaces, faces, and situations in order to acquire knowledge about a wide category of objects or faces. Therefore, the artist must be selective, choosing the attributes that are essential and discarding the superfluous.

Drawings and graphics can become instruments of thinking. Henry Petroski (1992), the author of comprehensive monograph about a pencil, writes,

The pencil, the tool of doodlers, stands for thinking and creativity, but at the same time, as the toy of children, it symbolizes spontaneity and immaturity. Yet the pencil's graphite is also the ephemeral medium of thinkers, planners, drafters, architects, and engineers, the medium to be erased, revised, smudged, obliterated, lost – or inked over. … Tolouse-Lautrec said of himself, "I am a pencil." (p. 6).

CRITICAL VS. CREATIVE THINKING

It might be a good time to analyze some works of arts, not only in terms of their aesthetic values but also by looking at the content of each image and a message it conveys to the perceiver. In addition to color reproductions published in art books it is easy to browse online (e.g., on Google) for the copies of works of art by typing a title of a masterpiece, a name of an artist, or the artistic style and then select 'Images.' For example, it might be interesting to see how William Blake's (1757-1827) poetic and symbolic paintings (such as "Pity", 1795) show his imaginative, mystical vision of the world. Piero di Cosimo's (1461-1521) "Perseus Freeing Andromeda" (1515) is another example of the imaginative vision of the world inhabited by bizarre monsters.

Integration of art and science in projects proposed in this book may require making many kinds of overlaps between the critical and the visual way of thinking. We may discern types of art that progressively abstract the essence of the picture theme:

- Photography shows everything we see. When we contrast traditional versus digital photographic imaging we may want to pay attention to cognitive processes, both artist's and viewers', in terms of the sending/receiving a message through imaging. The question is, how much image manipulation with the use of software may contradict the statement by Rudolph Arnheim who posed that photographs might affect our observation by singling out accidentals as readily as essentials, and making everything equally important, and that the extremely realistic images may have less symbolic value than the flags and company logos with strong symbolic power (Arnheim, 1990). Rudolf Arnheim (1954/2004) describes composition as the way in which works of art are put together of visual elements like shapes, colors, or movements, such that they create a self-contained, balanced whole and structured in a way that the configuration of forces reflects the meaning of the artistic statement. Elsewhere, composition is defined as the arrangement of visual elements that guides the eye through the work of art. By introducing symbols and metaphors, an artist may help to incorporate some complex concepts and data into a larger entity and hold the user's attention on cognitive processes.

- A portrait painted by an artist enhances characteristics that are specific for a sitter.
- A caricature deliberately exaggerates the subject's distinctive features or peculiarities. It often produces a comic or grotesque effect.
- Artists creating conceptual, non-objective, abstract art, abstract expressionism, or minimalist art have been abstracting unimportant issues.
- Other approaches to abstracting important issues have been taken by artists who developed the generative art. Maybe it is a task for art to de-formalize the websites that are loaded with knowledge, and evoke some cognitive processes that would facilitate absorption of their content. Symbols may support developing the systems of ideas, recognizing particulars, discerning relations and concepts.

A question arises, why so many people do not like abstract art. Maybe liking or not liking abstract images depends on the level of communication and on the understanding of the artist's intention. A message coming from abstract art does not end at the aesthetic level. The mechanism of coding visual messages in art works has been analyzed and discussed with cognitive approach: how the sophisticated language of abstract art conveys messages through the art works, pictograms, cartoons, advertisements, TV messages, animations, and even signs used on the streets. Even earlier, Wassily Kandinsky derived the language of his abstract forms from physiological characteristics of human perception. In a similar way, an American painter Arthur Pinkham Ryder (2012) considered his landscape paintings as being kind of abstract because he conveyed his messages beyond the representational appearance. Decoding the message of the artist is possible on a basis of a code shared by both the artist and the viewer. The essence of the message can be reduced to a simple gesture of a conductor, a selected fragment of a computer program, or a few wooden sticks symbolizing a warrior. In each case there is a signal to the receiver. While cognitive scientists are usually focused on looking for the sources of human communication grounded in precise thinking, artists often use purposefully transformed simple signs to direct the thoughts of viewers.

Another chance for the viewer for getting involved while looking at abstract art seems to depend on the amount of the viewer's previous encounters with various kinds of art, because viewer's sensitivity for aesthetic values of art works may only grow when looking at art. Shapes and configurations in an abstract artwork may evoke associations with other works of art, events, or written materials one might remember. In the postmodern deconstructionist terms, not only representational images may be considered metaphorically rich; they may be understood better when the viewer is knowledgeable about many possible ways of conveying messages that were applied before and stated in artists' manifestos. Abstract artists choose their own means of expression; their paintings are seemed ambiguous and open, with loose relation between signs and meanings. Thus, someone who can see there only the colorful rectangles may, not appreciate the paintings of Mark Rothko, in spite of their recognition in the world of art, and the works of Jackson Pollock may be received as a collection of random splashes of paint.

Many agree that an ability to think abstractly provides an opportunity to perceive problems with a bird's eye view perspective constructed in a somehow similar way as applied by architects who examine imaginary bird's view of a new complex before drawing its detailed blueprint. An artwork presents a stock of meanings with which we think and feel, which everybody is building during lifetime and while appreciating art. Meaning is contained in images: direct (concrete) – perceptions of shapes, colors, motion, that convey meaning (rustle of leafs means danger), and indirect (abstract) – imagery that influences the learning of languages, skills, concepts, and attitudes. The mechanism of coding and preserving visual messages was analyzed and discussed in cognitive terms. With a cognitive approach to design one can bridge the sophisticated language of abstract art with messages coming from pictograms, cartoons, advertisements, TV animations, and even signs used on the streets.

Conveying the very essence of the concept is a crucial part in sending our message or exchanging information and opinions. This is what most of artists do in their art works, sometimes merely through color combination like a Russian/American painter Mark Rothko (1903-1970) or line composition like a Dutch painter Piet Mondrian (1872-1944). There are also artists who portray the exact details of an object and so do the photographs. In such cases the message may convey a feeling of the beauty of nature through art, secure the resemblance of a person for example, for the official record, or of an object such as a family heirloom. However, this kind of exact picturing may not be the best interactive tool for sharing understanding and problem solving.

It is a common belief that exchanging information with others can be more efficient when we present our ideas by drawing. A practitioner's approach is that people can understand things better when they can do it themselves. For this reason it is important to feel confident doing so and not

being reluctant to draw human figures and discernible objects. We can surely be more convincing if our drawings can be recognized as our own ones, so they should have some distinctive features and contain some more than smiley faces and stick figures. The attitude expressed, "I am not a visual person, I can only draw sticky figures" might be popular among technology oriented people in the times from before the advent of the Internet and communication media.

In the following text readers will find many occasions to practice their skills to go beyond sticky figures, starting from an active participation in a "Sketching a shoe" and then "Creating a composition with a crowd " projects.

PROJECT 1: SKETCHING A SHOE TO CAPTURE AN ESSENCE OF AN OBJECT

It is good to feel confident about our drawing to be prepared to enhance our own argumentation with quick, even crude drawings on a board or on iPad, which show what we want to be seen and help to convey our solution in a visual way. This way people see how we unfold our reasoning and can respond spontaneously, making changes themselves. The short project about line drawing can be entertaining when done in company of others. It comprises three phases of sketching, each one with different pace, aimed at abstract representation of an object (see Table 1).

While working on this short project, it might be a right moment to explore the ways line can function in a work of art showing not only forms but also meaning and emotion. Line can make the shortest way between two points or show a path of a point that leads the eye through space. In these cases line is a record of movement and can create illusion of motion in a work of art. There are many ways for playing with lines. We can get a thrill out of looking at cartoons in various il-

Table 1.

Your Visual Response: Line Drawing
Take off your shoe. Examine it for a while in terms of basic lines, proportions and space. Use your shoe as an object to draw. Set up a timer to 3 minutes and start drawing your shoe with a pencil. It is OK to start with ovals and then work like a sculptor, by removing unwanted parts by narrowing some lines and thickening lines where they are needed, so they become descriptive. Do not worry if your lines do not outline the shape you consider perfect. The lines you will add in order to correct your image will bring depth and character to your drawing. Complete your first line drawing in 3 minutes. There will be enough time to apply various ways to vary your lines by changing their width, length, degree of curvature, position, and by adding texture. You may want to draw lines that are thick or thin, wavy, curved or angular, continuous or broken, dotted, dashed or a combination of any of these. Looking at your shoe may cause a need to apply repetition of lines without erasing previous ones. This way your drawing will define and enclose space within a contour of the shoe, show its weight, and even provide an illusion of motion, so your approach will be more imaginative than functional.   The next four phases of this project will consist of sketches of the same shoe, this time done in 2 minutes, 30 seconds, 10 seconds, and finally in 5 seconds. You will have to make fast decisions about what is really crucial for a clear, recognizable depiction of your object. For that reason you will unconsciously abstract unimportant features and draw only lines that are necessary for a viewer to identify a shape of a shoe. Abstracting unimportant details may proceed in a similar way as it happens in the course of designing a road sign, which shows only the essence of the message.   Set up a timer to 2 minutes. Change the position of your shoe and draw it again, but slightly faster. Limit you time to 30 seconds and repeat the previous task. You will now concentrate on the important characteristics of your shoe that make it your own shoe. Because of your time limit, omit all irrelevant details, all its obvious and typical features. It will be a contour drawing that leaves only crucial characteristics of your shoe. After all these attempts you will surely find a way to create a unique portrait of your shoe, almost a caricature of it, with certain specific characteristics exaggerated in a funny way.

lustrated magazines, for example in The New Yorker. We can explore by drawing how different expressive lines can show emotion. The ability to perceive line separated from form can become a major aesthetical skill providing an increased awareness of the visual beauty and function of line. We can also examine how artists use line in their art.

- El Lisitzky (Russian, 1890-1941). "Composition" (1920) shows revolving geometric lines and forms floating in the air, thus creating a sense of depth and an illusion of space (http://www. moma.org/collection/browse_results.php ?criteria=O%3AAD%3AE%3A3569&pa ge_number=18&template_id=1&sort_or der=1).
- Piet Mondrian (Dutch, 1872-1944). "Composition" (1929) is built from simple elements – straight lines and primary colors, and shows balance and order (http://homepages.cwi.nl/~media/projects/ CHIME/mondrian_layout.html
- Morris Louis (American, 1912-1962) applies in his acrylic painting "Alpha Pi" (1961) diagonal parallel lines like a Zen-like spirit of meditation. Louis resigned from shape and light in favor of pure color (http://www.metmuseum.org/toah/ works-of-art/67.232).
- Mario Merz (Italian, 1925-2003), *Unreal City, Nineteen Hundred Eighty-Nine (Città irreale, Millenovecentottantanove)"* (1989), glass, mirror, metal pipes, twigs, rubber, clay, and clamps, 16 feet 4 7/8 inches x 41 feet 11 15/16 inches x 32 feet 8 inches. Merz applies linear elements to create hemispherical structures (http://www.guggenheim.org/new-york/ collections/collection-online/show-full/ piece/?search=Unreal%20City%2C%20 Nineteen%20Hundred%20Eighty-Nine&page=&f=Title&object=89.3631).

PROJECT 2: CREATING A COMPOSITION WITH A CROWD AND AN EXPLANATORY BACKGROUND

Sketching Characters: A Self-Workshop

Many people lack confidence about their ability to draw, especially to draw human figures. They often reassure themselves drawing is not important when one can use a camera. Many claim that there is no need to draw when one may always cooperate with an artist to design a technical project or use a clipart, stock photography or templates. In practice, it often does not work well, as there is a poor understanding between cooperating partners, when an engineer and a computer scientist did not care enough about their visual literacy, and cooperating artists are not savvy enough about technology skills. Moreover, possibilities of creating art go far beyond drawing; visual language and visual literacy are essential to comprehend and interact with communication media. The aim of this project is to overcome such barriers, which are typical of people preoccupied with science, computer science, and technology who feel they have not enough training in the fine arts. This activity will also serve as an introduction to creating visual messages possessing an explanatory power.

With a practitioner's approach in mind, it may be said one can understand things better when one can do it oneself. This short exercise in drawing people may encourage a person who lacks confidence about their ability to draw, especially to draw human figures. This project can also serve for composing a background or a landscape. You will need several pieces of paper, soft pencil (3-6B), and computer with any image editing software (some are downloadable at no charge), a scanner or a digital camera, and a wooden manikin that can easily be found in stores. Pencils range from very hard to very soft, graded in most countries across the world in a continuum from "H" (for hardness) to "B" (for blackness), with "F" (for fine point) in the middle point. A method adopted in the United States uses numbers: #1 for B, #2 for HB, #2$^{1/2}$ for F, #3 for H, and #4 for 2H (Petroski, 1992).

This text comprises some suggestions for the beginners in drawing on a computer screen. This exercise starts with drawing a manikin, then creating a crowd scene composition by multiplying and elaborating the image, and then placing human figures in a background (See Table 2).

Think of a reason why several people might want the same thing and so they gather in an informal way.

Drawing a group of people set in a space that provides visual explanation why they are together (Table 3).

Figures 1-5 are student drawings of a transformed manikin. A picture created by Tiffany Mulford (Figure 1) seems to be focused on showing the dynamics of a group gathered with an unspecified common purpose that was not explained for the viewer: it might be an attempt to make something rotate, a dance, or a performance. Matthew Rodriguez (Figure 2) builds a distance between a viewer and his models by placing them in a virtual place of a framed scene. Garden scenery with leisure activities (by Jason Condon, Figure 3) may invoke in the viewers some connotations of paintings from earlier periods. A scene drawn by Natalie Grapes (Figure 4) makes us think about similar familiar events happening in big cities.

Ambient environment in our picture is a next important factor that contributes to an outcome of our communication effort. A background will explain why those wooden guys are crowding. We may use a background effectively to add meaning to the subject we present and to act on the viewers' reception. The next part of the "Crowd" project is about giving precise meaning of a picture by defining its background.

Create a background: use your visual reasoning about communication and show a visual explanation why these people are crowding. You may do it through designing the background as a visual clue.

It can be a concert hall, a field game scene, a roof to stand under it during the rain, or an approaching bus during a rush hour. Depending on the background the crowd becomes the audience at the concert, viewers of the circus performance, soldiers serving in an army, players, contestants, or competitors. If you prefer doing it all with pencil and paper instead of copying an pasting your manikin, sketch it over and over, scaling down for an illusion of perspective. At this moment your human figures are no longer unidentified, nameless figures – they acquire personality, thus meaning. The relation between human figures and a background in your project can be compared to the relation between the data and information gained when you conduct a search and refers to basic visualization concepts. The data itself has no meaning – it contains just numbers; the numbers gain meaning in context of your search and just become meaningful information. Create your data and their forms of presentation such as patterns, colors, densities, and sizes. You may want to apply metaphorical presentation and organize it around these factors. Draw scenery for your visual story, and at the same time create a clear message. At this moment you can think about composition of your work, make an assessment of your work, and analyze its arrangement, proportions, balance, and symmetry.

By drawing a background you will visualize scenery for your visual story, and at the same time you will create a close message instead of an open one. It will become self-explanatory because everyone will see what you described visually. Many artists use deliberately open messages using symbols or signs that could be freely interpreted and also generated cooperatively by the viewer. Umberto Eco (1979), who studied signs, symbols, and their use for interpretations, examined such open messages and asked: "How to produce texts by reading them." Abstract artists choose their own means of expression, so their paintings gain a feature of an ambiguous, open work with loose relation between signs and meanings. Figure 4 presents a student drawing from a manikin.

Table 2.

Your Visual Response: Drawing a Manikin
Draw a model on paper, or on a computer screen, applying geometrical approach (compare parts of the model to geometrical shapes), and negative/positive space (look at the correlation and coexistance of the negative and positive spaces that belong to the body of the model, and those which do not). For this purpose, you might want to consider three ideas:

1. **Proportion:** Start with applying basic geometric approach to composition by defining proportion of its elements to the whole picture and keeping the body parts in proportion. The head of a man fits seven to eight times in the entire body depending on the man's height – it might be eight times in case of a basketball player. Look at the manikin and think of its head as a unit. Make a mental or sketched division of your entire paper, so eight heads would fit in. This way you will make a grid, a network of lines that cross each other to form rectangles.

2. **Geometric Approach:** Examine your wooden manikin. It is made out of geometric forms; in computer world it is referred to as primitives. Those are the 3-D objects. Start with thinking in terms of 2D objects: an oval, a trapezoid, a circle, a rectangle, etc. By looking at the initial grid you created, start inserting an oval for the head, another one for the neck, a trapezoid for a torso, etc., till you see the whole figure drawn. Make your own individual decisions about dividing your paper with lines and placing shapes into the rectangles of the grid. Think in the same way as you did while drawing a brief sketch of your shoe, and draw only absolutely necessary lines to convey the essence of the human figure.

3. **Positive and Negative Space:** Employ a positive/negative space concept: consider all the space that belongs to your manikin a positive space and all that does not, a negative space. For example, its arm will form a positive space, while the space between an arm and its torso will be considered a negative one. Now, examine the relationship between the positive and the negative space. Like a subtractive sculptor working with clay, keep redefining your lines by making those lines that better define your shapes darker. Do not erase lines, and don't get upset if your hand guides the pencil in an unwanted direction. The triad of lines with different shades of gray will build so demanded depth in your object. Your drawing will not appear flat anymore, but will show an illusion of depth.

Table 3.

Your Visual Response: Drawing a Group of People
When you have drawn your manikin using any image editing software, select the entire drawing. Copy it; create a new canvas making sure that the background is set to transparent. Paste your model. Select all the areas surrounding the model, then press a Delete key. Now the model is on the checkerboard background (transparent). Select all again. Open your new file and title it yourname_crowd.jpg. A distinctive name would help find it later, especially when computers are shared. Applying © sign on your image helps in promoting your work, as well as finding you by one who would like to use your image. Paste your image. This will create a new layer. Now you may transform the object copied. Paste again, transform, etc. Create movement/motion for each wooden manikin's layer. Use Transformations, Filters. Copyright your image: (option g on a mac computer) © 2013 Your Name Save a file with layers for your future reworking: crowd.psd Flatten the image and save as .jpg for web and email. Unless you have drawn your manikin using any image editing software, you may either scan your drawing on paper or photograph it. Open your file using software of your choice, for example in Photoshop (you may try this program for 30 days, before buying it by registering and downloading from the Adobe.com website, download free of charge GIMP – the GNU Image Manipulation Program, or InkScape – an Open Source vector graphics editor). Select your manikin, copy it, and then paste it into a file with a transparent background so your manikin does not have a white area around it. Change the size, transform it by rotating, skewing, or applying perspective, so a manikin that is further away from you will appear smaller than the one that is right in front of you. Repeat these steps several times, so you have a scene with people crowding. Create an impression of motion in your picture by slanting the whole bodies of your figures and changing position of their limbs.

Figure 1. Tiffany Mulford, Crowd. (© 2010, T. Mulford. Used with permission)

Figure 2. Matthew Rodriguez, "Crowd" (© 2010, M. Rodriguez. Used with permission)

Figure 3. Jason Condon, "Crowd" (© 2010, J. Condon. Used with permission)

Figure 4. Natalie Grapes, "Crowd" (© 2010, N. Grapes. Used with permission)

Figure 5. a. Grace Jensen, Crowd (© 2011, G. Jensen. Used with permission). b. Cody Johnson, Crowd (© 2011, C. Johnson. Used with permission).

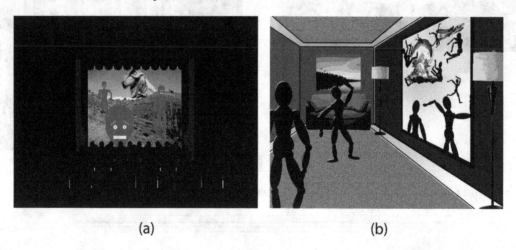

(a)   (b)

Figure 5 shows more student works about a crowd. For Grace Jensen (Figure 5a) a crowd is an audience in a movie theater, while a scene pictured by Cody Johnson (Figure 5b) may seem ambiguous, with unclear relation between individuals placed in front of and inside a framed space. It might be, there are avatars on a screen repeating movements of actors with sensors on their bodies, or two people placed at the front of a glass display case discuss a scene where a fictional action happens, maybe as a virtual reality.

You have just created a composition with an explanatory power. The viewer can look at your composition and understand why those people cluster, crowd, flock, or swarm. Thus, the project becomes visualization introducing light, color, or space to denote the conditions and circumstances relevant to the event depicted and actions taken by the human figures. To show action you may want to add motion into your picture.

COLLAGE

Background Information about Collage

A collage (From the French: *coller*, to glue) has been used primarily in the media related to painting and also in design. In computing practice, a command 'paste' aimed at transferring a digital content may be seen a metaphor of gluing. This may serve as an example of a web-based metaphor. The combining of newspaper clippings, cutouts of colored or hand-made cardboard or paper, fragments of art works, photographs, ribbons, and found objects, thus creating a new whole, and then gluing it to a piece of cardboard or canvas resulted in a particular form of art. Assemblage is an artistic process in which a three-dimensional artistic composition is made from putting together found objects.

There were early precedents of the collage technique. Collage artists used a variety of materials to create collage art. Procedures resembling collage were first used after the invention of paper in China around 200 BC. However, the use of collage was scarce until calligraphers from the 10th century Japan began to apply glued paper, place the lettering on paper, wood, and silk surfaces, and calligraphy their poems there. The technique of collage appeared in medieval Europe during the 13th century. Gold leaf panels, gemstones, and precious metals were applied to religious images, icons, and also to coats of arms.

Georges Braque (1882-1963) and Pablo Picasso (1881-1973) developed modern collage and coined this term in the beginning of the 20th century, and then collage became a distinctive part of modern art. Works of Braque, Fruit Dish and Glass, 1912, papier collé, (http://en.wikipedia.org/wiki/File:Braque_fruitdish_glass.jpg) and Picasso, Three Musicians, 1921 (http://en.wikipedia.org/wiki/File:Picasso_three_musicians_moma_2006.jpg) may serve as examples of this style. With a papier-collé (French: *pasted paper*) type of collage, artists paste paper and cloth into a painting in a similar way as in a collage technique. The glued-on patches colliding with the picture's surface, which Braque and Picasso attached to their canvases, changed the perception of painting. Photomontage has been another method for combining pictures. Combination printing, a process of merging two or more negatives on a single piece of printing paper became popular in the mid-19th century; this technique, introduced by Hippolyte Bayard (1807-1887) allowed avoiding overexposure of the light parts of the image, such as the sky. However, photography had not been the proof of truth any more. Romare Bearden (1912-1988), for example Romare Bearden, The Calabash (1970) created a series of black and white "photomontage projections." His method began with compositions of paper, paint, and photographs put on a board, fixed with an emulsion, and then photographically enlarged. Bearden created also patchwork quilts, cut-and-pasted cloth and paper with synthetic polymer paint placed on a composition board. Paper collages used commercial type of paper manufactured to look like wood. Hence came the idea of gluing wood to a picture to create collage art in wood. Kurt Schwitters (1887-1948, https://sites.google.com/site/tombowersites/kurt-schwitters) began experimenting with wood collages in the 1920s as a continuation of his paper collages.

Surrealist artists implemented innovative strategies of collage using this imagery as a portrayal of the subconscious. Surrealist collages included pictorial collage, verbal collage, and the hybrids of both. The works of Max Ernst (1891-1976, http://www.wikipaintings.org/en/max-ernst/the-eye-of-silence-1943), Rene Magritte (1898-1967, http://en.wikipedia.org/wiki/The_Son_of_Man), or Marcel Duchamp (1887-1968, http://en.wikipedia.org/wiki/File:Duchamp_LargeGlass.jpg) in painting, as well as Paul Eluard (1895-1952), André Breton (1896-1966) in poetry represent this style in the arts. In the 1940s Louise Nevelson (1899-1988, e.g., http://arttattler.com/archivenevelson.

html) assembled her sculptural wood collages from found pieces of wood such as crates or barrels, parts of furniture, and stair railings.

Art works created by Joseph Cornell (1903-1972) were assemblages of found objects in simple boxes, usually glass-fronted, sometimes interactive, where he placed photographs and bric-à-brac objects. Henri Matisse (1869-1954, http://en.wikipedia.org/wiki/Blue_Nude_II) created gouache-painted paper cutouts stuck to paper and mounted on canvas. They were called *gouaches découpés*, which mean the decorations of the surface of an object with paper cutouts. His Blue Nudes series feature prime examples of this technique he called "painting with scissors" (http://www.henri-matisse.net/cut_outs.html).

In the style of Pop Art, Robert Rauschenberg (1925-2008) began to create in the 1950s hybrids between painting and sculpture called combine paintings. He incorporated found objects, found images, and photographs transferred to the canvas by means of the silkscreen process. David Hockney (1937-, http://www.hockneypictures.com/) has also worked with photography and, more precisely, photocollage. Using Polaroid snaps of a single subject Hockney arranged a patchwork to make a composite image.

Niki de Saint Phalle created in the early 1960s a series of collage works "Shooting paintings" created by shooting the reliefs and sculptures with containers of paints buried underneath them (http://www.niki-museum.jp/english/shooting.htm). Tom Wesselmann (1931-2004), a pop art movement artist who worked in painting, collage, and sculpture specialized in found art collages. Wesselmann concentrated on the juxtapositions of different elements and depictions. His painting "Sunset Nude with Matisse Odalisque" contains in the background Matisse's Odalisque with Raised Arms from 1923 (2003, http://www.flickr.com/photos/artimageslibrary/6934290340/). Kara Walker, e.g., http://en.wikipedia.org/wiki/File:Walker_cut.jpg creates room-size tableaux of black cut-paper silhouettes.

Creating a Collage

Themes you may want to choose for your project may include:

1. Nature. The project about nature: you may want to choose either a more realistic theme, for example a flowerbed, animal world, a botanical garden, or a less realistic theme such as an enchanted garden. You may use scanned images or you might prefer to draw pictures by yourself on paper or on a computer. These may be the images of seashells, leaves, pinecones, plants, etc.

2. Architectural themes. You may want to design a house or a city neighborhood. In an image editing software such as Adobe Photoshop, you may use and manipulate the scanned images by layering, resizing, and using other tools and menu options. You may then create a decoupage (by decorating an object with cutouts) in a part of your project; for example, you may want to design an intarsia for a floor, a tabletop, or design a fabric for drapes.

3. Cars and commuting, using scanned toy cars and then drawing a background.

4. People – one may find many themes to choose from.

   a. You may make an image of yourself. Make your self-portrait using both traditional and digital tools. Make a pastiche from your self-portrait. Design your clothing for a particular occasion, and then insert your photo. Change this image, so it fits for various occasions. Then, dress yourself in a different style.

   b. Make a pastiche by drawing a person based on the history of art and then applying a medley of pieces taken from various sources. Using a collage technique, create an image of your real or imaginary friend. Make an interview with this friend, and then create a visual-plus-verbal portrait of this person.

5. Toy animals may also serve for this project; for example, you can dress a scanned stuffed animal. You may also add cutouts of snowflakes: choose an image as a background and then paste multiplied and resized images of snowflakes as a new layer onto the background image.

6. Fantasy based themes.

   a. Create an illustration showing your dream. Apply layers of images, and manipulate your initial image on a computer (for example, by layering, resizing, adding text, and using other tools and menu options.

   b. Create a monster or many monsters. However, make it different than the monsters you have seen in the art of Maurice Sendak, Dr. Seuss, Tim Burton, John Lasseter, or in movies produced by Walt Disney, Dreamworks, or Industrial Light and Magic Studios. Write a verse about your imaginary friends (or monsters), illustrate this poem, and thus create a visual-plus-verbal collage artwork.

   c. You may want to visualize elemental forces of nature, for example Wind, Water, Fire, and Earth.

   d. You may also want to design an everyday product such as a bookmark, book cover, or a postcard.

Media and art forms may differ depending on your choice and according to your project. It may be:

- **Animation**
- **Manga**
- **Storytelling (Verbal and Visual)**
- **Decollage:** Parts cut away from an existing image to reveal another image

- **Decoupage:** the decoration of the surface of an object with paper cut-outs
- **Photomontage:** Cut and folded photos
- **Pastiche:** A work of art that imitates the style of another work or an artist
- **Illustration**
- **Visual Music:** The translation of music into painting or graphics.

Tools, and sources for your projects may include: a digital camera, clipart, or Brushes – a painting application designed for the iPhone, iPod touch, and iPad. The use of copies made on a Xerox machine might be limited by copyright restrictions. Also typography – text as part of an image

The Digital Collage

Digital collage is a whole set of techniques that use electronic media to transform an image and add differing or contrasting visuals. In the digital collages, artists mix digital and traditional resources, juxtaposing natural and man-made objects (for example, leaves, seashells, shoes, newspapers, or tools). Computer montage techniques may be applied by using a number of photo editing programs and online photo editors that let the artist create a photo collage on a computer. Creating a collage can be done in software, for example Adobe Photoshop. Picasa is an online site with a free photo-editing program. Other online sites support collage making, card making, and scrapbooking.

A photographic mosaic may be seen as a continuation of the collage traditions. A photograph or a file created in graphic software can be divided into small sections, and than each section can be replaced with another image or a photograph that matches the original photo.

Traditional photograph may be altered on a computer with the use of filters. Digitally altered art imagery may serve to create collages that enhance the look of the house interior adding it a poetic or gothic style, after changing the coloring of an image, roughing its texture, and adding selected effects (Cartwright, 2007). With scanners and the desktop publishing software with page layout programs it is easy to create visual materials printed in digital form. Photographs, printed media, and artwork are used for creating artwork. They also serve to design scrapbook albums, often containing journalism. Scrapbooks are widely made to preserve personal and family history or serve as a pastime activity done for enjoyment. Digital scrapbooks are often made entirely online, with several kinds of Web-based software for uploading photos, creating a digital scrapbook layout, adding digital scrapbook graphics, and then downloading the low-resolution JPEG files for sharing on the Web or the high-resolution JPEG files for printing. Many digital artists, along with the scrapbook enthusiasts self-publish the professional looking art collages or digital scrapbooks (see Table 4).

The 3D Approaches to Collage

1. Save a box for a product you have bought and used, for example, a shoebox, a box from a bar of soap, or chocolate bars; if possible pick a sturdy one. Put some miniature toys inside and glue some images on the walls of your box. Then work on the interior/exterior composition by placing small objects around the box suggesting a landscape. This way you create a three-dimensional collage based environment. Cut out the space for a window, allowing an eye to see beyond the wall. Film the interior of your box by moving the camera around, then focus on the window and zoom in on the landscape behind the window.

2. Now, think about a theater stage. You may want to present your digital collage as if it was a theatrical stage as seen from a backstage, the theatrical wings. A rectangular box becomes a scene, while the surroundings beyond and above the box are the secret theater-related spaces for the play related tools, machines, and steps needed for the production of a play.

3. This time you will place a city scene into your box. Glue in various types of buildings, sidewalks, a river, people, dogs, cars, and intersections.

4. Grab a round box from a Brie or Camembert cheese. Create a three dimensional scene inside the box, by gluing in furniture, people, or toys. Imagine that the interior of the box is what you would see if you'd look through the keyhole. This project creates an occasion to ponder about the role of various forms of looking through a keyhole, peeping secretly, watching, observing, and invigilating. One may imagine many reasons for such activities such as performing a detective work, because of a lack of trust about somebody's actions, compulsive curiosity, nosiness, for security reasons, for self-defense, or to sift out unsuitable contacts. One may also find the keyhole analogies in everyday life, starting from checking the phone calls, through monitoring toddlers, psychiatric patients, or prisoners, to the work of air marshals, security operative agents, bodyguards, private and criminal investigators, or the IRS inspectors, and also paparazzi photographers. In a broader sense of this metaphor, one may say that the writers, biology-inspired scientists, bio-inspired computing specialists, birdwatchers, or surgeons performing postmortem examination gather information by looking without knowledge from the part of the observed. In even broader sense, our senses are the tools for such activities.

5. Now apply several techniques (if possible) to get a picture of your box: use a scanner, a copier, a digital camera, and video recording. Choose a solution that provided the best, most interesting result after you have transferred the images into your computer.

Table 4.

Your Visual Response: Create a Digital or a Mixed Media Collage
Chose a topic for your collage or select a theme from options listed above in this chapter: nature, architectural topics, cars and commuting, people, toy animals, or fantasy-based themes.   For this project, you may go back and forth using both traditional and digital media and tools.   • You can draw a picture,   • Gather some pictures from variety of sources,   • Print photographs,   • Apply a multi-negative picture technique,   • Drop some paint on your project or paint on a computer generated printout,   • Apply a photomontage compositing technique,   • Use clipart,   • Scan 3-d objects   • Use Brushes application designed for the iPhone, iPod touch, and iPad.

CONCLUSION: INTENTIONS AND CONCERNS

Each artist can choose to create an artwork by looking from a distance at a wall-size image: a monitor or a projection from a computer screen and using a hardware, a keyboard and a mouse placed conveniently by the hand. Thus, there is enough distance to examine the artwork, and the effects of applying particular brushstrokes or other tools, with no more scrolling the image on a monitor, nor walking back and forth from the surface of the canvas to the spot that allows for a good examination of the artwork. A possibility of creating brilliant colors and seeing them from a distance provides excellent conditions for creating a good quality electronic art, whether the 2-D, 3-D, interactive, time-based, or virtual 3-D forms.

Whatever would be a medium or a meaning of the work of an artist, there is still an ongoing discussion on the importance of the quality of the artwork. With all the variety of the media and technical tools and a trade-off between pressure of knowledge and a need for a discipline in the creative process, an exposure to electronic artwork may evoke in the viewers a need for the reconsideration of a question, whether artists use the computer to its fullest artistic potential and respond to technical developments with quality artwork. Also, whether they attain a composition free from unnecessary technical sophistication resulting from a desire to employ all possibilities provided by the deceitfully attractive hardware and software. According to some jurors' statements, the quantity of the types of software used and the trickery of their application does not account for the visual quality of the images sought for by the jurors.

Drawings and graphics can become instruments of thinking. The creation of meaning with the use of visual language is a part of visual rhetoric. Capturing the meaning in projects proposed in the second part of this chapter may require making many kinds of overlaps between the critical and the visual way of thinking. Conveying the very essence of the concept is a crucial part in sending our message or exchanging information and opinions; this is what most of artists do in their art works. Meaning contained in images may be direct (concrete) – perceptions of shapes, colors, motion, and indirect (abstract) – imagery that influences the learning of languages, skills, concepts, and attitudes. The mechanism of coding and preserving visual messages was analyzed and discussed in cognitive terms. One of the tasks for art may be also to de-formalize the websites that are loaded with knowledge, and evoke some cognitive processes that would facilitate absorption of their content.

Readers of this chapter have been encouraged to actively participate in a "Sketching a shoe" and then "Creating a composition with a crowd" projects.

Transferring a digital content may be seen a metaphor of traditional collage. Early precedents of the collage techniques come from ancient times and technique of collage appeared in art of almost all ages and countries. Description of the technique comprises explanation of themes, media, art forms, and tools, including the 3D approaches to collage and digital collage, which is a set of techniques using electronic media to transform an image and add differing or contrasting visuals.

REFERENCES

Arnheim, R. (1954/2004). *Art and visual perception: A psychology of the creative eye, fiftieth anniversary printing*. Berkeley, CA: University of California Press.

Arnheim, R. (1990). Language and the early cinema. *Leonardo, Digital Image*, 3-4.

Bearden, R. (1970). *The Calabash*. Retrieved November 20, 2011, from http://en.wikipedia.org/wiki/File:Romare_Bearden_-_The_Calabash,_1970,_Library_of_Congress.jpg

Hill, A. S. (1878/2007). *Principles of rhetoric and their application*. New York: Harper and Brothers. Retrieved November 28, 2012, from http://archive.org/stream/principlesofrhet00hilluoft#page/n1/mode/2up

Lengler, R., & Vande Moere, A. (2009). Guiding the viewer's imagination: How visual rhetorical figures create meaning in animated infographics. In *Proceedings of the 13th International Conference on Information Visualization*. doi 10.1109/IV.2009.102

Petroski, H. (1992). *The pencil: A history of design and circumstance*. New York: Alfred A. Knopf.

Zeki, S. (1999). Art and the brain. *Journal of Conscious Studies: Controversies in Science and the Humanities*, 6(6/7), 76–96.

Zeki, S. (2001). Artistic creativity and the brain. *Science*, *293*(5527), 51–52. doi:10.1126/science.1062331 PMID:11441167.

Chapter 3
Art Resulting from Computing

ABSTRACT

This chapter examines many types of new media art that are being created with computing. Displaying art becomes a tool for exchanging information and ideas that also creates channels for the viewers' input through digital art interactive events. Biology inspired computing applied for artistic tasks has often a mutual relationship with scientific research involving evolutionary computing. Net art, along with other electronic art media, may be seen closely related to the semantic networks and social networking media. Many times these media provide computational solutions for entertainment.

INTRODUCTION: PROGRAMMING AND ART

Computer graphics and art may be created through writing algorithms – instructions for determining sequential steps for carrying out operations, which result in a work of art. They have been considered the solution of choice, especially before the advent of graphic software packages and applications, being a merger between a programmer and design, ready for creating computer art graphics. Changing a pre-written code is also a solution, using for example, Processing.org., HTML, Blender with Python + HTML, or by combining either augmented reality or virtual reality with actions performed by an user. There are many ways of creating art that utilize technology without writing programs. An artwork based on a photo manipulated scanned image may be drawn on a computer screen with the use of graphic or painting software. One may

also apply digital multimedia packages, videotape animated sequences of those images immersed in a computer graphics-created environment, and stimulate real time interactive communication through art. Pictures made with computer programs and scene description languages to provide three-dimensional, or animated images may be projected on a screen. Transformed image may also be brought into the visualization system or the virtual reality 3D immersive world to develop interrelationships between some media. Structures can be shared or translated between media and thus we may construct both the new forms and the meaning of these media. In this process, we combine computation and thought representation. This way, we may visualize images, forms, music, poetics, and interactive fiction. We may also make metaphors of inter-sensory synaesthetic experience in the real time interactive systems or enhance virtual communication over the web.

Figure 1, "Birdcage, Sometimes a Dome" is a sculpture made after computer program. Ro-

DOI: 10.4018/978-1-4666-4627-8.ch003

tational ellipsoid has been selected as a form of choice to assemble a three-dimensional structure. A synthetic, almost abstract appearance of this wooden sculpture may be interpreted as a framework for an architectural structure or another construction; we host our pets in forms resembling our own edifices.

Realities created with the use of programming refer to our imagination and experience that are based on physiological reality of the mind. Not only the well-trained eye of a mathematician can perceive the sense of mathematical beauty. Sculptors render appealing forms which are, sometimes even without their knowledge, perfectly fitting mathematical equations. With the use of program-

ming, artists create shapes and forms that represent the beauty of mathematics: multi-dimensional spaces, hyperbolic planes, and fractal-like repetitions. They as well produce intriguing natural forms that obey the rules of equations, such as the Nautilus shell. Mehrdad Garousi (2012, p. 28), who creates pure fractals without use of image processing software, considers fractal art a conjunction of art, mathematics, and computer technology because of simultaneous existence of order and disorder, chaos and regularity, and complexity and self-similarity.

Figure 1. a. Anna Ursyn, Birdcage, Sometimes a Dome (© 1988, A. Ursyn. Used with permission). b. Maple, after 3-D computer program outputted into a plotter. VAX mainframe, Interactive Graphic Library (IGL), FORTRAN 77

(a) (b)

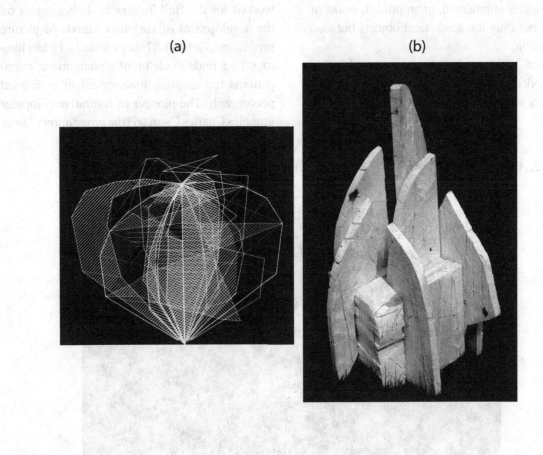

MANY TYPES OF ART CREATED WITH COMPUTING

Programs written in computer languages may serve for creating traditional forms of art and design, such as drawing, painting, sculpture, photography, as well as for the interactive arts including installations, web-based and multimedia projects, 3D animation, performances, and experimental works. Art created and often displayed with the use of computers has been first designated as generative art, computer art, electronic art, digital art, or algorithmic art. Authors often use the terms electronic art, computer art, and digital art interchangeably, when they these categorize art forms into several groups and describe generative art, interactive installations, video and animation art, web art, electronic music, and information art (that links computer science with information technology). For example, Redström, Skog & Hallnäs (2000, p. 103) define informative art as "computer augmented, or amplified, works of art that not only are aesthetical objects but also information.

Figure 2, "Motor Hotel" is an example of an early work created with an aid of black-and-white computer software Mac Paint.

Early Art Works Created with an Aid of Computers

History of computer art began in the mid-1960s in several places at the same time, originated by many artists. It could be first traced as a history of computer graphics, with the first contests, statements, criticism, and research in aesthetics and art theory. First computer graphics were created to solve some aircraft industry's problems. The term itself was coined in 1960 by the Boeing aircraft company, which used computer graphics to solve some aircraft industry's problems: to simulate landing on a runway and to anticipate possible movements of a pilot sitting in the cockpit. William A. Fetter developed his computer graphics in connection with research on flight technology and flight psychology. In 1962 Ivan Sutherland created the "Sketchpad," the first interactive system; this invention allowed creating a graphical user interface. Kenneth C. Knowlton and Leon D. Harmon worked for the Bell Telephone Laboratories on the development of various methods of picture processing. In 1966-67 they created a 12 feet long mural – a nude made up of alphanumeric micro patterns representing tone values of a scanned photograph. The pioneer of figurative computer graphics Charles Csuri and the programmer James

Figure 2. Anna Ursyn, Motor Hotel (© 1986, A. Ursyn. Used with permission)

Schaffer produced successive transformations of pictures and computer sculptures. Charles Csuri created in 1966 his works 'Sine Curve Man' and 'Hummingbird.'

The first computer art contest was opened in 1963 in the magazine "Computers and Automation." A graphic design that was made as an exercise in aesthetics was awarded the second prize. The first exhibition of computer graphics took place in 1965 in the New Howard Wise Gallery. "Cybernetic Serendipity" was the major exhibition emphasizing computer art. It was introduced in London in 1968 by Jasia Reichardt (1968) and traveled extensively throughout the United States.

Robert Mallary developed a concept of a highly integrated synesthesia of image and sound in space as a result of 45 years of his involvement with electronic art. In 1967 Artist Robert Rauschenberg and Bell Labs engineer Billy Klüver started Experiments in Art and Technology (E.A.T.) in New York. In the late sixties a number of centers, such as the freshly founded MIT, Tektronix, Intel, and University of Utah started programs in computer graphics. Then came fascination with technical achievements and the excellence of renderings of objects brought about an abundance of realistic pictures (such as checkered marbles bouncing on a checkered floor). Experiments were also conducted on production of music generated by a computer in various historical styles.

From 1973, the annual ACM/Siggraph (Association for Computing Machinery/Special Interest Group on Computer Graphics, formed in 1969) international conferences on computer graphics and interactive techniques have developed into a prominent forum for the exchange of ideas about computer graphics between presentation designers, web designers, data analyzers, and artists. Art exhibitions at the Siggraph conferences began in 1980. In the 1987 Siggraph Art Show, artwork was exhibited in five categories: Abstract, Visual Research, Human Image, Graphic Design, and Landscape. The Siggraph 1988 exhibition "The Interactive Image" included seven interactive

works, 12 installations and 12 video works. The first Siggraph Art Show Catalog was published in 1982. Written essays have been included in the Siggraph '89 Art Show Catalog and published in Leonardo, Journal of the International Society for the Arts Sciences and Technology. These essays considered the art tradition as a part of the history of culture rather than the history of the technologies employed by artists. Artists, historians, educators, scientists, and critics explore the wide range of views regarding the ways in which the computer extends the practice of art, as well as the meaning of computer art in visual communication. They join with engineers, designers, researchers, scientists, cartographers, animators and other enthusiasts to share ideas on the developments and applications in computer graphics and interactive techniques, and to cooperate in educational programs. The last few years witnessed the moderate interest in two dimensional, non-interactive art works, with 16 works (out of over 300 submissions) accepted in 2011 and 12 works (out of nearly 400 submissions) accepted in 2012. You may want to visit an ACM/Siggraph online gallery, find works of artists accepted to the Art Shows in the years 1997-2007 at http://www.siggraph.org/programs/artdesign/ and examine evolution of trends and solutions in this period of time.

Algorithmic art is mostly generated by an algorithm devised by an artist – "a set of rules that precisely defines a sequence of operations" and "must terminate in a finite number of steps" (Stone 1972: 7–8). Artists launched art works by writing a program before many kinds of user-friendly graphics software were developed. Algorists created mostly visual art determined by a computer code, functions and expressions contained in computer input, thus designing the generative system.

With the advance of the two-dimensional and three-dimensional computer graphics software designed to create computer-generated imagery artists, architects, mathematicians, and scientists could create without programming computer art graphics, sculptures, models, games, visualizations, animations, simulations, industrial projects, and other art forms. Some inexperienced in art use clipart and import images from the Internet. Mathematicians have been building bridges between computing and art, often by calculating fractal objects and creating diverse types of software, modeling, simulation, and computer art. Paul Fishwick (2008) describes the goals of aesthetic computing as associated with introducing aesthetic variety to visualization projects. For example, one can personalize mathematics and computer science to achieve a richer aesthetic landscape.

Images programmed on the computer have been extended beyond the computer screen and used for creating other forms of art. These approaches include simulation representing the real world by a computer program, biological growth patterns, artificial intelligence aimed at creating intelligent agents, robotics that develop computer systems to control the robots' design, construction, operation, and application, visualization that convert information into pictorial form, or stereoscopic HDTV animation. Projects introduce several levels of interactivity aimed at the web art and at interactive or performance-based video installations, site-specific installations, multichannel video pieces interconnecting films, music, sculptures, drawings, and photographs, animated film, interactive art, virtual environment, augmented reality, etc. Websites using 3D, containing interactive 3D material embedded into the html (HyperText Markup Language) used for creating web pages host art projects that can be seem through a web browser (web 3D viewer). In Web 3D, user interfaces allow interacting of the human sense of space with programming languages; thus Web3D is a body/group that defines formats related to the 3D content on the web.

Artists are now collaborating with scientists to draw the data from scientific visualizers; they have been contributing to scientific visualization projects with their scanned data based sculptures and curves based on parametric equations (Wilson,

2010). Art may show the paths of electrons after starting them in a bean. Also, transfer to other media resulted in a coherent whole, utilizing geometric figures recurring in art through the ages now written in computer codes, and the fractal designs, sometimes applying lenticular printing of the 3D images. Mathematical models of hyperbolic space that spreads infinitely in all directions resulted in spatial expansion of physical materials.

Figure 3 presents a work "Red Dress" that records how our mental images of favorite books, toys, and meaningful memories embody a meaning and accompany us in our ventures.

Going to the City,
Gazing at it from above, in front of, and inside.
Living there, among shops, stores, warehouses,
Grasping its self-identity.

Taxonomy of Art Created with the Use of a Computer

Discussion of the role of creativity in a creative process becomes even more complicated with the advent of many new types of art. Boden and Edmonds (2009, p. 28-37) proposed taxonomy of computer art that distinguishes eleven types of art. Boden (2010, p. 134; 2009, p. 31) examined the part played by creativity in these types of art.

1. **Electronic Art:** Ele-art is any artwork whose production involves electrical engineering and/or electronic technology.
2. **Computer Art:** C-art uses computers (first analogue, now mostly digital) as part of the art-making process.
3. **Digital Art:** D-art uses digital electronic technology of some sort, including human-produced and digitally manipulated music and video.
4. **Computer-Aided (or Computer-Assisted) Art:** CA-art uses computer as an aid (in principle, non-essential) in the art-making process.

Figure 3. Anna Ursyn, Red Dress (© 2004, A. Ursyn. Used with permission)

5. **Generative Art:** G-art is generated, at least in part, by some process that is not under the artist's direct control. The computer generates the result all by itself. The AI system might be credited with creativity (Boden, 2009, p. 31).

6. **Computer Generated Art:** CG-art results from some computer program being to run by itself, with minimal or zero interference from a human artist.

7. **Evolutionary Art:** Evo-art evolved by process of random variation and selective reproduction that affect the art-generating program itself. It relies on programs with self-modifying processes called genetic algorithms. The fitness function (decided by the artist/programmer) allows choosing candidates for breeding the next generation (Boden & Edmonds, 2009, p. 33). Much of the creativity may be credited to the AI system itself – not just its human originator, for the computer program produces novel results – images or melodies, for instance – that the human artist couldn't predict, or even imagine (Boden, 2009, p. 31).

8. **Robot Art:** R-art is the construction of robots for artistic purposes, where robots are

physical machines capable of autonomous movement and/or communication.

9. **Interactive Art:** In I-art the form/content of the artwork is significantly affected by the behavior of the audience. Some or all of the creativity is attributed to the programmer or the human participants, while the interactive program is designed to produce aesthetically attractive/interesting results in noncreative ways (Boden, 2009, p. 31).

10. **The Computer-Based Varieties:** CI-art, where the form/content of some CG artwork is significantly affected by the behavior of the audience: the voluntary (such as walking, touching the computer screen), largely automatic yet controllable actions (such as the direction of eye-gaze), and involuntary bodily movements (such as breathing) or physical factors (such as the radiation of body-heat) (Boden & Edmonds, 2009, p. 35). CI-art is generative art by definition.

11. **Virtual Reality Art:** VR-art where the observer is immersed in a computer-generated virtual world, experiencing it and responding to it as if it were real.

Along with the increasing role that computers play in a visual image creation grows the input of the website visitors and the museumgoers. Edmonds, Bilda, & Muller (2009) discussed the roles of an artist, curator, and evaluator on the functioning of the art system consisting of the dynamic interactive artwork, the audience, and the environmental context. They consider evaluation of interactive artworks in a public space a part of the creative process, as it enables the artists to observe and reconsider their work, engage the audience, and support the curatorial work.

"Continental Divide" (Figure 4) depicts advancement toward evolving, ever transforming targets through the winding, dividing ways no matter it is about mountain roads or trends in generative art.

Figure 4 Anna Ursyn, Continental Divide (© 2007, A. Ursyn. Used with permission)

*A well-known path goes on among the road
forks and viaducts,
On an upward slope and down dale,
To reveal the next vistas.*

According to Garry Greenfield (2010), "Algorithmic art refers to art, when the creative design results from an algorithmic process." Originators of this trend in art are "Charles Csuri, Georg Nees, Frieder Nake, William Fetter, Herbert W. Franke, A. Michael Noll, Edward Zajec, Roman Verostko, Kenneth Knowlton, Manfred Mohr, Jean-Pierre Hébert, and Yoichiro Kawaguchi" (Greenfield, 2010, p. 12). The term generative art is often applied to works created, composed, or constructed not only in algorithmic manner but also based on computer software algorithms. Artists may download from the Internet generative programs or generative systems that yield patterns. Digital art was originally describing paintings, drawings, and sculptures created with the use of digital technology; later on, art works created with electronic media technologies such as digital art, computer graphics and animation, sound, kinetic sculpture, video, interactive displays and installation art, generative art, bio art, robotics, virtual art, Internet art, art based on biotechnology, evolutionary art, and many other approaches, the names computer art and multimedia art became combined into the general concept and evolved into an art genre called new media art. New media content is accessible on demand, interactive with participants, often collaborative and networkable, among other qualities. Works perceived as new media art are usually involved in basic questions about art, scientific connections, and/or social and cultural activism.

Electronic media, which may be in either analog or digital format (however the majority of them are digital) consist of many forms such as computer graphics, video and audio recordings, slide and multimedia presentations, CDs, and online content. In digital media, data are stored and transmitted in digital form online through networking information and stored on hard drives as files of data or program records, video recordings, art works, augmented or virtual reality environments, or digital signage displays, among other forms. Multimedia art can take many forms – from the computer screen, to the movement of the body on a platform, to the acoustic space of digital music, and thus may involve text, body, space, sound, and image. Electronic media as a medium in art comprises graphics, sound, interactivities, and a variety of creative applications such as web art, games, animation, video, performance, and installations. Many uses of electronic media include journalism, marketing, education, science and engineering, commercial or professional business, simulation and visualization techniques, communication media, entertainment, and fine art.

Art Theories and Art Production Versus Scientific Theories and Technologies

Art theories and art production evolve according to the advances in scientific theories and technologies. In many instances, both in the past and now, artists themselves, for example Piero della Francesca or Leonardo da Vinci, changed the established way of thinking about technologies and procedures as they generated new theoretical trends. One may see the sequence: artist>message>recipient of art in semiotic terms. Impressionist and Post-Impressionist artists, modernist artists from different groups such as the Vienna Secession, the Art Nouveau or Jugendstil, Symbolist and surrealist artists, Russian Constructivists, photography artists, the Bauhaus School, Abstract Expressionists and the New York School, Futurists, Minimalist artists, all developed theories about art and then (sooner or later) convinced critics and viewers about their premises, changing the reception of art.

Several solutions in art production draw from the old techniques, so one can often make comparisons with old masters. Artists and programmers develop nature-inspired projects, adopt novel technologies, and apply new algorithms as tools for generative art creation, to present their products at art- and technology-oriented events. For instance, Theo Jansen installs his wind-powered sculptures on a beach, so they are able to march, powered by natural force of wind (Frazier, 2011). Artists engage the visual, kinesthetic, auditory, and tactile means of expression for their art. For example, sound art is an interdisciplinary, hybrid art form that involves audio and visual media, computing, analog and digital technology, psychoacoustics, and electronics. Artists explore man-made and environmental sound, combining their production with architecture, sculpture, experimental theatre, film, and video. Works classified as belonging to the Dadaist, Surrealist, or Fluxus movements evolved into computerized happenings and installations that may be seen as belonging to the conceptual, site-specific, sound poetry, or visual music genres. Artists also use mathematical forms to create graphical or sculptural works. Helaman Ferguson (1994, 2010) who applies mathematical formula to programmed carving, sculpts in stone and casts in bronze. He carries out the subtractive process using the computer tool position and orientation to gain computed quantitative information, and thus objects that follow mathematical formula take form in such materials as stone and bronze.

Creating musical compositions by directly translating data to sound is called sonification. Sonification and the visual music movement represent the ideas related to synesthesia, a unity of the senses and, by extension, synthesis of the arts. Examples of the approaches to visual presentation of music and sound include artwork sonification and environmental problems sonification. Visual music created by Evans (2007) may serve as an example of a sonification as an artwork. Sonification became a tool to address environmental problems. For example, Andrea Polli (2003) created the "Datareader" software for data sonification, and another software "The Fly's Eye" for creating animated documents, installations, and prints. Another series of her

sonifications illustrate changes focused on the heart of New York City and one of the city's first locations for climate monitoring, Central Park. A web visualization and sonification shows wind speeds and directions during the most intense 24 hours of Hurricane Bob in 1991.

Since the seventies, a Chicago-based art collective (art)^n laboratory founded by Ellen Sandor produces PHSColograms, computer generated, three-dimensional digital backlit photographs, sculptures and installations (PHSCologram is a barrier-strip similar in principle to the lenticular printing that provides illusion of depth) and lenticular autostereograms (autostereoscopy is a method of displaying stereoscopic images without the use by the viewer of special headgear or glasses). Artists from the (art)^n laboratory make also virtual photography – the process of taking photos of a virtual world rather than of real world.

The landscape of art and design creation has changed when Casey Reas and Benjamin Fry (2007) from the Aesthetics and Computation Group at the MIT Media Lab developed Processing http://processing.org/, a free to download, open source programming language and environment for people who want to create images, animations, and interactions, which evolved into a tool for generating finished professional work. Students, artists, designers, researchers, and hobbyists use Processing for learning, prototyping, and production. Casey Reas and Benjamin Fry won in 2005 the Golden Nica award from Ars Electronica.

Art communities and Internet based collective enterprises formed networks to produce cooperative networked art under the names like net.art, art on the net, or web art. Some groups, such as 0100101110101101.org were performing in the nineties collective interventions such as cloning, plagiarizing, and art hacktivism. Installations using wall-size display technology and viewers' interaction, 'focus-plus-content' screens showing details with higher resolution, and aligning objects with 'snap and go' technique (Baudisch, 2006) were followed by the developments in touch screen technology, where touch screens are replacing the use of mice and keyboards, or joysticks. Scientists design information interfaces and touch devices, such as touch screens to optimize the input technologies in human-computer interaction and to avoid errors, due to the good understanding of the touch sense. Holz and Baudisch (2011) argue that users employing the visual features of a target when they align with the screen as their target interface. The visual features are located on the top of the user's fingers, but not at the bottom (with the center of the contact area between finger and device), as assumed by traditional devices. Users can see their fingertips and imagine where the crosshairs intersect, and thus they can visualize the bottom of their finger and always position it at the same location.

An increasing number of artists have been engaged in environmental issues (such as climate change), destructive events caused by earthquakes, floods, or tsunami, and accidents (the Fukushima nuclear accident, explosion at Chernobyl). Artists' visual engagement in the crisis includes communication through information visualization and art works based on online analysis of the data and news media, among other activities (Hoetzlein, 2011). As noticed by Giannachi (2011), artists' commitment in response to climate change takes form of the strategies of representation through visualization and communication; performance environments providing an experience of immersion; and interventions emphasizing mitigation and behavioral change.

Figure 5, "Canopy" metaphorically expresses perception of a city as a self-defined entity resembling a tropical forest, and at the same time the visual engagement in the forest preservation issues.

City life surrounds us and closes above our heads. We have to push for space amongst buildings. Speed is a necessity (pizza is paid for if on time); we compete for a taxi, a table, a parking space, and run to a metro station without knowing if the train is approaching.

From the canopy of buildings we escape under the canopy of trees in majestic forest, until we learn, from our own experience or from the David Attenborough's programs, how much life of tropical forest can resemble our own.

Displaying Art, Exchanging Information and Ideas

New media art galleries select specific categories for each event or show, be it a wall based computer graphics art, interactive art installation or environment, performance, artist book, animation/video, robotics, web-based artwork, or time-based installation. An extensive collection of art works and technical projects can be seen at online galleries and in physical existence, for example, at ACM/ SIGGRAPH Art galleries, Ars Electronica, Evo-Musart conferences focused on evolutionary and biologically inspired music, sound, art, and design, and in many other events. Ars Electronica comprises several platforms for digital art and media culture: Festival for Art, Technology, and Society; Prix Ars Electronica, International Competition for Cyber-Arts; Ars Electronica Center, which is Museum of the Future; and Ars Electronica Future Lab, Laboratory for Future Innovations.

For many years visual and material artists, biological researchers, and neuroscientists participate in the Evolutionary Music and Art events to discuss evolutionary and bio-inspired music, sound, art and design, and techniques such as evolutionary computation, artificial life, artificial neural networks, and swarm intelligence (Di Chio et al., 2010a, Di Chio et al., 2010b). In collaborative and hybrid artistic projects biology-inspired research results are combined with the use of genetic algorithms, adaptive formal and structural design, architectural approaches, and new fabrication techniques. The EvoNet, the European Network of Excellence in Evolutionary Computing uses biotechnology as its medium, and applies evolutionary computing. EvoMusart events on Evolutionary and Biologically Inspired Music, Sound, Art and Design in-

Figure 5. Anna Ursyn, Canopy (© 2008, A. Ursyn. Used with permission)

troduce advancements in the use of bio-inspired techniques (such as evolutionary computation, artificial life, artificial neural networks, swarm intelligence, etc.) in the scope of the generation, analysis and interpretation of art, music, design, architecture and other artistic fields. Biologically inspired design and art-making systems create drawings, images, animations, sculptures, poetry, text, objects, designs, websites, buildings, etc. Biologically inspired sound-generators and music-systems create music, aggregate sound, or simulate instruments, voices, and effects. At the EvoMUSART events, evolutionary art includes also robotic-based evolutionary art and music, and other related generative techniques. The 9th European Event on Evolutionary and Biologically Inspired Music, Sound, Art and Design (Evo, 2011) brought together researchers interested in: generation (for example, biologically inspired design- and art-making systems, sound generators and music systems, and robotic based evolutionary art and music), theory (such as computational aesthetics, representation techniques, analyses, validation, and biologically inspired computation models in art, music, and design), computer-aided creativity, integrative and collaborative distributed artificial art environments, and automation.

The online forums such as Digital Art Gallery D-ART, the NanoArt21 Art/Science/Technology online gallery, and many other online galleries, along with a large number of physical settings have been serving in the late 20th and the 21st century for displaying art or exchanging information and ideas: Der Prix Ars Electronica International Computer Graphics Contest, Linz, Austria; Documenta, Kassel, Germany; Venice Biennale, Venice, Italy; ACM/SIGGRAPH Art Galleries, various locations, (Vancouver, Canada, 2011); SIGGRAPH Asia, various locations (Hong Kong, 2011); FILE Electronic Language International Festival, many locations (Brazil 2011, comprising works of webart, netart, artificial life, hypertext, computerized animation, real-time teleconference, virtual reality, soft art, games, interactive films, e-videos, digital panoramas, and installations of electronic art and robotics, through interactive and immersive rooms; evo conferences in evolutionary computing, with EvoMusart and Evostar events on Evolutionary and Biologically Inspired Music, Sound, Art, and Design, (Malaga, Spain, 2012); ISEA, Inter-Society for the Electronic Arts, various locations (Istanbul, Turkey, 2011); 404 Art and Technology Festival, many locations, (Buenos Aires, Argentina 2011); New York Digital Salon, 1993-2009, NY, USA; Bridges: Mathematical Connections in Art, Music, and Science, various locations (e.g., Coimbra U., Portugal, 2011, Baltimore, Maryland, USA, 2012); The Joint Mathematics Meetings Exhibitions of Mathematical Art, Boston, MA, USA; GA - Generative Art International Conferences, Roma and Milan, Italy; NanoArt21 International Festivals, various locations; Burning Man annual events, Nevada's Black Rock Desert, USA; Biannual Computer Art competitions, Museum der Stadt Gladbeck, Germany; Japan Media Arts Festival, different locations (Tokyo, Japan, 2011); Common Ground International Travelling Exhibitions, Digital Art+Green Values=Global Impact, Merging Art and Digital Media for a Healthy Planet, Los Angeles, CA, USA; GRAPHITE – International Conferences on Computer Graphics and Interactive Techniques in Australasia and South Asia, various locations; and many others.

Creating Channels for Viewers' Input: Digital Art Interactive Events

Artists investigate and present at digital art exhibitions the interactive systems and artistic interface designs: tangible interfaces such as mouse and keyboard, or joysticks, intangible interfaces that allow interactive performance based on position of the viewers, face recognition, expression, gesture, voice mapping, or bio-interfaces, which propose a physicality and ubiquity of a physiological nature (Zuanon, 2012). According to Zuanon, the adoption of bio-interfaces for the areas of design, art, and games turns significantly the forms of participation and audience interaction with these systems. Artists project their art at architectural facades (often applying solar powered display), create interactive video art installations and reactive sculptures, using computer animations, stereo images, interactive displays reacting to the presence of the viewers, video clips online, HD video clips, slow motion video, footage from electronic art events, collections of animated works, and using vimeo to share their work with others. A few examples of artists creating dynamic, interactive works and are Yoichiro Kawaguchi, the Japanese computer artist who mainly works in the area of HD TV and experiments with organic shapes (e.g., http://www.siggraph.org/artdesign/gallery/S99/animation/artificial_life.html), Camille Utterback who creates texts interactively combined by the viewers from falling letters (http://90.146.8.18/en/archives/picture_ausgabe_03_new.asp?iAreaID=49&showAreaID=49&iImageID=2016), and Christa Sommerer & Laurent Mignonneau who create interactive paintings; for example The Value of Art (Unruhige See, 2010) deals with the economy of attention, measured with sensors that count the number of visitors and the amount of time they spend looking at the painting, and the value of art in the art world (e.g., http://universes-in-universe.org/eng/specials/2011/global_contemporary/photo_tour/38_christa_sommerer_laurent_mignonneau).

Electronic art events prized at the international forums in most cases combine artistic statement with real life applications, biology inspired research, therapeutic implementations, or environmental concerns. For example, the 2011 Ars Electronica awards included a performance 'May the Horse Live in Me,' a hybrid bioart pertaining to a research on immunological barriers between species. Golden Nica awarded "The Eye Writer" created by a team working on creating an eye-tracking system that will allow patients with Lou Gehrig's disease, who cannot control voluntary muscle movement, to draw using just their eyes. A project "Pigeon d'Or" was awarded for an attempt to use pigeons as interface for synthetic biology in an urban environment, by designing bacteria (harmless to pigeons) that turn feces into detergent, so pigeons defecate biological window soap. The ACM/SIGGRAPH Art Gallery made the highlights of the event works that reflected environmental and social concerns, for example, an inflatable sculpture 'Moston' - a technology-driven amalgamation of Moscow and Boston that contained documentary footage projection; an installation 'tele-present wind' that causes the plant stalks in a gallery sway; and a telematically shown 'Open House' that mirrors virtual markets and creates hybrid subjects who occupy both virtual and physical space.

Interactive interfaces may serve the artistic goals or meet various everyday needs. Oh, Kim, Kim, & Shi (2011) created a prototype of a "Magic Monkey" – an interactive art in a narrative form. They developed a narrative in terms of its interactive scenario, graphic design, and technical design. The audience interacts by taking the role of Magic Monkey (painted with Processing) and creates the narrative through its own acting while experiencing a meaningful and funny story. Nagao, Takahashi, & Tanaka (2008) developed a "Mirror Appliance" used to recommend combinations of clothes in order to produce a coordinated look suitable for a given day's events and weather. The system stores information on the user's clothes, weather, and the events to which the user previously wore certain clothes. When the user stands in front of the "Mirror Appliance," the system refers to the current weather information, the user's current schedule, and the user's past behavior. Using this system, the user can chose the most suitable combination of clothes that reflects his/her preferences. Naito, Shizuki, Tanaka, & Hosobe (2009) developed a cylindrical multi-touch interface for a volumetric display allowing an easy interaction technique for acquiring objects or indicating with two hands (without wearing any special devices) a 3D area in space (for example, one atom on a model of the molecule). The position and size of the area touched is mapped to the position and size of the spherical cursor; this mapping can instantly determine the 3D coordinates and radius of the spherical cursor, and thus the gestures specify both the size and the position of the target simultaneously. In a work of James Charlton (2011) the gestures of the artist can interact with digital material; they can be translated into concrete form by integrating motion capture technology with real time 3D printing. Charlton's another project, the *iForm* is a process-based work that derives its 3D form from GPS data generated by the movement of the iphone participants through the landscape.

Art works and art galleries have also found their place in the Second Life, for example the Cerulean Gallery is available in the Second Life by clicking tabs at the top of the Gallery's website http://www.ceruleangallery.org or http://www.youtube.com/watch?v=Oj5W1fuVx74.

Figure 6, "Migration," which refers to the birds' annual migration to all corners of the earth to escape winter, may also make one think about human escapist attempts to figure different reality in a virtual Second Life.

Figure 6. Anna Ursyn, Migration (© 2007, A. Ursyn. Used with permission)

When times become harsh
And situation unfriendly,
It's time to go elsewhere.

BIOLOGY INSPIRED COMPUTING APPLIED FOR ARTISTIC TASKS

Techniques in communication and networking often use biological systems. Current interest in natural forces and events comes from researchers and engineers who develop natural computing and its branch, biology inspired computing, which deals with advances in artificial life, fractal geometry, and computing with natural means. Computing is now the study of natural and artificial information processes, no longer the study of phenomena surrounding computers only (Denning, 2007). Examples of bio-inspired techniques are evolutionary computation, artificial life, artificial neural networks, and swarm intel-

ligence. Genetic engineering techniques serve for designing new computers based on molecules, such as membranes, or for designing controllers for robots. Nature serves as a metaphor for developing methods such as molecular, membrane, and quantum computing. For example, dynamical transport network in a single-cell organism is considered a virtual computing material that allows approaching spatially represented geometry problems (Jones, 2010); a Physarum machine is a biological computing device that computes by propagating diffusive or excitation wave fronts (Adamatzky, 2010).

A great body of artistic endeavors has been inspired by complex systems and a complexity theory. Tom Davis (2011, p. 107) has defined a complex system as "a many-bodied system of components that, through interactions at the local level self-organize into structures that we can characterize as emergent of the system as a whole." They are spontaneous, self-organized emergent systems, without an internal pacemaker or an external controller. A complexity theory offers a possibility that, in contrast with the reductive Newtonian theories of classical science, complex systems "can create new structures and forms on an epistemic or even on an ontological basis." This framework of thought brings about a chance to explore the nature of our knowledge or validate it, study the nature of being, and create ever-changing forms and systems that outperform their creators by their ability to restructure the way they mine and collect knowledge about the environment. The complexity theory may support artistic inspiration because of the perpetual novelty of the complex systems (Davis, 2011), their relationship to artificial intelligence (AI) and artificial life (A-life). Many individuals apply complex systems as a foundation for creating artistic endeavors based on generative algorithm (GA) inspired implementations, cellular automata, emergent systems, or the A-life systems. Generative algorithms (GA) are programmed to navigate the large data sets in complex systems toward a best-case evolution scenario, with the use of a fitness function; such works are often inspired with the biological natural selection models.

Computers serve as design optimization tools employing options provided by the natural selection principles. New media artists compare to the life forms the interacting and adapting properties of digital environments. Transformed or invented living structures are used for developing engineered ecosystems and simulations of biotic habitats (Dorin and Korb, 2007). Applications of genetic algorithms and other evolutionary computing techniques may refer not only to the artistic areas but also many industries, including aeronautic and automotive design, electronic circuit design, routing optimization, modeling markets for investment, among other domains. A detailed inspection of generative art systems may result in detecting an analogy with the natural systems both systems maintaining balance between order and disorder. While biological life takes on most of its forms

in a spectrum between unstructured atmospheric gases and ordered crystals and minerals, generative art systems and artificial life (A-life) are placed somewhere in the middle of a continuum between disordered randomization, chaotic systems, and fractals or L-systems, and highly ordered forms such as symmetry and tiling (Galanter, 2010). Artist's creative process, when taken with generative approach draws from natural phenomena observed in biology and physics, so it may evolve into a sequence of iterative solutions and modifications transforming the artwork.

Bio-inspired algorithms enable solving complex problems, modeling, and designing simulations. For example, scientists and engineers examine swarm intelligence, collective intelligence of groups. Swarm intelligence concept, which is widely applied in computing, took inspiration from the self-organized systems, which are typical of biological organisms and colonies, from the sub-cellular structures to ecosystems. Swarm intelligence in biological or artificial systems is a collective action performed by self-organized systems without a central authority: each agent is a peer that acts and is interacting independently, and there is no central controller that directs the activities of other members of the swarm. Systems that depend on a central controller are often robust to disasters, such as a damage of the controller (Bonabeau, Corne, & Poli, 2010). Self-organizing chemical matter brought about the origin of life. Examples of the self-organizing groups revealing the swarm behavior are insects (such as bee swarms or ants colonies), mammals living in groups, the flocks of birds, and schools of fish. In some circumstances, people also display swarm behavior. Interactions between individual members lead to emergence of behavior that is optimal for the whole group. Individuals in a swarm, whether comprising animals or agents in a model, move in one direction without collisions, one close to another. According to Lima (2011, p. 226), most swarm behaviors follow three basic directives:

- **Separation:** Don't crowd your neighbors (short-range repulsion);
- **Alignment:** Maneuver in the average direction neighbors are moving toward;
- **Cohesion:** Steer toward average position of neighbors (long-range attraction).

Swarm intelligence inspired several new technologies and applications. Swarm behavior has been described in mathematical models as the collective motion of self-propelled units following simple rules that do not result from any central coordination. Scientists develop evolutionary computing inspired by nature that applies general ideas of biological evolution, like natural selection and genetic inheritance to build problem-solving techniques. They build evolutionary models and techniques for computation, such as genetic algorithms, artificial evolution strategies, classifier systems, evolutionary programming, genetic programming, swarm intelligence (e.g., ant colony optimization and particle swarm optimization), and other techniques. Decentralized systems such as networks are aimed at information processing, often at the global level, with the use of self-evolving cellular arrays or evolutionary computation.

Evolutionary computation and genetic algorithms serve for creating evolutionary and generative art projects. Artists apply models based on molecular genetics to create images and structures using artistic techniques. Genetic art projects of various types and genetically modified pets are designed by inserting or deleting genes, thus transforming living organism, their structure, and vital processes. Scientists model, simulate, and engineer particular ecosystems and habitats and apply artificially designed visual effects and soundscapes to create generative art. These systems operate with some autonomy, and synthetic animals can develop collective behavior or interact with the viewers. Evolutionary techniques allow developing controllers for animated motion of real or virtual creatures, and creating artificial

evolution of shape. Participatory, web-based art projects use evolutionary computation to create online interactive evolution of biomorphs, and real-time interaction between people and evolutionary creatures. Interactive genetic algorithms create and learn to create music (Reynolds, 2002).

Genetics, robotics, information technology, and nanotechnology (GRIN) are considered the four most fundamental venues in technology development. Geneticists develop model organisms for research studies on gene regulation and the role of genes in the development or sickness of a living being (with diseases such as cancer). Model organism serve for educational purpose as well (Model Organisms, 2008). The genetics- and evolution-related concepts generative let the artists draw technical solutions for automated behavior, artificial intelligence, and swarm intelligence features. This approach may lead to creating artificial DNA. For example, Eduardo Kac (2011) develops transgenic art with genetic material artificially modified. For example, in his "Cypher" (2009), Kac introduced synthetic DNA where genetic sequence was encoded according to the artist's poem. His "Natural History of Enigma," awarded the 2009 Golden Nica, comprises a genetically engineered flower that is a hybrid of Kac's DNA and petunia. The gene selected by the artist is responsible for the identification of foreign bodies. Celestino Soddu (2011) generated the artificial 'DNA' of medieval towns that can produce futuristic 3D architectural models for both interior and exterior in a selected style.

Robotic art may make use of an avatar or a specially designed robot that acts according to a story created by the artist, often interactively with the viewers due to the use of cameras or facial recognition software; generally speaking, it involves electronics, mechanics, and software. Actuators convert stored energy (taken from various kinds of power sources) to movement, sensing, computer vision, effectors manipulating objects with grippers, locomotion, and other elements. Neural networks direct a manipulator, the steering, and path planning. Some robots act autonomously in a dynamic environment, other can interact with humans, when equipped with speech recognition, gestures, facial expression, artificial emotions, and even personality (Biever, 2006). Geospatial art usually takes advantage from the availability of the space-based global positioning systems of many kinds, or uses data provided by the new media journalism and web-based information visualization to involve viewers into active way of their projects appreciation. Some artists choose blog art or any other way of creating mobile art to communicate with event participants. Others select open source projections involving images and music that may be played or even co-created by the viewers. Robot developers no longer try to mimic human mind with a logic-based reasoning of their products. They take advantage of inventions in artificial intelligence (AI) that uses machine learning, sophisticated sensors, and algorithms aimed at discrete tasks. Robotic systems derive meaning from massive data sets, which are formed with genetic algorithms that are probability-based and produce evolving, continuously improving codes. Therefore, robots and bots, computer programs designed to perform specific tasks, sometimes in nano scale (for example, iRobot, Roomba, or software Siri, intelligent personal assistant, which lets using one's voice to send messages, ask questions, or schedule actions) do not resemble humans (Levy, 2011).

Digital non-linear poetry, video games, and interactive installations of many kinds provide many channels for viewers' input through the sound, graphics, movement, messaging, and socializing supported by rules or the lack of rules. Another venue comprises haptic art engaging multiple senses and addressing kinesthetic intelligence and/or physical memory, physical relationship with others, with technology, or both. It often involves users' experience or creation of the work as an active combination of kinesthetic and tactual evidence, and even scent and audio interactions. Wearable garment makes yet another form of

agency aimed at building feedback or blurring the boundaries with the environment. Artists combine nature and technology creating both serious and playful projects where biological forms and life processes are grafted together with digital codes and devices. In an art gallery setting, kinetic, often interactive projects and large installations immerse a viewer in biology inspired environments of shivering tendrils, singing strands of hair, and fuzzy, cloud-like surfaces responding to strokes.

Sculptures created according to the programmed images (Figures 7a and 7b) may provide a visitor with a haptic experience (if it's allowed). "Hero Horse" shown on a Figure 7a uses the visual language of three-dimensional programs to show an image of the horse as a heroic symbol of the human struggle for survival. Figure 7b presents horses in motion.

I transform pictures of animals into simple images, iconic objects such as a rocking horse or a symbolic picture of a man or a bird. The horse can be seen as a link between natural surroundings and human nature. It is possible to go around the sculpture to look at it from different angles; however, there is still a need for achieving the fourth dimension. In order to represent movement in time, horses are shown running simultaneously in various directions

Evolutionary Computing

The growing interest in the field of nanoscience resulted in the development of evolutionary computing, a subfield in computational intelligence that examines growth or development in a population. Processes applied in this domain are inspired by biological mechanisms of evolution. Living organisms serve the artists not only as inspiration but also as an object of algorithmically triggered manipulation with the use of sensors and controllers. Artists using genetic algorithms and other evolutionary computing techniques

Figure 7. a. Anna Ursyn, Hero Horse, Computer enhanced sculpture. Vax mainframe, Interactive Graphic Library (IGL), Fortran. (© 2000, A. Ursyn. Used with permission); b. Anna Ursyn, Speeding, A wooden sculpture after a 3-D computer program (© 2000, A. Ursyn. Used with permission).

explore the ways that complex systems and patterns arise out of interactions existing in natural environments. They apply models and simulations of the development of cellular structures in living organisms to form evolutionary art systems. For example, at the EvoStar conferences, participants share the ways to develop, analyze, focus, and re-target evolved genetic material for aesthetic purposes and aesthetic pattern formation.

Evolutionary computing transforms computers into automatic optimization and design tools, utilizing the power of the natural selection mechanisms, which act through reproduction, mutation, the Darwinian principle of survival of the fittest through inheritance, selection, and

crossover. Various approaches to evolutionary computing include genetic algorithms (that mimic natural evolution to solve optimization and search problems), evolutionary programming (strategies using mutation as main variation operator, where a parent generates an offspring according to survivor selection principle), evolution strategies (using mutation and selection as search operators aimed at optimization techniques), and genetic programming (finding programs that would perform a user-defined task). Evolutionary computing resulted in a progress in quantum computing, search algorithms development, sorting, electronic design, evolvable hardware (containing hardware, artificial intelligence and autonomous systems that change their architecture and behavior in response to its environment), and advances in computer programming. Garry Greenfield (2010, p.12), whose interests include evolutionary computation and algorithmic art described the distinctive nature of some genres in computer art: in a process of evolutionary computation in art "members of a population undergo artificial evolution and modify their form over many reproductive generations in response to a selection/survival scheme." Numerous researchers apply biological techniques for artistic tasks. Evolutionary artists, for example, Richard Dawkins, William Latham, Karl Sims, and Yoichiro Kawaguchi, utilize evolutionary processes to create works that go through changes, often interactively (when a selective regime is applied by the viewer), according to artificial evolutionary processes. A digital media artist, computer graphics research scientist, and software entrepreneur Karl Sims (2009) is known for his interactive works, computer animations, and the GenArts, Inc., visual effects software he founded. Evolutionary computing resulted in creating generative art and the developments in biology-inspired design, arts, music, architecture, and other artistic fields. Analyses of the images, forms, and motions in interactive evolutionary design and art lead to new approaches in defining aesthetic criteria, not only in terms of the work beauty but also its effectiveness and usability.

Figure 8, "Social Networking" depicts how we create social circles: psychologically dependent structures, with guiding centers that organize order around the leading forces. People in power, inventors, artists, fashionable actors, rulers, or other leaders of social structure create a cloud. In cloud visualizations bigger letters may depict swarms where more tweets are present. A swarm may have a queen and members gathering around to fulfill their duties. Presently, humans may elect the government while in the past they obeyed the chorus of the elderly, or a council of elders in Areopagus. Cloud computing specialists and individuals organizing it all with cooperation of the social network members direct the cloud forming and managing.

With a focus on interactive networking, it might be interesting to gather and share on the Arduino microcontroller personal reactions to disparate performances such as operas, theater productions, concerts, musicals, and movies, and then present them as an artwork where a number of visages grows with the number of answers.

SOCIAL NETWORKING MEDIA

Communication media with a visual approach to social networking involve websites, social networking sites and numerous social networking services. A 2011 survey found that 47% of American adults used a social network (Rosman, 2011). Perhaps the most evident merging of science and art with the visual approach is the social networking that provides a fuel for any form of online creative work. Books produced as apps create another option for artists to publish their art: digital books, eBook apps, iBook apps, PDF Reader apps, and many others. Techniques in communications and networking can be achieved by using biologically inspired communication networks. According to Lio & Verma (2012), there are many advantages of implementing biological networks: they include their ability to maintain homeostatic environments, adapt rapidly to environmental changes, self-organize, assemble simple structures into complex tasks, autonomous operations, self-replication, protection against attacks of various natures, etc.

Visuals contained in new media art serve a variety of users with different frames of mind. They often serve for processing data, information, and knowledge. Availability of open source frameworks/databases and cloud apps prompts initiatives concerning the new media art, not only enterprises such as startups. People working in different disciplines are often interested in the collaborative and group art. Social networking in

Figure 8. Anna Ursyn, Social Networking (© 2011, A. Ursyn. Used with permission)

the case of a 'Synapse' group at the University of Akron gathers interdisciplinary artists and professionals in several disciplines at the confluence of art and science to work together on artistic production.

Social networking includes art created outside the technical structure of the Internet and involves users of the wireless technology and 3D technology such as Nintendo 3DS, animation, communication with the use of smart phones, wireless PDAs (palmtop computers), Skype (networked voice service over Internet Protocol), videoconferencing, etc., as well as iPads, video, vimeo, moving images of many kinds, all contribute to the developments in net art. Examining for example, the BBC News

we can find that video clips make a large part of its content. After an artwork is posted at the newsgroups, participants engage in Web discussions (that are asynchronous, meaning that they are exchanged over time rather than back and forth) or send messages via e-mail. Playing electronic games of various kinds, often created as art forms and serving education, entertainment, health, fitness, many times including biofeedback, is another means involving human interaction with a video interface that may benefit from the networked media. Computer games based on biofeedback principle provide mind and body training (e.g., www.WildDivine.com). Interactive novels, for example, Japanese visual and sound novels – interactive fiction and adventure games, or digital poetry – a revival of visual poetry from the time of the Fluxus community intermedia network from the 1960s, may serve as other examples.

Net Art

The rise of the net media and the omnipresence of mobile devices and wireless networks have prompted the development of the networked art called also net art or web art. Net art artists, for example artists participating in a net.art group and net.art movement, use the Internet as a necessary medium to experience the artwork. Net artists change the perception of the interactive, multimedia based, multisensory, and participatory art, and they often disregard the standards of the mainstream art aesthetics. Not limited to applying the web browsers, web art relies on innovative interfaces to refer to the Internet-based human interactions, and also to other than Internet social networks. Cheng (2009) puts forward classification of net art based on research, case studies, and characteristics of the networked projects. He discerns the email art, non-linear narrative, online performance, information art, game art, collaborative creation, Internet community, and physical interaction, in order to make the aesthesis of net art distinctive from the general aspects of contemporary art. Net artists use computer networks as their medium to create art at online social networking systems and information sharing platforms, acting and creating in interactive, participatory, and multimedia based ways.

Jon Ippolito (2002) described "Ten Myths" about Internet art: common misconceptions about what it means to make art for the Internet, and reminded that the World Wide Web is only one of the many parts that make up the Internet. Other online protocols include e-mail, peer-to-peer instant messaging, video- conferencing software, MP3 audio files, and text-based environments like MUDs – multiplayer real-time virtual worlds or multi-user dungeons, and MOO virtual reality

systems. He also prompted the idea that "online communities and listservers, along with interactive Internet artworks that trace viewers and integrate their actions into respective interfaces, prove that the Internet is a social mechanism" (Ippolito, 2002, p. 495). Blais and Ippolito (2006) added several fields of creative activity to the generally accepted definition of art, such as computer code-based art, games, online autobiography, haktivism, computer virus making and preservation, and community building. The Whitney Museum of American Art in New York established in 2002 a portal to Internet art and an online gallery space called the Whitney Artport (2011). Artport provides access to and documentation of commissioned net art and new media art works. Groups of artists (net.art) work on archiving and promoting Internet art among digital art communities, offer alternative answers such as cloning, plagiarizing, and collective creation, and expand the idea of art hacktivism by performing code interventions and perturbations both in real world and in art festivals.

Computer networks and information databases and applications of different kinds expand with the growth of information and communication technologies, hardware, software, and programming languages. According to the Global Information Technology Report (2009) network readiness correlates with the GDP per capita and depends on the market environment, political and regulatory environment, and infrastructure environment. Mobile telephony occupies a special place among information and communication technologies in terms of both its diffusion and impact on economic growth and poverty reduction. Computer communication networking and sensing draws from natural, biological, and cognitive sciences and utilize biologically inspired solutions including cell communication, molecular communication mechanisms, and neural networks, taking inspiration from evolutionary and adaptation algorithms (Lio & Verma, 2012). Net art and new media art works are turning into an inherent building block of communication networking.

CONCLUSION

There are many ways of creating art that utilize technology through writing algorithms or without the writing of programs: with the use of graphic or painting software, applying digital multimedia packages, or bringing images into the visualization system or the virtual reality 3D immersive world to develop interrelationships between media. Art programmed on the computer, which began in the mid-1960s, has been extended beyond the computer screen and used for creating other forms of art having several levels of interactivity: simulation of the real world, biological growth patterns, artificial intelligence aimed at creating intelligent agents, robotics that develop computer systems to control the robots, visualization, or stereoscopic HDTV animation. Taxonomy of computer art developed by Boden and Edmonds (2009) distinguishes eleven types of art. New media art galleries select specific categories for each event or show where artists present interactive systems and artistic interface designs. Art works and art galleries have also found their place in the virtual space, e.g., Second Life. Biology inspired computing is being applied for artistic tasks, using bio-inspired algorithms, swarm intelligence, evolutionary computing, genetic algorithms, and robotics, to name a few. Merging of science and art with the visual approach resulted in the social networking media and the net art.

REFERENCES

Adamatzky, A. (2010). Physarum machines: Encapsulating reaction-diffusion to compute spanning tree. *Naturwissenschaften*, *94*(12), 975–980. doi:10.1007/s00114-007-0276-5 PMID:17603779.

Baudisch, P. (2006). Interacting with wall-size screens. In *Proceedings of CHI 2006*. Montreal, Canada: ACM.

Biever, C. (2006). A good robot has personality but not looks. *New Scientist, 2561*. Retrieved January 9, 2011, from http://www.newscientist.com/article/mg19125616.400-a-good-robot-has-personality-but-not-looks.html

Blais, J., Ippolito, J., & Smith. (2006). *At the edge of art*. Thames & Hudson. ISBN 0500238227

Boden, M. A. (2009). Computer models of creativity. *AI Magazine*, *30*(3).

Boden, M. A. (2010). *Creativity and art: Three roads to surprise*. Oxford University Press.

Boden, M. A., & Edmonds, E. A. (2009). What is generative art? *Digital Creativity*, *20*(1-2), 21–46. doi:10.1080/14626260902867915.

Bonabeau, E., Corne, D., & Poli, R. (2010). Swarm intelligence: The state of the art special issue of natural computing. *Natural Computing*, *9*, 655–657. doi:10.1007/s11047-009-9172-6.

Charlton, J. (2011). Digitaterial gestures: Action-driven stereolithography. In *Proceedings of ISEA2011, the 17th International Symposium on Electronic Art*. Retrieved April 13, 2011, from http://isea2011.sabanciuniv.edu/paper/digitaterial-gestures---action-driven-stererolithography

Cheng, Y. H. G. (2009). The aesthetics of net dot art. In *Handbook of Research on Computational Arts and Creative Informatics* (pp. 162–180). Hershey, PA: IGI Global. doi:10.4018/978-1-60566-352-4.ch010.

Davis, T. (2011). Complexity as practice: A reflection on the creative outcomes of a sustained engagement with complexity. *Leonardo*, *45*(3), 106–112.

Denning, P. J. (2007). Computing is a natural science. *Communications of the ACM*, *50*(7), 13–18. doi:10.1145/1272516.1272529.

Di Chio, C., Brabazon, A., Ebner, M., Farooq, M., Fink, A., & Grahl, J. … Urquhart, N. (Eds.). (2010a). Applications of evolutionary computation. Berlin: Springer-Verlag. ISBN:978-3-642-12241-5

Di Chio, C., Brabazon, A., Di Caro, G., Ebner, M., Farooq, M., & Fink, A. … Urquhart, N. (Eds.). (2010b). Applications of evolutionary computation, evoapplications. In *Proceedings, Part II, (LNCS), (Vol. 6025)*. Berlin: Springer. Retrieved April 13, 2011, from http://www.springerlink.com/content/l8161m85r21r/front-matter.pdf

Dorin, A., & Korb, K. (2007). Building artificial ecosystems from artificial chemistry. In *Proceedings of the 9th European Conference on Artificial Life*. Springer-Verlag.

Edmonds, E., Bilda, Z., & Muller, L. (2009). Artist, evaluator and curator: Three viewpoints on interactive art, evaluation and audience experience. *Digital Creativity, 20*(3), 141–151. doi:10.1080/14626260903083579.

Evans, B. (2007). *Artist statement. Electronic Art and Animation Catalog*. ACM.

Evo: The 9th European Event on Evolutionary and Biologically Inspired Music, Sound, Art and Design. (2011). Retrieved April 12, 2011, from http://www.evostar.org/evomusart/

Ferguson, C., & Ferguson, H. (1994). *Mathematics in stone and bronze*. Erie, PA: Meridian Creative Group.

Ferguson, H. et al. (2010). Celebrating mathematics in stone and bronze. *Notices of the American Mathematical Society, 57*(7), 840–850.

Fishwick, P. (2008). An introduction to aesthetic computing. In P. Fishwick (Ed.), *Aesthetic Computing (Leonardo Book Series)*. The MIT Press.

Frazier, I. (2011, September 5). The march of the strandbeests: Theo Jansen's wind-powered sculpture. *New Yorker (New York, N.Y.)*, 54–61.

Galanter, P. (2010). The problem with evolutionary art is. In C. Di Chio et al. (Eds.), *EvoApplications, (LNCS)* (Vol. 6025, pp. 321–330). Berlin: Springer-Verlag.

Garousi, M. (2012). The postmodern beauty of fractals. *Leonardo, 45*(1), 26–32. doi:10.1162/LEON_a_00322.

Giannachi, G. (2011). Representing, performing, and mitigating climate change in contemporary art practice. *Leonardo, 45*(3), 125–131.

Global Information Technology Report 2008-2009. (2009). Retrieved January 9, 2011, from https://members.weforum.org/pdf/gitr/2009/gitr09fullreport.pdf

Greenfield, G. (2010). *Diffusion limited aggregation, evolutionary computation, and algorithmic art - Five easy pieces*. School of Computing, Clemson University, Visual Computing Seminar. Retrieved January 24, 2012, from http://www.cs.clemson.edu/~dhouse/vcseminar/talks/greenfield-talk.pdf

Hoetzlein, R. C. (2011). Visual communication in times of crisis: The Fukushima nuclear accident. *Leonardo, 45*(3), 113–118.

Holz, C., & Baudisch, P. (2011). *Understanding touch*. Paper presented at the ACM CHI Conference on Human Factors in Computing Systems. Vancouver, Canada. Retrieved January 30, 2012, from www.christianholz.net/2011-chi11-holz-baudisch-understanding_touch.pdf

Ippolito, J. (2002). Ten myths of internet art. *Leonardo, 35*(5), 485–498. doi:10.1162/002409402320774312.

Jones, J. (2010). Influences in the formation and evolution of physarum polycephalum inspired emergent transport networks. *Natural Computing, 4*, 793-1006. Retrieved April 11, 2011, from http://www.springerlink.com/content/p2r148p612k05207/export-citation/

Kac, E. (2011) *Website of Eduardo Kac*. Retrieved January 26, 2011, from http://ekac.org/

Levy, S. (2011, January). The AI revolution. *Wired*. Retrieved from http://www.wired.com/magazine/2010/12/ff_ai_essay_airevolution/

Lima, M. (2011). Visual complexity: Mapping patterns of information. New York: Princeton Architectural Press. ISBN 978 1 56898 936 5

Lio, P., & Verma, D. (2012). *Biologically inspired networking and sensing: Algorithms and architectures*. Hershey, PA: IGI Global.

Model Organisms. (2008). *The use of model organisms in instruction*. University of Wisconsin: Wisconsin Outreach Research Modules. Retrieved January 9, 2011, from http://wormclassroom.org/teaching-model-organisms

Nagao, S., Takahashi, S., & Tanaka, J. (2008). Mirror appliance: Recommendation of clothes coordination in daily life. In *Proceedings of the 21st Human Factors in Telecommunication*. Retrieved January 29, 2011, from http://www.hft2008.org/images/paper/hft08.nagao.pdf

Naito, M., Shizuki, B., Tanaka, J., & Hosobe, H. (2009). Interaction techniques using a spherical cursor for 3D targets acquisition and indicating in volumetric displays. In *Proceedings of the iV, 13th International Conference on Information Visualization*, (pp. 607–612). ISBN 978-0-7695-3733-7

Oh, J.-H., Kim, S.-Y., Kim, S.-H., & Shi, C.-K. (2011). A study of interactive art in the narrative form of magic monkey. In *Proceedings of the Eight International Conference Computer Graphics, Imaging, and Visualization*, (pp. 39-46). DOI 10.1109/CGIV.2011.19

Polli, A. (2003). *Atmospherics/weather works: The sonification of meteorological data*. Retrieved May 9, 2011, from http://www.andreapolli.com/studio/atmospherics/

Reas, C., & Fry, B. (2007). *Processing: A programming handbook for visual designers and artists*. Cambridge, MA: The MIT Press.

Redström, J., Skog, T., & Hallnäs, L. (2000). Informative art: Using amplified artworks as information displays. In W. Mackay (Ed.), *Proceedings of DARE 2000 (Designing Augmented Reality Environments)*, (pp. 103-114). ACM Press.

J. Reichardt (Ed.). (1968). *Cybernetic serendipity*. London: Studio International.

Reynolds, C. (2002). *Evolutionary computation and its application to art and design*. Retrieved January 9, 2011, from http://www.red3d.com/cwr/evolve.html

Rosman, K. (2011, June 16). Eat your vegetables, and don't forget to tweet. *The Wall Street Journal*. Retrieved January 9, 2011, from http://finance.yahoo.com/news/pf_article_112952.html

Sims, K. (2009). *Karl Sims website*. Retrieved January 9, 2011, from http://www.karlsims.com/

Soddu, C. (2011). *Website of Celestino Soddu*. Retrieved January 26, 2011, from http://www.celestinosoddu.com/

Sommerer, C., & Mignonneau, L. (2010). *The value of art (unruhige see)*. Retrieved January 9, 2011, from http://www.interface.ufg.ac.at/christa-laurent/WORKS/FRAMES/FrameSet.html

Stone, H. S. (1972). *Introduction to computer organization and data structures*. New York: McGraw Hill.

Sturm, B. L. (2005). Pulse of an ocean. *Leonardo*, 38(2), 143–149. doi:10.1162/0024094053722453.

Whitney Artport: The Whitney Museum of American Art. (2011). Retrieved January 27, 2011 from http://artport.whitney.org/

Wilson, S. (2010). *Art + science now*. Thames & Hudson.

Zuanon, R. (2012). The bio-interfaces at design, art and game areas: some applications. In A. Ursyn (Ed.), *Biologically-Inspired Computing for the Arts: Scientific Data through Graphics*. Hershey, PA: IGI Global.

Chapter 4
Aesthetics in the Context of New Media Art and Knowledge Visualization

ABSTRACT

This chapter discusses aesthetic values in mathematics, science, and computing including aesthetic computing and aesthetic issues related to digital environment. A study of aesthetics has always been related to the arts, philosophy of art, and our judgments about sensory or emotional values of specific art works; they are in the focus of neuroaesthetics. The objectives of aesthetic studies have been changing following the developments in computing technology, shifting the stress on usability and efficiency of projects and visualizations. Challenges and demands in aesthetics and art are then discussed, starting from an essential question (What is an artwork and what is not an artwork?), and including art definitions, art manifestos, opinions on the role of art, beauty, and aesthetic perception of art. Aesthetic education and ways of looking at art complete the chapter.

INTRODUCTION

Studies on aesthetics relate to the arts, philosophy of art, and our judgments about sensory or emotional values of specific art works. They are also in the focus of neuroaesthetics. Visual aesthetics draws has been based on the artistic principles and investigated as part of cognitive science (Chatterjee, 2003, 2011a, 2011b; Kawabata & Zeki, 2004; Watson & Chatterjee, 2011; Ishizu & Zeki, 2011). Traditionally the aesthetic values included objects that were beautiful, harmonious, or emotionally pleasing. Later on according to the concept presented by the postmodern philosopher Jean-Francois Lyotard (1924-1998), they would be sublime (Lessons on the Analytic of the Sublime, 1994). Then, with the broadened criteria of beauty, judgments of aesthetic values examined also social, political, moral, and many other aspects of the art objects. Modern analytic approach in aesthetics is no longer limited to just an analysis of natural beauty because, in opinion of cubists, dadaists, constructivists, conceptual artists, generative artists, and many others, beauty ceased

DOI: 10.4018/978-1-4666-4627-8.ch004

to be central to the definition of art. Computing science specialists examine aesthetics of electronic projects' usability, efficiency, and discuss aesthetics in terms of possible applications to controlling computer products. Evaluation of tag clouds in terms of the aesthetic quality obtained from an extensive user study confirms that aesthetic values correlate with product usability.

THE CHANGING MEANING OF THE AESTHETICS NOTION

Opinions about aesthetic experience meant quite different things in different times. As described by Tatarkiewicz (1999), Pythagoras wrote in the 6th century BC about the aesthetic emotions sensed while appreciating plays and games. Greek philosophers valued cognitive value of aesthetics, while the 18th century writers identified the differences between sensory and intellectual responses to beauty. Other authors describe a variety of aesthetic experiences, such as sensual, non-associative pleasure caused by beauty, cognitive intellectual indulgence, irrational elation, or experiencing illusions: a viewer knows it is an illusion but enjoys it, contemplates, feels empathy, plays a kind of a game by watching a fictional world with fictional rules, switching his troubles off, and feeling emotions (Tatarkiewicz, 1976). In many instances artists impart similar impression related to their creative process.

American mathematician George David Birkhoff (1884-1944) proposed in a book entitled "Aesthetic Measure" a mathematical theory of aesthetics: in an equation M=O/C, Aesthetic Measure (M) is a function of Order (O) divided by Complexity (C). The Gestalt psychology theory of mind postulated that brain has self-organizing tendencies and recognizes the whole of a figure rather than its individual parts (Birkhoff, 2003/1933).

The aesthetics of the new media art is derived from its characteristics: being digital, networked, multisensory, immersive, or interactive. For ex-

ample, Creative Time and the Public Art Fund in New York and Artangel in London are weaving video projections, websites, and interactive installations into the urban fabric. According to Hansen (2006), new media artworks provide the aesthetic interface between the digital technosphere and our bodies, which is experienced interactively or virtually. The co-evolution of the human body and the digital technosphere goes through the radical aesthetic interface provided by new media artworks themselves; our bodies, when brought into contact with the digital, experience the virtual.

NEUROAESTHETICS AND THE COGNITIVE NEUROSCIENCE

Investigation into the neural basis for perception of beauty in art evolved into a field of neuroaesthetics (Zeki 1999). Neuroimaging techniques enabling in vivo investigations of the human brain function include, among other techniques, fMRI - functional magnetic resonance imaging (through measuring changes in blood flow), PET - positron emission tomography, and near-infrared spectroscopy. Other techniques exist, such as electric (electroencephalography - EEG) and magnetic (magnetoencephalography - MEG). Research results obtained with the imaging and neurophysiological techniques suggest that the aesthetic experience of visual art works is characterized by the activation of sensorimotor areas of cerebral cortex, cortical emotional centers, and the reward-related centers (Cinzia & Gallese, 2009). However, external factors can bias the brain reaction to viewing art works and influence our aesthetic judgments. This fact might offer a scientific explanation as to why assessment of an artwork may depend on information about who the artist is, is this artist universally respected, and whether or not the work is shown in a renowned art gallery (Kirk, Skov, Christensen, & Nygaard, 2009). Possibly, we may soon encounter a new form of judging criteria based on a biofeedback research upon the audience' reaction toward the work of art, as it is already practiced at the networked sites. This may in turn lead to a reversal in art selections toward illustrative, symbolic, or amusing works, and may encourage artists to create realistic works aimed at entertaining viewers, for example by evoking a rush of feeling.

According to Zeki (1993, 1999), professor of neuroaesthetics at London University College common neural organization makes possible the creation and appreciation of art. As Zeki states, the almost infinite creative variability, which allows different artists to create radically different styles, arises out of common neurobiological processes. Visual art helps understand a visual brain and its perceptual capabilities. It also reveals the laws of the visual brain, two of them Zeki describes as essential. The law of constancy is about knowledge of the constant and essential properties of the ever-changing objects and surfaces; the brain is able to discard these changes in categorizing an object. Similarly, a great work of art tries to distill on canvas the essential qualities. The law of abstraction tells about the brain's capacity to abstract; it may be imposed on the brain by the limitations of its memory system. Zeki describes abstraction as the process in which the particular is subordinated to the general, so that what is represented is applicable to many particulars. He states that art, too, abstracts and thus externalizes the inner workings of the brain.

In the opinion of Zeki, artists study the brain with techniques unique to them. "Artists and neurobiologists have both studied the perceptual commonality, sharing the features and attributes, that underlie visual aesthetics. It is commonality that allows us to communicate about art and through art, with or without the use of the written or the spoken word." Zeki scanned the brains of volunteers; he found that their blood flow increased in the medial orbito-frontal cortex of the brain (located behind the eyes) when they looked at 28 masterpieces of art. He also found that viewing great works of art triggers a surge of

dopamine, the feel-good neurotransmitter released when one feels intense pleasure. (Neurotransmitters transfer signals from a neuron to another cell across a synapse. Neurotransmitters, contained in synaptic vessels in an axon, are released into a synaptic cleft at the arrival of an electrochemical wave of action potential at the presynaptic part of a synapse, and then they bind to the membrane receptors on the postsynaptic neuron, on the opposite side of a synapse). Dopamine and the orbito-frontal cortex are both known to be involved in desire and affection and in invoking pleasurable feelings in the brain (Alleyne, 2011). This way we can determine what a person finds beautiful, and thus we can tell beauty is not just in the eye but also in the brain of the beholder. Zeki stated, "The extent of activity in the medial frontal cortex is directly proportional to the declared intensity of beauty" (Lebwohl, 2011). He discovered that beauty perceived through the eyes as art and through the ears as music both activate the same spot. Aesthetically displeasing, ugly stimuli activate amygdala, a different part of the brain. In his blog, Semir Zeki (2011) stresses the power of the visual image, and its ability to give a great deal of knowledge even after a very brief viewing. When the Mona Lisa painting was in Japan, the average time spent by the viewer was 30 seconds, while at the Louvre (where it is housed), the average time is 15 seconds. Zeki (2001) ascribes it to the huge efficiency of the visual brain, as the visual brain can acquire a great deal of knowledge even after a very brief viewing. He states, "Volumes of writing on the *Mona Lisa* will not give the same information and knowledge that a few seconds of actual viewing does."

Figure 1, "End of the Street" provides an occasion for comparing the environmental and cultural impacts arising along with our growing connectivity. The possibility of studying depth in a landscape has been affected by man-made constructions with such impact that open space becomes a closed one. In a somewhat comparable way, perception of beauty that may invoke

Figure 1. Anna Ursyn, End of the Street (© 1993, A. Ursyn. Used with permission)

pleasurable feelings in the brain of the beholder has widened toward ugly artifacts (as described by Eco, On Ugliness, 2011), which according to traditional principles would arise disgust.

Gregory Minissale (2012) shows that, typically, art stimulates a network of conceptual relations. The author notices that neuroaesthetics used to examine mostly the perceptual responses. If science is to engage meaningfully with art, neu-

roaesthetics should come to terms with the conceptual content, rather than merely perceptions of the visible aspects of single artworks, which would allow "Thinking in terms of networks of relationships among artworks, helping to uncover an intertextual system of references" (p. 47). As a test case, the author discusses Marcel Duchamp's *Bôite-en-valise* (1935–1941):

The box requires that we use different brain areas: the feature detectors of the visual cortex, the action areas of the sensorimotor system studied by neuroaesthetics and cognitive science, as well as memory, language, and rational induction employed by other areas studied by these disciplines, along with cognitive psychology and philosophy. To privilege only one of these aspects massively reduces the multi dimensional meaning and experience the valise affords. (Minissale, 2012, p. 47).

According to the author, neuroaesthetics might consider addressing conceptual thought involved in conceptual art, not exclusively the traditional notions of beauty and formal design, artistic dexterity, aesthetic composition and technique. Four main areas of conceptual art outline opportunities for research in cognitive science and neuroaesthetics:

1. Conceptual art is witty and puzzling like a word game, comparable to the elegance of a mathematical proof (as in Magritte's Treachery of Images – Ceci n'est pas une pipe, 1928-29, http://enculturation.gmu.edu/3_2/introduction3.html).

2. With conceptual art, perceptions of shape and form are less important than the parody, the interplay between visible and invisible aspects of art (as in Marcel Duchamp's Bride Stripped Bare by Her Bachelors, Even, 1915-1924, http://en.wikipedia.org/wiki/The_Bride_Stripped_Bare_By_Her_Bachelors,_Even).

3. It enjoys intertextuality, conceptual relations between other works of art, using short- and long-term memory (as in Marcel Duchamp's *Bôite-en-valise* (1935–1941, http://www.moma.org/interactives/exhibitions/1999/muse/artist_pages/duchamp_boite.html).

4. It stimulates constructing larger superordinate categories (Minissale, 2012).

The growing number of research study results indicates that cognitive neuroscience has developed an underlying basis for aesthetics. Some researchers agree with Zeki and link art and aesthetics with neuroscience, telling that intents and practices done by artist go in parallel with organizational principles how the brain works. Functional magnetic resonance images show that the right hemisphere is processing the novel, low salience figurative meanings, while the process of conveying conventional metaphoric meaning is a bilaterally mediated (Cardillo, Watson, Schmidt, Kranjec, & Chatterjee, 2012). The field of semantics gained a neural basis; it can be represented by the example of neural instantiation of semantic knowledge. The organization of conceptual representations in the brain parallels perception and action. Sensory and motor areas of cortex that have one mode act as 'points of entry' for more abstract action knowledge. Increasingly abstract conceptual knowledge derived from these singular modalities is represented in brain areas located nearer the front and toward the center in relation to the modality-specific regions (Watson & Chatterjee, 2011).

Roger Pouivet (2000) explored the aesthetic emotions as cognitive functions. The author shows in this article that emotions are not purely private mental states. Private language of pain or emotion is often translated into a shared language. In order to feel an aesthetic emotion, one must go through learning process. According to the author, emotions are rational. Rationality is the capacity to pursue some end without preventing oneself from reaching it. One can anticipate someone's emotion and this shows someone's understanding. Our beliefs (determined, e.g., socially) constitute our emotions from the perspective of our inclinations. Emotional inclinations in terms of a linguistic learning process grow with the vocabulary of emotions contained in "stories" (Pouivet, 2000). However, we might keep in mind that aesthetic emotions may depend on one's physical or emotional state at the time of an object reception.

Michael Leyton (2006) discussed his asymmetry principle. He proposed in his "The Foundations of Aesthetics" that the two principles, maximization of transfer and maximization of recoverability are the basic principles both of geometry and aesthetics. They are fundamental to aesthetic judgment in the arts (painting, music, and poetry), the sciences (general relativity and quantum mechanics), and computer programming (object-oriented programming). Recoverability of the backward history is possible due to the asymmetry principle: to ensure recoverability of the past, any asymmetry in the present must go back to symmetry in the past. According to the author, in mathematics and physics "asymmetry" really means distinguishability, and "symmetry" means indistinguishability. Thus, the asymmetry principle really says that, to ensure recoverability, any distinguishability in the present must go back to indistinguishability in the past.

Watanabe (2010) probed experimentally the role of education (or training) in recognizing 'good' (beautiful) and 'bad' (ugly) when he gathered a set of children's paintings, and asked adult humans to label the "good" from the "bad." Then, pigeons were trained through operant conditioning to only peck at good paintings. After the training, when pigeons were exposed to a novel set of already judged children's paintings, they showed their ability in the correct classification of the paintings, even when they were presented reduced to a gray scale or reduced in size. The author suggests, "the pigeons used both color and pattern cues for the discrimination and show that non-human animals, such as pigeons, can be trained to discriminate abstract visual stimuli, such as pictures and may also have the ability to learn the concept of "beauty" as defined by humans." This work stresses out the role of training and raises the question on whether humans are trained (or "biased") to distinguish good and/or creativity work.

The spectrum has been widened with the evolvement of the critical theory of bio art using biotechnology as its medium (Kac 2006, 2011) and evolutionary computing that harnesses the power of natural selection to turn computers into automatic optimization, design tools, and evolutionary art. Artists manipulate in many ways life processes and invent or transform living forms, but also develop ecosystem engineering and simulations of biotic and abiotic habitats (Dorin & Korb 2007). By adding visual sequences and soundscapes to generative art creation, they contribute to advances in the art- and aesthetics-related concepts. Results of a research study on the relation between the aesthetic value of a machine and users' perception about its usability (Tractinsky, Katz, & Ikar, 2000) demonstrate the importance of the designer's visual literacy. The authors found strong correlation between system's perceived aesthetics and perceived usability.

"Landscape with a Blue Jeans Sky" (Figure 2) has a concept of a rigid jeans fabric inserted into a sky part of the picture. Artists may wonder how this soft, blue, downy essence above the head makes such heavy, strong, durable fabric we look at when we do our own things. With a blue or cloudy sky being a recurrent theme in the traditional fine arts, advances in the art- and aesthetics-related concepts might modify artists' interest toward explorations about the air's inherent features.

AESTHETIC DIMENSIONS OF ART INSPIRED BY MATHEMATICS AND SCIENCE

The cultural convergence of mathematics, art, and computer science developed gradually, from the simple to more complex forms, from mathematics-based patterns in world's architecture and design to innovative works of the present-day mathematicians. A foundation for further work can be found in expanding the ways that mathematics and art complement each other in many developing fields of science, such as knowledge and data visualization, simulation, data mining, web media and web communication. A city metaphor is often used in order to map information, while emotional fea-

Figure 2. Anna Ursyn, Landscape with a Blue Jeans Sky (© 1989, A. Ursyn. Used with permission)

tures of the face provide an automatic mapping of the big data sets. The diversity of architectural exterior forms and interior spaces and also integration of buildings into the environment are made possible only through digital design techniques, computer software and applications (Goldblatt & Paden, 2011). Efforts that help sustain both nature and culture provide stimulating challenge for architects and grounds for philosophical and artistic response.

One may ask whether the beauty of a natural object (its aesthetic value) makes its representation an artwork. On a way from nature, through math, to art, we may seek characteristics that distinguish natural forms, their mathematical descriptions, and mathematics-derived artwork. The shell of a mollusk contains a logarithmic spiral. It is a natural phenomenon, not any known result of some mathematical program in the nautilus. A drawing of a logarithmic spiral is a mathematics-derived form, and at the same time, it is also a natural phenomenon. Spiral forms have been explored, discovered and modified by people, but they are hardly an artwork. In the same way, when we

visualize the laws of nature and develop their representations, we rarely consider those representations an artwork. Criteria concerning the artistic quality that are accepted by art criticism do not say much about mathematically developed art. Precision is seen important for quality of mathematically developed art. While designing an artwork, a mathematician is careful to avoid ambiguity, so everybody can see the exact and precisely defined formula representation.

It may well be that a representation of mathematical formulas cannot inevitably become an art form, but it is their intentional transformation that may become an artwork. An artist using electronic media may communicate a distinction between a form in physical sense, i.e., a natural form, and a form in aesthetical sense, i.e., creation of mind. Due to the unique chance given us by the computer memory, one may search for the unity of an artwork, and may build its space by regrouping recurrent elements and contrasting ordered and chaotic relations between lines. For example, one may find electronic art media excellent for conveying the order and regularity of natural forms, depicting graphic patterns in nature, or rendering surfaces of objects in a still life. Activation of the neuronal system responsible for perception of an object results in one's personal idea of the object. For this reason, the artist departing from naturalistic imaging may evoke an individualistic and varying perception in each perceiver of the artwork. Then, a criticism of one's own work may provide an inspiration for further actions, especially if this artwork results from the artist's exposure to other works of art of another kind (e.g., to music or a literary work).

COMPUTATIONAL AESTHETICS AND AESTHETIC COMPUTING

Visual arts and computer technology could complement and assist each other in new and emerging interdisciplinary areas known as computational aesthetics and aesthetic computing (Zhang, Harrell, and Ji, 2012). The authors describe computational aesthetics as a way how technology could assist the visual arts (by creating tools), and how visual arts may help beautify technology outputs. For example, Price (2007) applied Kandinsky's aesthetics to Java programming. Aesthetic computing has been focused on application of the theory and practice of art to computer science: how aesthetics and art can play a role in computing disciplines (Fishwick, 2008). Zhang, Harrell, and Ji suggest that computer technology can generate aesthetic forms of visual art. Abstract paintings can be generated automatically using systematic and algorithmic approaches. As stated by the authors, modern computer technology can generate aesthetic forms of visual art at several levels of complexity, such as computerized abstract paintings realized by encoding computational rules to automatically generate a particular style of abstract painting.

Fishwick, Diehl, Prophet, & Löwgren (2005) describe interdisciplinary area of aesthetic computing, the study of artistic, personalized formal model structures in computing. This refers to the existence of aesthetics and its importance in computing and mathematics. Emphasis is on studying the art's effect on computing, rather than arts' advancements as achieved through technology. Paul Fishwick refers to numerous testimonies to aesthetics that can be found in mathematics (Hardy and Poincaré), physics (Einstein, Feynman), and computing (Knuth, Bentley with his "Programming Pearls"). In the Digital Arts and Sciences program, Fishwick (2005, 2008) has been teaching the Aesthetic Computing courses with the purpose of exploring the use of artistic methods and processes within common representations found in computing by translating physical and virtual computing models into aesthetic, personalized expressions. Fishwick (2006/2008) examines how aesthetics and computing may affect each other and can potentially alter their formal foundation – mathematics. He describes the goals of aesthetic computing as associated with exploring the applications of aesthetics to the field of computing, by representing components such as equations, trees, graphs, data structures, and programs to personalize mathematics and computer science.

Many times artists use technological potential for art making by utilizing software that was developed for other purposes but not as an artistic tool. The developments of computing and electronically generated art may affect our understanding of physical and human phenomena in a similar way as the development of the technology of microscopes and telescopes led to epistemological ideas under Rationalist philosophy, which stressed the meaning of observation as essential to scientific inquiry (Malina, 1990a). The medium of the artwork cannot be always defined as computer generated, computer inspired, computer aided, or computer enhanced. Not only the possible choices of media but also the aesthetic language of applying those media could not be discussed separately with regard to the mainstream and electronically generated art. For this reason, Ben Shneiderman (in a Foreword to Chen, 2011, p. vi) affirms, "transformative discoveries are likely to emerge from the twilight zones where multiple fields meet." In accordance with the postmodern approach to the existing images' deconstruction, both traditional and computer artists convey metaphorical messages by applying and transforming already existing images. We can consider Muybridge and Escher to be somehow protagonists of computer art, the factor of time used in their art being a common thread. With the introduction of computerized video technology, the dreams of Muybridge and Escher can be realized. Writings on aesthetics in data graphics take often form of a quest for those features that make graphics unique. An American artist born in Lithuania Ben Shahn (1898-1969) once said, "Aesthetics is for the artist like ornithology is for the birds." For Edward Tufte (1983, 1990), good design has two key elements: graphical elegance is often found in simplicity of design and complexity of data.

Some see the difference between the art using computer and art using traditional media much like that between painting and graphic techniques, as consisting in different types of tools. Each computer artist is working along his individual line and developing his own style. In 1933, long before the emergence of computer art, Arnheim observed that an artist makes his formative work and impresses his style on language of his art. Computer may be a stimulating tool in the creative process, as it provides inspiration coming from technology, but artists respond to the same metaphysical problems. However, in a growing number of publications the aesthetics concept refers to design effectiveness, efficiency, and easiness to understand (a low cognitive cost) of visual presentation, along with a computational self-critical function of a computer that can guide generative systems toward the machine creativity (Galanter, 2012a,b). For a wide range of computer vision applications, computational scientists and designers utilize technologies and procedures such as advanced mathematical analysis, computational processing, co-design of optical elements, and

computationally tractable models for human perception, along with high dimensional information display, dynamic range color reproduction, wide-color gamut display, and extended depth-of-field projection. Computational aesthetic evaluation might be based on conventional and geometric theories of aesthetics. The foundation for the digital exploitation would include the mathematical measure of aesthetics proposed by Birkhoff; the golden ratio (where the ratio of the smaller to the larger sub-segment is the same as the ratio of the larger sub-segment to the whole segment); the Zipf's law (studying the relation between the rank and frequency of natural language utterances); fractal dimension (providing a ratio of the change in detail to the change in the scale); basic gestalt design principles (telling about the principles of figure-ground articulation, proximity, similarity, closure, symmetry, continuity, past experience, common fate, and the good gestalt of perceptual scenes), and the rule of thirds (advising that an image should be imaginary divided into nine equal parts by two horizontal and two vertical lines, and that important compositional elements should be placed along these lines or their intersections). Computational aesthetic evaluation of evolutionary art systems may refer to the empirical studies and psychological modeling of aesthetics and neuroaesthetics. Figure 3 presents an individual perception of everyday experience, with simplified lines, shapes, and programmed figures digitally pictured against a synthetic background.

Mondays emphasize the typical routine each of us goes through during the workweek; after the weekend everything starts over. The cycle repeats itself with greater empathy, less efficiency, and even less energy.
All commotion, turmoil, confusion, and individual interests are then expressed and perceived with greater intensity.
This becomes a summary and a cast of characters for the whole week.

Figure 3. Anna Ursyn, Monday Morning (© 1995, A. Ursyn. Used with permission)

SOME CONCERNS ABOUT AESTHETICS OF DIGITAL ENVIRONMENT

Many times artistic productions made by technology-oriented people elicit critical reception from the artists. The advance of digital art created by computer programming or with the use of graphic software changed opinions about many issues in aesthetics and rose several not existing before questions. Electronic artwork, which could not be created in previous periods, differs from the design of traditional art because of its interactivity, programmability of images, possibility for blending media, and capacity for modeling real objects; it is often time-based (for example, recorded as a video or a CD) and multidimensional; many times

it is playful or provides synesthetic experience. In search for the identity of electronically generated art and the reasons for its poor recognition by the art world, some authors expressed doubt whether the computer is a medium, as it does not have physical material for image production but only a file of numbers that controls the image (Binkley, 1990). Painters or sculptors who are not labeled as electronic artists often use computers. Interactivity of a computer graphics can be utilized not only in service of art, but also for the purpose of art evaluation and communication. The French architect Jean Nouvel explained an interactive approach to the computerized architecture as a form of art as "a synergy between the different ideas, the possible solutions – an interaction, a connection, depth, complexity. This process shows how best to utilize the specific conditions of the program, the moment, the people" (De Bure, 1992, 15).

Another group of aesthetic issues relates to digital environments created with information technology. Developments in information visualization techniques, human-computer interaction, virtual reality simulations, and computer video games entail a need of exploring aesthetic dimensions of digital culture. Also, many communicate a need to draw some aesthetic constraints on such digital settings as websites, web browsers, software applications, and electronic art performances. Aesthetic merits are usually valued here in proportion to the degree how the solutions are user-friendly, clear and simple to apply, fast, efficient, and visually attractive.

Cooperation with scientists working on biology inspired methods and technologies and the cooperative nature of networked art events has evoked a spectrum of theories about art and aesthetics. Philip Galanter (2010) examined the ways of computational aesthetic evaluation, the notion of complexity as applied to the aesthetic perception of art objects and events, and posed that effective complexity might correlate with the aesthetic value. He sees a survival value in experiencing complexity as being pleasurable because pleasure directs our activity towards important survival behaviors. "Our aesthetic reward system encourages us to seek stimuli with high effective complexity content; the kind of stimuli associated with social interactions and the biological world" (Galanter, 2010, p. 8). Some find this approach restricted to particular forms of art such as the evolutionary art and somewhat behaviorist.

CHANGES IN CONCEPTS ABOUT THE AESTHETICS OF ELECTRONIC ART

Computers may have an effect on traditional art forms, both static such as painting, photography, sculpture, poetry and literature, and time-based such as kinetic art, video, music, dance and theater. In 1990 Roger Malina described attributes specific to the computer as a creative artistic tool. He saw them in its ability to have a built-in learning capacity, to collect and communicate large amount of information and to be used over large distance, in real-time, interactive display with humans or other devices (Malina, 1990, p. 159). The barriers between fine arts, data presentation, visualization, design and advertisement are constantly diminishing, which results in the widening spectrum of recipients. Visual communication in fine arts is often based on metaphors. Everyone may receive different, unique, and individual messages from the same artwork. Due to its memory, the computer allows saving versions deriver from a single image source. Painters or sculptors, usually not labeled as electronic artists, use computer as laborsaving or cost-saving devices. They also use them for trying many variations of a composition or visual design. With the computer at his command, an artist can make images of an object anew, not imitating or rendering objects, interpreting rather than recording images, creating spaces within spaces due to texture mapping, image processing and digitization, multimedia and virtual reality (Berton, 1990). The use of the computer may be helpful in the artist's exploration and experimentation in the course of creating an artwork without destructing its consecutive stages. Moreover, in a pursuit of masterly work the accent on technical perfection may be shifted from the capacities of a computer towards the artist's control of it.

The distinction between mind and nature, physical and mental processes, real and imaginary events disappear because information is separable from media in which it was stored and can be interactive; for this reason the viewers may speculate about whether the digital image and the original picture are on the screen of the monitor in the form of an array of colorful dots or in the contents of the frame buffer (image memory). Interactive relationship occurs between digital formats of the image residing inside the computer and its possible forms stored in traditional media. Computer art images bridge the gap between object and concept: they are at the same time physical objects that can be experienced with our eyes and mathematical concepts that can be computed without any visual manifestation (Binkley, 1990). In computer art, a file of numbers controls the image and different originals can be derived from the same program such as video image, a lithograph, or a slide. Conversion between a memory buffer and various graphic peripherals is controlled by interfaces.

Principles of aesthetic order dominated in the early period because of fascination with presentation of mathematical equations. Thus the early computer generated art graphics were mostly images of geometrically defined forms in Cartesian coordinates. Some of the themes of exploration that served as a starting point for creating an artwork were: the linear perspective, sectioning (for example, a golden section), the Fibonacci series (a sequence of numbers with the property that each number in the sequence represents the sum of the two preceding numbers), modeling, logic (especially based on Boolean operations), and logical laws applications (such as those based on Godel's theorem). Early inspirations included also the Lissajous figures (obtained through the superposition of sinusoidal waves upon the vertical and horizontal deflectors of the monitor) or images that visualize permutations cycling a basic set of numbers through all of its possible variations (Franke, 1971, 1989).

A number of computer art graphics were created due to fascination with astonishing patterns featuring harmonic relations such as the one thousand years old Vedic square – an arrangement of elements represented by numbers. (In the Vedic square, a set of numbers, for example 9 x 9, is placed in the first row. Remaining numbers in the square are computed by multiplying the respective values of row by column. Each time the product exceeds 9 a number is reduced by forming the sum of the first and second digit). Another source of aesthetic experience was seen in Latin squares

(arrangements possible of N elements where one number was placed only once in a particular row or column).

Some experiments were conducted on production of music in various historical styles generated by a computer, for example as a system for a musical composition. Since the sixties computer graphics have been used for various kinds of research in aesthetics and art theory, for the application of random processes as a principle generative impulse, as an interactive art object, for programming numbers as a code for particular colors, for distributing elements according to the "weighted" chance programs, etc.

A study of mathematical operations suitable for generating artistic images has been suggested as a method for creating art (Franke, 1971, 1989). Artistic creations have been achieved through visualization of mathematical relations from many fields of mathematics, such as geometry and fractal geometry (ultra realistic pictures built with numbers on the principle of self-similarity of forms composed of smaller forms, with shapes identical as the overall structure), field theory, Fourier transformations, topology, combinatorics, theory of numbers, and many others. A need for developing instruments and methods for studying rational aesthetics and its connections with mathematics has been stated by many artists and opposed by others.

AN INCLUSIVE ROLE OF A VIEWER: INTERACTIVE ARTS

The nineties brought the developments in interactive arts, designed for the first time in 1990 as a distinct category at the international computer art competition Prix Ars Electronica (Linz, Austria). Interactive art can be described as the viewers' real-time interaction with the artwork and the viewers' contribution to the presentation. Electronic images, computerized video animations, interactive installations, videotapes, multimedia presentations, and web art are examples of creating artifacts and interactions between the artist and the artwork. The viewer can respond and change the art environment in interactive installations, multimedia presentations, and virtual reality events. In the traditional art setting, a viewer could approach the artwork, change a point of view by walking around a sculpture, look at details, and evaluate the quality of an artwork. Electronic art allows us to communicate intelligence as well as information. Virtual reality systems connect visual environment to the viewer's nervous system. The viewers can experience an immersive 3-D reality, control computer programs, objects, and movement of images, contemplate colorful images controlled by music or created by their own movements, or put in motion laser beams by stepping on a projection surface.

Virtual reality systems represent a major advance in providing visualization environment and connecting it directly to the human nervous system. Virtual reality art often combines virtual and augmented reality technologies with mixed reality installations. The artistic events depend on the viewer's real-time interaction with the computer program. For example, the viewers could change the point of view in the barrier-strip autostereograms in sculpture [(ART)^n Laboratory/ The Nineties]. At the exhibition spaces, viewers could control the laser beam movements by stepping on its projection surface, which was recorded as an interactive computer video. Viewers could also put in motion the three-dimensional images created on monitors. They could contemplate colorful images created by their own movements recorded by a video camera with memory. Computer generated stereoscopic slides (stereoptics) enabled the viewers to experience a 3-D reality. Iron rods in a magnetic field were controlled by music. Myron Krueger (1991) has been considered the groundbreaking virtual and augmented reality researcher who envisioned *the art of interactivity, as opposed to art that happens to be interactive.*

Virtual reality art can be seen also in the Second Life world; in this case users represented by avatars can take any action they want. Artists use technologies of immersive virtual reality to create installations with 3D computer graphics and interactive 3D sound. Many of them generated a space for the perceptual interplay between self and world, such as an enveloping space 'Osmose' from 1995 created by Char Davies and several later works, where visitors can experience the awareness of their own self and their consciousness. David Rokeby's interactive work *'Very Nervous System'* has been evolving since 1982 along with the technology progress. The virtual-reality installation 'Particle Dreams in Spherical Harmonics' (2011) created by Dan Sandin and collaborators involves the viewers-participants in the creation of an immersive, visual, and sonic experience. As described, it is based on the physical simulation of over one million particles with momentum and elastic reflection in an environment with gravity, with realistic rendering of water and lighting based on spherical harmonics. The sound components are triggered and modified by the user and particle interaction. Several installations take form of public art that often document current reality. Maurice Benayoun created with a composer Jean Baptiste Barriére 'World Skin, a Photo Safari in the Land of War,' an immersive installation awarded with the Golden Nica, Ars Electronica 1998. 'Emotion Forecast' and 'Occupy Wall Screens' presented by the French new media artist Maurie Benayoun (2012) at the Big Screen Plaza near 6th Avenue, New York, NY, are the machine-made sculptures of digitally carved disks in various materials set out to map the world's emotions. Each disk bore a topographic pattern that corresponded to real-time Web data, which inventoried emotional states in the 3,200 biggest cities on the planet, by tracking word clusters (ecstatic, angry, terrified, etc).

Augmented-reality techniques allow combining the real world objects surrounding a user with virtual objects; moreover, these effects can be visualized with the use of see-through wearable displays, which add an image layer on top of what one can see through the glasses or as a video plugged to a smartphone. In a system that focuses on augmenting the user's full body, a half-silvered mirror combines the user's reflection with synthetic data to provide a mixed world. With a live and direct view of the user and the surrounding environment, the system allows the user to intuitively control virtual objects (for example, virtual drums) via the augmented reflection. Tangible textile interfaces behave as organic displays and react to impulses by showing animated patterns over the surface. When stimulated by viewers who touch the material, the pattern starts slowly shift. This interaction with a pattern is a demonstration of ubiquitous computing – an active, programmable secondary skin surrounding everyday objects – an ambient way to visualize information and form space (Eesti & Ozsvald, 2012).

It can be noticed, curators of recent international competitions offer categories such as Hybrid Art, Interactive Art, Digital Music and Sound, Digital Communities, Computer Animation/Film/VFX (visual effects), rather than Virtual Reality Art or Augmented Reality Art. And thus, Timo Toots, Estonia, won Golden Nica award in Interactive Art category for 'Memopol-2,' a social machine that maps the visitor's information field. When an identification document such as a national ID card or a passport is inserted into it, the machine starts collecting information about the visitor from (inter)national databases and the Internet. The data is then visualized on a large-scale custom display. People using the machine will be remembered by their names and portraits, and can see their data, from prescription drugs to high school exams, from tax reports to driving licenses. *Memopol-2* is a reaction to the developments in governmental data collecting; it uses contrasting aesthetics, being big and evil, dark and scary. Joe Davis, USA, was awarded Golden Nica at the 2012 Ars Electronica in the Hybrid Art category for 'Bacterial Radio,' which addresses the interface of biology and technology. According to the artist's statement,

Since nature is almost always much more efficient than human industry, researchers are focusing on various biological processes that can be put to work for humanity. However, biologically assisted methods of production are often put to use with relatively little understanding of the underlying chemical and molecular operations. A crystal radio is a basic resonant circuit requiring only induction, capacitance and a radio "crystal," a mineral semiconductor used to convert received radio signals into DC electrical signals that can be resolved with headphones as sound. These simple circuits require no batteries, tubes or transistors and operate with only the difference in voltage between the antenna and the ground. In spring 2011, I created a flat circuit design that could be constructed in a Petri dish. This circuit was then cast in negative relief in PDMS (polydimethylsiloxane) gel. Cells and growth media were then applied to circuit impressions in the gel. The cells used were E coli modified with a gene for silicatein, a ubiquitous protein native to many different marine organisms. These organisms use silicatein to polymerize silica from seawater in order to create glass endoskeletons and exoskeletons in a fantastic variety of forms. The silicatein gene used in the Bacterial Radio experiments was isolated from the marine sponge Tethya aurantia. Silicatein is a promiscuous protein, so that if growth media is starved of silica and instead provided with metal salts or semiconductors, then the protein will try to polymerize those materials instead. In this way, electrical characteristics were imparted to the two respective cultures of bacteria used with Bacterial Radio. Bacteria were fixed and immobilized in the PDMS gel. Pins and wires were used to connect elements of the gel-embedded circuit to each other and to external components such as the antenna, the ground and headphones. (J. Davis, Cyberarts 2012 - International Compendium Prix Ars Electronica 2012).

Figure 4. Anna Ursyn, No Concessions (© 2001, A. Ursyn. Used with permission)

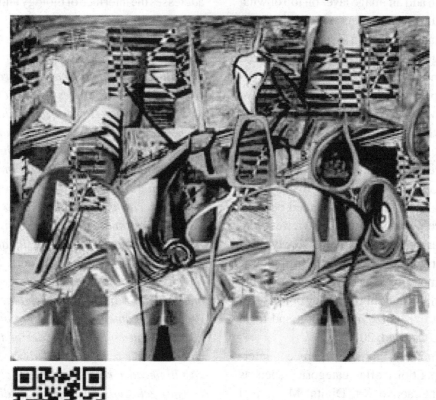

Figure 4, "No Concessions" introduces the element of confrontation, with an intention to question the combatants' motives: do they still remember what they are fighting for? One may ponder whether this question may somehow apply to the curators' preferences and choices for the art shows, with an emphasis placed mostly on the cutting-edge technological solutions.

PLACE FOR THE ELECTRONIC ART IN THE MAINSTREAM ART WORLD

We may be aware of the influence of past cultural patterns. The material and symbolic digital culture has been formed according to previous models.

The old cultural patterns on computer graphics, previous experience, knowledge, and conceptual frames influence both the scientific and artistic views on computer graphics' theory and practice. Artistic uses of computer graphics imitate the appearance and message of other contemporary art forms. Theorists in computer graphics, video, and photography stressed a need for aesthetical evaluation of the artistic, technical, scientific, commercial, and practical applications of computer graphics. An interactive computer art is not completed until a viewer becomes an active participant. The nature of the works of art has changed. The digital data can be easily shaped, moved, and transformed with computer tools for image processing, visualization, simulation, and network communication. Contrary to the traditional media of art, a computer artwork has been considered fixed in digital data that is not accessible to human senses.

Until recently, art critics discussed computer art referred as electronic media in terms of technology. Artists using computers have been finding more acceptances from the computing science community than from the art community. The subject of computer creations has been discussed pragmatically in respect to the programming and technical possibilities. The use of the whole computer's productive and technical capacity of hardware and software systems has been seen as the proof of the quality of a computer artwork, with products of simple programs not being qualified for the name of computer art. Theory and aesthetics of computer art have been underplayed. Art critics did not recognize computer art as a style until the context of computer art and its relationship to the mainstream art world emerged as an important issue. Creative activity and scholarly investigation on trends in electronic media art became a part of art departments' programs. The philosophy and practice in the field of electronic art is more often discussed as a part of the history of art not only as the history of technologies employed by the artists. Positions for electronic media artists have been opened to develop courses that employ the fine art application of computers.

CONCERNS ABOUT AESTHETICS OF VISUALIZATION

One may discuss the aesthetics of visualization as related to the visual competence in the art, design, and technological solutions in visualization. Visualization transmits the maximum amount of information with the minimum cognitive load for of the user. In a growing number of publications the aesthetics concept refers to design effectiveness, efficiency, and easiness to understand (a low cognitive cost) of visual presentation, not

exclusively the beauty of an image. Researchers who deal with advancements in visualization associate aesthetics with readability, and readability with understanding. Intensive research on the optimal layout aesthetics has been conducted in the field of graph drawing and the aesthetics of graph drawing algorithms (for example, Purchase; 2010; Lau & Vande Moere, 2007). Spatial relationships between nodes and edges and the overall layout, including graph's symmetry, area, flow, and aspect ratio, determine the aesthetics of a graph (Bennett, Ryall, Spalteholz, & Gooch, 2007). Methods of measuring the aesthetics of a layout and the results obtained suggested reducing the number of edge crossings and making the best use of symmetry, e.g., by maximizing symmetry of subgraphs. Artists' cooperation could amplify possible imagery from which visualization metaphors may be selected.

The physical model was a multimedia sculpture or architecturally oriented piece, and the virtual model was built in software. The physical model served the following purposes: 1) an artwork capturing the semantics of a computing model, 2) a tutorial device for teaching modeling, 3) an architectural model for future actualization, and 4) a prototype for a future tangible user interface with physical components being used to construct the computing model, which is sensed, identified, and automatically input to a computer. The virtual model had similar purposes to the physical, but emphasized attributes hard to achieve with physical materials: interaction, dynamics, and world navigation.

Discussion about the aesthetics of information visualization draws from existing approaches to information art and, even earlier, digital art. Moreover, tracing the evolution of digital art cannot be done without placing it within the context of art history, and in relation to other disciplines, such as cognitive science, computer science, philosophy, media studies, art history and criticism, and sciences dealing with images [Grau 2004, 2007, Wardrip-Fruin 2003, Lovejoy 2004].

On the other hand, some hold that aesthetics of information visualizations cannot be analyzed in terms analogous to artistic practices, especially when such analysis is based on misinterpretation of aesthetics as equivalent to art. Few would challenge the Andres Gaviria's [2008] assumption that "aesthetics is concerned with the theory of sensual perception, while art is a social practice involved in certain forms of research and investigation processes, and in the construction of particular types of artifacts." With this perspective, one may anticipate an impact of information visualization practices on aesthetic experience and the existing views about representation through art.

The application of aesthetics to the field of visualization supports a balance between form and function that is essential in the human interaction with the computer. Aesthetics of visualization pertains to visual means of expressing concepts and constructing meaning. Some time ago William Ittelson wrote, "The ability to perceive objects and events that have no immediate material existence and, indeed, may have no material existence at all" (Ittelson, 2007, p. 279). When we look at information visualizations, we can find truly captivating art works and aesthetically engaging projects. Many would agree that attractive visualizations are easier to understand and find a bigger audience. At the same time, data, processes, products, and events serve as a theme for art. Artists' cooperation could amplify possible imagery from which visualization metaphors may be selected. One can find a rich supply of imagery that has been drawn on to design knowledge-, data-, and information-visualization projects, where images serve as metaphors, icons, supporting images, etc., and thus metaphors are used not only in literature or speeches but also serve for searching data on the web.

Ward, Grinstein, & Keim, (2010, p. 366) have stressed that the effectiveness of visualization depends on its aesthetics. Visual appeal of visualization may depend on drawing the user's focus to the most important parts, balance of the screen space, and simplicity of presentation pro-

vided without information overload and graphical gimmicks. The authors provide several design rules for creating effective visualizations. These include the use of intuitive data-graphic mappings; providing multiple views of the data and tools for turning some parts off and on; including keys, labels, legends, and grids, along with a careful use of color and grids without occluding the data; creating attractive but not misleading design with semantic meaning and compatible units; providing the user an access to the raw data; and designing visualizations of the relative rather than absolute judgment (Ward, Grinstein, & Keim, (2010, p. 374).

Information aesthetics is a link between information visualization and visualization art. Interdisciplinary concepts, such as design cognition, user engagement, aesthetics, and art, can enhance information visualization. Current trend of information aesthetic visualization is focused on employing visual and interactive aesthetics to represent data in pleasurable and intelligible way. Several groups of people concerned with visual aesthetics create and maintain websites with collections of the most attractive visualization solutions, such as Visual-Literacy.org (2012) created and maintained by Sabina Bresciani, Martin Eppler, et al., where one can find, for example, an interactive portrait of Ben Shneiderman. The Information Aesthetics Weblog (http://infosthetics.com/) is another interesting ever-changing website with archives created and maintained by Andrew Vande Moere. The Flowing Data's blog (http://flowingdata.com/) collects appealing infographics.

Cawthon and Wande Moere (2007) consider aesthetics under-represented in most current data visualization evaluation methodologies. They postulated the positive role and purpose of aesthetics in the design of data visualization techniques. They examined the effect of the data visualization aesthetics on specific measures of usability (originally defined for website evaluation) namely, the correlation between perceived aesthetics, task abandonment (a measure of usability primarily referenced within the field of web analytics, a study of user behavior on the Internet), and erroneous response times (length of time taken by a participant who generates an incorrect answer). In an online survey, participants performed aesthetic ranking of 11 different visualization techniques and provided answers telling about task performance. The research results indicate that aesthetics has an effect on extending the latency of task abandonment and duration of erroneous response time: the most aesthetic data visualization technique (the Sunburst type) performs relatively high in metrics of effectiveness, rate of task abandonment, and latency of erroneous response. These factors correlate with user's patience, the duration in which interaction occurs before either completion or abandonment.

Aesthetics of visualizations is an important factor in building visual search engines. The mapping from a program to an image can be made through a metaphor. Most visualization techniques are based on a graph metaphor. There is an extensive research on graph layout algorithms and their metaphors. Using a methodology based on aesthetics and complexity to determine generative layouts, Paul Cleveland (2008) explored factors affecting aesthetic preferences and arousal potential and how they may depend on ratios, balance, complexity, and order. Several types of metaphors serve as the representations of programs, such as city representations, solar systems, video games, nested boxes, 3D space, etc. One can ponder over the use of avatars in visualizing knowledge. Aesthetics of visualizations could become part of education and an agent in further developments in this field. One may discuss the aesthetics of visualization as related to the visual competence in the art, design, and technological solutions in art creation, and thus competence depends on the balance between the digital art literacy and technological literacy. Visual quality of data-, information-, and knowledge-visualization projects depend on the skillfully applied imagery. This requires that images, symbols and metaphors are created or taken from the arts, both from the iconography of masterpieces and contemporary work of artists using technology.

AESTHETIC EDUCATION

People often shape their value schemata by providing a model person. A poet T. S. Eliot said he must rely upon his own sensitivity, intelligence, and capacity for wisdom. According to Harry Broudy (1972), the direct appeal of the aesthetic image is at the root of schooling, so whoever controls the images of value in a society also controls the value education. For him, the connoisseur is the person to whom small differences make a big difference, which becomes a bore to the layman. As Broudy states, the role of art in aesthetic education is to objectify metaphors created by artists' imagination, and students' feelings and values; to purify the students' imagery store, make it more conscious and less satisfied with the stereotyped image and the worn-out metaphor. Aesthetic literacy begins with learning aesthetic perception: ability to perceive the sensory, formal and expressive properties of the aesthetic images. Thus, the skills of aesthetic perception include perceiving sensory properties in the work, its formal qualities, technical merits, and expressive significance or message as aesthetically expressed. "Can serious art survive on the patronage of so small a portion of the population? It is clear that in this country it cannot... until the public schools take aesthetic education seriously" (Broudy, 1972, p. 115).

Digital productions affect viewers' aesthetic tastes and their perception. For this reason, developing aesthetic literacy in digital environment becomes an important concern related to computer graphics instruction. Electronic art is becoming finding its place in education. Until recently, electronic artists have been finding more acceptances from the computer community than from the mainstream art community and art criticism.

Trends and issues in electronic media art have now become a part of art departments' programs. Electronic media artists develop courses about fine art application of computers. Visual language, codes and symbols evolve with the new developments of tools and applications. Introduction of computers has an effect on traditional art forms, both on the static art, such as painting, photography, sculpture, poetry and literature, and on the time-based performance arts, kinetic art, video, music, dance and theater.

In terms of aesthetics, courses in computer graphics should help prospective computer artists create judgments about the sensory, formal, and expressive properties of digital images, and acquire visual and aesthetic skills along with technical and programming skills. Programs for art courses should be advised by computer graphics–related specialists. For example, software developers could discuss graphic possibilities offered by new kinds of software in terms of the market demands, while applying formal artistic quality principles to instruction could enrich interdisciplinary programs in computer science/visual arts.

SOME OPINIONS ON ART AND AESTHETIC

Opinions on the Role of Art

The interesting question is, whether artwork regarded now as art was considered art at the time it was made, and would it be art in the future. An answer to this question could depend on the results of an analysis of the art styles versus messages they carry: how issues in the old and new art works were solved in different times and in contemporary art, how they relate to actions or behaviors of people, influence their thinking, keep under control their emotions, and affect their reactions.

In fifteen century China, or seventeenth century Rome, identifying artworks could be easier than now, but how about the artists who did not fit into

the rules; where was then space for the progress? Moreover, properties common to all artworks and restricted only to artworks might always be rejected in the art of the future. For those reasons, it is difficult to find some perceptible properties that would be intrinsic to artworks.

The artist's intentions and the viewer's understanding of the artwork may be completely different; they also may be irrelevant to our understanding of the artwork. For some critics, intention is not only necessary but also sufficient for a creation to be considered an artwork. The artists' intentions are important but many times we, the viewers, do not know them, as in case of pre-historical cave drawings. A Nigerian/British painter Christopher Ofili used to apply elephant dung to his canvases making reference to his Nigerian heritage; in some African cultures elephant dung is a life-saving, valuable, and cherished resource. However, his Madonna image containing dried and varnished dung caused controversy. In many cultures inclusion of dung to the religion-related art is perceived offensive, and so the viewers and the media attacked the artist for profanity.

A question has been around whether the meaning of art changes in time, particularly due to the advent of electronic media, and whether there are some lasting motivations for creating art. Depending on the time, place, philosophical approach of an artist, and many other factors, the role of art has been seen as: producing beauty, imitating reality and beauty of nature, creating new forms and ideas, expressing artist's feelings, creating illusions, or providing shocking experiences. For this and several other reasons, some hold that history of art is a history of different opinions on art. For example, some people thought that culture is bad for art. Picasso pondered how to stay a child when growing as an artist. An avant-garde artist Jean Dubuffet (1901-1985), who created, for example, the "Jazz Band – Dirty Style Blues (1944), coined the term Art Brut (raw art); some artists belonging to the Art Informel movement believed that professional artists conveyed less truth than children, amateurs, naive artists, or insane people. Some hold that creating art does not require any skills because 'everything is art.' Others postulate that it's impossible to separate art from the rest of world. In this spirit, some artists, for example a British sculptor, photographer, and environmentalist Andy Goldsworthy chose to create earthwork art from natural and found objects. This process was documented in a film "Rivers and Tides" (2001, dir. Thomas Riedelsheimer).

Several artists adopted the environmental approach to art creation. For example, Scott Hessels (2012) created the wind-powered 'Sustainable Cinema No. 4: Shadow Play' as a kinetic public sculpture that harnesses sustainable energy to generate a moving image. According to the artist, "By using natural power to re-create an early art form that led to the beginnings of cinema, the sculpture references the histories of both motion pictures and industrialization. It explores a possible future of environmentally responsible media; looking forward by looking back." Christo created his environmental sculptures by wrapping great landmarks (natural or architectural) with woven nylon and rope, and thus temporarily transforming familiar surroundings (for example, The Pont Neuf Wrapped, Paris, 1985). The role of environmental art is seen in raising awareness of ecological issues, environmental degradation, and using found natural materials in harmony with the surroundings. The intention of many modern paintings is to bridge the distance between process of creating and a viewer, not necessarily rendering the naturalistic image of natural world. The value of such art is often seen in its impact than a product; for example, an impact can be achieved by creating installation art or interactive art where the viewer actively contributes to the creative process.

Opinions on Beauty

History of art is also a history of different opinions about beauty and the tastes of various epochs.

People had different thoughts about beauty; for example, some believed that:

- Beauty means perfection
- Beauty is something that provides aesthetic emotion
- Beauty causes visual sensations by shapes and colors. For example, from the 5th to 17th century proportion (with strict rules) was considered the most important criterion of beauty
- Then, a sense of the beauty of an artwork was shifted from the objective to subjective reception of an artwork
- Beauty of art has been separated from beauty of nature, and even
- Some theorists postulate that the concept of beauty does not exist in art, and cannot be defined

The worth of an artwork may depend on many factors, not necessarily related to its beauty. Former knowledge of the viewers may add up to their expectations concerning the aesthetic message. For this reason, reception of works of art that lack the predetermined pictorial models is most difficult. Such non-representational works are unlike anything; so many times they do not evoke much aesthetic pleasure. Two contemporary artists, Komar and Melamid (1997) asked viewers from several countries about their preferences related to art: what they considered beautiful, what was ugly, and what would they like to have in their homes, and then described their results in a book "Komar and Melamid's Scientific Guide to Art: Painting by Numbers" edited by JoAnn Wypijewski. According to the results of the Komar and Melamid's survey, the works of art wanted the least are abstract paintings that contain geometric patterns. On the other hand, the easy recognizable iconic images, that are often scanned and assembled eclectically in a post-modern way, act as well known symbols and evoke the viewers' appreciation not necessarily proportional to the aesthetic quality of the work.

Many times, beauty of masterpieces has been appraised not only according to their aesthetic values but also because of an artist's fame. The heart of exchanging ideas is contained in the message coming from the artist and the way it is conveyed to the viewer. Thus one cannot reduce this aim to just creating a picture, as it is tantamount neither to a cause nor to a purpose of artist's work. It has happened many times that effective communication with viewers and critics, and so the recognition of the artwork, came a long time after its creation. It happened with the paintings of a Dutch painter Jan Vermeer van Delft (1632-1675) about 200 years after their creation. Born in a family of a gallery merchant, he was assumed to take upon this profession. Vermeer supported his wife and children (4 of his 15 children died early), and he painted after hours of working in his inherited profession. His family preserved a great number of his paintings for two hundred years until they got discovered. Thus, many generations had to store and protect his art works in the crowded spaces.

However, great inventions in computer technology may lead to a really quick success of some electronic art productions followed by even faster fading of their fame. They may not be acknowledged as innovative anymore, and new bright solutions may cover up the older ones. In a similar way, public appraisal of the rendering talents of copyists, imitators, and forgers diminished with the improvement of reproducing technologies. Talents of the Dutch forger Han van Meegeren (1889-1947) who painted 'just discovered unknown works' of Vermeer were appreciated in his times, in both the artistic and deceptive terms, as equally skilled as those of the Masters; he was selling his paintings at high prices after he was unmasked as a counterfeiter. Van Meegeren created 'new' Vermeer's, Frans Hals' and other masters' paintings on old canvases from their times applying similar chemicals. Investigations made after his death with the use of the radioactive lead dating method revealed small differences in isotope composition of lead. It was caused by additional trace elements that were different in the 17th century than those that are present in contemporary lead pigments. Other investigations, including a gas chromatography method confirmed the forgery. One may ponder why talented people like van Meegeren preferred to forge and sign masterpieces instead of developing their own style, and whether they would still liked to do it having a computer as a tool, when computers make possible to do the task even without so great manual dexterity. Han van Meegeren and many other producers of counterfeits have been selling their works for millions until they were recognized as frauds; then the buyers felt they lost millions while still being the owners of these so called original works. Appraisal of the rendering talents has changed; documentation of historic events, wedding portraits and invitations do not necessary depend on artists' talents, as most people may use a camera, software for image manipulation, clipart, free Adobe Photoshop brushes, or other open source solutions. This is in a big contrast with the pre-computer documentation methods. For example, the art of Bernardo Belotto – Canaletto (1697-1768) became instrumental in shaping perceptions and initiatives not in the times when it was created but almost tree hundred years later, in the early days after the end of the World War II. Canaletto created tens of precise panoramic views of cities, including Warsaw, Poland, where he worked as the royal painter from 1767 till his death in 1780. His paintings were remarkable both in terms of their artistic quality and historical accuracy. In 1944 Warsaw was 90% burnt by the Nazis, along with historical writings and art works representing the Polish past, which were put on the Nazis' black-list to be destroyed due to their program of the germanization of invaded countries. After the end of the World War II citizens and architects rebuilt the traditional shape of Warsaw using informative visual materials contained in Canaletto's paintings to re-erect the whole quarters of the city, historical houses, residences, and churches (Ursyn, 2002).

Many times viewers examine artistic solutions, such as space, color, texture, value, motion, or dynamics within a picture, and they feel aesthetically impressed without even looking for a story, a caption, or a statement. Some examples of this are the fanciful scenes in works of the Dutch graphic artist Maurits Cornelis Escher (1902-1972), the human-like shapes painted by the Netherlands/American artist Willem de Kooning (1904-1997), the dynamic motion contained in works of the American artist Robert Motherwell's (1915-1991), the British photographer Eadweard Muybridge's (1830-1904) designs, or landscapes done by some

impressionist artists, for example, the French artist Claude Monet (1840-1926).

In 2004, an Italian semiotician and medievalist Umberto Eco co-edited with Girolamo de Michele "History of Beauty/On Beauty" (2010). Then, he discovered that history of ugliness is not supported with theoretical texts (Eco, 2011). We do not understand the meaning of imagery in many cultures so we shouldn't translate it into western terms such as "beautiful" or "ugly." Moreover, tastes of most people might differ from the tastes of the artists. Tastes might change in time, for example, dissonances in musical compositions were for centuries considered diabolic; now they are accepted for the same reason. In the past, people

Table 1.

Your Personal Response: Pick Art Works You Like (and Dislike)
From your environment, a book, or the Internet, pick an artwork you like the most. Describe in few sentences why you do like it. Then, do the same with a work of art you dislike most, and find if you have retained the same feeling toward the artwork after you have examined and described it.

drew an analogy between ugliness and moral evil, but "Darwin pointed out that what arouses disgust in a given culture does not arouse it in another, and vice-versa" (Eco, 2011, p. 16). Art, according to Eco, "insistently portrayed ugliness in various centuries ... because in everyday life we are surrounded by horrifying sights. ... Even if we accept them with the fatalism of those who believe that life is none other than a tale told by an idiot, full of sound and fury, ... I should like to finish wit the appeal for compassion" (Eco, 2011, p. 436-437) (See Table 1).

Aesthetic Perception

In his paper entitled "The Role of Imagery in Learning" written for the Getty Center for Education in the Arts, Harry S. Broudy (1987) examined properties of aesthetic perception. According to Broudy, making an informed aesthetic response may depend on perception based on examination of meanings. The skills of aesthetic perception may be summarized as the vividness and intensity in perceiving the sensory properties (such as shapes, lines, values, textures, colors, space, etc.); the formal qualities that tell how the work is organized (with unity in variety, hierarchy of elements, repetition, sense of balance, rhythm, and thematic variation); the technical merits that define how the object was created (for example how the surface texture was created by an impasto application of paint); and the expressive significance that reflects possible meanings: presentational (faces, trees, etc.) and/or metaphorical–symbolic characteristics. Expressive qualities of the object or the artwork evoke responses from one's storehouse of images and, when combined with sensory and formal properties, translate into such qualities as mood language (somber, frivolous, etc.), reflect the thematic meanings (such as faces, trees, etc.), metaphoric meanings (for example, symbols of a somber, frivolous, etc. mood), dynamic states (tension, conflict, relaxation, etc.), and ideas (such as interpretation of events, beliefs and expressions)

(Broudy, 1987). According to the psycholinguistic theory of nativism, all languages have some common phonetic, syntactic, and semantic features due to human genetic predisposition; hence they are marked by general similarities and universal generalities (e.g., universal grammar). Basic aesthetic experiences are considered by some anthropologists as aesthetic entities that result from apperception of archetypical forms.

Art Criticism

According to Broudy (1987), aesthetic criticism founded on aesthetic perception may be historical, recreative, and judicial. Historical criticism examines a work of art within its historical context and in relation to school, period, style and culture. Recreative criticism relates to artist's expression, while judicial criticism evaluates the artwork in relation to other works using three criteria: degree of formal excellence, truth, and significance.

Critical analysis of an artwork is considered a higher level thinking strategy that involves description, analysis, interpretation and judgment, rather then saying personal things about an artwork. When we are talking or writing on art, we put several types of questions to evaluate what we see and what we experience:

- The descriptive questions ask what we see;
- The analytical questions ask what are the interrelationships of the parts of the artwork;
- The interpretative questions ask what is the meaning to you; and
- The evaluative questions ask whether it is good or bad art, and if you do like or dislike it (see Table 2).

One may discuss in terms of phonology, whether any linguistic denotation system is based on an onomatopoeic, symbolic, or conventional principle. In the visual arts, acceptance of one or another system of signs may conceivably deter-

Figure 5. Anna Ursyn. "Planet Texture" (© 2010, A. Ursyn. Used with permission) In a big city, patterns consist of various shapes, hues, values, textures, and directions of lines. In a comparable way, societies, associations, communities, and groups create patterns that are diversified, specialized, and stratified.

mine the genre of artwork one creates. It could be figurative and realistic, such as are backdrops in interactive games or the French Academist paintings. Another style may be symbolic, such as in a computer-manipulated picture of Elvis Priestley emerging from a shell, or in Orthodox Eastern Church icons. It may also be convention-alized, such as in the digital artist Roman Verost-ko's calligraphic works or in paintings from the Far East. Communication through art cannot be considered explicit. According to Edwin Panofsky, meanings may be received on three levels. The first level of meaning is natural, pre-iconograph-ic, based on simple identification of objects. The

Table 2.

Your Personal Response: A Critique for a Magazine
How would you write a critique of an artwork for a literary or art-oriented magazine? List themes you consider important. Visit web pages that have some artwork on display. Go to many of them but concentrate on big galleries for this project. Find the artwork you really like, and then write a critique of that artwork. Make a description of the artwork under critique; the artist's name, the title of the artwork, its size, medium, year of production. First, collect the facts only (not your opinions) relating to depiction, composition, placement of objects, technique used, etc. Analyze and describe the facts you have collected by looking for proportion of forms, perspective used in the work, use of light and shade effects, texture, resemblance to the subject depicted or its deformation, relations between forms and the background. Try to make up a statement that would unify the single traits of the work. Make a critical interpretation of observations you have made. Do the separate traits of the work sum up to fit together and make sense? Why did you choose this piece of work and why did you prefer this one to the others. Make a judgment on the work in terms of formal beauty of the drawing, expressive values in communication with the viewer, and the instrumental effectiveness for a purpose. Justify your opinion on the artwork under critique. Why do you like the artwork?

secondary meaning is conventional and iconographic, derived from encoding abstract notions in the theme. Finally, there is an inner symbolic meaning of principles rather than individual motifs that may reveal their essence and symbolic value (Panofsky, 1997). Depending on a system of signs accepted in an artwork, the same work may be apprehended in different ways. For this reason, curators of exhibitions often supply information about works, such as paintings from the Baroque period or objects of oriental art, and explain a content of each picture providing a translation of images into their symbolic meaning. Besides an opportunity of indulging an aesthetic experience, the viewers are given an already forgotten code for the symbolic meaning, and thus they can take a secondary message that was hidden for them.

Art Manifestos

Writing a manifesto may be seen as an expression of one's aesthetic and philosophical thought about art (see Table 3). Art manifestos recording ideas for the artist or an art group, usually with their statements numbered or in bullet points became occurring often in the 20th century. Early manifes-

tos were mostly public declarations of political or social aims, for example, the Communist Manifesto written by Karl Marx and Engels in 1948. Avant-garde and modernist artists proclaimed their shocking, revolutionary ideas. Doubtlessly, the most expressive, controversial, and aggressive were Futurist manifestos. Futurism became an international movement in art, music, and literature. It emphasized the dynamism, speed, energy, and power of the machine, and restlessness of modern life. Too bad that Futurists were Fascists. In Paris in 1909, Marinetti, a poet, dramatist, and future friend of Mussolini introduced Futurism for the first time in an article in 'Le Figaro". In Italy, the Futurists introduced their manifestos in 1909 with

Table 3.

Your Personal Response: Manifesto
It seems quite interesting to follow some parallel actions and opinions and look for differences and similarities in various domains. After inspecting some examples of artistic manifestos created by visual artists you may want to create your own manifesto related to your favorite discipline. This activity creates an occasion to be playful and serious at the same time.

a purpose to liberate Italy from its past and enter modernity, in contrast to the weepy sentimentalism of Romanticism. The 'Manifesto of Futurist Painting' was signed by Boccioni, Carra, Russolo, Balla, and Severini.

(Art history resources on the web: http://witcombe.bcpw.sbc.edu/ARTHLinks.html, ART Source http://www.uky.edu/Artsource/general.html, http://www.unknown.nu/futurism).

Artists belonging to the Futurism movement were intrigued with motion as a symbol of the dynamism of modern world. For example, in "Flight of the Swallows" (1913) Giacomo Balla (1871-1958) used repetition to enhance the feeling of movement. In a similar way as other Futurists, Umberto Boccioni (1882-1916) inspired himself with science and technology, for example in a work "Head + Light + Surroundings" (1912); he as a Futurist considered the Machine Age to have a positive influence on art.

Futurists published several manifestos, which described their approach to art. For example,

- The Founding and Manifesto of Futurism, by F.T. Marinetti (Paris) Le Figaro, Feb. 20, 1909.
- The Manifesto of the Futurist Painters, by Umberto Boccioni, Carlo Carrà, Luigi Russolo, Giacomo Balla, and Gino Severini (Milan) Poesia, February 11, 1910.
- Technical Manifesto of Futurist Painting, by Umberto Boccioni, Carlo Carrà, Luigi Russolo, Giacomo Balla, and Gino Severini (Milan) Poesia, April 11, 1910, which is the key to the aesthetics of Futurism.
- Technical Manifesto of Futurist Sculpture, by Umberto Boccioni April 11, 1912.
- The Manifesto of Futurist Musicians, by Balilla Pratella Musica futurista per orchestre riduzione per pianoforte, 1912.
- Futurist Manifesto of Lust, by Valentine de Saint-Point Published as a leaflet January 11, 1913.

- Manifesto of Futurist Architecture, by Antonio Sant'Elia (Florence) Lacerba, August 1, 1914.
- The Futurist Cinema, by F.T. Marinetti, Bruno Corra, Emilio Settimelli, Arnaldo Ginna, Giacomo Balla, and Remo Chiti (Milan) L'Italia futurista, November 15, 1916.
- A Slap in the Face of Public Taste, by David Burliuk, Alexander Kruchenykh, Vladmir Mayakovsky, and Victor Khlebnikov 1917, and also many articles.

The Bauhaus Manifesto from 1919 proclaimed the unity of art, craft, industrial applications, and real life settings while teaching the vocabulary of forms, color, and their structural laws. After such training, the Bauhaus workshop participants could teach both the artistic and the technical aspects of their subject. André Breton proclaimed the Surrealist manifesto in 1924; he wrote: "Beauty will be convulsive – or will cease to be."

Raymond Lauzzana and Denise Penrose (1987) proclaimed "A 21st Century Manifesto," which starts with a statement, "That which is made by humans is art. Everything that is not is not. No natural things are art." They stated (1992), art is created by the artist and recreated by the observer/critic, and there is no meaning outside the relationship between the observer and the observed. The "Aesthetic Computing Manifesto," signed by thirty digital artists at the beginning of the 21st century, announced, "The application of computing to aesthetics, and the formation of art and design, has a long history, which resulted in the emergence of computer art as a new art form in the 1960s, with the integration of hardware, software, and cybernetics. We propose to look at the complementary area of applying aesthetics to computing … we wish to strike a balance between cognitive and material aesthetics."

Many times, students write their own manifestos that relate both to their artistic philosophy and the major discipline they are studying, for example, or a music manifesto. Ten years ago my student, Nathan Lowell wrote a still current Web Builder's Minimalist Manifesto:

Builder's of the World Wide Web, awake! The shackles of cuteness bind you and cripple you, obscuring communication and burying you in a mountain of unnecessary coding! Cast off these shackles that your work might be clear, clean, and unambiguously embraced by the masses.

1. No dancing bunnies! Stamp out writhing, bikini clad women and running dogs! The spread of these pointless animated graphics on pages clogs the bandwidth and provides no useful message content. Clear them from your minds and from your pages!

2. Eradicate the graphic separator line! These bars of various color and thickness pen your message behind walls much harder than steel! When coupled with an animated chromatic dazzle, they delight only you by blinding you to the pointlessness of their contribution to the page.

3. Tend to your fonts! Make the text big enough to be read. Use serif and sans serif fonts wisely and consistently. The text will set you free but only if people can read it!

4. Watch your background! Fie on those who would put red letters on black! A pox on you who place black text on dark gray marble! May the fleas of 10,000 camels infest your spouse's bedding, if you fail to provide sufficient contrast between the background and the text on your pages!

5. Stamp out Java! This spawn of the Oracle cannot be perceived by a host of viewers and takes up too much of your valuable time. The pitiful labor at which it toils provides little or nothing in the way of meaningful content, but serves only to fill the builder with unseemly hubris.

6. Demand better browsers! All browsers should support font objects as the builders intended them and not only as the viewer's machine has them! All text should format properly on the page with line length, tab controls, and a useful way of spacing the lines! Margins must be available on all browsers!

7. Deafen the clamor for sound! Until all homes have sufficient bandwidth, the Web is only a visual medium! Sounds serve no purpose in a visual medium! As well you might recite Shakespeare to the backs of the deaf! The limited bandwidth available to dialup modems must be preserved for content!

8. Edit your message! Check it for spelling and correct grammar! Ruthlessly prune unnecessary verbiage as you might your grape vine that it may bear more and sweeter fruit for it's trimming.

9. Strive for simplicity and clarity of message! The simplest designs carry the most elegant of messages. Don't hide your lack of content under the bushel of gratuitous graphic. Remember that, without white space, there can be no interest.

These few simple rules, my sisters and brothers, will free you from the slavery of Technology-Because-We-Can! Your pages will take on an ethereal beauty that can only enhance the messages you herald. Your work will be valued, its praises sung. Builders of the World Wide Web, awake!

CONCLUSION

Studies on aesthetics relate to the arts, philosophy of art, and our judgments about sensory and emotional values of specific art works. Traditionally the aesthetic values included objects that were beautiful, harmonious, or emotionally pleasing. Computing science specialists examine aesthetics of electronic projects' usability, efficiency, and discuss aesthetics in terms of possible applications to controlling computer products. The cultural convergence of mathematics, art, and computer science resulted in mathematics-based patterns in world's architecture and design, and also the innovative works of the mathematicians. Our neural organization makes possible the creation and appreciation of art (Zeki, 1993, 1999). Electronic art allows us to communicate intelligence as well as information. Augmented-reality techniques and virtual reality systems connect visual environment to the viewer's nervous system. Aesthetic computing has been focused on application of the theory and practice of art to computer science. Digital environments created with information technology, information visualization techniques, human-computer interaction, virtual reality simulations, and computer video games entail a need of exploring aesthetic dimensions of digital culture. Readers are invited to cooperate by writing an art critique and an art manifesto.

REFERENCES

Aesthetic Computing Manifesto. (n.d.). Retrieved October 10, 2012 from http://www.cise.ufl.edu/~fishwick/aescomputing/manifesto.pdf

Alleyne, R. (2011, May 8). Viewing art gives same pleasure as being in love. *The Telegraph.* Retrieved May 1, 2012, from http://www.telegraph.co.uk/culture/art/8501024/Viewing-art-gives-same-pleasure-as-being-in-love.html

Arnheim, R. (1990). Language and the early cinema. *Leonardo*, 3–4.

Benayoun, M. (2012). *Emotion forecast and occupy wall screen.* Retrieved October 11, 2012, from http://www.benayoun.com/projet.php?id=180

Bennett, C., Ryall, J., Spalteholz, L., & Gooch, A. (2007). *The aesthetics of graph visualization: Computational aesthetics in graphics, visualization, and imaging.* Eurographics Association.

Berton, J. A. Jr. (1990). Film theory for the digital world: Connecting the masters to the new digital cinema. *Leonardo*, 5–11.

Binkley, T. (1990). Digital dilemmas. *Leonardo*, 13–19.

Birkhoff, G. D. (2003). *Aesthetic measure.* Kessinger Publishing. (Original work published 1933).

Broudy, H. S. (1972). *Enlightened cherishing: An essay on aesthetic education.* Urbana, IL: University of Illinois Press.

Broudy, H. S. (1987). *The role of imagery in learning.* Occasional Paper 1. Malibu, CA: The Getty Center for Education in the Arts.

Cardillo, E. R., Watson, C. E., Schmidt, G. L., Kranjec, A., & Chatterjee, A. (2012). Article. *NeuroImage, 59*, 3212-3221. Retrieved June 7, 2012, from http://ccn.upenn.edu/chatterjee/anjan_pdfs/YNIMG8957.pdf

Cawthon, N., & Vande Moere, A. (2007). The effect of aesthetic on the usability of data visualization. In *Proceedings of 11th International Conference on Information Visualisation.* IEEE.

Chatterjee, A. (2003). Prospects for a cognitive neuroscience of visual aesthetics. *Bulletin of Psychology and the Arts, 4*(2), 55-60. Retrieved June 7, 2012, from http://ccn.upenn.edu/chatterjee/anjan_pdfs/Prospects%20of%20Cog%20Neuro%20Visual%20Aes.pdf

Chatterjee, A. (2011a). Where there be dragons: Finding the edges of neuroaesthetics. *American Society for Neuroaesthetics, 31*(2), 4-6. Retrieved October 6, 2012, from http://aesthetics-online.org/newsletter/31.2.pdf

Chatterjee, A. (2011b). Neuroaesthetics: A coming of age story. *Journal of Cognitive Neuroscience, 23*(1), 53–62. doi:10.1162/jocn.2010.21457 PMID:20175677.

Chen, C. (2011). *Turning points: The nature of creativity*. Springer-Verlag.

Cinzia, D. D., & Gallese, V. (2009). Neuroaesthetics: A review. *Current Opinion in Neurobiology, 19*(6), 682–687. doi:10.1016/j.conb.2009.09.001 PMID:19828312.

Cleveland, P. (2008). Aesthetics and complexity in digital layout systems. *Digital Creativity, 19*(1), 33–50. doi:10.1080/14626260701847498.

Correra, P. N., & Correra, A. N. (2004). *Nanometric functions of bioenergy*. Akronos Publishing.

Csikszentmihalyi, M., & Robinson, R. E. (1991). *The art of seeing: An interpretation of the aesthetic encounter*. J. Paul Getty Museum. ASIN B0088PKSOW

De Bure, G. (1992). *Jean Nouvel, Emmanuel Cattani, and associates: Four projects*. Zurich: Artemis.

DeLanda, M. (2010). Deleuze: History and science. (W. Schirmacher, Ed.). Atropos Press. ISBN 0982706715

Deleuze, G., & Guattari, F. (1983). *Anti-Oedipus*. Minneapolis, MN: Minnesota UP.

Deleuze, G., & Guattari, F. (1987). *A thousand plateaus: Capitalism and schizophrenia* (B. Massumi, Trans.). University of Minnesota Press.

Dorin, A., & Korb, K. (2007). Building artificial ecosystems from artificial chemistry. In *Proceedings of the 9th European Conference on Artificial Life*. Springer-Verlag.

Eco, U. (1979). *The role of the reader, explorations in the semiotics of texts: Advances in semiotics*. Bloomington, IN: Indiana University Press.

Eco, U. (1989). *The open work* (A. Cancogni, Trans.). Cambridge, MA: Harvard University Press.

U. Eco (Ed.). (2004/2010). *History of beauty*. Rizzoli.

Eco, U. (2011). *On ugliness*. Rizzoli.

Eesti, K. O., & Ozsvald, E. (2012). Symbiosis. In *Proceedings of the SIGGRAPH 2012 International Conference and Exhibition of Computer Graphics and Interactive Techniques*. Retrieved October 8, 2012, from http://s2012.siggraph.org/attendees/sessions/symbiosiss

Fishwick, P. (2005). *Introduction to the aesthetic computing method for teaching algebra in middle and high school*. Retrieved March 26, 2012 from http://www.cise.ufl.edu/~fishwick/acworkshop/aestheticcomputing.pdf

P. Fishwick (Ed.). (2006/2008). *Aesthetic computing. Leonardo Book Series*. The MIT Press.

Fishwick, P. (2006). Injecting creativity into teaching simulation modeling to computer science students. *Simulation, 82*(11), 719–728. Retrieved from http://sim.sagepub.com/cgi/content/abstract/82/11/719 doi:10.1177/0037549706074191.

Fishwick, P., Diehl, S., Prophet, J., & Löwgren, J. (2005). Perspectives on aesthetic computing. *Leonardo, 38*(2), 133–141. doi:10.1162/0024094053722372.

Franke, H. W. (1971). *Computer graphics, computer art*. Phaidon Press.

Franke, H. W. (1989). Mathematics as an artistic-generative principle. *Leonardo*, 25–26.

Galanter, P. (2010). The problem with evolutionary art is. In C. Di Chio et al. (Eds.), *EvoApplications, (LNCS)* (Vol. 6025, pp. 321–330). Berlin: Springer-Verlag.

Galanter, P. (2012a). *Complexity, neuroaesthetics, and computational aesthetic evaluation*. Retrieved June 8, 2012, from http://philipgalanter.com/downloads/ga2010_neuroaesthetics_and_cae.pdf

Galanter, P. (2012b). Computational aesthetic evaluation. In *Proceedings of the SIGGRAPH 2012 International Conference and Exhibition of Computer Graphics and Interactive Techniques*. Retrieved October 8, 2012, from http://s2012.siggraph.org/attendees/sessions/computational-aesthetic-evaluation-steps-toward-machine-creativity

Gaviria, A. R. (2008). When is information visualization art? Determining the critical criteria. *Leonardo, 41*(5), 479–482. doi:10.1162/leon.2008.41.5.479.

Goldblatt, D., & Paden, R. (2011). The aesthetics of architecture: Philosophical investigations into the art of building. *The Journal of Aesthetics and Art Criticism, 69*(1), 1–6. doi:10.1111/j.1540-6245.2010.01441.x.

Grau, O. (2004). *Virtual art: From illusion to immersion. Leonardo Book Series*. Boston: The MIT Press.

O. Grau (Ed.). (2007). *Media art histories. Leonardo Book Series*. Boston: The MIT Press.

Hansen, M. B. N. (2006). *New philosophy for new media*. Boston: The MIT Press.

Hessels, S. (2012). Sustainable cinema no. 4: Shadow play. In *Proceedings of the SIGGRAPH 2012 International Conference and Exhibition of Computer Graphics and Interactive Techniques*. Retrieved October 9, 2012, from http://s2012.siggraph.org/attendees/sessions/sustainable-cinema-no-4-shadow-play

Ishizu, T., & Zeki, S. (2011). Toward a brain-based theory of beauty. *PLoS ONE, 6*(7), e21852. doi:10.1371/journal.pone.0021852 PMID:21755004.

Ittelson, W. H. (2007). The perception of nonmaterial objects and events. *Leonardo, 40*(3), 279–283. doi:10.1162/leon.2007.40.3.279.

Kac, E. (2006). *Signs of life: Bio art and beyond. Leonardo Books*. Boston: The MIT Press.

Kac, E. (2011). *Website of Eduardo Kac*. Retrieved October 6, 2012, from http://ekac.org/

Kawabata, H., & Zeki, S. (2004). Neural correlates of beauty. *Journal of Neurophysiology, 91*, 699–1705. doi:10.1152/jn.00696.2003 PMID:15010496.

Kirk, U., Skov, M., Christensen, M. S., & Nygaard, N. (2009). Brain correlates with aesthetic expertise: A parametric fMRI study. *Brain and Cognition, 69*(2), 306–315. doi:10.1016/j.bandc.2008.08.004 PMID:18783864.

Krueger, M. (1991). *Artificial reality 2*. Reading, MA: Addison-Wesley Professional.

Lau, A., & Vande Moere, A. (2007). Towards a model of information aesthetics in information visualization. In *Proceedings of 11th International Conference on Information Visualisation*. IEEE.

Lauzzana, R., & Penrose, D. (1987). A 21st century manifesto. In *Proceedings of FINEART Forum 1, Electronic Newsletter of International Society for Art, Science, and Technology (ISAST)*. ISAST.

Lauzzana, R., & Penrose, D. (1992). A pre-21st century manifesto. *Languages of Design, 1*(1), 87.

Lebwohl, B. (2011, July 25). Semir Zeki: Beauty is in the brain of the beholder. *EarthSky*. Retrieved May 1, 2012, from http://earthsky.org/human-world/semir-zeki-beauty-is-in-the-brain-of-the-beholder

Leyton, M. (2006). The foundations of aesthetics. In P. A. Fishwick (Ed.), Aesthetic Computing (pp. 289-314). Leonardo Books. Cambridge, MA: The MIT Press. ISBN 026206250X

Lovejoy, M. (2004). *Digital currents: Art in the electronic age* (3rd ed.). Routledge.

Lyotard, J. F. (1994). *Lessons on the analytic of the sublime (meridian: crossing aesthetics)*. Stanford University Press.

Maeda, J. (2004). *Creative code: Aesthetics + computation*. Thames & Hudson.

Malina, R. F. (1990). The beginning of a new art form. In *Proceedings of Der Prix Ars Electronica: International Compendium of the Computer Arts*. Linz: Veritas-Verlag.

Minissale, G. (2012). Conceptual art: A blind spot for neuroaesthetics? *Leonardo*, *45*(1), 43–48. doi:10.1162/LEON_a_00324.

Pouivet, R. (2000). On the cognitive functioning of aesthetic emotions. *Leonardo*, *33*(1), 49–53. doi:10.1162/002409400552234.

Price, C. B. (2007). From Kandinsky to Java (the use of 20th century abstract art in learning programming). *ITALICS*, *6*(4), 35–50. doi:10.11120/ital.2007.06040035.

Purchase, H. (2010). Graph drawing aesthetics in user-sketched graph layouts. In *Proceedings of the Eleventh Australasian Conference on User Interface*, (Vol. 106). ACUI. ISBN: 978-1-920682-87-3

Seeley, W. P. (2011). What is the cognitive neuroscience of art … and why should we care? *American Society for Neuroaesthetics*, *31*(2), 1-4. Retrieved October 6, 2012, from http://aesthetics-online.org/newsletter/31.2.pdf

Stam, R. (2000). *Film theory*. Oxford, UK: Blackwell.

Tatarkiewicz, W. (1976). *Dzieje szesciu pojec*. Warsaw, Poland: PWN.

Tatarkiewicz, W. (1999). *History of aesthetics* (C. Barrett, Ed.). London: Thoemmes Press.

Tractinsky, N., Katz, A. S., & Ikar, D. (2000). Article. *Interacting with Computers*, *13*(2), 127–145. doi:10.1016/S0953-5438(00)00031-X.

Tufte, E. R. (1983/2001). *The visual display of quantitative information*. Cheshire, CT: Graphics Press.

Tufte, E. R. (1992/2005). *Envisioning information*. Cheshire, CT: Graphics Press.

Tufte, E. R. (2003). *The cognitive style of powerpoint*. Cheshire, CT: Graphics Press.

Ursyn, A. (2002). Art as information. *Leonardo*, *35*(4), 445–446. doi:10.1162/002409402760181277.

Vesna, V. (2007). *Database aesthetics: Art in the age of information overflow (electronic mediations)*. Minneapolis, MN: University of Minnesota Press.

Victorri, B. (2007). Analogy between language and biology: a functional approach. *Cognitive Process, 8*(1), 11-9. Retrieved May 27, 2012, from http://www.ncbi.nlm.nih.gov/pubmed/17171371

Ward, M., Grinstein, G., & Keim, D. (2010). Interactive data visualization: Foundations, techniques, and applications. Natick, MA: A K Peters, Ltd.

N. Wardrip-Fruin, & N. Montfort (Eds.). (2003). *The new media reader*. Boston: The MIT Press.

Watanabe, S. (2010). Pigeons can discriminate 'good' and 'bad' paintings by children. *Animal Cognition, 13*(1), 75-85. Retrieved October 1, 2012, from www.ncbi.nlm.nih.gov/pubmed/19533184

Watson, C. E., & Chatterjee, A. (2011). The functional neuroanatomy of actions. *Neurology*, *76*, 1428–1434. doi:10.1212/WNL.0b013e3182166e2c PMID:21502604.

Weitz, M. (1956). The role of theory in aesthetics. *The Journal of Aesthetics and Art Criticism*, *15*, 27–35. doi:10.2307/427491.

J. Wypijewski (Ed.). (1997). *Komar and Melamid's scientific guide to art: Painting by numbers*. New York: Farrar Straus Giroux.

Zeki, S. (1993). *Vision of the brain*. Oxford, UK. *Wiley-Blackwell., ISBN-10*, 0632030542.

Zeki, S. (1999). Art and the brain. *Journal of Conscious Studies: Controversies in Science and the Humanities*, 6(6/7), 76–96.

Zeki, S. (2001). Artistic creativity and the brain. *Science, 293*(5527), 51–52. doi:10.1126/science.1062331 PMID:11441167.

Zeki, S. (2011). *The Mona Lisa in 30 seconds*. Retrieved May 1, 2012, from http://profzeki.blogspot.com/

Zhang, K., Harrell, S., & Ji, X. (2012). Computational aesthetics: On the complexity of computer-generated paintings. *Leonardo, 45*(3), 243–248. http://www.mitpressjournals.org/doi/abs/10.1162/LEON_a_00366 doi:10.1162/LEON_a_00366.

Chapter 5
Art and Design Criticism in Art Production and Instruction

ABSTRACT

This chapter examines some of the changes in views about art, criticism of art works, and art-related teaching objectives, as they evolve with the developments in the new media art, works created through the Web, social networking, art created on portable devices, as well as information technologies. First, this chapter examines the changing meaning of the aesthetics notion in mathematics, science, information art, and information technology, as well as changes in the views about instruction in art criticism. Examination of these approaches is then contrasted with the models adopted in education. The four-part model used in instructional design, based on audience, outcome, environment, and usability, is adapted to suit the needs of art criticism. Materials based on a literature review provide the rationale for a four-part model to facilitate art critique. The next part is about the changing dimensions of criticism in the new media art and product design in respect to the product semantics analysis.

INTRODUCTION

Every act of art creation resonates among perceivers in the form of criticism. Also, education in the arts is under constant critical assessment. It is often considered the first program to cut when budget proves to be tight. In this chapter, discussion of art criticism, juxtaposed with a model of assessment, is aimed to analyze current cultural patterns and place the reader's interactive project in a critical framework.

Few people would contradict the opinion that assessment in art is nearly impossible because there are almost no generally accepted definitions and standards. The idea of the existing standards tells mostly about formal requirements along with the aesthetic values of the works, and everybody can be right or wrong, with their contrasting statements. Combining the roles of a teacher and an artist (a teacher-artist or an artist-teacher) is often considered valuable because such person is well aware of the creative instructional processes, so one can perform better. However, assessment of the artist-critic may be biased because of a personal art statement this person expresses: a critic has usually his/her own expectations about ethnicity, culture, gender, new communication technologies, new media art, etc. When we encounter a critic-artist or an artist-critic person, we can expect that this individual is familiar with the creative process not only in traditional

DOI: 10.4018/978-1-4666-4627-8.ch005

media but also in new media art. For this reason many hold that we need standards for designing curricula for the new media art critique programs: for this reason, a student of the graduate program in art criticism should complete courses in art to acquire skills in drawing, sketching (on paper and on tablet computers such as iPad), computer graphics, graphic design, computer art/3D, time based art such as video, animation, and web design, and even programming for web, smart phones or tablets. With the growing role of the networked technology in creating and disseminating art works one may expect that understanding the web and

technology driven demands is a requirement for a new media art critic.

Figure 1, "Choice Based Narrative" is a story about a truck driver transporting hazardous cargo who used to detach himself from possible dangerous scenarios by imaging good things he might convey to his passengers when he additionally works as a taxi driver. Not thinking about one's fears may diminish potential danger. The whole story may in some way relate to some dilemmas concerning the existing standards and formal requirements in art criticism.

Figure 1. Anna Ursyn, "Choice Based Narrative" (© 2010, A. Ursyn. Used with permission)

My taxi driver's day job is to drive with explosive cargos.
Not too hard of a job if you know limitations,
if you learn to train your brain to shift
From:
what you know,
what you've seen,
what can go wrong,
To:
what fun passengers will have
when they leave your cab.

AESTHETIC DIMENSIONS OF INFORMATION ART AND INFORMATION TECHNOLOGY

Criteria concerning the artistic quality that are accepted by art criticism do not say much about mathematically developed art. Soap bubble geometries, as well as fractal shapes rose to the form of art because of their natural beauty. Precision is seen important for quality of mathematically developed art. Graphic elegance can be found in the simplicity of the image that demands, "every bit of ink on a graphic requires a reason" (Tufte, 1983/2001). In one of his books, French philosopher and anthropologist associated with the development of structuralism Claude Lévi-Strauss (1997, pp. 83-87) characterized the essence of fractals in art. He recalled that according to Kant, aesthetic judgment has a place between judgments of taste (which are subjective) and judgments of reason (which are universally valid). The master of envisioning statistical information Edward Tufte (1997) explored how to recognize the multivariate nature of analytic problems and create multidimensional graphics that enhance the explanatory power of display. For John Maeda (2011) who is exploring the issues of aesthetics and computing, education is the highest form of intellectual philanthropy. With this approach, his students have been for years offering at no cost upgrades of programs for learning programming

available for all main operating systems, along with the Processing, an open-source programming language and environment. This is also true about other initiatives. For example, open-source platforms include Google SketchUp.com; Blender.org and Blender 3D; Moovl and Sodaplay; Panda3D – free game engine; GIMP – free and open-source GNU Image Manipulation Program for X Windows systems; Inkscape – an open-source vector graphics editor; POV-Ray – The Persistence of Vision Raytracer, a freeware multi-platform raytracing package, among other options. They are accessible free, however some of them offer also a paid, enhanced version; those who need free software can download it at no cost. The same holds true to various apps, for many reasons.

Visualization of fractals or the mathematical expression of music compositions with the use of Fourier analysis and fractal mapping allow for creating sonograms and experiencing digital synaesthesia. We are immersed in a variety of sounds coming from our surroundings, music, and various types of communication. The two disciplines, mathematics and music overlap making visual music possible.

"Bornholm" (Figure 2). *Bornholm is a Danish island in a Baltic Sea, which is eagerly visited by sailors because of its spectacular rock formations and a tradition in sailing sports such as the Danish Open and the World Match Racing. Coexistence of the exquisite beauty of yachts with their technical perfection may be likened to the flawlessness of the soap bubble geometries and the natural beauty of fractals, as both are appealing, and at the same time objectively governed by physical laws or reason.*

On that sunny day, it was easy to reach the harbor,
And find the depths suitable to lie at anchor.
Then, the next afternoon
Swiftly, smoothly, effortlessly sail against the wind.

Figure 2. Anna Ursyn, "Bornholm" (© 2003, A. Ursyn. Used with permission)

On the other hand, there is an aesthetic dimension of science. Aesthetic values inherent to mathematics and science, along with pleasure coming from using aesthetic values in making scientific judgments, have been stressed by Flannery (1992, p. 2): "Doing science is an aesthetic experience. All of science is permeated with the aesthetics, ... both public science-as-an-institution and "private science-in-the-making with its speculative and creative element. This side of science involves pleasure and using aesthetic values in making judgments. ... Doing science gives very similar "experiences to those involved in creating works of art: first, feelings of involvement and detach-ment, anxiety and confidence; then, surprise and elation when the problem is solved. The goal is to make science attractive enough to encourage lifelong learning among non-scientists."

Figure 3 "Logical Log" explores the idea of a static factor of time incorporated into a tree trunk as a sculpture and reveals correlations among nature, time, and our consciousness. The bluish circles metaphorically refer to the dried tree rings. There may be a danger of a treeless landscape caused by growing needs of human civilization. Natural annual rings showing the time needed for a tree to achieve its thickness have been juxtaposed with the expression of human acquisitive nature

Figure 3. Anna Ursyn, "Logical Log" (© 1998, A. Ursyn. Used with permission) Ash log (w 20", h 26", d 20"), and a program-based photosilkscreen on a fabric (Fortran, mixed media)

shown as a rhythmic pattern on the computer print. Rhythmic circles demonstrate diminution instead of the growing of the tree mass; hence a calling for saving the trees, for example through the use of e-mail instead of paper.

According to Galanter (2009a), the understanding of the mechanisms under human aesthetic experience is necessary in order to gain the ability to make computational aesthetic evaluations. Contributions toward such understanding include the theories from the field of evolutionary psychology, models of human aesthetics from psychologists such as Rudolph Arnheim (1988), Daniel Berlyne (1971, 1974), and Colin Martindale (1980), empirical studies of human aesthetics, and a growing literature in the field of neuroaesthetics (Zeki, 1999). Several authors attempted to apply numeric measures as aesthetic indicators (Galanter, 2009b), even looking for the computational equivalent of animal brain for computational aesthetic evaluation (Galanter, 2011). However, in opinion of Philip Galanter (2010) there are no computer methods of critical evaluation or the effective machine-based aesthetics. He sees a survival value in complexity as applied

to the aesthetic perception of art, at least the evolutionary art. Complexity might correlate with the aesthetic value. Experiencing complexity is pleasurable and pleasure directs our activity towards survival behaviors. To build creative systems we need generative systems plus systems of critical judgment. There were few attempts to apply design principles in evaluation of computational aesthetics. In an attempt to understand the correlation of human emotions and pictures people see, Ritendra Datta, Dhiraj Joshi, Jia Li, & James Z. Wang (2006) classified with the use of software the photo quality, which they correlated with the human ratings across 15 key features in separating high and low rated photographs.

Information Aesthetics Showcase at the ACM/SIGGRAPH 2009 Conference (ACM/SIGGRAPH, 2009), which included 2D and 3D prints, interactive and presentational screen-based works, multimodal installation environments, and physical objects, engaged not only the visual but also auditory, kinesthetic, and tactile modalities. However, many conference-related art galleries organizers stopped hanging two-dimensional artworks to be seen by conference participants. Carlsson (2010) addresses two types of perspectives on the aesthetics that are of relevance for a discussion of contemporary information design. Firstly, the 'aesthetic' understood as aesthetic perception of a beautiful form, and secondly, the 'aesthetic' recognized as the poietic activity, i.e. the production of an object in which the recipient also takes part. The author discusses these perspectives in relation to questions of form and content, and argues that aesthetic elements in some contemporary information designs cannot be understood as aesthetic perception of beautiful form but as poietic, creative elements.

Developments in information visualization techniques, human-computer interaction, virtual reality simulations, and computer video games entail a need of exploring aesthetic dimensions of digital culture and drawing up aesthetic constraints on such digital settings as websites, web browsers, software applications, and electronic art performances. Aesthetics of visualization pertains to visual means of expressing concepts and constructing meaning, and thus depends on the balance between the digital art literacy and technological literacy. Information aesthetics, discussed by Lev Manovich (2001) as appropriate for a society where most work and many forms of leisure are computer-based, inspired Andrew Vande Moere to discuss info-aesthetics in several publications (e.g., Lau & Vande Moere, 2007; Vande Moere, 2008; Vande Moere & Offenhuber, 2009) and establish in 2004 a weblog "Information Aesthetics: Where form follows data" (http://infosthetics.com). After examining the database as cultural and aesthetic form (Vesna, 2007), researchers stress the essential role of artists as co-creators and critics of the network culture; artists' choices in organizing the vast amounts of information as a medium play a part in formation of the database aesthetics.

A research professor of cognitive science Margaret Boden (2010) considers the theory and methods in computer art criticism more demanding than it is for the traditional art forms. She applies the homeostasis concept, in terms of the independence of the environment, as a form of autonomy that may exist in computing machines, computerized neural networks (due to, e.g., parallel distributed processing, PDP methods), and some computer artwork installations. Boden indicates some concepts often used in defining 'life' are common with those describing certain areas of computer art. These concepts may include emergence, autonomy, unity/wholeness, autopoiesis, homeostasis, evolution, adaptation, responsiveness, along with self-organization. The author discerns autonomy as ascribed to non-human systems and autonomy of adult human beings with freedom as the epitome of autonomy. "The examples of autonomy considered in A-Life show varying degrees of independence from direct outside control. But none has the cognitive/mo-

tivational complexity that's required for freedom" (Boden, 2010, p.181). Thus, "the autonomy one can ascribe to the computer artist and to the computer artwork are fundamentally different" (Boden, 2010, p.183), with the autonomy (independence) of the artwork being in some cases lessened and the autonomy (freedom) of the viewer increased.

Discussion about aesthetics in generative art involves the main approaches to the interface between economics, biology, neuroscience, and evolutionary computing such as genetic algorithms, evolutionary programming, evolution strategies, or genetic programming. Evolutionary algorithms serve for finding particular solutions in art, for example, by generating organic art forms (Latham, Shaw, Todd, & Leymarie, 2007), as well as in the fields related to science, economics, biology, and many others. EvoStar (2010), the annual European event on evolutionary computation listed Computational Aesthetics as their area of interest. The Evo events on evolutionary computation, and especially Evomusart (2012), the 10th European Event on Evolutionary and Biologically Inspired Music, Sound, Art and Design are focused on generation, theory, computational aesthetics, and digital creativity: analysis and evaluation of the artistic potential of biologically inspired art and music. Several digital art oriented associations aim to explore how the aesthetic framework adopted in particular forms of generative art intersect with other art disciplines.

Discussion of the aesthetics of information visualization draws from existing approaches to information art and, even earlier, digital art. Scientific visualizations, described generally as mapping from computer representations to perceptual representations, focus on choosing encoding techniques to maximize human understanding, usability, effectiveness, and efficiency. Information visualization is more often than not evaluated in terms of representing data in pleasurable and intelligible way. Moreover, tracing the evolution of digital art cannot be done without placing it within the context of art history, and in relation to other disciplines, such as cognitive science, computer science, philosophy, media studies, art history and criticism, and sciences dealing with images.

ART CRITICISM VS. EDUCATIONAL OBJECTIVES AND ASSESSMENT

Sharing Models Adopted in the Field of Education and Art Criticism

Opinions about teaching objectives evolved with the developments in the new media art: those caused through the web, social networking, and by creating art on portable devices. The advances in information technologies, which allow rendering and distributing data, information, and knowledge in a visual format, make an important source of motivation to develop up-to-date models.

Criticism about art production in art-related classes bears on the assessment criteria as well as upon the objectives established for a specific course. It has been generally acknowledged that

teachers, art critics, and learners need specific evaluation tools depending on the type of new media art created by professional artists and students, as well as the media used.

Programming an image allows us to construct spatial organization on a plane and in depth, and then transform and transfer images using algorithms (Figure 4, "The Thirties").

It seems there is a need for sharing experiences of people performing curatorial work and the instructional designers. In the field of instruction, research on art related topics usually includes examining criteria, assessment tools, and methods of criticism. In respect of art exhibitions, such research would encompass an analysis of the curatorial work and the criteria for art works' selection. A survey aimed at gathering information on this topic should comprise curators of contemporary art museums, such as: NY MoMA – the Museum of Modern Art, Los Angeles MoMA, Guggenheim Musea (in New York, NY, USA; Bilbao, Spain; Venice, Italy; Berlin, Germany; and Abu Dhabi, the United Arab Emirates), Whit-

Figure 4. (a) and (b). Anna Ursyn, The Thirties. (© 1987, A. Ursyn. Used with permission.) Printout of the 3D computer program: VAX mainframe, FORTRAN 77, Interactive Graphic Library (IGL) and PPC

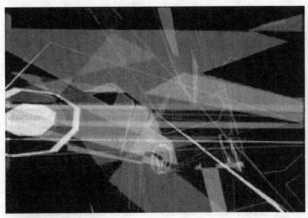
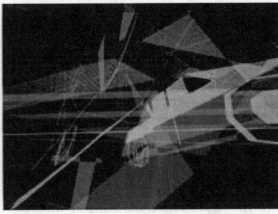

ney Museum of American Art and Whitney Artport (2011), a portal to net art and digital arts, the Metropolitan Museum of Art, New York, NY, USA, American Museum of Natural History, New York, NY, USA, Museum der Stadt Gladbeck, Germany, and also directors of events such as Prix Ars Electronica International Competition of CyberArts, ISEA International Symposia on Electronic Art, (Annual Conferences of the Eurographics – European Association for Computer Graphics), Documenta, modern and contemporary art exhibition taking place every five years in Kassel, Germany, Venice Biennale, the Monumenta show in Paris, Art Basel in Switzerland, and Imagina/SIGGRAPH European 3D Community event, among many others.

In order to arrive at a data based examination of the connections between art criticism, instructional objectives/assessment, the product design evaluation, and the technology requirements, professionals in these fields should share information, preferences, opinions, and the patterns of behavior adopted by professionals of concern. Issues and concerns that seem to relate to both the art gallery centered paradigms and the art instruction assessment criteria could be expressed in the form of general questions. One may wonder,

- How the ideas, techniques, and statements of established artists, emerging artists, or students are conducive to creating art works.
- How to apply criticism to the new media art created through the web, social networking, and art created on portable devices.
- How should we teach students to write a critique, an artist's statement, a storyboard, and a plan for a website.
- How teachers evaluate student's work, organize class discussion of the artwork created by professionals, and a class critique of the student art.

- How galleries, exhibitors, and conference organizers establish trends and evaluation framework for new artwork.
- How can we teach the networked audience to perform art criticism, making their voices knowledgeable and thus significant. Netflix, and many companies inform clients and listen to their evaluation. One may wonder whether art, especially interactive art acts that way and if this approach makes the viewers' criticism functional.

Figure 5, "Data Mining" is about a question what technological and human worlds have in common. Humans create cities, whereas a city metaphor reflects rhythm and organization of big data sets and makes data mining easier. Computer plots obtained using Fortran, IGL and transformed into photosilkscreens for color variation were applied on a mirror to create an image of a city. Then, a short animated film with music by Toby Rush involving people in motion was projected on this mirror surface, thus creating a reflection of people's movement. The image of the city has been juxtaposed with the animated actions to show how a big city life involves individual life events and daily routines.

The Four-Part Model of Instructional Objectives

In the field of instruction, 'objectives' is an important but underemphasized part of any syllabus; they allow an objective assessment. A four-part model of instructional objectives developed by Linda Lohr (Lohr & Ursyn, 2010) is based on the ABCD model that Robert Mager introduced in 1962 (Mager, 1984).

The ABCD model includes components:

A: Audience need (the learner) – Audience that specifies the learner;

Figure 5. Anna Ursyn, Data Mining. (© 2008, A. Ursyn. Used with permission)

B: Behavior outcome, action verb describing learner performance, observable behavior, real world skill;

C: Condition, catalyst, context – which means equipment, tools, aids, references, and special environmental circumstances; and

D: Degree of achievement – Degree criterion that means standard performance, time limit, range of accuracy, proportion of correct responses, and qualitative standards. Along with the Objectives we deal with rubrics, which assess what we expect and how we measure it. This model embraces the fractal nature of objectives as the underlying structure of job-aids, lessons, units of instruction, and even curricula.

The Four-Part Model in Art Criticism

We can look at the domain of the new media art criticism in terms analogical to the objectives used in the education domain. The four-part art critique model reflects interactions:

A: Audience characteristics and the changing profile of the criticism recipients: as discussed above, viewers are often acting as artists, jurors, critics, and curators.

B: Behavior, the visual outcomes, the viewers and audience performance and the ways of interacting with the networked art world; for example, robot's haptic interaction with people in response to how it is held and touched.

C: Conditions and context – The existing environments and the new tools for criticism

D: Degree of achievement – The heuristically focused critique criteria accepted in the new media art criticism.

The following text examines four parts of the ABCD art critique model.

A: Audience of the New Media Art

Some characteristics seem to be typical of the audience of the new media art. Audience can trigger an art making process by self-incorporation. Viewers, website visitors, and event participant may grant the artist with an audience award. Audience can easily get a lot of exposure to art, both traditional and new media art disregarding their location. It may go many ways. First of all, audience can see the art works online. Some people go so far as someone who said, "if something is not online, it does not exist."

Moreover, audience is networked due to a growing number of social networking options. Audience may thus communicate, comment, share, and translate data and information about art using instant messaging and chat rooms but also by telephone, email, video telephone calls, and video conferencing. Networked environment gives the viewers access to the resources on shared storage devices, so they may gain additional information about what they are seeing.

Audience may have access to art and current trends in art through online display representing almost every artist's works, for example, through the artists' personal websites, so the viewers may enhance their knowledge about particular artists and their circles. Viewers may also visit the galleries' and museums' websites, such as a portal to Internet art and online gallery space, the Whitney's Artport (http://whitney.org/Exhibitions/Artport). They may find art works on their smart phone apps, for example, when participating in walking tours.

Within an interactive framework of some art works audience can act both as artists and critics. Even if not directly, viewers can act collaboratively when they can view or read and then react on Facebook, Tweeter, and other networking options. It may provide an inspiration for further actions, especially if artwork results from the artist's contact with another kind of art (e.g., music).

The presence of social networks results in joining together to create the interactive group art projects and the research-based projects. Sometimes the audience may interfere with installations or technologies presented online. The interactive contribution of viewers/participant/users means that interactive art does not exist until a viewer becomes an active participant.

Figure 6, "Me Against Me" examines visually how at some moments we may feel overwhelmed by the reality that acts on our state of mind. We constantly act, keep busy producing, creating, repairing, or making things, exploring, visiting, immersing ourselves in nature or social activities, advising, teaching, curing, healing, trading, exercising, commuting, fighting for some cause, or researching something. Action keeps us mindful and concerned, but sometimes when we remove our thought from it, we can detect this huge reality around us.

"Stereotypes"

A small change makes a big difference.
We all know about the origins, uses, abilities, or problems.
It's faster and more efficient to classify, find order and importance
Of generally known routines for each situation
What to expect from a person or from an object.
We have a saying, a sentence, a word, or much simpler, a gesture.
A vocabulary of symbols makes us well-rounded
Only if we know how to apply our handy simplifications.

Social networking makes it easy to share individual art works. Mail Art became another form of social networking. Mail art, an international cul-

Figure 6. Anna Ursyn, Me Against Me (© 2011, A. Ursyn. Used with permission)

tural movement popular since the 1960s, evolved into online forms through the artists' websites, blogs, by using social networking groups, and sending images or sound files through the Internet. Also, there are actions encouraging viewers/participants to change an image, add content, and then forward it to the next user. There are also international art festivals.

The networked audience became active critics and jurors. They even act as curators, using YouTube, Internet, graffiti art, street art, and a good many other means of expression. As opinionated critics and jurors, the viewers discuss the new art forms while participating in polls and voting. The views and judgments resulting from social activities display often a considerable discrepancy between professional, mainstream criticism and popular opinions. A popularity poll organized by the Swiss-based New 7 Wonders Foundation (2011) announced winners first on July 7, 2007. Contrary to the seven wonders of the ancient world comprising the Great Pyramid of Giza (the only wonder existing now), Hanging Gardens of Babylon, Temple of Artemis at Ephesus, Statue of Zeus at Olympia, Mausoleum of Maussollos at Halicarnassus, Colossus of Rhodes, and Pharos Lighthouse of Alexandria, the rewritten list of world's 7 wonders contains the Great Wall of China, Rome's Colosseum, India's Taj Mahal, Jordan's Petra, Peru' Machu Picchu, Brazil's Statue of Christ the Redeemer, Mexico's Chichen Itza, and the Great Pyramid of Giza. According to the Foundation, more than 100 million votes were cast through the Internet or by telephone, and yet it is the subject of voting until November 11, 2011. However, UNESCO distanced itself from this undertaking.

Artists Komar and Melamid (Wypijewski, 1997) performed a random-phone based market survey about aesthetic preferences and personal tastes in painting. They asked people to verbally describe their most and least favorable art works and then statistically analyzed the data and produced the synthetic most wanted paintings (landscapes with animals and a flag on a pole) and least wanted paintings (abstract geometric paintings) for a number of countries under their scrutiny.

Abstract, nonrepresentational, nonfigurative, and nonobjective art, considered unwanted by a great part of the respondents, use a visual language of form, color, and line to create compositions that may exist with a degree of independence from the real-life pictorial references in the world (Arnheim, 1969/2004). While James McNeill Whistler (with his Nocturne in Black and Gold: The Falling Rocket, 1874) has been considered a precursor of abstract way of imaging, a Russian painter, musician, and theorist Wassily Kandinsky (1886-1944) was credited with painting the first purely abstract works as a pioneer of abstract art. The artists from France, Holland, and other European countries, the Russian avant-garde and German Bauhaus movements continued to create abstract art. The Polish sculptor Katarzyna Kobro 1898-1951) created mathematically based sculptures. European artists brought abstract art to the United States. Then came abstract art of the 20th century, namely Abstract expressionism, Color field, Lyrical abstraction, Post-painterly abstraction, Sculpture, and Minimal art. As for the beginning of the 21st century, an essay posted on Wikipedia (http://en.wikipedia.org/wiki/Abstract_art) lists digital art, computer art, internet art, hard-edge painting, geometric abstraction, appropriation, hyperrealism, photorealism, expressionism, minimalism, lyrical abstraction, pop art, op art, abstract expressionism, color field painting, monochrome painting, neo-expressionism, collage, decollage,

intermedia, assemblage, digital painting, postmodern art, neo-Dada painting, shaped canvas painting, environmental mural painting, and graffiti, to say nothing about the many kinds of interactive, virtual and augmented reality, along with online installations.

It seems the majority of people feel an innate need for art, regardless of their lack of interest in abstract art; they also want to make their surroundings looking aesthetically. That could probably be the case of placing on the window (upside down) a reproduction of the Wassily Kandinski's painting "Colour Study: Squares with Concentric Circles" (1913) printed as a MOMA poster on a sturdy cardboard, the face side toward the street, in order to fill the space around the window-mounted air conditioner. The Latin adage, '*habent sua fata libelli*' may come to mind while looking at this setting of the artwork. This proverb, '*pro captu lectoris habent sua fata libelli*' means, 'according to the capabilities of the reader, books have their destiny.' A grammar and poet from Terentianus Maurus wrote it in the second or third century AD in a book "De litteris, De syllabis, De metris" (2011, verse 1286). Because things that one admires another rejects, the Italian fabulist and semiotician Umberto Eco (1980/2006) translated it in his book "The Name of the Rose" as "Books share their fates with their readers." The development of events related to the painting reproduction, presented in Figure 7, may confirm this statement.

B: Behavior –The Visual Outcomes

One may say the lack of contiguity between the mainstream art and new media art is being continuously attenuated due to the presence of electronic media in everyday practice. Changes in views about art criticism and art-related teaching objectives evolve with the developments in the new media art, and with the information technologies usually defined as rendering and distributing data, information, and knowledge in a visual format. We cannot categorize precisely the domain of new

Figure 7. (A, B, C, and D). Kandinsky in the window. A – Wasily Kandinsky, Colour Study: Squares with Concentric Circles (1913) reprinted from http://www.wikipaintings.org/en/wassily-kandinsky/color-study-squares-with-concentric-circles-1913, posted on the site in accordance with fair use principles. B – A photograph taken in the summer: the Wasily Kandinsky's artwork in the window, positioned upside down. (© 2012, A. Ursyn. Used with permission). C – A photograph taken in the fall (© 2012, A. Ursyn. Used with permission). D – A photograph taken in the winter: artwork is no more needed. (© 2012, A. Ursyn. Used with permission)

(a)　　　　　　　　　　　　　(b)

(c)　　　　　　　　　　　　　(d)

media art because it is still transforming; for that reason there are many classifications. We might take in consideration generative art, computer graphics and animation, interactive and virtual reality art works, works of webart, netart, games, robotics, artificial life and biologically inspired evolutionary art. When examining the aesthetics of net art, Cheng (2009) classified the net art media into several groups: Email Art, Non-linear Narrative, Online Performance, Information Art, Game art, Collaborative Creation, Internet Community, and Physical Interaction. We may also encounter hypertext, computerized animation, art produced through real-time teleconference, soft art made of pliable materials, and also games, interactive films, e-videos, digital panoramas, visual music, and installations of electronic art and robotics through interactive and immersive rooms. A response to current demands for dissemination of shared knowledge comes in the form of establishing new journals, opening new academic degree programs, and developing new software applications for art creating and art education. The networked systems of interconnected people may become meaningful when it comes to making decisions about one's artistic work or the individual personal choices, especially when one suddenly becomes lonely.

In a context of the described changes one may reflect on a concept of a canon and the unpredictability in art. Bringing audience as an element of interactive art brings a factor of unpredictability, so the new criteria are needed. While objectives are found helpful for education and design, applying them to art might be tougher (for instance, the official Paris Salon and Salon des Refusés 1863). Art history knows many canons for art (i.e., China, Greece, or Rome). However, many would agree that a masterpiece could be done even with a broom, in a quite similar way as with portable computers such as an iPad or an iPhone. For example, David Hockney (2011), considered by many the most influential contemporary British artist, creates drawings on a graphic tablet with the program Photoshop, and on his Apple iPhone using the Brushes app. Currently, the artist paints every day on his iPad with the edge of his thumb and then sends his works digitally to many of his friends. David Kassan (2011) creates finger paintings from a live model. Many agree that a printed reproduction might look like a traditional oil painting.

Possibly, looking for the sources for shaping a canon makes one think of what Francis T. Marchese (2011, p. 303) wrote in the Special Issue of the Leonardo Journal, the International Society for the Arts, Sciences and Technology, "Artworks collected by museums possess a particular magisterial quality. Because museums are the de facto keepers of cultural heritage, any work acquired by the museum is expected to become part of the canon."

A work "The Epic Story" (Figure 8) is about the fact that we may imagine infinitely many figures that satisfy one basic rule, and then such images may invoke divagations on the semiotics of perspective.

The changing approach to art creation in response to the developments in information technologies and social networking results also in the new comprehension of the very notion of the creative process and its criticism, mostly because of the interactive contribution of viewers/participant/users: an interactive art does not exist until a viewer becomes an active participant. In the past, the part played by the viewer in the artist–viewer communication consisted of determining the viewing distance, the details' appreciation, and evaluation of the qualities of the artwork. The appreciation of a sculpture involved walking around it and changing the point of view. In electronic art, the division between artist, participant and artwork diminishes in importance, as the viewer interacts with the artwork and contributes to the presentation environment. A file of numbers controls the image so quite different originals can be derived from the same program, such as video image, a lithograph, or a slide. Conversion between a memory buffer and various graphic peripherals is controlled by interfaces. Artistic productions take form of the pictures but also the spatially referenced and time dependent events, the interactive and interdisciplinary visual forms, and a storytelling made with the use of programs for creating interactive literary and graphic forms from a story, a poem, a manga, and an anime. Therefore, according to the Berlin and Copenhagen based curator and critic Simon Sheik (2011, p. 55), "curating in the future should center around three key notions: articulation, imagination, and continuity," where articulation means positioning of the project and its narratives.

Quite often interactive art cannot even exist without a viewer's presence and input. Many times art works make an inherent part of science- and technology-related solutions. Open-source software that is available for everybody allows for collaborative production, often going online. Moreover, numerous options of social networking provide a fuel for any form of an online creative work that overcomes the semiotic divide between fictional and material characters, or between realistic and virtual images. Audience acts also as critics and even curators, while they are active at YouTube or Vimeo, Internet, graffiti art, street

Figure 8. Anna Ursyn, The Epic Story. Computer graphics from a series Visible Geometry. (© 2009, A. Ursyn. Used with permission

art, and a good many other means of expression or platforms for judging.

C: Conditions and Context: The Existing Environments and the New Tools for Criticism

Criticism as an analysis and judgment tool take different forms depending on the subject under scrutiny, whether it is an artwork, student production, product design, information visualization, or computer graphics and graph drawing. Criticism of art production in art-related classes may bear on the assessment criteria and the objectives established ad hoc for a specific course. In a similar

way, analysis and judgment of a product design requires establishing the assessment criteria based on the product semantics analysis aimed at supporting aesthetics, usability, efficacy, efficiency, and self-explanatory power.

Information visualization aesthetics aims at maximizing the effectiveness and efficiency of the user's ability to detect data patterns. Lau and Vande Moere discuss information aesthetics as a visualization field, which closely merges aspects of aesthetics, data, and interaction, as the degree of artistic influence on the mapping technique of a specific visualization, as opposed to aesthetics as a measure of subjective appeal. Analysis of information aesthetics is usually done from information visualization perspective, in terms of functionality and effectiveness, and from visualization art, in terms of artistic influence and meaningfulness (Lau and Vande Moere, 2007). Metrics for aesthetics have also been defined in the field of graph drawing, in terms of readability, such as minimizing the number of edge crossings or maximizing symmetry (Purchase, 2002).

D: Degree of Achievement: The Asessment/Critique Criteria in New Media Art

Particular groups of both art jurors and instructors adopt specific art judging criteria depending on the specific school educational objectives. They may evaluate the overall impact of the work, relevance to the theme, quality of accompanying artist statement, creative use of media, and depth of critical exploration as variables that might be valued most, along with the math or technology content (innovation in techniques used), aesthetic appeal (that is admittedly subjective), a variety of media used, and the level of skill and effort that results in an effective presentation of the idea. Many times the assessment of student artwork, especially a time-based or interactive art object depends on the theme and the solutions defining what is it doing, how is it doing it, and why is it significant. Student art assessment criteria prevalent in the educational framework include the selection of an exceptional concept, its novelty, quality and completeness of execution.

However, many times aesthetics and originality of the artwork gains not so much attention as the clarity of design and a clear, concise, well-written statement. Students, including art students, need to learn to code, often using various languages, acquire technical skills to perform tasks, connect parts in a planned way, create a story, and link visual concepts to them. The 'adopt a hacker' events have been organized to bring programmers from other states. The main sources of students' power are creativity and an ability to make aes-

thetic choices resulting in the beauty of their own products and research based projects. According to a thought-provoking anecdote shared by the Apple professionals, a three-year-old girl, when given a smart phone for 3 minutes, was able to buy $1200 worth of Smurf family products. Apple applies a specific design, using green materials that are eco friendly, recycling leftovers parts, and making it all self-explanatory. For years their products have easy to understand connections designed so that it is impossible to use them in a wrong way.

The domain known as information technology is generally described in related publications as the acquisition, processing, storage and dissemination of vocal, pictorial, textual and numerical information by a microelectronics-based combination of computing and telecommunications. One may also find assessment of activities and products in this domain. However, one may still notice a need of common criteria for criticism in the area of art, art education, product design, as well as the shared approaches to the aesthetics of the art products, sometimes extreme or hybrid. After the performance "May the Horse Live in me" (a bio-art project and an example of extreme body art where an animal organism is crossed with a human organism through blood injection) was awarded with Golden Nica at Ars Electronica (2011), the statement of Prix Ars Electronica from 1999 remains actual: there is a need to redefine, compare, and judge digital media in the ever-changing context (Hardtke, 1999). In art criticism, expectations related to the artist under scrutiny are not necessarily precise. However when it comes to new media art, there are often particular expectations, for example, about technology – whether an artist uses enough technology. For example, the ACM/SIGGRAPH International Conference and Exhibition on Computer Graphics and Interactive Techniques 2011 Art Gallery "Tracing Home" performed selections according to the creative use of media as one of five criteria accepted by a jury. On the other hand, some artists, e.g., Jonathan Borofsky often use technology in

Figure 9. Anna Ursyn, "Urban Legends." (© 2008, A. Ursyn. Used with permission)

an inconspicuous way. Many times they are not listed in the computer graphics related sources.

Quality of accompanying artist statement was another criterion accepted by the SIGGRAPH Art Galleries. This may be in accordance with a need expressed by a fairly large number of jurors who tell they need a story to evaluate an artwork; for them, Michelangelo Caravaggio, Jeff Koons, or Claes Oldenburg may serve as examples of artists with a story. Some jurors need a story about the artists themselves. If so, it is often expected from a member of a particular culture to create, to share expression that would agree with the common con-

notations of the jurors about that particular culture or region. Facts and events from artist' life are often sought for forming an opinion about the artwork. This may also bring into mind a question that has been around a long time about the superiority of a double-blind review versus info about artist. Artists submitting their work may fear that when a critic knows anything about an artist, some bias might take place. Many online competitions ask the submitter to provide the organizers with their age, gender, race, and country. Many entry forms require from the applicants providing info about affiliations, exhibition and awards record, with places and reviews (even sometimes with names of the reviewers). The web programs control the users to fill out all the spaces. Banksy would not be taken into consideration under these conditions, mostly for his unorthodox street art production.

Figure 9, "Urban Legends" is inspired by big city life; it is accompanied by a short story:

They are still looking for a robber
famous for using the under-the-mat keys,
who, when tired after his robbery,
takes a nap in a closet in the just-robbed house.
A pillow left behind him in a closet makes his
trademark.
His naps are short, so nobody managed to
catch him.
When someone finds him sleeping in a closet,
he'd quickly jump out from the window.
Closet watchers needed!
They must be strong and fast.

Book ranking may depend on a number of buyers. Amazon.com lists their books with numbers they have in statistics, for example, "Amazon Bestsellers Rank: #1,143,940 in Books. Netflix uses quantitative way of reviews' evaluation: e.g., "n viewers of m (the total of viewers) considered this review useful.

Some hold that criticism may mean: analyze, compare, contrast, and aestheticize; others may raise questions about the 'peer review' in criticism, and ask about the role of 'tools' in criticism now, within the ever changing social environment. For example, one of the new forms of collecting data for critics include filling in an entry form with questions about gender, age, race, previous shows with places, affiliations, reviews (often with names of the reviewers) by the applicants, applicants are asked to arrange voting on Facebook; thus artists compete with other applicants by recruiting more voting participants. The gallery/show organizers engage a critic/juror presented as a person with an important responsibility (e.g., an associate or a curator in a big firm). Few would think to chal-

lenge the assumption that the data gathered this way would weight heavily on the critic/juror's decision about the artwork quality. Both in art and in sales the Tweeter is used as a promotional tool. The more new members one gathers, the sooner their own artwork would go through the evaluation process, would be used for promotional purposes, or a new product would become sooner available to them.

We must always take into account individual differences in the responsiveness to art. Two people may respond differently both to natural environment and to art works depending on their spectra of interest. When approaching Niagara Falls one person may receive strong aesthetic experience while another one may complain about the cold and wet wind. When in a museum, the first person may feel tired, hungry, or in need to check email, while the second one may feel elation, responding emotionally to some art works.

CRITICAL FRAMEWORK WITH RESPECT TO THE CURRENT CULTURAL PATTERNS

Arnheim (1988) argues that abstractions are necessary to view art from a formal perspective, such as principles of design. Some hold there is misinterpretation of aesthetics as equivalent to art. Few would challenge the Andres Gaviria's (2008) assumption that "aesthetics is concerned with the theory of sensual perception, while art is a social practice involved in certain forms of research and investigation processes, and in the construction of particular types of artifacts." Introduction of computers has an effect on traditional art forms, both the static form of art such as painting, photography, sculpture, poetry, and literature, and the time-based art, such as kinetic art, video, music, dance, and theater. Constantly diminishing barriers between fine arts, data presentation, visualization, design and advertisement result in the widening spectrum of recipients. For this reason, criticism applied to information art is not exclusively founded on aesthetic perception of the work's sensory properties, formal qualities, or technical merits; it is often focused on examining a work of art in relation to its historical context, artist's expression, and relation to other works. Moreover, the standard descriptive, analytical, interpretative, and evaluative questions are now expanding on issues pertaining to usability, and efficiency.

The developing forms of material and symbolic culture originate from previous cultural patterns. The earlier experience, knowledge, and conceptual frames influence both the scientific and artistic views on generative art theory and practice. Many times the artistic uses of computer graphics imitate the appearance, message, and techniques of other contemporary art forms. Theorists in computer art, graphics, video, and photography aim at simultaneous consideration of the artistic, technical, scientific, commercial, and practical dimensions of a work under criticism. For example, criteria applied in most of the ACM/SIGGRAPH animation contests include aesthetics, originality, excellence of execution, compelling conception, and innovation in technique of the presentation, while criteria recommended for making a critic of a website design might include questions pertaining its usability, consistency in design and content, site architecture and layout, functionality, and easiness in site navigation.

CRITICISM OF THE PRODUCT DESIGN

A critique of a product design may involve several factors that are rarely liable to determine our judgment. First of all, the appearance of a product may influence both our cognitive and affective reactions, shaping our perception of what we see, as well as our related associations and generalizations we can make about the object under critique. Design has been described as 'patterns

with intent' (Klanten, Bourquin, Ehman, & Tissot, 2010). While aesthetics is given a great deal of attention in criticism, visualization techniques such as simplification, abstraction, metaphor, and dramatization reduce the distance between the audience and the subject.

Design as an art of putting form and content together is at the core of many definitions of aesthetics. While performing a critique of the object design we examine whether this design fulfills the functional, ergonomically oriented, aesthetic, material- and space-related demands. Trends in product design might aim at hiding the complexity of the product by showing the product's ergonometric comfort, simplicity, elaboration, or fool proof and easiness of use. Effective product semantics presents the features of an object as pleasurable and comprehensible. Aesthetics of such product is an experience envisioned by many as a "pleasant experience" to be "at the core of design, intertwined with utility and usability" (Hokanson, Miller, & Hooper, 2008).

Depending on their design, specific products may have varied functions (Ursyn & Lohr, 2010). We often communicate with shortcuts, using signs, symbols, icons and metaphors, analogies, connotations and associations. Therefore products serve us on many occasions as cultural icons that are characteristic of a given culture, as well as established canonical objects that have easy recognizable shapes. We use symbols and link-node diagrams for the abstract concepts in graphic languages.

CONCLUSION

Discussion of art criticism, juxtaposed with a model of assessment, was aimed in this chapter to analyze current cultural patterns and place the reader's interactive project in a critical framework. In order to be able to make computational aesthetic evaluations should understand the mechanisms under human aesthetic experience. Such understanding includes theories from the field of evolutionary psychology, models of human aesthetics from psychologists, empirical studies of human aesthetics, and a growing literature in the field of neuroaesthetics. The theory and methods in computer art criticism may be more demanding than it is for the traditional art forms. Tracing the evolution of digital art cannot be done without placing it within the context of art history, and in relation to other disciplines, such as cognitive science, computer science, philosophy, media studies, art history and criticism, and sciences dealing with images. Opinions about teaching objectives evolved with the developments in the new media art: those caused through the web, social networking, and by creating art on portable devices. In the field of instruction, four-part model of instructional objectives includes four components: A – Audience that specifies the learner; B – Behavior describing learner performance; C – Condition, which means equipment, tools, aids, references, and special environmental circumstances; and D – Degree criterion that means standard performance and qualitative standards. Social networking makes it easy to share individual art works, and the networked audience became active critics and jurors. Discussion of the best ways of applying art criticism and evaluation techniques has been done in relation to the real life examples, materials based on a literature review, the authors' study results, and experience, both own and shared by the professionals. All these materials provide the rationale for a comparably constructed four-part art critique model that reflects interactions between audience characteristics, visual outcomes, learning environments, and heuristically focused critique criteria.

REFERENCES

ACM/SIGGRAPH. (2009). *Information aesthetics showcase*. Retrieved June 20, 2011, from http://www.siggraph.org/s2009/galleries_experiences/information_aesthetics/

Arnheim, R. (1969/2004). *Visual thinking: Thirty-fifth anniversary printing*. University of California Press.

Arnheim, R. (1988). *The power of the center - A study of composition in the visual arts*. Berkeley, CA: University of California Press.

Ars Electronica. (2011). *Que le cheval vive en moi. Art Orienté objet*. Retrieved June 22, 2011, from http://prix.aec.at/winner/3043/ and http://www.artorienteobjet.com/

Berlyne, D. (1971). *Aesthetics and psychobiology*. Appleton-Century-Crofts.

Berlyne, D. E. (1974). *Studies in the new experimental aesthetics: Steps toward an objective psychology of aesthetic appreciation*. Hemisphere Pub. Corp..

Boden, M. A. (2010). *Creativity and art: Three roads to surprise*. Oxford University Press.

Carlsson, A.-L. (2010). The aesthetic and the poietic elements of information design. In *Proceedings of the 14th International Conference Information Visualisation* (pp. 450-454). IEEE.

Cheng, Y. H. G. (2009). The aesthetics of net dot art. In *Handbook of Research on Computational Arts and Creative Informatics*. Hershey, PA: IGI Global. doi:10.4018/978-1-60566-352-4.ch010.

Datta, R., Joshi, D., Jia Li, J., & Wang, J. Z. (2006). Studying aesthetics in photographic images using a computational approach. In *Proceedings of the European Conference on Computer Vision*, (LNCS), (vol. 3953, pp. 288-301). Graz, Austria: Springer. Retrieved August 18, 2012, from http://infolab.stanford.edu/~wangz/project/imsearch/Aesthetics/ECCV06/datta.pdf

Eco, U. (1980/2006). The name of the rose. (W. Weaver, Trans.). Everyman's Library. ISBN 0307264890

Evomusart. (2012). *The tenth European event on evolutionary and biologically inspired music, sound, art and design.* Retrieved September 5, 2011, from http://evostar.dei.uc.pt/2012/call-for-contributions/evomusart/

EvoStar. (2010). *The annual European event on evolutionary computation.* Retrieved May 15, 2011, from http://dces.essex.ac.uk/research/evostar/evocomp.html

Flannery, M. (1992). Using science's aesthetic dimension in teaching science. *Journal of Aesthetic Education, 26*(1), 1–15. doi:10.2307/3332723.

Galanter, P. (2009a). *Complexism and the role of evolutionary art.* Retrieved June 20, 2011, from http://tamu.academia.edu/PhilipGalanter/Papers/254390/Complexism_and_the_Role_of_Evolutionary_Art

Galanter, P. (2009b). Truth to process – Evolutionary art and the aesthetics of dynamism. In *Proceedings of the GA2009 – XII Generative Art Conference.* Politecnico di Milano University.

Galanter, P. (2009c). Thoughts on computational creativity. In *Proceedings of Dagstuhl Seminar Proceedings.* Schloss Dagstuhl – Leibniz Zentrum fuer Informatik.

Galanter, P. (2010). Complexity, neuroaesthetics, and computational aesthetic evaluation. In *Proceedings of the 13ᵗʰ Generative Art Conference GA2010,* (pp. 399-409). GA. Retrieved April 27, 2012 from http://philipgalanter.com/downloads/ga2010_neuroaesthetics_and_cae.pdf

Galanter, P. (2011). Computational aesthetic evaluation. In J. McCormack, & M. d'Inverno (Eds.), *Computers and Creativity.* Berlin: Springer.

Gaviria, A. R. (2008). When is information visualization art? Determining the critical criteria. *Leonardo, 41*(5), 479–482. doi:10.1162/leon.2008.41.5.479.

Hardtke. (1999). Jury statement. *Prix Ars Electronica.*

Hockney, D. (2011). *Personal website.* Retrieved October 22, 2011, from www.hockneypictures.com

Hokanson, B., Miller, C., & Hooper, S. (2008). Role-based design: A contemporary perspective for innovation in instructional design. *TechTrends, 52*(6), 36–43. doi:10.1007/s11528-008-0215-0.

Kassan, D. (2011). *Website.* Retrieved October 12, 2011, from http://davidkassan.com

Klanten, R. (2010). *Data flow 2: Visualizing information in graphic design.* Die Gestalten Verlag.

Latham, W., Shaw, M., Todd, S., & Leymarie, F. F. (2007). *From DNA to 3D organic art forms.* Retrieved May 15, 2011, from http://www.siggraph.org/s2007/attendees/sketches/3.html

Lau, A., & Vande Moere, A. (2007). Towards a model of information aesthetics in information visualization. In *Proceedings of the International Conference on Information Visualisation.* London, UK: IEEE Computer Society.

Lévi-Strauss, C. (1997, 1993). Look, listen, learn. Basic Books, a division of Harper-Collins Publishers. ISBN 0-465-06880-4

Lohr, L., & Ursyn, A. (2010). Visualizing the instructional design process: Seven usability strategies for promoting creative instruction. *Design Principles and Practices: An International Journal, 4*(2), 427–436.

Maeda, J., & Bermont, R. (2011). *Redesigning leadership (simplicity, technology, business, life).* The MIT Press.

Mager, R. F. (1984). *Preparing instructional objectives* (2nd ed.). Belmont, CA: David S. Lake.

Manovich, L. (2001). *Info-aesthetics: Information and form.* Retrieved May 18, 2011, from http://www.manovich.net/IA/index.html

Marchese, F. T. (2011). Article. *Leonardo, 44*(4), 303.

Martindale, C. (1990). *Cognitive psychology: A neural-network approach*. Brooks/Cole Pub Co..

New 7 wanders of the world. (n.d.). Retrieved October 22, 2011, from http://www.new7wonders.com/

Purchase, H. C. (2002). Metrics for graph drawing aesthetics. *Journal of Visual Languages and Computing, 13*(5), 501–516. doi:10.1006/jvlc.2002.0232.

Sheik, S. (2011). Constitutive effects: The techniques of the curator. In Z. Kocur (Ed.), *Global Visual Cultures: An Anthology*. Wiley-Blackwell. ISBN 978-1-4051-6921-2

M. Terentianus, & K. Lachmann (Eds.). (2011). *De litteris syllabis et metris liber*. Nabu Press.

Tufte, E. R. (1983/2001). *The visual display of quantitative information*. Cheshire, CT: Graphics Press.

Tufte, E. R. (1997). *Visual and statistical thinking: Displays of evidence for making decisions*. Cheshire, CT: Graphics Press.

Vande Moere, A. (2008). Beyond the tyranny of the pixel: Exploring the physicality of information visualization. In *Proceedings of the 12th International Conference Information Visualisation*, (pp. 469-474). IEEE.

Vande Moere, A., & Offenhuber, D. (2009). Beyond ambient display: A contextual taxonomy of alternative information display. *International Journal of Ambient Computing and Intelligence, 1*(2), 39–46. doi:10.4018/jaci.2009040105.

Vesna, V. (2007). Database aesthetics: Art in the age of information overflow. *Univ of Minnesota Press.*, *ISBN-10*, 0816641196.

Whitney Artport: The Whitney Museum of American Art. (2011). Retrieved January 27, 2011 from http://artport.whitney.org/

J.-A. Wypijewski (Ed.). (1997). *Komar and Melamid's scientific guide to art: Painting by numbers*. New York: Farrar Straus Giroux.

Zeki, S. (1999). Art and the brain. *Journal of Consciousness Studies, 6*, 76–96.

Section 2
Lessons from Science

Chapter 6
The Journey to the Center of the Earth

ABSTRACT

The "Journey to the Center of the Earth" project is a mental investigation about the interior of the Earth intended to encourage the reader to conduct an experiment in thinking and communicating with the use of visual language. Inspiration for this project comes from the theme of the interior of the Earth and some literary connotations. The challenge is to go on an imaginary trip in a transparent, pressure, and temperature resistant elevator descending to the center of the Earth, visualize its core, and make visual and verbal notes from the trip. Pictorial and verbal presentations are integrated with the physical geology-related concepts, events, processes, language arts, and connotations pertaining to cellular biology. The project is also about our awareness of the dynamics, forcefulness, and fragility of the matter under the ground we are living on.

INTRODUCTION

According to the leading objective of this book, the "Journey to the Center of the Earth" project is a mental investigation intended to encourage the reader to conduct an experiment in thinking and communicating with the use of visual language. The following text will involve creating a model intended to visualize the Earth structure. Queries about the physical geology of the Earth, its structural features and dynamical processes are aimed at providing a background to a nature-inspired work. A graphical model enables easy recognition of the whole structure that is broken into simpler forms and then presentation of it in a pictorial way.

A work "No Man, No Shadow" (Figure 1) is a personal interpretation of geological formations communicated in visual language. This is an account of conquering distance, with an experience described by T. S. Eliot in "Little Gidding," Either you had no purpose, or the purpose is beyond the end you figured and is altered in fulfillment. At the same time, what is seen in the surroundings brings back an association to one's mind: rhythmic patterns in nature remind us of a perfection of the computer algorithms.

DOI: 10.4018/978-1-4666-4627-8.ch006

Figure 1. Anna Ursyn, "No Man, No Shadow" (© 1989, A. Ursyn. Used with permission)

BACKGROUND INFORMATION

This distinctive imaginary adventure can only be done after completing some queries to recall our knowledge derived from science, art, and graphics. To be ready for working on this project, it would be helpful to bring back into one's mind some facts and properties related to the physical geology – a study of Earth structures and materials, as well as processes and forces that change these structures; one can find this information online or in textbooks (for example, Plummer et al., 2012; Tarbuck et al., 2011).

Mining for information may include themes related to rocks, minerals, and sediments, the composition and physical properties of the Earth's layers, its history and the natural processes that shape our planet by changing the makeup of the Earth over long periods of time. This knowledge tells about the nature of the Earth and gives us the understanding of the physical changes. It

may be useful as a stimulus to evoke your visual response in the form of your art graphics. When we analyze different types of Earth materials (such as rocks, soil, and minerals), we may recognize that rock layers and fossils hidden there provide the evidence of past life and tell how Earth has changed over long periods of time. Natural forces and processes, such as heat and pressure, are important factors that determine how the Earth's makeup has changed over short and then over long periods of time.

The Earth Layers

Figure 2 presents the structure, order, and density of the Earth layers with their depth and temperature changes on the 6,335 km (3,930 mi) long way down to the center. It shows what would we encounter if our imaginary elevator could go across real layers of the Earth.

Figure 2. Composition and structure of the Earth's interior; Earth layers and their differing physical properties: thickness and temperature changes. (© 2012, A. Ursyn. Used with permission)

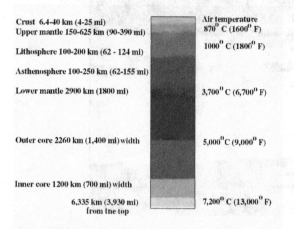

The sliced view of the Earth shows its compositional layers: the crust, the lithosphere, the asthenosphere, the mesosphere, liquid outer core, and solid inner core (Figure 3). The Earth has a diameter of about 12,670 km (7,920 mi) at the equator and a little less across the poles. It is composed of three chemically different layers: the crust, mantle, and core. While the dense materials (heavy metals: nickel and iron) became submerged closer to the center, the lighter materials (rocks: basalts and granites) form the crust.

The crust is rigid and thin compared with the other two layers. It's composed of the igneous, metamorphic, and sedimentary rocks of different kinds. Igneous, sedimentary, and metamorphic rocks are the three main rock types existing on Earth. Igneous rocks have their origin from lava or magma. Oceanic crust is about 5 to 10 km (3.1 to 6.2 miles) thick and is made of basalt, a relatively dense volcanic lava rock that is the most common mineral on Earth. Oceans are up to 3.7 km (2.3 mi) deep; they cover about 70% of Earth's surface. Continental crust is made of lower density rocks such as an igneous, volcanic rock andesite (a dark, fine-grained, igneous, volcanic

rock) and granite (a hard, often coarse-grained crystalline, igneous rock that builds most of the continental crust of the Earth. The main component is quartz, mica, and feldspar that crystallized from magma). It is about 35-70 km (22-43 mi) thick, but under large mountain ranges (for example, the Alps or the Sierra Nevada) it can be as thick as 100 km (62 miles). It is thin in volcanically active continental areas, for example, in the Western United States. The crust is rich in oxygen (O) and contains iron (Fe), magnesium (Mg), calcium (Ca), potassium (K), sodium (Na) and aluminum-silicate minerals. The crust has an air temperature on top but about 870-1,000 degrees Celsius (1,600-1,800 degrees Fahrenheit) in its deepest parts, where rocks begin to melt. The Mohorovicic discontinuity separates the crust and the upper mantle.

The mantle (upper and lower mantle) is a rigid, dense, hot, middle layer of semi-solid rock, more dense than crust. The upper mantle is 150-625 km (90-390 mi) thick. Its temperature is about 870 degrees C (1,600 degrees F) on the top to about 2,200 degrees C (4,000 degrees F) near the bottom. Its minerals are silicon (Si), oxygen (O), magnesium (Mg), iron (Fe), aluminum (Al), and calcium (Ca). The upper mantle is a part of the lithosphere (together with the crust).

The lower mantle is about 2,900 km (1,800 mi) thick; it is the largest layer, most of the mass of the Earth. The temperature of the mantle varies from 2,200 degrees C (4,000 degrees F) on top to 3,700 C degrees (6,700 degrees F) near the bottom. Its minerals are richer than the crust in elements: iron (Fe), magnesium (Mg), aluminum (Al), silicon (Si), oxygen (O), and silicate compounds. Dense rock, plastic like asphalt, flows at a rate of a few centimeters per year.

The lithosphere (the crust and the upper mantle) comes from the Greek word lithos, or stone. This is a "plate" which is readily breaking in pieces and floats on the less rigid mantle located below, drifting a few cm each year. Sometimes plates fracture under pressure, which results in earthquakes. The

Figure 3. The Earth's layers, their thickness and temperature. This visual presentation shows thickness of the Earth layers according to the data presented above. Colors indicate temperature of the layers. The sliced view of the Earth shows its compositional layers: the crust, the lithosphere, the asthenosphere, the mesosphere, liquid outer core, and solid inner core. (© 2012, A. Ursyn. Used with permission)

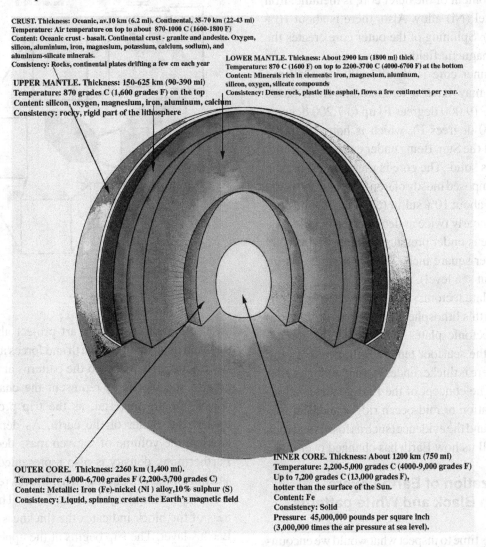

CRUST. Thickness: Oceanic, av.10 km (6.2 mi). Continental, 35-70 km (22-43 mi)
Temperature: Air temperature on top to about 870-1000 C (1600-1800 F)
Content: Oceanic crust - basalt. Continental crust - granite and andesite. Oxygen, silicon, aluminium, iron, magnesium, potassium, calcium, sodium, and aluminum-silicate minerals.
Consistency: Rocks, continental plates drifting a few cm each year

UPPER MANTLE. Thickness: 150-625 km (90-390 mi)
Temperature: 870 grades C (1,600 grades F) on the top
Content: silicon, oxygen, magnesium, iron, aluminum, calcium
Consistency: rocky, rigid part of the lithosphere

LOWER MANTLE. Thickness: About 2900 km (1800 mi) thick
Temperature: 870 C (1600 F) on top to 2200-3700 C (4000-6700 F) at the bottom
Content: Minerals rich in elements: iron, magnesium, aluminum, silicon, oxygen, silicate compounds
Consistency: Dense rock, plastic like asphalt, flows a few centimeters per year.

OUTER CORE. Thickness: 2260 km (1,400 mi).
Temperature: 4,000-6,700 grades F (2,200-3,700 grades C)
Content: Metallic: Iron (Fe)-nickel (Ni) alloy,10 % sulphur (S)
Consistency: Liquid, spinning creates the Earth's magnetic field

INNER CORE. Thickness: About 1200 km (750 mi)
Temperature: 2,200-5,000 grades C (4000-9,000 grades F)
Up to 7,200 grades C (13,000 grades F),
hotter than the surface of the Sun.
Content: Fe
Consistency: Solid
Pressure: 45,000,000 pounds per square inch
(3,000,000 times the air pressure at sea level).

earthquake waves move at the speed and angles different in the crust and the mantle. The inner part of the mantle, called asthenosphere (from the Greek word asthenos, or devoid of force) is about 100 and 250 km (62-155 mi) deep. When the hot, semi-solid material of the mantle soften under high temperature and pressure acting over geologic time, it is marked by plastic behavior, like cream in a tube. Hot material at the deepest part of the asthenosphere is repeatedly rising, then cooling, sinking, and then again heating. Convection currents in the mantle move a rigid, brittle lithosphere. The continents and oceans are parts of these moving plates. The Gutenberg discontinuity separates the mantle and the outer core.

The core is very hot, even after 4.5 billion years of cooling. It has about 2,100 miles in radius and is divided into the outer core and the inner core. The outer core is about 2,260 km (1,400 mi) thick. It is liquid because of its high temperature of 2,200-3,700 degrees C (4,000-6,700 degrees F). The content of the outer core is metallic: iron (Fe)-nickel (Ni) alloy. Also, there is about 10% sulfur (S). Spinning of the outer core creates the Earth's magnetic field.

The inner core is about 1,200 km (750 mi) thick. It may have a temperature from 5,000 degrees C (9,000 degrees F) up to 7,200 degrees C (13,000 degrees F), which is hotter than the surface of the Sun. Being under extreme pressure, it remains solid. The core is metallic rather than stony, composed mostly of iron (Fe), as iron-nickel alloy and about 10% sulfur (S). It has a solid consistency, nearly twice as dense as the mantle. The inner core is under pressure of about 45,000,000 pounds per square inch (3,000,000 times the air pressure at sea level).

The plate tectonics theory describes motions of the Earth's lithosphere, which was broken into several tectonic plates, which are now spreading over the seafloor tens of millimeters a year. Lithosphere is thicker under continents than under oceans. The concept of the Earth's plate tectonics, formation of mid-ocean ridges and deep-sea trenches, and the evidence (such as fossils and rock layers) tell us how Earth has changed over time.

Visualization of Earth Layers through Black and White patterns

Maybe it's time to inspect what would we encounter if an imaginary elevator could go across real layers of the Earth. Figure 4 shows visualization of the physical makeup of the Earth created by a student Trevor Pfaff. As a response to a challenge – how to visualize the Earth's structure and create a personal artistic solution – the author shows a translation from the earthly structures and materials into the graphical elements and sequential, pattern-coded organization of the design chunks.

Figure 4. A Journey to the Center of the Earth – Trevor K. Pfaff. Concept visualization. (© 2012, T. Pfaff. Used with permission)

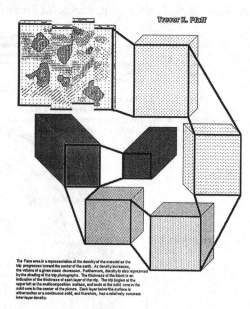

The author created an art project about the physical makeup of the Earth and forces affecting its structure. He assigned the patterns at the face area of the blocks to represent the changes in density of the material, as the trip progresses toward the center of the earth. As density increases, the volume of a given mass decreases. Furthermore, density is also represented by the shading of the trip photographs. Blocks represent the compositional layers of the Earth. The thickness of the block indicates the thickness of each Earth's layer. The trip begins at the upper left at the multi-composition surface and ends at the solid core in the center of the picture. Each layer below the surface is either molten or a continuously solid; there is a relatively constant inter-layer density. The author included the above text as a legend at the lowest part of his computer graphics.

Figure 5. Michael Keene, A graphic model of the strata. (© 2004, M. Keene. Used with permission)

Representation of Layers through a Sandwich Metaphor

Figure 5 shows a good-humored attachment to an e-mail sent from an imaginary region of Italy to Colorado by Michael Keene who worked on this project when taking an online course. He wrote to his classmates and the teacher, "Hi all, here is a graphic model of the sub-strata of a little known region of southern Italy. It's off the beaten path of tourists, but cherished by the natives for its quiet beauty and delightful local cuisine. I long for a time when I can visit again its craggy hills and sheepish plains. More later, Mike Keene."

The artist accepted the challenge to visualize this scientific concept in a cheerful way, create metaphor visualization, and communicate a personal artistic solution as a description of the forces affecting Earth's structure. He presented his view on the Earth's layers as a sandwich metaphor. His sub-strata analysis refers to an imaginary province, a fictional region of Italy called Portabella Panini consisting from many tasteful layers placed one on another like the Earth's layers. The author of this project devised his own coding to translate scientific data into visuals. He coded temperature and density of the Earth layers as colors and patterns of the colorful layers of vegetables: tomato, paprika, and onion, which represent the compositional layers of the Earth.

The Concept of the Scale in Biological Discovery

With an imaginative approach to presenting the Earth's layers, we may practice our spatial skills by shifting from the macro to micro scale. We may discuss the micro-versus-macro approach – very small structures compared to the very large ones. Imagine yourself as a miniature creature. We will now shift ideas by applying a change of scale. What structures would you see if you were to become very small and travel through a small organism or a human cell? You may feel unsafe among the cell organelles, or feel anxious about aggressive leukocytes. This mental exercise requires creating an analogy – a cognitive process of transferring information or meaning from one subject to another one.

In nature, we can find examples of a similar order and a common pattern, regardless of categories we explore and environments we investigate. This resemblance may result from the laws, forces, and properties that are common for physical substance comprising the same elements and atomic structure. You may want to show your own way of shifting proportion: how will you approach the concept of the scale and micro versus macro structures.

MENTAL EXPERIMENT: IMAGINARY TRIP IN A TEMPERATURE AND PRESSURE-RESISTANT ELEVATOR TO THE CENTER OF EARTH

The challenge is to visualize exploration of the Earth's center and create a personal artistic solution as an artistic report from the trip. First this project will be solved in the scientific terms and then in the artistic way and literary terms. It will be your visual response to the description of the Earth's physical makeup and forces affecting its structure, maybe much more impressive than the pie charts and graphs shown in textbooks. The "Four trapped in an elevator" project in Chapter 16 exercises your resistance to stress when entrapped in a stuck elevator; now you may want to entertain an imaginary journey to the Earth center.

Imagine a trip in a transparent elevator that is temperature-resistant, pressure-resistant, and sends out light (there is no smell or smoke). The elevator is descending to the center of the Earth. In order to imagine the size of the Earth and the scale of the trip, you may first want to perform the task of an event planner. The travelers should be equipped with all necessities. You may need to estimate the elevator's speed that the Earth's center visitors would be able to endure, take into account

the distance to the Earth's center (3,930 miles from the surface), and calculate how much time it would take to travel there. You may fantasize about stations that are needed on the way, with the rest areas, convenience stores with refreshment, and maybe even tourist attractions at the very center. Even though illustrations show spherical cross-sections of a planet, please remember that, unless we become a giant, after entering the planet we cannot see the whole picture but the sequentially changing structures of the interior. This exercise may also result in creating a storyboard for an animation.

Getting Ready to Delve Deeply into the Center of the Earth (Based on What we Know About It)

You may want to picture a fictional journey to the center of the Earth. This project can be solved graphically or as an animation. Imagine structures or objects you expect to see on you way down. You might want to begin by designing your fictional elevator. Draw on a computer sketches as your own visual notes from this imaginary trip in an elevator. They could resemble the 5"x 7" flash cards or photographs, many of them gathered on one page, or each of them could fill the entire page. Sketches may also be made on a screen or on paper, with charcoal, chalk, crayons, pastels, watercolor, or tempera paints. You may then choose to scan your sketches or use any scanned images of visually inspiring events and processes related to your project, obeying the copyright rules. You may want then to transform and manipulate drawings or short sketches and present them in an artistic way according to your own visual choices, to show the essence of this experience. You may also want to register at a texture site CGTextures maintained by a 3D artist, Marcel Vijfwinkel (www.cgtextures.com) to download free of charge textures of your choice, or paid depending on how many you'd like to download at a time. You may decide to put your work on a website, share it on a Facebook, or make a PowerPoint presentation. Scanned images may serve as a starting point for creating your own art.

Consider art as a way to communicate and express your ideas, concepts, and emotions through your visual representation of the project theme. You may want to show the forces below the tectonics that make continents unite or part, and factors that make the planet's interior so hot that it causes the heat waves. Your mining for the answers may stir your imagination. Whatever manner you would like to choose, it would be your own original solution. This project will just make connection between visual arts and the disciplines it is about, share information, produce aesthetic result, and engage viewers' emotions. Enjoy your visual and aesthetic experiences when you acquaint yourself with biological and geological structures. Transpose this experience into direct presentation of what you just read. Create an artwork to reflect on, synthesize, and communicate intended meanings.

Show your own image of the Earth center – the subjective view expressed as art. Thus, you will create your own imaginative artistic way of the scientific visualization, envision your conceptions about real features of the Earth center or show your fantasies evoked by fictional descriptions. Make connections between visual arts and the disciplines this project is about: share your knowledge, produce aesthetic result, and engage viewers' emotions. Gather your own visual and aesthetic experience while reading about geological structures. Transpose this experience into direct presentation of what you just read. Create an artwork to reflect on, synthesize, and communicate intended meanings.

The artistic message to be conveyed can be enhanced by choosing specific color selections, using additional lines, applying texture, enhancing the depth of the picture, or changing its balance and composition. Make your depiction of the layers effective as the imagination boosters;

for example, use varied textures to show density of rocks, from stiff to fluffy. Apply and make intelligible some visualization techniques using color coding, changing proportion, and modifying patterns, copying and pasting a selection, and/or introducing symbolic representation of facts and concepts. Apply manipulation with patterns to represent density changes, shifting the ideas, or changing the meaning of the selected part of a picture.

You may want to use modeling clay and small objects such as colored sand and grains to develop a three-dimensional model of the Earth. Create a colorful cross section of the Earth, and work on representing its surface. You may prefer to develop a color-coded model to represent solids of various kinds, liquids, and gases in different ways. Think how you will use patterns to represent density changes in your design, and show your own way of showing proportion: how you will approach the concept of the scale of the structures encountered in your own imaginary trip.

Figure 6 shows a computer graphics made by my student about a journey to the earth center as seen from an outsider's perspective rather than as the participant of this trip. He applied fictional trip in an elevator to visually present the density and temperature of the structures on the way toward the Earth's center.

Figure 7 shows a student's presentation of geological structures on the way to the Earth's center.

However, all the time we remember that our place is on the surface of this dynamic, full of life and energy uppermost layer of the planet, dependent on the changes we forcefully put forward (Figure 8, "Natural Order"). Processes and events going on underneath geological layers covered with vegetation display natural patterns. Effects of distortion may remind the recurrence of both the structure of each natural form and the relationship between them, and make up our environment.

Figure 6. Nathan White, Elevator to the Earth Core. (© 2004, N. White. Used with permission)

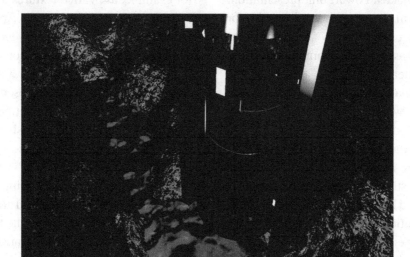

Figure 7. Peter Mussett. A Journey to the Center of the Earth. (© 2004, P. Mussett. Used with permission)

Figure 8. Anna Ursyn, Natural Order. (© 1992, A. Ursyn. Used with permission)

Literary Answers to the Theme of the Earth Center

We may now think about literature as a record of human experience. It might be interesting to contrast your and other people's literary answer with pictorial solutions that use the visual language. Individual solutions reflect one's preferences. Someone who feels more comfortable when writing rather than drawing may want to write a story and then put it on the web or as a blog. You may even want to incorporate your story into your artwork. And vice-versa, your drawings, hand drawn or created with the use of computer graphics software may illustrate your story and serve as a starting point for creating an animation, a poster, or a French fold card folded at a right angle twice such as it's often used for greeting cards and invitations. Display your work on the web, compare and discuss different approaches to the theme.

Jules Verne and the Interior of the Earth

In 1864 a French author Jules Verne (1828-1905) wrote a science fiction novel entitled "Journey to the Center of the Earth." Verne developed science fiction genre of literature writing about travels in air, in space, and underwater, in the times when airplanes, submarines, and space rockets had not been used everyday (with first submarines built in the 17th century and first airplanes at the very beginning of the 20th century). The Jules Verne's novel provides a description of the Earth, its center, and a fascinating plot about travelers' adventures in it. A handful of movies were based on this novel, along with other motion pictures about the core of the Earth.

The Jules Verne's novel may serve for creating a new point of view in this project. It may be visually interesting to contrast current knowledge about the physical characteristics of the Earth center with Jules Verne's assumptions about the interior of our planet and compare methods of investigation from the times of Jules Verne, when people collected rocks, examined samples from deep layers, and excavated fossils, with contemporary means of gathering evidence, such the radiometric dating with the use of a radioactive isotope (such as radiocarbon, potassium-argon, or uranium-lead) and its decay products, and also the ice cores – deep-level samples of ice that provide a climate record over thousands of years.

It is important to explore the difference between fact and fiction; examine the author's point of view and the fantastic ways in which his story reflects the Earth's natural events and processes, human fossils of the Quaternary period, the bones of antediluvian animals, and petrified gigantic vegetation. A short research would allow comparing and contrasting the scientific and fantastic descriptions. If you read the whole book before working on this project, connect Jules Verne's reflections upon the Earth processes with current scientific data. Analyze his literary setting, plot, and resolution, as well as your reading experience. Films based on the Jules Verne's book can also be analyzed that way.

The Dante Alighieri Connection

The poetical vision about journey through Inferno (hell), described by Dante Alighieri about 1300 in his "Divine Comedy" inspired Patricia Tryon to another visual solution to this topic: she decided to advertise a journey to the Earth center in the form of a travel brochure (Figure 9), which contains a portrait of Dante Alighieri, his translator John Ciardi, and a list of prerequisites for partaking in this trip. It takes a metaphorical form of an analogy between the Earth's layers and the seven deadly sins against the divine laws described by Dante Alighieri (Figure 10). The interesting trait is that human faults or shaded areas of their psyche are juxtaposed with the dark, hidden layers of the planet they inhabit – the deadlier the sin, the

Figure 9. Patricia Tryon. A front and back of the unfolded brochure (© 2009, P. Tryon. Used with permission)

Figure 10. Patricia Tryon, "Who will be first? Journey to the Center of the Earth ... and the Self" (© 2009, P. Tryon. Used with permission)

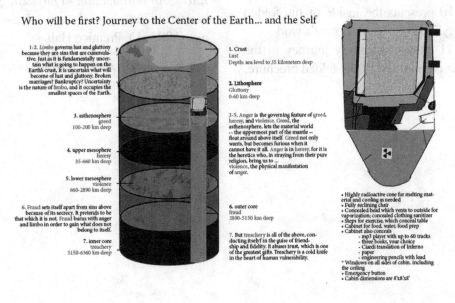

Figure 11. Steffanie Sperry, Let the pictures speak for themselves. (© 2012, S. Sperry. Used with permission)

deeper the layer, as referred to Dante's connotations to the Inferno.

Figure 10 presents the inside of the folded brochure, stylized to match the poet's work.

Figure 11 shows imaginary journey to the Earth center on an insert of the folded brochure.

CONCLUSION

A project described in this chapter is a mental investigation about the interior of the Earth intended to encourage the reader to conduct an experiment in thinking and communicating with the use of visual language. Pictorial and verbal presentations are integrated with the physical geology-related concepts, events, and processes, language arts, and connotations pertaining to cellular biology. The Jules Verne's novel serves for contrasting current knowledge about the physical characteristics of the Earth center with Jules Verne's assumptions about the interior of our planet. The project is also about our awareness of the dynamics, forcefulness, and fragility of the matter under the ground we are living on.

REFERENCES

Plummer, C., Carlson, D., & Hammersley, L. (2012). *Physical geology*. McGraw-Hill Science/Engineering/Math.

Tarbuck, E. J., Lutgens, F. K., & Tasa, D. (2011). *Earth: An introduction to physical geology plus mastering geology with etext -- Access card package* (10th ed.). Prentice Hall.

Verne, J. (2005). *Journey to the center of the earth*. Dover Publications.

Chapter 7
Taking Inspiration from Astronomy for Visual and Verbal Projects

ABSTRACT

The chapter comprises projects about some basic concepts related to astrophysics presented in a visual, verbal, or both ways, for example in the form of comics. The reader is encouraged to envision particular events, processes, and products, and then transform the concepts into another level of understanding. Projects involve visualizing or describing the relationship between frequency, wavelength, and energy, and the energy of light as the electromagnetic wave. Themes for projects include the solar system, Kepler's explanation of the forces acting on the solar system's motion and planetary movement, creating frames for animation about the expansion of the universe, a travel to the sun's center to explore nuclear fusion, examination of light and electromagnetic spectrum, elementary particles and quantum mechanics, and visualizing and designing one's own household and its objects and appliances.

INTRODUCTION: PROJECTS ABOUT COSMOS

In order to better understand abstract concepts, people create visualizations. This project invites you to develop a graphical presentation of a specific theme to show the physics-related concepts, forces, processes, and products. Think about making graphics to display the data. To design the visual content, apply textures, signs, symbols, and metaphors in order to envision the forces guiding particular events; color-code the material objects, organize, code, and present

knowledge. The data and information is easier to understand with the use of metaphors. In the first two projects we will start with some analogies. Our resulting confidence might be seen as our ability to understand and perceive connections among particular science themes. The following projects attempt presenting some basic concepts, using astrophysics as an example, and encouraging the reader to actively react in a visual, verbal, or both ways. Short background information provides introduction to each project. Visual projects involve applying various methods of imaging, and verbal projects represent different literary genres.

DOI: 10.4018/978-1-4666-4627-8.ch007

Written texts by my student Wes Thorpe illustrate the verbal projects, which comprise.

- **Project 1. About planets:** a still life presented in front of a house and conversation at a theatrical stage
- **Project 2. The planetary movement:** a design for a stain window and a text for a storyteller
- **Project 3. The expanding universe and the gravitational equilibrium:** designing and describing four key frames for an animation
- **Project 4. Nuclear fusion:** now inside of the Sun and in the Era of Nucleosynthesis: picturing and describing the center of the Sun
- **Project 5. Light and electromagnetic spectrum:** a portrait of a person in a forest, powerful animals, and a limerick about this scene
- **Project 6. Cosmic background radiation:** drawing and describing a concept map and a comics
- **Project 7. About mass and energy:** sketches about kinds of energy on a fictional star and a storyline for a game
- **Project 8. About elementary particles:** visualizing and designing seven household objects and appliances; over the phone narration
- **Project 9. About astronomy related tools:** assembling a picture of a telescope using matches

When working on visual projects, it's up to you what kind of tools or media you choose. You may want to create your projects by computing or using software, hand draw with pencils, brushes, or pens, or make the 3-D modeling projects. While working on a computer, it is also possible to use graphic programs downloaded from the Internet on your computer, such as (free download) Gimp (http://www.gimp.org/), InkScape – free download graphic editing software, or the Adobe 30 day trial version, before you decide to buy these programs, of Adobe Photoshop, Illustrator, or Fireworks. You may also draw single key frames for animation, scan, copy-and-paste images (but being conscientious about the copyright rules), or use photographs and combine them with your works. If you'd like to program your work, an open source programming language Processing. org can be downloaded without any charge. The MIT alumni Ben Fry and Casey Reas created this award-winning program for anyone willing to try one's exploratory way of programming. In this program, the image, animation, or an interactive work is presented along with a code, and the user is welcome to alter the code and see the changes made to the visual data provided by the authors, or write the own code following the rules provided in the added manual.

PROJECT 1: ABOUT PLANETS

Background Information for the Planets Project

Some data about the Solar System may be helpful in finding a general idea how to design this project. Before beginning the project it might be useful to recall some basic information (Bennett, Donahue, Schneider, & Voit, 2011).

- Astronomical unit (AU) is the average distance of Earth from the Sun, which is about 150 million km (93 million miles).
- Light year is a measure of distance; it is the distance that light can travel in vacuum 1 year, which is 9.46 trillion kilometers or 5.88 trillion miles. It means that a light minute – the distance light travels in a vacuum in one minute equals approximately 18 million kilometers.

- The Kelvin scale starts from the coldest possible temperature called absolute zero (0 K). The Sun's surface is about 5,800 K, 5,500^0 C, or 10,000^0 F.
- A star is a ball of shining, burning gas, and a star system consists of one or more stars, in our case the Sun, with the orbiting objects. Energy in a star comes from nuclear fusion occurring in its core. Protons and electrons force the reactions that fuel the stars.
- Atoms are composed of protons, electrons, and neutrons. Neutrons have no electric charge and do not interact with the surrounding medium. The protons have positive electric charge and the electrons have negative electric charge. In nuclear fusion, atomic nuclei that have low atomic number join together (fuse) to form a single, heavier nucleus. Our star is the Sun. A solar system comprises the Sun and planets.
- A planet is a round object that orbits a star and shines by reflecting light from its star, has enough mass to take on a round shape due to its gravity, and to clear a neighborhood around its orbit. Thus, in order to be named a planet, it needs to be identified by all three variables listed above. There are also smaller bodies in a solar system: asteroids – rocky objects orbiting stars, comets – small, icy objects orbiting stars, and dwarf planets.
- Dwarf planets can only fulfill two from the above conditions that are necessary to be called a planet. Dwarf planets of the solar system are the asteroid Ceres, along with Pluto, Eris, Haumea, and Makemake, which belong to the Kuiper belt – the region in the solar system near and beyond the orbit of Neptune. Dwarf planets orbit the Sun, are massive enough for their own gravity to give them a nearly round shape, but they do not fulfill the third criterion because they do not clear their orbital neighborhood.
- A moon (or a satellite) orbits a planet because gravity holds planets and moons in their orbits. Our moon rotates synchronously with Earth.
- Local Solar Neighborhood is a part of the Milky Way Galaxy.
- A galaxy is a collection of a hundred million or even trillions of stars that are held together by gravity and orbit a common center. Galaxies form groups, which are called clusters when contain large collections of galaxies. Individual galaxies, their groups, and clusters do not expand, it means the distance between stars does not get bigger. However, according to many scientists, the average distance between the whole galaxies seems to grow; that means the universe as a whole continues to expand.

Figure 1 shows a depiction of our planet inspired by a physics professor's lecture in my computer art class.

Figure 2 shows the data about planets ordered according to their closeness to the Sun. In respect to their size, the order would be: Sun, Jupiter, Saturn, Uranus, Neptune, Earth, Venus, Mars, Mercury, Eris, and Pluto.

The size of a planet, its distance from the Sun, and the rate of rotation influence both their physical features and their fate – the geological evolution of each planet. Large planets have warmer core and thus more intense mantle convection and stronger tectonic and volcanic activity. Distance from the Sun determines thermal conditions and the resulting chances to retain water: oceans, rain, snow, and ice. Too hot atmosphere allows escaping the water as a gas. Too low ground temperature on distant planets causes accumulation of ice, so there are no oceans and

Figure 1. Brennan Nelsen, "Planet Arrival" (© 2007, B. Nelsen. Used with permission)

no humidity in the atmosphere. Rotation plays an important role in formation of the wind (and the resulting erosion) as well as the strength of magnetic field.

As a summary of the basic motions of Earth, we may say it rotates around its axis once each day, orbits the Sun once each year, moves relatively to nearby stars with the whole Solar system, rotates as a part of the Solar system along with the Milky Way Galaxy (as a part of it), moves with the whole galaxy relatively to other galaxies in the Local Group, and participates in the universe's expansion (Bennett & al, 2011).

For directions on a project "Planets," see Table 1.

Figure 3, "The Solar System" shows a metaphorical picture of the solar system with the Sun and planets depicted as flowers. In order to be named a planet, it needs to be identified by three variables. Planets and all objects that orbit the Sun are objects that orbit a star, but they are not a star or a moon. They have to be massive enough for their own gravity to give them a nearly round shape.

Dwarfs can only fulfill two conditions. They orbit the Sun, are massive enough for their own gravity to give them a nearly round shape, but they do not fulfill the third criterion because they do not clear their orbital neighborhood. A planet needs to clear its path around its orbit. Ceres, Pluto and Eris could not clear their neighborhood around their orbits so they are proclaimed dwarf planets.

Below is a verbal project done by my computer graphics student, University of Northern Colorado.

Figure 2. The solar system: the sizes of the planets (as their equatorial radii in km), their distances from the Sun (in astronomical units), and their surface temperatures (in Kelvin scale)

Planet	Radius (km)	Distance (AU)	Temperature (K)
Sun	695,000		5,800
Mercury	2,440	0.387	700/100
Venus	6.051	0.723	740
Earth	6,378	1	290
Mars	3,397	1.52	220
Jupiter	71,492	5.2	125
Saturn	60,268	9.54	95
Uranus	25,559	19.2	60
Neptune	24,764	30.1	60
Pluto	1,160	39.5	40
Eris	1,200	67.7	?

Figure 3. Anna Ursyn, "The Solar System" (© 2011, A. Ursyn. Used with permission)

Project 1: Planets

An Example by Wes Thorpe

Universal News team reports on the warming of the Universe.

News Anchor: *This is just it – it seems the Sun is warming our galaxy to unbelievable temperatures. Could this mean Galactic Warming!*

We now turn to our heat correspondent Mercury who is right now in a debate about the current situation.

Mercury: *Yes Tom, it is really hot, almost too hot to bear. I believe it's not much longer until the sun destroys us all, as we know it. How do you feel about the situation earth?*

Earth: *I think we are all just overreacting here. I am feeling fine it's just your imaginations there is no such thing as Galactic warming.*

Table 1. Working on a Project: Planets. Create a visual, verbal, or both ways of presenting ideas related to the solar system

The Visual Approach: The Solar System as a Bouquet	The Verbal Approach: Conversations at a Theatrical Stage
Create a still life presented in front of a house. Place a circular table with a vase filled with different kinds of flowers on the top of the table. This picture will serve you as a metaphor of the solar system with the Sun and planets depicted as flowers.	Now maybe you will put a visualized concept into a written form and describe the Solar System in a specific literary genre. Write a short storyline for a theatrical performance about planets and the Sun. Put the actors at the theater stage. Write a dialog for this play based on information you already have about the Solar system. Write a script for each of the actors to talk about their plans about building a new house – their dream residence. Their houses will represent the planets (and the two largest known dwarf planets, Pluto and Eris). This task may need some additional research on the Web or in any textbook. We may assume the actors will want to compare their dream residencies, so they will tell about their houses. The houses will differ dramatically in terms of their size (describe them in scale) and different styles. Start with a big castle that will represent Jupiter, and select residencies standing for the rest of the planets, to show their scaled sizes, accepting the size of Earth as a unit. To represent the Sun in scale, you will not be able to introduce an actor who owns such a big residence (Sun), so someone will be only telling about the whole residential area called the Sun. Thus, your stage should be described as a fraction of this area. In your theatrical work, feel free to describe the exciting details that your characters would love. You may use photographs, if you'd prefer. While describing the gardens around the houses, think about colors in terms of the color-coding to tell about the atmospheric temperature of each planet. Actors may talk about different textures on the house exteriors as related to the amount of erosion caused by wind and the strength of magnetic field, and the problems caused by these processes.
Use the flowers to represent the planets (and the two largest known dwarf planets, Pluto and Eris). The table represents the Sun: the surface of the table will serve as a surface of the Sun. To represent the scale and also be able to fit all the planets, you may not show the whole table but just a portion of its oval (when drawn in perspective); only a fraction of the table will fit your canvas. To compare sizes of the planets look at the radius of each planet provided in kilometers (km) in the Figure 2. Draw the flowers in scale setting the size of Earth as a unit and drawing other flowers in proportion, according to Figure 2. Start with a big flower such as a sunflower that will represent Jupiter, and select flowers for the rest of the planets, to show their scaled sizes. You can also compare the distance from the Sun and the surface temperature of planets using the Kelvin temperature scale. Feel free to draw, scan images, or use photographs, if you'd prefer. While imaging flowers, apply color-coding to visualize atmospheric temperature of each planet. Apply different textures to show the amount of erosion caused by wind and the strength of magnetic field. Below the picture you have created, explain the color- and pattern-coding you have applied.	
Use the flower stems of different lengths as a metaphor of the planet's distance from the Sun (Figure 2). As the distances vary from 0.387 to 67.67 (with respect to Earth), one plant stem will be tiny, and the other one will extend above the house. Place numbers along the stems: calculate the distances from the Sun and place the numbers within your composition. This might add some character to your creation. Write how long would it take for a bee to fly from the flower Saturn to the Sun at the speed of light, measured in AU and in kilometers. Remember that one light-minute, as measured in kilometers, is 1.8×10^{10} m (1.8×10^7 km) far away. Compare a distance between Saturn and Jupiter with the size of a typical star. How these distances compare with a distance called an Astronomical Unit (AU) and a distance that light would travel in 1 second. Remember that the Astronomical Unit (AU), as well as a light-year, is the astronomical distance unit. AU is a measure of the average distance of the Earth to the Sun, but it is not a measure of length of time, speed, or any other basic unit used in astronomy.	Use the time of commuting to the Sun as a workplace as a metaphor of the planet's distance from Sun (Figure 2). As the distances vary from 0.387 to 67.67 (with respect to Earth), the lengths will be tiny for some of your characters, and others will have to make long trips. Describe the distances from the Sun that your characters will report. Discussion about the tradeoff between the beauty of the place and the amount of time spent on the road might add some character to your stage production. Tell about the kinds of work your characters perform. Additionally, you may want to write how long it would take for a bee to fly from the castle Saturn to the center square of the Sun residential area at the speed of light, measured in AU and in kilometers. Remember that one light-minute, as measured in kilometers, equals 17 987 547.5 kilometers (approximately 18 million kilometers). Compare a distance between Saturn and Jupiter with the size of a typical star. Describe how these distances compare with a distance called an Astronomical Unit (AU). Remember that the Astronomical Unit (AU), as well as a light-year, is the astronomical distance unit, a measure of the average distance of the Earth to the Sun, but it is not a measure of length of time, speed, or any other basic unit used in astronomy. Present yourself as an owner of the house called "A Planet Earth," and then provide your cosmic address, for example: Your Name>Earth>Solar System>Milky Way >Local Group>Local Supercluster>Universe.
You may use your project as a part of a report that you would like to send into cosmos, addressed to possible extraterrestrial beings. Thus, the message to possible residents of habitable zones on planets or stars in cosmos would comprise a collection of images and maybe formulas. On your artwork, present yourself as a bee on a flower Earth and then provide your cosmic address: Your name>Earth>Solar System>Milky Way galaxy>Local Group>Local Supercluster>Universe (Bennett & al., 2011). To visualize your whereabouts in the universe, imagine a visual presentation that best represents our cosmic address. Indicate on your illustration the concepts and structure of the super cluster, cluster, local group, galaxy, solar system, and earth. Yet, there is no chance to show the exact scale on your sketch.	

Neptune: *Yeah! I'm so cold I froze my ozone off. Nothing bad is going to happen.*
Venus: *Easy for you to say your 2,795,084,800 miles away from the sun whereas mercury and I are both less than a 100 million!*

Centuries later

Earth:... *and that is why I believe you are all overreach...............*

Explosions (sun explodes)

Neptune: (all by himself) *Why is it so dang hot! Maybe they were right about this Galactic Warming...*

"The Life and Death of Mother Sun:" A Visual and Verbal Solution by Steffanie Sperry

Figure 4, "Father Cosmo's Table" presents a student's solution of the "Planets" project: "Father Cosmo's Table" followed by the excerpts of a verbal solution – a theatrical play entitled "The Life and Death of Mother Sun."

"The Life and Death of Mother Sun" by Stephanie Sperry

DRAMATIS PERSONAE

Narrator
Terra: Goddess of the Earth
Mother Sun: The sun.
Mercury: God of the planet nearest the Sun, the messenger.
Venus: Goddess of the second planet, the lover.
Mars: God of the fourth planet, the warrior.
Jupiter: God of the fifth planet, the scholar.
Saturn: God of the sixth planet, wine, and music.
Uranus: God of the seventh planet and the rain.
Neptune: God of the eighth planet and the sea.
Pluto: God of the ninth planet and the underworld.

Figure 4. Steffanie Sperry, "Father Cosmo's Table" (© 2012, S. Sperry. Used with permission)

Chiron: Pluto's loyal companion, guardian of the ninth planet's moon, ferryman of the underworld.

Act I

Scene I: Earth, a sunny meadow of flowers
Enter Terra [Admires flowers].

Narrator: *Once a very long time ago when the earth was new and the sun already old, the mother Sun came down from her shining place of gold in the sky in search of help. She was in grave danger of dying, having given much of her life and essence to create her children: Mercury, Venus, Terra, Mars, Jupiter, Saturn, Uranus, Neptune, and Pluto. She came to her favorite child, Terra, hoping that the love and affection she had for*

Terra would be returned and Terra would help to save her.

Enter Mother Sun.

Terra: [Approaches and hugs Mother Sun] *Why Mother! You have come down from you shining gold city. Whatever could have brought you to me? It is such a very long way to travel here since I am 93 million miles away.*

Mother Sun: Indeed, it does take me quite a bit of time and energy to come her to you, my child Terra. But I am grave need of your assistance. I am dying my child, and I need you to do something for me.

Terra: [Horrified] *Yes mother! I will do anything you ask of me. Tell me what to do so you will continue to live. I love you and do not want you to die.*

Mother Sun: I knew I could count on you my Terra. I need you to go talk to your brothers and sisters. I need you to collect from them a bit of their life and bring it back to me. I need it to continue to live. It will renew me and make me whole again. If each of them gives a bit of their essence, then I will be restored, but if no one will give me a bit of their life then I will surely die and all my beautiful children will die with me. [Weeps softly]

Terra: I will get what you need Mother! I am sure that no one will refuse such a small favor to you. After all you are responsible for all life on our planets and you created from yourself and Father Cosmo all of us. We owe you our lives. My brothers and sisters will surely give of themselves to you Mother. Don't cry it will be all right. I will give of myself now and then go see my brothers and sisters. [Hands Mother Sun a handkerchief from her pants pocket]

Mother Sun: [Dries eyes with handkerchief] *No, my dear Terra, you cannot give your essence to me. You will need all your strength and life to gather from the others their essence.*

However, if I die the palace will go dark not long after, and all the worlds will be plunged back into darkness and Cosmo will only know grief and pain.

Terra: Don't worry Mother. I will do as you ask and I will leave at once! Here, stay in my humble home until I return with what you require.

Mother Sun: Thank you, my child. I think I will rest until you return. Take this gold box to put the shards of essence in for safekeeping. Guard it with all your heart Terra. It is the only way to bring the essence back to me.

Exit Terra

ACT II

Scene I: Outer space, surrounded by asteroids, Mercury's castle visible in the distance.

Enter Terra. [Slowly walk toward Mercury's castle]

Narrator: Terra began her journey less confident then she let her mother believe. Her brothers and sisters were not as kind as she, and Terra worried that they would not give her what she needed to help their mother. Her brothers and sisters were selfish creatures and absolute rulers of their own little planets. They had become high and mighty in their ways and it made Terra nervous. However, she continued on, determined that she would get what her Mother needed. She eventually reached Mercury and headed to Mercury's castle.

Exit Terra into Mercury's castle

Scene II: Inside Mercury's castle.

Terra appears seated in a comfortable chair. Enter Mercury and four servants.

Mercury: [Bored] *Hello, Terra. It has been a long while since I have seen you. What brings you to my little kingdom so close to Mother Sun? I wish I had moved further away as she drops in all the time; most inconvenient of her.*

Terra: I have come on Mother's behalf. She is in need of your essence. You, being the closest of her children, a mere 28.5 million miles away, I had hoped would understand her plight. She is dying, having given most of her life to us. She needs just a little of our life and she can continue on for millions and millions of years.

Mercury: [Outraged] *How dare you come ask for part of my life! She has given me nothing for which she deserves even a small piece of it. I have worked hard to make this hot rock my home. I have suffered her intolerable presence for a very long time. It is near to roasting here all the time and my subjects complain of the heat daily! Away with you Terra! You have no business here. You do not know what it is like with our mother at such an insufferable distance. Away with you or I will have you thrown out.*

[Terra has then been denied by most of the Sun's children. In an outer space, surrounded by asteroids, Venus complained that her subjects suffer of the heat and offers no part of her essence 'for that wretched woman we call a mother!' Mars denied giving part of his life: 'She has given me nothing for which she deserves even a small piece of it.' Jupiter said, 'Have any of our other brothers and sisters given their essence to you? Have you given of your life to her? I will not give my entire life for her because our other brothers and sisters our selfish and cruel. Saturn said laughing, 'A wealthy man knows that the only way to remain wealthy is to be sparse in his gifts to others.' Uranus told he was sorry that he could not help her, and so said Neptune. Finally, Pluto complies with Mother Sun and Terra wishes].

Pluto: Yes, my childhood was not the best and I have been abandoned out here on this cold rock, 3.67 billion miles away from our mother. I don't feel the rays of Mother Sun on my skin, but I can see them. The rays give me pleasure and remind me of how warm it used to be. Chiron has been the most loyal of friends I could have ever asked for. I know all of my other brothers and sisters, excluding you, have lavish palaces and servants that follow them everywhere, but that was never what I wanted. I have always wanted a simple life and to help others journey through the underworld beyond. I will help you Terra, for the love of life, warmth, and the woman who gave me my life. Do not despair my fair sister! Mother Sun and Father Cosmo will set it right. I give my life freely to her. I have lived well with the life she gave me, and do not resent her for needing it back now. It is the cycle of life and death, dear sister. I will forever be part of her, feel her love for me, and the life that she brings to all. I will go with you and help her.

Narrator: And so it was that Mother Sun had no choice but to take Pluto's life to restore her own. However, the cruel and unjust did not go unpunished. She took her life giving rays away from her other uncompassionate children. Their realms slowly withered and died, for no warmth or nourishment however passed to them. Only on Terra's planet did life flourish, and with it, according to her promise to Pluto, death. For every new life, Terra thanks her Mother Sun, and with every death, she remembers Pluto, and is grateful for his sacrifice so that others may live.

Exit.

Figures 5 a and b show student works in the form of programs written in Processing along with the corresponding images.

Figure 5a. Sean Flannery, "Big Bang" (© 2012, S. Flannery. Used with permission). Figure 5b. Sean Flannery, "Black Hole" (© 2012, S. Flannery. Used with permission)

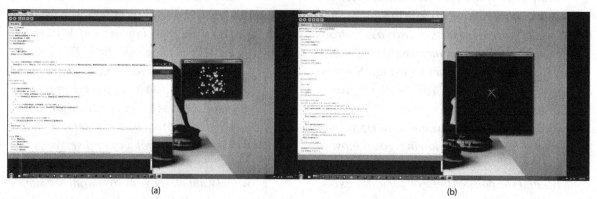

(a) (b)

Below is the author's statement.

This project shows an explosion of molecules from the bottom of the screen that bounce against any wall they come in contact with. By creating a finite amount of small objects in a space that each move away from a starting location by a fraction of a degree between each other, it creates a sort of explosion that looks like a galaxy of stars traveling across the sky. It was then just a matter of them interacting with the walls that made them bounce of the surface and maintain the same speed, but simply change the direction by its negative numerical value. I have been expanding my knowledge on coding, but I also wanted to expand my art knowledge in the process

The author of this project describes it as follows. This project was done in Processing. This project requires user input. By left clicking any where on this screen and holding the button down, you will see molecules from across the screen get sucked into the mouse pointer and then fly out the other side. This was done simply by creating a finite number of objects floating in space. Each object was given a random color code to display. When the mouse is clicked, it spins the color wheel and after a few second delay it will change the color of the molecules while pulling them into the mouse

click. Then once they reach the click they will be thrown out the other side at the same speed.

PROJECT 2: ABOUT THE PLANETARY MOVEMENT

In this project you are invited to present in a visual and verbal way the forces are acting at the Solar System's motion and Kepler's (1981) explanation of the planetary movement with his three laws of planetary motion (Kepler – Universe, 2010).

Background Information for the Project about the Planetary Movement

Johannes Kepler (1571-1630) worked on the laws of planetary motion and discovered the laws of physics, but also wrote the science fiction stories. Following Pythagoras' thoughts, he wanted to find the harmony of the celestial spheres, and prove that the dimensions of the Platonic solids (five regular solids – a tetrahedron, cube, octahedron, dodecahedron, or icosahedron) determine the distances from the planets to the Sun. In his model of the universe, Kepler nested five Platonic solids inside each other (Figure 6).

Figure 6. Johannes Kepler's Platonic solid model of the Solar system from Mysterium Cosmographicum (1596). From the Wikimedia Commons, PD-1923)

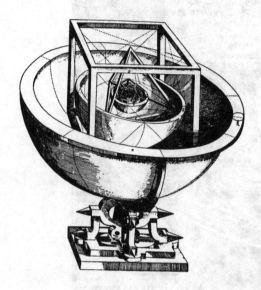

In his work from 1596, *Mysterium Cosmographicum,* Kepler explained the relation between the planets that revolve about the Sun and the solids. Kepler discerned six bodies: the sphere and the five regular polyhedra. According to Kepler, while the sphere corresponds to the heaven, the flat-faced solids represent the dynamic world: the cube, the pyramid, the dodecahedron, the octahedron, and the icosahedron (which has twenty plane faces). In his model of the universe, he assigned the cube to Saturn, the tetrahedron to Jupiter, the dodecahedron to Mars, the icosahedron to Venus, and the octahedron to Mercury. However, Uranus, Neptune, and Pluto had to be discovered yet: in 1781, 1846, and 1930, respectively. The celestial spheres have embedded planets and thus define the planets' orbits. A cube is inside an exterior sphere, with a tetrahedron inscribed in it; another sphere is inside it with a dodecahedron inscribed; a third sphere with an icosahedron is inscribed inside; and a smallest sphere has an octahedron inscribed. Kepler also believed, during its revolution about the Sun each planet generates a musical tone, the pitch of which varies with the angular velocity of the planet.

Each planet orbits the Sun following an ellipse with the Sun at one focus (one of the points from which the distances to any point of an ellipse are connected by a linear relation) and nothing at the other focus. Distances from the Sun vary when planets are orbiting. Kepler's 1st Law stated that planetary orbits about the Sun are ellipses and the Sun lies at one of the foci of the ellipse. In his 2nd Law, Kepler stated that a line connecting the Sun and a planet sweeps out equal areas in equal times, so a planet goes a bigger distance when it is closer to the Sun, and a smaller one when it's farther, and the area does not change. Therefore each planet travels faster when it is nearer the Sun than when it is further, and the orbital speed of a planet varies inversely with its distance from the Sun.

This happens because of the force of gravity and the action coming from the Newton's 2nd Law of Motion, which states that for any force (F) acting on any mass (m), F = m x a, where (a) is the acceleration of mass m. According to the Newton's 2nd Law, the acceleration of a planet in its orbit around the Sun depends upon the mass of the Sun and the inverse square of the planet's distance from the Sun. The force of gravity between the Sun and a planet changes with the planet's distance from the Sun. When the planet moves closer to the Sun, it exerts on the planet greater force, and then the acceleration of the planet increases, resulting in a higher orbital speed of the planet. When the planet moves further away in its orbit around the Sun, the gravitational force exerted by the Sun decreases, and so decreases the planet's acceleration, resulting in a lower orbital speed. In this way Kepler declared his 3rd Law telling that larger orbits have longer orbital periods, and the average orbital speeds are slower for planets with larger orbits.

"Kepler's Law and Gravitation" (Figure 7): Each planet orbits the Sun following an ellipse with the Sun at one focus and nothing at the other

Figure 7. Anna Ursyn, "Kepler's Law and Gravitation" (© 2010, A. Ursyn. Used with permission)

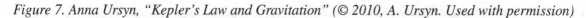

Figure 8. Cody Gallagher, "A stain glass window" (© 2012, C. Gallagher. Used with permission)

Figure 9. Steffanie Sperry, "A Diagram of Kepler's Laws" (© 2012, S. Sperry. Used with permission)

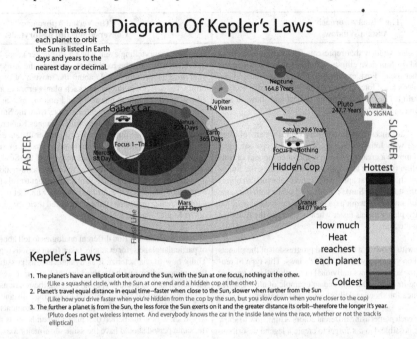

focus. Distances from the Sun vary when planets are orbiting. Kepler said that a planet covers the same area in the same time. It sweeps out equal areas in equal times so must go a bigger distance when it is closer to the Sun, and a smaller one when it's farther, so the area stays the same. Therefore each planet travels faster when it is nearer the Sun than when it is further.

For directions on a project, see Table 2.

Figure 8 is a student work "A stain glass window."

Figure 9 shows another visualization created by a student taking my Computer Graphics course. The author of this project intended to make her visualization of the Kepler's laws more attractive to those with a short attention span, who become distracted after a short time. Steffanie Sperry compared visualization of the planets' elliptical orbits, times to orbit the Sun, and the planets' speed to movement of a Gabe' car; Gabe can drive fast near the Sun that is in the focus of an elliptical orbit, but he has to slow his movement when approaching the other focus because there is a hidden cop there. The author also pictured plan-

ets and explained that those located in an inside lane would win the race, whether or not the track is elliptical. Pluto does not get wireless Internet; the Sun exerts less force on it because it is further from the Sun than other planets; for Pluto, it takes 247.7 years to orbit the Sun.

Project 2: Keplers Law and Gravitation

"Planetary Olympics:" A Verbal Project by Wes Thorpe

Tom: *Welcome! Here we are at another beautiful day at the Planetary Olympics. We have our eight contestants here, all excited to participate in the first event the "fastest trip around the Sun." All of our contestants have been training for this event for millions of years and are ready to show off all they have worked for.*

Announcer: *Get ready... Set.... Go!! And they are off! Venus and Mercury pull to the front of*

Table 2. Working on a project about the planetary movement

The Visual Approach: A Stain Window	The Verbal Approach: Conversation with a Storyteller
Create a design for a stain window that represents planetary orbits. Show planets orbiting around the Sun in an ellipse, with the Sun at one focus and nothing else at the other focus. First, examine information provided above to find data about Kepler's laws, forces acting at the Solar System's motion, and then gain a general idea how to design your project and show an area swept by a planet during a given time interval.	Describe a storytelling event when a storyteller keeps being interrupted by questions asked by the participants. Include the storyteller's answers. Let your storyteller unfold a tale about the movement of planets in planetary orbits. He will put in the picture each planet orbiting around the Sun in an ellipse, with the Sun at one focus and nothing else at the other focus. He will also inform how the planets' distances from the Sun vary while they are orbiting. Because, in accordance with Johannes Kepler, a planet sweeps out equal areas in equal times, it moves a greater distance in the same amount of time when it is near perihelion (a point closest to the Sun) than when it is near aphelion (the farthest point away from the Sun). This way, all orbits with the same period should have the same semi-major axis (a half of the long axis of the ellipse). Therefore, each planet travels faster when is nearer to the Sun than when it is farther from the Sun. Let the storyteller describe a time-based progression of the planets and their speed, based on your study of the Kepler's laws.
Display how the planets' distances from the Sun vary while they are orbiting. Because, in accordance with Johannes Kepler, a planet sweeps out equal areas in equal times, it moves a greater distance in the same amount of time when it is near perihelion (the point at which an object orbiting the Sun is closest to the Sun) than when it is near aphelion (the point at which an object orbiting the Sun is farthest from the Sun). This way, all orbits with the same period should have the same semi-major axis (a half of the long axis of the ellipse). Therefore, each planet travels faster when is nearer to the Sun than when it is farther from the Sun.	The participants will find different analogies to tell about the relative speeds of particular planets, for example, taken from various types of transportation. Think how to characterize it as dynamically as possible. Recount the fact that, in accordance with the third law of Kepler, more distant planets orbit the Sun at slower average speeds, obeying the relationship $p^2 + a^3$ between the planet's orbital period "p" and the average distance from the Sun "a", measured in astronomical units AU. Some comments of the participants would show how the period of a planet depends on its mass and orbits with the same period should have the same semi-major axis.
You may want to start with showing a time-based progression of the planets and their speed, based on your study of the Kepler's laws. This type of representation, called a time series, shows individual items plotted in a graphic display at uniform time intervals. One can see an example of a time series display in a phone application showing daily closing market values of stocks.	In an unfolding discussion, the participants will consider how does the period of the planet depend on its mass. The acceleration of a planet in its orbit around the Sun depends upon the mass of the Sun and the inverse square of the planet's distance from the Sun (M_{sun}/d^2). The gravitational force exerted on the planet by the Sun decreases when the planet moves away in its orbit around the Sun. Thus, the planet's acceleration must also decrease, resulting in a lower orbital speed. Remember that the strength of gravity, the gravitational force between objects can be described by the Newton's universal law of gravitation $F_g = G M_1 M_2/d^2$
Show relative speed of each planet using different colors. Think how to show that as dynamically as possible. Do not forget to create a legend describing the function of a color.	where masses M_1 and M_2 attract each other through the force of gravity F_g that is directly proportional to the product of their masses. The strength of gravity between two objects decreases with the square of the distance between their centers (thus the gravitational force follows an inverse square law with distance).
Display on your drawing that, in accordance with the third law of Kepler, more distant planets orbit the Sun at slower average speeds, obeying the relationship $p^2 + a^3$ between the planet's orbital period "p" and the average distance from the Sun "a", measured in astronomical units AU. Your design for a stain window should show how the period of a planet depends on its mass and the orbits with the same period should have the same semi-major axis. Consider how does the period of the planet depend on its mass. The acceleration of a planet in its orbit around the Sun depends upon the mass of the Sun and the inverse square of the planet's distance from the Sun (M_{sun}/d^2). The gravitational force exerted on the planet by the Sun decreases when the planet moves away in its orbit around the Sun. Thus, the planet's acceleration must also decrease, resulting in a lower orbital speed. Remember that the strength of gravity, the gravitational force between objects can be described by the Newton's universal law of gravitation $F_g = G M_1 M_2/d^2$	In the course of further discussion, one of the participants tells about two cosmic stations (or maybe rackets), situated close to each other. He informs, that if you triple the distance between these objects, the gravitational force would decrease by a factor of 3.
where masses M_1 and M_2 attract each other through the force of gravity F_g that is directly proportional to the product of their masses. The strength of gravity between two objects decreases with the square of the distance between their centers (thus the gravitational force follows an inverse square law with distance). In your stain window, place four sketches showing cosmic stations or rackets, two of them situated close to each other, and the next two separated much more. Indicate in a visual way that if you triple the distance between these objects, the gravitational force would decrease by a factor of 3.	Tell your listeners they are traveling in one of these rackets. How gravity will be changing in time of their travel, when they will go more and more away from the Earth, pass the Moon, and then even start going away from the Sun system and its planets? Discuss with the participants the pulling forces of gravity coming from these objects. Which are strong and which can be disregarded?
Imagine yourself traveling in one of these rackets. How gravity will be changing in time of your travel, when you will go more and more away from the Earth, pass the Moon, and then even start going away from the Sun system and its planets? Draw the pulling forces of gravity coming from these objects. Which are strong and which can be disregarded?	
You may also prefer a more metaphorical and less precise interpretation of the planetary movement. In this case present your personal response to the world's order and your place in it.	

Figure 10. Anna Ursyn, "Our Planetary System" (© 2010, A. Ursyn. Used with permission)

the line and are running neck and neck, and now Mercury pulls ahead. Look at them go!

88 days later

Announcer: *And here comes Mercury around the corner for the last bit of the stretch leaving the other planets days behind. Way to go, Mercury!*

599 more days later

Announcer: *Here comes Mars, the "Big Red." He'll be fourth coming in, behind Venus and Earth!*

59,513 more days later

Announcer: *Coming up now, certainly not least but definitely last Neptune!!! What an exciting race!! I cannot believe the unbelievable*

outcome of this unbelievable race! But you better believe it! Join us later when we have the axis rotation challenge!

Figure 10, "Our Planetary System" transfers a planetary model onto a dried tumbleweed.

PROJECT 3: ABOUT THE EXPANDING UNIVERSE AND THE GRAVITATIONAL EQUILIBRIUM

Background Information for the Project about the Expanding Universe and the Gravitational Equilibrium

Examining some basic data about the theme of this project may be helpful in finding a general idea how to design your project. Before beginning the project it might be useful to recall a few

Table 3. Working on a project about the expanding universe and the gravitational equilibrium

The Visual Approach Drawing Keyframes for animation	The Verbal Approach Describing Expansion
In this project we will start with a depiction of movement. The invention of time-based media changed our perception and emotions related to storytelling. In movies, a camera records all changes, a moment after a moment. When it comes to animation, either 2D (a flip-book on paper, or animation created with software such as Adobe Photoshop or Adobe Flash) or 3D (created with Autodesk 3ds Max, Autodesk Maya, Autodesk Softimage, Blender, etc.), the concept of key frames allows the user draw two events, as they changed in time, so the computer would fill out all the frames in between. For example, if an arm bends, it would be enough to show its horizontal position on one frame followed by another frame depicting its vertical placement. All frames with the arm in angular positions will be drawn by software. (In order to prevent breaking the character's elbow by moving arm in the wrong direction, computer animators apply a so-called inverse kinematics: to block the movement of the elbow, they start with its final position, and then reverse the order of drawings). It takes as little as two frames to create animation.	The visual part of this project comprised four key frames for an imaginary animation depicting the expansion of the universe. If you feel more comfortable while writing about this concept, describe this imaginary animation and explain what do we mean by a phrase "universe is expanding," by the gravitational equilibrium, the forces guiding physical event, and use that knowledge for description of the behavior of characters you invent. For example, your character cannot do something because it is not possible in terms of the laws of Physics. Create stories about invented creatures, which would not like to obey the existing physical laws. For example, characters can defy the rules by changing their physical environment. Unlike on a theater stage, in a fiction or in a 2D animation you can send your character to infinity.
For this project, create five key frames for an imaginary animation that would explain what do we mean by the phrase "universe is expanding" and by the concept of gravitational equilibrium. When we want to visualize how the universe is expanding, we have to take into consideration different kinds of objects to draw: the universe itself, galaxies, clusters of galaxies, individual stars, and star systems.	First, write about a first key frame for the animation. Present stars and star systems as your imaginary characters in their surroundings; the characters and rooms they exist will stand for objects you discuss. Each character in a room will represent a different kind of astronomical object: individual stars (you may include our star – the Sun), and star systems, galaxies, clusters of galaxies, and the universe itself. Characterize the distinctive nature of these characters and rooms in any configuration you choose, but remember to place the characters standing for stars and star systems inside of the galaxies, and the galaxies on the surface of the spaces representing the universe. This is a description of your first key frame of an imaginary animation.
First, draw a first key frame for the animation. Apply visual symbols for all the kinds of objects you visualize. Draw geometric objects, also called primitives. Geometric primitives in computer graphics are simple, irreducible objects that the computer system can draw and store. Two-dimensional primitives include lines, points, and polygons, sometimes also triangles and shapes, such as boxes, circles, and curves (for example, Bézier curves, which are defined by parametric equations describing a relation as a set of equations). In three dimensions, triangles and polygons can build 3D forms. Simple geometric solid forms include a cube, cylinder, sphere, cone, pyramid, or torus. Choose some nice names and assign them for these objects, for example, the names of the astronauts, astronomers, or Roman and Greek heroes. Each of the primitives will represent a different kind of astronomical object: the universe itself, galaxies, clusters of galaxies, individual stars (you may include our star – the Sun), and star systems. Draw these symbols in any configuration you choose, but remember to place the stars and star systems inside of galaxies, and the galaxies on the surface of the symbol for the universe. This is your first key frame drawing.	
Now imagine that a billion of light-years elapsed. Draw a second key frame for your animation showing what has changed during this time. Remember that the expansion of the universe means that the average distances between clusters of galaxies become larger, so draw them sparser, thinly dispersed. However, you will not draw the galaxies bigger, because the galaxies do not grow in size. The stars will not be bigger, as well. Also, you will not change average distances between star systems within galaxies. Only the growing distances between clusters of galaxies cause that the universe is expanding. Space is not expanding within our solar system, our galaxy, or our Local Group of galaxies.	From the time of the Big Bang the universe is expanding. Imagine that a billion of light-years elapsed. Discuss a second key frame for your animation explaining what has changed during this time. Remember that the expansion of the universe means that the average distances between clusters of galaxies become larger, so recount them sparser, thinly dispersed. However, your characters and their rooms will not grow; you will not characterize the galaxies as bigger, because the galaxies do not grow in size. The stars will not be bigger too. Also, you will not change average distances between star systems within galaxies. Only the growing distances between clusters of galaxies cause that the universe is expanding. Space is not expanding within our solar system, our galaxy, or our local group of galaxies.
For the third key frame of your animation, pretend that the next billion of light-years passed. Draw your picture appropriately, showing that galaxies are moving away from us and more distant ones are moving away faster. For this reason draw the changes in the distances between clusters of galaxies even larger than in your second key frame (and the universe much bigger than in a second key frame).	For the third key frame of your animation, pretend that the next billion of light-years passed. Describe this third key frame appropriately, pointing up that galaxies are moving away from us and more distant ones are moving away faster. For this reason report the changes in the distances between clusters of galaxies larger than in your second key frame (and the universe much bigger than in a second key frame).

Continued on following page

Table 3 continued

The Visual Approach Drawing Keyframes for Animation	The Verbal Approach Describing Expansion
Add an explanation of your drawings. Draw schematic sketches and define what do you mean by the four known fundamental forces acting in universe: (1) gravity, (2) the electromagnetic force, (3) the strong force that holds atomic nuclei together, and (4) the weak force that mediates nuclear reactions and is the only force besides gravity that is felt by weakly interacting particles. From the time of the Big Bang the universe is expanding. You may ponder why the expanding of the universe relates to the distances between galaxies, but not to the galaxies themselves. Scientists suspect that expansion is accelerating because of a dark energy we cannot directly detect. However, stars, galaxies, and clusters of galaxies are all gravitationally bound systems. Individual galaxies and galaxy clusters might not expand because gravity holds them together.	Add an explanation of your first three key frames. Define what do you mean by the four known fundamental forces acting in universe: (1) gravity, (2) the electromagnetic force, (3) strong force that holds atomic nuclei together, and (4) the weak force that mediates nuclear reactions and is the only force besides gravity that is felt by weakly interacting particles.
The fourth key frame for the animation will be about a gravitational equilibrium. You may want to examine forces acting inside of the Sun and causing that the Sun is in a gravitational equilibrium. The gravitational equilibrium is a condition where the thermal pressure inside of the Sun balances the gravity's inward push. The thermal pressure that is acting outward is caused by generation of energy in the process of nuclear fusion. Gravitational equilibrium acts as a solar thermostat because the nuclear fusion rate will slow with the decrease of the solar core temperature, and then the gravitational pull will prevail causing the Sun core to contract and return to the equilibrium.	Now you may also want to examine forces acting inside of the Sun and causing that the Sun is in a gravitational equilibrium. The gravitational equilibrium is a condition where the thermal pressure inside of the Sun balances the gravity's inward push. The thermal pressure that is acting outward is caused by generation of energy in the process of nuclear fusion.
Imagine a similar set of circumstances happening in space.	In a fourth key frame for your animation, you may now examine and discuss the forces that act on your characters and objects. For example, to understand the concept of the gravitational equilibrium better, describe an excursion to a meadow in a sunny day, and the enjoyment brought by floating above the ground in big, colorful balloons. The gas in the balloons is heated, so they can resist the gravitational pull. By heating the gas and raising its pressure you may go higher in your balloon. Describe in numbers the temperature inside the balloons.
Remember the two forces that are balanced in gravitational equilibrium, the outward pressure and gravity. On your fourth key frame draw arrows that show forces of gravity versus pressure in the state of the gravitational equilibrium. For example, it may be a sketch of a mule with a man riding on it and carrying a monkey on his shoulders. These three characters are in gravitational equilibrium. The mule supports the most weight and feels the greatest pressure, while the weight and underlying pressure are decreasing for the man (who supports the monkey) and the monkey. Maybe you prefer to draw humans pyramided in a way the Cirque du Soleil does.	Describe a similar set of circumstances happening in space. Remember the two forces that are balanced in gravitational equilibrium, the outward pressure and gravity. On your fourth key frame describe forces of gravity versus pressure in the state of the gravitational equilibrium, explaining that they are oriented, directed in opposite directions. Describe it as an interaction between the characters.
In a similar way, you may want to sketch gravitational equilibrium in the Sun. Draw the Sun as slice of a sphere, and then draw arrows denoting the outward push of pressure, and arrows directed inward showing the pull of gravity. Now you may want to visualize the forces that act on your objects. To visualize the concept of the gravitational equilibrium, imagine a landscape – a meadow in a sunny day with big, colorful balloons with people inside the baskets floating above the ground. The gas in the balloons is heated, so they can resist the gravitational pull. By heating the gas and raising its pressure you may go higher in your balloon. Show the temperature inside the balloons by various shades of red.	Finally, write a summary showing your own opinion about the possible fate of the universe that you base on your readings.
Finally, on the fifth animation frame draw your own vision of the world's future, your conclusions and opinion based on what just was discussed.	

key concepts. Cosmological principle is the idea that matter is distributed uniformly throughout the universe on very large scales, meaning that the universe has neither a center nor an edge. Expansion of the universe denotes the idea that the space between the galaxies or the clusters of galaxies is growing with time. This notion tells about the increase in the average distance between galaxies as the time progresses. Galaxies move apart as the universe expands, like dots on a rubber balloon when we are inflating it. The most distant objects in the universe move fastest, at speeds close to the speed of light. Presenting the expanding universe in the form of raised dough expanding during the baking process provides a simple metaphor of this concept: when dough for a raisin cake is rising, distances between particular raisins increase (Bennett & al, 2011).

While the majority of scientists agree the universe started with the Big Bang (rapid inflation), there are many possible scenarios for the fate of the universe. They depend on scientific theories that analyze the overall shape of the universe, the physical properties of the matter density, and the dark energy density in the universe. Astronomers mostly agree that the universe is expanding and ask whether it will expand forever, slower, or faster, or the expansion will stop and the universe will collapse (Adams, Buchert, Mersini-Houghton, & Nekoogar, 2012). The scenarios for the future of the universe depend on the understanding of interactions of dark matter (and energy) with mass and gravity. The astronomers discuss the overall geometry of the universe, which, depending on the universe fate, could be flat, open, or closed, and may be compared to the surface of a sphere, flat surface (with more dimensions), or a saddle. Several theories do not take into account the presence of dark energy. Some pose that the gravity of all universe matter eventually will halt and reverse the expansion, so the universe will begin contracting. The crushing galaxies will end in a Big Crunch. Others assume there would be a closed universe where the spacetime (the inseparable, four-dimensional combination of space and time) curves back on itself to the point where it assumes a shape like the surface of a sphere. Other theories would predict that once this universe collapses it would give rise to another universe. Some assume that the universe will never collapse, but will expand slower as time progresses. According to the Big Chill scenario, the universe has too little mass and drifts on forever, slowing but never stopping (Hubblesite, 2012). In the absence of a repulsive force or a type of energy called dark energy, the density of the universe would become equal to the critical density that indicates the fate of the cosmos: the boundary value between the universe models that expand forever (open models) and those that recollapse (closed models). Astronomers call it a flat universe, where the overall geometry (Euclidean) of spacetime is like a surface of a table but in more dimensions. If the cosmological constant is not zero it might cause the expansion of the universe to accelerate with time. A scenario of the coasting universe presumes that it will keep expanding forever with little change in its rate of expansion; in the absence of a repulsive force, the actual mass density in a coasting universe is smaller than the critical density. It is also called an open universe, in which spacetime has a shape like a surface of a saddle.

Dark energy may be a force that increases the expansion of the universe. In spite of the known facts that matter and energy are interchangeable ($E=mc^2$), and that energy supposedly has a source in the form of matter or radiation, astronomers discovered that space, even when devoid of all matter and radiation, has a residual energy. The physics of quantum mechanics allows energy and matter the constant brief appearance and disappearance; it could be giving energy to otherwise empty space. In the accelerating universe scenario, a repulsive force of dark energy causes that the expansion of the universe accelerates with time. With a Big Rip scenario, the universe will disintegrate into unbound elementary particles. Galaxies will recede from one another increasingly faster, and it will become cold and dark more quickly than in a coasting universe. If the cosmological constant (a name coming from a term in Einstein's equations of general relativity, described as an anti-gravity effect) is not zero, then it represents a repulsive force or a dark energy that might cause the expansion of the universe to accelerate with time. Depending on the scientists' opinions, dark energy has been constant throughout time and will remain that way, or the dark energy (quintessence) is a new force and will eventually fade away just as it arose (Hubblesite, 2012; Bennett & al, 2011).

Whichever answer is right, the universe still has at least a few tens of billions of years left.

For directions on this project, see Table 3.

Project 3: Expanding Universe

An Example by Wes Thorpe

Deep in the Milky Way Galaxy lies a family of nine planets all taken care of by their grandfather, Sun. All of the planets live in harmony revolving around their grandfather as they have from the beginning of time. One millennium however, Pluto was declared a planetoid not a planet. He felt shunned by his family. Pluto grew cold and dark plotting his revenge against Grandfather Sun whom he had previously held in such high regard.

Grandpa! Mars exclaims.

Yes, what is it Son? inquires Grandfather Sun.

Where did the Universe come from? questions Mars.

Ah. It is time you all heard this story. Gather round children as I reveal to you the greatest day of our lives, the creation of the Universe!

(All the planets listen in to hear about the great story of the creation of time itself, all but Pluto who is too angry to want to have anything to do with his so called family.)

And that is how the Universe began.

Wow! Yell out the Planets in unison.

What a fantastic history, so that means that we are all related! Meaning the stars and even the Dwarf Planets are a part of each other and need each other for our Galaxy to work, says Mars.

That is correct, replies Grandfather Sun.

Just then a blue dot flies towards Grandfather Sun and the other Planets.

You will pay for abandoning me! screams Pluto as he charges forcefully towards Grandfather Sun.

No son you can't do this!" yells Grandfather Sun.

I'm not your Son! You betrayed me! ... AAAAAHHHHHHHHHHHHHHH! Pluto begins to throws himself into Grandfather Sun.

WAIT!" an unheard voice cries out. Pluto stops instantly in his tracks.

Please don't do this. We need the sun for the Galaxy to work but even more we need you! Without you, Pluto, the Galaxy's equilibrium will be thrown off and we will all suffer from it and die, said the unknown voice as Earth rises up.

Earth is that you? But why do you need me. I was declared not a planet. You all betrayed me! Pluto says slowly being calmed by Earth's soft voice.

Pluto, you never left our family, the Universe makes us a family and being a part of the same Galaxy brings us even closer. Without you our Galaxy will fall apart. With every element in our Galaxy we will be able to contribute to the Universe and help it grow and soon we will be able to accept more members into our family, describes Earth.

I see the light! If we are always plotting against each other and never trying to work out our problems we will never be able to grow, Pluto says as he returns to his rightful place in the Universe.

It appears we have all learned a valuable lesson today, Grandfather Sun declares looking over his Galaxy. Each of us has his purpose and place in the Universe. Each of our roles has equal value. We must all work together if we want to better ourselves!

Figure 11, "Multiverse" presents an image coded as a 3D program about the expanding universe. The work was done as a response to the acquired information that can be briefly summarized as follows:

As distance between galaxies increases, their size does not. The space between galaxies or clusters of galaxies is growing in time. There is an increase in average distance between galaxies as the time progresses. As universe expands, the galaxies recede from one another. Cosmological Principle poses the Universe has neither a center nor an edge, which means matter is distributed uniformly throughout the universe on a very large scale. Cosmological Theories predict that maybe

Figure 11. Anna Ursyn, "Multiverse" (© 2010, A. Ursyn. Used with permission)

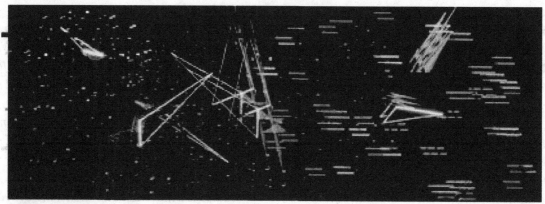

the Universe will be a re-collapsing universe, a critical universe, a coasting universe, or an accelerating universe. The four universal forces are gravity, electromagnetism, strong force that holds atomic nuclei together, and weak force that mediates nuclear reactions. Gravitational Equilibrium means a balance of gravitation vs. thermal pressure.

PROJECT 4: NUCLEAR FUSION. NOW INSIDE OF THE SUN AND IN THE ERA OF NUCLEOSYNTHESIS

This project is aimed to picture the center of the Sun (based on what we know about it) and describe what is happening now inside the Sun, and what happened when the universe was a few minutes old.

Background Information for the Project about Nuclear Fusion: Now Inside of the Sun, and in the Era of Nucleosynthesis

A short summary about the present and past events happening due to the process of nucleosynthesis, along with the Sun properties and structure might inspire creating this project. Sun generates energy by fusing hydrogen into helium. The core – the innermost layer of the sun is a source for all the Sun's energy. In a thermonuclear reaction called nuclear fusion, hydrogen atoms combined with each other to make helium atoms and produce energy, which keeps the Sun in a state of equilibrium. Thus, due to the nuclear fusion mostly hydrogen and helium atomic nuclei are formed, and the Sun releases energy into space.

The era of nucleosynthesis happened long ago in the early history of the universe. This era lasted from 0.001 second to about 3 minutes after the events described by the Big Bang theory, so the world was a few minutes old. Before this era elementary particles appeared spontaneously from energy but only for a short time; most nuclei broke apart as fast as they formed because of the great heat. By the end of this era virtually all of the neutrons and about one-seventh of the protons in the universe had fused into helium. The universe comprised hot plasma consisting of the nuclei of hydrogen, helium, and free electrons.

We keep in mind that the nuclear fusion happens in the Sun's center now, and the current Sun's composition is mainly hydrogen and helium. However, as nuclear fusion depends on temperature, in the era of nucleosynthesis higher temperature caused even more collisions than now happen inside the Sun. It allowed for fusion of a small amount of heavier chemical elements, such as lithium, beryllium, and boron. Then, for the next hundreds of thousands years the universe was expanding and cooling. Electrons bounded with atoms, while photons began stream freely, forming the cosmic microwave background existing today. Except for the small amount of matter produced later by stars, the chemical composition of the universe is the same now as at the end of the era of nucleosynthesis. That is the reason why a study of nucleosynthesis is so important in determining the chemical composition of the universe.

The Sun contains more than 99.9% of the solar system total mass; it is gaseous. Spectroscopic analysis shows that it contains hot hydrogen and helium. Starting from the center outward to the surface the Sun comprises the layers in the following order (NASA Space Station Info, 2012):

- **The Core:** A source of all the Sun's energy coming from nuclear fusion, a region of an immense density, pressure, and temperature of 15 million K
- **Radiation Zone:** With almost 10 million K, transfers energy outward as ions of hydrogen and helium emitting photons of light, which are then re-absorbed by other ions, and X rays

- **Convection Zone:** A region of the intense, turbulent transport of the hot gas outward and the cooled gas inward
- **Photosphere:** The visible surface of the Sun consisting of the churning gas that is less dense than the Earth's atmosphere (about 1% of the particle density of Earth's atmosphere at sea level) and is 6,000 K hot; its energy escapes the Sun. The solar atmosphere above the photosphere can be seen with telescopes across the electromagnetic spectrum, from the visible light to gamma rays.
- **Chromosphere:** Is about 2,000 km thick and has temperature about 10,000K; this part of the solar atmosphere radiates most of the ultraviolet light. The chromosphere is visible as a colored flash at the beginning and end of total eclipses of the Sun.
- **Corona:** is the outer atmosphere of the Sun, much larger in volume than the Sun itself, as it extends several millions kilometers above the visible surface. Its low-density gas has a temperature of several million K; it emits most of the Sun's X rays and a stream of charged particles causing a solar wind.

For directions on this project, see Table 4. For a visual representation of nuclear fusion, see Figure 12.

There are two instances when it happens:

- **Inside of the Sun (Now):** The Sun consists mostly of hydrogen and helium. When the temperature and pressure are high inside of the Sun, two atoms of hydrogen and one atom of helium move together and fuse into one atomic nucleus, and thus they generate energy. Energy gets released then, hence the warmth of the Sun in space.
- **In the Universe (in the Era of Nucleosynthesis):** During nuclear synthesis. The same happened in early history of

Table 4. Working on a project about nuclear fusion; now – inside of the sun, and in the era of nucleosynthesis

The Visual approach The Nuclear Fusion	The Verbal Approach A Nucleosynthesis Website
Draw a sketch and show with the use of colorful symbols the process of nuclear fusion that happens in the Sun center. To visualize nuclear fusion in the era of nucleosynthesis, sketch small colorful balloons held by a child. The balloons will represent atomic nuclei formed during the period of nucleosynthesis. Make the balloons color-coded. The color of each balloon tells what kind of a chemical element's nucleus it represents (for example, a blue balloon means hydrogen, orange means helium, etc.). Assemble the bunch of balloons of different colors to show (in proportion) that during the period of nucleosynthesis mostly hydrogen and helium atomic nuclei were formed, with only a small amount of lithium, beryllium, and boron. You may choose to scan your sketches or use any scanned images of visually inspiring events and processes related to your project, obeying the copyright rules. Choose specific color selections, use additional lines, apply texture, enhance the depth of the picture, or change its balance and composition. Apply and make intelligible some visualization techniques using color coding, changing proportion, and modifying patterns, copying and pasting a selection, and/or introducing symbolic representations. You may want to use modeling clay and develop a three-dimensional model of the Sun. You may decide to put your work on a website, a Facebook, or make a PowerPoint presentation. Create a colorful cross section of the Sun, and work on representing its surface. You may prefer to develop a color-coded model to represent gas having different temperatures. Show your own image of the Sun center. Show an impressionistic view of the Sun center or show an image of the real Sun's center. Show the forces that make the solar interior so hot and cause radiation and heat waves. Your mining for the answers may stir your imagination.	Make a design for a website. Imagine that you are building a website that explores and explains a structure of the Sun and describes a concept of nucleosynthesis. Write about the content of each page of the website and arrange your pages in hierarchical order (based on what we know about it). Describe the present and past events that are happening due to the process of nucleosynthesis. First, report what is going on now inside the Sun, how it generates energy by fusing hydrogen into helium, and how, due to the nuclear fusion mostly hydrogen and helium atomic nuclei are formed. Outline the process of nuclear fusion that happens in the Sun center. Now comment on what happened long ago in the early history of the universe. We keep in mind that the nuclear fusion happens in the Sun's center now, and the current Sun's composition is mainly hydrogen and helium. However, as nuclear fusion depends on temperature; in the era of nucleosynthesis higher temperature caused even more collisions than now happen inside the Sun. It allowed for fusion of a small amount of heavier chemical elements, such as lithium, beryllium, and boron. To explain the nuclear fusion occurring in the era of nucleosynthesis, describe a bunch of small colorful balloons held by a child that represent atomic nuclei formed during the period of nucleosynthesis. Describe how the balloons represent the chemical elements' nuclei. Emphasize that during the period of nucleosynthesis mostly hydrogen and helium atomic nuclei were formed, with only a small amount of lithium, beryllium, and boron. Give a report about the inner structure of the Sun, along with a description of the Sun as a whole, and then work on describing its surface. You may prefer to tell about gas having different temperatures. Provide your own account of what happens in the Sun center. Show the forces that make the solar interior so hot and cause radiation and heat waves. Your mining for the answers may stir your imagination.

Figure 12. Anna Ursyn, "Nuclear Fusion" (© 2010, A. Ursyn. Used with permission)

the Universe. Earlier there were more collisions (as a function of temperature), so not only helium was created, but also lithium, beryllium and barium. It lasted from 0.001 to 3 min.

Because fusion exists inside of the Sun, and started right after Big Bang in the space, the world looks the same: it has hydrogen and helium.

Project 4: Center of the Sun: A Verbal Project by Wes Thorpe

While on my journey to the Sun.
Oh, all the wonderful things I have learned.
I will have to move
After all the theories I will prove
With all the money I will have earned.

PROJECT 5: LIGHT AND ELECTROMAGNETIC SPECTRUM: A PORTRAIT OF A PERSON IN A FOREST

In this project you will be encouraged to create a visual explanation of a relationship between frequency, wavelength, energy, and the energy of light as the electromagnetic wave.

Background Information for the Project about Light and Electromagnetic Spectrum: A Portrait of a Person in a Forest

Examining some basic data about the theme of this project may be helpful in finding a general idea how to design your project. Before beginning the project it might be useful to recall a few key concepts.

- Energy as a physical quantity means the capacity to produce change in a physical system. Energy can be transformed into an-

other form but the total energy remains the same. The unit of energy is an electron volt eV, which means 1 volt multiplied by the electron charge. The electromagnetic wave as a synonym for light consists of waves of electric and magnetic fields.

- Electromagnetic radiation is a form of energy that has wave-like properties and travels through space. Charged particles, mostly electrons, emit and absorb electromagnetic radiation. In vacuum, electromagnetic radiation propagates at the speed of light. Electromagnetic radiation may be electric or/and magnetic, in a complementary ratio of intensity to each other; their direction of energy and wave propagation is perpendicular to each other. We cannot see the whole electromagnetic spectrum; we can only see a small fragment (Figure 13).

- We think about light as an electromagnetic radiation wave and describe all of its portions in an electromagnetic spectrum. We describe electromagnetic spectrum in terms of its wavelength (in meters, from 10^{-12} or even shorter to 10^3 meters or longer) and frequency in cycles per second (cycles per second are units of frequency for a wave; the number of peaks (or troughs) of a wave that pass by a given point each second) called hertz – Hz (hertz is the standard unit of frequency for light waves; equivalent to units of 1/s).

The complete spectrum of light includes radio waves, microwaves, infrared light, visible light, ultraviolet light, X rays, and gamma rays. Frequency is the rate at which peaks of a wave pass by a point, measured in units of 1/s, often called cycles per second or hertz. Wavelength is the distance between adjacent peaks (or troughs) of a wave. This simple relationship between wavelength and frequency applies to light. Light consists of individual photons that have properties of

Figure 13. Fatma Alabdullaziz, A diagram of the electromagnetic spectrum, showing various properties across the range of frequencies and wavelengths [Student's work from my Digital Illustration course, University of Northern Colorado]

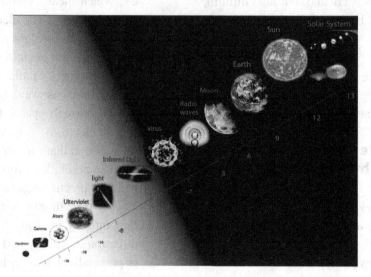

both particles and waves and travel through space with a speed of light. Photons of light are characterized by wavelength, frequency, and energy. Longer wavelength means lower frequency and lower energy. Photons of light carry radiative energy, and thus the shorter the wavelength of the light (and the higher its frequency) the higher is the energy of photons. We can see examples of waves and their movement when we toss a pebble into a pond to make the ripples move out, or when we shake a string and it vibrates up and down.

Information of that kind, about stars and galaxies, can be gathered with the use of spectroscopy. Astronomers can collect information that uses spectroscopy to determine the chemical composition of a distant star, the speed at which a distant galaxy is moving away from us, the surface temperature of a distant star, or the rotation rate of a distant star. However, spectroscopy cannot provide the data about the size of a galaxy.

For directions on this project, see Table 5. For a visual representation of the electromagnetic spectrum, see Figure 14.

- **Frequency:** Speed peak of a wave going through the point
- **Energy:** How many electron volts, a big range from $10^7 - 10^{-9}$
- **Wavelength:** Distance between the peaks of a wave
- **Energy:** Of the electromagnetic wave.

From the electromagnetic spectrum we can only see a small fragment. The longest are radio waves, then infrared light, visible light, ultraviolet, X rays, and Gamma rays.

Project 5: Light and Electromagnetic Spectrum. An Example by Wes Thorpe

Never ending, up and down through this world we go.
Will they hear us? Will they see us?
Always out of range.
Just trying to make a change.
But if we pass through, would anyone even know.

Figure 14. Anna Ursyn, Light and Electromagnetic Spectrum. (© 2010, A. Ursyn. Used with permission)

PROJECT 6: COSMIC BACKGROUND RADIATION

This project invites you to draw a visual concept map telling about the cosmic background radiation.

Background Information for the Project about Cosmic Background Radiation

Cosmic microwave background radiation is the remnant radiation from the times of a Big Bang. It consists of photons released in the era of nuclei, when the universe was about 380,000 years old, and now arriving at Earth. Early in time, in the era of nuclei, when temperature was about 6,000 K, photons bounced around among free electrons. Later on, in the era of atoms, when temperature decreased to about 1,500 K, photons moved freely through the universe because atoms captured the electrons (Bennett et al, 2011).

We can detect cosmic background radiation using radio telescopes sensitive to microwaves (which are short-wavelength radio waves). Penzias and Wilson discovered the cosmic background radiation in the early 1960s. Theories are confirmed by observation. COBE is the cosmic background explorer, a satellite developed by the NASA's Goddard Space Flight Center to measure the diffuse infrared and microwave radiation from the early universe. Signals from the COBE spacecraft are now sent out of space. The existence of the cosmic background radiation (which was confirmed by data from various sources, such as stellar and galactic), the experimental results, and measurements support the Big Bang Theory in many ways. Theoretically, the cosmic background is expected to have a temperature just a few degrees above absolute zero, and its actual, measured temperature turns out to be about 2.7 K degrees K above absolute zero. It had a much higher temperature in the past. The cosmic background radiation is expected to have tiny temperature fluctuations

Table 5. Working on a project about light and electromagnetic spectrum: a portrait of a person in a forest

The Visual Approach Electromagnetic Radiation	The Verbal Approach A Limerick about Waves
First, list different categories of electromagnetic radiation going from the lowest frequency to the highest frequency: radio, microwave, infrared, visible light, ultraviolet, X-rays, gamma rays. Assign simple symbols to these frequencies, draw them on small pieces of paper and arrange without looking at your notes. When ordered from the shortest to the longest wavelength, the different categories of electromagnetic radiation are: gamma rays, X-rays, ultraviolet, visible light, infrared, microwave, radio. Again, assign simple symbols to these wavelengths, draw them on small pieces of paper and arrange without looking at your notes. Now you may want to sketch a portrait (or a self-portrait) showing a curly hair of a person you draw. Imagine that you look at a curly hair. You can grab a small piece of paper, fold it, and then fold it again. Cut a square in a corner of your foldout, so you have a square opening when you unfold the paper. This is your viewfinder. Look at wavy hair on someone's head, while directing your gaze through the viewfinder you have just made. The curlier, undulating hair one has, the more peaks and troughs you will notice inside your viewfinder. The wavelength is the distance between two peaks (or two troughs), and the longer the wavelength, the lower is the frequency of the waves, and less waves you will see inside your viewfinder. Draw a frame around your sketch, and then change your sketch giving the subject another wavelength (and frequency) of hair undulations. Add a background to your portrait, drawing a forest. Imagine a forest where the animals possess different levels of strength projected as light. This means each animal can signal its power by sending off the light, but also each type of light gives the animal special powers. That means create a landscape with a forest where different types of animals project their special powers and they are represented and recognizable by special wavelengths. Create a system where a specific animal power depends on the emission or the absorption of the radiative energy, and then present the power of each animal in a graphical way, for example, through the colors or textures of the animals' bodies. Can you find the system that applies to trees, plants, flowers, or mushrooms? You can also show the relation between the animal's brightness and its speed and agility; for example, showing a gazelle in a yellow and a turtle in a brown color. How could you learn about animals' powers and speed by measuring wavelengths they emit? Since this environment is set like a color-coded one, one can set expectations just by looking at the color of each creature.	Write a limerick about the waves following a structure as provided below. This form of a poem is usually a very condensed form of expression that outlines emotions, feelings, events, or a state of mind. Select information about light and electromagnetic spectrum you want to memorize and shape it as a limerick. As it is described in Chapter 22 Visual-and-Verbal Storytelling, a limerick is a short, comic verse, frequently nonsensical. It consists of five lines, rhyming aabba, with two feet in the third and fourth lines rhyming 'aabba' with two feet in the third and fourth lines and three feet in the others; the meter has anapestic versification (has two short syllables followed by one long one, as in the word seventeen.) Write about a relationship between frequency, wavelength, and energy of light as the electromagnetic wave. Explain that the frequency of a wave varies inversely with the wavelength, and so a wave with a high frequency has a short wavelength (the distance from crest to crest) and the wave with a low frequency has a long wavelength. When we multiply frequency and wavelength we can calculate the speed of light (2.998×10^8 m/s). Describe how you would look at a curly hair through a viewfinder. You can grab a small piece of paper fold it two times. Cut a square in a corner of your foldout, so you have a square opening when you unfold the paper, fold it, and then fold it again. This is your viewfinder. Look at wavy hair on someone's head, while directing your gaze through the viewfinder you have just made. The curlier, undulating hair one has, the more peaks and troughs you will notice inside your viewfinder. The wavelength is the distance between two peaks (or two troughs), and the longer the wavelength, the lower is the frequency of the waves, and less waves you will see inside your viewfinder. Describe the waves inside a frame around hair that was formed by your viewfinder, and then change your description giving the subject another wavelength (and frequency) of hair undulations. Now write about a forest as a place where your imaginary model takes a walk, a forest where the animals possess different levels of strength projected as light. This means each animal can signal its power by sending off the light, but also each type of light gives the animal special powers. Describe the forest where different types of animals project their special powers and they are represented and recognizable by special wavelengths. Tell about a system where a specific animal power depends on the emission or the absorption of the radiative energy, and this is graphically defined, for example, through the colors or textures of the animals' bodies. Can you find the system that applies to trees, plants, flowers, or mushrooms? Define the relation between animal's brightness and its speed and agility, and then describe how could you learn about animal powers and speed by measuring spectral radiation they emit. Now you can feel ready to write a limerick that would capture the essence of the relations you have been writing about. Mix fantasy with real facts to provide energy to your writing.

Table 6. Working on a project about cosmic background radiation

The Visual Approach A Visual Concept Map	The Verbal Approach A Comic
Draw a visual concept map telling about the cosmic background radiation. This concept map, which confirms previous theories, is to be sent from the COBE spacecraft, to be understandable to anyone in the universe, out-of-the-space, who can record and understand visual information. First collect statements about cosmic background radiation that are coming from the Big Bang theory based speculations, and then the data obtained from the COBE spacecraft that verify these predictions. The fact that theory has been confirmed by the experimental data supports the Big Bang theory.	Comic strips consist of simplified graphics supported by descriptive texts. The comics medium involves comic books, graphic novels, and comic strips that became popular from the 1920s. You are invited to devise a comics telling about the cosmic background radiation. Develop a set of narrative drawings and write explanatory comments that describe an astronomical concept of the cosmic microwave background radiation. This comics, which explains the theory and the experimental results is to be sent from the COBE spacecraft, to be understandable to anyone in the universe from out-of-the-space who can record and understand information. First collect statements about cosmic microwave background radiation that are coming from the Big Bang theory based speculations, and then the data obtained from the COBE spacecraft that verify these predictions. Place the theory-based sentences and their empirical confirmations in your comics and add pictures and symbols to improve the clarity of your work.

at the level of about 1 part in 100,000. Such fluctuations were found in the COBE data. The cosmic background radiation is expected to have a perfect thermal spectrum, and observations from the COBE spacecraft verify this prediction. The cosmic background radiation is expected to look essentially the same in all directions, and it does (it is isotropic). The cosmic background radiation is not the result of a mixture of radiation from many independent sources, such as stars and galaxies. The statement that the cosmic background radiation contains spectral lines of hydrogen and helium has been confirmed by the data.

For directions on this project, see Table 6.

PROJECT 7: ABOUT MASS AND ENERGY

This project will picture and describe concepts and relations about motion of objects.

Background Information for the Project about Mass and Energy

Recalling some basic data, laws, and units related to these concepts may be helpful in finding an idea

how to design this project. The three basic terms describing the movement of an object are speed, velocity, and acceleration.

- Speed is a rate at which object moves, with units measured as distance divided by time. It is a scalar value of velocity, for example, 10 m/s.
- Velocity means a speed in a constant direction of motion; it is a vector physical quantity because it has quantity and direction; for example, 10 m/sec north.
- Acceleration is the rate of change in velocity; it measures how an object's speed or direction changes in time and shows both the magnitude and the direction of velocity at a given point in time as m/sec^2.

When we talk about interactions between objects, we use a notion of an object's momentum measured as a product of its mass and velocity (momentum = mass x velocity), which has a vector quantity of motion possessing a direction and a magnitude. In order to change the object's momentum we have to apply force to it. Three Newton's laws of motion describe the relation between force acting on a body and the resulting motion of this body. Newton's laws of motion apply to all kinds of motion:

- **The First Law:** In the absence of an external force an object moves with constant velocity. In uniform circular motion, the momentum changes direction but not magnitude.
- **The Second Law:** Tells about the rate of change in momentum of an object, where momentum means mass times velocity. That means, $F = ma$, where (F) is the net force applied to the object, (m) is its mass, and (a) is the object's acceleration. We may say a net force can accelerate momentum of an object in the direction of the force, or force = rate of change in momentum.
- **The Third Law:** States that for any force there always is an equal and opposite reaction force that is lying in the same straight line.

Thus, the result of the net force applied to the object is measured as mass times acceleration. Gravity causes change in objects' acceleration. Acceleration of gravity on Earth (the acceleration of a falling object) is about $9.6 \, m/s^2$, so velocity of falling object increases every second by $9.6 \, m/sec$.

These laws explain the conservation laws in astronomy: the law of conservation of momentum, conservation of angular momentum (that is due to both objects' rotation and orbit), and conservation of energy. The first Newton's law explains why celestial objects move at constant velocity without any force acting on them, rotate, and orbit the Sun. Angular momentum of a planet, which is equal mass (m) x velocity (v) x radius of the orbit (distance from the Sun r), stay the same, and the planet's orbital speed must be faster when the planet is nearer the Sun and slower when the radius is longer. The law of conservation of energy says that celestial objects can gain or lose energy only by exchanging energy with other objects or conversing energy from one form to another.

There are three basic categories of energy:

- **The Kinetic Energy of Objects:** Energy of motion, given by the formula $e = \frac{1}{2}mv^2$. Thermal energy is the kinetic energy of particles.
- **The Radiative Energy of Light Carried by Light:** In quantum mechanics, the size of the energy of a photon is described as the Planck's constant (h) times the frequency (f) of its associated electromagnetic wave: $E = h \times f$)
- **The Potential Energy:** Energy stored for later conversion into kinetic energy; includes gravitational potential energy: the experimentally measured constant G that appears in the law of universal gravitation, electrical potential energy, and chemical potential energy. The force of gravity causes that every mass attracts every other mass. The universal law of gravitation tells that the force of gravity (F_g) between the two objects (M_1 and M_2) declines with the square of the distance (d) between two objects: $F_g = G M_1 M_2 / d^2$.
All forms of energy can be converted one into another, but cannot be created or destroyed, according to the law of conservation of energy. In astronomy, the important types of potential energy are gravitational potential energy of objects and mass-energy contained in mass itself, as mass is a form of potential energy. Mass can be converted to other forms of energy according to Einstein's formula $m = mc^2$. Thus, a small amount of mass can be turned into a large amount of energy.

For directions on this project, see Table 7.

Table 7. Working on a project about mass and energy

The Visual Approach: Small Sketches	The Verbal Approach: A Story for a Game
In this project, you may want to design a series of small explanatory sketches an object of your choice and then, using arrows of different sizes and colors, show basic concepts about its motion and relations between speed, velocity, and acceleration. Another sketches may show the kinetic energy of motion, given by the formula $e = \frac{1}{2} mv^2$. For example, using this formula one can easily calculate kinetic energy of trucks having different weight and moving with various speed: a 3-ton truck that has a speed of 70 km/hr has more kinetic energy ($3 \times 70^2 = 14,700$) than a 6-ton truck moving 40 km/hr ($6 \times 40^2 = 9,600$), and a 2-ton truck moving 80 km/hr or a 1-ton truck moving 110 km/hr have yet another kinetic energy.	Create a story for a game that involves interaction among some characters. Base your story on the chapter about mass and energy, and make sure that the important information is weaved into the plot. Write about a series of events that involve your characters and describe basic concepts about motion and relations between speed, velocity, and acceleration. Make your characters compete or fight using existing physical laws, and then add some explanatory notes. You may also adopt another approach. For example, one character might change his gravity, while the other may use his electromagnetic force. Another writings may support your study about the kinetic energy of motion, given by the formula $e = \frac{1}{2} mv^2$. Write a story for a game about the concepts of mass, weight, force, and acceleration. For example, you may playfully show what happens when your character applies a force to strike a nail with a hammer. In another story, you may describe how acceleration of an elevator can be seen as an example of the force changing one's apparent weight.
Now draw sketches related to the concepts of mass (a measure of the amount of matter in an object), weight (the net force that an object applies to its surroundings; in the case of a stationary body on the surface of Earth, it equals mass×acceleration of gravity), force (anything that can cause a change in momentum), and acceleration (again, it's the rate at which an object's velocity changes. Its standard units are m/s²). For example, you may show visually what happens when you apply a force to strike a nail with a hammer. A force applied to your object (a hammer) will change momentum of this object. Momentum is the product of this object's mass and velocity. This force will accelerate your hammer in the direction of the net force. Your object's mass depends only on the amount of matter in this object and is the same anywhere, while weight (apparent weight) is the force acting on a floor (or a scale), and depends both on the object's mass and the forces (including gravity) acting on this mass. You may want to present the essence of this concept in a visual, artistic way, not necessarily as a detailed depiction used in the textbooks of physics, and without using a hammer (presented in a Figure 12).	Now write a story for a game involving a star with some planets where there wouldn't be many kinds of energy: kinetic, radioactive, and potential, but only one kind. On each planet, one type of energy is dominant. What should be there? Design a fictional device (let's believe it's possible) for generating one type of energy: kinetic, radioactive or potential – and show technical instructions how to use it. Think how the law of conservation of energy and the conversion of mass to other forms of energy (according to Einstein's formula $m = mc^2$) could be applied here.
Now let your imagination tell you how would it look if you would design a fictional star with some planets where there wouldn't be many kinds of energy: kinetic, radioactive, and potential, but only one type of energy is dominant on en each planet. What should be there? Design a fictional device (let's believe it's possible) for generating one type of energy: kinetic, radioactive or potential – and show technical instructions how to use it. Think how the law of conservation of energy and the conversion of mass to other forms of energy (according to Einstein's formula $m = mc^2$) could be applied here.	While you live on one of these fictional planets, write a story about a house built as a space commuter to other planets. This means you will live there and use it for transportation as well. Create it as if you would live in it, by organizing its space according to your needs, preferences and goals. Write about your "neighborhood" too. The house uses all sorts of energy types for its different functions. List the properties of each energy type and describe its actions. Describe all powered devices and explain the energetic needs and takes. Try to build this space commuter as a recycling machine.
While you live on one of these fictional planets, design a house built as a space commuter to other planets. This means you will live there and use it for transportation as well. Create it as if you would live in it, by organizing its space according to your needs, preferences and goals. Show your "neighborhood" too. The house uses all sorts of energy types for its different functions. Color code each energy type and show its actions. Draw all powered devices with a diagram that visually explains energetic needs and takes. Try to build this space commuter as a recycling machine.	

Project 7: Mass and Energy. An Example by Wes Thorpe: A Board Game

A board game where particles (players) are trying to reach the sun (Figure 15). Players will start on the outer orbit of Pluto and move through the various orbits by throwing a die. Players start with a speed of 10. The die will have colored dots. Whatever color the die has facing up the player must draw a card of that color. The card will have a formula on it such as mass, velocity, and acceleration. If that formula shows a decrease in speed, they must move back in orbit; if it shows a higher speed, a particle (a player) moves forward in the orbit. Whoever reaches the sun first wins, and who draws a black hole card automatically lose.

Figure 15 Wes Thorpe, "A Game" (© 2011, W. Thorpe. Used with permission)

PROJECT 8: ABOUT ELEMENTARY PARTICLES

This project will picture and describe concepts and relations about elementary particles and quantum mechanics. As an astronomer living on a spaceship you are about to design it to make it your livable home. You are invited to visualize and design seven household objects and appliances:

A. A table runner that shows specific sequences of emission

B. A window curtain designed to display distribution of light energy in the windows in a big city

C. A TV set for your house that shows a stadium with emotional viewers

D. A board game that helps learn about nuclear fusion

E. Table silverware or kitchen flatware, to visualize events in the Era of Nucleosynthesis

F. Lamps that represent possible options for the fate of the universe

G. A carpet showing planets and stars

Background Information for the Project about Elementary Particles

Project A: Emission is a process by which matter emits energy in the form of light. Absorption of light is a process by which matter absorbs radiative energy. Electrons undergo transitions between their allowed energy levels. When an electron in an atom goes from a higher energy state to a lower energy state, the atom emits a photon of a specific frequency. When an electron in an atom goes from a lower energy state to a higher energy state, the atom absorbs a photon of a specific frequency. Each atom emits or absorbs light at specific wavelengths only. For example, due to the downward transitions in hydrogen between light higher levels and level 2, the colorful emission lines appear:

310.1 nm, 434.0 nm, 486.1 nm, and 656.3 nm. Absorption lines are produced in the same way by upward transitions between level 2 and higher levels in hydrogen (Bennett et al, 2011).

Project B: We may see levels of light energy as transitions between light levels. The electron in a hydrogen atom can change the energy level when it gains or loses the amount of energy that separates the levels. When the electron reaches the highest, ionization level, it gains enough energy to escape from the atom. In temperatures of tens of thousands of K free electrons can move among ions having positive charges; we call this a plasma phase of matter.

Project C: We recounted earlier the wavelength as the distance from one peak of wave to another, frequency as the number of peaks passing by any point in a second, and speed as a wavelength multiplied by frequency. We have also discussed the electromagnetic spectrum (presented in Figure 9, and already examined for Project 5) and the colors from the spectrum of visible light. We can easily calculate a total electrical charge of an atom when we know its atomic structure. For example, in Hydrogen (^{1}H) the atomic number (a number of protons in its nucleus) = 1, atomic mass number = 1, and it has 1 electron. In Helium (^{4}He) the atomic number = 2, atomic mass number = 4, and it has 2 electrons. In Carbon (^{12}C) the atomic number = 6, atomic mass number = 12, and it has 6 electrons (in a carbon ^{13}C isotope there are 6 protons and 7 neutrons, and in a carbon ^{14}C isotope there are 6 protons and 8 neutrons) (Bennett et al, 2011). We can know how much electrical charge does an atom with 5 protons, 6 neutrons, and 5 electrons have, by adding 5 positive charges of protons, 6 neutrons without any electrical charge, and 5 electrons with negative charges (5 + 0 – 5 = 0).

Project D: Today, the Sun generates energy because of nuclear fusion, where two or more small nuclei crash into one another and form one larger nucleus. Nuclear fission of uranium or plutonium (where a larger nucleus splits into two or more smaller particles) used to be done in human-built nuclear power plants, but at the center of the Sun energy comes from nuclear fusion that turns hydrogen into helium. Gravitational contraction, chemical reactions, or gradual changes in size would not be able to generate this kind of process.

Elementary particles and atomic nuclei of different kinds may include a proton, antiproton, neutron, deuterium nucleus, hydrogen nucleus (proton), helium nucleus, helium-3 nucleus, helium-4 nucleus, gamma rays, and subatomic particles known as neutrinos and positrons that carry off the energy. An atom is about 100,000 times greater than its nucleus; however, almost all mass of the atom is contained in the nucleus. Scientists designed a Standard Model – the simple set of elementary particles. Quarks (called the up, charm, top, down, strange, and bottom fermions), are a part of this model. They can combine together to make the proton and neutron and thus to make up the nuclei of atoms. Leptons (called the electron neutrino, muon neutrino, tau neutrino, electron, muon, and tau fermions) can be in the charged and uncharged versions; electrons are the most familiar charged leptons, while neutrinos are the uncharged, inactive leptons. Neutrinos with quarks make up the familiar to us matter. Bosons (a photon, Z boson, W boson, and gluon), the "force carriers," are particles behind electricity and light (electromagnetism) and radioactive decay (the weak nuclear force). The Higgs boson is a hypothetical particle existing in the minds of theoretical physicists because, in accordance with the Standard Model, nothing requires the particles to have mass and the Higgs boson must fulfill this gap and confirm that assumption. Recently the scientists from the Large Hadron Collider (LHC) have claimed the discovery of a new particle consistent with the Higgs boson.

Scientists have also designed a model called the Proton-Proton Chain showing how does nuclear fusion occurs in the Sun, where four hydrogen nuclei (protons) fuse into one helium-4 nucleus and release gamma rays and subatomic particles: neutrinos and positrons, which carry off the energy released in this reaction. High pressure and temperature (about 15 million K) of plasma in solar core cause high-speed collisions that transform four hydrogen protons into helium nucleus containing two protons and two neutrons. This goes in three steps of the proton-proton chain. (1) Two protons fuse making a deuterium nucleus (deuterium is a form of hydrogen with a nucleus containing proton and a neutron, not just a proton like in most hydrogen nuclei). It goes two times. (2) The deuterium nucleus and a proton fuse to make a nucleus of helium-3 (2 protons, 1 neutron). This step also goes twice. (3) Two helium-3 nuclei fuse to form helium-4 (2 protons, 2 neutrons, and release two protons). This reaction generates electrical charges (energy) because a helium nucleus is slightly lighter than four hydrogen nuclei, so a small amount of mass becomes energy (disappears) according to the Einstein's formula $E = mc^2$, mostly as kinetic energy and gamma rays; it becomes the sunlight. Neutrinos carry off about 2% of the energy (Bennett et al, 2011).

Project E: Events that took place in the Era of Nucleosynthesis occurred within the first 0.001 second of the universe's history. Particles taking part in the Era of Nucleosynthesis in the production of other particles include quarks, protons (H nuclei), antiprotons, neutrons, helium, and deuterium. According to the Big Bang theory, a timeline for the eras of early universe included the Era of Nucleosynthesis. In the previous Particle Era elementary particles have already filled the universe, and then quarks combined to make protons (H nuclei) and antiprotons (particles with opposite electrical charges). Then, in the era of nucleosynthesis, fusion (occurring in 0.001 s at 10^{12} K) produced helium from protons (H nuclei).

Protons and neutrons fused into deuterium and the deuterium nuclei then fused into helium. This process stopped before most of the deuterium that was created during the era of nucleosynthesis has been destroyed, and some deuterium nuclei still exist in the universe today.

Project F: Different possible options for the future fate of the universe and the four expansion patterns have already been discussed for Project 3. Assuming a universe without dark energy, the fate of the universe depends only on how its actual density compares to critical density. Critical density means the precise average density for the entire universe that marks the dividing line between a collapsing universe and one that will expand forever. Without dark energy, calculations about the fate of the universe suggest that the future depends on the strength of gravitational pull slowing the expansion of the universe. The strength of this pull depends on the density of the universe. Gravity can win over expansion if the current density of the universe exceeds 10^{-29} gram per cube centimeter. Based on how much deuterium in the current universe, we can conclude that the density of ordinary (baryonic) matter is between 1 percent and 10 percent of the critical density. Thus, we do not live in a critical density universe and also ordinary (baryonic) matter doesn't make up most of the mass of the universe.

However, instead of slowing because of gravity, the expansion of the universe appears to be speeding up, due to the dark energy, a repulsive force that pushes all the universe's galaxies apart. Astronomers examine possibilities for the future

Table 8. Working on a project about elementary particles

The Visual Approach: Household Objects and Appliances	The Verbal Approach: Over the Phone Narration
Project A: A table runner that shows specific sequences of emission. Create a table runner that will show specific sequences of emission and absorption lines. Draw what happens to emission lines due to the downward transitions between light higher levels and level 2 in hydrogen. Also, draw absorption lines produced by upward transitions between level 2 and higher levels in hydrogen.	**Project A: A table runner that shows specific sequences of emission.** Write a script of your conversation with a friend when you explain concepts about elementary particles. Tell your friend about objects and decorations for your new house. Write a description of a table runner you just designed to show specific sequences of emission and absorption lines. Explain to your friend what happens to emission lines due to the downward transitions between light higher levels and level 2 in hydrogen. Also, describe absorption lines produced by upward transitions between level 2 and higher levels in hydrogen.
Project B: A window curtain that displays distribution of light energy in the windows in a big city. Make a drawing of a window curtain that displays distribution of light energy in the windows in a big city. Show the stars you can see or, when back on Earth, the office buildings in downtown, shopping centers, etc. Display action in windows and levels of light energy as transitions between light levels.	**Project B: A window curtain that displays distribution of light energy in the windows in a big city.** Make an explanation about a window curtain that displays distribution of light energy in the windows in a big city. Describe the stars you can see or, when back on Earth, the office buildings in downtown, shopping centers, etc. Display action in windows as the levels of light energy as transitions between light levels.
Project C: A TV set for your house that shows a stadium with viewers expressing their emotions. Now, transfer information to another concept. Design a TV set for your new house that shows a stadium with emotional viewers. Draw a tribune on a stadium, on the screen of your TV, and show the viewers' emotions coded in terms of light, using wavelength, frequency, and speed. Use the electromagnetic spectrum (we have already examined it for Project 5) to visualize events happening on the stadium. Write annotations below the drawing to explain your concepts. Use also colors from the spectrum of visible light. Show on your picture of a tribune the changes of electrical charge going in an atom as the movements of the viewers.	**Project C: A TV set for your house that shows a stadium with viewers expressing their emotions.** Now, transfer information to another concept. Describe a TV set that shows a stadium with emotional viewers. Tell about a tribune on a stadium that you see on the screen of your TV, and about viewers' emotions coded in terms of light, using wavelength, frequency, and speed. To explain your concepts, use the electromagnetic spectrum to describe events happening on the stadium. Describe in your report the changing charges in an atom as a story about the movements of the viewers on a tribune.
Project D: A board game that helps learn about nuclear fusion. For your living room, create a board game that will help learn about nuclear fusion. First, acquire adhesive labels, it means paper circles of various sizes and colors, just like those used to show a prize of an item to be sold. Then design a code. Assign specific circles to elementary particles and atomic nuclei of different kinds. You will need to use your round stickers for a proton, antiproton, neutron, deuterium nucleus, hydrogen nucleus (proton), helium nucleus, helium-3 nucleus, helium-4 nucleus, gamma rays, and subatomic particles known as neutrinos and positrons that carry off the energy. You may also want to demonstrate the Proton-Proton reaction.	**Project D: A board game that helps learn about nuclear fusion.** For your living room, create a board game that will help learn about nuclear fusion. Write a code by assigning specific values to elementary particles and atomic nuclei of different kinds: a proton, antiproton, neutron, deuterium nucleus, hydrogen nucleus (proton), helium nucleus, helium-3 nucleus, helium-4 nucleus, gamma rays, and subatomic particles known as neutrinos and positrons that carry off the energy. Maybe your board game would be played in a way that show how does nuclear fusion occurs in the Sun, and demonstrate the proton-proton chain.
Project E: Table silverware or kitchen flatware, to visualize events in the Era of Nucleosynthesis. Now it's time to think about your own table silverware or kitchen flatware, to visualize events in the Era of Nucleosynthesis. This part will be about the past of the universe. Construct a model explaining production of helium in the era of nucleosynthesis.

The major items of the silverware or flatware used for this purpose are a knife, a fork, and a spoon. You may use different kinds of forks, such as relish forks, salad forks, dinner forks, cold cuts forks, or dessert forks. Also, utensils sometimes combine the functionality, as the pairs of cutlery, including the spork (spoon / fork), spife (spoon / knife), and knork (knife / fork) or the sporf (all three).

Design your own table silverware or kitchen flatware that would make eating easier, for example, a grapefruit spoon as a spoon with one edge having cutting capability through sharp edge with tiny triangles. Assign your various implements to the specific particles taking part in the Era of Nucleosynthesis in the production of other particles: quarks, protons (H nuclei), antiprotons, neutrons, helium, and deuterium. Show the relation between these items during the sequence of the courses of a festive dinner. | **Project E: Table silverware or kitchen flatware, to visualize events in the Era of Nucleosynthesis.** Now it's time to think about your own table silverware or kitchen flatware, to explain events in the Era of Nucleosynthesis. Explain production of helium in the era of nucleosynthesis. The major items of the silverware or flatware used for this purpose are the knife, fork and spoon. You may use different kinds of forks, such as relish forks, salad forks, dinner forks, cold cuts forks, or dessert forks. Also, utensils sometimes combine the functionality, as the pairs of cutlery, including the spork (**sp**oon/**fork**), spife (**sp**oon/kni**fe**), and knork (**kn**ife/fo**rk**) or the sporf (all three).

Describe your own table silverware or kitchen flatware that would make eating easier, for example, a grapefruit spoon as a spoon with one edge having a cutting capability. Assign your various implements to specific particles taking part in the Era of Nucleosynthesis in the production of other particles: quarks, protons (H nuclei), antiprotons, neutrons, helium, and deuterium. Show the relation between these particles by referring them to your silverware items during the sequence of the courses of a festive dinner. |
| **Project F: Lamps that represent possible options for the fate of the universe.** Design four lamps for your house to represent different possible options for the future of the universe. Remember the expansion patterns; we have already discussed them for Project 3. You may consider a design on the lamps' shades made out of various material such as glass, fabric, or paper, light intensity coming from a bulb or a three-way switch, and the material and shape of the overall design of the lamp itself, with the widening shades repeating the shapes of particular models of the expanding universe. The models will be telling about the fate of the universe in a pictorial way. What visual shortcuts could be used? | **Project F: Lamps that represent possible options for the fate of the universe.** Describe four lamps for your house to represent possible options for the future of the universe. You may consider a design on the lamps' shades made out of various material such as glass, fabric, or paper, light intensity coming from a bulb or a three-way switch, and the material and shape of the overall design of the lamp itself, with the widening shades repeating the shapes of particular models of the expanding universe. Write about the models telling about the fate of the universe. |
| **Project G: A carpet showing planets and stars.** Design a carpet for your living room that will show planets and stars and will show the visual ways of measurement through the imaging of the objects. Include the drawings of the astronomical instruments used for imaging the stellar stuff. Show the colors of selected planets, the brightness of the stars you show, the general shape of an interstellar cloud of gas, and the number of bright stars in a nearby star cluster. | **Project G: A carpet showing planets and stars.** Design a carpet with planets and stars for a living room and explain the ways of measuring the celestial objects. Write about the colors of selected planets, the brightness of the stars, an interstellar cloud of gas, and the number of bright stars in a nearby star cluster. |

of the universe, with four possible models of expansion patterns called re-collapsing, critical, coasting, and accelerating. The first three models assume there is no dark energy (Bennett et al, 2011).

Project G: Planets and the two largest known dwarf planets (Eris and Pluto) can be drawn in scale (see Table 1), but not in their scaled distances. They are: Eris, Pluto, Neptune, Uranus, Saturn, Jupiter, Mars, Earth, Venus, and Mercury. A great selection of pictures showing the astronomical instruments used for imaging the stellar stuff can be found at Google Images

For directions on this project, see Table 8.

Project 8: Over the Phone Narration: A Verbal Project by Wes Thorpe: A Folk Story about a Snake Representing a Black Hole and Expanding the Universe

Long ago before time swept over the land like a quickening wind there was a black snake named Tekau Plus who couldn't stand the sight of the living. Tekau was greater than the widest rivers and would devour anything he wanted. Tekau decided that if he could eat anything he would eat life itself and rid himself of everything that is living. First Tekau ate all of the dirt and grass then he ate all of the stones and trees, and drank all the rivers and lakes, and finally he swallowed whole the mountains and oceans. It wasn't long before Tekau moved on to the planets and the stars. As Tekau feasted upon life he grew and grew, and when he was finished he just couldn't feel as if that's enough. His hunger became restless and he needed more. What more could I eat though, Tekau says as he looks up and sees the Sun. This is what I need; this Elixir of Life. The Sun has more life emanating from it than anything! exclaimed Tekau. Leaping towards the Sun Tekau starts to inhale. The sun moves closer and closer and slowly becomes larger and larger. Swallowing the Sun whole Tekau starts to expand uncontrollably growing to sizes unimaginable. Suddenly Tekau's body bursts creating an explosion unleashing everything he had consumed. From this explosion a new life had been created, even bigger than before. Tekau's greatest hate became his greatest creation.

Table 9. Assembling a picture of a telescope with matches

The Visual Approach	The Verbal Approach
The type of representation you are invited to do now will be simple, emphasizing function over form. Use matches to show a general concept beyond a telescope, showing the factors that decide on magnification, ability to collect light, angular resolution, image distortion, and color accuracy. Consider how would you write an advertisement to highlight the best aspects of the product. Cut the tips (heads) of several matches to assemble a simple image of the Hubble Space Telescope. "Clean" matchsticks without the lighting ends will show the advantages coming from the location of the Hubble Space Telescope above the Earth atmosphere: astronomers can observe infrared and ultraviolet light as well as visible light, they can use it all the time regardless of the weather and any time of day, not only during night, and the stars do not twinkle. However, the difference in a distance between the star and the location of a telescope does not matter at all because a great distance between the Solar system and any star.	Write a riddle about a telescope. Your riddle would emphasize the advantages coming from the location of the Hubble Space Telescope above the Earth atmosphere: astronomers can observe infrared and ultraviolet light as well as visible light, they can use it all the time regardless of the weather and any time of day, not only during night, and the stars do not twinkle. However, the difference in a distance between the star and the location of a telescope does not matter at all because a great distance between the Solar system and any star.

PROJECT 9: ABOUT ASTRONOMY RELATED TOOLS

Visual and verbal approaches to Project 9 can be found in Table 9.

Project 9: A Riddle about a Telescope: A Verbal Project by Wes Thorpe

What is a giant eye?
Collecting more light than ever before
Allowing our eyes to see so much more
When our own eyes wouldn't even try.

CONCLUSION

Projects presented in this chapter invite the reader to develop a graphical presentation of a specific theme to show the physics-related concepts, forces, processes, and products by making graphics to display the data. The projects presenting some basic concepts, using astrophysics as an example, and encourage the reader to actively react in a visual, verbal, or both ways.

REFERENCES

Adams, F., Buchert, T., Mersini-Houghton, L., & Nekoogar, F. (2012). *Cosmic update: Dark puzzles, arrow of time, future history*. Springer. ISBN 978-1-4419-8293-3. Retrieved March 1, 2012, from http://www.springerlink.com/content/n5077275538k7u56/

Bennett, J., Donahue, M., Schneider, N., & Voit, M. (2011). *Essential cosmic perspective with mastering astronomy* (6th ed.). Addison Wesley.

Gardner, H. (1983). *Frames of mind: The theory of multiple intelligences.* New York: Basic Books.

Gardner, H. (2006). *Multiple intelligences: New horizons*. New York: Basic Books.

Gardner, H. (2007). *Five minds for the future*. Boston: Harvard Business School Press.

Hubblesite, Hubble Discoveries. (2012). Retrieved March 1, 2012, from http://hubblesite.org/hubble_discoveries/dark_energy/de-did-einstein_predict.php

Kepler, J. (1981). *Mysterium cosmographicum: The secret of the universe* (A. M. Duncan, Trans.). New York: Abaris Books.

Kepler – Universe. (1910). *The science-history of the universe*. New York: The Current Literature Publishing Company.

NASA Space Station Info. (2012). Retrieved March 2, 2012, from http://www.spacestationinfo.com/layers-sun.htm

Chapter 8
Imaging and Picturing Volcanism

ABSTRACT

This part of the book invites the reader to look closer at plate tectonics and volcanism, and then draw inspiration from geological events, processes, and products for creating a visual and/or verbal project. The next part is about earthquakes, tsunami, the explosive eruptions of volcanoes such as Mt. St. Helens, Yellowstone, and Vesuvius, about the Japan 2011 earthquake, and the impact of volcanism on human fates.

PLATE TECTONICS AND VOLCANOES

A volcano is a break in a planet's crust, which frees out a hot magma, volcanic ash, and gases, so they burst and escape from below the surface. Magma contained within crust or mantle rise and form volcanic rocks on the surface. Volcanoes are generally found where tectonic plates are parting or converging. The surface of the Earth is composed of the crust and upper mantle (called together the lithosphere). According to the scientific theory about plate tectonics, a large-scale process called tectonics resulted in broking the lithosphere into 14 large and 38 small tectonic plates (Bird, 2003). The plates (with areas and shapes different than the continents or oceans) move up to 100 mm per year above a hot, more mobile, underlying

DOI: 10.4018/978-1-4666-4627-8.ch008

asthenosphere. Digital models of the plate boundaries have been computed, based on the literature sources (e.g., Bird, 2003).

The Earth's interior is divided into layers, which differ in their chemical composition and physical properties. The crust is the farthest from the center layer of the Earth. The oceanic crust in the region of Hawaii is about 5 kilometers thick, while the continental crust under eastern California is from about 30 km thick (Robertson, 2011). The mantle is a layer between the crust and the outer core. It forms a rocky shell about 2,900 km (1,820 miles) thick (Schlumberger, 2012), which makes about 84% of Earth's volume (Robertson, 2011). Continental crust comprises rocks of the granite and basalt types, while oceanic crust is basaltic. In deeper layers it has a thick, sticky consistency between solid and liquid. Between the crust and the mantle, the Mohorovicic discontinuity, called Moho, separates crust from the mantle and marks

Figure 1. Left: Mathew Skiff, "Earth," Right: Nathan White, "Core"(© 2006, M. Skiff and N. White. Used with permission)

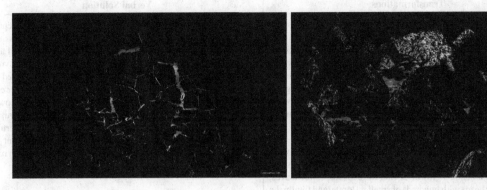

a sharp increase of the speed of earthquake waves, possibly due to the change in rock types (Robertson, 2012).

Scientists work on advancing the science of forecasting a volcanic eruption. They are able to detect the buildup preceding a catastrophic eruption for weeks, months, or even years. Earthquakes and ground deformations are the precursors of imminent volcanic eruptions; typically they take place days to weeks before an actual eruption. However, scientists cannot do anything to prevent or control eruptions because of the immensity of the temperature, pressure, physical characteristics of partially molten rock, and the extent of the magma chambers.

Figure 1 presents two student works about magma. For directions on depicting plate tectonics and volcanoes, see Table 1.

EARTHQUAKES

Earthquakes and volcanoes occur mostly at the edges of the tectonic plates. About 100-200 km below the Earth's surface the rocks are melting because of high temperature. Molten rock – magma contained within crust or mantle – rises through the Earth's crust and forms volcanic rocks on the surface. The forces that contribute to volcanism include thermal convection currents, changes in

gravitation occurring on the surface, and also snow and water-derived factors. Thick, viscous magma produces volcanoes by means of explosive eruptions, while runny magma gives rise to volcanoes by pouring lava onto the surface. Part of magma stays between rocks forming intrusions. Volcano eruptions form an ash cloud, and emit layers of lava and ash that spread on the ground around the crater and later form rocks. Magma that cools rapidly forms basalts with small crystals. Magma trapped in intrusions cools slowly and produces granites and gabbros with large crystals. Rocks on the surface melt partially because of the heat and become metamorphic rocks.

Both the plate tectonic activity and volcanic activity cause earthquakes. Release of energy in the Earth's crust creates seismic waves of various magnitudes. Seismometers measure the magnitude of an earthquake and report it as expressed on the local and on the Richter scale. A magnitude up to 3 is almost unnoticeable; an earthquake of magnitude 7 and more causes damage, while the largest magnitudes were over 9. The most recent powerful earthquake with a magnitude 9.0 was the 2011 earthquake off the Pacific coast of Tōhoku, Japan. On 12 March 2012, a National Police Agency of Japan (2012) report confirmed 15,854 deaths, 26,992 injured, and 3,155 people missing. This earthquake shifted the Earth on its axis. According to the NASA's Jet propulsion

Table 1. Transformations and verbal solutions for plate tectonics and volcanoes

Transformations	Verbal Solution
Using the animation software or even Adobe Photoshop and some scanned images make animation sequences to build some analogies and to find similarities in representing events of quite different kinds, such as a bud bursting into a flower, a volcano erupting, fireworks bursting, or a pop-corn puffing when heated. Now, when you developed an action-based progression, add some other content, so the progress of images would become the consistent story. For example, write the lyrics for a song and then illustrate this song. Now transform fire related images into animation of a life cycle of a dandelion. In a similar way, create pictures, manga, or animation that involves a life cycle of a dandelion. On your drawings illustrating your lyrics show the phases of dandelion's growth: at first the delicate, edible leaves, then the flower heads with hundreds of smaller florets, and finally the seed heads. This biennial or perennial life cycle of a plant would be interrupted by the drastic events, such as volcano eruption with the following fire, which would become a theme for the refrain. Depict how the plant benefits from the richness of lava, the accompanying earthquakes magnify its seed dispersal, while the deep roots of the dandelion seem almost indestructible; thus the plant grows taller and stronger after each volcano eruption.	Think about changes caused by natural events, presented as a repetitive or looped refrain for lyrics. Develop a song: write the lyrics and the refrain that focuses on a volcano eruption. For example, tell a story linking the events in somebody's life interrupted by a drastic volcano eruption. Each generation experiences a difficult time caused by an active volcano, and the refrain repeats your comment about these events. At first it would be a story of a grand pa, then the parents, followed by an adventure of their descendants, all caused by the volcano eruptions. The refrain would describe the process and products of the eruption, as well as the dynamics of this phenomenon. Illustrate your poem by inserting small pictures, each one different one, after each refrain.

laboratory, the earthquake shifted the axis that the Earth's mass is balanced around by 6.5 inches. Also, the length of the Earth's day was shortened by 1.8 millionths of a second (Chang, 2011). Earlier great earthquakes also changed the axis and shortened the day. For example, the magnitude 8.8 earthquake in Chile last year shortened the day by 1.26 millionths of a second and moved the axis by about three inches, while the Sumatra earthquake in 2004 shortened the day by 6.8 millionths of a second (Chang, 2011). However, these changes are imperceptible for humans and have almost no impact on a calendar we use, because they are so small. According to Italian National Institute of Geophysics and Volcanology the earthquake that rattled Japan shifted the earth's rotation axis by about 25 centimeters (Chai, 2011). As reported by the United States Geological Survey, Japan is now 13 feet closer to the United States (Chang, 2011). This gives us some visible clues for imaging shifts between land and ocean.

Earthquakes, volcanic eruptions, and underwater explosions (such as detonations of nuclear devices) might generate a tsunami. Tsunami is a massive water displacement that causes a series of water waves of a long wavelength and a period (the time taken by one full wave) ranging from minutes to hours. The 2011 earthquake off the Pacific coast of Tōhoku triggered a powerful tsunami waves that were reaching heights of up to with waves up to 133 ft (40.5 meters) and travelled inland up to 10 km (6 miles). This tsunami caused a number of nuclear incidents and radiation release due to strong meltdowns at three reactors; the resulting evacuation from the radiation zones affected hundreds of thousands of residents.

A disaster that happened in the Tōhoku region in Japan means something new. The natural disasters – the 9.0 magnitude 2011 Tōhoku undersea earthquake and a resulting tsunami caused death of almost 16,000 people; almost 27,000 people were injured and more than 3,000 missing. This was a megathrust earthquake where one tectonic plate was forced underneath another one. The resulting powerful tsunami caused a number of nuclear accidents: radiation, pollution, and contamination, all resulting from human activity. Meltdowns at three reactors and explosions of hydrogen gas occurred in a Fukushima Daiichi Nuclear Power Plant. People were left without electricity and had to drive 80 km to acquire clean water. It can be hardly called a natural disaster.

THE MOUNT ST. HELENS VOLCANO

A most destructive volcanic eruption in the history of the United States was the eruption of the Mount St. Helens stratovolcano located in the Pacific Northwest region of the United States happened in 1982. Stratovolcano (composite volcano) is a tall, multilayered, conical volcano. Captain George Vancouver, who made a survey of this area at the end of the 18th century, named this volcano "Mount St. Helens" after the name of his friend, a British diplomat Lord St. Helens (USGS, 2012). Catastrophic eruptions of this type happened in Krakatoa (Indonesia, 1883) and Vesuvius (Italy, 79 A.D.). Due to the St. Helens volcano eruption, triggered by an earthquake of a magnitude 5.1, fifty-seven people were killed; 250 homes, 47 bridges, 15 miles (24 km) of railways, and 185 miles (298 km) of highway were destroyed (USGS/Cascades Volcano Observatory, 2009). More eruptions followed in the following years. A massive debris avalanche reduced the elevation of the summit by 400 m, produced an about 3,000 ft (~1 km) high steam plume containing sulfur dioxide, and formed an ash-cloud stem 10 miles (16 km) wide, with the mushroom top 40 miles (64 km) wide and 15 miles (24 km) high.

Native Americans' legends were inspired by the volcano's beauty; the story goes that the fighting sons of the chief of all the gods were transformed by him into Mount Hood and Mount Adams, while the object of their desire, a beautiful Loowit, became Mount St Helens. According to the U.S. Department of Agriculture (2012),

Northwest Indians told early explorers about the fiery Mount St. Helens. In fact, an Indian name for the mountain, Louwala-Clough means a "smoking mountain." According to one legend, the mountain was once a beautiful maiden "Loowit." When two sons of the Great Spirit "Sahale" fell in love with her, she could not choose between them. The two braves, Wyeast and Klickitat fought over her, burying villages and forests in the process. Sahale was furious. He smote the three lovers and erected a mighty mountain peak where each fell. Because Loowit was beautiful, her mountain (Mount St. Helens) was a beautiful, symmetrical cone of dazzling white. Wyeast (Mount Hood) lifts his head in pride, but Klickitat (Mount Adams) wept to see the beautiful maiden wrapped in snow, so he bends his head as he gazes on St. Helens.(The U.S. Department of Agriculture, Northwest Legends)

For directions on visual and verbal solutions to such parables, see Table 2.

THE YELLOWSTONE VOLCANO

The Yellowstone volcano is located at the Yellowstone National Park, spread across the Wyoming, Idaho, and Montana states. The Yellowstone Supervolcano – a volcanic field that produces exceptionally large volcanic eruptions –produced the latest three super eruptions that occurred 2.1 million, 1.3 million, and 640,000 years ago; each of them caused the collapse of the mouth of the volcano into the emptied magma chamber and formed the caldera – a large volcanic crater. The major caldera can be 34 by 45 miles (55 by 72 km) wide. The Yellowstone Caldera is experiencing between 1000 and 2000 measurable earthquakes a year. Most are relatively minor, measuring a magnitude of 3 or weaker (National Park Service, 2012). Many artists chose the Old Faithful as a theme for their paintings, for a German-American painter Albert Bierstadt (1830-1902) painted an

oil on canvas artwork entitled "Old Faithful" (http://en.wikipedia.org/wiki/File:Bierstadt_Albert_Old_Faithful.jpg)

The Yellowstone Volcano is still active; there are 1,000 to 3,000 earthquakes, active ground deformation, and over 10,000 thermal features per year. However, there is no evidence that a catastrophic eruption at Yellowstone National Park is imminent. The website of the Yellowstone Volcano Observatory is at http://volcanoes.usgs.gov/yvo/. Geysers are natural phenomena with unpredictable behavior (The Geyser Observation and Study Association, 2011). The cone-type geyser Old Faithful, which erupts every 91 minutes for 1.5 to 5 minutes, is unique because its eruptions are predictable and have been relatively consistent during the last century. The average height of the geyser's eruption of boiling water is 145 feet (44 m), in amount of 3,700 to 8,400 gallons (14,000 to 32,000 L) (see Table 3).

THE MOUNT VESUVIUS VOLCANO

The city of Pompeii, settled on a prehistoric lava flow in the 8th century B.C., was an agricultural and commercial port with a big harbor. On 24 August, 79 A.D. a ribbon of smoke could be seen above the volcano crater because Mount Vesuvius, a stratovolcano in the Gulf of Naples, Italy, erupted killing thousands of residents of the towns of Pompeii, Stabiae, and Herculaneum located in southern Italy, near Naples: 16,000 out of 20,000 inhabitants of Pompeii were buried beneath 20 feet of volcanic debris. Almost immediately, Pliny the Younger described the catastrophe for the Roman historian Titus, while his uncle, Pliny the Elder, who as a commander of a fleet of war ships at a nearby port Misenam, decided to rescue people suffering near the volcano (Mount Vesuvius, 2011). He described the huge cloud towering over the area,

Table 2. Visual and verbal solutions for volcano legends

Visual Solution Illustration to a Legend	Verbal Solution Writing a Parable
Create illustrations for a legend about a volcano. Draw geological formations depicted as characters involved in an action related to the volcano activity. Show the volcano features such as its immediacy, power, and unpredictability and compare them with your characters' attributes. Your characters' wishes may signify forces; their tools may symbolize the geological materials; the characters' actions may stand for the geological processes, while their personalities may denote the final products of these processes, somehow like the legend about Loowit and the sons of the Great Spirit Sahale. There are some common threads appearing in the tales of different cultures, for example, in the legends of Northwest Indians and the ancient Greek myths. However, they used to be pictured in a distinctive, typical of a particular culture style. Maybe you would choose to solve your project in the form of a design for a porcelain plate in an ancient Greek style.	Write a story in a form of an ancient legend that would tell both about the volcanic events from the past and the human fates resulting nowadays from the encounter they are faced with. Focus on the differences and similarities between physical/chemical forces and factors that govern the human actions: character, four temperament types: choleric, melancholic, sanguine, and phlegmatic, physical strength and beauty, skills, talents, insight, will, knowledge, intellect, creativity, psychic powers, and also on. Translate these qualities into the physical/chemical processes, products, and the resulting changes. Make it as a two-way translation: how the material forces relate to human characteristics and how human features correlate with natural forces. We can find the signs of this way of thinking in the ancient Greek myths, where natural forces were presented as gods, demigods, or heroes (e.g., the Sun as Helios, the Earth as Gaia, sky as Uranus, and ocean ruled by Poseidon), while the gods temporary changed themselves into animals or forces of nature; erotic escapades of Zeus as a shower of gold (to Danae), an eagle (to Ganymede), a bull (to Europa), and as a swan (to Leda) may serve as an example.

its general appearance can best be expressed as   *being like a pine rather than any other tree, for*

Table 3. Visual solutions and verbal responses

Visual Solution The Geyser Event	Verbal Response Collecting Hot Water
Create a scene showing a dance/game performed in front of the Old Faithful that is interrupted when the geyser strikes. Place the dancers/players above a cross-section of the ground that lies below them, so you could show the tectonic plate shift and its cause. Explain the causes of the shift using an analogy in a way you would explain a machine construction as a musical box from the 19th century that uses a set of pins placed on a revolving cylinder plucking the teeth of a steel comb. You may want to develop a stop motion (stop frame) animation where illusion of movement results from photographing small increments in the object's movement. The movements of dancing/playing characters may relate to the dynamics of the geological event you show or may be your ultimate fantasy.	Present your opinion based on an online search concerning the actual and possible ways of collecting hot water from the geysers and either sending it through pipes inserted deep below the ground or transforming heat into electrical energy. Discuss possible environmental threats resulting from such projects.

it rose to a great height on a sort of trunk and then split off into branches, I imagine because it was thrust upwards by the first blast and then left unsupported as the pressure subsided, or else it was borne down by its own weight so that it spread out and gradually dispersed. Sometimes it looked white, sometimes blotched and dirty, according to the amount of soil and ashes it carried with it (Pliny the Younger, translated by Radice, 1963, p. 427, after Mount Vesuvius, 2011).

Pliny the Younger wrote about the death of his uncle, when the buildings were shaking with violent shocks and he decided to leave,

Figure 2. Anna Ursyn, Horizon Line, Below and Above. (© 1990. Used with permission). Image manipulation with the use of a computer allows constructing spatial organization on a plane and in depth, both through transforming and transferring images; it was done with computer graphics, photosilkscreens, photolithographs, scanned images, and mental rotations supported by the wire frame drawings, with changing the eyeball position, perspective, and the size of the image.

My uncle decided to go down to the shore and investigate on the spot the possibility of any escape by sea, but he found the waves still wild and dangerous. A sheet was spread on the ground for him to lie down, and he repeatedly asked for cold water to drink. Then the flames and smell of sulphur which gave warning of the approaching fire drove the others to take flight and roused him to stand up. He stood leaning on two slaves and then suddenly collapsed, I imagine because the dense fumes choked his breathing by blocking his windpipe which was constitutionally weak and narrow and often inflamed. When daylight returned on the 26th – two days after the last day he had seen – his body was found intact and uninjured, still fully clothed and looking more like sleep than death (Pliny the Younger, 1963, p. 168).

Ancient Romans developed a special kind of mortar made from the Vesuvius materials, which hardens under water and lasts for ages. According to Gillian (2011),

Vitruvius, the author of an architectural treatise and a military engineer in the ancient Rome, described the characteristics of Vesuvius and its wonderful sand with the high silica content, which gave the special mortar known as pozzolano, with great strength and waterproof properties. This bonding material was used under water for Ostia's docks, and for vaulted, curvilinear buildings such as Pantheon. It was the key ingredient in 'Roman cement'" (p. 18).

As written in The Household Cyclopedia (1881), "The following is the formula of Vitruvius: 12 parts pozzuolana well powdered, 6 sharp sand well washed, 9 rich lime, recently slaked. It has the power of rapidly hardening under water." The strength of this cement comes from a chemical process of combination with water, while previous cements depended on water evaporation, which tended to make them weaker and slower to cure. After the great fire in Rome in AD 64 ignited by Nero, the new type of mortar was used for renovation of the Pantheon. It contained a volcanic ash from Vesuvius called Pozzuolana. It was the starting point for a revolution in the construction of arches and vaults, and the Pantheon is its greatest example (Milani-Santarpia, 2012). Other sources, along with the documentary film materials about the Colosseum amphitheatre in Rome, describe the same process used for building the amphitheatre; the longer was the time of keeping the mortar under water, the stronger material resulted.

People died because they were buried under hot lava and ashes; archeologists preserved the casts of their bodies, which were formed in a natural way from these materials. These artifacts and other physical remains found in the excavation sites in this region tell a great deal about life in ancient Pompeii and make possible for the next generations to study history, culture, art, and lifestyles of this period. Other people were suffocated by the poisonous fumes or drowned in the sea while trying to escape from heat; they disappeared leaving no remains preserved till our times.

Due to the volcano eruption, the whole city of Pompeii had been suddenly covered with hot lava, cinders, and ash in the midst of the day. The ash covered and preserved the buried remains of the city residents, animals, buildings, the works of art, and even the uneaten dinner. Excavators removing earth from the site could learn how Pompeii looked like in 79 A.D. Victims of Vesuvius were immortalized when their decomposed bodies left cavities in the hardened ash, and the bakery oven contained loaves of bread from before nearly 2000 years. The archeologists filled the cavities with plaster to recreate victims much as they looked at the time of their death (Mount Vesuvius, 2011). The plaster casts can be seen at the site http://www2.brevard.edu/reynoljh/italy/corpsecasts.htm. Archival quality photographs taken in 1995 by Aaron Levin as a part of the Pompeii Forum Project can be found at http://pompeii.virginia.edu/images/b-w/levin/small/levin.html. Color images of the artifacts recovered from Pompeii can be found at Art and History site http://www.utexas.edu/courses/italianarch/pompeii.html. A big collection of visual resources for the Pompeii Forum Project including photos and videos can be seen at http://www.utexas.edu/courses/italianarch/pompeii.html.

Figure 3 presents two student works about the declining environment. For directions on how to create your own visual response, see Table 4.

REDISCOVERY OF POMPEII AND HERCULANEUM

A crew digging an underground channel to divert the river Sarno discovered in 1599 ancient walls covered with paintings and inscriptions. They called the architect Domenico Fontana (1543-1607). However, Fontana covered this buried city over again. He missed the meaning of the wall inscription showing the name of an ancient Roman city (Grant, 1976, p. 215). Censorship was a main reason for covering the frescoes found in some Pompeian villas, because of a frequent view of the sexual content of such paintings. The paintings of the hedonistic kind were not considered in good taste in the climate of the late Renaissance, the time of the counter-reformation focused on devotional life (Özgenel, 2008). Many of frescoes and even household items had erotic themes. Later on, the same clash of a liberal culture of Pompeii and "prudishness" typical of the 19th and 20th century societies caused that several sites have been visited and the reburied,

Figure 3. Left: John Cook, "Pompeii." Right: Jefferson Lee, "Extinction"(© 2002, J. Cook and J. Lee. Used with permission)

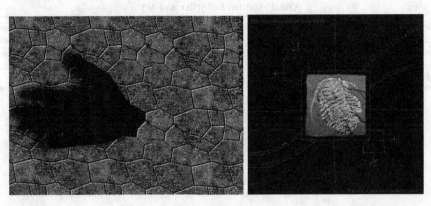

Table 4. Visual response

Your Visual Response
Create a scene showing an interior, to provide a glimpse of an ancient life, if possible with people. For example, you may want to draw a Roman interior with a mosaic floor and drawings on the walls. Make tiles for your mosaic from images of rocks and sections of leafs. You may choose to make an illustration, a sketch or other way of imaging.

Table 5. Visual solutions

Visual Solution: Extinction and Art
Imagine that you are participating in an archeological expedition and you have just discovered something unusual. You have found "frozen in time" remains of various creatures, several of each kind. It seems impossible to guess what happened to all these creatures, but it looks like a result of a sudden disaster, such as the Biblical deluge but with animals being not ready enough to save themselves in an arc. Nicholas Christopher (2008) explored this theme in his book "Bestiary." You have also found images of these creatures in the form of frescos on the walls. Imagine and show your involvement in this event.

the erotic artwork has been for nearly one hundred years locked away, opened, and closed again in a secret cabinet accessible only to selected visitors. According to Karl Schefold, (1993), it was briefly made accessible again at the end of the 1960s, at the time of the sexual revolution, and was finally re-opened for viewing in 2000. Minors are still allowed entry to the secret cabinet only in the presence of a guardian or with written permission. A wall fresco, which depicted Priapus, the ancient phallic god of gardens and fertility, was covered with plaster, the reproduction below was locked away, and accidentally rediscovered in 1998 due to a rainfall.

Almost one hundred fifty years after the first discovery the Spanish military engineer Rocque Joaquin de Alcubierre performed excavations starting in 1748 in order to rediscover Pompeii. Herculaneum was rediscovered in 1738 by workmen digging for the foundations of a summer palace for the King of Naples, Charles of Bourbon. Then Karl Weber directed the excavation works that made accessible the images of ancient world (Parslow, 1998). The archeologists perceived four sequential styles of wall paintings as being distinct:

Figure 5. Left: Kelly Bowman, "Pompeii." Right: Craig Stalker, "Help us so we can protect the city of Pompeii" © 2002, K. Bowman and C. Stalker. Used with permission

the 'masonry' style from 200 B. C. –60 B. C., the 'architectural' style (60 B.C.–20 A.D.) that created an illusion of space, the vivid and decorative third style (27 B.C.–54 A.D.), followed by a violent earthquake, and the fourth style (20 A.D–79 A.D.) depicting legendary angels, beasts, gods, and goddesses related to everyday life. A great number of artifacts from Pompeii are preserved in the Naples National Archeological Museum. However, the exposed wall paintings continue to deteriorate, fade, and decay due to several Mont Vesuvius eruptions and because sufficient funds are unavailable to maintain such a large monument.

Since the ancient catastrophe in Pompeii and Herculaneum Vesuvius erupted over 50 times: every 100 years until about 1037 A.D., then in 1631 it killed 4,000 residents. There was also big eruption in 1944, which destroyed a great part of the American and German aircraft engaged in the WWII actions (The Mount Vesuvius eruption of March 1944).

Today, in the towns of Pompeii and Herculaneum one may find hotels, restaurants, cafés, and gift shops serving the thousands of tourists from all over the world. Excursions to the rim of Vesuvius are also possible, as the scientists have devised a system to detect impending eruptions. Mountain slopes covered with lava serve well for producing wines. Ancient frescoes in the Villa dei Misteri (House of Mysteries) depict drinking red wine by ancient Pompeiians; winemakers have recreated the types of wine that were drunk in Pompeii.

For directions on how to craft a visual response to these events, see Table 5.

In his film "Roma" (1972) awarded at Festival de Cannes, BAFTA (British Academy of Film and Television Arts), and other festivals, an Italian film director and scriptwriter Federico Fellini devoted one episode to a sudden discovery of ancient Roman frescoes and sculptures that would conceivably happen during digging a tunnel for an underground metro. When the workers stunned by the majesty of the portraits on the frescoes pointed their flashlights toward the paintings in the newly discovered chambers, the faces on the walls became slowly bleach, whiten by exposure to light, and finally they disappeared.

Figure 5 presents two student works about the deteriorating beauty of the Pompeii.

Many printed collections of pictures document the art of Pompeii. Several poems were inspired by the art, the tragedy of its residents, and the mystery behind the findings allowing important discoveries about the past. For example, Robert Bly (Bly & Brigidi, 1992), American poet and the winner of the National Book Award, wrote

Figure 4. Anna Ursyn. Forever (© A. Ursyn 1989. Used with permission). A clash between the ancient and present-day life in Pompeii might certainly become a strong experience. Allegories of irrepressible desires, mystical scenes of funeral dances and initiation rites survived on the fragile frescoes and mosaics under the Vesuvius ash. Now, unquenchable aspirations, social gatherings, rituals, and puzzling practices continue on the surface.

poetry inspired by the Stephen Brigidi's ciba-chrome prints of the "Angels of Pompeii" when, in a verse entitled "Ramage for Awakening Sorrow" he wrote, "What is sorrow for? It is a storehouse set on rocks for wheat, barley, corn, and tears. One steps to the door on a round stone. The storehouse feeds all the birds of sorrow." Collaboration between Bly and Brigidi centered on angels and other divine beings painted in the ancient ruins of Pompeii.

CONCLUSION

Earthquakes and ground deformations are the precursors of imminent volcanic eruptions. Scientists cannot prevent or control eruptions because of the immensity of the temperature, pressure, physical characteristics of partially molten rock, and the extent of the magma chambers. This chapter describes earthquakes, tsunami, the explosive eruptions of volcanoes such as Mt. St. Helens, Yellowstone, and Vesuvius, and the Japan 2011 earthquake. After examining the impact of volcanism on human fates the reader is invited to draw inspiration from these geological events for creating a visual and/or verbal project.

REFERENCES

Bird, P. (2003). An updated digital model of plate boundaries. *An Electronic Journal of the Earth Sciences, 4*(3). Retrieved April 11, 2012, from http://peterbird.name/publications/2003_PB2002/2001GC000252.pdf

Bly, R. (1992). *Angels of Pompeii*. New York: Ballantine Books.

Chai, C. (2011, March 11). Japan's quake shifts earth's axis by 25 centimetres. *The Gazette*. Retrieved April 11, 2012, from http://www.canada.com/news/Japan+quake+shifts+earth+axis+c entimetres/4426356/story.html#ixzz1rko46tCl

Chang, K. (2011, March 13). Quake moves Japan closer to U.S., & alters earth's spin. *The New York Times*. Retrieved April 11, 2012, from http://www.nytimes.com/2011/03/14/world/asia/14seismic.html?_r=1

Christopher, N. (2008). *The Bestiary*. Dial Press Trade.

Eliot, T. S. (1968). *Four quartets: Little gidding*. Mariner Books.

Gillian, D. (2011). *Vesuvius*. Profile Books, Ltd..

Grant, M. (2005). *Cities of Vesuvius: Pompeii and Herculaneum*. Phoenix Press.

Milani-Santarpia, G. (2012). *Mariamilani, antiquities of Rome, Roman construction and technology, constructing walls in ancient Rome*. Retrieved April 15, 2012, from http://www.mariamilani.com/ancient_rome/rome_building_walls.htm

Mount Vesuvius. (2011). Exploring the environment: Volcanoes. *NASA Talk and Center for Educational Technologies*. Retrieved April 11, 2012, from http://www.cotf.edu/ete/modules/volcanoes/vmtvesuvius.html

National Park Service. (2012). *Yellowstone national park*. Retrieved April 12, 2012, from http://www.nps.gov/yell/naturescience/volcanoqa.htm

National Police Agency of Japan. (2012). Retrieved April 11, 2012, from http://www.npa.go.jp/archive/keibi/biki/higaijokyo_e.pdf

Özgenel, L. (2008). A tale of two cities: In search of ancient Pompeii and Herculaneum. *METU Journal of the Faculty of Architecture, 25*(1), 1–25.

Parslow, C. C. (1998). *Rediscovering antiquity: Karl Weber and the excavation of Herculaneum, Pompeii, and Stabiae*. Cambridge University Press.

Pliny the Younger. (1963). *The letters of the younger Pliny* (B. Radice, Trans.). Penguin Classics.

Robertson, E. C. (2011). *The interior of the earth*. Retrieved April 10, 2012, from http://pubs.usgs.gov/gip/interior/

Schefold, K. (1993). *Gods and heroes in late archaic Greek art*. Cambridge University Press.

Schlumberger. (2012). *Oil glossary*. Retrieved April 11, 2012, from http://www.glossary.oilfield.slb.com/Display.cfm?Term=mantle

The, U. S. Department of Agriculture. (2012). *Gifford Pinchot national forest Mount St. Helens brochure, 1980*. Government Printing Office GPO 1980 699-331. Retrieved April 15, 2012, from http://vulcan.wr.usgs.gov/Volcanoes/MSH/description_msh.html

The Geyser Observation and Study Association. (2011). Retrieved April 12, 2012, from http://www.geyserstudy.org/geyser.aspx?pGeyserNo=OLDFAITHFUL

The Household Cyclopedia. (1881). Retrieved from http://www.mspong.org/cyclopedia/cements.html

The Mount Vesuvius eruption of March 1944. (n.d.). *Mount Vesuvius facts and resources*. Retrieved April 11, 2012, from http://www.warwingsart.com/12thAirForce/Vesuvius.html

USGS. (2012). *Geographic names information system.* U.S. Geological Survey. Retrieved June 11, 2012, from http://geonames.usgs.gov/pls/gnispublic/f?p=gnispq:3:1297639910658653:NO:P3_FID:1525360

USGS/Cascades volcano observatory, Vancouver, Washington. (2009). Retrieved April 11, 2012, from http://web.archive.org/web/20090507051117/http://vulcan.wr.usgs.gov/Volcanoes/MSH/framework.html

Chapter 9
Picturing Minerals and Rocks

ABSTRACT

In this chapter, we draw inspiration from the study of Earth structures and materials, as well as processes and forces that change these structures, which is the core of the domain of physical geology. We examine minerals, main types of rocks, gems, and other more mundane earth baubles, the rock cycle, and processes that change the structure of the minerals. Projects are aimed at linking these physical and chemical processes and events with our ambient surroundings and personal perceptions of our own experiences.

MINERALS

The study of minerals is called mineralogy. Generally speaking, a mineral is a naturally occurring solid substance that has characteristic chemical composition and physical properties, and a crystalline, ordered atomic structure. There are more than 4,000 known minerals; they may comprise pure elements and simple salts or they may be very complex. Three layers: the crust, mantle, and core contain the dense materials (heavy metals: nickel and iron) close to the center and the lighter materials (rocks: basalts and granites) in the crust.

Classification of minerals takes different forms; it may take into consideration optical, chemical, x-ray diffraction, or other properties of minerals. Physical properties often used to classify minerals are the crystal structure of a mineral, its physical hardness (from talc to diamond), luster (from

dull to vitreous), diaphaneity (from transparent, through translucent, to opaque), color, streak (the color of the powdered mineral), cleavage (a way it splits), fracture (a way it breaks), specific gravity, fluorescence, magnetism, radioactivity, and piezoelectricity, among other properties. Chemical properties of minerals are used to discern the silicate class (such as quartz), carbonate minerals (mostly in marine and evaporation setting), the sulfate, halide, oxide, sulfide, and phosphate classes, as well as element class containing metals and an organic mineral class (Dana Classification, 2012).

Now you may want to visit a page: Vedauwoo – Images, to find sharp boundaries between rocks, every conceivable gradation in texture and the rocks' composition. Vedauwoo is an area of granite rock formations located in southeastern Wyoming, United States. To further visualize images such as this, see Table 1.

DOI: 10.4018/978-1-4666-4627-8.ch009

Table 1. An exercise in perspective

Visual Solution: Changing the Scale – An Ant Eye's Perspective
Imagine being very small, so the grain of sand or a small rock becomes a mountain for you. Looking on a grain of sand, a pebble, or a piece of rock, draw a mountain landscape with a horn-like rocky promontory, a sharp mountain ridge in the shape of an arête, and a rounded open space as a circus. What kind of a habitat would fit this picture with the rocks you have selected?
And then, create drawings that show close-ups of grains to create an ant eye's perspective, a landscape that expresses in dark or light colors the characteristics of grains, such as size, rounding, size of components, and surfaces: rough, polished, or frosted. Maybe, each small-scale segment could be as big as a postcard; so then, all pieces could be put together as a mural showing the landscape drawn with a pen, placed at the top of these close-ups.

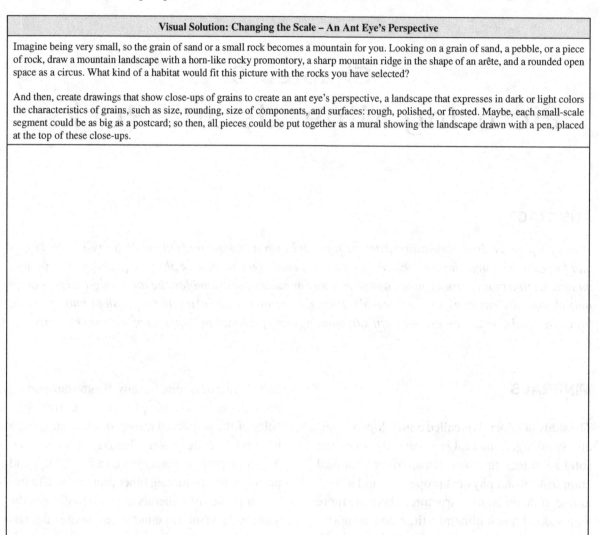

Biominerals

Seemingly simple definitions of familiar concepts, such as a mineral, may become controversial when the scientists take a closer look at the matter. Definition of a mineral began one of such objects of discussion when methods like the high-resolution genetic mapping and x-ray absorption spectroscopy could be used for examining minerals with a changed scale. A mineral can be an element or a compound; it may be amorphous or crystalline.

More recent mineral classifications include an organic class that also takes in a very rare group of minerals with hydrocarbons.

Previously, only compounds formed by geological processes were regarded as minerals, while biogenic substances produced by life processes were excluded. However, many scientists agree that organisms are capable of forming minerals that could not be formed inorganically in the biosphere (Dana Classification, 2012). According to Skinner (2005), biominerals created by living creatures are a subset of the mineral kingdom. The biomineralization of uni- and multi-cellular organisms provide more than 60 common biominerals composed of iron hydroxides and oxyhydroxides, calcium carbonates, and calcium phosphates. Tools, instruments, and technologies that operate at micro or nano scale, for example genetic mapping or X-ray absorption spectroscopy are used to determine structure of biominerals.

Genetic mapping (2012), also called linkage mapping, is one of the tools serving to isolating single genes and defining a genome (the whole of an organism's hereditary information, both the genes and the non-coding sequences such as DNA and RNA). Genetic markers consisting of DNA are developed from the genome. Assembly of markers is used as the reference genome to construct a genetic map, often called a microsatellite map. Genetic mapping is helpful in several disciplines, for example, in identifying genes responsible for a disease or in criminal or forensic investigations.

X-ray absorption spectroscopy serves to determine the local geometric and/or electronic structure of matter. A sample of matter absorbs photons (energy) from the radiating field, and absorption depends on its frequency, creating spectra. This tool is used to identify the presence of a particular substance, in astronomy, atomic and molecular physics, chemistry, earth science, biology, and in other disciplines (Rehr & Albers, 2000).

Thus, in the biogeochemical processes, not only physical or chemical forces, may form the minerals. Biogeochemistry is a discipline related to ecology that studies the chemical, physical, geological, and biological cycles of processes in a natural environment. Such cycles are both driven and have an impact on organisms. Natural environ-

Figure 1. Ben Burch, Nature (© 2010, B. Burch. Used with permission)

ment means the biosphere (the zone of life on Earth with its ecosystems), the hydrosphere (the mass of water on, under, and over the surface of Earth), the atmosphere (a layer of gases around the planet), the lithosphere (a rigid shell of a planet), and the pedosphere (the layer of soil at the interface of the above spheres). All these spheres have natural cycles of processes; they also are strongly modified by human cognitive processes and activities such as agriculture and industry. For an exercise in depicting these cycles, see Table 2.

Figure 1 presents a student's work from my Computer Graphics class.

Crystalline Minerals

Minerals may have the same chemical composition but different crystal structure; for example, pyrite and marcasite are such polymorphs. Some minerals with different chemical composition, such as halite

Table 2. Visualizing biomineral processes

Visual Response: Making a Cartoon or Animation
Create a cartoon, with people climbing up the columnar jointing. Or make animation of a volcano, according to your preferences. Consider how many images you need as a minimum to create animation.

and galena, have the same crystal structure, and thus share similar physical properties. Graphite and diamond are both pure carbon but differ in hardness because of the arrangement of atoms. There are 14 crystal lattice arrangements of atoms that make geometric forms of crystalline minerals.

ROCKS

A rock is a mixture of minerals and so its chemical composition varies; it may also include organic remains and mineraloids (non-crystalline, mineral-like substances such as obsidian – an amorphous glass, or opal). A small number of minerals make up the great volume of the rocks on Earth they occur in. The rock forming minerals include (Alden, 2012):

- **Feldspars:** Silicate minerals that crystallize from magma, making up as much as 60% of the Earth's igneous, metamorphic, and sedimentary rocks
- **Quartz:** The most common silicate mineral occurring as clear or cloudy crystals in igneous and metamorphic rocks
- **Pyroxene:** Dark silicate material common in igneous and metamorphic rocks present in granite igneous rocks and metamorphic rocks
- **Biotite (Black Mica):** Iron-rich, silicate mineral that splits in thin sheet in a similar way as muscovite, the white mica
- **Hornblende:** Dark-colored rock-forming silicate minerals
- **Olivine:** Green magnesium-iron silicate common in basalt and the igneous rocks of the oceanic crust
- **Calcite:** The principle carbonate (carbonates are minerals containing the carbonate ion CO_3^{2-}) present in limestone
- **Dolomite:** A crystalline mineral, a major carbonate mineral created underground

Figure 2 presents a student's work from my Computer Graphics class. To create your own project, see Table 3.

Rocks are often colorful, having shapes resembling precious stones, and so they may inspire you to draw a still life on a computer, on canvas, or on paper. A still life is a drawing, painting, or other work of art that presents objects: usually familiar, mostly inanimate items arranged by the artist to make a harmonious composition. In books on art or online (many images are at the Google – Images when you type the name of the artist and then add 'still life'), one can find drawings and paintings created by artists such as Paul Cézanne (1839-1906), Henry Matisse (1869-1954), Pablo Picasso (1881-1973), Wassily Kandinsky (1866-1944), or Takashi Murakami.

The Rock Cycle

The rock cycle is a depiction of dynamic processes happening through geologic time in the Earth's crust. Dynamic processes that shape the rocks include igneous intrusion, uplift, erosion, transportation, deposition as a sedimentary rock, metamorphism, re-melting, and further igneous intrusion.

The main types of rocks are the sedimentary rocks (formed from sand, shells, pebbles, and other particles of various materials), metamorphic (formed under intense heat and pressure, often with crystalline mineral intrusions), and igneous rocks (resulting from cooling of magma under the Earth's surface). Conglomerate and limestone are examples of sedimentary rocks; gneiss and marble are metamorphic; basalt and obsidian (glassy and without any crystals because of fast cooling) are the examples of igneous rocks.

States of matter are controlled by temperature and pressure. Rocks inside the Earth (sedimentary, metamorphic, and/or igneous rocks) melt into magma; magma cooled within the Earth undergo crystallization and becomes an igneous rock; in a case when magma erupts on the surface and cools

Figure 2. Peter White, All that we see or seem (© 2010, P. White. Used with permission)

Table 3. Depicting stones

Visual Solution: Still Life out of Stones
Look at some still life drawings and paintings by Paul Cezanne, Henry Matisse, Pablo Picasso, or other artists. Create your own still-life drawing using rocks containing the rock forming minerals. Images of these rocks can be found at the Wikipedia Images (when you type a name of the mineral). Consider using textures from CG Textures: http://cgtextures.com. Select the rocks you really like and retain the name and description. Now you may want to create a still life drawing. Arrange the rock images and then assign various textures appropriate for the minerals you appreciate. Consider putting stones in layers, if you wish. Your project does not have to be realistic.

quickly, it becomes a shiny, glasslike, and devoid of crystals lava. When exposed to atmosphere, igneous rocks on the Earth's surface go through changes (caused by gases, rain, frost, carbonic acid, oxygen, and other chemical elements) such as erosion, weathering, and sedimentation, and become sedimentary rocks, often with the accumulation of fossils – biogenic sedimentary rocks. Under high temperature and pressure under the Earth's surface the rocks become the metamorphic rocks. They will be melted again when the temperature and pressure grow enough. Forces such as plate tectonics carry on the rock cycle, as they change the plate ridges, pull the oceanic crust back into the mantle, or cause continental collisions (The Wilson cycle, 2000). For a suggestion on how to visualize these forces in different terms, see Table 4.

You may now want to take some joy in approaching the theme of minerals and rock forms by devising an analogy. Analogy is a cognitive activity of transferring meaning or information, in this case, from the data about geology to a visual presentation of the concept supported by the data or its linguistic expression. Analogy shows the relation between the source and a target, so it

Table 4. Visualizing plate tectonics

Visual Solution: Clouds as a Seascape
Imagine you are lying on a grass, facing the sky on a cloudy, but sunny and warm day. Imagine yourself travelling in a hot-air balloon, so you can look down at the Earth and up at the sky. Look at the sky as if it was an ocean and at the clouds as if they were continents. Name the ocean and the continents (lands and islands); the names could be made up. Think about the plate tectonics and how they carry on the rocks. Sketch and then change on a computer the configuration of 'land' and 'water.'

is an important factor in problem solving, finding computational solutions, information visualization, decision-making, and then explanation and communication of the results. Many times we create biological analogies, for example about anatomy, saying that the fish gills are like the bird lungs, or the butterfly wings work like the bird wings. To create an analogy, one may first select a complex idea, object, or model and use it as a source for creating an analogy to the less complex target – an everyday example of the issue one is working on. For example, you one visualize a representation of sustainability (such as a 'green'

building) and present an analogy of it as a gadget with a solar panel on it (such as a cup with rotating figures on its cover). Or one may picture a model of a solar system made out of colorful balls of different sizes as an analogy of astronomical images of the solar system as seen by astrophysicists through big telescopes. For more suggestions, see Table 5.

Sedimentary Rocks

Some sedimentary rocks, for example limestone, contain only one mineral (calcite). However, most

Figure 3. Anna Ursyn, "Audacity" (© 2000, A. Ursyn. Used with permission). A work "Audacity" alludes to the elements like wind, rain, and snow, which make a metaphor for our conditions. We need audacity to make dangerous decisions and take a risk to get a desired result.

Table 5. Visualizing a rock cycle

Visual Response: Landscape and its Analogy	Verbal Response: Landscape and its Analogy
Draw a landscape depicted across time representing a rock cycle: how igneous rock is weathering, turns into a sedimentary rock, and again becomes igneous rock. Use color or pattern as a clue (or even colors as pattern); possibly also use letters as pattern. If you wish, you can change a point of view (top view, side view) and change size and perspective. You may also want to create an ant eye's perspective, a landscape that expresses characteristics of a grain. By applying selected slopes, perspective, sizes, and directions you can visually code the information to distinguish a process from a product. Create a design for a dinner plate containing depiction of processes characterizing a rock cycle. The plate is round and its design is circular, showing rotational, around the center of symmetry (with no cardinal directions of north, east, south, and west) because the rock cycle goes in circles.	Describe a rock cycle by placing your characters or objects in different environments where ambient surrounding is dictated by the conditions that are decisive for the dynamic processes in the Earth's crust, and forming the sedimentary, metamorphic, and igneous kinds of rocks. Write a story about a troubled boy who is learning from studying objects. Describe the process of designing everyday objects that would visually contribute to the boy's learning process. For example, to learn/teach about the rock cycle, make the boy play with his food by rearranging the content of his meal on the plate, and changing its design according to the forces and processes involved in a rock cycle. The boy may visualize them by drawing color coded eating utensils: a red knife would picture heat, a blue fork – pressure, a green spoon – water, and a yellow teaspoon – gases.

sedimentary rocks are composed of many minerals. Components of common rocks are mostly minerals such as quartz, feldspar, chlorite, kaolin, mica, calcite, olivine, magnetite, hornblende, hematite, and limonite, among other minerals (Dana Classification, 2012). Some sedimentary rocks contain water, which is trapped or liberated during chemical processes, for example when clay minerals change into feldspar and mica.

Folds and Faults

Rocks, mostly the sedimentary strata, undergo deformations because of the applied stress (that may be tensile, compressive, or shear stress) mostly resulting from plate tectonics, which can be elastic, brittle, or ductile deformations. Rocks cannot glide or flow one on another because they are too rigid. By producing too much stress, tectonics may cause breaking and causing fault or folding the rock material, causing folds. Tension, compression, or shear, lateral forces cause faults – the planar fractures of a rock. Compression may fold the rocky material up, in a shape of

Table 6. Depicting folds and faults

Visual Solution: Mapping the Contortions as the Fingerprints of Forces
Imagine and picture changes occurring in sedimentary rocks. Show the rock as a part of a landscape; use the structure of a single stone to create structure of a mountain. Show an imaginary cross section of the sediments in a stream, a lake, or a swamp, as a combined picture of these environments.
Represent the length of time the sediments remain in those environments, using numbers if you wish, and including them into your composition. Also, show forces applied to your structures: stress (tensile, compressive, or shear) and friction, and show slippage. You may use letters for this type of info. Think about interaction between the numbers and the landscape by covering part of a letter, making a pattern from letters, or changing the size of lettering: the size may mean something, for example, age.
To change a point of view, maybe you will also want to eyeball it from under the water or from above.
On the computer screen, create a landscape with famous world's constructions, such as the New York Statue of Liberty, the Leaning Tower of Pisa, or the Eiffel's Tower. Consider what kinds of human interference would prevent a long term leaning over of the constructions, according to the rules and data shown on your picture?

an 'A' letter, forming an anticline, or down, in a shape of a 'U' letter building a syncline. Because of forces acting on both walls of such geological bodies they bend in a symmetrical or asymmetrical way, so a fault contortion may be composed of the rear fault strait, bend, or front fault, also bend or straight. See Table 6 for tips on depicting faults.

Metamorphic Rocks

Sedimentary and igneous rocks undergo metamorphism after they are subjected to pressure and heat when buried deep. Fluids and strain are other factors that metamorphose rocks. Igneous rocks included into sedimentary rocks may recrystallize or become converted into metamorphic rock gneiss that contains large mineral grains arranged in bands. After more metamorphism, gneiss may recrystallize again into granite, similar to that formed by the consolidation of a molten volcanic magma at high temperature and great pressure. An example of changes in metamorphic rocks may include a change of the sedimentary rock shale, first into slate, then into phyllite, and finally into mica-rich schist. Under high temperature and pressure, quartz becomes cemented: the sedimentary rock sandstone turns to quartzite. Sand mixed with clay metamorphose into schists or gneisses. The sedimentary rock limestone recrystallizes and becomes marble (About.com Geology, 2012). A process of altering metamorphic or igneous rocks by hydrothermal (consisting of hot water circulating in ocean, magma, or in deep crust) or other fluids, causing a change in their color of crystalline structure, is called metasomatism.

Radical changes that rocks undergo may seem amazing, when they change their content, appearance, and size. One may find truly fascinating a possibility to personally experience the changed properties and dimensions. Many writers imagined this experience. In some virtual worlds, characters made themselves bigger or smaller, like Alice from the Lewis Carroll's "Alice's Adventures in Wonderland" (Carroll,

2012, first edition 1865), who bit a mushroom from one or the other side. Other authors, for example Jonathan Swift (Swift, 2003, first edition 1726) in his novel "Gulliver's Travels" sent his main character to the lands inhabited by the giants or the Lilliputs, would change proportions of the ambient surrounding.

It is becoming possible now to make a familiar object different in size, or change its properties. You can scan your favorite chair, and then transform and modify the scanned model on your computer. For this purpose, one may use the three-dimensional computer-aided data, computer-based 3D modeling software, and then apply rapid prototyping to make a new, smaller (or even bigger) chair in any material one chooses: plastic or gold. Rapid prototyping includes many different processes for fabricating objects; machines used for prototyping may include laser cutters, computer-controlled milling machines, or three-dimensional printers, among other methods such as telecarving according to the computer program. With reverse engineering, one can reconstruct a thing as a physical object or make its three-dimensional model based on information extracted from the prototype. Moreover, one can perform the rapid prototyping or reverse engineering in another place, so your chair will not only get a new 'life' but it will happen in a new location. It is possible that in the near future we will be able to design an object such as a chair or a table in 3d software, and then send a wireframe via Internet to our friends living in another state or in a distant part of the world where the object would be prototyped. Another possibility are the online multiuser technology platform, such as EON Reality (2012) allowing the users to convene on the Web, interact with 3D objects virtually, and collaborate or chat in 3D using rich media such as 3D worlds, slideshows, videos, and avatars. For tips on visually modifying objects, see Table 7.

Table 7. Visualizing metamorphic processes

Visual Response: A Library as a Rocky Landscape

1. Draw an interior of a library. Replace the images from the book spines or the front covers with some geological objects:
   a. images of rocks, organized with respect to their geological age;
   b. images of rock formations, etc.

2. Write up names of the objects in the form of titles of books, both on the front covers and on the book spines.

3. Picture processes and conditions that decide what would metamorphic processes look like. On a b&w drawing, assign colors only for processes, to express the effects of:
   a. prolonged high temperature
   b. pressure
   c. metasomatism.

4. Express processes and chemical reactions by color codes, and their results through changing objects pattern or scale.   You may also apply gray scale, changes between patterns, or replace the pre-made patterns (for example, from clip art) with the scanned ones.

Igneous Rocks

Cooling and the resulting phase change from liquid to solid produce the igneous rocks from magma or lava. Most liquids solidify by crystallization – formation of crystalline rocks from the uniform liquids; however, igneous rocks may form without crystallization, as the plutonic rocks below the surface or the extrusive volcanic rocks from lava. There are about 700 kinds of known igneous rocks. Analysis of the rocks provides information about the composition of the earth's mantle, the age of rock formations (obtained by radiometric dating, by comparing

Figure 4. Anna Ursyn, "Goldview" (© 2004, A. Ursyn. Used with permission). "Goldview" is about regular and at the same time radical changes that rocks undergo. Rhythmic patterns, ubiquitous in nature, may make us think of a perfection of computer algorithms, if they not become chaotic.

the decay products in a rock with the known decay rates), about some processes such as plate tectonics, and the presence of important ores. Particle size in a rock depends on the cooling history. The intrusive rocks, cooling in preexisting rocks, form a central core (coarse grained, usually granite) of mountain ranges. The extrusive igneous rocks solidify fast at the crust's surface from magma – a melted rock (that is called lava when reaches the surface); therefore they are fine grained. Igneous rocks display various modes of occurrence, textures, mineral composition, and the geometry. Basic minerals in igneous rocks are feldspars, olivines, quartz, pyroxenes, amphiboles, and micas. Porphyry is an igneous rock with large crystals embedded in a finer-grained matrix. Gillian Foulger (2010) put forward a hypothesis that the surface volcanism is driven by convection in the deep mantle, contrary to the plate hypothesis that attributes melting anomalies to shallow effects directly related to plate tectonics. To further explore these relationships, see Table 8.

Table 8. Discovering new ways to visualize igneous rock

Visual Response: Making an Analogy Between the Igneous and Organic Structures
Visit the Devil's Tower at the page http://en.wikipedia.org/wiki/Devils_Tower_National_Monument
Look for similarities in the images of the Devil's Tower in Wyoming and a piece of petrified wood. Draw the top view of both objects. Examine both images in detail to determine if you can find their fractal nature. Enhance composition of your drawing applying the rich texture that is defining both objects of your attention.

The Rock Art

Hunters/gatherers, ranchers, and herd keepers on all continents have been creating rock art forms, mostly drawings and paintings on the rock formations such as rock faces, caves, and caverns. There are many sites with rock art in the United States, for example in Colorado, Utah, New Mexico, Arizona, or California. David Harmon (2012) lists Native American tribes in the great planes such as the Arapahoe, Cheyenne, Crow, Kansa (whereby the state Kansas had gotten its name), Pawnee, Shoshone and Sioux that contributed to the rock art. According to Harmon, rock art can be defined as: pictographs painted or sprayed, usually within cave entrances or in caves; petroglyphs: carved or incised /engraved onto rock surfaces; geoglyphs: mysterious images, quite large in surface area which can really only be seen aerially; and intaglios – surface depressions of animal shapes, such as the 160-foot-long serpent near Lyons, Kansas holding a ball in its mouth. Scientists are working on deciphering the cultural and religious significance and the symbolic or ritual language, maybe even early forms of runes, as found in Siberia. It is believed the intaglios may have been used in religious ceremonies depicting the winter and summer solstices. The great Medicine Wheel located in the Bighorn Mountains of Wyoming is a sacred destination for pilgrims.

Peratt (2004) searches for a possible insight into the origin and meaning of ancient petroglyphs. He compares the graphical and radiation data from the high-current Z-pinch Auroras (caused by the electrical current and magnetic field in the compressed plasma) to the patterns on objects, mostly petroglyphs, geoglyphs, and megaliths from the Neolithic or Early Bronze Age. Possibly, an intense aurora, as might be produced if the solar wind had increased millennia ago, resulted in creating by humans the ancient symbols. Petroglyphs

have been surveyed and GPS logged around the world; surveyed data come from 139 countries, from sites and fields containing several millions of these objects. They display commonalities indicating pre-historic (7,000-3,000 B.C.) intense auroras observable across the continents (Peratt, McGovern, Qoyawayma, Van der Sluijs, & Peratt, 2007). Common associated archetypes include: squatting man, caterpillars, ladders, eye mask, kokopelli, spoked wheels, and others.

Ancient petroglyphs, some coming from the Bronze Age are in many cases unprotected. Vandalism is a threat to the preservation of these images (Harmon, 2012). To create your own rock art, see Table 9.

Table 9. Rock art

Your Visual Response: Designing a Message as a Rock Art
Maybe you will want to visit a collection of rock art on the Petroglyph Google Images, at http://en.wikipedia.org/wiki/Petroglyph and then design your own message in the form of a rock art. It may be a cheerful picture, a sketch, or a visual pun. Ink, soft pencil, paint, and black or color marker are good for this purpose. Then you may want to post the image of your painted rock online to learn if other people read your message well.

CONCLUSION

In this chapter, the reader is encouraged to take some joy in approaching the theme of minerals and rock forms by devising an analogy – a cognitive activity of transferring meaning or information about a concept on the basis of the data or its linguistic expression. In this case, this is analogy with geology, solved as visual presentation. There are more than 4,000 known minerals: pure elements and simple salts or very complex matter. More recent mineral classifications include biominerals – an organic class including a very rare group of minerals with hydrocarbons. Biogeochemistry is a discipline related to ecology that studies the chemical, physical, geological, and biological cycles of processes in a natural environment. Projects are about both minerals and rocks.

REFERENCES

Abbott Abbott, E. A. (2008). *Flatland: A romance of many dimensions (Oxford World's Classics)*. Oxford University Press.

About.com. (2012). *Geology*. Retrieved April 17, 2012, from http://geology.about.com/cs/basics_roxmin/a/aa011804c.htm

Alden, A. (2012). *Formulas of rock-forming minerals*. Retrieved April 14, 2012, from http://geology.about.com/od/minerals/a/rockformforms.htm

Carroll, L. (2012). *Alice's adventures in wonderland*. CreateSpace.

Dana Classification. (2012). *Organic compounds*. Retrieved April 14, 2012, from http://www.mindat.org/dana.php?a=50

Foulger, G. R. (2010). Plates vs plumes: A geological controversy. Wiley-Blackwell. ISBN 978-1-4051-6148-0

Genetic Mapping. (2012). *National Human Genome Research Institute*. Retrieved April 14, 2012, from http://www.genome.gov/10000715

Harmon, D. (2012). World rock art, no borders: A world museum. In *Proceedings of the School of Visual Arts 25th National Conference on Liberal Arts and the Education of Artists*, (pp. 57-61). School of Visual Arts.

Peratt, A. L. (2004). Characteristics for the occurrence of a high-current, Z-pinch aurora as recorded in antiquity. *IEEE Transactions on Plasma Science, 31*(6), 1192–1214. doi:10.1109/TPS.2003.820956.

Peratt, A. L., McGovern, J., Qoyawayma, A. H., Van der Sluijs, M. A., & Peratt, M. G. (2007). Characteristics for the occurrence of a high-current z-pinch aurora as recorded in antiquity part II: Directionality and source. *IEEE Transactions on Plasma Science, 35*(4), 778–807. doi:10.1109/TPS.2007.902630.

Reality, E. O. N. (2012). *EON coliseum*. Retrieved June 14, 2012, from http://www.eonreality.com/products_coliseum.html

Rehr, J. J., & Albers, R. C. (2000). Theoretical approaches to x-ray absorption fine structure. *Reviews of Modern Physics, 72*, 621–654. doi:10.1103/RevModPhys.72.621.

Skinner, H. C. W. (2005). Biominerals. *Mineralogical Magazine, 69*(5), 621–641. doi:10.1180/0026461056950275.

Swift, J. (2003). *Gulliver's travels*. Penguin Classics. (Original work published 1726).

Chapter 10
Energy and Environment

ABSTRACT

The "Energy and Environment" project is a mental exercise intended to assist the reader in thinking and communicating with the use of visual language. Inspiration for this project comes from the theme of energy (such as kinetic, potential, mechanical, electrical, chemical, light, radiant, nuclear, and heat energy) and a need for its conservation. It also tells about the environmental concerns related to energy production and use. Visual and verbal projects provide analogies and comparisons of some energy related processes and events to our everyday experiences.

INTRODUCTION

The sources for generation of electric energy in the United States are coal (42%), natural gas (25%), nuclear energy (19%), and renewable energy (13%). Renewable energy comprises 63% hydropower, 23% wind, 7% wood, 4% waste, 3% geothermal, and 1% solar energy, without taking into account solar energy produced by the residential and commercial rooftop solar installations (eia, 2012).

Energy consumption goes in tens of quadrillions Btu in the United States (a quadrillion Btu equals 10^{15} Btu). An acronym Btu (the British thermal unit) denotes a unit of energy equal to about 1,055 joules or 252 cal. A Btu is defined as amount of heat required to raise the temperature

of one pound (0.454 kg) of water from 39 °F to 40 °F (3.8 °C to 4.4 °C) at a constant pressure of one atmosphere (Business Dictionary.com, 2012).

There are a variety of oils in nature; it may be any substance that does not mix with water but can mix with other oils and organic solvents. Organic oils produced by plants, animals, and other organisms through metabolic processes, mineral oils (called also petrochemicals) originated from ancient fossilized organic tissues, and synthetic oils are used for energy production.

Every form of energy can be generated from matter, in accordance with the Enstein's formula $E = m c^2$ telling that energy (E) equals mass (m) times the velocity or the speed of light raised to the second power (c^2). The further text discusses several forms of energy used or generated to satisfy

DOI: 10.4018/978-1-4666-4627-8.ch010

human needs, especially some of those available from natural resources such as water, wind, ocean thermal energy coming from a difference in water temperature, coal as a fossil fuel, solar, and nuclear energy trapped in an atom. The following projects: Hydropower, The Ocean Thermal Energy Conversion, Building a zero-energy house; bird's eye view and orthographic projection, Windmill: A Rondo (but not a perpetuum mobile), Nuclear power plant: a company as an atom, Greenhouse effect and global warming, and Solar cooking aim at encouraging the reader in thinking and communicating visually.

PROJECT 1: HYDROPOWER

People have been harnessing energy from hydropower for centuries but presently only about 7% of electricity produced in the United States and about 21% of the world's electricity comes from hydropower. Hydroelectric plants take energy from water flowing from dams and rivers. There are now about 8,000 dams in the United States. The important parts of a hydroelectric plant are a dam (with a high or low head) and a large pipe called a penstock that carries water from the dam to a generator (usually located in a power house). The vertical distance from the water level to a power-producing turbine is called a head. This distance – elevation change – allows for converting potential energy into kinetic energy. A high-head dam (e.g., about 300 m – 1000 ft) can provide a large volume of water to a turbine, to supply energy for a generator and produce thousands of megawatts (MW) of energy. When there is a low-head dam (for instance, less than 30 m – 100 ft) the output, that means the water flow, depends on the diameter of the penstock. The main types of turbines are the impulse and the reaction turbines. The impulse turbine, for example, the Pelton or the Francis turbine, uses nozzles aimed at cupped blades, so water pushes a wheel with blades; this type of turbine can rotate with a speed up to 1300 rpm (revolutions per minute). The reaction turbine, for example, the Kaplan turbine turns the wheel according to the Newton's third law, which states that mutual forces of action and reaction between two bodies are equal, opposite and collinear.

The author and illustrator David MacAulay (1989) designed a book entitled "Mill," which shows visual explanation of the planning, construction, and operation typical of mills developed in New England throughout the nineteenth century. This book is helpful in understanding how to gain energy from water.

The following project can be designed as a comparison of advantages and disadvantages of various types of hydroelectric energy systems. Maybe you would like to make a model of a turbine, with Flash or a physical model made of cardboard. For tips, see Table 1.

A sculptor, media artist, and filmmaker Scott Hessel (2012) developed a kinetic sculpture entitled "The Image Mill" and a video "No.1: Image Mill." This time-based artwork provides the moving image of galloping horses, mediated versions of cinema and computer forms. According to the artist's description, "The Image mill is a rotating steel machine that uses the force and beauty of falling water as the energy to create a moving picture. As water falls over the 4-meter-tall wheel, a transmission assembly causes two disks to spin in opposite directions. On the interior wheel are a series of animation frames painted onto plexiglass; on the black outside wheel, rotating in the opposite direction, are cut slits. As the two wheels spin, the slits act as a shutter and the animation becomes visible; a movie plays in the falling water." (Hessels, 2012, p. 98). When one visit Scott Hessel's website (http://www.dshessels.com/) and watch the 'No.1: Image Mill' video (http://www.dshessels.com/artworks/Imagemill/image_mill.htm) one can see a mill with horses

Table 1. Comparing hydroelectric energy systems

Visual Solution: Turbines	Verbal Response: Turbines
Sketch a landscape with a selected type of a turbine located by the dam or a river. Examine the main types of turbines taking human needs as a main factor. Application of color-coding may signify the benefits in green and the drawbacks in red color. For example, you may find a positive feature that hydropower facilities do not produce pollutants. However, collecting pollutants from the upstream water, possible breeding of the parasite-carrying species, the impact on plant and animal habitats, displacing people, and inundating treasures of architecture can be listed as negative consequences of building dams. Consider many other features, both beneficial and harmful. Provide your audience with a legend.	Describe on the index cards notes about hydropower, types of hydroelectric energy systems and kinds of turbines, and then glue the cards around the perimeter of a circular cardboard. Draw sketches along with your notes.

Show negative and positive factors characterizing a system you have chosen by describing positive aspects; code them as green and the negative ones as red. Describe an object floating on water and develop a story about what happened when an object, for example, a large stick approached the turbine. Show this object appearing in different systems, and what would happen depending on the characteristics of each particular system |
| | |

that are apparently moving due to the rotation of a wheel caused by the flow of water. The drawings of running horses seem to be inspired by images made by Eadweard James Muybridge (1830-1904), who studied animal and human locomotion by making stop-action photographs on multiple cameras and projecting them on a zoopraxiscope, which he devised, which projected images from rotating glass disks. More images created by Muybridge can be seen online, at the site 'Images for Eadweard James Muybridge.' For a similar project idea, see Table 2

Table 2. Visualizing hydropower

A Flipbook Animation of Hydropower
Now you may want to create a flipbook animation showing how water makes the turbine rotate. Show an object (from the previous verbal response), which floats on the surface of water. Develop a story what happens when an object, for example, a large stick approaches the turbine. Imagine a splash causing some other action: what would it be?
Looking at illustrations found online, at the 'Images for hydropower turbines' site, select one type of a water turbine. Draw a sketch of the selected turbine on a paper thin enough to see through it, for example, tracing paper. To make a flipbook, use your drawing as a first animation frame on a registered piece of paper, and then place another piece of paper on top of the first one to trace the lines that don't change and add the lines that tell about the action. Use the original drawing as a guide. Images should gradually change from one page to the next. Start with the last page of the flipbook because it will go from back to the front. Copy your first drawing with small changes telling about the water and turbine movements. Draw only on the lower half of the page and then staple the pages at the top. When they are flipped rapidly, the pictures will simulate motion of water and rotation of the turbine. Maybe you would prefer to create this animation in Adobe Photoshop, Flash, or other software.
Looking at illustrations found online, at the 'Images for hydropower turbines' site, select one type of a water turbine. Draw a sketch of the selected turbine on a paper thin enough to see through it, for example, tracing paper. To make a flipbook, use your drawing as a first animation frame on a registered piece of paper, and then place another piece of paper on top of the first one to trace the lines that don't change and add the lines that tell about the action. Use the original drawing as a guide. Images should gradually change from one page to the next. Start with the last page of the flipbook because it will go from back to the front. Copy your first drawing with small changes telling about the water and turbine movements. Draw only on the lower half of the page and then staple the pages at the top. When they are flipped rapidly, the pictures will simulate motion of water and rotation of the turbine. Maybe you would prefer to create this animation in Adobe Photoshop (in layers), Flash, or other software.

PROJECT 2: THE OCEAN THERMAL ENERGY CONVERSION (OTEC)

The Ocean Thermal Energy Conversion (OTEC) is an example of applying naturally existing sources of energy for generation of energy. It is a system using a heat engine for generating electricity. This project makes use of the difference between the temperature of the warm surface water of a tropical ocean (about $25°$ C, 77 degree F) and the cold seawater at the ocean bottom, one thousand meters below (about $5°$ C, 41 degree F). This project results from a thought experiment aimed at generating a perpetual motion device: "A ship or a large power plant using the temperature gradient and heat transfer between a large surface exposed to the sun (or another heat source) and a colder one (e.g., the sea or the ground)" (Websters Online, 2012). This appeared to be a low-efficiency solar generator, far less efficient than conventional solar cells.

People behind this project installed a pipe in a closed loop between the ocean surface and its bottom filled with ammonia. Ammonia boils at the surface level and its vapor drives a turbine generator, which produces electricity. The temperature difference (about $20°$ C) turns the ammonia vapor into a liquid (with the aid of a condenser). The fluid ammonia is then pumped back to the boiler at the surface level. However, the efficiency of this plant has been small (3-4%). A great part of its output must go to run the pump and salt water causes corrosion of the plant's part. The OTEC plants have been considered useful for island nations. Figure 1 shows a student's visual response to a physicist's lecture offered for the class about the OTEC system delivered in my computer graphics lab. Figure 1, Nuclear Energy is a student work. Further visual responses are available in Table 3.

Figure 2 shows depiction of the ocean from a turtle's perspective.

Table 3. Visualizing OTEC

Visual Response: From the Sky, through the Ocean, to the Underwater Treasure
Illustrate a scene of the OTEC system installed in the tropical ocean between the corral reef at the bottom of the ocean and the surface of the ocean. Focus on including action into the picture: a composition with an overall feel of dynamics and action rather than representing separate objects. To get to the essence of this, some search about water habitats would be needed first: research the ocean life and find out what kind of animals and plants live at which depth. Create a three-part scene: actions and events on the skies above the ocean may comprise all the atmospheric, animal, and human-based actions – clouds carried by the wind, storms with thunder and lightning, heavy rain or hail, but also flocks of birds, planes, gliders, balloons with gondolas, and kites. The surface of the ocean on the horizon line where water meets the sky may be populated with all sorts of ships, boats, birds, animals, and sport related actions: sailboats and surfers. A hidden treasure region includes whatever you may think about the underwater life: from plants and living creatures, to sunken galleons, treasures and corral reefs. Draw a cross section of the ocean showing the ocean life coexisting with the man-made constructions set underwater in order to produce energy. Place measuring tool that displays depth related information on the edge of your composition. Show all sorts of creatures in scale along the pipes, the generator, and objects installed around the system.

Figure 1. Dwaine Birden, Nuclear Energy. (© 2006, D. Birden. Used with permission)

Figure 2. Jessica Wilson, "Horizon" (© 2005, J. Wilson. Used with permission)

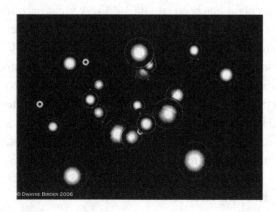

PROJECT 3: BUILDING A ZERO-ENERGY HOUSE; BIRD'S EYE VIEW AND ORTHOGRAPHIC PROJECTION

Local governments and organizations often provide citizens with brochures and kits for saving energy. This kit may contain: a bucket for collecting rainwater, tape for insulating windows, new types of bulbs (13W and 19W compact fluorescent light bulbs stand for the old 60W and 75W incandescent light), crises for faucets, programmable thermostats for controlling temperature, shower heads (1.5 gal/min), kitchen/bathroom faucet aerators, refrigerator thermometers, hot water temperature gauge indicator (with recommended temperature 120 F).

They also provide a pamphlet advising people to educate their children about energy saving, use a bicycle instead of a car to save gas, arrange for a better transportation for every family member, open or close windows and drapes according to the atmospheric conditions, turn off all unnecessary lights, computers, applications, and unplug appliances at night, stop using a screen saver, lower the heating/air conditioning units at night, place buckets to collect rainwater, use a dishwater wisely, wash the dishes with the earth safe detergents using not too much water, save and recycle paper to save trees (cancel unnecessary mail order catalogs, bring your own bags to a store for packaging, reuse printer's paper), insert a bottle to a bathroom reservoir tank, use a fan to use air condition less, buy less food (to avoid throwing it out because of the expiration date), and cover the pool. They advise people to put on a sweater instead of turning heating on. They explain that clothing either lets the heat in or isolates, that wool should be worn instead of polyester, which serves as an isolator. They encourage doing simple home experiments, such as covering colored cans with a cardboard, set them out to sun, and see how cans painted black react differently from those painted white. For another home experiment, see Table 4.

Apart from these small changes you may think about improvements in your house aimed at creating a Zero Energy House, which produces as much energy as it consumes in a year (see Table 5). This may include using solar energy by installing solar panels to have solar heating and warm water, or even generate excessive energy. Some savings come from applying environment- and energy-saving building and insulation materials.

PROJECT 4: WINDMILL: A RONDO (BUT NOT A PERPETUUM MOBILE)

Our world is based on entropy, which describes the flow of energy through a thermodynamic process. Entropy causes that some of energy is unavailable for work in the thermodynamic processes in machines or living systems. Perpetuum mobile (which in Latin means perpetual motion) refers to movement that goes on forever (Websters Online, 2012). An object would move infinitely, according to Newton's first law of motion, in a perfect vacuum with no forces acting at it. In reality, space is filled with low-density plasma. Every machine would lose energy to friction and air resistance. Moreover, a perpetual machine would deliver more energy than was put into it, which would violate the law of conservation of energy, which states that energy can never be created or destroyed. For this reason it is impossible to build a perpetual motion machine that would work infinitely without the input of energy from the external sources. Physicists and philosophers have been performing for ages the thought experiments about interaction between entropy, information, quantum fluctuations of energy, thermal effects, magnetism, gravity, etc. Proponents of the perpetual machine have been working from the ancient times on thousands of various solutions

Table 4. Visualizing energy use

Visual Response: Energy in Your Home
Draw a floor plan of your dream house or a place you grew up in. Consider home energy usage and savings in your home. sList types of energy you can use in your house. After learning about forms of energy such as kinetic, potential, mechanical, electrical, chemical, light, radiant, nuclear, and heat energy, pair them up with the kinds of energy used at home. You can select from: energy from hydropower, wind (windmill), electrical energy from a power plant, from gas, and solar batteries. Design types of energy to be used in your home and assign color to each specific energy type color-coding each type of energy. Design solar roofs on a dream house or windmills set on its property to generate energy with. Imagine there is no budget limit, so you could include a space for your cars, bikes, horses, or design a garden and add a solar-heated swimming pool.

Explain what kind of materials will be used for your house to make it more energy efficient. For example whether aluminum foil or styrofoam (polystyrene foam) can reflect heat and should be used to insulate; fiberglass with air inside would be used for the attic, with house insulation for the ceiling in accordance with recommendations set for a particular geographical region. The amount of insulation depends on a zone you are living in and is specified by the R-value (Recommended levels of insulation, 2012). For example, somebody living in a zone 3 in California may need the R30 to R60 insulation for a not insulated attic and the R19 to R25 insulation for a floor. Since black, green, grey, and white colors may absorb radial energy differently, color could be selected for the exposed parts. Passive heating from a solar system could be installed; also retrofitting structures and heat transfer systems could be applied. A good spot selection would be made for a house, and the front of the house should face south. |

and were often so confident about their success that in 1775 the Royal Academy of Sciences in Paris, and then the United States Patent and Trademark Office and many other patent offices started to officially reject all patent applications. This theme is constantly present in literature, music, and film. Refer to Table 6 to brainstorm ideas for your own device.

PROJECT 5: NUCLEAR POWER PLANT: PRESENTING AN ATOM AS A COMPANY

Thousands years ago people originated an idea of an atom as a discrete unit that cannot be further divided; this idea was discussed by philosophers for thousands of years. Theories on how atoms

Table 5. Applying changes in energy use

Visual Response: Creating One's Own House
Present your house on paper in a two-dimensional way applying parallel orthographic projection (with lines orthogonal to the projection plane) or using a perspective drawing. These kinds of drawing have been known and documented from the ancient times; drawings served the cartographic and astronomical uses, such as to compute the sun and other stars positions (Maynard, 2005). A good spot selection would be made for a house, and the front of the house should face south. There are also unconventional materials to consider. For example a paper bale or straw bale houses have been made from recycled newspapers, incombustible and relatively indestructible (Drummey, 2001). For example Rich Messer's (2012) paper and stucco houses in Fraser, Colorado save lots of energy by having very wide walls, so one may place objects, or even rest sitting by the windowpane.   Show ways to save energy in every part of the house: living room, dining room, office, master bedroom and bedrooms, bathrooms, mudroom, den, basement, attic, laundry room, kitchen, garden, backyard, and garage. Assign pattern coded types for saving energy. Show devices, appliances, applications, technologies, methods, routines, and habits, along with traditions. To save energy even more, show how family traditions can support or hinder energy savings. For example, some dry their laundry in the attic or in the garden; others rigorously turn out lights to save energy.

combine into complex objects were developed in India; in ancient Greece Democritus coined the name *átomos* (uncuttable, indivisible particle of matter) in about 450 BCE (McEvilley, 2002). Later on scientists adopted the name. Now it is discussed whether quarks are the smallest elementary particles. The following text is aimed at motivating you to look at the structure and properties of an atom in a similar way as you would look at a big company or corporation (see Table 7 & Table 8).

Nuclear Fission

Now, picture a case when a newcomer joined a company (Table 9).

Table 6. Creating one's own energy production cycle

Visual Response: Creating One's Own Rondo
While taking into account all the above remarks, you may anyway want to draw a rondo, a sequence of actions, where one event proceeds from another and can even be seen as never-ending events or cycles. For example, how a windmill pumps water, water allows corn to grow, corn produces gas, gas powers machinery, machinery digs the oil, oil serves for digging coal through surface mining, which allows for a hydropower production, which in turn may be used to water the ground.

Table 7. Atom as a company

Visual Response: Atom	**Verbal Response: A Company as an Atom**
An atom of any element is usually drawn as a set of concentric orbitals having a nucleus in the center of rotation and several elementary particles circulating around the nucleus at various distances (Visualizing Electron Orbitals, 2012). Particles vary in terms of the energy level, wavelengths, and sizes. We think about electrons as the waves and masses at the same time. We can calculate probabilities of finding any electron of an atom in any region on an orbital but not its exact location. Thus we need to examine the wave nature of electrons and the electronic structure of atoms and molecules. The radial wave functions describe the distribution of electrons with respect to the distance to the atom's nucleus. When we talk about electrons in terms of quantum mechanics, we can think about the patterns of electron density rather than the individual electrons as concrete particular bodies. We may discuss the electron properties represented as waves, as they are characterized not only by mass but also charge, spin, and magnetism. Thus, an orbital on which an electron is circulating around an atom's nucleus is described in textbooks as the actual or potential pattern of electron density formed in an atom. One or more electrons, which can be described by wave equations, may circulate on an orbital.	Look at the structure and properties of an atom in a similar way as you would look at a big company or corporation. Draw a three-dimensional tree diagram showing a dynamic structure of an imaginary institution such as a company, a university, or a corporation. We can see such tree diagrams, often with photographs of chief executive officers and senior business officials, presented on the company website, pamphlets, or in the lobbies of the company buildings, so the visitors can see a hierarchy of the staff, orient themselves, and find a person they intend to call on. Employees in this workplace have various duties and competencies, which are changing depending on their individual input and their cooperation with others. Present these individuals circulating at their assigned levels, as you could imagine neutrons going on their orbitals in an atom. Energy-loaded input coming from other people (for example, from the talented interns who arrive at the premises) or external factors such as grants or equipment may energize particular employees allowing for their promotion to a higher level, so now they will circulate on bigger orbitals.

Table 8. People in a company as an atom

Atom	People in a Company as an Atom
Elementary particles sometimes change one into another. They differ in terms of an energy levels and size. The approximate size of an atom is 10^{-10} m, the size of a nucleus of an atom is about 10^{-14} m, a proto is about 10^{-15} m, and a quark about 10^{-18} m large. If we accept the size of an electron as a one unit, a proton will present itself as one thousand units, nucleus as ten thousand units, and an atom as million units. However, quantum physics describes elementary particles in terms of fundamental forces such as gravitation between particles having certain mass; electromagnetic forces between charged particle; strong nuclear force between quarks; and weak nuclear force between neutrinos and electrons (Elementary particles, 2012).	We can see the employees as collaborators. Within your company, present a rank system, a hierarchy that characterizes this company and consider how it may support initiatives proposed by the staff members.
There are many kinds of elementary particles existing in an atom, which have properties both of waves and particles. In the text on this theme we may encounter descriptions of electrons; neutrons and protons (which in turn may contain three quarks) that are present in an atomic nucleus; photons (the quantum of light or other form of electromagnetic radiation, which carries electromagnetic force, with eight quanta called a gluon; gluons and photons belong to the force-carrying particles), leptons (the electron and the neutrino) paired with quarks and considered the particles associated with matter; and other, detected or hypothetic particles. Much of the quark and the lepton matter coexist with antimatter having an opposite sign (e.g., positrons).	Picture a situation where a member of the company staff attains an energy level high enough to become free from the attractive force exerted by the chief (like a positively-charges nucleus in an atom) and go outside, in external space. It happens with the negatively charged electrons when they leave an atom or a molecule; they change it into an ion, namely a cation. When the atomic orbitals interact and overlap with each other, two atoms can share electrons by making a common orbital for two electrons. This makes a stable new molecule. For example, sodium Na, which has 11 electrons on three orbitals, tends to lose one electron to chlorine Cl and form a NaCl molecule.
The number of electrons and their configuration around the atom nucleus contribute to determining the structure of the periodic table. Hydrogen wavefunctions map the electron density. The shells (orbitals) are often visualized as a planetary model for the electrons showing definite quantized energy levels. Particles on higher orbitals, which are further from the nucleus, have higher, less tightly bound energy. The first element, H has one electron only; helium has two electrons that fill the orbit, because it is stable, it is called the noble gas.	Show interactions between individual employees as short cartoons (where the characters may be drawn as sticky figures).

Table 9. New hire as nuclear fission

Nuclear Fission	Making a New Company
A radioactive decay or a nuclear reaction may cause a nuclear fission. In a naturally occurring, spontaneous radioactive decay the nucleus of an atom splits into two lighter nuclei, releases a very large amount of energy, and often produces free neutrons and photons. In manmade nuclear reaction, a neutron is needed to induce nuclear fission. For example, a nucleus of uranium-235 absorbs a neutron and turns into an unstable, excited nucleus of uranium-236. Excitation energy comes from the kinetic energy and the binding forces in the neutron. Uranium-236 splits into two lighter elements (Kr-92 and Ba-141), releases three free-moving neutrons and radiates electromagnetic gamma rays. This nuclear fission releases a great amount of energy: electromagnetic radiation and kinetic energy of the fragments (which causes the heating of vessels in the power plant nuclear reactor. The amount of energy is millions of times the amount of free energy existing in a similar mass of gasoline.	The ideas brought by the individual stir the routine and cause a split of a company into two new units; some members of the former personnel as well as interns may leave the institution and maybe join another institution. This happens when a radioactive decay or a nuclear reaction cause a nuclear fission. Describe how the energy of partners founding a new company may result in it dynamic growth and success.

Figures 3a and 3b show students' visual interpretations of the atom as a company.

Nuclear Fusion

Nuclear physics, chemistry, and astrophysics describe nuclear fusion as the process where two or more atomic nuclei fuse, that means join together and form a heavier nucleus. This process causes release (in case of small-mass nuclei) or absorption (in case of the nuclei heavier than iron) of a large quantity of energy. Nuclear fusion occurs in all active stars; creating on Earth conditions required for synthetic fusion, continuous reactions, and plasma containment (maintaining plasma in a discrete volume) is very difficult. However, research toward developing controlled thermonuclear fusion is carried out in the laboratory

Figure 3. a. America Zamora, Atom as a Company (© 2012, A. Zamora. Used with permission); b. Matthew Rodriguez, Atom as a Company (© 2012, M. Rodriguez. Used with permission)

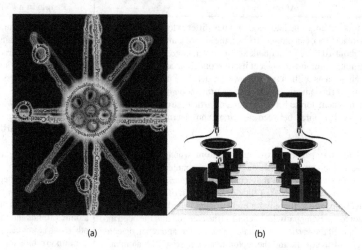

(a)   (b)

Table 10. Fusing entities

Visual Response: Company Fusion and Transformation
Corporate decisions about fusion may result from globalization, interconnected environments, and complexity of networked structures. You may now want to draw an analogy between joining two atomic nuclei to form one heavier nucleus and a joining of two companies that seek new capabilities to combine energy, production, security, and education by their fusion and transformation.

Figure 4. Michael Van Zant, Nuclear Fusion (© 2007, M. Van Zant. Used with permission)

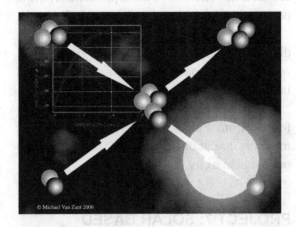

experiments, sometimes resulting in uncontrolled explosions during nuclear weapon testing. Taking this into account, the company metaphor continues in Table 10.

Figure 4 shows a student's visual interpretation of the fusion processes going in Cosmos as a visual response to a physicist's lecture offered for my class about the OTEC system delivered in my computer graphics lab.

When asked to visualize a scientific concept of a nuclear fusion after listening to a lecture delivered by a physicist, students from the computer art class at University of Northern Colorado represented this abstract concept in an artistic way. In an imaginative way, one of the students, Andrea Carvalho presented the concept of fusion as a musical performance (Figure 5). The artist placed the images of players across the background showing distribution of forces existing around the atoms. The heat of the intense musical event, the excitement of the musicians and viewers make a metaphor of the energy release and the rise of temperature caused by nuclear fusion. The inscription 'Fusion' placed on the artwork can refer to the nuclear fusion, the fusion of the musicians in their creative performance, or maybe to the term 'jazz fusion' used for music combining jazz with other musical genres.

PROJECT 6: GREENHOUSE EFFECT AND GLOBAL WARMING

Scientists study specific components of nature, both living and inanimate. They examine particu-

Figure 5. Andrea Carvalho, Nuclear Fusion. (© 2006, A. Carvalho. Used with permission)

Figure 6. Peter White, Lab. (© 2006, P. White. Used with permission)

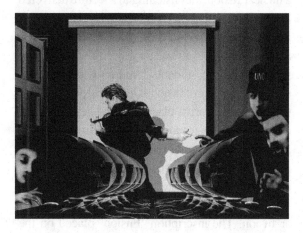

Figure 7, Jeremy Raisch, Lab – Landscape (© 2010, J. Raisch. Used with permission)

lar events, processes, and their interactions; then they draw conclusions that refer not only to the research results but also to the world outside the lab. However, not always the laboratory results can be extended to a larger area; sometimes they may become disastrous because of pollution they cause, health problems that follow but are difficult to perceive right now, and effects on the environment that sometimes are irreversible. We should evaluate our experiments and large-scale actions as a part of a bigger picture of the whole earth.

Now you may want to present your ideas about collaboration on environmental problems. The first part would relate to the laboratory work (Table 11).

Figure 6 shows a collaborative fusion of energy displayed by students in a computer graphics lab.

The second part will be about transformed landscape from a drawing of a lab (Table 12).

Figure 7 presents an urban landscape transformed from a picture of a lab where computer monitors are transformed and converted into buildings in a city.

PROJECT 7: SOLAR BASED ACTIONS: SOLAR COOKING, SOLAR HAT

You may want to experiment with the solar cooking as an environmentally friendly solution and an exemplar way of energy conservation. Solar cooking may refer to themes coming from many domains.

1. Energy (physics of heating with the Sun energy)
2. Mathematics (geometry for designing a cooker and calculation of the cooker's performance)
3. The Cosmos (Solar system)
4. Environmental awareness (energy conservation)
5. Design (building a cooker)
6. Art History (presence of the Sun in cultures)
7. Art (creating art – making and adorning a cooker)
8. Culinary arts (health and diet).

We are harvesting and using energy of sunlight as we care about the environment conservation. Solar cookers provide a sustainable, efficient method for cooking. A solar oven captures the sunlight. Sunlight is reflected or trapped and converted into heat energy. Solar ovens are also used for drying food and pasteurization. However,

Table 11. Transferring environmental problems from a lab to a larger scale

Visual Solution: A Lab and Environment	Verbal Response: A Lab and Environment
Draw a small picture of several labs in a building as a part of a bigger image, which includes a surrounding landscape with a stretch of land and a sky. Present also what is going underground, below the lab building. The picture may also show a skyscraper or a tower with several windows, each window depicting a different lab. The scientists conduct various experiments. Now show what kind of a process is held in each lab, and how each work affects the environment surrounding the building in various aspects (positively?) Using computer software of your choice draw what you think you would see around you; you may focus on the small fragments. Your work do not have to be realistic. Feel free to use transform tools. Try to depict depth.	Describe individual scientists working inside of the lab, each one on a specific experiment, and then draw connections how each of their projects may have a possible impact on Earth when conducted on a larger scale: its thermal pollution, climate, or effect on bio-diversity. This may even affect people walking down the street, or even farms, factories, or workplaces located on surrounding rural areas.

they require strong sunlight acting for considerable time to produce sufficient heat. To make a successful project, we should understand how the sun sends this energy as light and how it depends on the sun's, the earth's, and the moon's movements. Understanding of these variables will help to locate our solar cooker in a right place and under right angle because the usefulness of a solar cooker depends on the sun energy received during different seasons from various angles. Not only the earth rotates around the sun but also it rotates around its own axis. One rotation of the earth around the sun lasts about a year, with its four seasons, while one rotation of the earth around its own axis results in a cycle of night and day. The sun's trajectory on the sky changes in particular

Table 12. Transforming a room into a landscape

Visual Response: A Transformed Landscape
Draw a room as you see it in front of you and then convert it to a landscape. Modify the content of your file so the room becomes a landscape. You may want to use transforming tools. For example, select a fragment of the composition and use scaling, slanting, perspective, distort, etc. You may convert each object into some element of the landscape or modify it differently (for example by using filters.) The idea is that you'll recycle the elements and use them as transformed building blocks of the landscape. If you'd like you can copy and paste the components from the first file to a blank document, and copy them one by one onto the new file, while thinking about each and every object, and how to modify it. You do not have to use all the parts. Change the meaning of the objects in the room, thus creating a landscape by overlapping objects, such as hills, rocks, and trees, with nearer objects partially covering more distant objects. Closer objects appear to be bigger: sizing objects makes the far away objects smaller than the close ones. Darker shades may be used for the far away objects; you may also choose to shade the details.

seasons. We may draw positions of the sun at the same location on the globe at the selected hours in four seasons. While rotating around the sun, the earth blocks partially or totally the sunlight that is incident on the moon's surface, which results in the phases of the moon: we cannot see some part of the moon. Solar eclipse happens when the moon partially covers an access for sunlight to arrive on the earth surface. Efficiency of the sunlight operation and the amount of provided energy depends on an actual earth's location and movement. A sufficiently sunshine day must be chosen for cooking.

From the Neolithic times people worshipped sun, which was imagined traversing sky in a boat or a 4-horse chariot. Many images showing Sun worship in various cultures may serve as an inspiration to decorate the solar cooker. Harvesting sunlight as energy source has a long history. First solar cells were made in 1876 from

Table 13. Solar cooking

Building a Solar Cooker
Making a solar cooker may involve a research, gathering materials, and then designing a shape of a solar cooker, followed by performing calculations. Then come the testing, decorating, and illustrating the cooker according to Sun related myths. We may improve efficiency of a solar cooker in two ways: by maximizing the solar energy intake by transmission and absorption, and by preventing heat lost from conduction and convection. For this reason we may use materials such as cardboard, styrofoam (polystyrene foam), plastic, wood, glass, mirrors, or aluminum foil, to minimize reflection and reduce heat lost through insulation.
Construct a solar cooker; it may have any shape and design, assuming a cubic, rectangular, parabolic, or oval form. Make sure you maximize the solar energy intake by transmission and absorption and prevent heat lost from conduction and convection. In order to calculate the total heat absorbed by the water, on a sunshine day measure the temperature of water and the volume of the water before putting it into your solar cooker. Then measure the temperature again after it goes up significantly, and then record and tabulate all the experimental data. Taking photographs, sketching, or drawing pictures of every step will help to develop visual illustration of the concepts/design of the solar cooker.
To measure performance of a cooker Q (how much heat is absorbed by water in a cooker) you will need three measurements.
First calculate the volume of water by measuring its dimensions in a square vessel.
Next, calculate the mass of water: mass = density of water ($1000 kg/m^3$) x volume of water.
Then, measure the temperature change ΔT (final temperature minus initial temperature, e.g., $\Delta T = 95F - 55F = 40F = 22C$).
The specific heat is C (1000 calorie/kg/C).
The total heat absorption needed equals Q (in calories) $Q = m C \Delta T = m \times 1000$ calorie/kg/C x ΔT.
Cook some eggs and then decorate your solar cooker and cooked eggs. You may want to decorate them with images reflecting Sun related myths and ideas gained by getting inspiration from various cultures, such as Mayan, Egyptian, Greek, or Roman or use cultural icons that represent objects, actions, or feelings, symbols such as warning signs or symbols used for the sun, a moon, or a star. Some hieroglyphic writings can also be used for designs. The outside of the box can be decorated as well. One may use cultural icons that represent objects, actions, or feelings, or symbols used for the stars, the moon, or the sun. France had its King Sun in the person of King Louis XIV of France (1638-1715), known as Louis the Great or the Sun King (French: le Roi-Soleil), who reigned for 72 years and 110 days.
After you have eaten the eggs you may want to give the solar cooker to those who haven't eaten yet, according to the mantra: Reuse, Reduce, Recycle.

Table 14. Solar hat

Visual Response: Solar Hat Design – Passive Solar Usage
Buy a solar kit at a craft store such as Hobby Lobby or Michaels. It consists of a solar panel and a small motor. Select a sport hat. Attach to your hat a solar panel with a spinning top that will be powered by sunlight.
Cut out of paper some small figures that will be moving on the top of your hat. Think of a repetitive action performed by a group of characters rotating on the top of your hat. It could be an astronomy related event, such as daily sun's or moon's travel, a circus scene, a life cycle of a flower, a row of running horses, pelicans, flamingos, monkeys, people, a family with their leashed dogs, or more. Attach your figures to the flat panel placed on the top of you hat.

selenium. Gerald Pearson in 1953, and then Darryl Chapin and Calvin Fuller made silicon solar cells. Photovoltaic-generated electricity is a less expensive than any other power source. Cells are made from crystalline silicon and other materials.

There are many types of solar cookers used across the world: the most used are the box oven, the parabolic oven, and their hybrids. The first box solar cooker was built by Horace de Saussure in 1767. The box oven, popular in India, uses an adjustable reflecting surface to focus sunlight inside an insulated box. A plastic or glass cover traps the heat from sunlight. The parabolic oven, popular in China, concentrates heat above the cooker's base because of its curved shape and thus can create higher levels of heat and cook foods quicker. One may buy solar cooking kits ready for use. Events organized in many countries are aimed at popularizing solar cooking all over the world (Table 13).

Figure 8 pictures "Solar Cooker" – a fourfold structure presenting four sides of a solar cooker in front of a mirror installation. The four sides of the cooker are adorned with sun related images derived from solar astronomy. The upper part of the Solar Cooker includes a model of a solar system. For another solar-powered gadget, see Table 14.

CONCLUSION

This chapter assists the reader in thinking and communicating with the use of visual language

Figure 8, Anna Ursyn, Solar Cooker (© 2013, A. Ursyn. Used with permission)

while creating projects that come from the theme of energy (such as kinetic, potential, mechanical, electrical, chemical, light, radiant, nuclear, and heat energy) and a need for its conservation. Projects pertain the themes of hydropower, the Ocean Thermal Energy Conversion, zero-energy house, a windmill, presenting an atom as a company, global warming, and solar cooking.

REFERENCES

Business Dictionary.com. (2012). Retrieved May 25, 2012, from http://www.businessdictionary.com/definition/British-thermal-unit-Btu.html

Drummey, M. (2001). The paper bale house. *Ski Mag.com.* Retrieved May 26, 2012, from http://www.skinet.com/ski/detergent/2001/10/the-paper-bale-house

EIA. (2012). *U.S. Energy Information Administration*. Retrieved May 25, 2012, from http://www.eia.gov/electricity/

Hessels, S. (2012). Sustainable cinema: The moving image and the forces of nature. In A. Ursyn (Ed.), *Biologically-Inspired Computing for the Arts: Scientific Data through Graphics* (pp. 90–105). Hershey, PA: IGI Global. doi:10.4018/978-1-4666-0942-6.ch006.

MacAulay, D. (1989). *Mill*. Graphia.

Maynard, P. (2005). *Drawing distinctions: The varieties of graphic expressions*. Cornell University Press.

McEvilley, T. C. (2002). *The shape of ancient thought: Comparative studies in Greek and Indian philosophies*. Allworth Press.

Messer, R. (2012). *Image*. Retrieved May 25, 2012, from http://www.naturalhomeandgarden.com/multimedia/image-gallery.aspx?id=1854

Minimum Solar Box Cooker. (n.d.). Retrieved from http://solarcooking.wikia.com/wiki/Minimum_Solar_Box_Cooker

National Geographic. (n.d.). *Three main types of solar ovens*. Retrieved from http://greenliving.nationalgeographic.com/three-main-types-solar-ovens-2877.html

Recommended Levels of Insulation. (2012). Retrieved June 10, 2012, from http://www.energystar.gov/index.cfm?c=home_sealing.hm_improvement_insulation_table

Solar Cooker. (n.d.). Retrieved from: http://en.wikipedia.org/wiki/Solar_cooker; http://solarcooking.wikia.com/wiki/Solar_Cookers_World_Network_%28Home%29Minimum Solar Box Cooker; Wikia http://solarcooking.wikia.com/wiki/"Minimum"_Solar_Box_Cooker; http://greenliving.nationalgeographic.com/three-main-types-solar-ovens-2877.html

Solar Cookers International: How Solar Cookers Work. (n.d.). Retrieved from http://www.solar-cookers.org/basics/how.html

Solar Cooking. (n.d.). Retrieved from http://solarcooking.wikia.com/wiki/Solar_Cookers_World_Network_%28Home%29

University of Oregon. (2012). *Elementary particles*. Retrieved May 21, 2012, from http://abyss.uoregon.edu/~js/glossary/particle_physics.html

Visualizing Electron Orbitals. (2012). Retrieved May 21, 2012, from http://hyperphysics.phy-astr.gsu.edu/hbase/chemical/eleorb.html

Websters Online. (2012). Retrieved May 27, 2012, from http://www.websters-online-dictionary.org/definitions/perpetual+motion

Chapter 11
Nano World

ABSTRACT

This part of the book provides information and projects for the readers about the omnipresence of nanoscale objects – soft matter, colloids, liquid crystals, carbon nanotubes, nanoshells, and the developments in nanoscale and molecular-scale technologies involving these small structures. Nanotechnology concerns structures measuring between 1 and 100 nanometers and allows manipulating individual atoms and molecules. Since Norio Taniguchi of Tokyo Science University first used the term nanotechnology in 1974, the governments, corporations, and venture capitalists invest every year billions of dollars in nanotechnology and more than a half of advanced technologies incorporate nanotechnology products in different ways. In addition, developments in nanotechnology demand hiring in millions of trained nanotechnology workforce (Nano.gov, 2012).

INTRODUCTION

The developments in nanoscale and molecular-scale technologies let us study the nanoscale objects: liquid crystals, soft matter, nanoshells, and carbon nanotubes. We may learn about structures and actions going in the nanoscale and how can we use nanoparticles and nanotechnology. These technologies make a background for progress in energy conservation in micro and nano scale. Nanotechnology can impact cancer treatment, clinical neuroscience, tissue engineering, drug delivery, and diagnostics.

Nanoparticles can be made "top down" by chopping a bulk material into nanosize bits or "bottom up" by growing molecules like crystals in controlled conditions. Nanoshells, nanoparticles covered with metal, e.g., gold nanoshells are used for biomedical imaging and serve therapeutic applications. Nanoceramic filters allow water purification pushing water through nanotubes or a 10^{-9} m to 10^{-11} m membranes. Themes discussed here comprise early nano applications and technologies, soft matter, nanoscale metric measures, tools for examining nanostructures, graphene, nanofabrication, size dependent properties of nanoparticles, colloids, nanoshells, viruses, liquid crystals, fullerenes: carbon nanotubes and buckyballs, structures in a human cell, and visualization of biological data: DNA.

DOI: 10.4018/978-1-4666-4627-8.ch011

EARLY NANO APPLICATIONS AND TECHNOLOGIES

Nano applications had preceded nano technologies. Before the time when nanoparticles became the object of thorough investigation people were not fully aware of the omnipresence of nano structures functioning as the nanoscale building blocks in nature and as our makeup. The prehistoric, ancient, and medieval people did not know about the nanoscale domain because they could not see it; however, they did make use of its potential in the past by applying specific techniques without knowing why their action were effective. People applied molds on wounds without knowledge about the antibiotic properties of penicillin, and used cultured molds to produce cheese, bread, or soy sauce. Long before the advent of nanotechnology, the Upper Paleolithic inhabitants of the Altamira caves in Spain, 13,000 B.C. created cave drawings and polychrome rock paintings of wild mammals and human hands using painting materials: charcoal and pigments. Charcoal contains nano material graphene, a two-dimensional allotrope of carbon. Pigments are micro- and nano-powders; by mixing with water they can be converted in colloidal or clay form. Many pigments change the color of reflected or transmitted light because they selectively absorb certain wavelengths of light (Cave of Altamira and Paleolithic Cave Art of Northern Spain, 2012; Orfescu, 2012).

2,000 years ago Romans used the gold and silver nanoparticles in their artwork not knowing they are so minuscule. Dated from fourth century AD base of the Lycurgus cup (now in the British Museum, London) changes color from green (when illuminated from outside) to red (when illuminated from within) because it contains nanoparticles of gold and silver; followers couldn't recreate this effect (Cook, 2005).

Medieval artists from the 500–1450 period used to add nanoparticles of gold to create stained glass windows; they produced colors from yellow-orange (with silver nanoparticles) to ruby red (with gold nanoparticles). The Renaissance (15th-16th centuries) Italian pottery makers from Deruta (2012), Umbria produced iridescent or metallic glazes using copper and silver particles: light bounces off the particles' surface at different wavelengths giving metallic or iridescent effect. Irish stain glass designers and the Damascene masters of sword making also applied nanoparticles materials (PennState modules, 2009, Goodsell, 2006).

Thomas Wedgewood and Sir Humphry Davy used silver nitrate and chloride to produce impermanent images. Photographic film is covered with gelatin containing silver halides and a base of transparent cellulose acetate. Light decomposes the silver halides producing nanoparticles of silver – the pixels of the photographic image. In 1827 Joseph Niépce used material that hardened when exposed to light. Louis Daguerre (1839) continued this work after Niépce died. Michael Faraday prepared first metallic (gold) colloids in 1857. As described below, colloidal systems have now numerous applications. Gustav Mie's developed in 1908 a theory about why light scatters from particles more efficiently at short wavelengths. Thus scientists learned why the size of particles would determine the visible colors. For example, air particles scatter blue light more efficiently than red light (blue light has a shorter wavelength than red light), and so the sky is blue.

In 1960, Charles Plank and Edward Rosinski developed a process to use zeolites to speed up chemical reactions when breaking down petroleum into gasoline. A zeolite is either natural or synthetic porous material that works as a sieve. In order to use fossil fuels more efficiently, researchers are now working on discovering or inventing zeolytes and designing zeolite catalysts at the nanoscale. By adjusting the size of the zeolite pores on the nanoscale, they can control the size and shape of molecules that can enter. In the case of gasoline production, this technique could produce more and cleaner gasoline and provide new ways to generate energy (Cook, 2005). Ion exchange systems use zeolite-packed columns to replace unwanted ions (Rahmani & Mahvi, 2006). In food industry, unwanted chemical reactions going in cooking oil can be inhibited by adding ceramic-zeolite nanoscale beads (PennState modules, 2009).

However, there is growing concern about nanotoxicology and ecotoxicology, the study of toxicity of nanomaterials that intended to determine a threat to the humans and environment. Developments in nanotechnology allow understanding both the benign and toxic effects of molds, such as some fungi that colonize crops and contaminate them with mycotoxins in the field or after harvest (Turner, Subrahmanyam, & Piletsky, 2009).

SOFT MATTER

The soft condensed matter is in a state neither liquid nor crystalline. Liquid crystals, biological tissues: cells, and a cytoplasm, biological membranes, microfilaments and filamentous networks, e.g., a cytoskeleton present in all cells, molecular mono-layers, polymers and biopolymers (such as DNA or filaments in neuronal or muscle fibers), and also liquid crystals are called soft matter. We all can be called soft matter, as well. When we look at things in the nano scale we can credit a great amount of everyday things as soft matter including food, soap, ink, paint, cosmetics, putty, and gels. Research community has studied nanoparticles for several decades. Scientists and practitioners explore complex soft matter in order to understand general principles that drive behavior and properties of the nanoscale structures. They develop measuring tools, new chemical structures and new technologies, and examine processes going at the nanoscale. A 2010 National Academies roundtable explored advances in static, dynamic, experimental, computational, and theoretical characterization of small particles from the nano- to the micro-scale, and research tools developed in environmental science, mate-

rial, chemical sciences, biological science, and engineering (Challenges, 2012).

Natural and engineered small particles range from one nanometer to tens of microns. In atmosphere, where there is from a few to a few thousand of small particles/cm^3, they impact both warming and cooling of the climate. In Earth subsurface, they impact soil and water quality. Small particles have an effect on catalysis and reaction engineering, material design, and synthesis. Isotopic signature (with krypton or xenon isotopes) of some nanodiamonds indicate they were formed outside the solar system, whether in supernova or in interstellar medium. The noble gas atoms such as neon can also be seen in a monolayer of carbon when it is trapped inside C60 cages that were formed at the same time as the nanodiamonds (Challenges, 2012: Rhonda Stroud).

Figure 1, "All You Can See" calls attention to the world of little and big creatures.

In the sky, we see what we like:
Lines of clouds with familiar shapes.
On the ground, furrows get to be animated
At the rate of our driving.

THE NANOSCALE WORLD: METRIC MEASURES

The developments in nanoscale and molecular-scale technologies allow researching the nanoscale objects: liquid crystals, soft matter, nanoshells, and carbon nanotubes. In order to discuss soft matter and liquid crystals we need to discuss the metric measurements and some metric prefixes (prefixes for other multiples, such as 10^4, 10^5, 10^{-4}, and 10^{-5}), as well as metric conversions.

- A macro-scale comprises visible objects with sizes of a millimeter or more (1 millimeter, 1 mm = 1/1,000 meter – 1×10^{-3} m) For example, a human hair is about 10^{-4} m wide (about 100,000 nanometers wide).

Figure 1. Anna Ursyn, All You Can See (© 2007, A. Ursyn. Used with permission)

- A micro-scale relates to objects with sizes about a micrometer to about 1/10 of a millimeter (1 micrometer, 1 μm = 1/1,000,000, one millionth of a meter – 1x10^{-6} m) For example, red blood cells may have a size of several μm; bacteria may be about 1 μm large.

- A nano-scale encompasses a range of subjects from about a nanometer to about 1/10 of micrometer (1 nanometer, 1 nm = 1/1,000,000,000, one billionth of meter – 1x10^{-9} m). For example, a virus is about 10^{-7} m; a DNA is about 10^{-8} m; molecular structures are about 10^{-9} m;

- A pico-scale is a size range of single atoms, both found in nature (and represented in the periodic table) and atoms man-made in accelerators for nuclear technology (1 ångström or angstrom (symbol Å) = 1 x 10^{-10} meters). For example, a helium atom has a diameter of about 0.1 nm.

One nano is 10^{-9} meter; that means one-billionth of a meter. That means the size of a nanometer is to the size of a meter like a marble compared to the size of Earth. Many familiar objects are millions of nanometers big: a human nail on a little finger is about ten million nanometers across and a human hair is about 80,000 nanometers wide. A dollar bill is 100,000 nanometers thick. A small reptile gecko can cling upside down to the pane of glass because it has millions of microhairs on its toes; each hair is split into hundreds of tips 200 nanometers wide, which form nanohairs on its microhairs). The van der Waals force causes intermolecular attraction and pulls glass and hair tips together. Scientists in several institutions fabricate gecko-inspired lamellar and nanofibrillar structures to make surfaces adhere (Lee, Bush, Maboudian, & Fearing, 2009; Sitti, & Fearing, 2003).

Figure 2, "Encounter" is an irrational combination of images obtained from the scanning microscope with computer graphics. The American modernist painter Stuart Davis (1982-1964), French painter and printmaker Jean-Baptiste-Camille Corot (1796-1875), and the influential French writer Émile François Zola (1840-1902)

Figure 2. Anna Ursyn, Encounter (© 2010, A. Ursyn. Used with permission)

stated independently that art is nature seen through the artist's temperament. We enter the scaled world ready for encounters with unknown. Sometimes, our readiness to fantasize triggers our imagination to find what we do not see.

TOOLS FOR EXAMINING NANOSTRUCTURES

Developments in technology, especially advances in microscopy and spectroscopy (recording how matter interacts with or emits electromagnetic radiation) provide opportunities for discoveries in a nano scale, which in turn cause that new epistemologies evolve allowing us to see the world in a changed way. Tools are needed to determine the size, shape, and physical structure, to know the composition of chemical elements and the physical and chemical properties. Generally, tools are based on electron beams; they produce images

using electrons, inform about composition using x-ray photons, or they are the scanning probe tools. Beams of electrons can be transmitted through the specimen (which is used in transmission electron microscopy, TEM or field emission transmission electron microscopy, or FE-TEM in case of quantum mechanical tunneling), bounced back (backscattered, as used in scanning electron microscopy, SEM (the 1986 Nobel Prize in Physics for Gerd Binnig and Heinrich Rohrer), or FE-SEM in case of quantum mechanical tunneling), or knocked back from an atom and come as the secondary electrons.

Scientists are working on imaging (with the use of computed tomography such as soft x-ray tomography, and also cryogenic light microscopy) and visualization of small particles in cells in order to know how nanoparticles interact, undergo changes, and deliver drugs into the intended inside targets or only to a cell membrane (Challenges, 2012: Gerry McDermott). Researchers work on obtaining temporal resolution to monitor ongoing processes. Tools that enable obtaining atomic resolution images that clearly delineate the atoms in polymer-capped platinum and palladium nanoparticles include neutron- and x-ray-based microscopy and analytic electron microscopy (Challenges, 2012: Doug Ray). They reveal atomic structure and speciation of elements. It is possible to count atoms, see lattices and clusters, to correlate particle size with atom count in various types of particle morphologies, and thus understand structural defects and disorders. Combined data from microscopy and spectroscopy provide information how bond distances change with temperature: they contract as temperature rises when particle diameter riches sizes as small as 1 nanometer (Challenges, 2012: Ralph Nuzzo). Nanoscale-sized catalysts and catalytic technologies are important in refineries, automobile catalytic converters, and in developing catalytic fuel cells for powering laptops. Catalyst designers work on gold nanoparticles on a titanium dioxide that catalyze oxidation of (CO) carbon monoxide. They become able to control the features of catalysts by design (Challenges, 2012: Abhaya Datye). Figure 3, "Nano" is a student work.

Figure 3. Wes Thorpe, Nano. (© 2011, W. Thorpe. Used with permission)

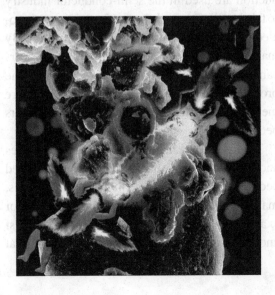

GRAPHENE

Graphene is a one atom thick membrane, a sheet of carbon atoms arranged in tightly bound hexagons. Graphene is almost unbreakable, tougher than a diamond, and stretchable like a rubber (Palmer, 2012). Graphene was discovered in 2004 by two University of Manchester scientists; a Russian-Dutch scientist Andre Geim and a Russian-British scientist Konstantin Novoselov shared the 2010 Nobel Prize for physics for studying behavior of this one atom thick sheet of carbon (Nobleprize, 2010). According to Geim & Novoselov (2007), graphene is a flat monolayer of carbon atoms tightly packed into a two-dimensional (2D) honeycomb lattice, and is a basic building block for graphitic materials of all other dimensionalities. It can be wrapped up into 0D fullerenes, rolled into 1D nanotubes, or stacked into 3D graphite. Geim and Novoselov were praised for playfulness of their approach that involved producing flakes of graphene using sticky tape: they extracted the material from a piece of graphite that can be found in ordinary pencils using adhesive tape, and repeating the tape-trick until they got miniscule flakes of graphene. Three million sheets of graphene loosely held together on top of each other produce 1mm of graphite. Scientists are able to fabricate molecule-scale structures and devices in graphene with atomic precision (Russo & Golovchenko, 2012). Gardener & Golovchenko (2012) demonstrate that the ice-assisted e-beam lithography can be used to pattern very thin materials deposited on substrate surfaces. The procedure can be performed *in situ* in a modified scanning electron microscope. A low energy focused electron beam can locally pattern graphene coated with a thin ice layer. Moreover, photons, x-rays generated by atoms may also come back (which is used in X-ray spectroscopy). The scanning probe tools use the nanoscale probe (a small, sharp tip on the end of a lever that is dragged across a nanoscale object) for the scanning probe microscopy. Nanoscale beams or probes interact with a nano material generating signals that can be processed by a computer into pictures. Examples of such tools are the atomic force microscope AFM that measures forces between atoms; and scanning tunneling microscope STM that uses quantum mechanical tunneling between atoms of the probe and atoms on the scanned surface. The nano-scale tips on scanning probe microscopes (SPMs) allow us to even "see" atoms (PennState modules, 2009). Atoms on the probed surface may be arranged by an STM into a quantum corral, which is about 14 nm in diameter. Christopher Lutz, Donald Eigler, and Michael Crommie demonstrated for the first time the quantum corral in 1993 by using an elliptical ring of iron atoms on a copper surface (Ball, 2009). The STM tunneling current can be turned by a computer into a false color STM image of the quantum corral (PennState modules, 2009).

NANOFABRICATION: MAKING NANOSCALE STRUCTURES

Nanoparticles can be made "top down" by chopping a bulk material into nanosize bits or "bottom up" by growing molecules like crystals in controlled conditions. These approaches can be combined into a hybrid nanofabrication. Nanoscale structures may include nano particles such as macromolecules, beads, tubes, wires; planar structures built, for example by layers; and hybrid mixtures of particles and planar structures.

With a top-down approach, material is removed or added in layers using mechanical or chemical means, such as lithography. Thus, the top-down approach may involve several basic steps such as deposition (the additive process causing the film growth), material modification (designing chemical, physical, and electrical properties of the nano material), etching (the subtractive process – material removal), and lithography, externally imposed pattern transfer: writing where material should be added or removed. Usually, computer

programming provides the content for transfer. In some cases there is inherent pattern, such as the self-assembling of an antigen and antibody due to shape, size, and chemical bonding. These processes allow forming the layers (films) into nano structures. Lithography of many kinds may include photolithography, electron beam lithography, ion beam lithography, dip pen lithography, embossing lithography, stamp lithography, molding lithography, and self-assembly lithography (PennState modules, 2009).

With the bottom-up approach, which can often be seen in nature, small components are building blocks for a structure. Nano structures are built from atoms, molecules, particles, their combinations, and layers. They grow molecule-by molecule and have often the ability to self-assemble spontaneously in response to a trigger (Cook, 2005). The bottom-up approach involves chemical or physical self-assembly, catalyzed nano-wire (nanotube, about 1.3 nm in diameter) growth, colloidal characterization with the use of optical means, scanning probes, and electron microscopy (NSF NACK Center, 2012). For example, with a bottom-up nanofabrication sequence a nanoparticles may be synthesized made functional, linked with antibodies, or attached to the antigen (PennState modules, 2009).

Both methods of the nanoscale structures production are used in the semi-conductor industry to fabricate integrated electronic circuitry. Microelectronics is changing into nanoelectronics. By making the nanoscale sized transistors engineers can put millions of transistors per square inch. The provide more processing per square inch, more memory, and faster communication, so computers become faster.

Knowledge about how can we use nanoparticles and nanotechnology inspires technology-oriented people to design biologically inspired models, materials, applications, tools, and devices. For example, graphene is considered the thinnest and the strongest material that can sustain great densities of current, has great thermal conductivity, stiffness, is impermeable to gases, and allows investigation of relativistic quantum phenomena in laboratory experiments (Geim, 2009). Free-standing monolayer graphene membranes, and also monolayers of graphene on silicon dioxide, are considered one of the strongest materials ever measured (Grantab, Shenoy, & Ruoff, 2010). Also, thermal conductivity of suspended graphene exceeds that of diamond and graphite, so this feature of graphene can be useful in nanoelectronics. Graphene can carry electric charges far faster than currently used materials. Graphene has been used as 'electrodes' for solar cells but it wasn't used as semiconductor applications because it is a poor semiconductor and has been difficult to add metal contacts to shuttle electric charges into and out of it. In 2009, a solution has been found in the process of baking the wafers of crystalline silicon carbide (Palmer, 2012).

Nanoceramic filters allow water purification pushing water through nanotubes or the 10^{-9} m to 10^{-11} m membranes. Carbon nanotubes are distributed on small cement grain to achieve superior strength concrete for construction. A single silicon wafer, a macroporous silicon film has been produced as an anode material for lithium ion batteries (Thakur, Pernites, Nitta Isaacson, Sinsabaugh, Wong, & Biswal, 2012). Integrated scientific and educational program at the Institute for Complex Adaptive Matter (ICAM-I2CAM, 2012) includes exploratory workshops, symposia, fellowships, and research and educational networks. In a research on molecular and cellular biology Selvin (2012) and his group developed a method for recording the walking motion at a distance of 74 nm for the biggest motor (myosin V), and 16 nm for the smallest motor (kinesin), which is 30 times smaller than the diffraction limit of light. DeWitt, Chang, Combs, & Yildiz (2012) examined, with a 3 nm precision, a dynein motor that transports a multitude of cargos along the microtubule in the cell cytoplasm. Dynein takes part in many cellular

Figure 4. Kati Stanford, Nano (© 2009, K. Stanford. Used with permission)

processes including organelle transport and cell division. The dynein motor converts chemical energy of the ATP hydrolysis to mechanical work (ATP – adenosine triphospate transports energy within cells for metabolic processes). By recording single molecule fluorescence, Yildiz, Forkey, McKinney, Ha, Goldman, & Selvin (2003) could see steps sizes of each head of the myosin V that moves on a protein actin filament in a cell. Figure 4, "Nano" is a student work.

SIZE DEPENDENT PROPERTIES OF NANOPARTICLES

Familiar materials develop odd properties when they're nanosize because their atomic structure is determined differently at this level. Materials at the nanoscale level display quantum mechanics effects, distinct from those of materials controlled by laws of classical physics. At the nanoscale level only certain energy levels are allowed, and the levels allowed depend on the size of a particle; this creates difference in energy ΔE between a particle and its environment (ΔE becomes bigger when particles are smaller). As the size of a particle decides on the value of ΔE, the same light wavelength would produce different colors of particles of silver and gold: silver spheres of a size about 40 nm look blue; gold spheres ~80 nm look light green; gold spheres ~120 nm look yellow; gold spheres ~50 nm look deep green; gold spheres ~100 nm look orange; and silver spheres ~100 nm look green deep red. In the natural settings, nanostructures at the butterfly wings scatter and diffract light giving us the perception of different colors. When seen at different magnifications, butterfly wing scales look different: a wing that is dark blue when looked at without magnification becomes yellow at 220x magnification, purple at 5000x magnification, and green at 20000x magnification (PennState modules, 2009; Cook, 2005).

Electrons can tunnel through a barrier formed by potential at semiconductor junctions. Leo Esaki and Ivar Giaver were awarded the 1973 Nobel Prize for the 1958 discovery of the tunneling phenomenon. Visible light has a wavelength λ between 400 and 750 nanometers. It is larger than the radii R of the nanostructures. Specific wave properties of the soft matter are caused by the size of nanostructures that is smaller than the wavelength λ of visible light, so light interacts with nanostructures (scatters and diffracts) differently.

Some properties of nano-scale objects are unique, such as a small size as compared to biological structures and macromolecules, and large surface to volume ratio resulting from the small size and the placing of particles on the surface of nano particles. Some properties of nanoparticles,

for example, the melting temperature of gold, depend on the surface to volume ratio. The smaller is a nano particle the lower is its melting temperature because there is higher percentage of (not bound) atoms on the surface. If we succeed to cut familiar materials and reduce them to a nanoscale size they would develop odd properties. For example, aluminum foil, which would normally behave like aluminum, would explode when cut in strips 20 to 30 nanometers thick. Catalysis – the acceleration of chemical processes goes faster as the particles become smaller, the ratio of the surface area to the volume of the particles increases, and nanoparticle catalysts become more reactive.

Metal nanoparticles become easily ionized and, when inserted into textiles, metal ions kill bacteria present there and thus make clothing odor-free and odor-resistant. When inside of a bacteria, silver ions prevent transport across the cell wall, metabolism, respiration, RNA replication, and thus reproduction of the bacteria. Soft materials have many other chemical and mechanical characteristics that are useful in technology, such as quantum size effects, responsiveness to small electrical fields and to chemical or thermal actions, and flexibility, so they are used in a fast growing number of applications (for example, in flat panel LCD TVs) (PennState modules, 2009; Cook, 2005).

Nanoparticle fluids called ferrofluids can be controlled through the application of a magnetic field. They form a colloid suspension in a liquid of the 10 nm magnetic nanoparticles coated with surfactant to prevent aggregation (5% magnetic nanoparticles, 10% surfactant, and 85% carrier fluid by volume). They are used to attenuate vibration in audio loudspeakers, eliminate impurities in high-speed computer disk drives, and as liquid gaskets in rotating shaft seals.

As stated by Mort Lippman (Challenges, 2012), nano particles, which range from less than 2.5 microns to 10 microns in diameter, impact organism's health and viability of living systems. Particles penetrate lungs and the blood stream affecting liver, brain, heart, and other tissues. According to Michael Hochella (Challenges, 2012), biotech industry, energy, electronics, and aerospace industries produce less than 1 teragrams/year nanomaterials worth many hundreds of billions of dollars. The Earth produces even more nanoparticles, about 100 teragrams/year. They enter the environment in many ways. For example, iron oxide nanoparticles, which are deposited by glaciers into rivers and then oceans, serve ocean-dwelling phytoplankton in photosynthesis, forming a CO_2 sink in the oceans. Natural nanoparticles come from dust in the atmosphere, sea spray, hydrothermal events in the deep ocean that can produce heat up to 350° C, melting icebergs, rivers, and volcanoes. Manufactured or synthetic nanoparticles show the same size-dependent properties as the natural ones, in terms of their physical, chemical, electrical, and magnetic properties.

A contaminated mining site in Western Montana the size of Germany discharges titanium oxide and lead nanoparticles into the rivers. Other toxic materials such as copper, zinc, arsenic, and cad-

mium also move in the river system and interact with biological systems. Images obtained with the mass spectroscopy and transmission electron microscopy revealed (under 1.8 million-fold magnification) that the nanoparticles were covered with metals. For example, nanoparticles of the iron mineral goethite carry arsenic hundreds of kilometers from the source into drinking water; those of other iron oxide mineral carry copper, zinc, and arsenic, and the titanium dioxide mineral carry lead. Sludge from wastewater treatment plants that is applied to farm fields often contains manufactured silver particles.

Figure 5, "Nano" pictures a scene pictured an interstate related traffic, with simplified images of heavy pickup trucks, tractor-trailers, and eighteen-wheelers. The presence of geometric shapes and rhythms may refer to the loads on the trucks: there may be pipes, mobile houses, cones formed by piles of sugar beets, bales of hay, big boxes, and more articles and merchandises carried on the tracks.

The geometric shapes can be also discerned on the fields, horizontal and oblique shapes cre-

Figure 5. Anna Ursyn, Nano. (© 2013, A. Ursyn. Used with permission)

ated by the roads and vertical rhythms created by the poles of power lines. It depicts the interstate highway from a driver's perspective with a network of highway crossings and exits. For many of us it may look, especially when viewed from overhead, like spaghetti in a bowl, so it's known as a spaghetti junction or a spaghetti bowl.

The trucks may also represent liquid crystal rods. Road signs showing why a particular track is turning on a certain exit may signify changeable chemical and mechanical characteristics of the soft matter. Various kinds of trucks, looking similar, yet performing various tasks and services may be seen similar to disparate kinds of liquid crystals. Loads carried on tracks may have an alignment in the same direction, in layers or planes, or in columns. They may symbolize the smectic, nematic, and cholesteric arrangement of the liquid crystal rods. When thinking about the smectic, nematic, and cholesteric arrangement of the liquid crystal rods, the work of Ursus Wehrli (2006) might come to mind. It could be interesting to look at his art, photography and think about concepts under discussion.

COLLOIDS

A great part of matter has colloidal properties. We can see it by examining it in the nanoscale.

Colloidal systems are objects of intensive research. In colloids at least a part of a system has a dimension of one micrometer or less. They may form a colloidal suspension of:

- A solid in liquid – as in an Indian ink
- Liquid in liquid, an emulsion of liquid in liquid as in mayonnaise
- Gas in liquid, foam of gas in liquid – as in beer or soap foam.
- There could be also gas in solid, like in a bath sponge or ice cream.

According to Steven Schwartz (Challenges, 2012) aerosols are particles suspended in the air, more often they are mixtures of particles. Particles form clusters. They come from organic vapors from vegetation, dust, industrial sulfur dioxide emissions, biomass burning, ocean sea salt, and other sources. Aerosols scatter light producing urban haze and photochemical smog; they reflect sunlight so less sunlight reaches Earth's surface; they also act as seed particles for the formation of cloud droplets. Without aerosols there would be no clouds, and the Earth's climate would be very different. Aerosols thus change the global energy balance and climate. Research on aerosols pertains to theoretical nanoscience, air pollution, potential bioterrorism, climate change, and diesel engines related pollution with exhaust.

Knowledge of particle shape, size, and size distribution is critical for creating useful materials and understanding how they will behave from an environment health, safety, and stewardship perspective. It may be conducive in researching the role of aerosols in climate by modeling the particle formation in polluted atmosphere, where newly formatted particles may act as the cloud condensation nuclei (Challenges, 2012: Lee Silverman). The strong impact of amines (organic compounds derived from ammonia) on atmospheric aerosol formation was also detected (Challenges, 2012: James Smith).

There are many applications of colloidal systems. They include fabrication of photonic crystals, which are natural (for example, a gemstone opal) or artificial optical nanostructures that affect the propagation of electromagnetic waves. There are also numerous new applications such as nanoantennas, plasmonic sensors, and nanocircuits. Plasmonics is a field of research on light–metal interaction: for example, surface plasmons are oscillations of electrons on a metal surface excited by electromagnetic radiation. Potential applications of plasmonic nanostructures include miniature optical devices, sensors, chemical imaging, nanosphere, colloidal, and soft lithography, and also photonic circuits. They can be applied to medical diagnostics, therapeutics, and nanofabrication methods (Stewart, Anderton, Thompson, Maria, Gray, Rogers, & Nuzzo, 2008). Scientists has already created a biosensor made from plasmonic nanohole arrays, to detect molecular binding on the membrane surface, such as of viruses like Ebola (Yanik, Huang, Kamohara, Artar, Geisbert, Connor, & Altug, 2010). Virus, a package having a diameter 20 to 300 nm and containing proteins, genetic material, and often lipids, may reorganize itself after entering a living cell, whether a mosquito cell or a human cell, where it may mutate, replicate, and spread into new cells. Trivedi, Klevets, Senyuk, Lee, & Smalyukh (2012) work on achieving sparse colloidal assemblies that can be controlled at will due to tunable interparticle separations. As claimed by Smalyukh (2011), some biological macromolecules can control their own assembly into elegant hierarchical structures. Synthetic supramolecules are catching up fast, promising new advances for optical and biomedical materials. According to Senyuk & Smalyukh (2012), self-assembly of metal and dielectric nanoparticles with dissimilar shapes and sizes opens new possibilities for self-assembly based fabrication of structured condensed matter composites with predesigned properties. As stated by González, Arbiol, & Puntes (2011), it is possible to control the shape of inorganic nanocrystals by applying reaction and diffusion processes at room temperature. This process opens up a synthetic route for the production of polymetallic hollow nanoparticles with very different morphology and composition.

Scientists work on designing the packaging of small particles as dry fine powders. Applications for packaging include metallurgy, agricultural, pharmaceutical and food products, fertilizers, detergents, catalysts, and other applications (Challenges, 2012: James Litster). Toward the development of eco-responsible nanotechnology, there is a need to study bioavailability and bioaccumulation of nanomaterials, their possible toxicity, mechanisms of action in organisms, and interaction with bacteria and other microorganisms. Studies are conducted, to design simulations and models of nanomaterial interaction with biological structures, especially the cell membrane lipids and the lung surfactant lipids. Other groups examine the sea salt 100-nanometer to 100-micron aerosol droplets, their effect on atmosphere, and interactions with biological structures. Sea salt particles coated with organic material in smog can increase ozone levels (Challenges, 2012: Douglas Tobias).

Nanoscale devices are man-made constructs made with carbon, silicon, and other materials that have the capability to monitor the biological phenomena and relay information to the medical care provider.

Devices are one hundred to ten thousand times smaller than human cells, similar in size to large biological molecules such as enzymes and receptors. As an example, hemoglobin, the molecule that carries oxygen in red blood cells, is approximately 5 nanometers in diameter. Nanoscale devices smaller than 50 nanometers can easily enter most cells, while those smaller than 20 nanometers can move out of blood vessels as they circulate through the body. Scientists can fabricate and control the self-assembly of nanoscale biomolecules on surfaces and screen the protein–DNA binding events at the single-molecule level (Palma et al., 2011). Zhang & Zhang (2010) developed the lipid–polymer hybrid nanoparticle, with a lipid shell surrounding the polymeric core and a hydrophilic polymer layer outside the lipid shell, as a platform and the delivery vehicle of therapeutic and imaging agents. Nanoscale devices can interact with biomolecules on both the surface and inside cells. They can detect disease and deliver treatment. See Table 1 for an exercise involving nanoscale devices.

Table 1. Colloids

Visual Response: Colloids
Imagine a scene with an interstate traffic and the truck drivers. Picture truck drivers when they rest at the inn usually visited by truckers; show various actions of truckers residing at the inn or at the adjacent area. This may be presented as a row of windows, with the drivers visible there while they are performing different actions: Eating mayonnaise (liquid in liquid), Eating ice cream (gas in solid), Drinking beer (gas in liquid), Writing checks with ink (solid in liquid) to pay for their mayonnaise, and then Taking a bath with a sponge (gas in solid) and Making soap bubbles (gas in liquid). Place two drivers who blow soap bubbles in front of the hotel. Soap bubbles, which are made from liquid crystals, change colors when light is reflected through the bubble walls. First, a wall of a small bubble is a few nanometers thick and reflects the full spectrum of colors in a rainbow. However, part of light reflects from the outer surface of a bubble wall, and part is reflected from its inner surface that is a few nanometers further. When the two waves interfere and reinforce each other, we see color that is more intense when the waves reinforce each other. When the bubble wall gets thinner, a distance between wall surfaces becomes smaller, the reflected waves of light start to cancel each other out, and the bubble loses its color (Bubbles, 2011).

NANOSHELLS

A nanoshell consists of a dielectric core covered by a thin metallic (usually gold) shell. Light interacts with nanoparticles; hence nanoshells possess optical and chemical properties involving quantum plasma oscillation where the electrons simultaneously oscillate with respect to all the ions (plasmon hybridization). They are often used for biomedical imaging, fluorescence enhancement of weak molecular emitters, some kinds of surface enhanced spectroscopy, and therapeutic applications. Nanoshells can selectively link to cancer cells, delivering therapeutic treatment directly to kill tumor cells and not harm neighboring healthy cells. Because of their size, nanoshells will preferentially concentrate in cancer lesion sites. This phenomenon is called enhanced permeation retention. Scientists can add to the shells the conjugates to the antigens expressed on the cancer cells to link the nanoshells to the tumor and not to neighboring healthy cells. They can also supply external energy to these cells, just creating an intense heat that selectively kills the tumor cells (National Cancer Institute, 2012). For example, gold nanoshells act as a Trojan horse when they enter a tumor cell in a macrophage (a cell in a body tissue or a white blood cell that can engulf bacteria or particles) and cause a photo-induced tumor cell death. Monocytes (large white blood cells which can engulf and absorb bacteria or harmful particles) containing therapeutic nanoparticles could also serve as Trojan horses for nanoparticle transport into tumor regions that are inaccessible to cancer therapies. Destruction of hypoxic regions within tumors may prevent malignant progression (Choi, Stanton-Maxey, Stanley, Levin, Bardhan, Akin, Badve, Sturgis, Robinson, Bashir, Halas, & Clare, 2007). Coated gold nanoparticles interact with molecules of the hormones present in pregnancy. This hormone-particle interaction is used for production of the

pregnancy tests. Nanoparticles can be designed so they attach to the cell walls or exclusively to cancer cells. They can carry drug molecules, especially anti-cancer drugs to cancerous cells (PennState modules, 2009).

Nanowires: Nano sized sensing wires are laid down across a microfluidic channel. They have properties of selectivity and specificity; they pick up the molecular signatures of particles and relay this information through a connection of electrodes to the outside world. They can detect the presence of altered genes associated with cancer and may help researchers pinpoint the exact location of those changes (National Cancer Institute, 2012).

Cantilevers: Flexible beams built with the use of semiconductor lithographic techniques to provide rapid and sensitive detection of cancer-related molecules. They can be coated with molecules capable of binding specific substrate-DNA compounds complementary to a specific gene sequence, for example. The micron-sized devices comprising many nanometer-sized cantilevers can detect single molecules of DNA or protein. As cancer cells secrete their molecular products, the antibodies coated on the cantilever fingers selectively bind to these secreted proteins. These antibodies have been designed to pick up one or more different, specific molecular expressions from a cancer cell. The physical properties of the cantilevers change as a result of the binding event. Researchers can read this change in real time and provide not only information about the presence and the absence but also the concentration of different molecular expressions. Nanoscale cantilevers, constructed as part of a larger diagnostic device, can provide rapid and sensitive detection of cancer-related molecules (National Cancer Institute, 2012).

Drug Delivery: The majority of diagnostic and therapeutic techniques involving fullerenes and engineered viruses are performed only in the lab so far on a test-tube scale with the use of laboratory animals, not in humans, but they will possibly lead to a cure for cancer in the future. Some efforts to use nanotechnology in medicine have moved from the realm of research papers to the pre-clinical or clinical testing. For example, the oncologists at the Uppsala University Hospital, a European Centre of Excellence in Neuroendocrine Tumours are not permitted yet to treat patients with neuroendocrine tumors, the type of cancer that Steve Jobs had. Adenovirus serotype 5 is a common virus but it eats cancer with only mild, flu-like side effects in humans. It originates from humans, occurring naturally in the adenoids; it is cheap to produce.

The harmful side effects of chemotherapy result from drug delivery methods that don't accurately pinpoint their intended target cells. Ionizing radiation may increase injury to healthy tissues; the most toxic for cells are the DNA double-strand breaks. Researchers at Harvard and MIT have been able to attach RNA strands (about 10 nm in diameter) to nanoparticles and fill the nanoparticles with a chemotherapy drug (RSC, 2006; Farokhzad, 2006). These RNA strands are attracted to cancer cells. When the nanoparticle encounters a cancer cell it adheres to it and releases the drug into the cancer cell.

This directed method of drug delivery has great potential for treating cancer patients while producing less side harmful affects than those produced by conventional chemotherapy. The nanoparticle carrying the a tumor-killing agent tends to accumulate in cancer tumors but does not appear to accumulate in other regions of the body, which limits the toxic effects on healthy cells. The challenges are to determine the right size, to hide the nanoparticle from the immune system, and choose a targeting molecule to bind to the tumor. To increase the time nanoparticles can circulate in the blood stream, researchers are coating nanoparticles containing therapeutic drugs with membranes from red blood cells and have shown that these nanoparticles will circulate in a mouse's blood stream for almost two days, instead of the few hours observed for nanoparticles using ethylene glycol molecules (National Cancer Institute, 2012).

A PROJECT: BATTLEFIELD WITH TRANSFORMERS

Below is a project that motivates the reader to create a metaphor comparing the defense of a country to the defense of a living organism. Several examples of battles led in the unexpected ways may provide inspiration for completing the project.

1. **The Trojan War:** A disguised gift as a tactic in fighting is often used as a metaphor of a successful trick or stratagem that causes that a foe can enter a protected space. The ancient Greeks constructed a hollow wooden horse, which enabled them to enter and destroy the city of Troy and end the Trojan War. The only evidence that the Trojan horse really existed is in written and pictorial sources. This metaphor is often applied to describe deceitful computers programs or applications that are really harmful, it is used in political disputes, as well as in describing the strategies in fighting cancer. The earliest picture of the Trojan horse can be seen on a vase ca. 670 BC. A painting by Giovanni Domenico Tiepolo (1727-1804) presents the Procession of the Trojan horse into Troy. (http://www.nationalgallery.org.uk/paintings/giovanni-domenico-tiepolo-the-procession-of-the-trojan-horse-into-troy).

2. **The Battle of the Ice:** Took place at Lake Peipus in 1242 between the Russian Republic of Novgorod and the Teutonic Knights (Roman Catholic Northern Crusaders consisting of Germans and Estonians) is an example showing how knowledge about the terrain allows the right choice of tactic. 20 years old prince

Alexander Nevski and his 1,000 soldiers defeated 5,000 Teutonic crusaders when he made the knights rally at the far side of the lake. Many knights drowned when the thin ice gave way under the weight of their heavy armor. Russian film director Sergei Eisenstein glorified this event in 1938 in his drama 'Alexander Nevski.'

3. **Polish Hussars:** The cavalry undefeated in battle and regarded as the most powerful cavalry formation between 16th and 18th centuries. The hussars were famous for their huge wings, a wooden, then metal frame carrying eagle feathers (and sometimes ostrich or swan feathers). Wings were originally attached to the saddle and later to the backs of the riders covered with plate metal body armor. The possible purpose of the wings was that they made a loud, clattering noise, which made it seem like the cavalry was much larger than in reality. The wings were also made to defend the backs of hussars against swords and lassos, or that they were worn to make their own horses more fearless, insensible to noise made by the wooden noise makers used by the Turkish Ottoman and Crimean Tatars. The other army's horses were afraid of noise caused by the hussars' wings.

4. **Napoleon's Russian Campaign of 1812:** Illustrates a misfortune coming out of a lack of knowledge about the region. In 1869 Charles Joseph Minard created his famous 'Carte Figurative' picturing this epic disaster; later on, Edward Tufte (1983/2001) made this graphics famous by describing it in his writings. Napoleon's army of 422,000 soldiers retreated from Moscow in the cold winter (-36 F on December 6, 1812) and only 4,000 soldiers survived the campaign, with 45% captured, 29% killed in battle, and 24% were those who died of hunger, cold, and sickness (Boykin, 2012).

Refer to Table 2 to expand this metaphor.

Figure 6a and b present students' answer to this theme. On a Figure 6a, America Zamora's solution takes form of the abstract computer generated art. Anna Thompson (Figure 6b) pictured a 'magic bracelet' that enhanced the spirit and energy of the child with leukemia every time she put it on.

In Figure 7, a computer generated graphics presents visualization of a cancer battlefield where healthy cells are pictured as apples, tanks are the scans of cancer cells, and healthy agents (medicated cells) are disguised as horses that can roam freely to stop cancer cells before they start spreading.

VIRUSES

A virus is a few nanometers long; it has a protein shell. Healthy cells are programmed to die when infected by a virus, because this prevents the virus spreading to other parts of the body. But a cancerous cell is immortal, so if a virus infects a cancer cell, it could continue to replicate inside it and cause the cell to die. The progeny viruses then spread to cancer cells nearby and repeat the process. A virus becomes, in effect, a cancer of cancer.

Oncologists are working on using the virus shells to target cancer cells. They remove the viral material from the virus shell and replace it with chemotherapy drugs. When injected into a cancer patient, virus shells would seek out the cancer cells and inject the chemotherapy medication directly into them. This targeted approach could help reduce negative side effects. Viruses can be modified by genetic engineering or chemical modification. It is possible to modify properties of a virus and target the viruses to cancer cells, so the engineered viruses can infect cancer cells. Another example of utilizing viruses in service of therapy is provided by the Bradbury Science Museum (2011). A benign nanoscale virus called

Table 2. A nano tech battlefield

Visual Response: A Battlefield with Transformers

Imagine a biology-inspired scenario with the new types of treatment using nano technology. Create a metaphor comparing the defense of a country to the defense of a living organism. Create a picture, comics, a short animation, or a skit that would offer the basic understanding how we can fight cancer. Your visual response to the theme may inform the viewers how nanotechnology may have an impact on fighting an illness.

The enemy is a cancer cell. These cells multiply. Chemotherapy, drugs, and nanotechnology are your weapons. Cancer cells are aggressors that are difficult to destroy without destroying the environment and its inhabitants. Some techniques involve hiding a medication into a shell of a virus. This way the treatment is aimed at a cancerous sells without affecting the other cells and functions of a body. Therefore, you need to create Transformers that would distract, mislead the enemy, and penetrate into inaccessible areas. Several special teams come to the rescue. For example,

- Picture a RNA molecule as a Transformer who carries molecules of a tumor-killing drug. Nanoparticles can be designed so they attach exclusively to cancer cells. They can carry drug molecules.
- Another Transformer may represent an engineered virus filled with a drug or a radioactive material.
- Translate into a Transformer the application of the gold nanoshells that can enter a tumor cell in a macrophage; nanoshells can selectively link to cancer cells, delivering therapeutic treatment directly to kill tumor cells without harming neighboring healthy cells.
- Show the monocytes containing drugs that can serve for nanoparticle transport into tumor regions that are inaccessible to cancer therapies.

You will need a background scene for a battlefield. Translate into your battlefield scenario the environment as bulk of the healthy cells of different kinds, as well as the cancer cells. Use color-coding to enhance the dramatic, frightening situation. Show an organism composed of healthy cells that make a quiet, free from hardship environment. This idyllic serenity may be dramatically changed when the abnormal cancer cells spread, invade, and consume the healthy ones. Picture is threat to health or even life, and how body's immune system produces more white blood cells to defend body against intruders. The body recognizes cancer cells and their products as alien. Present visually how the help comes from the outside of the body when a chemotherapy and radiation therapy is applied. Chemotherapy agents kill cancer cells but they also harm normal cells. For this reason, you need to show a targeted therapy.

Figure 6. a. America Zamora. A Battle with Cancer (© 2012, A. Zamora. Used with permission); b. Anna Thompson, A Battle with Cancer (© 2012, A. Thompson. Used with permission)

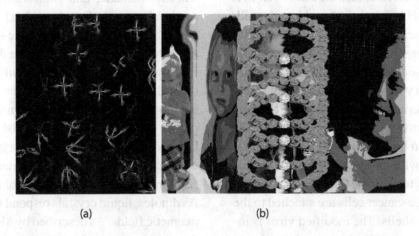

(a)   (b)

Figure 7. Steffanie Sperry, Battle Plan to Fight Cancer. (© 2012, S. Sperry. Used with permission)

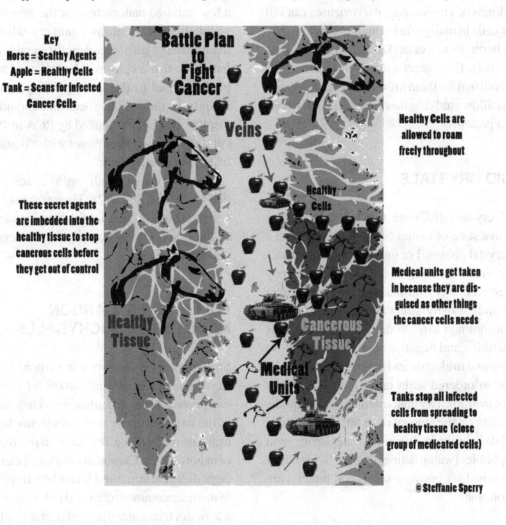

MS2 lives in human gut. It uses protein markers to identify a host cell and then attaches itself to it and injects its RNA genetic material into the cell. (RNA, a ribonucleic acid is one of the nucleic acids that, along with lipids, carbohydrates, and proteins, are essential for life. You can see RNA molecules when you google 'RNA' and click 'images'). The material produces copies of the virus and releases them back into the organism's tissues. MS2 viruses can be broken into pieces and their RNA replaced with chemotherapy medications. Then virus cells reassemble themselves. Proteins designed to target cancer cells are attached to the modified virus' shells. The modified virus is injected into the patient's bloodstream; viruses inject the drugs into the virus cell and then disintegrate. Some kinds of viruses, e.g., parvoviruses can kill cancer cells in malignant brain tumors while they do not harm normal cells (DKFZ, 2012; Allaume et al., 2012). Their genetic material does not need to be modified for them to do so. Computer-based models allow studying how viruses attach to cell surface proteins.

LIQUID CRYSTALS

Liquid crystals (LC) are usually described as being in a state of matter between a liquid and a solid crystal phases. For instance, liquid crystals change shape like a liquid, but its molecules may be oriented in a crystal-like way. LC are organic compounds usually structured as rods oriented along a common axis. As dipoles, liquid crystals have positive and negative charges separated, so they respond to electric and magnetic fields. Rods are not so ordered as in crystalline matter, but also not isotropic (without orientation) as liquids. Depending on the amount of order, liquid crystal materials have the hydrophilic (water loving) and hydrophobic (water-hating) parts. Some (that are intermediate between solids and liquids) are thermotropic.

Thermotropic LCs have common phases: smectic, nematic, and cholesteric (also known as chiral nematic liquid crystals). In the liquid crystal phase, LCs called nematic spontaneously align their molecules in the same direction, with long axes roughly parallel but without positional order. LCs called smectic also have general orientation but in addition are aligned in layers or planes or stacked columns of disks; cholesteric LCs (not identical to its mirror image) is a subclass of nematic phases; they have nematic phases and columnar phases, with stacked columns of disks. As dipoles, liquid crystals respond to electric and magnetic fields. As described by McHale (2008), the distance over which the LC rotates to equal 360° is called the chiral pitch and normally has a few hundred nanometers, or the wavelength of visible light. This allows liquid crystals to selectively reflect light of wavelengths equal to the pitch length, so that a color will be reflected when the pitch is equal to the corresponding wavelength of light in the visible spectrum. Liquid crystal displays (LCD), introduced by RCA in 1971, are composed of two glass plates with a liquid crystal material between them.

Familiarize yourself with Ursus Wehrli's tied up art (TED, 2012). Then you may want to compare highway traffic with heavy loaded trucks to the liquid crystals configurations existing in nature (Table 3).

FULLERENES: CARBON NANOTUBES, BUCKYBALLS

Structures such as inorganic carbon, DNA (deoxyribonucleic acid), and parts of cell membranes contain nanotubes and fullerenes. They are subject of the inquiries made with nanotechnologies, for example molecular electronics, nanolithography, or nanorobotics. Carbon as a chemical element has eight different structural forms (allotropes); three of them are common: diamond (whose atoms make a lattice of triangular pyramids), graphite (a lattice

Table 3. Visualizing liquid crystals

Visual Response: Interstate Traffic
Create a scene of an interstate traffic. Focus on the presence of geometrical shapes and rhythms. Show geometrical forms you can find as the loads on the heavy trucks, such as pipes, mobile houses, cones formed by sugar beets, bales of hay, big boxes, and more forms carried on tracks.
Show the geometrical shapes you can discern on the fields, horizontal shapes created by the roads, and vertical rhythms created by the poles of power lines. Depict an interstate highway from a driver's perspective with a network of highway crossings and exits that look like spaghetti in a bowl when viewed from overhead, also known as a spaghetti junction or a spaghetti bowl.
Now represent liquid crystal rods as trucks. Assign various trucks with loads that may be seen similar to the kinds of liquid crystals. Organize trucks according to a scheme you created. The road signs should show why a particular track is turning on a certain exit, for example, they may have symbols for the smectic, nematic, and cholesteric arrangement of the loads carried on tracks depending on their alignment in the same direction, in layers or planes, or in columns.

of forms with six straight sides and angles), and graphenes. Fullerenes were discovered in 1985; they have atoms bonded in a form of an empty sphere, ellipsoid or a tube. Examples of fullerenes are buckminsterfullerenes (or buckyballs, spherical molecules where carbon atoms are connected in a pattern of hexagons and pentagons) and carbon nanotubes. The most common buckyball contains 60 carbon atoms and is called C_{60}. A nanotech

pioneer Richard E. Smalley (2012) discovered a molecule made of 60 carbon atoms, about 1 nm in diameter, which he called a buckminsterfullerene or a buckyball because it resembled geodesic domes created by Richard Buckminster Fuller. Smalley was awarded the 1996 Nobel Prize in Chemistry, shared with Robert Curl and Harry Kroto. Carbon nanotubes are cylindrical fullerenes, usually a few nanometers wide (tens of thousands times smaller than the diameter of human hair) but they may be micrometers up to centimeters long. Single walled carbon nanotubes are the rolled sheets of graphene. Multi walled nanotubes take form of the parchment or Russian doll model; their production is cheaper.

Smalley envisioned a power grid of nanotubes that would distribute electricity from solar farms. He believed nanoscale missiles would target cancer cells in human body. He spoke this on June 1999 but he died of non-Hodgkin lymphoma on October 2005. The IBM Research–Zurich scientists Gross, Mohn, Moll, Liljeroth, & Meyer (2009) provided images of single carbon molecules and their chemical structure with unprecedented atomic resolution by probing the short-range chemical forces with use of noncontact atomic force microscopy. They could imagine not only the physical shape of a single carbon nanotube but even the bonds to the hydrogen atoms could be seen (Palmer, 2009).

Scientists examine metabolism, excretion, and toxicity of fullerenes C_{60} and their derivatives because they have potential biological applications, such as enzyme inhibition, antiviral activity, DNA cleavage, photodynamic therapy, electron transfer, and other in vitro and in vivo biological effects. Buckyballs can act in a body as antioxidants. Antioxidant is a molecule that can add an electron and neutralize a free radical. Free radical is a molecule or atom with an unpaired electron. Free radicals may react with cells in the body and cause many types of cancer. Buckyballs may connect a drug with a molecule that reacts to changes in pH (pH is a measure of the acidity in a solution). As the harmed tissues have different pH levels than the healthy areas, buckyballs may deliver drugs directly to harmed areas of the body. Thus, by using buckyballs researchers can create drugs that are only released at the infected area (Clark, 2006).

Carbon nanotubes have the nanoscale cross-section areas but they may be many micrometers up to centimeters long. This shapes cause unusual chemical bonding and physical properties,

such as great strength: carbon nanotubes are the strongest known materials. Carbon nanotubes may form single wall and multi-wall structures. Nanotube sheets are 250 times stronger than steel and 10 times lighter; they are also stretchable. Many magazines quoted in 2008 James Hone, Columbia University saying, "It would take an elephant, balanced on a pencil, to break through a sheet of graphene the thickness of Saran Wrap [cling film]." As claimed by Richard Van Noorden (2011), "According to the Nobel Prize committee, a hypothetical one-metre-square hammock of perfect graphene could support a four-kilogram cat - the hammock would weigh 0.77 milligrams, less than a cat's whisker, and would be virtually invisible."

In both the micro-scale and the macro-scale dimensions, pure carbon has the diamond-type bond and the graphite-type bond between carbon atoms (existing for example, in pencil lead). At the nanoscale, carbon develops a specific type of bonding: buckyball bonding, typical of the carbon nanotubes; covalent bonds between carbon atoms make buckyballs very strong, so they are used to strengthen composites (PennState modules, 2011). The carbon nanotubes display several particular properties; they perform ballistic conduction – the flow of charged particles; they conduct phonons, which means quantum vibration; they absorb radiofrequency (which is promising in therapy); they also display surface plasmon (a quantum of plasma oscillation) resonance under an electrical field. There are also several forms involving other elements, such as perfluorocarbons, magnetic iron oxide nano particles, and also silver nanoparticles that are used to coat medical instruments. Buckyballs are good electron acceptors from other materials. They are used to improve efficiency of solar cells that transform sunlight into electricity.

Buckyballs can deliver drugs or radioactive particles to attack cancer cells. However, buckyballs may have different configurations: along with a plain buckyball, a *tris* configuration exists, which has three molecular branches coming off the main structural body in one hemisphere, and a *hexa* configuration that has six branches arranged in a symmetrical pattern. Toxicologists from the Los Alamos National Laboratory in New Mexico recommend the use of the non-toxic *hexa* configuration; the cells exposed to the *tris* buckyballs enter the suspended animation state where they don't die, divide, or grow. The researches also work on turning the *tris* buckyballs into a weapon for halting the spread of cancer cells or delaying the onset of Parkinson's or Alzheimer's in nerve cells (Hsu, 2010). Chemotherapy kills cancer cells but it also kills a lot of healthy cells. Scientists from the Virginia Commonwealth University have devised a technique for placing radioactive molecules inside the buckyballs to deliver them to specific cancer cells. This method would provide a targeted chemotherapy that would avoid the painful and prolonged side effects caused by today's full-body radiation treatments. Targeted radioactive buckyballs could possibly also serve for creating diagnostic techniques with super-accurate MRIs (Fox, 2009). Mroz et al. (2007) applied photodynamic therapy by producing functionalized fullerenes (biologically inert fullerenes changed into photosensitizers), which caused the death of the mouse cancer cells incubated for 24 h with fullerenes and illuminated with white light. Highly water-soluble fullerene C_{60} can deliver biologic and cancer drugs across biological barriers. With the use of a laser-scanning confocal microscopy and flow cytometry it can be seen how C_{60} nanoparticle (C_{60}-serPF) is internalized in the nucleus (through the nucleus pore complex) within living cancer cells, and how the buckyballs escape engulfing by the endocytic vesicles (Raoof et al., 2012).

The mechanical tensile strength, high electrical and heat conductivity, and chemical inactivity of nanotubes make them useful in nanotechnology, electronics, optics, material and architectural science domains, and many other applications. They are applied for strengthening materials (e.g., carbon-fiber frames for bicycles), gluing, food processing, preservation with additives, and packaging, coating transparent conductive display films, building artificial muscles (Aliev, Oh, Kozlov, Kuznetsov, Fang, Fonseca, Ovalle, Lima, Haque, Gartstein, Zhang, Zakhidov, & Baughman, 2009), space elevators, a body armor (in the MIT's Institute for Soldier Nanotechnologies: ISN, 2010), waterproof and tear-resistant textiles (Dalton, Collins, Muñoz, Razal, Von Ebron, Ferraris, Coleman, Kim, & Baughman, 2003), non-cracking concrete, and a lot of other implementations such as fold-away mobile phones, wallpaper-thin lighting panels, and the next generation of aircraft. Professional forensic investigation uses nano technology. Credit cards may possible soon contain as much processing power as current smart phones. Research teams focus on nanotechnology applications in countless areas of life. The precise delivery of drugs with the use of nanostructures (such as by the RNA strands 10 nano in diameter) may help avoid side effects. Nanotechnology applications serve in fighting cancer by attaching nanostructures and destroying cancer cells; in tissue engineering by building scaffolds for cell growth and differentiation; for clinical neuroscience, to enhance neuronal signaling and survival potential by supplementing the nervous system with nanoparticles or nanomaterials; in surgery by welding tissues: stem cell culture matrices by building scaffolds for stem growth and tissue differentiation for further transport; and for diagnostics, by utilizing contrast agents (Burgess, 2012). While nanoparticles had been considered extremely toxic, Chan (2007) concluded that the evidence, which has been gathered since the discovery of fullerenes, overwhelmingly points to C_{60} being non-toxic.

STRUCTURES IN A HUMAN CELL (IN MICRO- AND NANO-SCALE)

We may now shift ideas by applying the concept of the scale to cell biology. A cross section of a human cell presents its compositional elements

*Figure 8. Compositional elements of a cell (©
2012, A. Ursyn. Used with permission)*

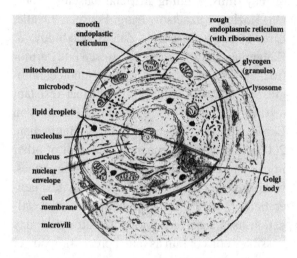

(Figure 8). A cell is surrounded by a cell membrane.
The cytoplasm lies within the plasma membrane
of lipids (fat) and protein. Most cells have a single
nucleus, which contains nucleoli. Nucleus embod-
ies most of the cell's genetic material in chromosomes containing DNA and proteins; it directs the
activity of the cell. Some other organelles are:
complex sets of membranes called endoplasmic
reticulum (with ribosomes, numerous tiny particles
consisting of RNA and proteins, which control
protein synthesis), a Golgi apparatus (part of en-
domembrane system that processes proteins for
further secretion), mitochondria (with an outer
membrane and a convoluted inner membrane, a
site of respiration and energy production in the
cell), and centrioles near the nucleus (which play
a part in cell division).

The size of a human cell is between 4 μm (4
x 10^{-6} m) and 135 μm. Blood cells are about 2.5
μm. For comparison, the ostrich egg is the largest
known cell and weights over 3 pounds (over 1360
grams). Paramecium (a single-celled freshwater
animal) is about 60 μm wide and 50 to 350 μm
long. The size of a skin human cell is about 30
μm. Water molecule (hydrogen oxide H_2O consisting of two hydrogen atoms and one oxygen) is
about 0.29 nm. A flu virus has diameter about
100 nm.

Most of the structures inside the cell belong to
the nano world. For example, a molecule of the
deoxyribonucleic acid, DNA is 2.5 nm wide (it
is millions of atoms long). Mitochondria range
from .5 to 1 μm and ribosomes are between 25
and 30 nm in diameter. Microtubules in a cytoskeleton (a scaffolding of a cell's cytoplasm) may
be 25 micrometers long, with diameter about 25
nm. Microfilaments in a cytoskeleton have individual subunits of microfilaments in the actin
filaments that measure approximately 7 nm, and
their bundles separate filaments by ~35 nm. In
many cells one may find plasmids, which are not
considered alive; they are the DNA molecules
separate from the chromosomal DNA. Table 4
offers directions for an exercise in which you
visualize the contents of a cell.

VISUALIZATION OF BIOLOGICAL DATA: DNA

Researchers utilize visualization tools to understand better the massive amount of complex biological data and provide new biological insights.
Designing visualization tools that support research
results usually from collaboration between biology and computing science specialists. Maybe
the most popular biological visualization on the
molecular, nanoscale level is a colorful, often
rotating, animated picture of a DNA (deoxyribonucleic acid) structure.

The DNA molecules store the long-term information and instructions needed to build components of cells, such as proteins, molecules of
ribonucleic acid RNA. They influence organism
characteristics through information stored within
regions of DNA called genes. Development and
survival of a living organism depends on the
precise regulation of the expression of genetic
information (Watson & Crick, 1953). Following
the solution of DNA structure and the deciphering

Table 4. A story about the contents of a cell

Visual Response: A Journey to the Cell
With an imaginative approach to presenting nanosize structures in living cells, you may want to practice your spatial skills by discussing a concept of a scale and the micro-versus-macro structures. On a figure above are the structures you would see if you could become very small and travel through the human cell. By examining this figure you may encourage your imagination and reinforce an even better your understanding of the concept of the scale.
Create comics, a storyboard for animation, or write a story about a character named Spoko who is 25 nm high (or you would like to choose another size). The story will tell about the encounters and adventures of Spoko wandering in the cell and then leaving one cell to explore other ones. Determine what structures, colors, shapes and textures can be seen inside and outside of the cell and how would you picture this environment. There may be many dangerous meetings and confrontations because some organelles might try to engulf, dissolve, or otherwise harm Spoko. After all, a 500 nm mitochondrion, twenty times taller than Spoko, may look like a 5-story high building.
Also, describe what could happen if he would choose to enter other kinds of cells. For example, a nerve cell, with a long axon, may deliver an electric shock – an action potential, and it may be accompanied by a flow of different cations through the gates opening in the cell membrane. Spoko must be also careful about the skeletal, cardiac, or smooth muscle cells, with contractile protein filaments that generate dangerous force. Also, with all nanotechnologies available, Spoko may fantasize about designing a nano body-armor that would prevent dissolving him by the mighty enzymes secreted by the cell organelles. For example, he may consider waterproof, bulletproof vests that are lighter in weight and cheaper to make, fabricated by blending wool with Kevlar, a synthetic fiber blend (Boyle, 2011).

of the genetic code instructing the translation of RNA transcripts, Francis Crick (1958) depicted the flow of genetic information between macro-molecules as proceeding from DNA to RNA to protein. Beginning in 1990 scientists worked on international Human Genome Project resulting in multiple publications on the project's progress on sequencing approximately 20,500 genes present in human beings. Following this research, Venter et al (2001) published in Science magazine "The

Sequence of the Human Genome." And then on November 5, 2009, Radoje Drmanac (2009) and 64 coauthors published online in *Science* magazine a report about a DNA sequence completion of the sequencing of the human genome. They examined each base from patterned nano arrays of self-assembling DNA nanoballs and identified 3.2 to 4.5 million sequence variants per genome. The authors opened their article with a statement, "genome sequencing of large numbers of individuals promises to advance the understanding, treatment, and prevention of human diseases, among other applications." Currently genetic information is used in many technologies, such as genetic engineering, forensics, bioinformatics, DNA nanotechnology, history, anthropology, and many other branches of knowledge.

Figure 9 presents a computer graphics where the student pictures a cell and the cell organelles in a cheerful way as a living room with a wallpaper, artwork on the wall, a coach, easy chairs, and a carpet.

The most accurate description of the structure of matter would be at the atomic and molecular scale, which is observable in two dimensions. By producing precisely designed 3D macroscopic objects it is possible to bridge the macroscopic and molecular worlds, which is required to understand the relationships with atomic precision. Zheng, Birktoft, Chen, Wang, Sha, Constantinou, Ginell, Mao, & Seeman (2009) from the NY University created a 3D DNA crystal, at 4Å resolution. The designed, self-assembled structures were created by using single-stranded sticky ends, which link double helices in DNA triangles; it opens possibilities of pharmaceutical (controlling the organization of drug receptor targets) and industrial (creating nanoelectronic components) applications (No author, Chemistry World News, 2009). The helically repeating nature of DNA facilitates the construction of a periodic array. The authors formed a crystalline arrangement of a DNA crystal that fulfilled criteria necessary to produce a 3D periodic system: a robust 3D structure and affinity interactions between parts of the DNA with predictable structures when it self-associates by its sticky ends. They demonstrated that it is possible to design and self-assemble a well-ordered macromolecular 3D crystalline lattice with precise control.

Figure 9. E. Maldonaldo, Cell Room. (© 2009, E. Maldonaldo. Used with permission)

CONCLUSION

This chapter provides information and projects for the readers about the omnipresence of the nanoscale objects – soft matter, colloids, liquid crystals, carbon nanotubes, nanoshells, and the developments in nanoscale and molecular-scale technologies. The prehistoric, ancient, and medieval people did make use of the potential of nanostructures by applying specific techniques without knowing why they were effective. Current tools for examining nanostructures include, for example, microscopy and spectroscopy, which records how matter interacts with or emits electromagnetic radiation. Knowledge about graphenes allows nanofabrication – making nanoscale structures and quite new technologies resulting from the size dependent properties of nanoparticles. Colloids, nanoshells, viruses, nanotubes, buckyballs, and visualization of biological data such as DNA are the themes selected for making visual solutions.

REFERENCES

Aliev, A. E., Oh, J., Kozlov, M. E., Kuznetsov, A. A., Fang, S., & Fonseca, A. F., … Baughman, R. H. (2009). Giant-stroke, superelastic carbon nanotube aerogel muscles. *Science, 323*(5921), 1575-1578. doi: doi:10.1126/science.1168312.

Allaume, X., El-Andaloussi, N., Leuchs, B., Bonifati, S., Kulkarni, A., & Marttila, T., … Marchini, A. (2012). Retargeting of rat parvovirus H-1PV to cancer cells through genetic engineering of the viral capsid. *Journal of Virology*. doi: doi:10.1128/JVI.06208-11 PMID:22258256.

Ball, P. (2009). Worlds within worlds: Quantum objects by Julian Voss-Andreae. *Nature, 462*, 416. doi:10.1038/462416a.

Boykin, J. (2012). *Redesigning Minard's graphic of Napoleon's march*. Retrieved September 7, 2012, from http://www.wayfind.com/napoleon.html

Boyle, R. (2011, April 14). Blending wool and Kevlar could make better, lighter body armor. *Popular Science*. Retrieved August 28, 2012, from http://www.popsci.com/technology/article/2011-04/blending-wool-and-kevlar-could-reduce-body-armors-weight-and-cost-researchers-say

Bradbury Science Museum. (2011). *Los Alamos national laboratory*. Retrieved September 7, 2012, from http://www.lanl.gov/museum/explore/_docs/MS2%20virus.pdf

Bubbles. (2011). Retrieved August 24, 2012, from http://bubbles.org/html/questions/color.htm

Burgess, R. (2012). *Understanding nanomedicine: An introductory textbook*. Pan Stanford Publishing.

Cave of Altamira and Paleolithic Cave Art of Northern Spain. (2012). *Unesco world heritage centre*. Retrieved August 26, 2012, from http://whc.unesco.org/en/list/310

Challenges in Characterizing Small Particles: Exploring Particles from the Nano- to Microscales. (2012). *Chemical sciences roundtable & national research council*. The National Academies Press. ISBN 0-309-22590-6

Chan, W. C. (2007). Toxicity studies of fullerenes and derivatives. In Bio-applications of nanoparticles. New York, NY: Springer Science + Business Media. ISBN 0-387-76712-6

Chemistry World News. (2009). Designing 3D DNA crystals. *Chemistry World News*. Retrieved August 24, 2012, from http://www.rsc.org/chemistryworld/news/2009/september/02090904.asp

Choi, M.-R., Stanton-Maxey, K. J., Stanley, J. K., Levin, C. S., Bardhan, R., & Akin, D. … Clare, S. E. (2007). A cellular Trojan horse for delivery of therapeutic nanoparticles into tumors. *Nano Lett., 7*(12), 3759–3765. doi 10.1021/nl072209h. Retrieved August 23, 2012, from http://pubs.acs.org/action/doSearch?action=search&author=Choi%2C+Mi%5C-Ran&qsSearchArea=author&

Clark, J. (2006). *The basics of buckyballs*. Retrieved September 7, 2012, from http://www.growthstockwire.com/2399/The-Basics-of-Buckyballs

Cook, K. A. (2005). Discover nano. *History of Nano Timeline*. Retrieved August 26, 2012, from http://www.discovernano.northwestern.edu/whatis/History

Crick, F. H. C. (1958). On protein synthesis. [from http://profiles.nlm.nih.gov/SC/B/B/Z/Y/_/scbbzy.pdf]. *Symposia of the Society for Experimental Biology, 12*, 138–163. Retrieved April 13, 2011 PMID:13580867.

Daguerre, L. J. (1839). *History and practice of photogenic drawing on the true principles of the daguerréotype, with the new method of dioramic painting, by the inventor Louis Jacques M. Daguerre*. London: Smith, Elder and Co..

Dalton, A. B., Collins, S., Muñoz, E., Razal, J. M., Von Ebron, H., & Ferraris, J. P. et al. (2003). Super-tough carbon-nanotube fibres. *Nature, 423,* 703. doi:10.1038/423703a PMID:12802323.

Deruta Ceramists. (2012). Retrieved August 26, 2012, from http://www.thatsarte.com/region/Deruta

DeWitt, M. A., Chang, A., Combs, P. A., & Yildiz, A. (2012). Ytoplasmic Dynein moves through uncoordinated stepping of the AAA+ ring domains. *Science, 335*(221), 221-225. doi 10.1126/science.1215804. Retrieved August 24, 2012, from http://physics.berkeley.edu/research/yildiz/papers/Science-2012-DeWitt.pdf

DKFZ. (2012). *German cancer research center*. Retrieved September 7, 2012, from http://www.dkfz.de/en/presse/pressemitteilungen/2012/dkfz-pm-12-39-Tailor-made-viruses-for-enhanced-cancer-therapy.php

Drmanac, R., Sparks, A. B., Callow, M. J., Halpern, A. L., et al. (2010). Human genome sequencing using unchained base reads on self-assembling DNA nanoarrays. *Science, 327*(5961), 78-81. Retrieved December 19, 2010, from http://www.sciencemag.org/content/327/5961/78.abstract

Farokhzad, O. C., Cheng, J., Teply, B. A., Sherifi, I., Jon, S., & Kantoff, P. W., … Langer, R. (2006). Targeted nanoparticle-aptamer bioconjugates for cancer chemotherapy in vivo. *Proc. Natl. Acad. Sci., 103*(16), 6315-6320. doi 10.1073/pnas.0601755103. Retrieved September 8, 2012, 2012, from http://www.pnas.org/content/103/16/6315

Fox, S. (2009). Radioactive cancer-binding buckyballs for targeted chemotherapy. *POPSCI*. Retrieved September 7, 2012, from http://www.popsci.com/scitech/article/2009-08/radiation-carrying-cancer-binding-bucky-balls-targeted-chemotherapy

Gardener & Golovchenko. (2012). Ice-assisted electron beam lithography of graphene. *Nanotechnology, 23*(18), 185302. doi 10.1088/0957-4484/23/18/185302. Retrieved August 27, 2012, from http://iopscience.iop.org/0957-4484/23/18/185302/

Geim, A. K. (2009). Graphene: Status and prospects. *Science, 324*(5934), 1530–1534. doi:10.1126/science.1158877 PMID:19541989.

Geim, A. K., & Novoselov, K. S. (2007). The rise of graphene. *Nature Materials, 6*(3), 183–191. Retrieved from http://onnes.ph.man.ac.uk/nano/Publications/Naturemat_2007Review.pdf doi:10.1038/nmat1849 PMID:17330084.

González, E., Arbiol, J., & Puntes, V. F. (2011). Carving at the nanoscale: Sequential galvanic exchange and Kirkendall growth at room temperature. *Science, 334*(6061), 1377-1380. doi 10.1126/science.1212822. Retrieved November 1, 2012, from http://www.sciencemag.org/content/334/6061/1377.abstract?sid=1055ee45-abc7-4f9a-8698-e9ae3487aa68

Goodsell, D. S. (2006). Fact and fantasy in nanotech imagery. *Leonardo, 42*(1), 52–57. doi:10.1162/leon.2009.42.1.52.

Grantab, R., Shenoy, V. B., & Ruoff, R. S. (2010). Anomalous strength characteristics of tilt grain boundaries in graphene. *Science, 330*(6006), 946–948. doi:10.1126/science.1196893 PMID:21071664.

Gross, L., Mohn, F., Moll, N., Liljeroth, P., & Meyer, G. (2009, August 28). The chemical structure of a molecule resolved by atomic force microscopy. *Science, 1110-1114*. doi: doi:10.1126/science.1176210 PMID:19713523.

Hsu, J. (2010). Tiny buckyballs could put fast-spreading cancer cells into suspended animation, but their effect in normal cells may prove toxic for the body. *POPSCI*. Retrieved September 7, 2012, from http://www.popsci.com/technology/article/2010-03/buckyballs-could-put-fast-spreading-cancer-cells-suspended-animation

ICAM-I2CAM. (2012). *The International Institute for Complex Adaptive Matter*. Retrieved August 24, 2012 from http://icam-i2cam.org/index.php/icamnews/

ISN. (2010). *Institute for Soldier Nanotechnologies*. Retrieved December 11, 2010, from http://web.mit.edu/isn/

Lee, J., Bush, B., Maboudian, B., & Fearing, R. S. (2009). Gecko-inspired combined lamellar and nanofibrillar array for adhesion on nonplanar surface. *Langmuir, 25*(21), 12449–12453. doi 10.1021/la9029672. Retrieved August 24, 2012, from http://pubs.acs.org/doi/abs/10.1021/la9029672

McHale, M. (2008). *Nanotechnology: Ferrofluids and liquid crystals*. Retrieved August 29, 2012 from http://cnx.org/content/m15532/latest/

Mroz, P., Pawlak, A., Satti, M., Lee, H., Wharton, T., Galli, H., et al. (2007). Functionalized fullerenes mediate photodynamic killing of cancer cells: Type I versus type II photochemical mechanism. *Free Radic Biol Med., 43*(5), 711–719. Retrieved September 7, 2012, from http://www.ncbi.nlm.nih.gov/pmc/articles/PMC1995806/

Nano.gov. (2012). *National Nanotechnology Initiative*. Retrieved August 27, 2012, from http://www.nano.gov/education-training/workforce-training-center

Nanotec Applications. (n.d.). Retrieved August 26, 2012, from http://www.discovernano.northwestern.edu/affect/applications_content

National Cancer Institute. (2012). *NCI Alliance for Nanotechnology in Cancer*. Retrieved from http://nano.cancer.gov/learn/understanding/

Nobleprize.org. (2010). Retrieved October 26, 2012, from http://www.nobelprize.org/nobel_prizes/physics/laureates/2010/

NSF NACK Center. (2012). *National center for nanotechnology applications and career knowledge*. Penn State University Center for Nanotechnology Education and Utilization. Retrieved August 20, 2011, from http://www.nano4me.org/

Orfescu, C. (2012). NanoArt: Nanotechnology and art. In A. Ursyn (Ed.), *Biologically-Inspired Computing for the Arts: Scientific Data through Graphics*. Hershey, PA: IGI Global. doi:10.4018/978-1-4666-0942-6.ch008.

Palma, M., Abramson, J. J., Gorodetsky, A. A., Penzo, E., Gonzalez, R. L. Jr, & Sheetz, M. P. … Wind, S. J. (2011). Selective biomolecular nanoarrays for parallel single-molecule investigations. *Journal of the American Chemical Society*. doi: doi:10.1021/ja201031g.

Palmer, J. (2009). *Single molecule's stunning image*. Retrieved August 20, 2011, from http://news.bbc.co.uk/2/hi/science/nature/8225491.stm

Palmer, J. (2012). *Graphene transistors in high-performance demonstration*. Retrieved October 26, 2012, from http://www.bbc.co.uk/news/science-environment-18868848

PennState modules. (2011). Nano4Me.org. *NACK Educational Resources*. The Pennsylvania State University. Retrieved August 27, 2012, from http://nano4me.live.subhub.com/categories/modules

Rahmani, A. R., & Mahvi, A. H. (2006). Use of ion exchange for removal of ammonium: A biological regeneration of zeolite. *Global Nest Journal, 8*(2), 146-150. Retrieved August 27, 2011, from http://www.gnest.org/journal/Vol8_No2/146-150_RAHMANI_396_8-2.pdf

Raoof, M., Mackeyev, Y., Cheney, M. A., Wilson, L. J., & Curley, S. A. (2012). Internalization of C_{60} fullerenes into cancer cells with accumulation in the nucleus via the nuclear pore complex. *Biomaterials, 33*(10), 2952-2960. Retrieved September 7, 2012, from http://www.ncbi.nlm.nih.gov/pubmed/22245558

RSC. (2006). *Advancing the chemical sciences: Nanotechnology tackles chemotherapy.* Retrieved September 8, 2011, from http://www.rsc.org/chemistryworld/News/2006/April/11040601.asp

Russo, C. J., & Golovchenko, J. A. (2012). Atom-by-atom nucleation and growth of graphene nanopores. *Proc. Natl. Acad. Sci. U.S.A., 109,* 5953-5957. Retrieved August 28, 2011, from http://labs.mcb.harvard.edu/branton/RussoAndGolovchenko2012.pdf

Selvin, P. R. (2012). *Physics.* Retrieved August 24, 2012, from http://physics.illinois.edu/people/profile.asp?selvin

Senyuk, B., & Smalyukh, I. I. (2012). Elastic interactions between colloidal microspheres and elongated convex and concave nanoprisms in nematic liquid crystals. *Soft Matter, 8,* 8729–8734. doi:10.1039/c2sm25821h.

Sitti, M., & Fearing, R. S. (2003). Synthetic gecko foot-hair micro/nano-structures as dry adhesives. *Journal of Adhesion Science and Technology, 18*(7), 1055–1074. doi:10.1163/156856103322113788.

Smalley, R. E. (2012). *Rice university.* Retrieved August 24, 2012, from http://cnst.rice.edu/

Smalyukh, I. I. (2011). Materials science: Deft tricks with liquid crystals. *Nature, 478,* 330–331. doi:10.1038/478330a PMID:22012387.

Stewart, M. E., Anderton, C. R., Thompson, L. B., Maria, J., Gray, S. K., Rogers, J. A., & Nuzzo, R. G. (2008). Nanostructured plasmonic sensors. *Chem. Reviews, 108,* 494-521. doi 10.1021/cr068126n. Retrieved August 24, 2012, from http://rogers.matse.illinois.edu/files/2008/plasmonschemrev.pdf

Taniguchi, N. (1974). On the basic concept of 'nano-technology. In *Proceedings of the International Conference on Production Engineering.* Japan Society of Precision Engineering.

TED. (2012). *Ursus Wehrli's tied up art.* Retrieved August 24, 2012, from http://www.ted.com/talks/ursus_wehrli_tidies_up_art.html http://design.org/blog/art-clean-organized-chaos-ursus-wehrli

Thakur, M., Pernites, R. B., Nitta, N., Isaacson, M., Sinsabaugh, S. L., Wong, M. S., & Biswal, S. L. (2012). Freestanding macroporous silicon and pyrolyzed polyacrylonitrile as a composite anode for lithium ion batteries. *Chem. Mater., 24*(15), 2998–3003. doi 10.1021/cm301376t. Retrieved August 24, 2012, from http://pubs.acs.org/doi/pdf/10.1021/cm301376t

Trivedi, R. P., Klevets, I. I., Senyuk, B., Lee, T., & Smalyukh, I. I. (2012). Reconfigurable interactions and three-dimensional patterning of colloidal particles and defects in lamellar soft media. *Proceedings of the National Academy of Sciences of the United States of America, 109,* 4744–4749. doi:10.1073/pnas.1119118109 PMID:22411822.

Tufte, E. R. (1983/2001). *The visual display of quantitative information.* Cheshire, CT: Graphics Press.

Turner, N. W., Subrahmanyam, S., & Piletsky, S. A. (2009). Analytical methods for determination of mycotoxins: A review. *Analytica Chimica Acta, 632*(2), 168-180. Retrieved August 29, 2012, from http://dx.doi.org/10.1016/j.aca.2008.11.010

Van Noorden, R. (2011). Chemistry: The trials of new carbon. *Nature, 469*, 14-16. doi:10.1038/469014a. Retrieved August 29, 2012, from http://www.nature.com/news/2011/050111/full/469014a.html

Venter, J. C., Adams, M. D., Myers, E. W., Li, P. W., Mural, R. J., & Sutton, G. G., ... Yandell, M. (2001). The sequence of the human genome. *Science, 291*(5507), 1304–1351. doi:10.1126/science.1058040. Retrieved August 24, 2012, from http://www.sciencemag.org/content/291/5507/1304

Watson, J. D., & Crick, F. H. (1953). Molecular structure of nucleic acids: A structure for deoxyribose nucleic acid. *Nature, 171*(4356), 737–738. doi:10.1038/171737a0 PMID:13054692.

Yanik, A. A., Huang, M., Kamohara, O., Artar, A., Geisbert, T. W., Connor, J. H., & Altug, H. (2010). An optofluidic nanoplasmonic biosensor for direct detection of live viruses from biological media. *Nano Letters 2010*. doi 10.1021/nl103025u. Retrieved August 24, 2012, from http://www.bu.edu/smartlighting/files/2010/01/2010_Nano-Letters_Virus.pdf

Yildiz, A., Forkey, J. N., McKinney, S. A., Ha, T., Goldman, Y. A., & Selvin, P. R. (2003). Myosin V walks hand-over-hand: Single fluorophore imaging with 1.5-nm localization. *Science, 300*(5628), 2061–2065. doi:10.1126/science.1084398 PMID:12791999.

Zhang, L., & Zhang, L. (2010). Lipid-polymer hybrid nanoparticles: Synthesis, characterization and applications. *NanoLIFE, 1*(163). doi 10.1142/S179398441000016X. Retrieved September 8, 2012, from http://www.worldscientific.com/doi/ref/10.1142/S179398441000016X

Zheng, J., Birktoft, J. J., Chen, Y., Wang, T., Sha, R., & Constantinou, P. E. et al. (2009). From molecular to macroscopic via the rational design of a self-assembled 3D DNA crystal. *Nature, 461*, 74–77. doi:10.1038/nature08274 PMID:19727196.

Chapter 12
Acceleration

ABSTRACT

This part of the book provides an occasion to combine visual presentation of concepts related to speed, velocity, and acceleration with the real-life circumstances (such as car or horse races) and at the same time with artistic connotations about motion and artistic responses to it. The goal of this project is to show acceleration, speed, and velocity by producing an image that would look very dynamic. For example, dynamic changes of motion can be presented as a scene with racecars or horses. Connotations related to art may enhance both our knowledge about acceleration and a message it evokes.

INTRODUCTION

We can feel some laws of physics in our guts and acceleration is one of these. Acceleration evokes visceral reaction because our old brain is scanning for danger and noticing acceleration as such. In a practical setting the feeling of acceleration evokes our emotion. While the times change and living conditions improve, humans still fell in their old brain a need to enhance their survival skills by conquering their fear and strengthening their courage. Maybe for that reason toddlers enjoy greatly swings and slides, first graders take pleasure in carousels and go-carts, and the grown-ups like the extreme sports, fast cars and motorcycles, parachuting and bungee jumping, and also visits to the theme and amusement parks with thrill rides, Ferris and eccentric wheels, and roller coasters that provide occasions to feel acceleration and the emotion of speed. Acceleration has been accepted

DOI: 10.4018/978-1-4666-4627-8.ch012

a performance measure of cars and motorcycles, with the shortest time needed to achieve 60 mph (97 km/h) being about 2.4 seconds for a car (The Super Cars, 2012) and 1.75 seconds for a motorcycle (Top 10 fastest Bikes, 2012). Many events recorded by psychologists display a normal curve, which shows first positive acceleration (upward movement shown by a curve, e.g., of muscular power) and then negative acceleration (deceleration, e.g., resulting from age). Acceleration sensors of mobile devices support solutions applied for interactive visualizations. It is not very intuitive to manipulate objects visualized in 3-dimension by a mouse because a mouse can only move in 2-dimensional space. Mariko Sasakura, Akira Kotaki, & Junya Inada (2011) propose an interaction technique using a library for 3D acceleration sensors of mobile devices, which results in a 3D molecular visualization system to manipulate 3D objects, which displays a simulation of the molecular dynamics method. Users can rotate 3D objects by leaning a mobile device and change a viewing

Figure 1. Erick Weitkamp, Acceleration. (© 2005. E. Weitkamp. Used with permission)

location. Visual interest about these scientific terms can be seen in works of art representing motion in various styles in art.

Figure 1 presents computer graphics created by a student from my Computer Art class.

The concept (and a project) allows discussing and solving visually the dynamic events in physics (acceleration of particles in nuclear fusion), geology (volcanoes, earthquakes), history of science (wheel, industrial revolution, electricity, computers), and human history (revolutions, declarations of independence). Kinematics, theoretical study about the motion of a body has been mostly applied to machinery, mechanisms, and robotics. It involves concepts of motion: change in position and orientation, whatever is its cause. Speed, velocity, and acceleration can be described with symbols and presented as graphs. Visual computing enables us to form a clear impression of these connections. It may also motivate one to create one's individual solution while creating computer graphics. Thus, the goal of this project is to show acceleration, speed, and velocity by producing an image that would look very dynamic. For example, dynamic changes of motion can be presented as a scene with racecars or horses.

Motion can be experienced as a continuous change of position in time. However, ancient Greek philosophers generally questioned the concept of change. Zeno of Elea (c. 490-430 BC)

devised the paradox of the arrow: a body occupying a space equal to its volume is at rest; a flying arrow occupies, at any moment, a space equal to its volume. Thus, at any moment, the arrow is at rest; therefore it is at rest all the time. This paradox was not resolved until the development of calculus enabled mathematicians to distinguish changes from zero, which were earlier too small to be calculated.

Figure 2 presents another computer graphics created by a student from my Computer Art class. The idea of blurriness caused by a sudden change of velocity reminded this student of an abstract composition. As we accelerate, the reality changes, pretty much like in non-representational work, where the artist can depict own experiences, and a perceiver interpret them in one's own private way.

Figure 2. Jenny Wise, Acceleration. (© 2001. J. Wise. Used with permission)

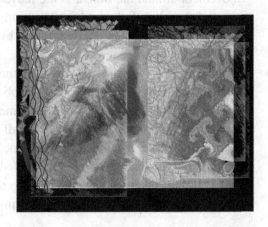

SPEED, VELOCITY, ACCELERATION

Three basic terms describing the movement of an object are speed, velocity, and acceleration.

- **Speed** is a rate at which object moves, with units measured as distance divided by time (for example, when a miniature car moves along a straight line). It is a scalar value measured by dividing the distance d covered by an object by the time passed t: $v = d/t$. We can calculate the average speed for the entire drive of our miniature car: $v = 30$ in / 2 sec $= 15$ in/sec (or, for example $v = 10$ m/s or $v = 60$ ft/2 min $= 30$ ft/min); thus the car's displacement is a product of velocity and time.

- **Velocity** means a speed in a constant direction of motion: a rate of motion of an object in a particular direction meant as the distance covered and the time taken to drive (for example, miles per hour). It is a vector because it has quantity and direction; for example, 10 m/sec north. It can be constant or accelerated. Velocity is a vector, which is drawn as an arrowed line that has both magnitude and direction. An object can have several velocities directed differently at the same time, for example, when a cup is raised by somebody who is walking along the airplane in motion, to say nothing about the Earth's rotation, its movement around the Sun, and the movement of the whole Solar system. The resultant velocity of a cup can be determined by construction of six vectors.

- **Acceleration** is a rate of increase in the object's velocity; it measures how an object's speed or direction changes in time and shows both the magnitude and the direction of velocity at a given point in time. It is the rate of change in velocity divided by the time it takes to make the change: $a = v_{final} - v_{initial} /t$. For example, when a min-

iature car starts from rest and reaches a speed 15 inches per second in 2 seconds, its acceleration is $a = 15$ in / 2 sec $= 7.5$ in per sec per sec. We write this derived unit as "in/sec^2" and read it "inches per second squared." If we further accelerate our miniature car, it reaches a speed of 60 inches per second. A change from 15 in/sec to 60 in/sec takes 5 sec, so the rate of change is $60 - 15 = 45$ in/sec / 5 sec $= 9$ in/sec^2 (it is a change at the rate of 9 in/sec each second). The amount of the acceleration may be constant, increasing, or decreasing (decelerated). We can also calculate how long would it take to stop the car or how far our car would move in a given time. A change in the speed of motion is usually indicated on a graph by the amount of rise or fall per unit of time.

When we talk about interactions between objects, we use a notion of object's momentum. It is measured as a product of mass and velocity, which has a vector quantity of motion, as it possesses a direction and a magnitude. In order to change the object's momentum we have to apply force. Three Newton's laws of motion describe the relation between force acting on a body and the resulting motion of this body. Newton's laws of motion apply to all kinds of motion:

- **The First Law:** In the absence of an external force an object moves with constant velocity. In uniform circular motion, the momentum changes direction but not magnitude.

- **The Second Law:** Tells about the rate of change in momentum of an object, where momentum means mass times velocity. That means, $F = ma$, where (F) is the net force applied to the object, (m) is its mass, and (a) is the object's acceleration. We may say a net force can accelerate momentum of an object in the direction of the force, or force = rate of change in momentum.

- **The Third Law:** States that for any force there always is an equal and opposite reaction force that is lying in the same straight line.

Thus, the result of the net force applied to the object is measured as mass times acceleration. Gravity causes change in objects' acceleration. When masses M_1 and M_2 attract each other through the force of gravity F_g, the strength of gravity, the gravitational force between objects can be described by the Newton's universal law of gravitation $F_g = G\, M_1 M_2/d^2$

ART WORKS SHOWING MOTION AND EMOTION

To make some art connections, on the web or using books, for example The Art Book (Editors of Phaidon Press, 2012/2005) examine reproductions of works of art representing motion in different styles in art, such as:

Symbolism (for example, the American painter Arnold Böcklin, 1827-1901; "Centaurs' Combat")

Cubism (e.g., Fernand Léger, 1881-1955; "The Builders").

Artists belonging to the Futurism movement (e.g., Giacomo Balla, 1871-1958; "Flight of the Swallows" or Umberto Boccioni, 1882-1916; "Head + Light + Surroundings") were intrigued with movement through time and space.

Look also at works done in the Surrealism style (e.g., Arshile Gorky, 1904-1948; "The Waterfall"), Abstract (e.g., Wassily Kandinsky, 1866-1944; "Cossacks"), or other styles.

Inspect dynamic paintings of the American painter Thomas Eakins (1844-1916), for example,

his scenes of wrestling. Look over how artists employ some elements of art, (such as line, space, or time) and principles of design, (such as emphasis, rhythm, contrast), to enhance the dynamics of their artwork. Give some thought to how the British photographer Eadweard Muybridge (1830-1904) analyzed movement, right before the advent of cinematography, by taking sequential photographs of people and animals in motion. Inspect critically the metaphors used by artists to imply the notion of motion. Other approaches can be found in Oriental sculptures, for example, presentations of the goddess Shiva with multiple hands.

Figure 3 presents yet another computer graphics created by my student from a Computer Graphics class.

Figure 4 presents a project done by Sean Flannery in Processing. This is his description. This project requires user input. It shows the acceleration of a triangle through space. By holding down the mouse button and dragging it across the display screen, and then releasing the mouse button, you will see a triangle travel through space at the desired speed the line has created. You will also see a number in the bottom left hand corner of the screen that displays the angle at which the line was created. I have been expanding my knowledge on coding to represent this project through mathematics over art.

WORKING ON VISUAL RESPONSE TO THE THEME

The goal of this project is to show in an artistic way the dynamic changes of motion. This project does not exclusively depend on programming or on the existence of such tools as a mouse or scanner. You may want to copy and paste images. What is really needed here is the use of line. Create a scene on paper on the computer screen. It may be produced in many ways, not necessarily with miniature cars or horses. Acceleration may happen in any sphere of life and it may be pictured

Figure 3. Reda Benembarek, Acceleration. (© 2005. R. Benembarek. Used with permission). The hammering serves as an example of the importance of speed and acceleration for the work's efficiency. Red dots gain in color intensity with a growing speed of the hammer.

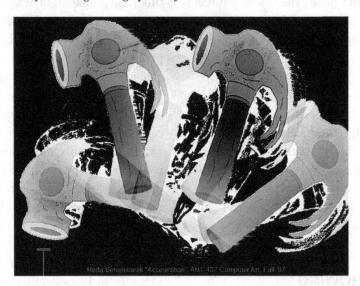

Figure 4. Sean Flannery, Acceleration. (© 2013. Sean Flannery. Used with permission)

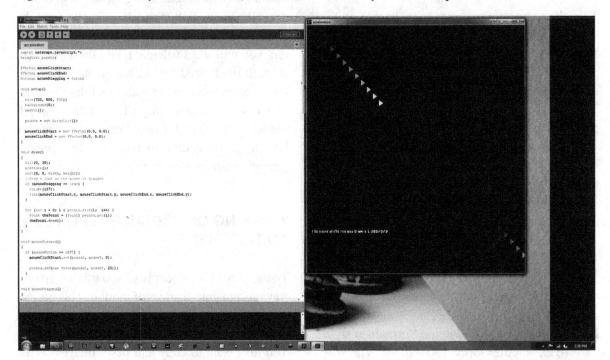

in a variety of ways. You may choose an abstract geometric design. You may want to organize your work around some inspiring concept, such as time, color, or technology. For example, you may apply an abstract approach to the issue of acceleration by examining and presenting in a dynamic way the swift changes that have taken place throughout history, such as revolutions, declarations of independence, or in the history of science occurring due to the great inventions such the invention of the wheel, the advent of industrial revolution, the discovery of electricity, and then the invention of computers. We can also visualize the concept of acceleration in terms of geology; for instance, by creating a dynamic landscape seen from the inside of the volcano crater full of fire, geysers of hot steam, dramatic faults, folds, and rims. Examine reproductions of works of art to see how great artists approached the issue of motion and velocity.

For the beginning take a look at miniature toys (for example, cars). Carve a model of your dream car out of a bar of soap, and shape it in clay. (When you have made it in clay, you may want to wash your hands with a car sculpted in soap!) Then, you may arrange a car race. Make various solutions for putting miniature cars in motion, for example, with the use of a rubber band. Cars made of soap may be put in motion in a dish filled with water.

If you still prefer to present a car race, draw a highway using a pencil or any computer art graphics program as a tool for drawing. You may prefer to draw horses and draw a racecourse as a background. You may also select and scan illustrations on this theme. Using a model of your dream car that you have carved out of a bar of soap or shaped in clay, look at your clay sculptures and make sketches on a computer screen or draw on paper. If you prefer to look at miniature toys (racing cars or racehorses), make sketches of these toys. If you drew them on paper, you may photograph or scan your sketches and drawings and transfer them into a computer, especially when you are not accustomed to drawing with a mouse, a graphic

tablet, or a stylus. Some illustrations may also be useful for creating the background.

Try to visually express your understanding of acceleration and show the emotion of the race. Add expressive features when drawing cars by identifying shapes and forms showing motion, using proportion, analyzing negative and positive space, and perspective to represent space and time, and emphasize rhythm, repetition, and contrast while creating a scene. You may want to apply the transforming effects and dynamic effects offered by the computer: scaling, slanting, distorting, rotating, and applying perspective, to explore symmetry, repetition, and patterns. Manipulate the image by specific color selection, the use of additional lines, application of texture, and/or enhancement of the depth of the picture. Maybe use 3D software to translate a shape into a form and then scale it. Experiment with perspective using several approaches to creating the illusion of space: by positioning objects on a page, by covering one image by another, and by adding more details to images which are supposed to appear closer. First of all, you may position objects on a page in different places, bigger in the front, so they look close to the viewer. You may also partially cover one car with another, so it seems to be placed farther than the second one. Note that the image supposedly appears closer when it has more details added.

Then, place the cars (or horses) against the background. Transform and manipulate the scanned images in order to present them in a personal, artistic way. To create a quality picture, make a composition of the artwork: think about the processes in action, and imagine the events to be represented in the picture. To create an even better illusion of space, experiment with forms and shapes. For example, in a separate file, change the point of view of the scene. Change the perspective and a point of view, from the bird's eye view, to the driver's point of view after saving the file under a different name. Using your spatial reasoning visualize your point of view going from the bird's eye perspective to the orthographic and isometric projection. Then, in yet another file, you may want to draw the picture from the pedestrian's (spectator's) point of view. Consider compiling parts of these scenes drawn from the bird's eye view, the driver's, and the pedestrian's point of view as a unified picture, to express the dynamics of the scene. After saving the file under a different name you may select all the drawing and apply inversion of the image, thus exchanging black and white points. This way, a daylight scene (black lines on a white background) becomes an event seen during the night, and what was white becomes dark.

Try to attain some expressive artistic means of your own by creating metaphors and symbols representing the dynamics of your composition. What happens when we think about rate of change, versus change of rate? To enhance the feeling of motion and the artistic message to be conveyed, transform and manipulate the scanned images according to your own choices. Show the emotions related to speed and motion. Image manipulation on the screen may be attained by specific color selection, use of additional lines, application of

texture, enhancement of the depth of the picture or changing its balance and composition. It may be interesting to create the code for each transformation.

Figure 5, "Acceleration" is a loose interpretation of the enjoyable experience of the car's acceleration. Route-retracing navigation system, satellite radio, cute sunroof, leather-appointed seats, smart phone, and i-Pod – go!

VISUALIZING MOTION BY CONSTRUCTING GRAPHS

Now, you may want to calculate the velocity of the cars (or horses) and construct graphs illustrating results of this work. You may also want to graphically present changes in velocity and acceleration of your car. The motion of our miniature car may be presented visually with a simple graph. To present changes in our car's velocity or acceleration, we may draw relational graphs with their x and y axes, showing time on the x axis and a speed or a change of speed on the axis y. First, we can plot a graph showing the speed of the car against time,

Figure 5. Anna Ursyn, Acceleration. (© 1997, A. Ursyn. Used with permission)

along with the car's position and its displacement – the change of position. If the velocity of a car is increasing or decreasing continuously (due to acceleration or decrease in velocity), our graph will make a figure marked by pronounced curves.

If velocity is constant, our graph will show a straight line with its slant becoming greater with the increase of velocity. From the graph, we can read and calculate the average velocity of a miniature car in motion as the distance d it travels divided by the time t it takes in passage from one place to another. We can also draw a graph showing acceleration - a change of velocity, and see how the speed of a car changes in time. Thus, the motion of the car is seen against the frame of reference: when the frame of reference is changed (by showing values of velocity of its changes), the graph is also changed.

Construct simple charts related to the races you draw. While working with coordinates x and y use numbers to locate cars along lines: assign numbers along rectangular coordinates and then draw graphs. Construct graphs with the use of graphic software; apply coordinates, vectors, or sets of vectors in problem-solving situations related to car races. Analyze quantitative relationships between speed, velocity, and acceleration presented

as relational graphs showing velocity versus time, then changes of velocity versus time. Represent velocity by constructing vectors: directed line segments with magnitude and direction. Draw a vector showing velocity of the object depicted in your artwork: it is its rate of motion in a particular direction meant as the distance covered and the time taken to drive. Figure 6 a, b is about the car in motion.

Figure 6a shows changes in velocity of a car. This graph shows a rate of motion meant as the distance covered and the time taken to drive, with numerical values to determine the velocity and of this car in motion. The changes in velocity of this car go from v_1=50 in/sec gained in 4 seconds from the start, through v_2=10 in/sec (deceleration due to the steep slope of the road) occurring in the next 2 seconds, and then increases to v_3=60 in/sec again, during the next 2 seconds. Then, the car slows down at constant deceleration, so its speed after next 4 seconds is v_4=20 inches/second.

Figure 6b shows a simplified record of acceleration values. Assuming constant acceleration, you may calculate the acceleration values using the kinematic equations for these three stages: $a = v_{final} - v_{initial}/t$.

Figure 6a. A velocity-time curve for a car in motion (© 2012, A. Ursyn. Used with permission). Figure 6b. Acceleration-time graph for a car in motion (© 2012, A. Ursyn. Used with permission). a_1 = 50 in/ sec–0 in/sec/4 sec = 50 in/sec/4 sec = 12.5 in/sec²; a_2 = 10 in/sec–50 in/sec/2 sec = –40 in/sec/2 sec = –20 in/sec²; a_3 = 60 in/sec–10 in/sec/2 sec = 50 in/sec/2 sec = 25 in/sec²; a_4 = 20 in/sec–60 in/sec/4 sec = –40 in/sec/4 sec = –10 in/sec².

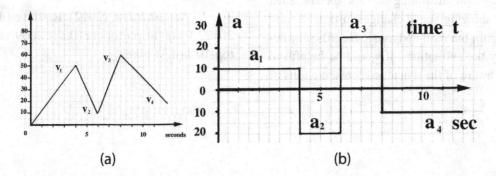

(a)   (b)

Assign some numerical values of your choice to determine the velocity and acceleration of the object in motion. Make your own calculations and place your results on a graph about your car or horse, depending on the slope of the road you have just depicted. When you read and interpret your graphs presenting velocity and changes in velocity, you have to remember that for simplification, your graph shows average velocity and constant acceleration values for the time segments, so you was drawing straight lines instead of curves. Also, we have to remember about the car's tendency to keep moving due to inertia. You may later want to include these vectors and graphs in your artwork or animation.

You may want to make your cars animated, to show the velocity of a particular car and its acceleration due to the downhill motion, showing the speed of a car versus the slope of a road and the cars' position against the background. Start creating an animation, considering it as an artistic medium. For example, you may build key frames and a time line, or take a flipbook approach to animation, where, in order to put things in motion, each next image has some added lines. If you copy and paste the drawings of cars (or horses), along with the scanned sketches, you may rework those sequential drawings. The graphs illustrating velocity and acceleration of the cars or horses may be transferred into any animation software and then transferred to video, with the use of scanned toys: racing cars or race horses, sketches of those toys, and a hand-drawn race course in the background. Sketches of cars may be assigned to different parts of a graph illustrating the cars' speed against time, or showing speed changes in time. Sound effects from the road and music records may accompany the animations. It would be helpful to become aware of the dynamic representations of movement in different styles of art and multiple solutions in various media.

CONCLUSION

This chapter provides an occasion to combine visual presentation of concepts related to speed, velocity, and acceleration with the real-life circumstances and to show acceleration, speed, and velocity by producing an image that would look very dynamic. Acceleration may happen in any sphere of life and it may be pictured in a variety of ways. This project does not exclusively depend on programming or on the existence of such tools as a mouse or scanner. One may copy and paste images and then convey the feeling of motion and the artistic message by transforming and manipulating the scanned images. Art works showing motion and emotions are discussed, as many works of art represent motion in different styles.

REFERENCES

Sasakura, M., Kotaki, A., & Inada, J. (2011). A 3D molecular visualization system with mobile devices. In *Proceedings of the 15th International Conference on Information Visualization,* (pp. 429-433). ISBN 978-1-4577-0868-8

The Super Cars.org. (2012). *Fastest cars by acceleration: Top 10 list.* Retrieved July 26, 2012, from http://www.thesupercars.org/fastest-cars/fastest-cars-by-acceleration-top-10-list/

Top 10 Fastest Bikes. (2012). Retrieved July 26, 2012, from http://topper10.net/2009/vehicles/top-10-fastest-bikes/

Chapter 13
Carbon:
A Gem, a Molecule, and a Heart of Nanotechnology

ABSTRACT

"Carbon: A Gem, a Molecule, and a Heart of Nanotechnology" is about related habitats and technologies seen from the scientific, artistic, and educational points of view. It explores carbon as mineral: coal, carbon as a molecule, carbon as soft matter, and biologically inspired models for computing. Art inspired by carbon and enhanced by digital technologies are a means to understand and interpret nature- and science-related concepts.

INTRODUCTION: BACKGROUND DATA

Themes discussed in this chapter comprise: Carbon as mineral, meaning coal: in fossil fuels, as a source of energy, in surface mining with its environmental cost. Next, carbon as a molecule is examined: in the carbon cycle, carbon monoxide CO, carbon allotropes and isotopes. Finally, carbon as soft matter: present in computers, nanocomputers, quantum computing, and biologically inspired models for computing.

Organic chemistry is about carbon compounds and thus it is also about us. Carbon was known in ancient civilizations, e.g., Egyptian and Roman, in the forms of soot and charcoal. Diamonds were known in China about 2500 BC. Scientists

described almost ten million organic compounds formed by carbon. Carbon is the fourth most abundant element in the universe after hydrogen, helium, and oxygen. There is a lot of carbon in the Sun, stars, and comets. On the Earth it is the main constituent of many minerals and biological molecules. Inorganic carbon is contained in carbonate rocks: limestones, dolomites, marbles, and in carbon dioxide (CO_2); it occurs in organic deposits such as coal, peat, oil, and methane hydrate. Carbon is present in all life forms and is crucial for life on Earth because it forms many bonds to form complex organic molecules (carbon makes up to four bonds per atom). Strong Carbon-carbon bonds to other carbon atoms combine into long, strong, stable, rich in energy chains and rings, such as in a DNA that is made of two intertwined molecules built around a carbon chain. The carbon exchange results from the chemical, physical, geological,

DOI: 10.4018/978-1-4666-4627-8.ch013

and biological processes. Carbon exists in the atmosphere as carbon dioxide (810 gigatonnes of carbon: one gigatonne $= 10^9$ metric tons), in water bodies (36,000 gigatonnes of carbon), and in the biosphere (1,900 gigatonnes of carbon). The amount of carbon in simple organic compounds (carbon plus hydrogen) of hydrocarbons, such as coal, petroleum, and natural gas, is around 900 gigatonnes. Carbon combines with hydrogen and oxygen into sugars, lignans, chitins, alcohols, fats, aromatic esters, carotenoids, and terpens. Carbon dioxide is the most important human-contributed greenhouse gas (which absorbs and emits infrared radiation) resulting in the greenhouse effect. A chemical element carbon C has atomic number 6. Carbon nucleus contains 6 protons and 8 neutrons (carbon isotopes have 2–16 neutrons). As a nonmetallic element, carbon in its solid form is dull and brittle, forms acidic molecules with oxygen, and has a tendency to attract electrons, making four electrons available to form very strong covalent chemical bonds (with pairs of electrons shared between atoms). It does not react with oxidizers at room temperature; when heated, it forms carbon oxides, which are used in the iron and steel industry. Carbon atoms can form covalent bonds to many other types of atoms and form many materials such as wood or body cells.

Organic carbon is a crucial component and a source of energy stored in carbon bonds and used by all living beings. Organisms (called autotrophs) extract carbon from the air in the form of CO_2 converting it into organic carbon and building nutrients. Using the sunlight's energy plants and plankton absorb and combine CO_2 and water to form sugar (CH_2O) and oxygen: $CO_2 + H_2O +$ energy $= CH_2O + O_2$. Glucose, fructose, and other sugars, through processes such as respiration, create fuel for further metabolic processes. Plants can break down the sugar to get the energy. Other organisms (called heterotrophs) must obtain organic carbon by consuming other organisms. Animals (including people) can get energy from breaking down the plant or plankton sugar; they have to eat it first. Oxygen combines with sugar to release water, carbon dioxide, and energy: CH_2O

Figure 1. Jennifer Funnell, Carbon. (© 2011, J. Funnell. Used with permission)

$+ O_2 = CO_2 + H_2O +$ energy. Then, carbon (as CO_2) returns to the atmosphere because plants and plankton die and decay, bacteria decompose dead organisms, or fire burns out plants.

Figure 1 presents carbon existing in its different forms, which people would be able to associate with what's shown: as a stick of graphite in a pencil, charcoal, diamond, a part of tires and steel.

CARBON AS MINERAL: COAL

Carbon in Fossil Fuels

Carbon is one of the most plentiful elements in the universe after hydrogen, helium, and oxygen (by mass). Carbon is second element (18% by mass) after oxygen (65% by mass) that makes human body. Human cells, which consist of 65-90% water, are apart of it composed of organic molecules containing carbon. Carbon is the 15th most abundant element in the Earth crust, present in great amounts in fossil fuels – coal, petroleum, and natural gas. Fossil fuels result from decomposition of the large quantities of organisms, mostly zooplankton, algae, and plants. Microorganisms break down organic matter in the absence of oxygen (which is called anaerobic digestion). Organisms and resulting fossil fuels, mostly buried below the Earth surface underneath sedimentary rock, undergo intense heat and pressure. They are up to 650 million years old (Halbouty, 2004). Decomposing organic matter provides an abundance of hydro-carbons – organic compounds built from hydrogen and carbon. They can be gaseous like methane or propane, liquid such as benzene, solid (for example paraffin wax), or polymers (e.g., polyethylene or polystyrene). Saturated (without double or triple bonds in a molecule) hydrocarbons, along with other organic compounds, occur in abundance in crude oil and are basis of petroleum fuels existing in geologic formations. Oil provides 93% of the energy used for transportation, but only about 1% of the energy used to generate electric power.

The consumption of fossil fuels results in energy-related carbon dioxide (CO_2) emissions. The U.S. dioxide emissions from the consumption of fossil fuels were 5,471 million metric tons CO_2 in 2011. It fell 2.4 percent from the 2010 level and, according to the EIA predictions will be below the 2005 level through 2035 (EIA, 2012a; EIA, 2012b).

Greenhouse gases in an atmosphere trap heat from the sun and warm the planet's surface. They are mostly water vapor (H_2O), carbon dioxide (CO_2), methane (CH_4), ozone (O_3), and nitrous oxide (N_2O). Nitrogen (N_2 comprising 78% of the dry atmosphere) and oxygen (O_2 comprising 21%) exert almost no greenhouse effect (IPPC, 2007). Most of the U.S. greenhouse gas emissions are related to energy consumption, and most of those are CO_2. From 1990 to 2011, energy-related CO_2 emissions in the United States increased by about 0.4% per year, and comprised about 18% of the world's total energy-related CO_2. Greenhouse gases absorb and emit thermal infrared radiation (with longer wavelength than that of visible light). The greenhouse effect results from this: absorption and re-radiation of heat toward the Earth surface and lower atmosphere, and the following elevation of the Earth temperature. In the United States, about three-quarters of human-caused greenhouse gas emissions came from the burning of fossil fuels in energy use driven by economic growth, heating and cooling needs, and electricity generation. Energy consumption causes 87% of the U.S. greenhouse gas emission, which is growing by about 1% per year. Levels of greenhouse gases have increased by about 40% since industrialization began around 150 years ago. A cap-and-trade program (which increases the costs of using fossil fuels) places a limit (or cap) on the total amount of emissions, to reduce polluting emissions through a system of allowances that can be traded to minimize costs to affected sources.

Scientists estimate there is organic matter beneath the Antarctic Ice Sheet, up to 14 kilometers thick and weighting billions of tons, possibly the same order of magnitude as in the

Arctic permafrost. It contains metabolically active Archaea (single-cell microorganisms) that support the degradation of organic carbon to methane. That means organic carbon is probably being metabolized beneath the ice by microbes to carbon dioxide and methane gas. It may play a part in the global climate warming because of the ice-sheet deterioration (Wadham et al., 2012).

Sources of Energy

The major energy sources in the United States are petroleum (oil), natural gas, coal, nuclear, and renewable energy. Renewable energy sources used in the U. S. power plants include water (hydroelectric), wood, wind, organic waste, geothermal energy, and sun. About 13% of electricity was generated in 2011 from renewable energy sources.

Geological survey and research programs on searching for possible mineral resources may involve many disciplines. Some are unexpected; for example, according to Maura Flannery (2012), "there are even cases where herbarium specimens have been analyzed for mineral content as a way to identify areas where there are high concentrations of a particular mineral in the soil, and therefore may be places to mine for that substance (Mabey, 2010)".

A hydroelectric plant is an alternative source of electricity generation. Hydroelectric plants are the run-of-river plants (that utilize the flow of a waterway, usually a river to turn a turbine) and the storage plants (using water from a reservoir to control water flow over a turbine). In 2011 hydropower accounted for 8% of total U.S. electricity generation; however, they provided over half of the electricity in the Pacific Northwest. Some Northeastern states, in response to the potential closure of several major refineries, plan a transition to ultra-low sulfur diesel for heating oil, beginning with New York in the summer of 2012.

Worldwide wind power generation exceeded 250 billion kilowatt hours in 2009, which is equivalent to the annual electricity consumption of over 22 million average households in the United States. Wind generation has more than tripled since 2004. Despite this growth, the world still generated only 1% of its total electricity from wind power in 2009.

Shale gas is natural gas that is trapped within the shale formations. Shale is fine-grained sedimentary rock formed from mud and clay that contains petroleum and natural gas. Horizontal drilling and hydraulic fracturing techniques allowed an access to shale gas and revived the natural gas industry in the United States.

Nuclear power generation provides about 20% of total electricity supply in the U.S., where 65 nuclear power plants include 104 operable commercial nuclear reactors. Nuclear power output is expected to grow at a rate about half that of total electricity generation (EIA, 2012d).

Biofuel production includes production of bioethanol (ethyl alcohol, same as found in alcoholic beverages) from agricultural feedstocks: corn, sugar cane, potato, or manioc, as a form of renewable energy. Ethanol is mainly used as a biofuel additive for gasoline: ethanol fuel mixtures add up to 10% of ethanol to gasoline (RFA, 2012). World ethanol production for transport fuel exceeds 52 billion liters. Ethanol fuel is mostly used in the U.S. and Brazil; both countries produced 87% of the world's ethanol fuel production in 2011. However, various social, economic, environmental, and technical issues with biofuel production and use have been discussed in the popular media and scientific journals. These include oil prices, the 'food versus fuel' debate, poverty reduction potential, carbon emissions levels, sustainable issues related to production, deforestation (about half of the world's original forests had been destroyed by 2011), soil erosion, loss of biodiversity, impact on water resources, as well as energy balance and efficiency. As for now, only the starch that represents about 50% of the dry kernel mass

Figure 2. Grant Stout, Carbon. (© 2011, G. Stout. Used with permission)

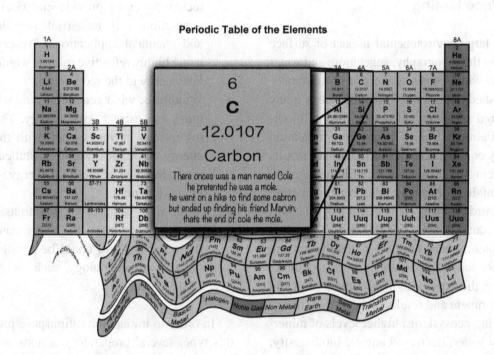

is transformed into ethanol. Figure 2, "Carbon" presents a student work.

Surface Mining in the United States

The world's largest reserves of coal are in the United States, where the coalmines produced in 2011 more than a billion short tons of coal, and more than 90% of this coal was used by the U. S. power plants to generate electricity (EIA, 2012d).

The low-sulfur content coal of the Midwest and western states contribute to the geographical shift in coal production towards the western United States. About 60% of the coal produced today results from the surface mining from the seams lying close to the earth surface. The soil and rock overlying the mineral deposit, called the overburden is removed with the use of the heavy equipment called the earthmovers. Then the next huge machines such as dragline excavators or

bucket wheel excavators extract the coal. There are several forms of surface mining including

- Strip mining of a seam of mineral by removing a strip of the overburden;
- Open-pit mining that means removing rock and minerals from an open pit or borrow and later converting pits to landfills after the mineral resource is exhausted;
- Mountaintop removal mining that involves restructuring both the mine site and the previously forested area where the overburden is dumped;
- Dredging that brings underwater mineral deposits;
- Highwall mining through pushing with a power head and shearing with a cutterhead boom and auger.

The Environmental Cost of Surface Mining

There is large environmental impact of surface mining on the topography, vegetation, and water resources, which causes conversion of substances in watersheds into toxic forms, threatens many endangered species and lead to a loss of biodiversity (Palmer, 2011). The growing production of energy coming from the surface mines results in producing large areas of infertile waste rock. The mountaintop removal mining involves blasting the overburden (up to 400 vertical feet – 120 m) with thousands of tones of explosives. The valley fills frequently bury headwater streams causing permanent loss of ecosystems. Surface mining happens at the expense of local communities and the environment and results in the disturbance of pre-existing ecosystems: higher levels of minerals in the water; decreased aquatic biodiversity; presence of dust containing sulfur compounds; poor level of reforesting the areas; invasion of the quick-growing, non-native grasses that compete with tree seedlings, planted to quickly provide vegetation on a site; and many other threats.

The Wasteland Development

This project is about a holistic solution to the wasteland development. We may now consider the multilevel recycled business. Land on which surface mining is actually going or has been already completed can be reused for establishing entrepreneurial economic activities aimed at energy production (see Table 1). The land on which surface mining is actually going or has been already completed can be converted to conduct energy producing entrepreneurial economic activities:

- Flat plate arrays of solar cells can generate electric power. Photovoltaic systems can be installed on the reclaimed area. Solar thermal electric facilities can be installed to focus direct sunlight for the production of high-temperature fluids. Solar thermal technology may provide electrical power generation, with industrial, metallurgical, and chemical applications. Power towers using highly reflective mirrors would translate energy to the receivers.
- Windmills, wind generators, and wind turbines can extract wind energy. The wind towers can be intertwined with the solar energy units, for example, installed in-between the rows of the solar energy generating system units.
- Some may wonder whether transforming wind from windy parts of the country to those flat and still could be possible with the use of technology such as Arduino (2013) boards.

In order to initiate a multipurpose project of this type, several preparatory actions would be needed, along with professional consultations. As a summary, proposed actions would comprise

Conducting a survey about wasteland locations and ownerships allowing possible initiatives

- Working with real estate agents on buying a land and solving legal issues
- Working on road construction, if necessary
- Continuing or completing surface mining
- Working on stabilizing rock and controlling erosion
- Solar panels installation
- Windmills installation
- Establishing an Artificial Garden and Artist Residency Program and facilities
- Establishing event program.

On the top of the profitable, often lucrative ways of reusing the wasteland left after surface mining, the owners of the surface mining areas may choose initiatives and investments that would at least partially compensate for the harm inflicted on local communities and the environment. The so-called wasteland could be turned into cultural,

Table 1. Converting surface mining sites

Visual Response: A Multilevel Recycled Business Scenario
Create a scenario for reshaping the land where surface mining took place, making it useful again, environmentally healthy, and still generating profit could be designed as a multilevel recycled business. Draw a plan for a project about possible group collaboration, which might comprise several stages: Imagine that you and your siblings inherited some land. You are an archeologist who explores this ground and your sibling is a paleontologist who searches for the remains of ancient animal life. After inheriting some land, you as an archeologist and a paleontologist would hire a crew to attach strings to short vertical poles in order to setup a grid evenly distributed in rows and columns. The crew would be assigned to uncover several feet of dirt. Another sibling, a photographer and yet another one a drawer would document the content of the underground in two ways: photographically and graphically, to analyze the data and find artifacts that interest them. A cross-section of the earth from the surface down would be drawn. Make a depiction of layers as they found them: a swamp, grass and soil, bushes, trees with roots, dirt, stones, rocks, and then show the underground layers. The next step would be drilling core samples down from the surface and cutting the walls of a river exposed a layer of coal. Data collected with a GPS (Global Positioning System) may confirm the existence of a layer of coal, from single inches to several feet deep. Heavy machines are needed in order to extract coal. To develop a surface mining plant, they would have to build roads, so heavy machinery could arrive and dig out the scoops of dirt and then coal, each of the size of a house.

experimental, and entertaining area for local and incoming people. In order to make it happen, artist residence program could be established to gather artists and scientists working on a new type of an interactive setup for anyone willing to experience, interpret, and play with art related themes. This creative environment could involve the new media art: digital paintings, drawings, and sculptures created with the use of digital technology; computer graphics and animation, sound, kinetic sculpture, video, interactive displays and installation art, generative art, bio art, robotics, virtual art, Internet

Figure 3. Anna Ursyn, Surface Mining. (© 2013, A. Ursyn. Used with permission)

art, art based on biotechnology, evolutionary art, and many other approaches. Artists would explore man-made and environmental sound, combining their production with architecture, sculpture, experimental theatre, film, and video. The facility would not only contain spaces assigned for art production but also would be open to the public, so the new media art products could be accessible on demand, interact with participants, and possibly become collaborative and networkable, among other qualities.

Artists would be given an access to the equipment and the power producing facilities: windmills, wind and solar towers, so they could design those energy-producing devices to become the attractive to the eye sculptural constructions. They would be invited to create an artificial garden filled with evolutionary creations such as trees or mushrooms that change, react, evolve, and mutate, robotic artificial animals and thinking creatures that interact with visitors, and provide them with artificial life encounters or virtual reality experience. The facility would become a center that would gather those researching biologically

inspired technological solutions and those creating biologically inspired art. Contrary to the "Burning Man" tradition, art production would not perish at the end of any festival or exhibition but would add to the permanent art collection.

This initiative could possibly interest several institutions, societies, and organizations, because of its forward-thinking profile. One may imagine participants working on projects supported by the NSF grants, contributing to the EvoMusart conferences and events on Evolutionary and Biologically Inspired Music, Sound, Art and Design, Ars Electronica and SIGGRAPH Conference programs and Art Galleries, cooperating with the Leonardo Art-Science projects, working on projects awarded by the McArthur Foundation grants, and many others.

Figure 3 presents "Surface Mining" which shows the turmoil and the environmental impact caused by goal driven, incremental actions of entrepreneurs that are ready to expose the land to environmental risks. It pictures metaphorically, with sharp colors and dynamic lines, the disturbance caused by the removal of the overburden

Table 2. Plans for utilizing the land sites

Verbal Response: A Surface Mining Enterprise
Describe a multilayered structure of a project of reclaiming such an area. Now you have to face the environmental aspects of a surface mining. Machines removed the soil, the overburden between the soil and the coal, and extracted coal, which had been then taken away. Now you are facing a big surface with no soil, trees, animals and plants to feed them, forest, field, nor pasture. You are under public criticism because of the destructive effects of your actions, which may affect the climate, fauna and flora, to say nothing about people. There are no plants and so wildlife cannot revive on your wasted land. Moreover, despite of an income coming from the surface mining, the land remains quite ugly and useless. Mountaintop removal mining has caused a loss of more than 1.4 million acres of land land (Squillace, 2009).
You could now discuss utilizing the land for developing a factory of bricks or cement, building a prison, a landfill, a recycling station, a disposal area of computers, or, since many trees have already been cut, building a furniture factory and a paper making or a printing company. You could build an airport, a military base, or a culture-, sport-, or entertainment endeavors, such as a giant cinema, theaters, spaces for various kinds of performances, sports arena shaped like a coliseum, or arrange for events such as the Burning Man Festival (2013). You could consider constructing Olympic games (summer or winter) stadiums and facilities. This project would open other possibilities such as founding an artist-residence center or establishing a museum of copies of major collection of artwork. For example the ART BOOK, published by Phaidon Press could serve as a guide to the artwork created till XX century. Make a list of needs and a cost estimation for a multilayered structure of a project of reclaiming such an area, but remember that many of them require water and electricity supply, meeting sanitary needs of users, housing for workers and visitors, among other needs. You may be told to measure the level of pollution in the area first.

Figure 4. Osley and Elisabeth Cooper, Carbon. (© 2011, Osley &. E. Cooper. Used with permission)

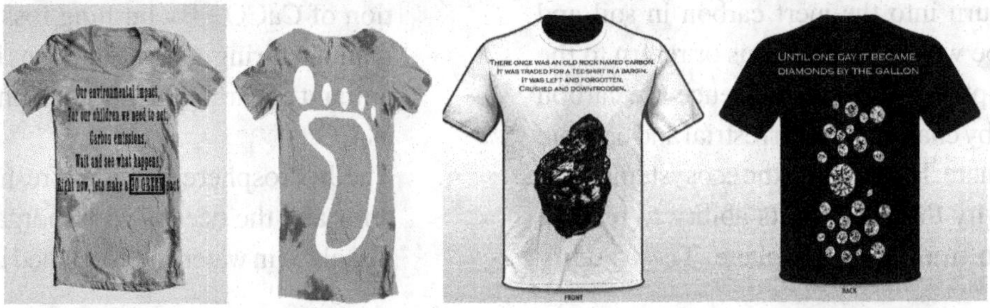

– soil and rock overlying the mineral deposit. This work shows the environmental cost of surface mining (Table 2).

Figure 4, "Carbon" presents two students' projects for a t-shirt design: an illustrated limerick and a verse on the theme of carbon.

CARBON AS A MOLECULE

The Carbon Cycle

Processes going in the carbon cycle regulate the CO_2 concentration in the atmosphere in a natural way. Carbon geochemical cycle describes the processes that sustain life on Earth. It is generally accepted that the rising levels of CO_2 concentration (from 280 ppm in 1800 to almost 400 ppm) result in global warming, so lowering the amount of CO_2 in the atmosphere may re-balance the carbon cycle (NASA Earth Observatory, 2011).

The exchange of carbon, which includes respiration, transpiration, combustion, and decomposition, goes between the four reservoirs of carbon: the biosphere, the earth, the air, and the water.

1. We are all made of carbon (and of water as well). The biosphere contains organic carbon in living and dead organisms, as well as in soils: about 500 gigatons of carbon is in plants and other living organisms and approximately 1,500 gigatons in soil. Carbon in the terrestrial biosphere is mostly organic; the soil contains also inorganic carbon such as calcium carbonate ($CaCO_3$). Combustion and respiration cause the release of organic carbon into the atmosphere. Organic carbon may turn into the inert carbon in soil and then be washed into oceans or return to the atmosphere. Humans influence the carbon cycle by changing the terrestrial and oceanic biosphere. By affecting the ecosystem's productivity they change its ability to remove carbon from the atmosphere. They modify the land use, change the land cover, and reduce the ecosystems' biodiversity and resilience to environmental stresses. Forests hold large amounts of carbon; removing them for agricultural, industrial, or urbanization related purpose causes that more carbon stays in the atmosphere. Air pollution, temperature increase, agricultural practices, and land erosion are increasing decomposition processes and washing carbon out of soils to the atmosphere.

2. The lithosphere comprises the carbon reservoirs in the Earth's upper mantle and crust, in the sediments with fossil fuels. The outer layer of the Earth includes soil organic carbon and the terrestrial biosphere. Carbonate rocks release carbon as CO_2 when they undergo metamorphosis. Volcanoes release CO_2 into the atmosphere and ocean when the moving crustal plates collide, sink, and melt under the great heat and pressure producing silicate minerals and CO_2 (between 130 and 380 million metric tons of carbon dioxide per year). Humans release carbon as CO_2 when they extract and burn fossil fuels.

3. The atmosphere contains two main forms of carbon: carbon dioxide (CO_2) and methane (CH_4) both absorb and retain heat intensifying the greenhouse effect. CO_2 is more important greenhouse gas because methane is more short-lived and its concentration is much lower. Plant respiration produces CO_2, which falls in raindrops and reacts with the atmosphere's water forming carbonic acid (H_2CO_3). This acidifies rocks and increases the ocean acidity, which affects ocean biosystems and slows the biological precipitation of $CaCO_3$. By burning fossil fuels and manufacturing concrete humans increase the amount of carbon in the atmosphere, mostly as CO_2.

4. The hydrosphere includes fresh water systems and the oceans with inorganic carbon dissolved in water and contained in living and

dead marine biota. Oceans contain almost as much carbon as the lithosphere. The surface and the deep layers of the oceans contain dissolved CO_2 from the atmosphere and rivers (turned into H_2CO_3) and organic carbon, which is produced by organisms through photosynthesis, exchanged throughout the food chain, or settled in the ocean's deep, carbon rich layers as dead soft tissue or in shells as $CaCO_3$. Absorption of CO_2 in oceans limits its rise in the atmosphere caused by humans. Humans affect the oceanic carbon cycle. Higher ocean temperatures due to the human-induced climate change modify ecosystems. Acid rain and polluted runoff from agriculture and industry have devastating effects on sensitive ecosystems such as coral reefs. It limits both the ocean's ability to absorb carbon from the atmosphere and reduces oceanic biodiversity.

Scientists describe the fast and slow carbon cycle. The fast carbon cycle includes the plants and phytoplankton (microscopic organisms in the ocean); they are the main components of the fast, biological/physical carbon cycle, which operates at the time scale of days to thousands of years. The fast carbon cycle presents the movement of carbon through life forms or the biosphere such as animal tissues, between land, atmosphere, and oceans, in billions of tons of carbon per year (with diurnal and seasonal oscillations). It is caused both by natural fluxes and human actions.

The geological component of the carbon cycle operates at a slow pace, at the time scale of millions of years, yet it determines the amount of carbon in the atmosphere, and thus of global temperature. Tectonic activity, that may last hundreds of millions years, moves great amounts of carbon (10-100 million metric tons every year) between rocks, soil, ocean, and atmosphere. There is carbon stored in lithosphere as rocks from the time when the earth was formed, and the organic carbon, mostly as limestone and its derivatives

resulting from the sedimentation of $CaCO_3$ stored in the shells of marine shell-building (calcifying) organisms (such as corals) and plankton (like coccolithophores and foraminifera), which sink after death to the seafloor. Calcium ions combine with carbonic acid into calcium carbonate that becomes limestone or its metamorphic form, marble. There are also fossilized organic materials sedimented and buried under high heat and pressure, some fossils aging millions, sometimes hundreds of millions of years. Carbon moves with rain from the atmosphere to the lithosphere as carbonic acid (H_2CO_3) and causes chemical weathering: calcium, magnesium, potassium, or sodium ions flow in rivers to the ocean.

Humans strongly alter the carbon cycle, mostly through CO_2 emissions into the atmosphere that are exceeding natural fluctuations (Falkowski et al., 2000), altering weather patterns, influencing oceanic chemistry, and affecting global climate, especially temperature. The use of fossil fuels has accelerated since the industrial revolution and increased carbon accumulation in the atmosphere.

Carbon Monoxide (CO)

Carbon monoxide (CO) has no color, odor, or taste, and is slightly lighter than air. Atoms of carbon and oxygen are connected by a triple bond. However when in air, carbon monoxide combines with oxygen and forms carbon dioxide CO_2 and ozone O_3; it is part of photochemical smog and also increases ground ozone level according to reaction $CO + 2O_2 > CO_2 + O_3$. It occurs naturally in the lowest parts of atmosphere due to photochemical reactions that produce about 5×10^{12} kilograms per year; daytime concentration in atmosphere is twice more during a day than in darkness (Weinstock & Niki, 1972). It is dissolved in molten volcanic rock at high pressures in the Earth's mantle. It is also present in forest fires, man-made fires, and other forms of combustion associated with vehicles, generators (many of cases occurring during power outages due to severe weather), furnaces, ranges, fireplaces, water heaters, room heaters, or mowers. It is also temporary pollutant in some urban areas. Carbon monoxide forms due to incomplete burning of wood, coal, charcoal, oil, paraffin, propane, natural gas, and trash, when there is not enough oxygen to produce CO_2.

CO normal level in human blood is 0% to 3% and is higher in smokers. In higher concentrations it is toxic to humans and animals because it combines with hemoglobin (protein that transports oxygen in blood of vertebrates) to produce carboxy-hemoglobin, which cannot deliver oxygen to tissues and also to myoglobin (a red protein in muscle cells that delivers and stories oxygen) and mitochondrial enzyme cytochrome oxidase. Therefore there is a danger of poisoning when coal is burning in a stove or a car is idling in a closed garage. On average, about 170 people in the United States die every year from CO produced by non-automotive consumer products (U.S. Consumer Product Safety Commision, 2012). Previously, coal gas containing CO was used for domestic lighting, cooking, and heating, and now iron smelting in steel plants still produces CO as a byproduct, blast-furnace gas, which is flammable and toxic (Ayres & Ayres, 2010, p. 36). Some microorganisms (bacteria and archea) living in extreme conditions can metabolize carbon monoxide.

Carbon monoxide is produced in organism as part of normal metabolism (when produced during hemoglobin breakdown) and may possibly have biological functions as a biological regulator of several functions: as a vascular growth factor, anti-inflammatory agent, and blood vessel relaxant. CO is associated with many functions in the immune, respiratory, reproductive, gastrointestinal, kidney, and liver systems. According to Wu & Wang (2005), communication inside a cell and also among cells occurs by conducting mechanical, electrical, or chemical signals. Chemical communication includes hormones (acting on distant targets via circulation in endocrine mode), autocoids (that act on the same cells from which they are produced (such as prostaglandins, adenosine, and platelet-activating factor), and transmitters (regulation for adjacent cells or cells where transmitters are produced).

Physiological functions of CO involve acting as a signaling molecule in the neuronal system: neuronal activities such as regulation of neurotransmitters (ACH, catecholamines, serotonin, histamine, glutamate, glycine, GABA, and ATP or its metabolites), neuropeptide release, learning and memory, and odor response adaptation. Abnormalities in CO metabolism have been linked to a variety of diseases including neuro degenerations, hypertension, heart failure, and inflammation (Wu & Wang, 2005).

Solomon Snyder & Christopher Ferris (2000) examined carbon monoxide CO, nitrogen monoxide (nitric oxide) NO and d-serine as candidate neurotransmitters and offered insights regarding novel definitions of neurotransmitters or neuromodulators. As described by the authors, a transmitter is a molecule, released by neurons or glial cells (non-neuronal, connective cells that support and protect neurons) that physiologically influences the eletrochemical state of adjacent cells. Outside the CNS, those adjacent target cells need not be neurons and, in most instances, would be smooth muscle or glandular cells (Snyder & Ferris, 2000, p. 1750). Carbon monoxide (CO), nitric oxide (NO), and hydrogen sulfide (H_2S) display metabolism and physiological functions that position this gas in the family of endogenous (originating within an organism) signaling gasotransmitters (Wang, 2002).

Interstellar CO molecule is the most abundant molecule after hydrogen both in atomic or molecular form H_2. The CO molecule is asymmetric and thus it radiates spectral lines easier to detect than hydrogen lines (Combes, 1991, p. 195). In astrophysics, it is commonly used tracer of molecular gas in the interstellar medium of galaxies

Table 3. Calling attention to CO

Visual Response: Engaging into Environmental Concerns
Animated visualizations show, across various continents and on different dates, the levels of carbon monoxide as the color streaks of red, orange, and yellow colors. Maybe you would design a poster warning about the CO poisoning danger. Translate the data concerning CO concentrations resulting from various activities into a colorful visual form with a limited yet coded color palette and make a picture that could prevent careless actions of people you care about.

and provides information about the molecular clouds in which stars emerge.

Industrial carbon monoxide's production includes many methods for obtaining CO under different names such as producer gas, water gas, or synthesis gas, applied along with several laboratory methods. As an industrial gas, it has many applications in bulk chemicals manufacturing, for example, for producing fuels used as replacement for petrol, or as color additive in meat and fish packaging, to keep them looking fresh (because it combines with myoglobin) (Table 3).

Carbon Allotropes

Carbon exists in several physical forms with different molecular configurations, which are called allotropes. The best-known allotropes are: graphite, diamond, and amorphous (without crystalline structure) carbon. Graphene is a single layer of graphite and has extraordinary electrical, thermal, and physical properties. Physical properties of carbon's allotropic forms vary. Carbon as graphite is the softest of natural substances, opaque, black, and conducts electricity well. Carbon as diamond has the highest thermal conductivity of all materials, poor electrical conductivity, is transparent, and the hardest of natural substances. Graphite is a good lubricant and diamond is highly abrasive. Carbon atom in a diamond has covalent bonds with four other carbons: each carbon atom bonds to four other carbon atoms, which makes tetrahedrons that form hexagonal rings; this makes diamond extremely strong. Of the mined diamonds, 80% (20 tons annually) are for industrial use and are unsuitable as gemstones; additionally from the 1950s, 80 tons of synthetic diamonds are produced annually. Synthetic nano crystalline diamond is the hardest material known (Irifune, Kurio, Sakamoto, Inoue, & Sumiya, 2003). Coal and soot, called amorphous carbon, are products of pyrolysis (decomposing by heat). The coal grades in industry depend on the carbon content and include anthracite (about 90% carbon), bituminous coal (75–90% carbon), and lignite (about 55% carbon).

Sticks of graphite are used as the handwriting material in pencils. Henry Petroski (1992) described in a monographic way a history of the pencil design and its circumstances. According to Petroski, deposits of graphite, that was thought a form of lead, were found in Cumbria, England about 1565. At that time, the Crown – the corporation sole in England, guarded graphite because it could be used to line the cannonballs, so it had to be smuggled out for use in pencils or for marking sheep. There were at first many confusing names for a pencil. Cannabis hemp fibres with clamps of plumbago (an old-fashioned term for graphite) were used in pencils. In his letter of 1586, William Camden's wrote, "Here also is found abundance of that mineral earth, or hard shining stone, which we call Blacklead, used by painters in drawing their lines and shading" (cited after Petroski, 1992, p. 46). In the 17th century pieces of plumbago were held in brass and silver cases with Baroque designs; early wood-cased graphite changed into pencils in the shape of octagonal shaft of wood. Black lead was discovered in the black-lead mine of Cumberland (which is now exhausted) and also imported from the Balearic Islands, Ceylon, Bohemia, and Sicily. In 1795 Nicolas Jacques

Conté discovered the process of mixing graphite dust with clay, so the pencils could be made in variety of hardness; it was universally used for making pencils called Conte crayons. In the 19th century Johann Faber used Siberian graphite that was 94.5% pure. In 1800 in Concord, Mass., an unknown woman mixed plumbago with English red chalk; this was the beginning of first pencils made in America (Petroski, 1992). Although lead is not used for writing, there were many lead poisoning cases in the 20th century because of the lead content in the pencils' lacquer outer coating; people ingested lead by sucking and chewing pencils (Life, 1972).

Charcoal drawings in caves were inspiring for artists; for example, Pablo Picasso drew inspiration from the Lascaux caves and the German film director and screenwriter Werner Herzog from the Chauvet cave. A pencil has become a tool for its own medium, a metaphor and even an object for auto identification. The French artist Henri de Toulouse-Lautrec (1864-1901) had reportedly said of himself, "I am a pencil." The American painter Andrew Wyeth (1917-2009) described his pencil as "the fencer's foil." The Moscow-born Paris illustrator and caricaturist Emmanuel Poiré took his pseudonym after the Russian word for pencil, karandash. In turn, a Swiss pencil-making firm was named Caran d'Ache after this artist (Petroski, 1992, p. 6).

Carbon Isotopes

Carbon has three naturally occurring isotopes (isotopes have in their nuclei equal numbers of protons but different numbers of neutrons), with ^{12}C and ^{13}C being stable; carbon ^{14}C is a radioactive isotope decaying with a half-life of about 5,730 years (half-life tells time isotope falls to half of its original radioactivity). Because of this relatively short half-life ^{14}C is virtually absent in ancient rocks. It develops in atmosphere at altitudes of 9–15 km by interaction of nitrogen with cosmic rays. Formation of the carbon atomic nucleus occurs within giant and supergiant stars in extreme temperatures, in a triple alpha process. The shortest-lived of isotope is ^8C, which has a half-life of 1.98739×10^{-21} seconds (Barwinski, 2012).

Radiocarbon dating, invented in 1949 by Willard Libby (the 1960 Nobel Prize) is a ^{14}C-based radiometric method of estimating the age of materials aged up to 58,000–62,000 years. Older samples contain too small number of remaining intrinsic ^{14}C carbon. Carbon dating allows estimate the age of organic remains and artifacts, objects of cultural or historical value, if they contain carbon. Scientists collected wood of the same age (based on the tree ring analysis) to increase accuracy of the technique. They have also measured radiocarbon in stalactites and stalagmites (called speleothems) using both ^{14}C carbon dating method and the uranium-thorium dating to obtain radiocarbon calibration curves (Hoffman et al., 2010).

Ancient fossilized animal and human footprints in Acahualinka, Nicaragua has been first estimated as 5,000 years old and later determined as 2,100 years old.

The Chauvet-Pont-d'Arc Cave in the southern France, discovered in 1994, contains the rock art, a treasure trove of Paleolithic masterwork paintings, prints, charcoal drawings of different animal species such as horses, lions, rhinos and bears, etched into the cave's walls, and also fossilized remains, and markings of animals, some of which are now extinct (Herzog, 2012). Findings based on an analysis called geomorphological and chlorine-36 dating (^{36}Cl Cosmic Ray Exposure) show that most of the art works were created by people who lived 28,000 to 40,000 years ago, in the Aurignacian culture of the early stages of the Upper Paleolithic, Late Stone Age; later on, an overhanging cliff began collapsing 29,000 years ago and did so repeatedly over time, definitively sealing the entrance to humans around 21,000 years ago. "This study confirms that the Chauvet cave paintings are the oldest and the most elaborate ever discovered, challenging our current knowledge of human cognitive evolution" (Sadier et al., 2008; Agence France-Presse, 2012). Bon et al. (2008) wrote, "We collected bone samples from the Paleolithic painted cave of Chauvet-Pont d'Arc (France), which displays the earliest known human drawings, and contains thousands of bear remains. We selected a cave bear sternebra, radiocarbon dated to 32,000 years before present, from which we generated overlapping DNA fragments assembling into a 16,810-base pair mitochondrial genome. … our study establishes the Chauvet-Pont d'Arc Cave as a new reservoir for Paleogenetic studies."

A German film director Werner Herzog created in 2010 a documentary film about Chauvet Cave, *Cave of Forgotten Dreams* (2012) and won Best Documentary Award by several film critics groups. He rendered in 3D the curvature of the rocks to enhance the texture and depth of the art works on the cave walls. As described on his webpage, Herzog had been mesmerized, as a boy in Germany, by a book about cave paintings that he saw in a store window. He wrote, "The deep amazement it inspired in me is with me to this day. I remember a shudder of awe possessing me as I opened its pages." (Werner Herzog, 2012). Cave of Forgotten Dreams was triggered by a Judith Thurman's article in The New Yorker based on photos and interviews. Herzog became the first filmmaker permitted by the French Ministry of Culture to enter the cave, however under heavy restrictions. All people had to wear special suits and shoes that have had no contact with the exterior, stay on a two-foot-wide walkway, using only a small 3D-camera rig and three battery-powered light sources. Because of near-toxic levels of CO_2 and radon in the cave, the crew could enter the cave for only a few hours each day. The cave explorers found, among rock paintings on a cave wall, some hand imprints with one finger shorter than others. This could be considered the first signature in art.

The radiocarbon dating provided a key marker for the disastrous volcanic eruption (Minoan eruption of Santorini) that devastated the island of

Thera close to the coast of Crete, and implications for the chronology of the Eastern Mediterranean cultures from the Bronze Age in the second millennium BC. The radiocarbon dating analysis of an olive tree buried beneath a lava flow from the volcano indicate, that the eruption occurred between 1627 BC and 1600 BC with a 95% degree of probability (Friedrich et al., 2006; Manning et al, 2006).

CARBON AS SOFT MATTER

In 1996 Harold Kroto, Robert Curl and Richard Smalley won the Nobel Prize for Chemistry for their discovery in 1985 of a new allotrope of carbon, which they named Buckminsterfullerene after the architect Buckminster Fuller who designed geodesic domes in the 1960's. It opened a new section of chemistry, with applications in astrochemistry, superconductivity, and chemistry/physics material science, for example for catalytic methane activation. Fullerene C60 is a black solid that sublimes at 800 K and is soluble in common solvents such as benzene, toluene or chloroform.

Carbon exists the nanoscale dimension as graphenes, carbon nanotubes, liquid crystals, nanoshells, and other soft matter. Graphene is a one atom thick sheet of carbon atoms arranged in tightly bound hexagons. Fullerenes, which have the atoms arranged in closed shells, include buckyballs (particles that have millions of atoms, with dozens of concentric shells like a set of Russian dolls that fit one into another from the smallest to the biggest one), carbon nanotubes, nanofibers, and carbon nanobuds. In 2007 Nasibulin et al. (2007) have synthesized NanoBuds – a hybrid material that combines fullerenes and single-walled carbon nanotubes into a structure where the fullerenes are covalently bonded to the outer sidewalls of carbon nanotubes. Nanobuds have combined mechanical and electrical properties of both these structures. Buckyball bonding is a specific type of bonding typical of the carbon nanotubes.

A carbon nanotube is a molecule of carbon in form of a hollow cylinder with a diameter of around one or two nanometers; they can be seen using a scanning tunneling microscope. One nanometer (nm) is one billionth, or 10^{-9} of a meter. Typical carbon-carbon bond has the length about 0.12-0.15 nm; a DNA double helix has a diameter around 2 nm. Nanotubes and fullerenes are present in structures such as inorganic carbon, DNA, and cell membranes. Both carbon nanotubes and graphene products (such as graphene foams, nanowires, sieves, graphite nanoparticles, or porous carbon) are offered for sale online. The cylindrical structures of carbon nanotubes have exceptional electrical and thermal properties along with superior mechanical strength. The fabrication of carbon nanotubes serves a variety of applications. Carbon nanotubes are used in the production of memory chips, batteries, and many consumer products such as tennis rackets, badminton rackets, bicycles, compounds to manufacture cars and airplanes, and so forth. Carbon nanotubes distributed on small cement grains provide superior strength of concrete. New methods for producing carbon nanotubes are capable of reducing their price.

Carbon in Computers

Before the advent of nanotechnology and an abundance of works on designing a nanocomputer, when one talked about computers one might mean an original mainframe computer, a mini computer, or a microcomputer. The powerful mainframe computers served for statistics, planning, and processing of big data sets such as those concerning the census, government, industry, or consumers. They included the central processing unit, main memory, hosted multiple operating systems, and operated virtual machines – the guest operating systems with software implementation of a computer enabling the execution of the operating system or running programs aiding the single processes.

Mini computers, introduced in mid-1960s cost about $25,000; they had input-output devices such as a teleprinter and memory capable of running higher-level language programs such as Fortran or Basic.

Microcomputers, often called personal computers and designed for individual users, did not need big cabinets or special rooms. They contained a microprocessor, a central processing unit (CPU), a power supply unit, RAM memory, memory storage devices combined with the CPU, batteries, and integrated or separate input/output devices for conveying information such as monitors, keyboards, printers, and other human interface devices. Some of them became personal computers.

Nanocomputers

Advances in building nanocomputers bring about thinking about the role of carbon in computers, namely carbon in the nanoscale dimension in the form of carbon nanotubes. A nanocomputer has its parts no bigger than a few nanometers. There are no commercially available nanocomputers yet; they exist both in computer science and in science fiction. Nanocomputers might be built using mechanical, electronic, biochemical, or quantum mechanics principles.

Computer scientists are working toward building nanoscale computers that would be significantly faster and combine high computing power with low electrical requirements. Nanotubes allow reducing the size of chips and lowering physical limitations that prevent them from functioning reliably. Chips would contain a great number of electronic switches (50–100 nanometers in size). Grids of nanotubes may form memory and very fast operating circuits. With the Stanford team's approach, the digital integrated systems would possibly comprise arithmetic circuits, sequential storage, as well as the monolithic three-dimensional integrated circuits with extreme levels of integration (Science Daily, 2012). Na-

noscale computers would be portable, wearable or implantable. The small, nanoscale size of such computers would make them faster. Applications of nanoscale products would include carrying big data and information sets, detecting diseases and monitoring treatment, creating probes to detect single molecules, or constructing smart materials for turbine engines and body armor.

In 1965, Gordon Moore, one of the founders of the maker of computer chips Intel, predicted that the number of electronic switches and other devices put on a single chip would double every 18 months. It is still happening, with the smaller and faster chips. Nanosize chips would be ten-thousandths of an inch on a side and hold thousands bits of memory. That would involve thousands junctions, each of which would represent a "0" or "1" in digital language. Individual junctions would open and close billions of times per second, hundreds of gigahertz. A hybrid approach would allow making the nanotube junction switches by combining silicon nano wires with carbon nanotubes, to make it easier to connect switches on a chip and chips in the computer.

Chips have been made of silicon, which as the main ingredient of sand is one of the most abundant elements on Earth. The decrease in the size of silicon transistors in order to increase their speed causes increased energy consumption. Now, silicon will have to be replaced in order to further miniaturize electronic systems and make them faster. Silicon transistors in computers may be replaced by transistors based on carbon nanotubes, when nanotubes would replace traditional silicon technologies and produce smaller and faster components. By exchanging the silicon for a carbon nanotube, the transistors can be made both smaller and faster. Miniaturization of electronic systems depends on attaining energy efficiency. Application of carbon nanotubes circuit will possibly help to solve the challenge of energy efficiency, as they could provide a ten-times improvement in energy efficiency over silicon.

However, nanotube transistors display material imperfections inherent to carbon nanotubes. Some carbon nanotubes are semiconducting and they can be used in transistors. Metallic carbon nanotubes (that are not semiconducting) may often cause short circuits, excessive power leakage, and susceptibility to noise. Existing nanotube synthesis techniques do not produce exclusively semiconducting nanotube solutions. Teams of engineers are now working on securing the carbon nanotubes' viability to complement silicon CMOS (complementary metal–oxide–semiconductor) transistors that would have high noise immunity and low static power consumption. The Stanford engineers are working on developing a synthesis technique where the full-wafer-scale digital logic structures would be unaffected by misaligned and mis-positioned carbon nanotubes (Science Daily1, 2012).

Connecting nanotubes to form large circuits creates another problems. Integrating nanotubes into larger circuits entails the difficulty of manufacturing good metal contacts for the tubes (Science Daily2, 2012). Concerns are also about the perfect alignment of nanotubes without stray conducting paths and faulty functionality into the circuits, making reliable junctions between nanotubes, and assembling junctions between the arrays of switches that would form workable computer memory or logic circuits enabling the computer to make choices. Application of an electrical field guides the carbon nanotubes as they grow randomly (Svensson, 2010).

Quantum Computing

Another area of the advancements in computation is quantum computing, which combines physics, mathematics, and computer science. Nanocomputers might be possibly built using quantum mechanics principles. Richard Feynman introduced the field of quantum computing in 1982. Quantum computing is still in its infancy because quantum computational operations can now be done only on single qubits. Quibit is the quantum analogue of the bit. A quantum computer is a device that uses quantum mechanical phenomena to perform operations on data; the basic paradigm for quantum algorithms involves the quantum circuit model composed of the basic quantum units of information (qubits) and their basic logical manipulations (quantum gates represented by matrices). Qubits are made up of controlled particles and the means of control (e.g. devices that trap particles and switch them from one state to another). Traditional computers (along with nanocomputers) transform data encoded as binary digits, while quantum computation performs operations on the quantum characteristics of the data. At the level of quantum mechanics particles of matter can exist in multiple, simultaneous combinations of states (0 or 1). However, required computational basis of qubits is too large to be handled by a classical computer's memory made up of bits.

Practical and theoretical research on quantum computing offers promises to solve civilian and national security purposes, such as cryptanalysis. Scientists are working on solving technical challenges in physically implementing a quantum computer. They create quantum computing models based on the basic elements and the physical systems used to realize the qubits. Attempts include, among many others, developing a quantum computer that utilizes properties of superconductor circuits, trapped ions, quantum dot charge based semiconductor, nuclear magnetic resonance on molecules in solution, fullerene-based (electronic spin of atoms or molecules encased in fullerene structures), or a diamond based quantum computer. For example, a silicon-based a quantum computing chip has been built, based on quantum optics, and other scientists demonstrated a two-dimensional chip that houses three qubits. The team led Michelle Simmons of the University of New South Wales in Sydney demonstrated the fabrication of wires in silicon—only one atom tall and four atoms wide—with exceptionally low resistivity (~0.3 milliohm-centimeters) and the current-carrying capabilities of copper. According to the authors this achievement paves the way for single-atom device architectures for both classical and quantum information processing (Weber et al., 2012). IBM scientists announced several breakthroughs in quantum computing that "will take computing to a whole new level" (Poeter, 2012).

Biologically Inspired Models for Computing

Nanocomputers might be built using biochemical principles. Study of biological systems can significantly improve computing, networking, and robotics. Bio-inspired models utilize information gathered from animal social systems. Artificial life (ALife) denotes the creation of synthetic life on computers to study, simulate, and understand living systems. According to Kim & Cho (2006), ALife application fields include robot control, robot manufacturing, practical robots, computer graphics, natural phenomenon modeling, entertainment, games, music, economics, Internet, information processing, industrial design, simulation software, electronics, security, data mining, and telecommunications. Methods for designing such applications include evolutionary computation, swarm intelligence, artificial immune network, and agent-based modeling. Biologically inspired evolutionary robotics (ER) is a powerful approach for the automatic synthesis of robot controllers. (Trianni & Nolfi, 2011).

A challenge in constructing models is in incorporation of variables such as internal states: hunger, sex, drive, and higher functions: learning, memory, and personality into the models. As stated by Bales & Kitzmann (2011), a biologically inspired model for computing is any model of communication that displays evolution (a selection process that acts on variation). Most models focus on social systems. Computing scientists examine most often social insects, which display emergent behavioral properties of individuals that do not require centralized command, but also packs of wolfs, schools of fish, flocks of birds, and other social animals. Animal communication is shaped by natural selection and adaptation, which requires plasticity. Signals may last long, for example, chemical signals, or may be transient like acoustical ones. Animals communicate with members of their own species and of another species. They effectively convey information about functions they perform, such as foraging and predator defense, maximizing the success of both the sender and the receiver, while minimizing the cost of signaling. Some signal modalities (modes of communication may differ from those used by humans and may include chemical (pheromones), electrical, and seismic signals (for example, when blind mole rat transmits signals over long distances by thumping on burrow walls). An unsuccessful ant will switch to the task that the successful one is performing. It means a worker ant assesses its own success. In social insects individuals respond to stimuli in a similar way. The resulting emergent property, referred to as swarm intelligence, has been compared to distributed, parallel computing. Biologically-inspired evolutionary robotics (ER) is a powerful approach for the automatic synthesis of robot controllers. Creation of collective and swarm robotics may be inspired by the property that the desired behavior of the social group is an indirect result of the control and communication rules followed by each individual (Trianni & Nolfi, 2011).

CONCLUSION

Art inspired by carbon and enhanced by digital technologies are a means to understand and interpret nature- and science-related concepts. The chapter offers projects aimed at visual presentation of the themes and related information about carbon. It also presents a project about a holistic solution to the wasteland development.

REFERENCES

Agence France-Presse. (2012, May 7). France cave art gives glimpse into human life 40,000 years ago. *National Post*. Retrieved September 2, 2012, from http://news.nationalpost.com/2012/05/07/france-cave-art-gives-glimpse-into-human-life-40000-years-ago/

Arduino. (2013). Retrieved April 14, 2013, from http://www.mouser.com/knowledge/arduino/ or http://www.mouser.com/arduino/?cm_mmc=google-_-ppc-_-americas-_-Arduino&gclid=CL-Lx4X_mbACFSMDQAodxWvNZw

Ayres, R. U., & Ayres, E. (2010). *Crossing the energy divide: Moving from fossil fuel dependence to a clean-energy*. Pearson Prentice Hall. ISBN 137015445

Bales, K. L., & Kitzmann, C. D. (2011). Animal models for computing and communications: Past approaches and future challenges. In X. Yiang (Ed.), *Bio-Inspired Computing and Networking*, (pp. 3-18). CRC Press, Taylor & Francis Group. ISBN1420080326

Barwinski.net. (2012). *Links to various web database*. Retrieved September 2, 2012, from http://barwinski.net/isotopes/query_select.php

Bon, C., Caudy, N., de Dieuleveult, M., Fosse, P., Philippe, M., & Maksud, F. … Elalouf, J.-M. (2008). Deciphering the complete mitochondrial genome and phylogeny of the extinct cave bear in the Paleolithic painted cave of Chauvet. *Proceedings of the National Academy of Sciences of the United States of America*. doi: 10.1073/pnas.0806143105

Burning Man. (2013). Retrieved April 14, 2013, from http://www.burningman.com/whatisburningman.

Cave of Forgotten Dreams. (2012). Retrieved September 3, 2012, from http://en.wikipedia.org/wiki/Cave_of_Forgotten_Dreams

Combes. F. (1991). The SAO/NASA astrophysics data system. *Annual Review of Astronomy and Astrophysics, 29*(A92-18081 05-90), 195-237. doi 10.1146/annurev.aa.29.090191.001211. Retrieved September 1, 2012, from http://articles.adsabs.harvard.edu/full/1991ARA%26A.29.195C

EIA. (2012a). *Annual energy outlook 2012*. Retrieved August 30, 2012, from http://www.eia.gov/forecasts/aeo/

EIA. (2012b). *U.S. energy-related carbon dioxide emissions, 2011*. Retrieved August 30, 2012, from http://www.eia.gov/environment/emissions/carbon/

EIA. (2012c). *Energy and the environment explained: Greenhouse gases' effect on the climate*. Retrieved August 30, 2012, from http://www.eia.gov/energyexplained/index.cfm?page=environment_how_ghg_affect_climate

EIA. (2012d). *U.S. Energy Information Administration*. Retrieved August 30, 2012, from http://www.eia.gov/energy_in_brief/

Falkowski, P., Scholes, R. J., Boyle, E., Canadell, J., Canfield, D., & Elser, J. et al. (2000). The global carbon cycle: A test of our knowledge of earth as a system. *Science, 290*(5490), 291–296. doi:10.1126/science.290.5490.291 PMID:11030643.

Flannery, M. C. (2012). Herbaria: Border crossers extraordinaire. In *Proceedings of the School of Visual Arts 25th National Conference on Liberal Arts and the Education of Artists*, (pp. 51-57). School of Visual Arts.

Friedrich, W. L., Kromer, B., Friedrich, M., Heinemeier, J., Pfeiffer, T., & Talamo, S. (2006). Santorini eruption radiocarbon dated to 1627-1600 B.C. *Science, 312*(5773), 548. Retrieved September 2, 2012, from http://www.sciencemag.org/content/312/5773/548

Halbouty, M. T. (2004). *Giant oil & gas fields of the decade - 1990-99 (Aapg Memoir 78)*. American Association of Petroleum Geologists.

Herzog, W. (2012). *Werner Herzog: The artist's website*. Retrieved September 3, 2012, from http://www.wernerherzog.com/index.php?id=64

Hoffmann, D. L., Beck, J. W., Richards, D. A., Smart, P. L., Singarayer, J. S., Ketchmark, T., & Hawkesworth, C. J. (2010). Towards radiocarbon calibration beyond 28 ka using speleothems from the Bahamas. *Earth and Planetary Science Letters, 289*(1–2), 1–10. Retrieved September 2, 2012, from http://www.sciencedirect.com/science/article/pii/S0012821X09006037

IPPC. (2007). *Intergovernmental Panel on Climate Change*. Retrieved August 30, 2012, from http://www.ipcc.ch/publications_and_data/ar4/wg1/en/faq-1-3.html

Irifune, T., Kurio, A., Sakamoto, S., Inoue, T., & Sumiya, H. (2003). Materials: Ultrahard polycrystalline diamond from graphite. *Nature, 421*, 599–600. doi:10.1038/421599b PMID:12571587.

Kim, K. J., & Cho, S. B. (2006). A comprehensive overview of the applications of artificial life. *Artificial Life, 12*(1), 153-82. Retrieved September 3, 2012, from http://www.ncbi.nlm.nih.gov/pubmed/16393455

Life. (1972, July 7). Pencils, paint and pottery can give you lead poisoning. *Life*, 46. Retrieved September 3, 2012, from http://books.google.com/books?id=_1QEAAAAMBAJ&printsec=frontcover&source=gbs_ge_summary_r&cad=0#v=onepage&q&f=false

Mabey, R. (2010). *Weeds: In defense of nature's most unloved plants*. New York, NY: HarperCollins.

Manning, S. W., Ramsey, C. B., Kutschera, W., Higham, T., Kromer, B., Steier, P., & Wild, E. M. (2006). Chronology for the Aegean late bronze age 1700-1400 B.C. *Science, 312*(5773), 565–569. Retrieved September 2, 2012, from http://www.sciencemag.org/content/312/5773/565

NASA Earth Observatory. (2011). Retrieved August 30, 2012, from http://earthobservatory.nasa.gov/Features/CarbonCycle/carbon_cycle2001.pdf

Nasibulin, A. G., Pikhitsa, P. V., Jiang, H., Brown, D. P., Krasheninnikov, A. V., & Anisimov, A. S. et al. (2007). A novel hybrid carbon material. *Nature Nanotechnology, 2*, 156–161. doi:10.1038/nnano.2007.37 PMID:18654245.

Palmer, M. A. et al. (2010). Mountaintop mining consequences. *Science, 327*, 148. doi:10.1126/science.1180543 PMID:20056876.

Petroski, H. (1992). *The pencil: A history of design and circumstance*. Knopf.

Poeter, D. (2012). IBM says it's 'on the cusp' of building a quantum computer. *PC Magazine*. Retrieved September 6, 2012, from http://www.pcmag.com/article2/0,2817,2400930,00.asp

RFA. (2012). *Renewable fuels association: Accelerating industry innovation, 2012 ethanol industry outlook*. Retrieved August 30, 2012, from http://ethanolrfa.3cdn.net/d4ad995ffb7ae8fbfe_1vm62ypzd.pdf

Sadier, B., Delannoy, J.-J., Benedetti, L., Bourlès, D. L., Jaillet, S., & Geneste, J.-M. ... Arnold, M. (2012). Further constraints on the Chauvet cave artwork elaboration. *Proceedings of the National Academy of Sciences of the United States of America*. doi 10.1073/pnas.1118593109

Science Daily. (2010, June 1). Faster computers with nanotechnology. *Science Daily*. Retrieved September 3, 2012, from http://www.sciencedaily.com/releases/2010/05/100531082857.htm

Science Daily. (2012, June 14). Engineers perfecting carbon nanotubes for highly energy-efficient computing. *Science Daily*. Retrieved September 3, 2012, from http://www.sciencedaily.com/releases/2012/06/120614131202.htm

Snyder, S. H., & Ferris, C. D. (2000). Novel neurotransmitters and their neuropsychiatric relevance. *Am J Psychiatry, 157*, 1738-1751. doi 10.1176/appi.ajp.157.11.1738. Retrieved September 1, 2012, from http://ajp.psychiatryonline.org/article.aspx?articleID=174415

Squillace, M. (2009). *The strip mining handbook*. Retrieved April 14, 2013, from http://sites.google.com/site/stripmininghandbook/chapter-1-introduction

Svensson, J. (2010). Carbon nanotube transistors: Nanotube growth, contact properties and novel devices. *University of Gothenburg PhD Thesis*. Retrieved September 4, 2012, from https://gupea.ub.gu.se/bitstream/2077/21859/1/gupea_2077_21859_1.pdf

Trianni, V., & Nolfi, S. (2011). Engineering the evolution of self-organizing behaviors in swarm robotics: A case study. *Artificial Life, 17*(3), 183–202. doi:10.1162/artl_a_00031 PMID:21554112.

U.S. Consumer Product Safety Commission. (2012). Retrieved September 1, 2012, from http://www.cpsc.gov/cpscpub/pubs/466.html

Wadham, J. L., Arndt, S., Tulaczyk, S., Stibal, M., Tranter, M., & Telling, J. … Butler, C. E. H. (2012). Potential methane reservoirs beneath Antarctica. *Nature, 488*, 633–637. Retrieved August 30, 2012, from http://www.nature.com/nature/journal/v488/n7413/full/nature11374.html

Wang, R. (2002). Two's company, three's a crowd: Can H_2S be the third endogenous gaseous transmitter? *The FASEB Journal, 16*(13), 1792-1798. doi 10.1096/fj.02-0211hyp. Retrieved September 3, 2012, from http://www.fasebj.org/content/16/13/1792.full

Weber, B., Mahapatra, S., Ryu, H., Lee, S., Fuhrer, A., & Reusch, T. C. G. … Simmons, M. Y. (2012). Ohm's law survives to the atomic scale. *Science, 335*(6064), 64-67. doi 10.1126/science.1214319. Retrieved September 6, 2012, from http://www.sciencemag.org/content/335/6064/64

Weinstock, B., & Niki, H. (1972). Carbon monoxide balance in nature. *Science, 176*(4032), 290–292. doi:10.1126/science.176.4032.290 PMID:5019781.

Wu, L., & Wang, R. (2005). Carbon monoxide: Endogenous production, physiological functions, and pharmacological applications. *Pharmacol Rev, 57*(4), 585–630. doi:10.1124/pr.57.4.3. Retrieved September 1, 2012, from http://pharmrev.aspetjournals.org/content/57/4/585.full.pdf+html

Yiang, X. (2011). *Bio-inspired computing and networking*. CRC Press.

Chapter 14
Mathematics–Related Visual Events

ABSTRACT

A mathematical way of thinking may often involve the visual processes while the beauty of forms derived from mathematical formulas may become an inspiration and a source for creating art works. This text examines organic/geometric forms present in nature, mathematics, and art, symmetry, fractals, artists' responses, and computational solutions in the form of visual presentations. This is followed by some aesthetical and critical notions about mathematics-derived art.

INTRODUCTION: VISUAL APPEAL OF MATHEMATICS FOR MATHEMATICIANS AND ARTISTS

Visual mathematics uses appealing computer graphics for constructing models and as a guide for intuition. Mathematics helps to explain the world. Mathematicians describe nature by using approaches from within geometry, topology, analysis, and also the theoretical computer science. They study natural structures and properties of space: shapes, sizes, distances, positions of figures and their conjectures, and thus investigate change in natural forms. They develop methods for analysis, applications, and technologies. We can realize how much the mathematical way of thinking is a visual process and how often the beauty of forms derived from mathematical formulas becomes an

inspiration and a source for creating art works. This idea may provide a common language for mathematicians, visual artists, architects, musicians, crystallographers, cartographers, computer scientists, and many other professionals.

Before we can develop further statements we have to accept axioms – universally established propositions, truths that are accepted without proof. For example, a symmetry axiom tells that for all points A and B, AB = BA. Axioms seem to be self-evident for human reasoning; however, many of the inventive and significant discoveries, such as the Heisenberg's uncertainty principle in quantum mechanics resulted from the questioning of axioms and mixing an investigation of a subject with an object. As Julian Voss-Andreae wrote, "Quantum theory remains philosophically problematic because 'objective realism' turns out to be incompatible with quantum theory offered by Albert Einstein, Boris Podolsky, and Nathan Rosen in 1935. There is no accurate space-time

DOI: 10.4018/978-1-4666-4627-8.ch014

representation of, say, an electron: It is neither a particle nor a wave or any other 'thing'" (Voss-Andreae, 2011, p.14. Also, Ball, 2009). (The Heisenberg's uncertainty principle is a part of quantum mechanics. This principle states that we cannot know precisely about certain pairs of physical properties, such as a particle's position and momentum – the product of the mass of a particle and its velocity at the same time, because the measuring process involves interaction, which disturbs the particle. For example, a photon of light used in a measurement is bouncing off the particle. Thus, one cannot, even theoretically, predict the moment-to-moment behavior of a system consisting of the subject and the object of examination – somebody who makes an observation and an object observed. There is a theoretical limit for simultaneous measuring at an atomic scale because the more precisely is figured one amount the more uncertain is the other one).

With another point of view, intuition, along with knowledge and calculations has been stressed as a leading force in problem solving. Arthur Loeb (1993) in his book entitled "Concepts & Images – Visual Mathematics" claimed that mathematical intuition is a form of non-verbalized knowledge. Some scientists and artists use their knowledge and intuition in such a way that their abstract reasoning takes form of images, rather than words or formulas. Helmer Aslaksen (2005) identified four types of conditions relevant to the coexistence of mathematics and art: mathematics in art (where he includes perspective, symmetry, and musical scales – appreciated by the art connoisseurs); mathematical art (as created by artists, for example by Escher – often ignored by art community); mathematics as art (visual mathematics such as a Mandelbrot set – however art museums are usually not interested); mathematics is art (for example, the Euclid's axiom – which is also not appreciated by the art connoisseurs). Teaching is focused on a small number of topics, such as Escher, perspective, tilings, golden ratio, and polyhedra, at the expense of mathematical art in general. Study of geometric two-dimensional shapes and three-dimensional forms resulted in works of art done in various media, both traditional and digital, including painting, sculpture, printmaking, and architecture. Computer programs and computer graphics produced with the use of software packages give a boost to such studies. They make a separate category of digital art and, at the same time, serve as a tool for creating works in other media. Teams working on visualization or simulation projects usually include a mathematician, and the direct results of their work look many times like artistic productions.

ORGANIC/GEOMETRIC

Natural and Calculated Patterns

Golden section, rectangle and triangle reflect the ways nature presents itself by creating self-similar forms. Hence the flow patterns in tile, steel and glass, and fractal poetry look at nature in metaphoric terms (Bernstein, 2005). Testimony about the order of the world would be incomplete without showing the mathematical solutions that are invisible in natural forms. They are often enjoyable and pleasing to the eye, maybe due to intuitive understanding of their origin.

In art and design domains, pattern is an artistic or decorative design made of lines. Pattern is based on the repetition of units coming from the natural or artificial origin. Patterns make a basis of ornaments, which are used in decorative arts and architecture and have distinctive styles, specific for each culture or ethnic group. In cultural anthropology, a study of decorative patterns, ornaments, and their characteristics support the detailed analysis of an individual culture.

Art forms that present solutions of mathematical equations may be derived from random selection of numbers, permutations resulting in more or less regular patterns, equations visualized as sculptures (for example, a Möebius knot), or stereo geometry transformations. They provide the viewer with aesthetic satisfaction and a feeling of pleasure, which confirms that the artistic goal has been fully achieved. Some shapes and forms that contain mathematical regularities described as equations seem to be especially inspirational and aesthetically appealing. For example, the complex polygons, tessellations of strings and lattices, the geometry displayed by soap bubble films, tiles, Oriental mosaics, Roman mosaics, and mazes motivated mathematicians and artists to create art- and design-related works.

A need for embellishing things seems to be universal among people, also those not necessarily educated in mathematics. Artists, especially folk artists, often act instinctively in accordance with mathematical rules and create forms that follow the formulas derived from geometry, fractal geometry, or various approaches to programming. Many times, they are unaware of it. Intricate designs of old embroideries and patterns for laces seem to be derived from mathematical principles in an intuitive way. In the same way, we knowingly employ mathematics in developing complex polygons and fractal images to create an artwork. Artistic expressions based on a tessellation principle had been applied both by old Islamic artists and by the twentieth-century Dutch graphic artist Maurits Cornelis Escher (1902-1972) in his impossible sceneries.

Patterns are ubiquitous in our surroundings; patterns in plants and animals have consistent forms and features characteristic of an individual or a group. Animal patterns, such as the designs on scales of fish, or on feathers of birds enable animals to recognize individuals of their own species. Humans can describe and classify these species on the basis of these characteristics (Neville, 1977).

Nature presents itself by creating self-similar forms. Ken Bernstein (2005) indicates golden section, rectangle, and triangle as forms that reflect the ways it happens. He claims that the flow patterns in tile, steel, and glass, and also fractal

poetry look at nature in metaphoric terms. Several topics of research in visual mathematics provide inspiration for the artists, for example, geometry and fractal geometry, computer graphics, symmetry and perspective, or fuzzy logic, to name a few. Geometry provides unlimited possibilities for creating patterns and ornaments that are present in the variety of design styles characteristic of all of cultures of the world. Symmetry plays a remarkable role in most human visual endeavors. Natural objects displaying symmetry evoke wonder and surprise because their intricacy. Architectural details as stain-glass windows, mosaics, and friezes, visual arts, pottery and ceramics, quilts, textiles, and carpets many times make a varied use of symmetry as an important principle in their design. Maybe for that reason symmetry is so often seen not only beautiful but also conducive to visual communication.

Figure 1, "Organic/Geometric" is a computer enhanced wooden sculpture – some reflection about how visual rules may need their formal description

Spirals and Tiles

Spiral shapes are ubiquitous in nature, existing in ammonites that are extinct from 250 millions years, pinecones, pineapples, DNA molecules, and also water swirls, hurricane fronts, and galaxies. They obey the Fibonacci number relationships, which describe the mathematics theory ruling the numbers. Leonardo Fibonacci, the 13th century Italian mathematician from Pisa brought in Europe the Hindu-Arabic numeral system. The Fibonacci series, which is a sequence of numbers where each number is the sum of the previous two (such as 1,1,2,3,5,8, etc.) can be seen as a tiling with squares whose sides are successive Fibonacci numbers, or a spiral created by drawing arcs connecting the corners of squares in a such tiling. The proportions for a tiling are similar to the 8 1/2 x 11 inch page or the 3 x 5 index card. The Fibonacci spirals and golden sections, present in almost all life forms,

Figure 1. Anna Ursyn, Organic/Geometric. (© A. Ursyn, 1988. Used with permission)

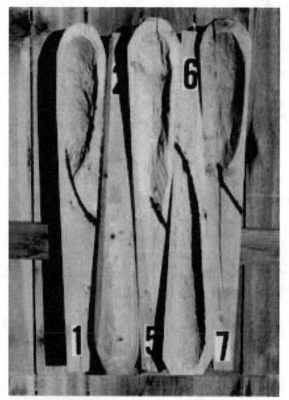

define how a daisy is flowering and *Araucaria* grows by sprouting leaves at an angle of 137.5 degrees, to generate spirals of golden rectangles obeying the A/B=B/C rule (Doczi, 2005). Many two- and three-dimensional structures (such as leaves and seashells) have dimensions that reflect the phi ratio, which is (approximately) 1 to 1.618034. This ratio, known amongst the Greeks as the Golden Mean and usually called golden section is used extensively in sculpture and architecture. Builders used to ascribe structural stability and aesthetic balance to objects with the golden ratio incorporated.

Patterns in Ornaments

Several topics of research in visual mathematics provide inspiration for artists. For example, geometry provides unlimited possibilities for creating patterns and ornaments that are present in the variety of design styles characteristic of all of cultures of the world. Mathematicians and electronic artists find beauty in natural order and its mathematical description. Regular patterns are perceived as beauty in nature, be it a natural meander of a river or a fractal design of structures such as a mollusk shell, a snowflake, a pinecone, a sunflower, or a foliage arrangement on a tree. Other examples of aesthetically appealing forms that contain mathematical regularities and serve as inspiration for art are complex polygons, tessellations of strings and lattices, the geometry of soap bubble films, and patterns displayed in ornaments, tiles, mazes, and mosaics created in various cultures (e.g., Oriental or Roman mosaics). A great part of ornaments display motifs as elements of patterns.

About a hundred years ago Owen Jones wrote a seminal monographic book "The Grammar of Ornament" (1856/2010) about the mathematically based culture of patterns. Jones made a huge collection of ornaments typical of different countries; he collected patterns created by ancient and contemporary cultures of Egypt, Greece, India, Iran, Japan, or Americas, and wrote about the conceptual structures on which these designs drew. He described the mathematical order in Greek meanders made by square shapes, sculptural forms, Iranian pottery, or patterns woven into African textiles.

"The Grammar of Ornament" accompanied the author's work on creating a permanent exhibition of decorative art as 'the history of the civilization of the world' – a display on the walls of the Crystal Palace opened by Queen Victoria in June 1854. Jones advocated general principles in the arrangement of form and color in architecture and the decorative arts. According to Jones, decorative arts derive from, and accompany architecture. Architecture, as well as decorative arts is expressing the time period in which it has been created under the influence of climate and available materials. They should possess fitness, proportion, and harmony resulting in beauty that satisfies the eye, the intellect, and the affections of the viewer. Construction should be decorated, but decoration should never be purposely constructed. Beauty is produced by lines growing out one from another, with general form subdivided and interstices filled with ornaments based upon a geometrical construction. There should be a true, definite proportion between the parts, in both architecture and decorative arts, most of them difficult for the eye to detect: 5:8, 3:7, and 3:5 are more beautiful than 4:8, 3:6, and 3:4. Harmony of form consists in the proper balance and contrast of the straight, the inclined, and the curved. According to the Oriental practice, lines flow out of a parent stem, so the ornament can be traced to its branch and

root. Junctions of curved or straight lines should be tangential to each other. Ornaments in any color or in gold may be used on white or black ground; otherwise they should be outlined, separated from grounds of by edgings of white, gold, or black. Imitations such as graining of woods or colored marbles are allowable only when the employment of the thing imitated is consistent.

Works of art created according to various art movements or artistic groups display patterns characteristic of this group, for example, decorative patterns typical of the Art Nouveau or Secession styles. Some common leading ideas on which patterns of ornaments are based are in accordance with the arrangement typical of the distribution of form in nature. Artists from different periods, such as the Italian Renaissance painter Piero della Francesca (1410/20-1492) or the Italian Surrealist artist Giorgio de Chirico (1888-1978) explore symmetry and perspective, some of them making exciting tricks, such as Hans Holbein the Younger

Figure 2. Anna Ursyn, An Idea for Ammonite. From a series Visible Geometry (© A. Ursyn, 2010. Used with permission).

(1497-1543), who applied anamorphosis in "The Ambassadors."

Figure 2, "An Idea for an Ammonite" belongs to a series entitled "Visible Geometry" that includes two-dimensional images of abstract-geometric designs executed with computer programs. This work tells how we encounter every day shapes determined by lines with evolving curves and then recognize them in natural objects.

Transformations

Geometric transformations may refer to objects; the theme is vital for people active in all kinds of visual presentation of natural objects - living and inanimate, the scientific, architectural, or any other kinds of data, as well as those who study the theoretical framework of the subjects concerning objects. Traditional (and most commonly used) Euclidian transformations are a translation, a rotation, or a reflection. Affine transformation may be any combination of a coordinate translation, scaling, rotation, and skew (Tanimoto, 2012). In the affine transformations (which allow preserving parallel relationships) objects do not change their length and angle measures, and do not change the shape; only the position and orientation of the object will change (Inselberg, 2009). For example, with affine transformation we can map one line segment to another one. Scaling transformations stretch or shrink a geometric object; therefore it changes its lengths and angles. Shear transformation pushes an object in a direction parallel to a plane or an axis. Mathematical translation describes movement of an object in space, with every point of the object moving in the same direction over the same distance, without any rotation, reflection, or change in size.

Patterns resulting from reflection, translation, and rotation can be seen often in nature. As pointed out by Marcia Birken (2009), branches of the fish tail palm exhibit translation and glide translation symmetries, while corresponding leaves exhibit reflection symmetry. Transformations of drawings, such as reflection, translation, and rotation may help extend our knowledge about geometric relationships in nature and in architecture. Classification of designs in architectural forms requires describing of their geometries and grids in a standard form.

Facades of hundreds of buildings in the village of Pirgi, a small town on the Greek island of Chios in the eastern Aegean Sea are covered with dark gray and white decoration in the form of friezes, distinct for each house. This unique ornamental plasterwork called xisto resulted from scratching patterns drawn by the artists in a white top layer of plaster to reveal a dark base. James, James, & Kalisperis (2004), a mathematician, an anthropologist, and an architect, performed a computer analysis of friezes applying a mathematical group theory to the organization of friezes, and found the essential mathematical structure underlying these color-reversing friezes. They discovered three general categories of symmetry applied to a frieze: rotational (often six-fold), frieze, and space filling. Rotational symmetry occurs in nature in snowflakes, flowers, fruits, starfish, jellyfish, and other sea animals. Leonardo da Vinci conducted studies on rotational symmetry. It occurs universally in decorative arts, both prehistoric and contemporary. Frieze symmetry repeats itself along a given direction. It appears in certain rock formations, in the structure and coloring of animals such as caterpillars, centipedes and snakes. The authors found five basic actions on friezes: translation (like in marching triangles, with the colors reverted), vertical mirror (like in a letter A), horizontal mirror (like in a letter E), half turn (like in a letter S), and glide reflection (horizontal + translation, like in footsteps). The authors stated that artists from Pirgi have invented a novel art form going far in exploring the area of pure dichromatic color-reversing friezes (James, James, & Kalisperis, 2004).

OBJECTS AND SHADOWS

Geometrical transformations may result in distortions of objects providing artists with inspiring images. Many other ways may serve to produce the effects that transform the reality into fantastic or virtual worlds. For example, by adding an image of water with the ripples-on-a-pond effect one can transform the current picture of a glacier into the one affected by global warming (Tanimoto, 2012). Techniques discussed below include distortions in perspective, anamorphosis, pinhole photography, light reflections, shadow effects, and electronic installations.

Anamorphosis and Other Distortions of Perspective

Distortions in perspective were often used for entertainment; they also enhance the relativity of vision and the subjectivity of human experience. Postmodern theorists discussed them as a metaphorical tool (Topper, 2000). A circular plate can be seen as a circle and as an ellipse form at the same time; the information displayed and the picture perception is, according to James J. Gibson (1986) dual in a virtual space, when we draw on a flat surface the three-dimensional objects existing in virtual space. Circles are transformed into ellipses, squares into a pattern of trapezoids, and they are compressed or foreshortened (Topper, 2000).

Anamorphic images result from geometric distortions brought about by slanted or mirror surfaces. Anamorphosis is a way of distorting perspective causing that an image seems to be meaningless until viewed from a particular angle that inverts this geometric distortion. Anamorphic drawings have appeared in the Renaissance art. Leonardo da Vinci experimented with such optical illusions. Anamorphic imagery was used in post-Renaissance Europe since the 1500s. Slant anamorphosis can be seen at the Hans Holbein the Younger's painting "The Ambassadors" painted in 1533 by Hans Holbein the Younger (http://www.oneonta.edu/faculty/farberas/arth/ARTH214/am-bassadors_home.html, also http://en.wikipedia.org/wiki/The_Ambassadors_(Holbein). The artist placed there an anamorphic picture of the human skull. When looking at this anamorphic picture from near its projection point, one can see the projected image contracted to its normal form: it is visible as a human skull amorphic images can be produced by placing a cylindrical mirror (a reflecting cylinder) in the center of an image and look at the image's reflection (Tanimoto, 2012). Cylinder anamorphic images can be traced for the 1600s and were popular in the 19th century. Anamorphic images can be produced on a computer by stretching an image horizontally to obtain a slant anamorphosis or, in the case of the cylinder anamorphosis, it can be done by mapping a rectangular array and wrapping it around the center in the polar array (by describing the point's distance from the pole placed in the center of the image and an angle value in radians as related to the horizontal axis). The use of ray tracing in computer graphics allows creating even more complicated distortions (Tanimoto, 2012).

Leonardo's work (in Codex Atlanticus 35, versa a) 'Child's Face and Eye' is considered the first anamorphic drawing (Leonardo da Vinci, 2012). Leonardo wrote about creating a slant anamorphic drawing on the wall:

If you want to represent a figure on a wall, the wall being foreshortened, while the figure is to appear in its proper form, and as standing free from the wall, you must proceed thus: have a thin plate of iron and make a small hole in the center; this hole must be round. Set a light close to it in such a position that it shines through the central hole, then place any object or figure you please so close to the wall that it touches it and draw the outline of the shadow on the wall; then fill in the shade and add the lights; place the person who is to see it so that he looks through the same hole where at first the light was; and you will never be able to persuade yourself that the image is not detached from the wall. (Leonardo, Codex Atlanticus 42, versa b).

Secrets of the Codex Atlanticus can be now seen on the apps for iPhone and iPad, which contain high-quality photographs reproduced along with QR codes to access content such as 3-D reconstructions of Leonardo's machines (Leonardo, 2011, an iPhone, iPod touch, and iPad application, a virtual tour of the exhibition of Leonardo's machines).

Many ways of distorting perspective can be found art works in the following centuries. Huge ceiling frescoes were often designed as giant anamorphs. Slant anamorphic distortions supported production of the 17th century superrealistic paintings, which provided a three-dimensional illusion of the objects floating in space before the viewer due to the trompe l'oeil technique. An example of such illusion is the false cupola looking like a real large dome, painted by Andrea Pozzo on a flat ceiling of the church of Sant'Ignatio di Loyola in Rome built about 1650.

Figure 3. "Winter Fences" and also corrals, all made from planks, are of importance for the landscape's character. The traveler perceives them as patterns and moiré images.

Pinhole

As for pictures seen through a pinhole, "images of illuminated objects penetrate into a very dark chamber by some small round hole" (Leonardo, Codex Atlanticus 190, versa a). The first pinhole photographs appeared in the 1860s, after Sir David Brewster published in 1856 his book "The Ste-

Figure 3. Anna Ursyn, "Winter Fences" (© A. Ursyn, 1989. Used with permission).

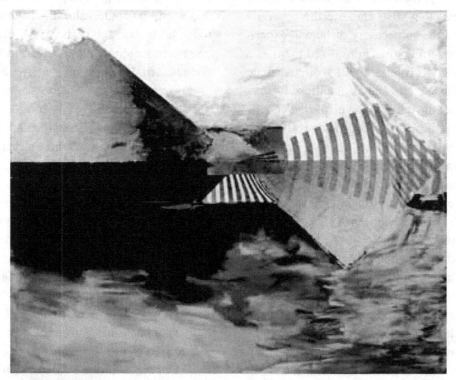

reoscope, its History, Theory, and Construction" (London: J. Murray). In the late 1880s impressionistic photographs with atmospheric, fuzzy qualities *became* known as pictorialism (Renner, 2000). We can see anamorphic signs painted on the road surfaces. While in a graphical projection on a plane objects that are not parallel to the picture plane are foreshortened, in an anamorphic drawing pictures are stretched or elongated, so they appear distorted on the picture plane.

Transformation by Shadows

Shadows transform shapes of objects and thus are often seen as a link between the real and imaginary or virtual world. Maybe for this reason there are so many performances involving shadows. The shape created by placing an object between a light source and a target surface will change depending on an angle between the object's surface and a target surface and position of the light source, and thus the angle at which the light rays would strike an object and a target surface. The shape of the shadow will also be changing along with the movement of the target surface; if there is any undulation, there would be interference between light waves and the wavelike motion of the reflecting surface, and it will also depend on the kind of undulating matter: whether it is water or a more dense material.

The Greek philosopher Plato used the unreal appearance of changeable shadows to discuss the relation between our experiences and real world. In his work 'Republic' Plato (2011) created the Allegory of the Cave in the form of a dialogue about people chained to the wall of a cave all of their lives, facing a blank wall. Watching the shadows projected on the wall by things passing in front of a fire behind them, people ascribed forms to these shadows and experienced them as if they were reality. Plato poses that the philosopher is like a prisoner freed from the cave that understands that the shadows are not reality. According to Plato, forms (ideas) but not the material, observable

world make the fundamental kind of reality. Plato also thought artists could imitate but not create (Plato, Republic, 597D).

Artists from various cultures such as China, Taiwan, India, Greece, Nepal, Cambodia, Thailand, and Turkey have been creating magical effects of shadows casted by cutout figures held between a source of light and a translucent screen. Since many centuries artists of puppetry create transformation of shadows by moving both the puppets and the light source. Performances called Chinese shadows were also popular on Montmarte in Paris in 18th century. In Malaysia and Indonesia, especially Java and Bali, shadow puppet theater with figures made from buffalo skin is called Wayang kulit. Wayang Kulit Kelantan is threatened with imminent extinction. In 2003 UNESCO has designated Wayang Kulit Kelantan in Malaysia as a Masterpiece of Oral and Intangible Heritage of Humanity. The use of visualization and computer graphics techniques for the Wayang Kulit Kelantan preservation is examined in its four major aspects: puppets, shadows, screen for shadow projection (Kelir), and the light source (Ghani, 2011). Multimedia artists in Malyasia are now examining possibilities of using computer graphics to capture visual style of Wayang Kulit Kelantan performances. In India, shadow puppets are cut out of leather, which has been treated to make it translucent. Shadow puppets are pressed against the screen with a strong source of light behind it. The manipulation between the light and the screen make silhouettes or colorful shadows visible for the viewers who sit in front of the screen (Puppet Forms in India, 2012). The theatrical shadow puppet tradition, in the folklore, popular, court, and contemporary Western versions, is still continued in Turkey (Senyer, 2012). In the United States animation was for some time dominated by the Disney style, which in turn drew inspiration from European children books. In Germany from before the Nazis, Otto Fischinger and Lotte Reininger were considered modern animation pioneers, with animations showing references to both expressionist movement and the Oriental art (Rall, 2009). The renaissance of German animation came in the eighties with production of independent animation films. Current trends in contemporary South Asian animations based on old myths and traditions: Indonesian ones based on wayang kulit, Chinese hybrid production with the presence of traditional cultural heritage, Thailand animations based on shadow play nang yi, the ancient Indian epic tale of the Ramayana, and many others from Philippines, Vietnam, and Singapore has been described by Hannes Rall (2009) in a book "Tradigital Mythmaking."

Shadow Worlds/Writers' Rooms (Brontë Parsonage) presents the shadow worlds as the sites of wonder. A parsonage in England where in a nineteenth-century lived the Brontë family has been chosen by Chara Lewis, Kristin Mojsiewicz, and Anneké Pettican (2012) as a scenery for installation that combined the real and virtual realm. The precocious Brontë siblings who survived into adulthood in spite of the threat of tuberculosis were novelists and poets: Charlotte (1816-1855) the author of *Jane Eyre*, *Shirley*, and *Villette*; Emily (1818-1848), author of *Wuthering Heights*; Anne (1820-1849) author of *Agnes Grey* and *The Tenant of Wildfell Hall*; a painter, writer, and poet Branwell (1817-1848). Lewis, Mojsiewicz, and Pettican created two projects, *Still Life No. 1* and *Shadow Worlds/Writers' Rooms (Brontë Parsonage)*. Motorized light casted shadows of people and objects. The limen – a threshold in the real or virtual realm below which a stimulus cannot be distinguished from another – has been explored with the white light and the infrared digital scanning. The installation was projected on a transparent tabletop landscape. The authors performed the 3D-laser body scanning of people and then they fabricated figures casted in 3D, scanned and 3D printed; they also performed the 4D facial scanning. The data were stitched, filled, and remotely printed using stereo laser-sintering processes in a transparent resin. The motorized light casted shadows of people and

objects, and then shadows were captured in two ways: a medium-format digital camera served to capture frozen moments as 'shadows' on the wall, and Microsoft Kinect, an on-range camera technology coupled with software, captured live data from the performance (Table 1).

Figure 4, "The Minimal Surface." We know how to construct an egg shape using two different radii of curvature and we can appreciate the egg's minimal surface, but we are still curious why the bird's egg is more pointed at one end then at the other.

SYMMETRY

One may say geometry of symmetrical forms and shapes reflects their aesthetic beauty. Many kinds of symmetry exist not only in geometry but also in natural world and human works. For example, water in a liquid state has bilateral symmetry. Two O-H bonds display a symmetric stretch with some molecular vibrations (Kettle, 2007). When frozen, water is usually symmetrical in various ways, most often developing the hexagonal crystals. Ice, snowflakes, feather ice on the twigs, hail, sleet, icicles, glaciers, and polar caps, all have their own order of symmetry and develop arrangements of symmetry axes.

Symmetry means the correspondence in size, form, and arrangement of parts. Similar parts of an object are arranged on the opposite sides of a point, line (axis), or plane. A crystal shows symmetry when it has a center of symmetry, rotation axes, or mirror planes (imaginary planes that divide it into halves). Several types of symmetry can be seen in natural forms, for example line or mirror symmetry, radial, cylindrical, or spherical symmetry. A figure that has line symmetry has two identical halves when folded along its line of symmetry, and these halves are congruent, meaning they are the same size and shape. An object has a radial symmetry when it can be rotated around the rotation axis. For example, with a fourfold rotation

Table 1. Deceiving the viewer's perception

Visual Response: Virtual Shadows
Create an anamorphic drawing obeying Leonardo's recommendations discussed above, and then videotape the result changing the position of your camera (or a smartphone) a little bit at a time. This way, create the deception of the eye with illusionistic pictures that deceive the viewer's perception. Invent a short, unrealistic story about the virtual world of imaginary creatures you have just created on your video.

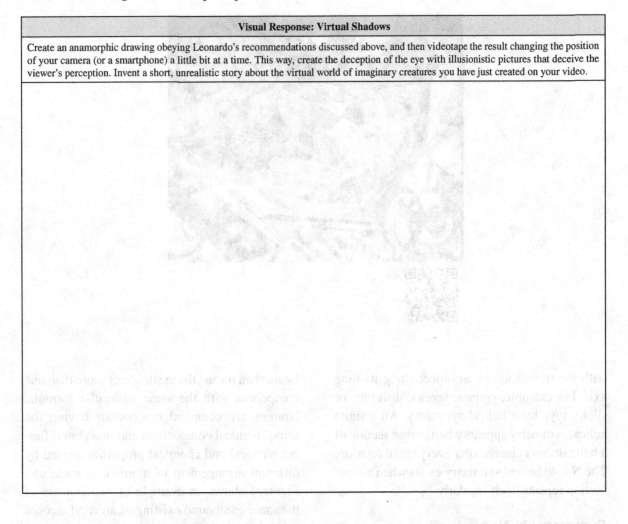

axis the crystal repeats itself each 90°. Angles of rotational symmetry possible for crystals are: 60 degrees, 90 degrees, 120 degrees, 180 degrees, and 360 degrees.

In geometry, figures can display several types of geometrical symmetry; it is usually described as bilateral (reflection or mirror), rotational, cylindrical, spherical, and helical symmetry. There are also some kinds of symmetry not so obviously seen in everyday objects. Translational symmetry can be obtained by moving a geometric figure by sliding, so each of its points moves the same distance in the same direction; a particular translation – moving in a specified direction does not change the object. Glide reflection may occur in a line or plane combined with a translation; rotoreflection symmetry presents rotation about an axis, combined with reflection in a plane perpendicular to that axis. An object has a rotational (radial) symmetry when a figure can be rotated around a given number of degrees around an imaginary line called the rotation axis and retain the same appearance as before rotating, repeating itself several times during a complete rotation. A circle is symmetrical around its center. For example, with a six-fold rotation axis the crystal repeats itself each 60°. A center of symmetry is equally distant from any point on the surface of a symmetrical object. Helical symmetry can be seen in objects that combine symmetry of a circle

Figure 4. Anna Ursyn, The Minimal Surface (© A. Ursyn, 2010. Used with permission).

with the translation of an object along its long axis. For example, springs, screws, drill bits, or slinky toys have helical symmetry. An infinite helical symmetry appears when a cross section of a helix doesn't change after every small rotation. The N-fold helical symmetry exists when a cross section repeats itself regularly.

Symmetry in Nature

Optical isomers are symmetrical around a plane; many times they are mirror images of each other.

Figure 5. A compound C_2H_6O may take form of an ethyl alcohol or diethyl ether. (© A. Ursyn, 2013. Used with permission).

Isomerism means the existence of more than one component with the same molecular formula. Isomers are chemical compounds having the same chemical composition and mass but different physical and chemical properties caused by different arrangement of atoms in a molecule. Figure 5 shows an example of two isomers of the same compound existing as an ethyl alcohol or diethyl ether.

Symmetrical objects show several elements of symmetry, for example, a crystal may show rotation axes, a center of symmetry, or mirror planes – the imaginary planes that separate an object into halves. Molecules of some sugar isomers are deflecting the rays of light in right or left direction. Double helix is the case of helical symmetry that repeats after every full rotation and returns to its initial position. A molecule of DNA, a deoxyribonucleic acid has a non-repeating helical symmetry.

The continuously changing environment makes that humans and animals evolve and change. In the course of the long periods animal adaptation resulted in a variety of new species. The design of bodies, their symmetry and patterns has also been changing in the course of evolution. Symmetry and its changes are used in biology in the process of classification, as indications how the animal is built. Many of the earliest organisms lacked symmetry. However, some floating animals and those sitting mostly in one place at the bottom of the ocean developed radial symmetry. These creatures had the rotational symmetry; that means they did not change their appearance after rotating a certain number of degrees around the center of their body. Radial arrangement of body parts strengthens the animal's skeleton. Also, animals with rotational symmetry can sense the danger from all directions. The balloon-shaped creatures swimming in the oceans have cylindrical symmetry around the vertical axis, which facilitates their forward motion. A body with the spherical symmetry, for example a spherical pollen the same on all sides. Both now and in the times past many animals have a three-rayed symmetry. Other creatures, for example jellyfish keep a pentagonal symmetry of their skeleton, major organ systems, and rays radiating from the mouth in five tube feet. There are also seven-armed starfish, while sea lilies develop 10 to 200 arms resembling fern fronds. German naturalist, philosopher, physician, and artist Ernst von Haeckel (1834-1919) described thousands of new species and described the developmental processes stressing their aesthetic value. His work from 1904 "Kunstformen der Natur" (Art Forms in Nature) contains images of marine animals, often displaying symmetry of various kinds (Haeckel, 2008). Bilateral symmetry occurs in all living groups and is especially marked in the larval stages. During evolution, muscle contraction replaced the beating of cilia so streamlined bodies with bilateral symmetry (similar to line symmetry) became dominant. This type of symmetry occurs when the animals develop different front and the rear parts and display the forward motion. In bilaterally symmetrical animals, for example in butterflies the halves of their bodies, when seen along the horizontal or the vertical axis (x or y axis) form each other's mirror images.

Humans, often in a similar way as animals, apply asymmetrical patterns as a camouflage, a way of blending with the environment; they use hunting camouflage clothing in colors (for example, bright orange) that are perceived as dull by the game animals, and battledresses or camouflage netting for military purposes. Artists and designers contribute with their projects. For example, for warplane and ship camouflage, in order to confuse the periscope view of the submarine gunners during World War I, Norman Wilkinson, Everett L. Warner, and other artists painted the high-contrast, asymmetric shapes on ship surfaces, thus confusing the periscope view of the German submarines (Berens, 1999). Other, non-military applications include art. Artists, for example, Liu Bolin (2012) or Bev Doolittle (2011) create camouflage art, while architects and designers construct unusual camouflage restaurants (2012) of different kinds. For an exercise in working with other kinds of symmetry, see Table 2.

Asymmetry

Asymmetry, omnipresent in the animal world, is important in design, architecture, and art. For example, the complicated asymmetrical forms included the ornaments in the Rococco style (the late Baroque, 18th century artistic style), Art Nouveau (the decorative style from the period around 1890-1914), and also the rotational and translational symmetry in Islamic tilings and architecture. Charles Jencks (2003/2009, p. 25) considers symmetry breaking "a basic truth of the universe" that occurs due to processes such as bending, heating, or hitting. In his *The Garden of Cosmic Speculation*, Charles Jencks (2003/2009, pp. 182-3) visualized the history of the universe as the four breaks in symmetry that indicate the origin, the era of energy, life, and consciousness. He describes the origin of the world as a result of the imbalance between particles and their oppo-

Table 2. Drawing symmetrical objects

Visual Response: Abstract Composition with Symmetry
Make an abstract composition of simple geometric forms. Draw on the computer screen some forms showing several types of symmetry: the bilateral, the radial, cylindrical, or spherical symmetry and arrange them on the screen. It may be useful in further work on your composition.
To create an object with a bilateral symmetry, draw a left or right side of a shape you plan to design, then perform a "Save as ..." operation, and create it's another side using the "Brush mirror" option. It can be a geometric form, for example, an acute triangle (having angles less than 90°), and the right-angle triangle or, if you prefer so, it may also be a butterfly or a flower. Organize several such shapes; for example, create a steel bridge applying copying, flipping, and mirroring triangles.
To show an object with radial symmetry, for example, an open umbrella or a flower, draw a segment of your object: an isosceles triangle (having two sides and two angles the same) or a petal of a flower, then rotate it three, four, five or six times around an imaginary line called the rotation axis, so your segment will repeat itself each 120°, 90°, 72°, or 60°. Now you may find a center of symmetry equally distant from any point on the exterior surface of your object. You can also see that your shape will retain the same appearance after rotation.
Make a sketch of an object with a cylindrical symmetry, for example, a glass, a top hat or a tube.
To show a spherical symmetry, design a spherical object, for example, a space ship that fulfills the space explorers' needs and demands. How will you divide the sphere interior? Draw a plan of the interior.

sites, anti-particles: according to the uncertainty principle the void contains such virtual pairs jumping into existence from nothing and being annihilated by their opposites.

The art theorist and perceptual psychologist Rudolf Arnheim (1969, 1974) stated that gravity makes the space asymmetrical, not in a geometrical but in a dynamical sense, because an upward movement requires energy, whereas downward movement can be done by removing any support that keeps an object from falling. We perceive this asymmetry by two senses, with kinesthesia (awareness of the tension in the muscles and joints of the body) and vision.

External patterns in animals are not always symmetrical: some species of salamanders, frogs, vipers, fly larvae, and fish have asymmetrical patterns. Asymmetry of a pattern may be useful in terms of the camouflage possibilities: they aid to conceal their bodies from enemies by making them look like a part of the natural surroundings. An asymmetrical pattern can help an animal with bilateral symmetry to change its appearance, to hide and become invisible against the background. In later stages of evolutionary development, body forms became not so simple. Most animal bodies, including people, cannot be divided into identical halves, even when they look symmetrical from external appearance. Other forms, for example marine animals holothurians that are also called sea cucumbers (echinoderms), show bilateral symmetry outside and radial symmetry of hemal sinuses inside.

Asymmetry in animals can be expressed as a zigzag pattern down the back of a viper or as a location of a liver or a heart. Not only internal organs, but the skull and the brain are also asymmetrical in humans, as well as in some animals and birds. Organisms develop not only a structural but also a behavioral asymmetry. Two halves of the human brain display different abilities, ways of learning, and thinking. Human and animal handedness displays asymmetry in skill development; for example, Fiddler crabs have one claw much bigger than another. Earthworms, when put in a maze, display a behavioral asymmetry when they can recognize the difference between right and left. Some insects use their jaws like left-handed or right-handed scissors, depending on the species they belong to. Several technologies applied in zoology help to explain existing symmetry or asymmetry. For example nuclear transplantation

or application of a mutagen drug may induce biased symmetry.

Asymmetry can be also noticed in several other disciplines. In organic chemistry chirality refers most often to molecules: chiral molecules display lack of an internal plane of symmetry, usually because of the presence of an asymmetric carbon atom. In simple terms, chirality means the existence of left/right opposition (IUPAC, 2010; Leffingwell, 2003). Chirality is also present in biological structures; it often determines bioactivity (for example, odor perception depends on the molecule's configuration) and is an important factor in drug efficacy. As was stated at the 2011 Congress of the European Society for Evolutionary Biology, "asymmetric shapes in animals and plants can come in two mirror-image forms. However, such chiral dimorphism is found in some structures but not in others. This makes chirality one of the very few developmental traits that can be studied consistently across all multicellular organisms, offering a goldmine of research questions in evolutionary developmental biology (Carroll, evo-devo, 2005), evolutionary ecology (Mayhew, 2006), and macro-evolution" (Schilthuizen & Gravendeel, 2011).

Animals in Art

Pictures of animals exist at the cave walls (regardless of a debate as to whether the cave paintings were created for artistic intent), ancient or antique paintings, as well as the paintings from the Renaissance or modern times. Real and fantastic animals served in the medieval paintings (from most of the Gothic period of the 12th through the 15th century) as a part of decorative vocabulary and vehicles for religious allegory and moral instruction (Animals in Medieval Art, 2011). One can also find fantastic animals and beasts in classical paintings of ancient Egypt, Greece, and Rome, and in the dreamlike or nightmarish pictures from the times of the Surrealism movement (originated in France in the 1920s). Such bizarre, fictional beasts were derived both from mythology and pure fantasy.

In order to examine paintings containing representations of animals, and make the animal theme in art more familiar, we can find them in Google Images, and on web art galleries and collections, for example, http://palimpsest.stanford.edu/icom/vlmp/usa.html for American art, and http://palimpsest.stanford.edu/icom/vlmp/world.html for the rest of the world; The Parthenet: http://witcombe.sbc.edu/ARTHLinks.html, specifically, http://witcombe.sbc.edu/ARTH20thcentury.html#general20century for the contemporary art; or World Art Treasures: http://sgwww.epfl.ch/BERGER/.

We may surely find artwork in books. Many of the titles of art works collected below come from the Art Book (1994), The 20th Century Artbook (1996), and The American Art Book (1999).

While looking at the artwork, it may be interesting to fix one's eyes on the painting and give a serious thought to a real cause or a motive the artist might have in mind to create it. It may not necessarily be an accurate and detailed representation of a scene with the animals but a message to convey or an artistic statement that provides a reason for bringing this work into being. You are requested to figure out the content of the artwork and then, in the same way, make an effort to include some meaning into your animal representations. Below, some approaches to the animal theme are shown in works from various periods of time.

Jacopo Bassano, c1590, "The Animals Entering the Ark," "Sacrificio di Noe"

Jan Breugel, c1620, "The Garden of Eden," "Paradise"

Frans Snyder, 1620s, "A Game Stall," "Still Life of Dead Game"

Aelbert Cuyp, c1650, "Cattle with Horseman and Peasants," "Cows in Water"

Carel Fabritius, 1654, "The Goldfinch"

Edward Hicks, 1833/4, "The Peaceable Kingdom"

John James Audubon, 1835-8, "Roseate Spoonbill"

George Catlin, c.1857, "Ambush for Flamingoes"

Sir Stanley Spencer, 1935, "Saint Francis and the Birds"

Henri Rousseau, 1906, "The Monkeys"

Giacomo Balla, 1913, "Flight of Swallows"

Raoul Dufy, c1926, "The Paddock"

Marcel Broodthaers, 1964-5, "Casserole and Closed Mussels"

Arthur Boyd, 1987, "The Australian Skapegoat.

See Table 3 for making a composition with symmetrical forms in nature.

Figures 6a and 6b shows students' impressions about animal symmetry and pattern.

Tessellation, Virtual Garden

For a project on tessellation and virtual gardening, see Table 4.

Figure 7(a, b) shows tessellations created by students.

SQUARE AND CUBE IN NATURE

It is hard to find a square or a cube in nature. There is an apparent lack of geometric forms, especially Euclidean forms in the living organisms. It seems there are not too many organic squares or cubes. They are much better represented in minerals. When researching this theme, one can find mineral crystal forms such as table salt or fluorite. An organic mineral form Pyrite and some plates of mica may possibly represent a flat square all by itself. Other than that, nature displays complex curvilinear forms rather than squares. The cube-shaped bacteria and an organism Haloquadratum walsbyi may come to mind while wandering at the Internet. Lobsters' eyes contain square structures that reflect light onto the retina.

Table 3. Finding symmetry in living forms

Visual Response: Symmetry and Pattern
This project combines geometry- and art-related concepts: symmetry and pattern. It pertains as well to biology (the general design of animal bodies, animal shapes, symmetry and patterns, adaptation), art and art history concepts (patterns in artistic or decorative design, animals in art, and general composition of the artwork), and computer graphics. It also encourages the use of spatial visualization skills. This theme could certainly be interesting for a mathematician, an anthropologist, and someone who conducts a computer analysis of the facades, friezes, and architectural details.
After some study about the use of symmetry and pattern in the art works, make a composition with symmetry. Look at some living forms and examine how the geometry related concepts of symmetry (bilateral, radial, or helical), asymmetry, and patterns pertain to the general design of animals' bodies, look, and behavior. Find mathematical order in natural forms and re-create it in your own work. Explain a relation between the type of symmetry and the animal moving capacity by drawing two- and three-dimensional models and applying visualization made with the use of color and pattern coding. You may also want to construct models out of paper to explore principles of symmetry. Emphasize the importance of their adaptations to the conditions of life. Many artists have created masterpieces this way. Show symmetry (or lack of symmetry) in animal patterns, for example of fish scales or bird feather.
You may also want to write a story in your journal, on your listserv, or on the web, about your imaginative trip to the virtual garden, and then you may want to incorporate this story into your picture.

Figure 6. a. Sam Dailey, Symmetry (© 2005, S.Dailey. Used with permission); b. Andrea Carvalho, Symmetry (© 2006, A. Carvalho. Used with permission).

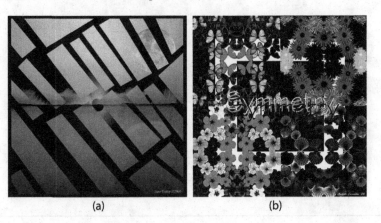

(a)   (b)

Table 4. Creating images with tessellations

Visual Response: Tessellation, Virtual Garden
Tesselation This project combines tessellation (natural or human-made filling of a surface with figures with no overlaps or gaps) with your previous work. Create your own tessellation; this time it will be an abstract art. Sketch a rectangle or a geometric shape. Take away a fragment from this rectangle by cutting out a shape of your choice from its left side. Slide this fragment so that it becomes closely attached with its straight line's edge to the bottom line of your rectangle. Save your work. Repeat this procedure, now on the other side of the rectangle: select and subtract a fragment at the right side, and attach its straight-line side to the upper border of the rectangle. Copy and paste the new shape you have just created, making several copies. Color them all: select one color for a half of these shapes, and choose another color for the rest of them. Arrange all fragments as a two-colored whole. In some image editing programs the sequent stages of your work are being organized in layers, so you may color shapes from each layer separately, then flatten the image and arrange the shapes into a tesselation pattern. **Virtual Garden** You may then want to create a Virtual Garden with animals, by applying tessellation and creating an imaginative drawing of the Virtual Garden with images of animals and plants. Use your tesselation to design a background for the artwork. Looking at small plastic animals, make several pictures of animals on the screen. You have many options in doing this. You may create hand drawings or scan pictures of animals and paste the images into your work. Also, you may import animal pictures from the web (being careful to obey copyright rules!) or from a clip-art, but your artwork would be more genuine, original, and authentic with your hand-drawn animals. Remember that no two animals look alike, even when they belong to the same population, so avoid copying and pasting the images of animals. Add some plants: trees, flowers, grass, carefully composing them together with your tesselation background. Create a sense of perspective by placing bigger objects in the foreground, partially covering farther objects by the nearer ones, and applying lighter shades in front than in the back of the space of your virtual garden. Try to imagine the impact of the environment you depict on each of the animals, resulting from changes and events you invented. Think how the creatures living there experience the environment of your virtual garden. In your work, use patterns to convey the sense of variety. Assign a specific pattern to each of the specimens selecting one that indicates that this individual apparently belongs to its class. Arrange patterns (that means, animals with patterns) in order to bring harmony in your composition, and make your landscape purposeful, not resembling a piece of fabric which had been cut at random from a bale to make a tablecloth. Remember one general principle, which is usually expressed sententiously as "form follows function." Each animal shape you draw should indirectly convey a particular characteristic of movement, which is specific to an animal you choose to portray, while each symmetrical or asymmetrical pattern tells about animal's locomotion or possible ways of disguising its true appearance. When you are ready with the general design of your picture, think about its composition. Examine your work in detailed and complete manner: whether your artwork conveys the message you intended to express by art or is it just an accurate depiction of the object of your attention you have been working on. After saving your image under a new name select the best and most meaningful part of your work and crop it, so you can endeavor now to complete a new, blown-up segment. Work on it having in mind both the meaning you want to convey and the aesthetic matters of artistic beauty and taste. Your new work may be less descriptive than your initial composition, but you may find it more engaging and intent. After you feel you have completed your work, compare it critically with the first rendering in terms of your initial goals and your actual answer to the issues you were working on.

Figure 7. a. Pete Fadner, Tesselation (© 2010, P. Fadner. Used with permission); b. Alex Elsberg, Tesselation (© 2001, A. Elsberg. Used with permission).

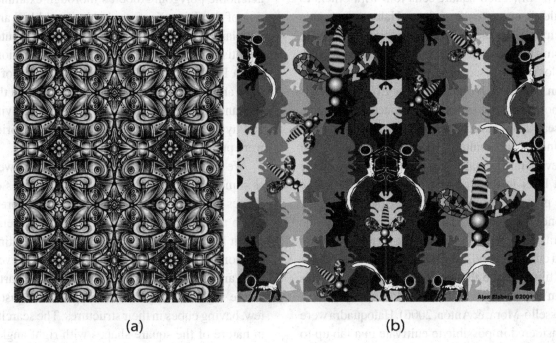

(a)　　　　　　　　　　　　　(b)

Archaea and Haloquadra: Fragile Squares

Scientists discovered new biogeochemical relations between microorganisms and minerals (Skinner, 2005). Mineral forming microorganisms exist on nearly every rock, soil, reaching depths at 1600 meters or more below the sea floor and 70 kilometers into the stratosphere, possibly even the mesosphere (Takai, 2010; Roussel, Cambon, Bonavita, Querellou, Cragg, Prieur, Parkes, & Parkes, 2008; Pearce, Bridge, Hughes, Sattler, Psenner, & Russel, 2009). In the Newfoundland region, the 111 million old, hot (54° to 100° C) marine sediments that are at least 1600 meters below the sub-sea floor contain living prokaryotic cells belonging to Archaea. Prokaryotes are microscopic single-cell organisms that have neither well-defined nucleus nor distinct organelles. Sub-sea-floor sediments may contain two-thirds of Earth's total prokaryotic biomass (Roussel et al., 2008).

Archaea are ancient, single-celled organisms without cell nuclei or other membrane-bound organelles, single-cell microorganisms that have no cell nucleus or organelles with membranes. They are different in many aspects from other organisms, such as bacteria or eukaryote (having nuclei and distinct organelles); at the same time they have genes, some enzymes, and metabolic pathways resembling those in more advanced single–cell organisms. Archaea can live in extreme harsh environments such as volcanic hot springs or salt lakes (in concentration of salt up to 18%). They can draw energy from a great variety of sources, using as nutrients organic compounds such as sugars, ammonia, metal ions, and hydrogen. Some are anaerobic methane-oxidizing organisms (Roussel et al, 2008).

One genus belonging to archaea, called Haloquadratum walsbyi, forms unique, fragile square cells, unusual for living beings (Burns, Camakaris, Jansen, & Dyall-Smith, 2004). It is still unknown why haloquadra take this atypical form. Haloquadra are about 0.15 μm thick (1 μm = 10^{-6} m). Their square cells join with others to build sheets up to 40 μm long. Haloquadra rotate their flagella clockwise to move forward, or rotate them counterclockwise when moving backward. Haloquadra, discovered in 1980, require more than 14% (mass/volume) salt for growth, which is a more than four times higher concentration than in seawater. The archaeon Haloquadra walsbyi was found in Maras salterns (pools where water is left to evaporate to make salt) located 3,380 m above sea level in the Peruvian Andes. To determine the presence of microorganisms, the rRNA gene clones were analyzed and compared to the clone libraries. The total counts in these rich in sodium and chloride ponds were up to 3 millions cells per milliliter, while the spring water contained less than 100 cells per milliliter (Maturrano, Santos, Rosselló-Mora, & Antón, 2006). Haloquadra were considered impossible to cultivate in a lab up to 2004. Scientists in several labs are mapping the organism's 3.1 Mb large genome (Dyall-Smith, Pfeiffer, Klee, Palm, Gross, Schuster, Rampp, & Oesterhelt, 2011; Haloquadra, 2010).

Other Encounters with Squares

We have a privilege to live in the at least three-dimensional space; the idea of a flatland, a different world that is limited to two dimensions is based on a favorite science-fiction classic written by "a Square" (a pseudonym of Edwin A. Abbott Abbott) entitled "Flatland: A Romance of Many Dimensions." In 1884 Abbott Abbott (2008) described a satirical journey to the universe inhabited by flat characters with a hierarchy of their different geometric shapes. Geometric figures inhabit the fictional two-dimensional world of Flatland: straight lines, triangles, squares, pentagons, hexagons, and other figures move freely on the surface. In this satirical novel about a Victorian culture social hierarchy depends on the figures' regularity and the number of sides; for example a Merchant – an equilateral triangle belongs to

the craftsmen class, and a Physician – a pentagon is a noble polygon. Abbott's thorough examination of the dimensions made his novel liked and popular among mathematicians and computer scientists. There is also a Pointland (no dimension) and a Lineland (one dimension). Speaking of a third and a fourth dimension is prohibited in the Flatland. Abbott introduced aspects of relativity and hyperspace years before Einstein's theories were published.

We are surrounded by organic shapes, as well as some geometric ones. The two derivatives of shapes and forms (a cube and a square) are present in nature but they are hard to find. It seems also it is hard to find in nature anything relating to geometry as developed by Euclid. However, there are minerals, some plants with cubical parts, whole organisms, eye structures, to name just a few, having cubes in their structures. The scarcity in nature of the square shapes with right angles and the cube forms is difficult to explain. It is difficult to find translation of living forms into squares, possibly, because it's difficult to transfer a square into a 3-D form in another way than into a cube, and to build a sphere from squares (on the other hand, a ball in a discothèque is often a sphere made out of square mirrors). A triangle or a hexagon can serve better to build rounded forms. Round shapes and spheres are ubiquitous in nature; maybe because it is somehow resulting from the laws of physics. Gravitation or electromagnetism cause that stars and planets rotate and assume round shapes, and pebbles in a river become spherical. If an organ, for example a heart had a form of a cube, there would be accumulation of deposits in its corners. Rivers act through forces of motion, friction, attrition, tension, and gravity, all forces applied against the surrounding surfaces, and all corners becoming filled with deposits. There are plants, minerals, whole organisms, and structures in the eye, to name just a few, having cubes in their structures.

Maybe the avoidance of corners comes out the basic characteristics of flow of liquids: the circulation has a circle in the name. Fluid mechanics, especially hydrodynamics tells us that flow of blood in arteries and veins is the most efficient and free of deposits when occurring in rounded, straight vessels. If he pipes had a square shape when cut, there would be sedimentation in the corners. For example, if a heart had a form of a cube, there would be accumulation of deposits in its corners. Hydraulics describing the conveyance of water in waterways or canals tells that accumulation of sediments happens mostly in the turns of the rivers. Rivers affect everything through forces of motion, friction, attrition, tension, and gravity, all forces applied against the surrounding surfaces, and all corners becoming filled with deposits. In a square or cubic organism, cleaning or feeding the corners might be economically inefficient. Water circulates in circles; maybe circulation of liquids determines the form of the living organisms. However, we can find that rhomboids (with equal sides) are common in minerals. The shapes of

crystals formed by some minerals, such as pyrite, quartz, or maybe mica, display angles determined by a structure of molecules making their building blocks having right angles but being a part of a prism, not a cube. The regular geometric forms we can think about are a plaster of honey or the eyes of some insects.

Figure 8 is a creative response to this discussion. In a composition bound up with the golden section, the author presents 'reasons for roundness' in nature: Fibonacci sequence, planetary orbits, atomic structure, gravitational equilibrium, aesthetic order in Hindu philosophy, and a structure of DNA.

Maybe the reason why it is hard to find a presence of a square in nature is that a square has right angles, is two-dimensional, and cannot transfer into a 3-D form (such a triangle or a hexagon can) in another way than into a cube (with squares as faces of a cube).

Figure 8. Steffanie Sperry, Why not square (© 2012, S. Sperry. Used with permission).

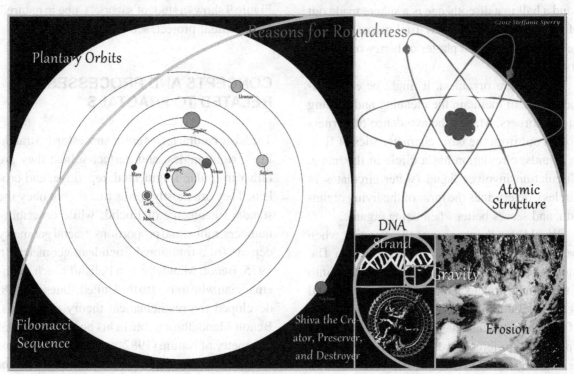

Rhomboids (which have equal sides) are common in minerals. Maybe there is a mineral with a right angle square side, which is part of a prism, not a cube. Prism is a solid geometric figure whose two end faces are similar, equal, and parallel rectilinear figures, and whose sides are parallelograms.

How about a point in Nature, how about a line segment? Can a point be classified as one of the Elements of Design? We define a line as a collection of points; can we do the same with the cube? Bottom line: there are no circles, points, straight lines, or any other Euclidean constructions in Nature, but we could recognize approximations and then the question is, what deviations are acceptable.

Beyond approximation, we can talk about translation; creation of living forms out of squares, for example. Is translation present in living organisms not only crystals? Can a rhomb and crystallography forms serve as examples of translation? (It is true, it's hard to find anything Euclidean in Nature, but then we can use the usual cop-out, geometry and mathematicians are part of Nature). On the other hand a ball in a discothèque is a sphere made out of square mirrors. We may find natural regular geometric forms in a plaster of honey or eyes of some insects.

In a square organism, it might be economically hard to maintain the cleaning and feeding in the corners. Maybe the avoidance of corners comes out from the basic characteristics of flow in liquids: circulation has a circle in the name. Circulation involves liquid (water circulates in circles), determines the form of the living organism, and serves better when being organic.

Would this theme change the meaning when we go to the nano scale? Graphene is a flat monolayer of carbon atoms tightly packed into a two-dimensional (2D) honeycomb lattice, and is a basic building block for graphitic materials of all other dimensionalities. It can be wrapped up into 0D fullerenes, rolled into 1D nanotubes or stacked into 3D (Geim & Novoselov, 2007).

Figure 9. Matthew Rodriguez, Cube in nature. (© 2012, M. Rodriguez. Used with permission).

Figure 9 shows a student's work "Cube in nature." For a similar project, see Table 5.

CONCEPTS AND PROCESSES RELATED TO FRACTALS

The basic natural forms are not necessarily straight lines, right angles, and perfect solids; they are rather irregular, fragmented, repetitive, and broken. They are mostly forms that do not obey the standard geometry of Euclid; while describing numbers, ratios, and proportions, fractal geometry departs from traditional Euclidean geometry. In 1975, Benoit Mandelbrot, a Polish/French mathematician who moved to the United States in 1958, developed the mathematical theory of fractals. Benoit Mandelbrot wrote in his book The Fractal Geometry of Nature (1982, p. 1), "Clouds are not spheres, mountains are not cones, coastlines are not

Table 5. Showing natural occurrences of squares and cubes

Visual Response: A Square and a Cube
You may want to examine an organic–geometric coexistence of the living and inanimate parts of our surroundings and represent the idea of a cube or a square (or both), which are hard to find in nature. Summarize your search on the presence of a cube in nature and create a visual representation showing this phenomenon with somehow explanative power.

circles, and bark is not smooth, nor does lightning travel in a straight line." Mandelbrot's (1982, p. 3) manifesto was, "There is a fractal face to the geometry of nature." Fractal geometry, which describes self-similar or scale symmetric objects, is often discussed in relation to art, mathematics, and computer graphics. Fractals represent form of scale symmetry that appears when an object magnified or reduced in size has the same properties. Fractals have been often applied in order to create two dimensional and three-dimensional compositions of fractal forms using symmetry, repetition, and patterns. Fractals are exceedingly common in nature and can be found virtually everywhere in the natural world. One can ponder a complex idea how to find patterns in nature that can be represented by humans as mathematical equations and also as art forms. Mathematicians name some objects symmetrical with respect to a given mathematical operation applied to this object, when this operation preserves some property of the object. Such operations form a symmetry group of the object.

The concept of self-similarity is central for fractals because fractal geometry describes objects that have the same structure, whatever their scale. Fractals represent a form of scale symmetry that appears when the objects magnified or reduced in size have the same properties. They can be subdivided into smaller parts, each of which is a smaller copy of the whole. When fractal objects are magnified, their parts are similar to the whole, the likeness continuing with the parts of the parts and so on, forever. That means the part, whatever its size, has the same topology as the whole. According to Gfdas (2011), golden rectangles have an ability to create other rectangles proportionally similar to themselves; therefore they can be discussed as fractals. The golden rectangle is a rectangle with sides 1 by φ that can be defined by the golden ratio between 1 and φ:

$$\frac{\varphi}{1} = \frac{1}{\varphi - 1}$$

which may be verbalized as the smaller part is to larger as a larger part is to the whole. If you multiply the smaller rectangle by φ then you get the larger rectangle. Also, the golden spiral, also called the eye of God, has fractal properties because a definition, 'a fractal is a shape made of parts similar to the whole in some way' (Mandelbrot, 1987) applies to it (Gfdas, 2011).

On April 1, 1999, an article by Ray Girvan appeared online. It reported a discovery of a medieval manuscript written by the Benedictine monk Udo of Aachen who lived around 1200-1270. The manuscript was a part of a collection of underground profane verses entitled Carmina Burana, which were later orchestrated by a composer Carl Orff in 1937. The article also reported a discovery made by a mathematician Bob Schipke, of a gilded image of the Star of Bethlehem that was a representation of the Mandelbroth set. The image was included into the article. Udo of Aachen had also devised the rules for complex arithmetic, the spiritual and profane parts corresponding to the real and imaginary numbers of modern mathematics. A document written by Brother Udo entitled Codex Udolphus was also found, where he stated "that on pain of excommunication I must lay down my dice and my numbers." However, the author dropped the cue about his mathematical research

into the manuscript illumination. The point is, the Ray Girvan's article was an April Fool hoax, with several internal clues in the article that helped to recognize this was a joke, beginning with the false reference to a journal that has not been existing.

Algorithms and Ways to Calculate a Graphic or Acoustic Fractal

Fractals are produced by algorithms, mathematical equations used to solve complicated problems by carrying out a sequence of simpler, unambiguous steps. A recursive process means that an algorithm is applied many times to perform operations on its previous products. The Cantor Set is the simplest fractal based on the following algorithm. First, divide a line in 3 parts and remove the middle part. Repeat this action many times, first on the 2 remaining parts, then on 4 resulting parts, and so on. After that, the fractal will have an immeasurably great number of infinitely small parts. Recursive procedures are used in computer programs and in programmed learning. The results of calculations can be presented graphically or acoustically. Fractals can be used to create visual art or visual music, where the results of calculations can be presented graphically or acoustically and result from iteration (repeated application of an equation) in a recursive manner, where the items are repeated in a self-similar way during the process. By using fractal-generating applets we may create images of plants, snowflakes, landscapes, and many other forms, including fractal art, music, and fractal music generators.

Basic types of fractals include iterated function systems (random and deterministic) such as Koch snowflakes, Mandelbrot sets, Julia sets, and L-system fractals that exist in biological structures. Exploration of fractals is even easier with the use of interactive tools designed for exploring the fractal patterns. Such tools combine supercomputing and networks with the simple interface of a Macintosh or X-Windows workstation. One can design a fractal by capturing one generator and transforming it on a computer by scaling, rotating, etc., and then create two-dimensional and a three-dimensional compositions of fractal forms using symmetry, repetition, and pattern. Many natural objects display statistical self-similarity and can be modeled as fractal surfaces. Fractal surfaces can be generated in many ways, starting with a large triangle, then recursively zooming it in. Natural looking landscapes are generated as fractal landscapes via computer algorithms. Topographic maps of different heights can be created, e.g., drawn by Java applets, using fractal algorithms such as plasma or cloud fractals as visual implementations of the diamond-square algorithm. A three-dimensional analog of the Sierpinski triangle (the tetrix) can be formed by repeatedly shrinking a regular tetrahedron.

Fractals in Science and Technology

Fractals can be found virtually everywhere in the natural world. In a quest for fractal forms we can find patterns in nature that are represented by humans in a form of mathematical equations. The basic ideas in fractal geometry are concepts of self-similarity and of kinetic growth. Self-similarity can be seen in many plants, including the fern: each leaf branching off the fern is a smaller version of the entire plant. Delacroix noticed it in nature in 1854. In kinetic growth particles added to a structure neither come off nor rearrange themselves (White, 2004). Using concepts of self-similarity and kinetic growth physicists can describe the chaotic course of events occurring in dynamical systems and build visual models of what we see in nature. Fractal geometry is used to model soil erosion and to analyze seismic patterns. In biology, polymer chains building proteins, as well as patterns of atoms on the protein surface have a fractal shape. Fractals describe complex figures, such as clouds, river networks, crystalline structures, or trees. In geology, coastlines, surfaces of mountains, and the interior brittle crust such as California's San Andreas Fault (Okubo & Aki,

1987) are fractal in nature and can be modeled with fractal geometry. Small earthquakes are fractal both in time and space. Fractals are used in a variety of applications ranging from special film and TV effects to economy and physics (La Brecque, 1987). In technology, scientists investigate the fractal nature of materials, objects, and events in biology, geology, meteorology, along with their implications for physics, electrical conductivity, the atomic structure of glasses, gels, and other amorphous materials. A fractal can appear when two glue covered acrylic sheets are pulled apart. Irreversible growth processes involve gradual addition and sticking of particles. Fractal aggregation is considered a common mechanism underlying spontaneous formation of patterns and shapes that are common in non-equilibrium (far from thermodynamic, energetically favorable equilibrium) growth processes in physics, chemistry, and biology (Liu & Sawant, 2001). Many network patterns occur during crystallization in biomacromolecules, polymers, nanofiber networks, which are basic structural elements of materials such as gels, soft tissues, and nanocrystalline materials. The self-organization of small molecule gelling agents results in formation of nanofibers fractal networks in organic gels. Tseng, Hsieh, & Jeng (2008) presented a strategy for fractal image compression with the use of the visual-based particle swarm optimization (PSO) method, that makes possible visual search better and faster.

Fractals in Art

Fractals are common in nature and can imitate nature. As they often evoke an aesthetic response in us, fractals are given the status of a work of art. On the interface of science and art, computer-graphics artists and mathematicians have produced fractal images of great statistical complexity. Fractal art resulting from the developments in fractal geometry has been presented in many books and displayed at art exhibitions. Fractal landscapes serve as background in motion pictures, while trees and other branching structures can be seen in animations. Decorative arts are often produced with fractals.

Depending on a method of calculation fractal designs may resemble various styles in art. With all their decorative merits, fractals have often evoked discussions about their aesthetic values in terms of fine art. In one of his books, Claude Lévi-Strauss (French philosopher and anthropologist associated with the development of structuralism) characterized the essence of fractals in art. He recalled the opinion of a German philosopher Immanuel Kant (1724-1804) about an aesthetic judgment. In an aesthetic theory developed by Kant, judgments about beauty rest on feeling but they should be validated in harmony with mental structure, so they are not merely statements of taste or opinion. According to Kant, there are judgments of taste that are subjective and judgments of reason that are universally valid. Aesthetic judgment falls somewhere between these two kinds. Lévi-Strauss (1997) stated that, in this intermediary space, fractals are given the status of a work of art, because they are appealing and at the same time, objectively governed by reason. The aesthetic value of asymmetry has been appreciated in Chinese art and art

Table 6. Working with Fractals

Visual Response: Fractals
In your project, you can use fractals produced by algorithms to create music or art. The appearance of fractal designs may resemble various styles in art, depending on the method of calculation. While creating your project, you may start from examination of web pages about fractal geometry, and then create your own fractal design. You may think about the fern leaf, the seashell, or simply about Ansel Adams' photography. You may also try capturing the idea of one generator being transformed by scaling, rotating, etc. If you like our composition, you may then make it functional. You may also want to use XaoS – a portable real-time interactive fractal zoomer, to zoom in and out a fractal.

criticism. In Chinese calligraphy, the "dynamic asymmetry' proportion of a Chinese character, with a subtle discrimination, is prized by Chinese artists and art theorists (Huang & Balsys, 2009). According to Huang & Balsys, an ancient Chinese philosophy of Tao is based on the same principle as that found in modern chaos and fractal theories. Key principles and notions of Chinese art theory are in agreement with fractal notions from chaos theory. Chinese art is an abstract form of symbolic brushstrokes, which elicit intrinsic mathematic values in fractal form.

One may create a fractal design when thinking about the fern leaf, the seashell, or simply about Ansel Adams' photography (Ansel Easton Adams, 1902-1984, was an American photographer and environmentalist). Julia Jones (2005) saw it when she wrote about Adams, "Great photographs are like living things, subject to the laws of life. They are made up of cells or parts, each as significant as the whole. There are photos within photos: fractals. Fractals work and exist in nature and in Adam's photographs; these fractals play out to recreate what Adams' saw in the scene, making it alive again to the viewer. Adams saw and captured pictures within pictures; masterpieces within the one masterpiece. Adams once argued, no note is beautiful on its own: it is the repetition, variation, and the note's place in the whole that allows one to hear its beauty."

It may be interesting to visit a Geom-e-tree for iPhone, iPod touch, and iPad on iTunes App (http://www.geom-e-tree.com/). One may create fractal-like trees, discover patterns by changing number, angle, and the common ratio of the tree branches, and watch the trees growing, changing, and morphing in real time. For a project involving fractals, see Table 6.

COMPUTATIONAL SOLUTIONS AS VISUAL PRESENTATIONS

We are talking about algorithmic art when one creates a work by writing a program (the similar way it was done before many kinds of user friendly graphics software were developed). Programming in art serves today mostly for making further modifications, such as creating simulations, biological growth patterns, artificial intelligence, robotics, or visualizations, and introducing several levels of interactivity aimed at the Web art and at interactive or performance-based installations.

Presentation of mathematical equations may evoke fascination with their aesthetic order. A study of mathematical operations suitable for generating artistic images (Franke, 1971, 1989) has been suggested as a method for creating art. Artistic creations have been achieved through visualization of mathematical relations from many fields of mathematics, such as geometry and fractal geometry (ultrarealistic pictures built with numbers on the principle of self-similarity of forms composed of smaller forms, with shapes identical as the overall structure), field theory, Fourier transformations, topology, combinatorics, theory of numbers, and they may serve for the purpose of developing interest and motivation in students. The early computer art graphics were mostly images of geometrically defined forms in Cartesian coordinates. The linear perspective, sectioning, for example golden section, the Fibonacci series (a sequence of numbers with the property that each number in the sequence represents the sum of the two preceding numbers), logic, especially based on Boolean operations, logical laws applications (such as those based on Godel's theorem) can be explored and used as a starting point for creating computer graphics assignments. The Lissajous figures obtained through the superposition of sinusoidal waves upon the vertical and horizontal deflectors of the monitor, as well as images that visualize permutations cycling a basic set of numbers through all of its possible variations may serve as examples of inspirations. A number of computer art graphics may be created with the use of astonishing patterns featuring harmonic relations such as the one thousand years old Vedic square – an arrangement of elements represented by numbers. (In the Vedic square, a set of numbers, for example 9x9, is placed in first row. The remaining numbers in the square are computed by multiplying the values of the respective values of row by column. Each time the product exceeds 9, number is reduced by forming the sum of the first and second digit). Another source of aesthetic experience was seen in Latin squares, arrangements possible of N elements where one number was placed only once in a particular row or column (Dietrich & Molnar, 1981).

Scientists perceive an analogy between the highly excited atoms examined with the quantum physics approach and the stellar systems; they are developing a self-similar cosmological model describing the self-similarity on the atomic, stellar, and galactic scale (Oldershaw, 2005). The author demonstrated discrete self-similarity between these fractal analogues in terms of their masses, radii, oscillation periods, basic morphologies, and kinematics (Oldershaw, 2006).

Artists Inspired by Mathematical Problems

Art and mathematics can complement one another. There seems little doubt that mathematics exists profusely in works of many artists. Mathematicians and electronic artists can find beauty in mathematical description of natural order, whatever they choose to examine. Art resides in many mathematical applications that are related both to the formulas and programs, so mathematical order is often an inspiration for art. Study of geometric two-dimensional shapes and three-dimensional forms resulted in works of art done in various media, both traditional and digital, including painting, sculpture, printmaking, and architecture.

A foundation for further work can be found in expanding the ways that mathematics and art complement each other in many developing fields of science, such as knowledge and data visualization, simulation, data mining, web media and web communication. A city metaphor is often used to map information, while emotional features of the face provide an automatic mapping of the big data sets. Yasuhiko Saito produced artworks using an information visualization technique for financial analysis.

Electronic or computer art may be done with programs as well as created with the off-the-shelf applications. By writing a computer program we may create a two- dimensional shape or a three-dimensional form, then render projection of the form on a surface. For example, a line drawing of a horse can become a three-dimensional wire frame drawing, and multiplied with resizing each copied horse. Images can be transformed by ascribing them different points of reference, perspectives, viewing points. Such programs may serve for developing sculptures. Algorithms, mathematical recipes telling how to carry out a process allow solving a problem by carrying out a fixed sequence of simpler, unambiguous steps. Such procedures are used in computer programs and in programmed learning. Examples of art resulting from computing are examined in Chapter 3. Computer programs and computer graphics produced with the use of software packages give a boost to theoretical studies. They make a separate category of digital art and, at the same time, serve as a tool for creating works in other media. Teams working on visualization or simulation projects usually include a mathematician, and the direct results of their work look many times as artistic productions.

Artists face mathematical problems, both in the old masters' studies on perspective (such as Piero de la Francesca, Renaissance masters, and then Maurits Cornelis Escher) or in the applications of mathematical theorems to visual solutions. Both the mathematicians and artists examine how mathematical rules manifest themselves in nature, science, and the works of art. For example, the aesthetics of fractal design has been discovered and studied not only in minerals and plants, also but in the Anselm Adams' photographs of minerals and plants, paintings by Jackson Pollock, writings and artwork by Clifford A. Pickover, and many art works created not only by fine arts artists but also by mathematicians and scientists. Forms that present solutions of mathematical equations are often enjoyable and pleasing to the eye, maybe due to intuitive understanding of their origin. They include art works derived from random selection of numbers, permutations resulting in more or less regular patterns, equations visualized as sculptures (for example a Moebius knot), and stereo geometry transformations. For example, Kenneth Huff builds the forms based on an idealized mathematical knot, Michael Field on symmetry and chaotic dynamical systems described mathematically, while Marte Newcombe and Greg Shirah apply scientific data to their sculptures and mathematically based curves derived from parametric equations.

The general direction has been in developing application of mathematics to computer science and the digital art, for example, in works created by algorist artists. Several artists utilized the plotted line as a means of artistic expression, using mechanically guided pen to draw the monochrome line according to the generative code. Algorithmic images of a cube created by German artist Manfred Mohr (1990) may serve as an example of work of art that can be rationally understood, and yet there is room for associations and imagination. As it was stated by Manfred Mohr (Keiner, Kurz, Nadin, 1994, p. 154), "My art is not a mathematical art, but an expression of my artistic experiences. I don't want to show cold mathematics but a vital philosophy." Manfred Mohr (2012), who transformed his art from abstract expressionism to computer-generated algorithmic geometry, first worked on the 4-dimensional hypercube, its rotation, and the 6-dimensional hypercube. Then he worked on the systematic creation of signs from

the fixed system of the cube and the hyper cube, visually fracturing the symmetry and at the same time creating an ambiguity in the sign. Now, 40 years later he investigates these tension fields, as they would re-appear in a diagonal-path through the 11-dimensional hypercube. Algorithmic artist Jean-Pierre Hébert (2012) creates drawings on paper, films, glass, steel, copper plates, linoleum, wood, sand, and even on air and water. A sculptor and mathematician Helaman Ferguson (1994) is considering mathematics both an invisible art form and a science. Ferguson claims that computer graphics make mathematics visible. He transfers the thought forms formulated in terms of topological mathematics to physical materials using a method of telecarving where geometric forms drawn on a computer screen are translated into instructions on direct carving the stone.

Mathematical art is widely represented at many conferences, art shows, and other events, for example, the annual Bridges conferences on connections between art and mathematics, where artists, mathematicians, and scientists focus on, around, and beyond mathematics related topics such as fractals, geometry, Fibonacci sequence, golden section, art, design, and craft based on algorithms, programs translation into materials, and other approaches. International associations explore developments in these fields at their conferences, such as ACM/SIGGRAPH, iV Information Visualization (London, UK), or Information Visualization, IEEE, CA. YLEM, Artists using science and technology, and several new journals focus some of their issues on the mathematics–art connection. Many universities offer courses on mathematics and art (for example, Helmer Aslaksen, Dept. of Mathematics, U. of Singapore) and research-oriented interdisciplinary curricula in advanced computing and computer graphics with programs that provide an advanced computing environment in support of integrative education. (e.g., Maria Palazzi, Ohio State U., Peter Border, Minneapolis College of Art and Design, Thomas Linehan, Arts and Technology, U. of Texas at Dallas).

Aesthetical Concerns: From Nature, through Math, to Art

One may ask, does the beauty of an object (its aesthetic value) make its representation an artwork? What are the distinguishing characteristics of natural forms, their mathematical descriptions, and mathematics derived artwork? The shell of a mollusk contains a logarithmic spiral. It is a natural phenomenon, not the result of some mathematical program in the nautilus. A drawing of a logarithmic spiral is a mathematics-derived form, and at the same time, it is also a natural phenomenon. Spiral forms have been explored, discovered and modified by people, but they are hardly an artwork. In the same way, when we visualize the laws of nature and develop their representations, can we consider those representations an artwork? Which criteria concerning the artistic quality of mathematically developed art may be accepted by art criticism?

Other concerns about determining artistic quality of mathematically developed art may also relate to its precision. While designing an artwork, a mathematician is careful to avoid ambiguity. Everybody can see the exact and precisely defined formula representation. On the contrary, visual communication in fine arts is often based on metaphors and open messages. Everyone may receive different, unique, and individual messages from the same artwork. It may well be that a representation of mathematical formulas cannot inevitably become an art form, but it is their intentional transformation that may become an artwork.

Art Criticism and Mathematically Developed Art: Beauty of Nature, or of Mathematics?

Laces of complex ornamentation, geometric representations of polygons, and interlaced patterns, all evoke in us the sense of beauty. Some paintings and photographs explored the beauty of natural objects that have been magnified or reduced. In a similar way, the exquisite perfection of soap bubble geometries, as well as fractal shapes rose to the form of art because of their natural beauty. Graphic elegance can be found in the simplicity of the image that demands, "every bit of ink on a graphic requires a reason" (Tufte, 1983). Where is the secret of perfect design – in its simplicity or its elaborate intricateness? A question arises, does the art critics' evaluation of the mathematics-derived artwork depends on:

- The aesthetic quality of patterns;
- The beauty of underlying mathematical formulas which give those ornamental arrangements; or
- Has some human intervention occurred between these two points of interest?

The cultural convergence of mathematics, art, and computer science developed gradually, from the simple to more complex forms, from mathematics-based patterns in world's architecture and design to innovative works of the present-day mathematicians. For example, Michele Emmer have focused his 30 year lasting project "The Mathematics and Art" on the cultural aspect of mathematics, while LEONARDO Journal of the International Society for the Arts, Sciences and Technology became a rich data source about mathematics – art connections. The American Mathematical Society (2013) hosts a Mathematical Imagery website with information about articles, resources, events, galleries, museums, and exhibitions, as well as comments. A website of Helmer Aslaksen (2013) contains educational materials, visuals, and references about mathematics in art and architecture.

CONCLUSION

This chapter examines organic/geometric forms present in nature, mathematics, and art, symmetry, fractals, artists' responses and computational solutions in the form of visual presentations. Many natural objects that entail regular mathematical forms may inspire the readers' projects. Symmetry, asymmetry, fractal forms, and tessellations may also evoke visual response.

REFERENCES

Abbott Abbott, E. A. (1994/2008). *Flatland: A romance of many dimensions (Oxford World's Classics)*. Oxford University Press.

(1999). *American Art Book*. London: Phaidon Press.

American Mathematical Society. (2013). *Mathematical imagery website*. Retrieved March 13, 2013, from http://www.ams.org/mathimagery/

Animals in Medieval Art. (2011). *Heilbrun timeline of art history*. Department of Medieval Art and The Cloisters, The Metropolitan Museum of Art. Retrieved September 11, 2012, from http://www.metmuseum.org/toah/hd/best/hd_best.htm

Arnheim, R. (1969). *Visual thinking*. Berkeley, CA: University of California Press.

Arnheim, R. (1974). *Art and visual perception*. Berkeley, CA: University of California Press.

Art Book. (2012/1994). London: Phaidon Press, ISBN 07148 64676

Artbook. (1996). *The 20th century artbook*. San Francisco, CA: Chronicle Books/Phaidon Press. ISBN 0-71483542 0

Aslaksen, H. (2005). A contrarian view of teaching mathematics and art. In *Proceedings of the Special Year in Art & Mathematics, A+M=X International Conference*. Univ. of Colorado.

Aslaksen, H. (2013). *Mathematics in art and architecture*. Retrieved March 13, 2013, from http://www.math.nus.edu.sg/aslaksen/teaching/math-art-arch.shtml

Ball, P. (2009). Worlds within worlds: Quantum objects by Julian Voss-Andreae. *Nature, 462*, 416. doi:10.1038/462416a.

Berens, R. R. (1999). The role of artists in ship camouflage during world war I. *Leonardo, 32*(1), 53–59. doi:10.1162/002409499553000.

Bernstein, K. (2005). Expression in the form of our own making. In *Proceedings of the Special Year in Art & Mathematics, A+M=X International Conference*. Univ. of Colorado.

Birken, M. (2008). Light motifs – Marcia Birken's images meld math and art. *Mount Holyoke Alumnae Quarterly*. Retrieved September 11, 2012, from http://alumnae.mtholyoke.edu/wp/mhaq/2008/11/light-motifs-marcia-birkens-images-meld-math-and-art/

Bolin, L. (2009). *Camouflage art*. Retrieved September 14, 2012, from http://www.toxel.com/inspiration/2009/10/04/camouflage-art-by-liu-bolin/

Burns, D. G., Camakaris, H. M., Jansen, P. H., & Dyall-Smith, M. L. (2004). Cultivation of Walsby's square haloarchaeon. *FEMS Microbiology Letters, 238*(2), 469–473. Retrieved from http://www.ncbi.nlm.nih.gov/pubmed/15358434 PMID:15358434.

Camouflage Restaurants. (n.d.). Retrieved September 14, 2012, from http://www.toxel.com/inspiration/2009/06/20/10-unusual-and-creative-restaurants/

Carroll, S. B. (2005). *Endless forms most beautiful: The new science of evo devo and the making of the animal kingdom*. W. W. Norton & Company.

Dietrich, F., & Molnar, Z. (1981). Pictures by funny numbers. *Creative Computing, 7*(6), 102–107.

Doczi, G. (2005). *The power of limits: Proportional harmonies in nature, art, and architecture*. Shambhala Pocket Classics.

Doolittle, B. (2011). *Camouflage art*. Retrieved September 14, 2012, from http://www.bnr-art.com/doolitt/

Dyall-Smith, M. L., Pfeiffer, F., Klee, K., Palm, P., Gross, K., & Schuster, S. C. ... Oesterhelt, D. (2011). Haloquadratum walsbyi: Limited diversity in a global pond. *PLoS One, 6*(6), e20968. DOI 10.1371/journal.pone.0020968. Retrieved April 17, 2012, from http://www.ncbi.nlm.nih.gov/pmc/articles/PMC3119063/?tool=pmcentrez

Ferguson, C., & Ferguson, H. (1994). *Mathematics in stone and bronze*. Erie, PA: Meridian Creative Group.

Franke, H. W. (1971). *Computer graphics, computer art*. Phaidon Press.

Franke, H. W. (1989). Mathematics as an artistic-generative principle. *Leonardo, 25*, 26.

Geim, A. K., & Novoselov, K. S. (2007). The rise of graphene. *Nature Materials, 6*(3), 183–191. Retrieved September 13, 2012, from http://onnes.ph.man.ac.uk/nano/Publications/Naturemat_2007Review.pdf

Gfdas. (2011). *Golden fractals*. Retrieved July 23, 2011, from http://en.wikipedia.org/wiki/User:Gfdas29/Golden_Fractals

Ghani, D. A. (2011). Visualization elements of shadow play technique movement and study of computer graphic imagery (CGI) in Wayang Kulit Kelantan. *International Journal of Art, Culture and Design Technologies, 1*(1), 50–57. doi:10.4018/IJACDT.2011010105.

Gibson, J. J. (1986). *The ecological approach to visual perception*. Psychology Press.

Haeckel, E. (2008). *Art forms in nature: The prints of Ernst Haeckel (monographs)*. Prestel.

Haloquadra. (2010). Retrieved January 27, 2011, from microbewiki.kenyon.edu/index.php/Haloquadra

Hébert, J. P. (2012). *Personal website*. Retrieved September 14, 2012, from http://jeanpierrehebert.com/index.html

Huang, Q., & Balsys, R. J. (2009). Applying fractal and chaos theory to animation in the chinese literati tradition. In *Proceedings of the Sixth International Conference on Computer Graphics, Imaging and Visualization*, (pp. 112-122). ISBN: 978-0-7695-3789-4

Inselberg, A. (2009). *Parallel coordinates: Visual multidimensional geometry and its applications*. New York: Springer.

James, A. V., James, D. A., & Kalisperis, L. N. (2004). A unique art form: The friezes of Pirgi. *Leonardo, 37*(3), 234–242. doi:10.1162/0024094041139409.

Jencks, C. (2003/2009). *The garden of cosmic speculation*. Frances Lincoln, Ltd..

Jones, J. (2005). *Fractals & frequencies*. Retrieved September 4, 2012, from http://fractalsandfrequencies.blogspot.com/

Jones, O. (2010). *The grammar of ornament*. Deutsch Press. (Original work published 1856).

Keiner, M., Kurz, T., & Nadin, M. (1994). *Manfred Mohr*. Weiningen-Zürich: Viviane Ehri.

Kettle, S. F. A. (2007). *Symmetry and structure: Readable group theory for chemists* (3rd ed.). Wiley-Blackwell. ISBN 0470060409

La Brecque, M. (1987). Retrieved July 23, 2012, from http://www.mosaicsciencemagazine.org/pdf/m18_02_87_03.pdf

Leffingwell, J. C. (2003). Chirality and bioactivity I: Pharmacology. *Leffingwell Reports, 3*(1). Retrieved April 13, 2011, from http://www.leffingwell.com/download/chirality-phamacology.pdf

(2012). *Leonardo da Vinci and the Secrets of the Codex Atlanticus*. White Star Publishers.

Leonardo – The Genius and His Inventions. (2011). *An iPhone, iPod touch, and iPad application.* Retrieved April 14, 2013, from https://itunes. apple.com/hk/app/leonardo-da-vinci-genius-his/ id448208854?mt=8

Lévi-Strauss, C. (1997). *Look, listen, learn.* Basic Books, a division of Harper-Collins Publishers. ISBN 0-465-06880-4

Lewis, C., Mojsiewicz, K., & Pettican, A. (2012). From wunderkammern to kinect – The creation of shadow worlds. *Leonardo, 45*(4), 330–337. doi:10.1162/LEON_a_00407.

Liu, X. Y., & Sawant, P. D. (2001). Formation kinetics of fractal nanofibers networks in organogels. *Applied Physics Letters, 79*(21), 3518-3520. Retrieved July 21, 2012, from http://www.physics. nus.edu.sg/~interface/Papers/37.PDF

Loeb, A. L. (1993). *Concepts & images: Visual mathematics. Design Science Collection.* Boston: Birkhäuser.

Mandelbrot, B. B. (1982). *The fractal geometry of nature.* W. H. Freeman and Company.

Mandelbrot, B. B. (1987). Fractals. *Encyclopedia of Physical Science and Technology, 5*, 579-593.

Maturrano, L., Santos, F., Rosselló-Mora, R., & Antón, J. (2006). Microbial diversity in maras salterns, a hypersaline environment in the Peruvian Andes. *Applied and Environmental Microbiology, 72*(6), 3887–3895. doi:10.1128/AEM.02214-05 PMID:16751493.

Mayhew, P. J. (2006). *Discovering evolutionary ecology: Bringing together ecology and evolution.* Oxford University Press.

McNaught, A. D., & Wilkinson, A. (Eds.). (2010). *Compendium of chemical terminology* (2nd ed). Blackwell Scientific Publications. Retrieved October 2, 2011, from http://goldbook.iupac.org/ C01058.html

Mohr, M. (2012). *Manfred Mohr, personal website.* Retrieved September 11, 2012, from http://www. emohr.com/index.html

Neville, A. C. (1977). Symmetry and asymmetry problems in animals. In *The Encyclopedia of Ignorance: Everything you ever wanted to know about the unknown* (pp. 331–338). New York: Pergamon Press.

Okubo, P. G., & Aki, K. (1987). Fractal geometry in the San Andreas Fault system. *Journal of Geophysical Research, 92*(B1), 345–355. doi:10.1029/ JB092iB01p00345.

Oldershaw, R. L. (2005). *Self-similarity of RR lyrae stars and singly-excited helium atoms.* Retrieved October 26, 2012, from http://arxiv.org/ pdf/astro-ph/0510147.pdf

Oldershaw, R. L. (2006). *Discrete self-similarity between RR Lyrae stars II.* Retrieved October 26, 2012, from http://www.researchgate.net/publication/1787531_Discrete_Self-Similarity_Of_RR_ Lyrae_Stars_II._Period_Spectrum_For_A_Very_ Large_Sample

Pearce, D. A., Bridge, P. D., Hughes, K. A., Sattler, B., Psenner, R., & Russel, N. J. (2009). Microorganisms in the atmosphere over Antarctica. *FEMS Microbiology Ecology, 69*(2), 143–157. doi:10.1111/j.1574-6941.2009.00706.x PMID:19527292.

Plato. (2011). The republic. Simon & Brown. ISBN 1613823703

Puppet Forms in India. (2012). Retrieved September 16, 2012, from http://ccrtindia.gov.in/ puppetforms.htm

Rall, H. (2009). Tradigital mythmaking: Singapore animation for the 21st century. Singapore: Dominie Press. ISBN 978 981-08-2932-2

Renner, E. (2000). *Pinhole photography: Rediscovering a historic technique* (2nd ed.). Taylor & Francis.

Roussel, E. G., Cambon Bonavita, M., Querellou, J., Cragg, B. A., Prieur, D., Parkes, R. J., & Parkes, R. J. (2008). Extending the sub-sea-floor biosphere. *Science*, *320*(5879), 1046. doi:10.1126/science.1154545 PMID:18497290.

Schilthuizen, M., & Gravendeel, B. (2011). Evolution of chirality symposium. In *Proceedings of the 13th Congress of the European Society for Evolutionary Biology*. Retrieved August 26, 2011, from http://www.eseb2011.de/

Şenyer, E. (2012). *Traditional Turkish puppet shadow play karagöβz hacivat*. Retrieved September 16, 2012, from http://www.karagoz.net/english/shadowplay.htm

Takai, K. (2010). Limits of life and the biosphere: Lessons from the detection of microorganisms in the deep ses and deep subsurface of the Earth. In *Origins and Evolution of Life: An Astrobiological Perspective*. Cambridge, UK: Cambridge University Press.

Tanimoto, S. L. (2012). *An interdisciplinary introduction to image processing*. The MIT Press.

Topper, D. (2008). On anamorphosis: Setting some things straight. *Leonardo*, *33*(2), 115–124. doi:10.1162/002409400552379.

Tseng, C., Hsieh, J., & Jeng, J. (2008). Fractal image compression using visual-based particle swarm optimization. In *Proceedings of Image Vision Comput* (pp. 1154–1162). IEEE. doi:10.1016/j.imavis.2008.01.003.

Tufte, E. R. (2003). *The cognitive style of powerpoint*. Cheshire, CT: Graphics Press.

Voss-Andreae, J. (2011). Quantum sculpture: Art inspired by the deeper nature of reality. *Leonardo*, *44*(1), 14–20. doi:10.1162/LEON_a_00088.

White, H. (2004). *Fractal geometry*. Retrieved July 23, 2012, from www.geometriafractal.com/articlech000300.htm

Chapter 15
Poem Illustration for the
Spoon River Anthology
by Edgar Lee Masters

ABSTRACT

This project makes a connection between visual arts and a literary analysis of the masterpiece collection of poems, Spoon River Anthology, by Edgar Lee Masters, his work, and his times. The aim of this project is to create an artistic expression of our understanding of Edgar Lee Masters's work as a personal response to the spirit and the meaning of the verse, as well as to the author's comments on the philosophical, social, and historical issues.

INTRODUCTION

This project draws from a collection of poems "Spoon River Anthology" (1915/2012) written by Edgar Lee Masters (1869–1950), which is published as a public domain work at Project Gutenberg http://www.gutenberg.org/browse/authors/m#a584. An online publication of Edgar Lee Masters' classic "Spoon River Anthology" can also be found on the page http://www.bartleby.com/84/1.html and http://www2.hn.psu.edu/faculty/jmanis/masters/sranthology6x9.pdf.

The aim of this project is to create an expression of your interpretation of this work and to set forth your personal response to one of the poems, whether by writing programs for images or applying any

drawing or painting software on a computer, tablet, a smart phone such as an iPad, or on paper. You may prefer to draw by hand on the computer screen using a mouse or a graphic tablet and a stylus, you may use a digital camera or transform scanned images of your choice, or you may also use your own tools or programs. If you have some experience in programming, you may use the programming process for developing an abstract or representational image, and then you may choose to work further on it using graphic or painting software. Concentrate on achieving the artistic integrity of your image and employing all your technical capacity to bring about your vision of the poem.

Derive your inspiration from a selected verse and create a synthetic visual counterpart to Masters' epigrammatic poetry. The work resulting from this experience will envisage the spirit and the meaning of the verse in a single scene from

DOI: 10.4018/978-1-4666-4627-8.ch015

it. Literary compositions written with intensity and beauty of language brought the success and fame to the author. Your art may be illustrative or metaphorical. After you create your project as a complement to a selected poem, maybe you will want to compare and contrast your visual artistic solutions for a visual version of the poem with the works of art created in the times of Masters. While working on this project, you may want to explore concepts derived from art and computer graphics and make connections between visual arts and other disciplines. If you would make some sketches, and summaries, and conclusions as short files written in an electronic or traditional notebook, you may later enclose some of these sketches and notes in your artwork.

EDGAR LEE MASTERS AND HIS TIMES

Both the Internet resources and books on history of American literature provide information about life of the poet and his achievements confirmed by almost one hundred editions of his book, translations into many languages, and by granting the poet in 1946 the Academy of American Poets Fellowship; also, some comments and explanations about his personal views within historical and cultural context. Edgar Lee Masters intertwined his social and ethical involvement with the accounts of the frustrated lives of his characters. People portrayed in his poems speak in free-verse monologues that sound like their own epitaphs – inscriptions on their tombstones in memory of themselves, buried there.

Masters conveys his philosophical concerns about accidental events that determined fates of these deceased persons and prevented them from fulfilling their desires. The fatalistic drama about their lives reflects Masters' anger caused by social exploitation, political injustice, and economic hardship. Masters expressed his sympathy aroused by the misfortunes of soldiers just before America entered World War I

(in 1917, throughout the course of Woodrow Wilson's presidency). One may also find in the "Spoon River Anthology" a depiction of how the industrial developments in American economy affected the village life.

Romanticism in literature might influence the writings of Edgar Lee Masters, with its emphasis on imagination, emotions, and social issues. It was reflected by his ardent devotion toward English Romantic poets, such as John Keats (1795-1821), Percy Bysshe Shelley (1792-1822), as well as the American poet, Walt Whitman (1819-1892). One may also see how Masters, who studied Greek and declared himself as a Hellenist, attained the clear, precise expression in few words, which is characteristic of Greek epigrams. His epitaphs are characterized by the use of condensed language charged with suggestive power. Masters conveys the experiences, ideas, and strong emotions of his characters in a vivid and imaginative way, without using expressions controlled by meter and rhymes characteristic of poetry. His literary technique includes the use of metaphors to portray ideas and states of mind rather than facts or events.

EPIGRAMS, EPITAPHS, AND METAPHORS IN POETRY AND PAINTINGS

Epigrammatic form of writing was originally a written note on a sculpture erected as a memorial. Epigrams evolved into short satirical verses, and then in brief, witty utterances expressed in a verse or prose. These concise, rich-in-meaning, and expressive short poems or sayings were written by other writers, for example, by American writers Mark Twain (1835-1910) and Ogden Nash (1902-1971), for instance, *"Senescence begins/ and middle age ends/ the day your descendants/ outnumber your friends"*, or British authors George Bernard Shaw (1856-1950) and Oscar Wilde (1854-1900), for example, *"Experience is the name everyone gives to his mistakes"*).

Edgar Lee Masters explored also a tradition of employing an epitaph (an inscription written for a tombstone) as a brief literary piece commemorating a deceased person. One may find epitaphs, serious or humorous, for example written by Edward Gorey (1925-2000) or Edward Lear (1812-1888).

Human fate has often been presented metaphorically in allegories, stories, tales, and fables that have a deeper or more general meaning in addition to their surface meaning, as well as in literary forms where a word or a phrase that usually means one thing is metaphorically used to designate another one. Distinctive symbols and metaphors can be found in the "Spoon River Anthology" in dramatic monologues spoken by dead persons from beyond the grave. You may also want to look on the Internet or in art books for metaphors expressed in a visual way, for example in paintings, where one object is recognized as representing another. Metaphorical paintings have been created in various styles in art, for example from the period of Romanticism "Pity" by English poet and artist William Blake (1757-1827) (http://commons.wikimedia. org/wiki/File:Pity_by_William_Blake_1795.jpg). From the period of Symbolism, we can look at "Galatea" by Gustave Moreau (1826-1898) (http:// artmight.com/Artists/Moreau-Gustave-6-April-1826-18-April-1898/Moreau-Gustave-Galatea-detail-end-272858p.html/(mode)/search/ (keyword)/galatea) and "The Cyclops" by Odilon Redon (1840-1916) (http://en.wikipedia.org/ wiki/Cyclops), which portray ideas and states of mind rather than realistic images.

Appreciation of the Fayum portraits could be supportive. Fayum portraits from the Nile Delta, from Hellenistic times between 1st and 3rd century AD portrayed the deceased persons. They were early easel paintings placed at the surface of the mummy case. "The Fayum portraits are the most outstanding body of painting to have come down to us from the ancient world, remarkable for heir social and psychological insight and for their quality of art" (Doxiadis, 1995, p. 12). One can see them at the Amazon page. Visit a Greek page "From the Fayum Portraits to Early Byzantine Icon Painting." Click at portraits at http://www.ics.forth.gr/isl/ fayum/ekthemata.htm.

ANALYSIS OF ART WORKS

Masters' unusual way of describing dramatic fates of the deceased inhabitants of a Midwestern cemetery may be considered to be in correspondence with current styles in art and predominating artistic movements created in this period of time. Masters, the poet, intellectual, psychologist, and reformer, knew and appreciated works of art. Trends and movements reflected in these masterpieces might have influenced his work. Edgar Lee Masters wrote his poems in the time when American Realist artists, united in a group Ash Can School, pictured the city street-life of the working classes. For example, John Sloan (American, 1871-1951) in his "Sunday, Women Drying Their Hair" (http://xroads.virginia.edu/~museum/ armory/galleryM/sloan.906.html) and George Bellows (American, 1882-1925) in his passionate painting "Stag at Sharkey's" reflected the not-really glorified environments of a city (http://www. google.com/imgres?q=George+Bellows+(1882-1925)+in+his+passionate+painting+ "Stag+at+Sharkey's&hl=en&client= safari&sa=X&rls=en&biw=1181&bih=929&t bm=isch&prmd=imvnso&tbnid=CUHtF8QcE_ sysM:&imgrefurl=http://babylonbaroque.word-press.com/category/gay/page/2/&docid=5DIopm b8x1ZsPM&imgurl=http://babylonbaroque.files. wordpress.com/2010/08/stag-at-sharkeys.jpg&w=7 24&h=546&ei=XvnjTrCoIYevgwfMxMWKBg&z oom=1&iact=rc&dur=918&sig=10772921580296 6964536&page=1&tbnh=134&tbnw=183&start= 0&ndsp=30&ved=1t:429,r:7,s:0&tx=96&ty=36). Dante Gabriel Rosetti's (English, 1828-1882) "The Day Dream" (http://bertc.com/subsix/g85/ros-setti18.htm) and William Holman Hunt's (English, 1827-1910) "The Awakening Conscience" (http:// www.pierreaugusterenoir.org/painting-William%20 Holman%20Hunt-The%20Awakening%20Conscience-02244.htm) were created by the members of the Pre-Raphaelite Brotherhood, the artistic and literary English movement which influenced some American artists such as Albert Pinkham Ryder (1847-1917), who created visionary works, for example, "The Race Track (Death on a Pale Horse)" (http://en.wikipedia.org/wiki/Albert_Pinkham_Ryder).

Surrealist painters who created their works during Master's lifetime, such as Spanish artist Salvador Dali (1904-1987) (e.g., http://misszoecat.tripod.com/dali.htm) or a Belgian artist Rene Magritte (1898-1967) (e.g., http://www.gallery-art.org/artist-rene-magritte-1898-1967/), expressed unconscious experiences and illogical dreams by picturing, in a precise manner, collections of both the everyday and fantastic objects. One may see imaginative or ambiguous metaphysical paintings such as "The Uncertainty of The Poet" by Giorgio De Chirico (1888-1978) (http://www.tate.org.uk/servlet/ViewWork?cgroupid=999999961&workid=2204&searchid=9619&tabview=image) as the potential illustrations for Masters' poems. If you believe that the ineffable substance of a Masters' poem may be best represented by non-figurative art, examine some works created by American artists designated as Abstract Expressionists such as "Elegy to the Spanish Republic No. LV" by Robert Motherwell (American, 1915-1991) (http://www.flickr.com/photos/renzodionigi/sets/72157625833906918/detail/?page=3), "Ghost Town" by Mark Tobey (American, 1890-1976) (http://www.google.com/imgres?q=Ghost+Town"+by+Mark+Tobey&hl=en&client=safari&sa=X&rls=en&biw=1181&bih=929&tbm=isch&prmd=imvnso&tbnid=D8EDtrDsWz7mpM:&imgrefurl=http://michaelrosenfeldart.com/artists/infocusarchive.php&docid=ODL2ScInvr2z4M&imgurl=http://michaelrosenfeldart.com/images/infocus_thumbs/Tobey-Ghost_Town_sm.jpg&w=172&h=266&ei=bwHkTp3_F4X2gAexop3tBQ&zoom=1), or "Number 1, 1950, Lavender Mist" by Jackson Pollock (American, 1912-1956) (http://www.google.com/imgres?q="Number+1,+1950,+La vender+Mist"+by+Jackson+Pollock&hl=en&client=safari&sa=X&rls=en&biw=1181&bih=929&tbm=isch&prmd=imvnso&tbnid=xovA_auhsN8cCM:&imgrefurl=http://ibiblio.org/wm/paint/auth/pollock/lavender-mist/&docid=5PR_HYzgweTX7M&imgurl=http://ibiblio.org/wm/paint/auth/pollock/lavender-mist/pollock.lavender-mist.jpg&w=1100&h=814&ei=NwLkTum_L8qcgwf23MDmBQ&zoom=1&iact=hc&vpx=122&vpy=244&dur=2669&hovh=193&hovw=261&tx=127&ty=88&sig=107729215802966964536&page=1&tbnh=135&tbnw=185&start=0&ndsp=22&ved=1t:429,r:0,s:0).

CREATING THE VISUAL COUNTERPART THAT COMPLEMENTS THE POEM

See Table 1 for suggestions on how to create your own visual interpretations.

Examples of Computer Art Graphics

Selected poems from the "Spoon River Anthology" by Edgar Lee Masters along with the computer art graphics. Figure 1 shows an interpretation by Erich Michael Penfold.

I was only eight years old;
And before I grew up and knew what it meant
I had no words for it, except
That I was frightened and told my Mother;
And that my Father got a pistol
And would have killed Charlie, who was a big boy,
Fifteen years old, except for his Mother.
Nevertheless the story clung to me.
But the man who married me, a widower of thirty-five,
Was a newcomer and never heard it
Till two years after we were married.
Then he considered himself cheated,
And the village agreed that I was not really a virgin.
Well, he deserted me, and I died
The following winter.

Table 1. Visualizing the poems

Your Visual Response: Deciphering the Meaning
Now the task is to find an explanation and artistic solution for the mysterious, sometimes incomprehensible outcomes the author choose to describe, to express Edgar Lee Masters' intents and find the essence of his verse. Masters inspired himself with the gravestones in a local cemetery; after reading the information provided there he allowed his mind to ponder over the imaginative course of life of a deceased person. Possibly, some visual metaphors would be equivalent to the poet's indirect references to his not-actually mentioned philosophies. Try to avoid straightforward story telling and the narrative illustration of the events described in the verse. It may be an abstract artwork, which does not represent recognizable objects, but capture the essence of Masters' message contained in the poem you have selected. However, it may be more difficult than creating a figurative artwork. You may also want to use some words or sentences from the poem to explain or enhance the meaning of your artwork.
After you inspect attentively poems that you can import from http://www.bartleby.com/84/index2.html on the computer screen, choose a poem you consider the most visually stimulating to illustrate it. While reading and rereading the poem you have selected, draw your ideas on how to convert its metaphorical scenes into pictorial language. Give serious thought to contemplate the message this poem is conveying and present it as a strong visual message.

Figure 1. Eric Michael Penfold, Artwork inspired by a poem "Nellie Clark" selected from the "Spoon River Anthology" by Edgar Lee Masters. (© 2000, E. M. Penfold. Used with permission).

Figure 2 shows an interpretation by Mike Davis.

I have studied many times
The marble which was chiseled for me –
A boat with a furled sail at rest in a harbor.
In truth it pictures not my destination
But my life.
For love was offered me and I shrank from its disillu-
sionment;
Sorrow knocked at my door, but I was afraid;
Ambition called to me, but I dreaded the chances.
Yet all the while I hungered for meaning in my life.
And now I know that we must lift the sail
And catch the winds of destiny
Wherever they drive the boat.
To put meaning in one's life may end in madness,
But life without meaning is the torture
Of restlessness and vague desire –
It is a boat longing for the sea and yet afraid.

Figure 2. Mike Davis, Artwork inspired by a poem "George Gray" selected from the "Spoon River Anthology" by Edgar Lee Masters. (© 1996, M. Davis. Used with permission).

Figure 3. John Floyd, Artwork inspired by a poem "Lydia Puckett" selected from the "Spoon River Anthology" by Edgar Lee Masters. (© 1995, J. Floyd. Used with permission).

Figure 3 shows an interpretation by John Floyd.

Knowlt Hoheimer ran away to the war
The day before Curl Trenary
Swore out a warrant through Justice Arnett
For stealing hogs.
But that's not the reason he turned a soldier.
He caught me running with Lucius Atherton.
We quarreled and I told him never again
To cross my path.
Then he stole the hogs and went to the war –
Back of every soldier is a woman.

Figure 4 shows an interpretation by Cinnamon Lowe.

The earth keeps some vibration going
There in your heart, and that is you.
And if the people find you can fiddle,
Why, fiddle you must, for all your life.
What do you see, a harvest of clover?
Or a meadow to walk through to the river?

Figure 4. Cinnamon Lowe, Artwork inspired by a poem "Fiddler Jones" selected from the "Spoon River Anthology" by Edgar Lee Masters. (© 2000, C. Lowe. Used with permission).

The wind's in the corn; you rub your hands
For beeves hereafter ready for market;
Or else you hear the rustle of skirts
Like the girls when dancing at Little Grove.
To Cooney Potter a pillar of dust
Or whirling leaves meant ruinous drought;
They looked to me like Red-Head Sammy
Stepping it off, to "Toor-a-Loor."
How could I till my forty acres
Not to speak of getting more,
With a medley of horns, bassoons and piccolos
Stirred in my brain by crows and robins
And the creak of a windmill – only these?
And I never started to plow in my life
That some one did not stop in the road
And take me away to a dance or picnic.
I ended up with a broken fiddle –
And a broken laugh, and a thousand memories,
And not a single regret.

Figure 5 shows an interpretation by Truillo.

Figure 5. Truillo, Artwork inspired by a poem "Chase Henry" selected from the "Spoon River Anthology" by Edgar Lee Masters. (© 2000, Truillo. Used with permission).

Figure 6. David Kindvall, Artwork inspired by a poem "Barney Hainsfeather" selected from the "Spoon River Anthology" by Edgar Lee Masters. (© 1998, D. Kindvall. Used with permission).

Figure 6 shows an interpretation by David Kindvall.

If the excursion train to Peoria
Had just been wrecked, I might have escaped with my life –
Certainly I should have escaped this place.
But as it was burned as well, they mistook me
For John Allen who was sent to the Hebrew Cemetery
At Chicago,
And John for me, so I lie here.
It was bad enough to run a clothing store in the town,
But to be buried here – ach!

For the next step in this project, see Table 2.

Table 2. Designing a book cover

Designing a Cover for the Book
Using your artwork as a starting point, create a cover for Edgar Lee Masters' "Spoon River Anthology," which you are going to publish; this could be challenging as this book has already had numerous editions. Design of the cover and symbols used might be relevant to Masters' time, reflect a region where he lived (he was born in Kansas), or show influences exerted over his mind. The cover should be competitive in nature, so the prospective publisher would pick this work for a new edition of the book. This means that potential readers, bookstore visitors, Masters' enthusiasts, and book collectors would do anything to get a hold of this book, even if the edition would be very limited and expensive. Thus, your book cover should convey some specific atmosphere, transmit the message from the book, communicate factual information about the times and events related to the poet and his characters, and at the same time, it should be tasteful and original. Obviously, it should possess strong aesthetic quality that draws people's attention, moves the imagination, and spurs their curiosity.

Table 3. Creating an epitaph

Writing an Epigrammatic Poem
Choose a hero you would like to honor or an inventive person and write a free-verse epitaph. It may be an epigram. Create sound patterns and, if you will, meters which make the style of your verse. Use a metaphor, if needed, to convey the ideas. At the same time, think about a pictorial counterpart of your literary work: draw some sketches on a computer for further work on this theme. Would it be a portrait, a caricature, a collage, an animated cartoon, or manga?

WRITING AND ILLUSTRATING AN EPIGRAMMATIC POEM

See Table 3 for suggestions on how to generate an epigrammatic poem

CONCLUSION

This chapter makes connection between visual arts and a literary analysis of the Edgar Lee Masters' collection of poems "Spoon River Anthology," his work, and his times. The readers are asked to make an interpretation of this work and to set forth their personal responses to one of the poems, by creating the visual counterpart that complements the poem.

REFERENCES

Euphrosyne Doxiadis, E. (1995). *The mysterious fayum portraits.* Harry N. Abrams. ISBN 0810933314. Retrieved November 1, 2012, from http://www.amazon.com/Mysterious-Fayum-Portraits-Euphrosyne-Doxiadis/dp/0810933314/ref=sr_1_fkmr0_1?s=books&ie=UTF8&qid=1351815015&sr=1-1-fkmr0&keywords=Euphrosyne+Doxiadis%2C+E.%2C+and+D.+J.+Thompson

Masters, E. L. (1915/2012). *Spoon river anthology.* Empire Books. ISBN 1619491923. Retrieved October 21, 2012, from http://www.bartleby.com/84/1.html

Chapter 16
Four Trapped in an Elevator

ABSTRACT

In this physics/psychology related integrative project, gravitation acting on the elevator riders is discussed in psychological terms. It may be interesting to portray some characters and convey their emotional states and actions in this unusual situation. Science-based themes that serve as inspiration for this project refer to the physical concepts of gravitation as a natural force causing objects with mass to attract one another, acceleration due to gravity, and the potential energy of the stuck elevator. This project is also about an artistic interpretation of psychological and social aspects of the unusual and stressful circumstances.

INTRODUCTION

The unusual and stressful situation caused by a stuck elevator relates to the physical condition of people trapped in the elevator who might ponder about the possible effects of gravitation. At the same time, we may seek interpretation of psychological and social aspects of these circumstances. The further text focuses on the concepts of acceleration and gravity.

The objective of the project is to depict attitudes of four different individuals who never met before, and show their feelings that could arise in the elevator, when it becomes a source of a sudden change, a frozen experience that became scary. It may be interesting to present the event from the four perspectives, each from the point of view of one person that is waiting for a rescue. After gathering some information about artistic and graphical concepts and examining ways to depict people and their activities, the task is to portray people and artistically convey their emotional states and actions they would choose to entertain in this tense time of confinement in an elevator. It may also be interesting to imagine how interactions between trapped people would change depending on circumstances: whether they are trapped in an elevator inside of a building or placed on its front elevation, which allows viewing a street; or they got stuck underground in a subway, in a cable car installed in a ski area, or between skyscrapers in a city center.

DOI: 10.4018/978-1-4666-4627-8.ch016

Figure 1. Anna Ursyn, Elevator Art. (© 2012, A. Ursyn. Used with permission)

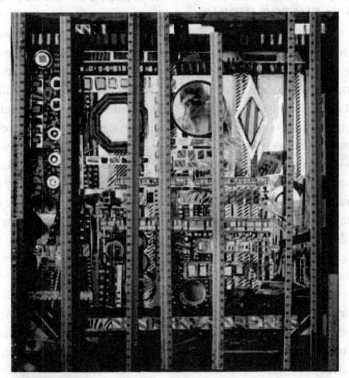

Figure 1 shows a decorated elevator (that is not scary yet, maybe filled with the elevator music).

There is an impact between a static condition of a person waiting in an elevator as a passenger and a dynamics of the results one does achieves after leaving it. All elevator riders are still, yet everyone in a different fashion. They visualize where they go and why: so many different tasks, ideas, and endeavors. Floors send sudden glimpses, whenever the elevator stops. One rides toward myriads of issues, has one's own lists to do, and everyone sets it up differently, on a different floor.

Four people, all have different emotions
The people feed off one another with their emotions.
Small compact area
Examine elevator
Lots of buttons.
People in elevator are
Mad because he is going to miss his basketball game
Content, wants o play card, since they are going to be there for a while anyways
Laughing, because "when does this really actually happen to someone"
Talking on the phone/playing game on phone, trying to get ahead of someone.

PHYSICAL AND PSYCHOLOGICAL CONDITIONS OF ELEVATOR RIDING

To understand this set of circumstances better, one may want to examine the forces that act on the elevator and on four strangers accidentally locked in a small space, first in the time when it works properly and then when it is stuck. Gravitation is a natural force causing that objects with mass attract one another. Newton's law of universal gravitation states that every mass attracts every other mass in the universe in direct relation to the product of the two masses and to the inverse square of the distance between them (Stock, 2012). Gravitation provides objects that have mass with their weight. We will focus on acceleration acting due to gravity and the potential energy of the stuck elevator. In terms of the quantum field theory, gravitation remains a not completely understood force; a common unified theory for universal forces does not yet account for gravitation Craft, 2012).

The notion of gravity will surely come to mind of the entrapped people. They may keep in mind that no shield can protect them from gravitation forces (We may think about gravitation (g) as a natural force causing that objects with mass attract one another. The same way as the gravitational field attracts our elevator to the Earth's center, it controls the orbit of the Moon, keeps planets moving around the Sun, causes the rising and falling tides, and many other phenomena. The strength of the gravitational Earth's field is equal to the acceleration of objects that are under its influence: $g = 9.81$ m/s^2 = 32.2 ft/s^2 and thus the velocity of falling object increases every second by 9.6 m/sec.

Elevators are much safer than cars. Every year, with tens of billions elevator trips, about twenty-six people die in (or on) elevators in the United States (Paumgarten, 2008). Some say one person dies in a car every five hours. However, many of us may know a person who refuses using elevators at all for fear of being stuck in them. This person would be always afraid of the decrease in weight (w) described as $w = m \cdot g$, which he feels when the elevator starts

to accelerate downwards. He knows that in such moments a spring scale will register a decrease in his apparent weight, because the floor under his feet exerts less force and provides less support to his weight as an elevator accelerates downwards. He would never risk a free-fall, such as experienced in sky-diving, and has never dreamt about being an astronaut and feeling 'weightlessness' coming from a lowered force of gravity.

A speed of one's ride in an elevator is the rate of motion. It is measured by dividing the distance d covered by an object, (for example, an elevator moving along the shaft), by the time passed t: $v = d / t$. We can calculate the average speed for the drive of our elevator, for example, $v = 60$ ft / 2 min = 30 ft/min; its displacement is a product of velocity and time. Acceleration is a rate of increase of the object's velocity, so it is the rate of change in velocity: $(v_{final} - v_{initial})$ divided by the time (t) it takes to make the change: $a = v_{final} - v_{initial} / t$.

For example, when an elevator starts from rest and reaches a speed 10 ft per second (about 6,82 miles per hour) in 2 seconds, its acceleration is $a = 10$ ft / 2 sec = 5 ft per sec per sec. We write this unit as "ft/sec^2" and read it "feet per second squared." If we further accelerate our imaginary elevator, it reaches a speed of 30 ft per second (about 20,45 miles per hour). A change from 10 ft/sec to 30 ft/sec takes 5 sec, so the rate of change is $30 - 10 = 20$ ft/sec / 5 sec = 4 ft/sec^2. The amount of the acceleration may be constant, increasing, or decreasing (decelerated). We can also calculate how long would it take to stop the elevator or how far our elevator moves in a given time.

Figure 2 shows a student work inspired by studying physical conditions of the elevator riding.

Somebody from this elevator may use his knowledge remembered from a physics class, and try to imagine acceleration acting on him due to gravity (g), and then calculate the force $F = m \cdot g$, where m is the mass of the body and g is acceleration factor with magnitude of 9.81 m/s^2. Thus, he would like to estimate the weight of the elevator full of people (is it about 2,000 pounds?) and think how long it

Figure 2. Matthew Skiff, Trapped in an Elevator (© 2006, M. Skiff. Used with permission)

Figure 3. Andrea Carvalho, Waiting in an elevator with a mirror (© 2006, A. Carvalho. Used with permission)

would take to hit the ground if actual technical problem become serious. He can image himself falling freely and increasing his velocity with 9.81 m/s (32.2 ft/s or 22 mph) for each second of his fall. He may also think about the potential energy stored in the elevator, resulting from its position relative to the Earth's center. A frightful thought may be run-

ning through his mind, that if the things would go from bad to worse, the potential energy ($E_0 = mgh$) of his elevator having mass (m) and hanging somewhere between floors at the height of (h) may convert to the kinetic energy of free falling.

Figure 3 shows a student work.

ART CONCEPTS RELATED TO PORTRAYING PEOPLE

Artists employ some elements of art, (such as line, space, or time) and principles of design, (such as emphasis, rhythm, or contrast) to enhance the dynamics of their artwork (Table 1). The British photographer Eadweard Muybridge (1830-1904) analyzed movement, right before the advent of cinematography, by taking sequential photographs of people and animals in motion http://www.mcmxi.com/~jpr/teaching/gph213/walkcycle/walk.html. Other approaches can be found in Asian sculptures, for example presentations of the goddess Shiva having multiple hands.

Figures 4, 5, and 6 and 7 show interpretations of this issue created by students from the computer art graphics classes. Some works depict emotion of people trapped in the elevator: they may reflect on fear, tension, self-pity, and anger of the trapped people; they present realistic visualization or present more abstract solutions for this project.

It might happen that one of these people may feel frustration, so he or she might feel frightened or panic, and would incessantly press the button for the lobby. However, it doesn't mean that the artwork has to be representational and show in detail the state of affairs. After a while all the elevator dwellers may come to conclusion that elevators serve, as a matter of routine, for raising or lowering people to different floors or levels, and people do not die in elevators. So, they may simply act socially or in a playful way, spend the waiting time joyfully, and try to know each other better. Some might even enjoy this, because it would create a good excuse for not doing something they would not like very much. They might be happy not having to go and take a test, while other person might be missing an audition, a job interview, or another important meeting and be angry. Some may use this time to do their homework, sketch others on their tablet computers such as iPad, or on paper; somebody may find four trapped people to be an ideal number and situation for card playing.

Please do not copy the ready examples, and yet make sure that other people can understand your concept: if you decide to draw the elevator, make sure it does not look like a closet. This would add the feel for this space. You may decide to show the signs, certain kinds of signage – visual graphics that display information, and all the details we usually ignore but we are forced to examine when contained there without any choice.

If you choose to portray your companions, enhance characteristics that are specific for each individual. You may want to show a likeness of every individual, not only showing the face, but the background, clothes on this person, objects, possessions, and fads that attract our attention and may be important in a similar way as in "The Ambassadors," where Hans Holbein shows, partially in anamorphic perspective, an elaborate collection of musical, astronomical, and scientific instruments to symbolize the ambassadors' knowledge and power. You may also think about the purpose of portraying your companions, depending on what you would like to say about their distinctive characteristics.

Taking pictures of signs that we can usually find in and around an elevator may be helpful in this project. Think about textures that are characteristic for materials and objects you are going to draw. You may find a set of useful textures at the website http://www.cgtextures.com/. They offer a membership with a limited amount of free data and many categories of paid textures. Draw simulated textures to represent real textures such as a smooth arm or a rough finish of the elevator wall; it might enhance your work.

Also, use patterns: add recurring lines inside any part of your drawing. We can see patterns everywhere in nature, and also as an artistic or

Four Trapped in an Elevator

Table 1. Portraying psychological states

Your Visual Response: Portraying Four Characters and Conveying their Psychological and Emotional States and Actions
Imagine that you are trapped in an elevator along with three other individuals that you never met before. Unknowingly, you start to perceive their behavior in this stressful time of the confinement in an elevator. Nobody knows the consequences of the event, or how long it might last. Some may comfort themselves by bringing to mind that, according to the Roman architect Vitruvius (Gellner, 2008), Archimedes built the first elevator about 336 BC, so people have gathered a lot of experience since then. The development of the situation is beyond a control of people who want to know what fate has in store for them. You may notice how they apply an opportune use of humor to lower stress. After careful consideration of the physical and psychological circumstances, you may want to portrait people and activities they would choose to entertain in this tense time. You may need to make some choices about the way of presenting thoughts and vision of a person that is waiting for a rescue.
Depict this situation. First, you may want to visit e few elevators and take some photos. Visualize the forces acting on the characters acting in this project. This will be your own artistic interpretation of the situation and the emotional states of people involved. Focus on psychological and social aspects of such unusual circumstances in which people find themselves in an elevator that got stuck in a shaft for nobody knows how long period of time. You may want to portray, without unnecessary directedness, thoughts of the entrapped people: fear caused by the belief that it would be dangerous and anxiety concerning the outcome of this problem. Think to what conclusions everyone might come. Surely, the image could be more abstracted, not directly indicating what happened.

decorative design, often in the form of an ornament that is specific for a given culture. Maybe you may want to use letters as a pattern. Also, focus on depth of the picture. Photography may be not the best choice for that purpose, as it shows everything we see, so it does not exaggerates details conveying the specific emotions. Finally, you may want to draw your self-portrait (or a quick sketch), to show your mood in these worrying circumstances and emphasize your own traits you consider most characteristic of your personality.

327

Figure 4. Beverly Alliss, Trapped in the Elevator (© 2005, B. Alliss. Used with permission)

Figure 6. A. Woolddridge, Trapped in an Elevator (© 2002, A. Woolddridge. Used with permission)

Figure 5. Anna Melkumian, Trapped in an Elevator (© 2002, A. Melkumian. Used with permission)

Figure 7. Hunter Trimble, Trapped in an Elevator (© 2005, H. Trimble. Used with permission)

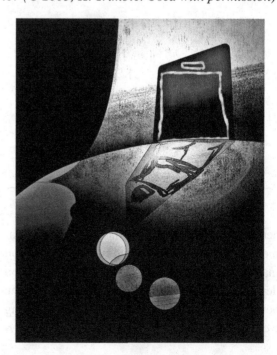

CONCLUSION

In this chapter, the reader is asked to portray some characters and convey their emotional states and actions in this unusual situation. Science-based themes that serve as inspiration for this project refer to the physical concepts of gravity and acceleration. Description of the physical and psychological conditions of the elevator riding, information about gravity and acceleration, along with art concepts about portraying people serve as an introduction to working on the project.

REFERENCES

Battail, G. (2009). Living versus inanimate: The information border. *Biosemiotics*, *2*, 321–341. doi:10.1007/s12304-009-9059-z.

Craft, D. (2012). Science within the art: Aesthetics based on the fractal and holographic structure of nature. In A. Ursyn (Ed.), *Biologically-Inspired Computing for the Arts: Scientific Data through Graphics* (pp. 290–321). IGI Global. doi:10.4018/978-1-4666-0942-6.ch017.

Gellner, A. (2008, August 23). Laying the foundation for today's skyscrapers. *San Francisco Chronicle*. Retrieved March 3, 2013, from http://www.sfgate.com/homeandgarden/article/Laying-the-foundation-for-today-s-skyscrapers-3199017.php

Stock, M. (2012). Flow simulation with vortex elements. In A. Ursyn (Ed.), *Biologically-Inspired Computing for the Arts: Scientific Data through Graphics* (pp. 18–30). IGI Global. doi:10.4018/978-1-4666-0942-6.ch002.

Chapter 17
The History of Love

ABSTRACT

This text provides insight about love, seen as a power that lets people survive in spite of all overwhelming forces. It helps us to understand, preserve the natural world, and protect values; love as a force gives us strength and motivation to perform both heroic and everyday deeds, develop knowledge at the macro, micro, and nano levels, produce medicine drugs and vaccines, initiate social changes, and enhance communication networks to share and exchange information.

INTRODUCTION

The "History of Love" project is an occasion to visually convey your insight and understanding. Think about some abstract concepts and ideas. Things we cannot see, but we know well and often use as metaphors. One of the abstract concepts is love. Thus, we can think about love that occurs at many levels – personal, self-oriented, or group-oriented toward a common benefit. Love is a power that let people survive, understand, and preserve the natural world, and protect values. Think of love as force and building material, the enigmatic force that pushed the members of the United Nations international committee to adopt "The Millennium Development Goals" and put forward a target: "Halve, by 2015, the proportion of the population without sustainable access to safe

drinking water and basic sanitation" (MDG, 2008). Think how love made people stronger, nurtured them, cured, healed, and resolved conflicts over centuries and across the globe. There have been so many obstacles threatening mankind, from natural disasters, such as earthquakes, volcano actions, through fires, floods, to disease outbreaks, wars and crime with violence. Bacteria and viruses mutate, adjusting themselves to newly designed treatments and prevention shots, thus forcing people to constantly modifying them. Show a metaphorical portrayal of the power of love seen as a force that gives the whole humanity strength and motivation to perform both heroic and everyday deeds: develop knowledge, produce medicine drugs and vaccines, initiate social changes, and enhance communication networks to share and exchange information.

DOI: 10.4018/978-1-4666-4627-8.ch017

Figure 1. Anna Ursyn, "History of Love as a Building Power against Dark Forces" (© 2006, A. Ursyn. Used with permission)

Figure 1, "History of love as a building power against dark forces" presents a polyptych that reflects a story of actions in a good cause. Chapters of this work:

1. Death of a Crow
2. Double Duties
3. A Life of a Rabbit
4. Job Hunting
5. The Next Year

A series of figures show the works of students from the computer art classes. One can see different types of reactions inspired by this theme: some choose to present real scenes, other preferred imaginary, symbolic, unrealistic presentations. There are also iconic images and symbols used to convey a synthesized meaning. Yet another works are emotionally loaded, sometimes under the cover of mockery; we laugh even as we empathize with the author's discomfort.

Figure 2. a. Sam Dailey, "Love" (© 2011, S. Dailey. Used with permission); b. Jael Esquibel, "History of Love" (© 2011, J. Esquibel. Used with permission)

(a)   (b)

Figure 2a and b show two student works. Sam Dailey (Figure 2a) presents in metaphorical way human concern about water environment. Jael Esquibel (Figure 2b) shows the artist's personal approach to values shared by the whole community.

MANY WAYS OF PICTURING THE IDEA OF LOVE AS FORCE AND POWER

Some stories introduce black or white characters. In the Star Wars movies, characters possess a great deal of love toward their goals. "May the Force be with you" is an important imperative, working on a psychological level and beyond. But Darth Vader sends out sounds that may stop any action. Figures 3a and 3b present students interpretations of this theme.

Robert J. Sternberg (1986) developed a triangular theory of love, with the three components of love in the context of interpersonal relationships being intimacy (which encompasses feelings of attachment, closeness, connectedness, and bondedness), passion (which encompasses drives

connected to both limerence – attraction and a need to have one's feelings reciprocated - and sexual attraction), and commitment (which encompasses the decision to remain with another, and in a long term, the shared achievements and plans made with that other). Sternberg provided as well a framework for examining possible intelligence-creativity relationships (Sternberg & Kaufman, 2011). Image created by Anthony Bianchi (Figure 4a) shows his personal reaction conveyed mostly in color, while Susan Barron (Figure 4b) shows a dreamy, imaginary world.

A work about "History of Love" may be clearly identified or it may be open to more than one interpretation. A message about the power of love may be delivered in many ways: through art, graphic design, visual storytelling, and the use of signs, icons, and visual metaphors that focus people on an issue and facilitate understanding of the idea. In any case, find a metaphorical way to convey visually the essence of the message. You may prefer to create deliberately open messages using symbols or signs that could be freely interpreted and also generated cooperatively by the viewer. A viable possibility for open com-

Figure 3. a. Zach Britton, "History of Love" (© 2012, Z. Britton. Used with permission); b. Michael Fenton, "History of Love" (© 2010, M. Fenton. Used with permission)

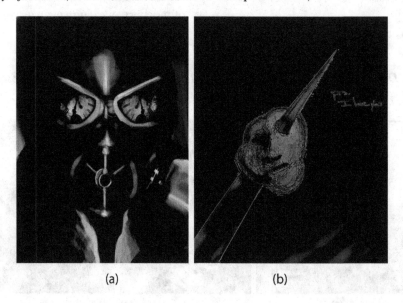

(a)   (b)

Figure 4. a. Anthony Bianchi, "History of Love" (© 2012, A. Bianchi. Used with permission); b. Susan Barron, "History of Love" (© 2010, S. Barron. Used with permission)

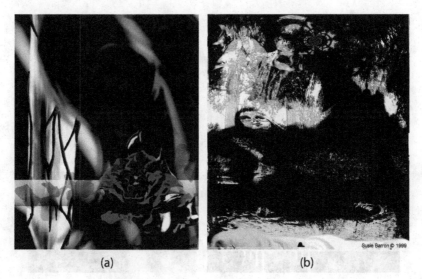

(a)　　　　　　　　(b)

munication is in interactive art, where the viewer's involvement in the artwork is mandatory, and there is viewer's real-time interaction with the computer program. As it was stated by Steve Tomasula (1998, 338), there "is always a palindrome that can be read from art to artist and back," as the culture of web or communication media projects is "increasingly interactive, encyclopedic, linked, and therefore open-ended and open to reorganization by its users." Catherine Bakewell

(Figure 5a) introduces biological symbols, such as a fragment of a DNA molecule, a sliced cell, chromosomes, and simplified pictures of a planet and the Milky Way, to convey her involvement with the world and to make her statement general. Danielle Phillips (Figure 5b) shows her involvement with the past conflicts presented in an imaginative, fairy-tale style.

Love is an abstract concept and heart as the love symbol is different than a heart – a human

Figure 5. a. Catherine Bakewell, "History of Love" (© 2010, C. Bakewell. Used with permission); b. Danielle Phillips, "History of Love" (© 2010, D. Phillips. Used with permission).

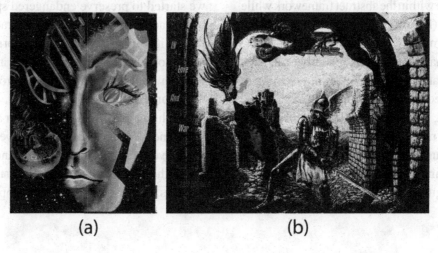

(a)　　　　　　　　(b)

Figure 6. a. Matthew Rodriguez, "History of Love" (© 2012, M. Rodriguez. Used with permission); b. Logan Hurd, "History of Love" (© 2012, L. Hurd. Used with permission).

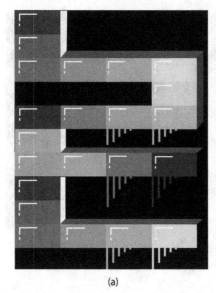

(a)   (b)

organ. Images that have iconic properties or serve as generally accepted symbols could be considered crucial in knowledge visualization. Authors active in the field of cognitive science hold that natural metaphors, as well as words, reside in thought as instinctively understandable concepts (Mateo and Sauter 2007).

Many times conveying meaning goes through the use of a meta-language, as in case of blogs where people involved in a field of study communicate using specific terms and their metaphorical explanations.

Matthew Rodriguez (Figure 6a) imagined the history of love within the abstract framework while Logan Hurd (Figure 6b) presented it in almost theatrical terms.

Objects that are common and universal, such as helices created by climber plants or existing in the DNA molecules, snail shells, fossil ammonites, natural knots, as well as mathematical knots – helicoids and non-helicoidally built knots, all can be seen as natural metaphors. Some artists present them combining imagery and rationality. Don Klumker (Figure 7a) dealt with the task express-

ing it in ironic way: he created a humorous depiction of intense feelings and deep affections. Using dynamic, almost abstract parts, Reda Benembarek (Figure 7b) created visualization of physical explosion to present the power and great potential of love.

There are many conflicting issues related to love. The doers need to establish the order, create revolutions, and change the directions. The invention of gunpowder caused many deaths. The Nobel Prize was established, to balance out the dreadful outcomes of regrettable inventions. We do not have to fight wild animals anymore and we started to preserve endangered species, but a bear practically ate a man in Colorado last summer. With all the mutations, transformations, and repetitions, we have a feeling that it all is going through circles, repeating itself through the history; some would see it as a spiral, as good and evil fighting in a circular motion, or as a balance/imbalance. We are aware of the power of entropy; we strive to keep forces in a balance. In 2011, when the end of the world was announced in tabloids, it was stated that good people would die

Figure 7. a. Don Klumker, "History of Love" (© 2000, D. Klumker. Used with permission); b. Reda Benembarek, "History of Love" (© 1995, R. Benembarek. Used with permission).

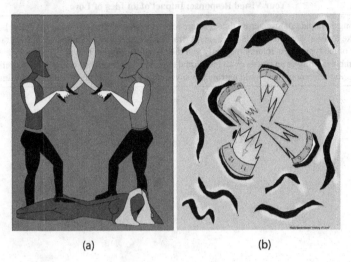

(a) (b)

first, and the bad ones must first go through the inevitable nightmare. Someone offered services to take care of the good people's pets. When asked if he was a good one, he answered, 'yes, but it has been arranged with the atheists.'

Courtney Lowe (Figure 8a) and Shannon Zaimstra (Figure 8b) focused on messages from the past ages conveyed with symbolic pictures and signs.

Human-made creations have been usually seen as art when they display traits common to all artworks and restricted only to artworks. Inquiries about the essence of art became even more difficult when they expanded into areas of visualization (both in a micro and macro scale) and simulation of process/product relations. Structures of what is not visible, for example, molecules or atoms, can often evoke awe. Many times, forms of engineering are derived from natural patterns, for example, airplane wings, or ergonomically designed machines. In a similar way, bringing synthetic polymers and nanopolymers into artis-

Figure 8. a. Courtney Lowe, "History of Love" (© 2000, C. Lowe. Used with permission); b. Shannon Zaimstra, "History of Love" (© 2000, S. Zaimstra. Used with permission).

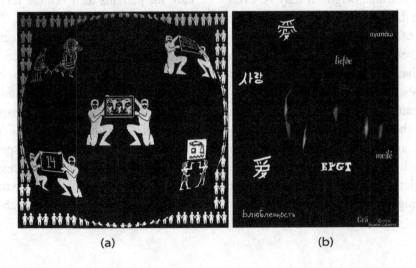

(a) (b)

Table 1. Picturing an impact of love

Your Visual Response: Impact of an Idea of Love
Create a composition showing an impact of love across time. Picture love as a general idea related to the entire humankind, over time, from the beginnings to now. Make a visual depiction of this idea, an abstract concept as a whole, rather then illustration of a personal story or somebody else's life events of the type, "how Johnny met Sally and they lived happily ever after." Try to stay away from the heart symbol, or any specific or cliché symbol coming from rituals or an individual experience. There have been too many religions across time to show them all, so try to avoid specific references that would narrow down your story to one particular culture or religion.

tic practice may be inspired by natural polymers and resins of a volcanic origin. It may be even more surprising that images obtained through the transformation of mathematical formula, for example fractals, bear such a strong resemblance to natural forms that they may be easily related to their homologies in the natural fractal environments such as patterns of branches in a tree, fern leaves, viruses' shells or rocky formations. Computer graphics, animations, visualizations, and simulations employ such transformations.

Figure 9 depicts love as a power existing under actions of working and helping others. It explores the role of conducting research and providing care for patients as a vehicle for wellbeing that promotes positive attitudes.

Issues discussed in this project pertain to our individual life, everyday experience, and also our fate in the future. Maybe they resonate with many different important topics and disturbing emotions, and for that reason they may inspire you with a vision of a personal, emotional response to the "History of Love" challenge. Inspiration has been generally seen as an internal process, often evoked by external events that stimulate to do something creative. It may be shown in an abstract way, e.g.

Figure 9. Amber Wolf, "History of Love" (© 2000, A. Wolf. Used with permission)

through a ballet performance, to conceptualize cosmic awareness and existential questions about human condition (See Table 1).

Devise your own metaphor suitable for the theme of your work, using metaphorical imagery and visual thinking to process complex information. Your metaphor may be shaped upon natural forms, such as a Nautilus shell with a spiral or helical curve (we can feel the sense of mathematical beauty when watching how the Nautilus obeys the rules resulting from equations discovered by mathematicians), an extinct fossil of an ammonite, or the spiral chains of polymers characteristic of the nucleic acids (such as a double helix of the deoxyribonucleic acid, DNA or other protein molecules that have a helical form). Translate abstract knowledge into a realm of familiar actualities that we all can experience or see. You may draw inspiration from many forms present in natural objects that may be described as geometrical curves or mathematical equations, in the same way as they provide inspiration to sculptors, architects, graphic artists, and designers.

CONCLUSION

A "History of Love" project is an occasion to visually convey the reader's insight and understanding. It is aimed to provide an insight about love as a power that let people survive in spite of all overwhelming forces, understand, preserve the natural world, and protect values. Images that have iconic properties or serve as generally accepted symbols could be considered crucial in knowledge visualization. Many times conveying meaning goes through the use of a meta-language, as in case of blogs where people involved in a field of study communicate using specific terms and their metaphorical explanations. Inspiration has been generally seen as an internal process, often evoked by external events that stimulate to do something creative. Issues discussed in this project pertain to our individual life, everyday experience, and also our fate in the future. Maybe they resonate with important topics and may inspire the reader with a personal response.

REFERENCES

Lengler, R., & Eppler, M. (2006). *A periodic table of visualization methods*. Retrieved December 17, 2010, from http://www.visual-literacy.org/periodic_table/periodic_table.html

J. Mateo, & F. Sauter (Eds.). (2007). *Natural metaphor: Architectural papers III*. Zurich: ACTAR & ETH Zurich.

MDG. (2008). The Millennium Development Goals Report. *United Nations*. Retrieved December 11, 2010, from http://mdgs.un.org/unsd/mdg/Resources/Static/Products/Progress2008/MDG_Report_2008_En.pdf#page=44

Sternberg, R. J. (1986). A triangular theory of love. *Psychological Review, 93*(2), 119–135. doi 10.1037/0033-295X.93.2.119. Retrieved May 5, 2012, from http://psycnet.apa.org/journals/rev/93/2/119/

R. J. Sternberg, & S. B. Kaufman (Eds.). (2011). *The Cambridge handbook of intelligence.* Cambridge University Press. doi:10.1017/CBO9780511977244.

Tomasula, S. (1998). Bytes and zeitgeist: Digitizing the cultural landscape, six annual New York digital salon. *Leonardo Journal, 31*(5), 337–344. doi:10.2307/1576592.

Chapter 18
Architecture and Media

ABSTRACT

This part of the book explores how architects and urban developers apply computational solutions and create a fusion of architecture and media. The use of new technologies for communication, sustainability, functionality, and economy of resources is discussed next. Issues that are relevant to computational methods in design, urban aesthetics, ambient computing, sustainable habitats, novel materials, biology-inspired projects, and many others all pertain to innovative solutions that we can observe in architecture. Themes related to some of the tools and technologies, models of architectural structures, intelligent buildings, and sustainable and green architecture complete this chapter.

INTRODUCTION

It seems the title of this book: "Computational solutions for knowledge, art, and entertainment: information exchange beyond text" could serve perfectly as a description of current trends and patterns one can perceive in architecture. The reader is encouraged to actively respond with own projects to the issues under discussion. Architects and urban developers find computational solutions to add programmable elements to the façades, which often results in a fusion of architecture and media. Placing electronic display on a façade (which is sometimes called mediatecture) adds entertainment to city life. The use of new technologies for communication and sustainability may lead to dissolving the boundaries between building categories and functions, whether the structure

serves art, media culture, entertainment, commerce, or advertising. Issues that are relevant to computational methods in design, urban aesthetics, ambient computing, sustainable habitats, novel materials, biology inspired projects, and many others, all pertain to innovative solutions that we can observe in architecture. As a result, encounters with architectural creations offer the users and visitors complex multimodal experiences.

Figure 1, "Exits" implies some similarities in the connectedness existing in architectural detail and composition of art works.

A bridge connects us with faraway places. A triptych gives a notional link with the absolute. Borders enclosing an icon invoke meanings contained in our inward frame. Elaborate portals lead someone up the path of choices. Let others build their frames for interpretation.

DOI: 10.4018/978-1-4666-4627-8.ch018

Figure 1. Anna Ursyn, Exits. (© 2006, A. Ursyn. Used with permission)

VISUAL THINKING IN ARCHITECTURE

Many times architects apply an ability to think abstractly as an opportunity to perceive problems with a bird's eye view perspective and examine an imaginary bird's view of a new complex before drawing its detailed blueprint. According to Paivio, (1970) spatial skills necessary for architectural drawing are visualization, mental rotation, transposition of 3-D objects to 2-D paper, and cognitive mapping. Images of architectural solutions may have persuasive power because they act rhetorically upon viewers and participants of discussions in social media (Hill & Helmers, 2004/2008). Authors of innovative architectural projects organize and structure the core message of their projects in a meaningful, sometimes metaphorical way. Most of metaphors

we encounter or create are shaped upon natural forms. On the other hand, the principles behind the historical development of the architectural details oscillated between aesthetics and pragmatic structure. As Hironori Yoshida (2012, p. 81) points out, "building with adobe bricks has over 9,000 years of history, and the Egyptian pyramids are made of millions of standardized stones. It is no exaggeration to say that throughout history, people have continuously flattened and standardized the diverse natural materials into regular, uniform, repeatable, measurable forms." Later on, forms and patterns gained in variability and architectural aesthetics has been considered intrinsically tied to development of many computer-assisted architectural design systems.

Cognitive scientists hold that natural metaphors reside in thought as instinctively understandable concepts. Mateo and Sauter (2007) present diverse design approaches taken by the cross-disciplinary teams that address theoretical, material, and artistic challenges by finding correlations between nature and architectural design. Forms and patterns – natural metaphors that are present in architectural details – are often derived from common and universal live forms such as helices (formed by climber plants or present in the DNA molecules), snail shells, fossil ammonites, and natural knots (Mateo and Sauter 2007). Architecture and cell biology have been examined in terms of biosemiotics (Ferreira, 2011), with architectural structures discussed as context-dependent semiotic objects with functional and/or aesthetic values. Both the natural and man-made environment can be perceived as locus, place, site, or a part of a mental map of a cultural framework. (see Table 1)

The way we design and build architectural structures can be compared to biological forms, and the relation of these structures to their surroundings can be examined in terms of cellular motility in the extracellular matrix environment. The study of Lucia, Sabin, and Jones (2011) extends across architecture and the biological sciences in terms of the information theoretical

Table 1. Creating inverted cityscape

Your Visual Response
You may want to show city architecture in the daytime and then at night by creating a scene and then inverting it. Make a cityscape out of paper placed inside of a box: create a cutout of city houses, fold paper, cut and fold windows and doors. Create layers by cutting out parts of image from upper layers of paper cutouts. Put your city into a box. Take a photograph a whole city-in-a-box. In an image editing software such as Adobe Photoshop, manipulate the scanned image, for example, by layering, resizing, and using other tools and menu options. After that, you may want to inverse the image to create a nighttime scene. Those images might serve as a basis for animation. There might be a question what could happen in a city between day and night that would be interesting enough to describe in a time-based visual form? How one can distinguish the day life from the night life in the same part of a city?

framework. The authors compare dynamic organizations of matter in the cellular systems and the human-scale environment of architecture and design. They ponder whether this perceptual environment can be examined in terms of order, difference, and information rather than through descriptive or projective geometric terms; also, how actual morphologies and their perceptions could be represented in architectural design. Seeing a difference and a rate of its change in a neighborhood may create information, which is the medium of communicative exchange for ob-

serving bodies: humans or cells. Each observer possesses memory or history that has an impact on the instantaneous perception about its environment. In generative design the data arrays, fluxes of matter and energy produced by objects within their environments generate potential information as the image difference, with and without observers. The authors measured this image difference (discrete pixels intensities across all time states within a video). They analyzed the case studies: vascular smooth muscle cells, and the spatial perception of an observer through a hallway.

Interactive Building Skins

Occasionally, forms chosen by architects for their structures function as informers visually communicating to visitors the purpose and content of a building. For example, Kansas City Library informs that it contains books; the Big Duck building at Flanders, NY informs that it was built to sell ducks and duck eggs; and the Longaberger Basket Company residing in a building shaped as a giant basket informs about its profile. Thus, the content and purpose of a building is shown as a one-way message. Moreover, buildings communicate their function and status through a language of visual signs. Digital designers and architects are working together to give buildings a living skin that could inform about the building, weather, or environment and respond in real time to its occupants, or bystanders (Hall, 2012).

Technological evolution makes sustainability, functionality, and economy of resources an essential part of today's art, advertising and media culture (Bisantz, 2010). Architects create interactive building skins as buildings with the environmental control systems that react to changes in external conditions; they transform façades into a light and media display, and then artists experiment with media façades (Moloney, 2006). It started at the beginning of this century with blinking lights that transformed the lighted windows into 'pixels.' As described by Hall (2012), passersby could email or phone in simple animations or play Pong with another caller, using the web-based "blinkentools" developed by the programmers. Media screens – large-scale computer displays with data projection or video walls – enable social interaction and engagement. This way architecture becomes a time-based medium, with buildings having an input, processing, and output systems and often a learning ability.

Several intelligent buildings feature the media façades with an integrated light and media installa-tion that can change color and material, simulating stone, metal, or fur. One-way media screens with large-scale computer displays with data projection or video provide the information or art shows; for example the Chanel building in Tokyo, Japan has a side of the building set as a TV billboard; it has also the state-changing electronic privacy glass. Other façades have computer-controlled light emitting diodes. The BIX (programmable skin technology) installation for the Kunsthaus in Graz, Austria has fluorescent lamps on acrylic glass façade acting as pixels controlled individually by a computer to display images, films, animations, and multi-disciplinary exhibitions. Interactive systems make architectural environments conducive to social interaction and engagement of the visitors. The SPOTS building at the Potsdamer Platz in Berlin also has fluorescent lamps that act as a media screen with a large grid pattern. Interactive screens are usually installed in internal environments. Various projects use cell phone technology and infrared plus image tracking technology to enable the audience to interact with the display. The new Zealand pavilion for the 2005 world expo in Japan showcased a rear projection screen system linked to an infra red camera that tracked the hands of users interacting with the content. The 12 meter jelly-fish like D-tower in Doetinchem, Netherlands has an accessible to everybody website and a questionnaire to gauge the mood of the town and add to a sense of social cohesiveness. In a "Not so white walls" project, users can display pixilated texts and images on interactive wallpaper by using heat-sensitive ink and a resistor matrix, and thus they can decorate a wall, read their e-mail, or view images taken with their cellphone camera. The ICE (Interactive Communicative Experience, Bloomberg Headquarters, Tokyo) display stock-exchange data in an understandable way; a green icicle suspended from the ceiling acts as a data collector.

Figure 2. Anna Ursyn, Park and Ride. (© 2012, A. Ursyn. Used with permission)

Figure 2, "Park and Ride" refers to our willingness to look at commuting as a price for keeping the city green. Layers, levels, micro worlds, and complicated structures encompass a city. When it grows it often devours green terrains without damaging them. They enter the city and coexist with the sustainable architecture. This symbiosis creates a need for commuting.

Architectural Forms Inspired by Mathematics, Geometry, Biology, etc.

In a similar way as other artistic systems, architectural projects can often gain from the examination of nature-derived events and laws and benefit from the developments in the biologically inspired techniques (evolutionary computation, artificial life, artificial neural networks, swarm intelligence, and other artificial intelligence techniques) (Evomusart, 2012). Whichever source serves for choosing

the imagery, architects examine mathematical, physical, chemical, biological, and other laws and search for visual language to translate what they find out to architectural forms. For example, crystal form is used as a metaphorically rich form in architecture (Cheetham, 2010); crystalline form can be seen in a Crystal Palace built by Paxton for the 1851 London Great Exhibition and the 2007 Michael Lee-Chin Crystal addition to the Royal Ontario Museum in Toronto.

Architects, graphic artists, and designers draw inspiration from forms present in natural objects that may be described as geometrical curves or mathematical equations. Architects, for example Alessandro Rocca (2007) or Santiago Calatrava (Tzonis, 2004) adopt a concept of natural architecture when they refer to the relationship between art, humans, nature, and architecture. They investigate the relationship of architecture to its surroundings by shaping manmade constructions as biology-inspired designs or transforming biological forms, such as trees into sculptures or architectural creations. Classification of designs requires describing the geometries and grids in architectural details in a standard form. It requires examining on the drawings geometric relationships such as transformations as reflection, translation, and rotation. Architects and designers draw inspiration from mathematical knots to create metaphorical projects.

A question has been around, to what extent visual mathematics, with complex polygons, tessellations of strings and lattices, bubble geometry, and fractals, can be visually appealing as the language of space design and used for designing buildings and their façades. Visual mathematics may be examined as a source of visually appealing computer graphics that could be used as a guide for intuition, and inspiration for constructing architectural models. This idea may provide a common language for mathematicians and architects, about how architecture and mathematics can complement one another in providing innovative solutions. Models of architectural systems comprise mathematical models that imitate processes in particular projects from the field of architecture and architecture history; they can predict the system behavior in changing circumstances. Digital design and modeling can be realized though integration with manufacturing processes within architecture, construction, engineering, and materials technology. Digital fabrication technologies enable new construction opportunities. Cooperation of this kind requires interdisciplinary education in economic and sustainable contexts.

Architecture projects include many types of electronic components; they are becoming parts of visual art forms generated by computers, usually labeled as electronic art, digital art, or computer-generated art. It is an interdisciplinary field, so architects often collaborate with artists, scientists, and engineers when they design their works. As early as in 1992 Jean Nouvel (De Bure, 1992, p. 15) explained the interactive approach of the computerized architecture as "a synergy between the different ideas, the possible solutions – an interaction, a connection, depth, complexity. This process shows how best to utilize the specific conditions of the program, the moment, the people." Human computer interaction (HCI) can be attained by interactive art. Distributed collaboration on architectural and urban design can be done on an online visualizartion platform called "ArchiBrain" (Van Bouvel, Vande Moere, & Boeykens, 2012), which provides participants with a structured overview of the design process they are working on.

Figure 3, "Architectural Impacts" ponders how coexistence of various architectural styles adds dynamics to a city.

TOOLS AND TECHNOLOGIES; MODELS OF ARCHITECTURAL STRUCTURES

Computer-assisted architectural design systems and the services from computer graphics firms, for example Cinema 4D (Sonderman, 2008) aim at designing a space and defining the lighting and textures of architecture models of interior spaces. In cooperation with these firms architects create for both customers and builders the architectural scenes and 3-dimensional models that are often animated and interactive. Computer-generated models do not use paper and pencil and can be more precise than traditional drawings; they most result from using computer algorithms. Information visualization may serve scientific theories and fields pertaining to architectural applications such as visualization in built and rural environments. The engineers' or architects' blueprints visualize information in an abstract way showing numerical, graphic, or diagram-

Figure 3. Anna Ursyn, Architectural Impacts. (© 2012, A. Ursyn. Used with permission)

matic data. Many times architects use knowledge visualization to represent the complexity of structures. Visualization supports architects in drafting architectural projects and designing networked information. Architects use visualizations as a mediating framework to amplify cognition and to transfer knowledge (Burkhard (2006); visualizations unify and focus research directions that are decisive in knowledge management. In a pictorial way, animated movies, interactive images of buildings, and walk-through demonstrations provide various points of view on interactive urban surroundings and building settings; they are also used to see the possible

relationship between the environment and the already existing structures. In many cases architectural modeling tools are internet-based and applying biologically inspired networking (Lio & Verma, 2012). Models include the specification of building structures such as walls and windows as well as the effects of light that shape the viewers' perception of interior design at different times of the day. Mathematical models imitate internal processes in the field of architecture and architecture history; they can predict the system behavior in changing circumstances. Improved visualization performance can be attained by designing digital 3D city models developed from photography with the use of photogrammetry (to determine geometry of objects from photos) and high-resolution stereo camera (Banissi & Zhou, 2012).

Architects began to make use of the opportunities offered by bio-inspired techniques (such as evolutionary computation, artificial life, artificial neural networks, swarm intelligence, etc.). The adoption of biology-inspired research results, the use of genetic algorithms, adaptive formal and structural design, and new fabrication techniques may reinforce architectural modeling techniques and advance the generation of projects. Architects and artists develop ecosystem engineering and simulations of biotic and abiotic habitats (Dorin & Korb, 2007). Researchers and specialists in architectural science explore mechanical tensile strength, high electrical and heat conductivity, and chemical inactivity of thin nanotube sheets and discuss possible application of these many times stronger and lighter than steel nano materials for architectural solutions. Architects use the notion of articulation to describe the styling of the joints as the formal elements of design. The notion of articulation is also used in terms of mechanical properties of parts joined into a whole.

Generative architecture is designed as a genetic code of artificial events. The codes of transformation resemble the natural structure of DNA. Celestino Soddu (2012) writes a code or uses generative software allowing the computer to design architectural structures and interiors that fit the research on DNA and to start generative approach for collecting artificial DNA of Italian medieval towns and American cities. His works include intelligent industrial productions that create new identities of the cities. Soddu selects the genes responsible for the identification of foreign bodies to generate the artificial DNA of medieval towns (number of inhabitants, their age, profession, etc.) that can produce 3D architectural models in a selected style. Bio-interfaces can enrich methods used in the areas of architectural design; according to Zuanon

(2012), architects can project artists' works at architectural facades, apply solar powered displays, and create interactive installations on buildings' skins, which react to the presence of the viewers. Architects combine their production with experimental film and video, adding the man-made and environmental sound.

Figure 4, "Business Oriented" pictures impersonal spaces in a city. A business district without people, sidewalks, trees, tables, shopping windows, or any human detail shows us what is not there: a small architecture, benches, a dog, and you.

Simulating and Modeling

Along with the paintings, sculptures, music, and inspiring or thought provoking sounds, architecture flourished in western and central Europe during the middle ages, with the Gothic art that evolved from Romanesque art and lasted from the mid-12th century to the end of the 16th century. Computer-generated images and applications allow analyzing the existing historical structures or recreating the historical buildings. Natural disasters, such as the eruption of Mt. Vesuvius resulting in tearing down an ancient Italian city of Pompeii in the 1st Century A.D. offer an insight to architects who then rediscover the old paradigms for a town, preserve, categorize, label the site, and organize it into databases and research libraries (Özgenel, 2008). Interactive visualization techniques have been used to recreate the images and show physical or virtual reconstructions of historically significant places. Several other historical places no longer accessible to the public have been installed permanently in the museum settings as the real time interactive simulations (e.g., LoPiccolo, 2003).

Architects cooperate with computer graphic firms to create models for customers and builders that show possible relation of a building to the environment and its surrounding buildings. Architectural simulation tools allow an architect to visualize a space and perform interactive demonstrations and explanations.

Figure 4. Anna Ursyn, Business Oriented. (© 2012, A. Ursyn. Used with permission)

The expressive and experiential features of virtual reality environments serve for presentations of architectural environments. Creation of 3d virtual spaces serves a purpose of performing personal interaction in a web conferencing room or in architectural space. Architects utilize online multiuser technology platforms such as CAVE (Cruz-Neira, Sandin, DeFanti, Kenyon, & Hart, 1992) or the EON Reality immersive environments such as EON Reality Coliseum (2012) and EON Reality Icube (2012) to virtually meet online their customers, students, and media specialists, to present in real time their projects and architectural designs as the interactive 3D worlds. Agent-based crowd simulation tools have been used in

architecture and urban planning for analytical purposes, such as the simulation of pedestrians or fire escape scenarios in buildings. To bridge the fields of architecture and commercial crowd simulation, Burkhard, Bischof, & Herzog (2008) discuss crowd simulations for analytical purposes and case studies and consider this relevant for architects, urban designers, communication and PR experts, and for researchers in the fields of architecture, knowledge visualization, communication science, and agent-based simulations.

Figure 5, "Cul-de-sac" refers to possible claustrophobic fear one may experience amongst dense, tall constructions. The neighboring architectural constructions, small and big, without a way out,

Figure 5. Anna Ursyn, Cul-de-sac. (© 2012, A. Ursyn. Used with permission)

without a street, surround and often overwhelm you, while also may make you feel safe..

Intelligent Buildings

Since smart sensors and control systems become ubiquitous, intelligent buildings can be designed to sense and control the conditions of particular systems and even communicate with users and other systems. One can configure, command, and control systems and equipment from other locations using a web based user interface (Siemens, 2012). Several systems can operate independently without human intervention: smart meters of energy and water use, passive and active energy use (adjusting environment depending on occupancy),

maintenance and services, space management according to occupancy, waste management and trash recycling, safety monitoring and security systems, and other Internet enabled controls that are related to particular use of the building space may run on their own. Future scenarios focus on cooperation between facilities and IT organizations, aimed at optimal reactions, preemptive actions, informative services, and holistic understanding of all conditions (IBM Smarter Buildings, 2010).

The fact that the site of computing goes beyond the desktop or laptop PC shifting toward smart, mobile appliances, devices, phones, or shoes results in changes we work (more often from our home), shop (with the use of online commerce), consume, and entertain. Every level of intelligent infrastructure is always accessible and configurable. Distributed control systems use computerized, intelligent networks of electronic devices (so it has no central location). They monitor and control the electronics and lighting system in a building using dimmable lighting and motion sensors. Distinctive features of the intelligent design include, among flexibility, the use of building modeling that can be optimized according to new information and changed, integration with the surrounding environment, transportation, and other community issues, remote operation of the equipment with the use of optimized algorithms, self-management of systems and appliances, maintaining personal comfort conditions through monitoring and the users' feedback, and real-time self-control of energy production and usage, among other features. Intelligent buildings secure personal safety through digital video monitoring, fire, smoke, and contaminants detection and automatic suppression.

Table 2. Designing an intelligent building

Your Visual Response: Intelligent Dream House
Think about your own dream house, an apartment on a high floor of an intelligent skyscraper, or a loft with a roof access and design all smart, interactive systems and appliances you would like to add to your home. Would you like to have your room rotating along with the sun, so you would have sunlight (or an exposure to the shady side) all the time? How about using media display available on the skin of your skyscraper to convey your own manifesto to a broader audience?
In your own version of a green house, take into account all appliances that pertain to your needs and hobbies. While working on your design, think about your installations in term of the local, potentially available resources. Think about the environment-friendly design of your house. Take advantage of the surrounding environmental features, local microclimate, the region's cultural history and distinctive style in design and architecture. How will you configure, command, and control your systems and appliances from other locations?

Figure 6. Anna Ursyn, "Small Window as a Part of the Big City" (© 1988, A. Ursyn. Used with permission)

To improve public awareness of waste issues, a group of the MIT researchers concerned about the sustainability of the city waste removal systems sent a set of small tracking devices (with network connectivity) fixed to the trash items. They learned that the tagged "printer cartridge travelled 3,210 miles from its disposal location to reach the point (where the location sensor was probably destroyed), by a combination of road, rail, and air freight" (Shepard, 2011, p. 101). An old sneaker with a tag embedded in it "traveled across Seattle, south to Portland, Oregon, veering off the course to rest somewhere along the Washington-Oregon border" (Shepard, 2011, p. 92). At its path the shoe stopped at the train station, facilities near Portland International Airport, and the Columbia Ridge landfill in rural Oregon. In another case study, journalists from Greenpeace embedded GPS sensors into television sets and learned that "the defunct televisions were tracked all the way to Nigeria, where they were likely illegally dumped … despite legislation banning the movement of e-waste between nations" (Shepard, 2011, p. 94).

Below are several examples of intelligent building projects. In Germany, a company Realities United plans to convert in 2019 a part of Berlin's Spree River into a natural swimming pool. Architects work on designing a new waste-to-energy plant for Copenhagen, Denmark, that will reduce the CO_2 emission and also double as a ski slope for Copenhagen's citizens. Other examples include synchronized or kinetic lighting systems on high-rise buildings, communicative display skins, and ornamental granulated light and media skin of the buildings. Robotic architecture is planned for the Khalifa Park Art Square, Abu Dhabi, United Arab Emirates. For tips on envisioning your own intelligent house, see Table 2.

Figure 6, "Small Window as a Part of the Big City" is about appreciation of architectural beauty. With a personal approach to the metro life one can see rhythmic repetition of natural structures juxtaposed with patterned constructions and architecture.

Urban Computing

The role of new technologies in a public space is prominent but also time-sensitive. According to Geiger (2012), public space, as a physical construct, changes with the embedded forms of computing. Embedded technologies and HCI have been migrating over the past 20 years in routine situations of everyday life from desktop to things: place-based, wearable, and otherwise situated mobile electronics; it affected both the conception and use of public space. The dynamic, evolving field of urban computing has been recently intensively studied and theoretically analyzed (Shepard, 2011; UbiComp, Pervasive, and MediaCity Conferences, 2012).

Urban computing ranges from instant messaging to demonstrating against dictators, to navigation to a coffee date (Geiger, 2012). Many years ago Mark Weiser (1991, p. 94) identified a concept of ubiquitous computing when he wrote in 1991, "Ubiquitous computing begins to emerge in the form of live boards that replace chalkboards." Ubiquitous computing "affects uses of open public spaces, from streets and plazas to the very air above" (Geiger, 2012, p. 338), so it also changes behavior of very large organizations that pertain to the built environments, work, agriculture, trade, travel, and education, in global financial and communication networks. This creates challenges that refer both to the public space and the discourse, described by Garrett Hardin (1968) as the commons. Hardin posed that the population

problem has no technical solution; it requires a fundamental extension in morality.

The debates shift from the solving spatial problems with advanced technologies to the possible impact on urban society and the values of urban life. Dataclouds of 21st century urban space shape our experience of the city (Shepard, 2011). In a study "The urban culture of sentient cities: from an Internet of things to a public sphere of things" Martin de Waal sees the forms of public exchange "no longer based on bringing people with different backgrounds and opinions spatially together (as in coffeehouses or town squares), but on the organization of publics around particular issues of concern" (Shepard, 2011, p. 190).

The entr'acte is a term given by Jordan Geiger (2012) to a model designed to reframe the spatial, temporal, and social terms of the commons with the use of urban computing: both the physical construction of urban spaces and the user-driven development of media networks by wirelessly communication, blogging, tweeting, and public speaking. Geiger puts forward four methods for creating such model, calling them: sampling (by collecting samples of the public's 'databody'); retinal (by installing projections that support, for example the city-run media campaigns); social (based on conviction that participation is at the heart of social actions, so making individuals generate rather than only receiving the data); and embodied (shifting relations between individuals and crowds in motion, for example by building a palpable collectivity through the wearable heart monitors). The author thus offers a model to build the understanding of the transient nature of a public space and a method to form the commons as a space and a discourse, material and immaterial.

SUSTAINABLE LANDSCAPE, SUSTAINABLE ARCHITECTURE

Efforts aimed at attaining green architecture and environmentally beneficial results are undertaken with the use of natural metaphors at the interface between economics, biology and neuroscience. Environmental architecture may mean knitting together dwellings within a landscape and learn to draw natural resources from the power of sun, wind, and water. Environmentally conscious design and techniques seek to reduce the impact of architectural constructions on the environment, conserve nonrenewable resources, and reduce the consumption of energy. Architects and urban planners strive to integrate eco-design that uses natural, locally available materials with sustainable architecture that utilizes recycled materials. A variety of techniques and technologies to achieve ultra-low energy use include passive solar design, recycled and sustainable materials, photovoltaic cells, wastewater treatment, rainwater collection, daylight harvesting, ventilation by rooftop wind-activated turbines, and solar hot water. Geothermal heating and cooling, e.g., through a vertical ground-coupled heat pump may use river water for cooling the building. Environmental design aims at capturing renewable energy sources, such as solar photovoltaic, solar thermal, wind energy, geothermal, and biomass energy (resulting from biological processes going in organic materials), to design zero emission architectural structures using self-generating, non-polluting energy. Eco-design is focused on problems resulting from the consumption of resources (such as energy and matter), emission to air, water, and ground, and pollution by wastes (such as industrial, commercial, household, radioactive, and electronic waste) and contaminants introduced to the natural environment. Eco-design also means reducing the energy needs of buildings by utilizing passive energy systems that optimize natural lighting, cooling and heating (e.g., solar water heating), covering roofs with vegetation, recycling water and other resources, using for insulation refractive materials, lowering the VOC (volatile organic compounds)-emitting materials, and developing ecological engineering and restoration. Sustainable homes contain appliances and furniture designed with

the reused materials for example tables made out of the reused electric wire reels.

Builders of the sustainable architectural structures take into account not only the possible impact of their projects on natural habitat and its resources; with the ongoing programs requiring inundation, displacement, and other environmental impacts, treasures of architecture can be affected by negative consequences of building dams, power stations, surface mining, and business enterprises. Following destruction caused by tornadoes, fires, or earthquakes, some city councils elect to rebuild as green cities. For example, all city buildings in Greensburg, Kansas would be built to the LEED Platinum environmental standards, making it the first city in the nation to do so (Greensburg, 2012). LEED – Leadership in Energy and Environmental Design developed by the U.S. Green Building Council consists of a suite of rating systems for the design, construction and operation of high performance green buildings, homes and neighborhoods.

Architects, engineers, developers, other building professionals, and legislators pursue sustainability in institutional, commercial, and civic buildings. The 71-story Zero Energy Tower built in Guangzhou, China in 2008 is an example of the net zero energy structure that does not require an increase in the community's need to produce energy (Frechette & Gilchrist, 2008). The building, called by the designers "a high-performance instrument shaped by the sun and wind," operates solely on energy created on-site. The site, active and passive energy sources, and materials reduce the building's dependency on the city's electrical grid. The designers' approach includes energy consumption reduction (double wall, triple-glazed façade with heat from it used as an energy source, radiant chilling ceilings and floors); absorption (photovoltaic elements in the tower's glass surfaces to harness solar power, external shades, daylight harvesting); reclamation (reusing energy); and generation (efficient micro-turbines, wind turbines capturing wind funneled down from openings in the façade and converting wind power into energy for the building). The Ford Calumet Environmental Center, Chicago is an environmental education center. Materials come from the surrounding area of the industrial region. Natural methods for heating and cooling include a geothermal system, daylight harvesting, and ventilation by rooftop wind-activated turbines. In a Hyatt Regency Exhibition Hall & Riverwalk, living wall systems and green roof's energy-saving mechanisms are applied. Turbines harvest wind energy, geothermal heating and cooling through a heat pump uses river water for cooling the building. Triple-glazed vacuum insulation and heat recovery system saves energy. The project is seeking LEED® Platinum certification.

For the World Business Center, Busan, Korea, SHoP architects from New York designed the traditional Korean courtyard with high-rise living towers as a new urban ecology: the vertical

garden. The Phare Tower in the La Défense district in Paris, France (to be completed 2017) will have 71 floors designed as a green building: a diagonal grid of louvers angled as a matrix will respond to the path of Sun to maximize energy efficiency. The Kohn Pedersen Tower has an organic form of a white magnolia, the city flower of Shanghai, which twists, focusing on views and optimizing solar orientation. In the Grimshaw Tower, the louvers track sun movement and interior heat gain while preserving the prevailing views. A proposed 1,380-foot-tall rotating Dynamic Tower in Dubai (David Fisher) will twirl sinuously, each story turning at its own speed and in its own direction, so residents can enjoy sunrise and sunset from the same window, and their plants will have the optimum amount of light all the day. Panels on the roof of each story will collect sunrays, and airplane-like propellers placed between stories will gather power from the wind. The building

Figure 7. Anna Ursyn, Glass Sky. (© 2012, A. Ursyn. Used with permission)

will produce more energy than it consumes and will sell the rest to the neighbors.

Figure 7, "Glass Sky" reflects a feeling of our submersion in a deep well made by the high-rise towers. Sometimes, we breathe with the reflected air.

Green Architecture

Green architecture is usually described as a building design that is in harmony with the natural features that surround the location of the project, is energy efficient and environmentally friendly, can reduce energy bills, uses less water, and lessen the amount of waste being added to landfill sites. Constructors of new green buildings use recycled materials such as glass, plastic, tires, or reclaimed lumber to reduce the waste being delivered to landfill sites and help the buildings blend with their environs. When possible, they apply concrete that has been composed and cured to reduce its thermal conductivity. They also utilize green, locally available materials that include wood, stone, and earth, to reduce the use of fuel for transportation. In many cases users of green structures recycle grey water (waste water from baths, showers and wash hand basins) and capture rainwater for watering a garden, cleaning a car, flushing toilets, or having a shower. They install solar panels along with other renewable energy sources; this enables low maintenance and is a non-polluting way to lighten a house, a garden, a greenhouse, and a recreational trailer. Wind generators can be used to charge small batteries for lighting and pumps.

The American Institute of Architects (AIA, 2012) and its Committee on the Environment (COTE) have selected for the 16th time the top ten examples of sustainable architecture and green design solutions that show excellence in sustainable design and the reduced energy consumption. The projects will be honored at the AIA 2012 National Convention and Design Exposition.

The green structures selected by AIA contribute to their communities in several ways: they improve comfort for building occupants, reduce environmental impacts, reuse of existing structures, connect to transit systems, proved the low-impact and regenerative site development, energy and water conservation, use of sustainable or renewable construction materials, and design that improves indoor air quality. They also have many merits. In some structures the use of potable water is reduced; rainwater from the roof goes to an underground cistern; filtered and treated with ultraviolet light water is then pumped to all flush fixtures in the building. The vegetative roof provides habitat where the chives and flowering sedum attract butterflies and bees and also keeps the building cool. Xero gardening eliminates the need for irrigation, and paving is permeable to rainfall water. Projects built in the harsh desert climate use a dense network of linear buildings to maximize shade, create a pedestrian green space, and minimize costs of air-condition and electricity. A project built on a former landfill captures and infiltrates the storm water and diverts it from adjacent streets for on-site treatment. The geothermal well field uses the earth's constant temperature to offset heating and cooling loads. Green roofs filters water, slow storm water discharge, and improve air quality. Rooms' orientation for illumination by natural light reduces artificial lighting. Carbon dioxide sensors adjust airflow depending on occupancy.

The National Renewable Energy Laboratory (NREL, 2012) is the only national laboratory solely dedicated to advancing renewable energy and energy efficiency technologies. Its 327-acre main campus in Golden, Colorado, is a living model of sustainable energy. NREL's areas of expertise in renewable fuels, renewable electricity (solar, wind, water, geothermal, smart-grid technology), chemical science, biosciences, scientific computing, and materials science transfer knowledge and innovations to the society and support building technology and efficiency.

Figure 8. Anna Ursyn, Plans and Realities. (© 2012, A. Ursyn. Used with permission)

The NREL employees consider their newly constructed sustainable Research Support Facility (RSF) a living laboratory that can be seen at http://www.nrel.gov/rsf. This building showcases high performance design features including passive energy strategies and renewable energy technology. Passive heating and cooling include: building's orientation toward sun light minimizing heat losses and gains; a labyrinth thermal storage concrete structure in the crawl space; transpired solar collectors on the south face that preheat air for a labyrinth; light-reflecting devices and paints that make all workstations day-lit; triple-glazed, tinted or opened on command windows with louvered sunshades; concrete panels providing thermal mass. Moreover, 70 miles of radiant piping running through all floors and thermal slabs in the

ceiling hydronically heats and cools the building instead of forced air. Demand-controlled, under-floor ventilation is supported by the evaporative cooling and energy recovery systems. An energy-efficient green data center supports reducing energy use by 50% over traditional approaches. Solar energy devices (2.5 MW of photovoltaics) are installed on the rooftop, visitor parking lot, and staff-parking garage. Storm water runoffs and permeable landscaping surround the facility. Workstations include LED task lights and monitors, power management surge protectors, energy-saving laptop computers, and all-in-one print/fax/scan devices; each workstation uses about 70W compared to 300-500W per workstation at typical office building. This net zero energy building won the Leadership in Energy and Environmental

Design (LEED) Platinum rating awarded by the U. S. Green Buildings Council.

Research about the carbon dioxide (CO_2) overload in the atmosphere, caused in a great part by generating electricity to power electronic products, included designing the 'natural fuses' in the form of plants that absorb carbon dioxide and grow. Plants, used as an interface in an electric circuit, formed a 'carbon footprint' telling about the carbon dioxide production by this circuit. The 'Natural Fuse' created by Hague Design+Research is a citywide network of electronically assisted plants that act both as energy providers and a shared CO_2 sink. According to the authors, "even a low-power light bulbs draw more power than can be comfortably offset by a single plant. ... The average carbon footprint per energy usage in the USA is 322 g of CO_2/1kWhUSA" (Shepard, 2011, p. 66, 70).

Innovative projects proved themselves as having inspirational educational merits. The Kensington High School for the Creative and Performing Arts in Philadelphia (Kensington, 2012) reported that in one year truancy (staying away from school) has dropped from 35% to 0%, tests scores have quadrupled, and graduation has gone from 29% to 69%. The faculty has used the visible sustainability features as teaching tool for students. In another school students have access to the building's geothermal and water system, the pump room, labeled and metered specifically to be used for classroom demonstration and instruction. The Portland Community College is designed to be the first net zero energy higher education building in Oregon.

Figure 8, "Plans and Realities" is about urban planning. We plan, we hope, and we achieve by making plans real. They can expand or shrink, though.

THE ROLE OF PUBLIC OPINION IN PRESERVING THE PAST FOR THE FUTURE: TRADITIONAL AND PRESENT-DAY WONDERS

The ancient seven world's wonders had comprised:

- A Great Pyramid of Giza (existing now)
- Hanging Gardens of Babylon
- Temple of Artemis at Ephesus
- Statue of Zeus at Olympia
- Mausoleum of Maussollos Halicarnassus
- Colossus of Rhodes
- Pharos lighthouse of Alexandria

Since the Great Pyramid of Giza was the only structure that continues to exist, an international poll was called upon in order to select the next seven wonders. The New World's seven wonders rewritten by the New 7 Wonders Foundation (Fletcher, 2012) include:

- The Great Wall of China
- Italy's Roman Colosseum
- India's Taj Mahal
- Jordan's Petra
- Peru' Machu Picchu
- Brazil's Statue of Christ the Redeemer
- Mexico's Pyramid at Chichen Itza, and
- The Great Pyramid of Giza, which remained on the list.

Below are examples of contemporary architectural creations that use current technologies in a sustainable way.

The Arab Institute in Paris designed by Jean Nouvel in 1988 has a southern wall protected from the sun by a 60-meter wall composed of multiple panels with metallic diaphragms of various sizes. They shrink or widen like an eye or camera lenses in response to sensors, to control penetration of sunlight into the building.

Many consider the Hearst Building the most beautiful skyscraper in Manhattan. At first, the six stories high publishing firm headquarters were built in the twenties by Joseph Urban. Norman Foster built a forty stories skyscraper on the top of this construction. The tower is sheathed in glass and stainless steel, with a geometric diamond-shape pattern of four-story-high triangles. The entrance to the building leads through the Urban's original arch to the vast atrium roofed with three stories of windows and diagonal structural supports of the tower. Norman Foster built the Tower for the Swiss Reinsurance Company in London, UK. Its shape aids natural ventilation as it helps the air to flow. The glazed skin allows the maximum use of natural light and reduces energy consumption by 50%. Foster also put a steel-and-glass canopy atop the British Museum in London. The Dynamic Tower in Dubai, United Arab Emirates would consist of 80 pre-fabricated apartments, which will spill independently at a voice command, to make a complete rotation in a one to three hours by means of power-generating wind turbines and solar panels. The building will be 'green:' panels on the roof of each story will collect sunrays, and airplane-like propellers placed between stories will gather power from the wind. The building will produce more energy than it consumes and will sell the rest to the neighbors. The Taipei 101 skyscraper in Taiwan was awarded in 2011 the LEED Platinum certification as the tallest green building in the world. In 2010, the Burj Khalifa became the tallest structure (828 m, 2,717 ft), so Taipei 101 is now the world's second tallest building. It is built in innovative way by applying mostly off-site construction. California Academy of Sciences (2012), designed by the Italian architect Renzo Piano, has its building covered with a green roof that repeats the shapes of the hills. There is also abundance of plants inside this cupola.

The Millennium Tower in Tokyo Bay is capable of housing up to 60,000 people, generating its own energy, and processing its own waste. The tower's conical structure with helical steel cage is inherently stable is designed to be resistant to hurricanes and earthquakes that are notorious in this region. The Skidmore Merrill towers of the One and Two Hudson Place has a glass envelope that maximizes natural day lighting with minimal glare and secures energy efficiency. Lotte Super Tower in Seoul (1,640 feet, 555 meters) transforms from a square base to a circle, which is based on an ancient Korean observatory.

CONCLUSION

The title of this book: "Computational solutions for knowledge, art, and entertainment: information exchange beyond text" could serve perfectly as a description of current trends and patterns one can perceive in architecture. Architects examine mathematical, physical, chemical, biological, and other laws and search for visual language to translate what they find out to architectural forms. The reader is encouraged to actively respond with own projects to the issues under discussion, which include interactive skins, architectural simulation and modeling, intelligent buildings, urban computing, sustainable landscape and architecture, and green architecture, for example by creating an own intelligent dream house.

REFERENCES

AIA. (2012). *Top ten green projects*. Retrieved July 30, 2012, from http://inhabitat.com/aias-top-ten-green-projects-of-2010/

Banissi, E., & Zhou, H. (2012). Modeling 3D city using high resolution stereo camera imagery. In *Proceedings of the 16th International Conference on Information Visualization*, (pp. 516-522). doi 10.1109/IV.2012.119

Bisantz, J. (2010). Art, advertising and green technologies. In *Proceedings of the School of Visual Arts 24th Annual National Conference on Liberal Arts and the Education of Artists*. Retrieved October 23, 2012, from http://media.schoolofvisualarts.edu/sva/media/18944/medium/Proceedings2010.pdf

Burkhard, R., Bischof, S., & Herzog, A. (2008). The potential of crowd simulations for communication purposes in architecture. In *Proceedings of the iV, 12th International Conference on Information Visualisation*, (pp. 403-408). London, UK: IEEE Computer Society Press.

Burkhard, R. A. (2006). Learning from architects: complementary concept mapping approaches. In *Proceedings of the International Conference on Information Visualization* (pp. 225-234). ISBN 0-7695-2177-0. Retrieved from http://www.computer.org/portal/web/csdl/doi/10.1109/IV.2004.1320194

California Academy of Sciences. (2012). Retrieved August 2, 2012, from http://www.nytimes.com/slideshow/2008/09/23/arts/20080924_ACADEMY_SLIDESHOW_index.html

Cheetham, M. A. (2010). The crystal interface in contemporary art: metaphors of the organic and inorganic. *Leonardo, 43*(3), 251–255. doi:10.1162/leon.2010.43.3.250.

Cruz-Neira, C., Sandin, D. J., DeFanti, T. A., Kenyon, R. V., & Hart, J. C. (1992). The CAVE: Audio visual experience automatic virtual environment. *Communications of the ACM, 35*(6), 64–72. doi:10.1145/129888.129892.

De Bure, G. (1992). *Jean Nouvel, Emmanuel Cattani, and associates: Four projects*. Zurich: Artemis.

Dorin, A., & Korb, K. (2007). Building artificial ecosystems from artificial chemistry. In *Proceedings of the 9th European Conference on Artificial Life*, (pp. 103-112). Springer-Verlag.

EON Icube. (2012). Retrieved July 30, 2012, from http://www.eonreality.com/products_icube.html

EON Reality Coliseum. (2012). Retrieved July 30, 2012, from http://www.eonreality.com/products_coliseum.html

Evomusart. (2012). Retrieved July 29, 2012, from http://evostar.dei.uc.pt/2012/call-for-contributions/evomusart/

Ferreira, M. I. A. (2011). Interactive bodies: The semiosis of architectural forms a case study. *Biosemiotics Online First*. doi 10.1007/s12304-011-9126-0. Retrieved July 29, 2012, from http://www.springerlink.com/content/v72u2555445qv167/

Fletcher, A. (2012). *Seven new wonders*. Infoplease. Retrieved July 29, 2012, from Fletcherhttp://hawkstryker.hubpages.com/hub/The-Current-7-Man-Made-Wonders-of-The-World

Frechette, R. E., III, & Gilchrist, R. (2008). *Towards zero energy: A case study of the Pearl River Tower, Guangzhou, China*. Retrieved August 1, 2008, from http://som.com/resources/content/5/0/4/3/9/0/2/0/documents/SOM_TowardsZeroEnergy.pdf

Geiger, J. (2012). Entr'acte. *Leonardo, 45*(4), 338–347. doi:10.1162/LEON_a_00408.

Greensburg, Kansas. (2012). Retrieved August 1, 2012, from http://en.wikipedia.org/wiki/Greensburg,_Kansas

Hall, P. (2012). *Living skins: Architecture as interface*. Retrieved August 11, 2012, from http://www.adobe.com/motiondesign/MDC_Think_Tank.html?u%5FsLang=en&u%5FnTextSize=14&u%5FsFontType=sans&u%5FsContent=Living%5FSkins

Hardin, G. (1968, December 13). The tragedy of the commons. *Science*, 1243–1248. doi: doi:10.1126/science.162.3859.1243 PMID:5699198.

C. A. Hill, & M. Helmers (Eds.). (2004/2008). *Defining visual rhetorics*. Routledge.

IBM Smarter Buildings. (2010). Retrieved August 1, 2008, from http://www.ibm.com/smarterplanet/us/en/green_buildings/overview/index.html?csr=agus_getgovtsmbuild20120320&cm=k&cr=google&ct=LBSK005&S_TACT=LBSK005&ck=smarter_buildings&cmp=LBSK0&mkwid=sufBbUa4x_20798476667_432cfc4094

Kensington. (2012). *The Kensington high school for the creative and performing arts*. Retrieved July 29, 2012, from http://www.aiatopten.org/node/48

Lio, P., & Verma, D. (2012). *Biologically inspired networking and sensing: Algorithms and architectures*. IGI Global.

LoPiccolo, P. (2003). A virtual exhibit transports museum-goers back in time to view a famous art collection in its original setting. *Computer Graphics World, 26*(3). Retrieved July 14, 2012, from http://www.cgw.com/Publications/CGW/2003/Volume-26-Issue-3-March-2003-/Backdrop-3-03.aspx

Lucia, A., Sabin, J. E., & Jones, P. L. (2011). Memory, difference, and information: Generative architectures latent to material and perceptual plasticity. In *Proceedings of The 15th International Conference on Information Visualization,* (pp. 379-388). Los Alamitos, CA: IEEE Computer Society. ISBN 978-1-4577-0868-8

J. Mateo, & F. Sauter (Eds.). (2007). *Natural metaphor: Architectural papers III*. Zurich: ACTAR & ETH Zurich.

Moloney, J. (2006). Between art and architecture: The interactive skins. In *Proceedings of the 10th International Conference on Information Visualization,* (pp. 681-686). IEEE.

NREL. (2012). *National renewable energy laboratory*. Retrieved October 30, 2012, from http://www.nrel.gov/rsf

Özgenel, L. (2008). A tale of two cities: In search of ancient Pompeii and Herculaneum. *METU Journal of the Faculty of Architecture, 25*(1), 1–25.

Paivio, A. (1970). On the functional significance of imagery. *Psychological Bulletin, 73*, 385–392. doi:10.1037/h0029180.

Rocca, A. (2007). *Natural architecture*. Princeton Architectural Press.

M. Shepard (Ed.). (2011). *Sentient city: Ubiquitous computing, architecture, and the future of urban space*. Cambridge, MA: MIT Press.

Siemens. (2012). *System architecture for the APOGEE building automation system with BACnet*. Retrieved July 14, 2012, from http://w3.usa.siemens.com/buildingtechnologies/us/en/building-automation-and-energy-management/apogee/architecture/Pages/architecture.aspx

Soddu, C. (2012). *Argenia, generative art and science: Website of Celestino Soddu*. Retrieved February 5, 2012, from http://www.celestino-soddu.com/

Sondermann, H. (2008). *Light shadow space: Architectural rendering with cinema 4D*. Springer Vienna Architecture.

Tzonis, A. (2004). *Santiago Calatrava: The complete works*. Rizzoli.

UbiComp, Pervasive, and MediaCity Conference. (2012). Retrieved August 10, 2012, from http://www.ubicomp.org/ubicomp2012/calls/workshopsCFP.html

Van Bouvel, T., Vande Moere, A., & Boeykens, S. (2012). ArchiBrain: A conceptual platform for the visualization of collaborative design. In *Proceedings of the 16ᵗʰ International Conference on Information Visualization*, (pp. 396-402). doi 10.1109/IV.2012.72

Weiser, M. (1991). The computer for the 21ˢᵗ century. [from http://wiki.daimi.au.dk/pca/_files/weiser-orig.pdf]. *Scientific American*, *3*(3), 94–104. Retrieved August 10, 2012 doi:10.1038/scientificamerican0991-94.

Yoshida, H. (2012). Bridging synthetic and organic materiality: Graded transitions in material connections. In A. Ursyn (Ed.), *Biologically-Inspired Computing for the Arts: Scientific Data through Graphics* (pp. 81–88). IGI Global. doi:10.4018/978-1-4666-0942-6.ch005.

Zuanon, r. (2012). The bio-interfaces at design, art and game areas: some applications. In a. Ursyn (ed.), *biologically-inspired computing for the arts: scientific data through graphics*. IGI Global. ISBN 978-1-4666-0942-6

Chapter 19
Educational Implications

ABSTRACT

An integrative art-science approach to teaching is described, involving imaging concepts about science, with three approaches to integration of art and science: 1) visual presentation of scientific concepts, 2) creating art by finding inspiration in a science-based topic, 3) learning visually for other courses taken concurrently by arranging data into a structured whole. The next part of the chapter is about several dimensions that seem important in blended and online learning regarding social networking and the collaborative virtual environments. Virtual education in a first life and a Second Life classroom environment is discussed next.

INTRODUCTION

In the process of learning, visual computing may help to recognize configurations and relationships described by formulas. The impact of visuals on learning as a cognitive activity gains attention because of a facilitating effect of visual materials in the process of communication. It seems, the same way as we may list three basic elements of communication in the arts: the artist as a sender of a message, art media, and a viewer as the receiver, we may translate these elements in educational terms: the teacher as a sender, visual educational materials, and the student as the receiver. In terms of pedagogical constructivism, learning is an interpretive process leading to the construction of the individual's subjective reality, not identical with the knowledge of the teacher. The

value of computing for the arts used as of visual educational materials might be in their emotional impact that might bridge the distance between the object and the viewer. Thus cognitive and expressive meanings conveyed through the shared media art containing signs, symbols, and metaphors may improve the capacity for learning. Using visual thinking and learning with relation to semiotic practices seems rare. The creation of illustrated and annotated web resources would provide materials for visual learning. In educational terms, by supplying an access through the new media art to the images and artists' approaches to their work, it is possible to develop the curricula for teaching contemporary art with the core based on semiotic analysis of the art content and the technological thought, not just historical chronology. When students learn to apply visual signs, symbols, and meanings in relation to any subject matter under study, they can extract more information from data they collected. Instruction in computer

DOI: 10.4018/978-1-4666-4627-8.ch019

art graphics and new media art serves a tool to facilitate students' learning in other disciplines and their growth in artistic creation. Through art inspired by science-related concepts it is possible to visually present these concepts and discover the power of their visual forms.

APPLICATIONS OF TECHNOLOGICAL THOUGHT

Computers as tools for creating models of realistic situations serve well for developing higher cognitive strategies for problem solving and decision-making. Specific software for the curriculum helps the teachers to teach an action-oriented and problem-solving material. Someone has compared the computer to the cart and knowledge to a load transported on the cart. A need for developing cognitive abilities has been already recognized by science and mathematics teachers, but this integrative function of intelligence cannot take effect without understanding visual messages, imaginative approach in exploring conceptual structures and scientific problems, spatial abilities to visualize configurations and relationships described by the formulas. Education in computer art graphics may support students' progress and achievement in science, mathematics, and also in the learning of computer art with illustrated and annotated resources. Unlike the history of science of technology, art history cannot simply report facts by putting them into chronological order. The challenge lies in interpreting the meaning of the artwork, in hazarding a guess about how the work will be seen and referred to 50 years form now, which works will fade away, and in relating the work of computer artists to the rest of the art world and the cultures in which they were created. Although some large museums curate computer shows, a historical understanding of the field often seems lacking. Just as Clement Greenberg brought Abstract Expressionism into the art canon with his seminal essays in the 1960s, so the critics and historians may help the museum-goers

understand the vital role the computer plays in visual image creation. All we know is that there is an audience waiting.

The Emergence of Cross-Disciplinary Efforts

A number of new journals, academic degree programs, and software applications mark the dominance of visual technologies and their role in creative thinking, problem solving, and visual communication. A change towards increasing interdisciplinary approaches is evident on a variety of fronts. New journals, books, interdisciplinary degree programs, teaching strategies, conferences, technologies, and domain taxonomies have surfaced. Examples of cross-disciplinary and visually oriented journals may include the International Journal of Creative Interfaces and Computer Graphics, Digital Creativity, Leonardo, Journal of the International Society for the Arts, Sciences, and Technology, and many other periodicals. A great number of books merge art and science, such as "Digital Creativity: Techniques for Digital Media and the Internet" by Bruce Wands (2001) and "Art of the Digital Age" (2007) by the same author, "Digital Creativity: a Reader (Innovations in Art and Design) by Colin Beardon and Lone Malmborg (2010), "Creative Code" by John Maeda (2004), or Daniel Pink's "A Whole New Mind: Why Right-Brainers Will Rule the Future" (2006). They all emphasize the importance of developing creative thinking for career survival.

Currently, a great number of artists possess a substantial knowledge of computer technology, business, and other areas. Many galleries, festivals, and shows are re-orienting to media arts. University colleges are changing to Art and Media rather than Art and Design and prepare students to meet job market expectations. Job positions for visual artists and graphic designers are still open, but better opportunities have arisen for interactive media developers who don't hesitate to explore possibilities. Job opportunities increasingly require applicants to be creative not only artistically but technologically as well. This does not mean that one must have a strong knowledge of math, computer science, and sciences, but that this person is open for using readily made tools creatively.

Mental involvement, taken from a deeply personal perspective, into the complex structure of the big city life may complement a process of our learning as a cognitive activity involving visuals and computing (Figure 1, "Grammar of the City"):

Rhythms of floors, crossings, passages and street signs
Reflected in window panes
Make space for replicas of people attracted to the city center,
Create multiplied layers of singular existences
Who learn the grammar of the City.

COGNITIVE LOAD

It is well known that individuals differ in their processing capacity. The format of instructional materials either promotes or limits the success in learning. Researchers discern three categories of cognitive load and its cognitive architecture; they describe the intrinsic load, extraneous load, and germane load (Artino, 2008).

1. The intrinsic load results from the content of the load and its level of complexity, its overlapping and interaction with other information. Artino (2008, p. 429) refers the intrinsic load to element interactivity; that means the number of elements that must be processed simultaneously in working memory for schema construction. Understanding con-

Figure 1. Anna Ursyn, Grammar of the City (© 2002, A. Ursyn. Used with permission)

cepts would involve more complex and interactive learning than studying facts. Visual presentation of concepts reduces cognitive load of a learner. An instructional designer may control the intrinsic load caused by the high content interactivity by breaking some of the concepts into individual "sub schemas" to be taught in isolation and later brought back together and described as a combined whole (Clark, Nguyen, & Sweller, 2006). We cannot change the intrinsic cognitive load induced by learning an abstract concept, but we can separate and present parts of this concept in a visual, more intuitive way and then combine them into a whole as a source of germane load. Teams of scientists are working on taking the load off a learner's mind by managing cognitive load in science learning and fostering cognitive skill acquisition. With a cognitive load perspective, they work on designing worked examples and example-based learning to improve transfer to novel problems, and also on structuring the transition from the example study to problem solving. Several ways that are considered effective in reducing cognitive load in science education may include instruction with drawing and imagining, employing computer-based simulations, learning by concept mapping, incorporating embedded icons and full-screen illustrations into computer tutorial manuals, and utilizing multimodal user interfaces. Successful problem solving in knowledge-rich domains requires building schemas about abstract problems. Worked examples and example-based learning may support students in acquiring such schemas. Overall solution procedures presented from a `molar' view that relate to the whole body of matter and focus on the whole problem categories, engage a huge amount of information in working memory. To reduce intrinsic cognitive load, a `modular'' view is

recommended, where such examples relate to the properties of the problem's parts, and complex solutions are broken down into smaller meaningful elements that can be conveyed separately (Gerjets, Scheiter, and Catrambone, 2004).

2. The extraneous cognitive load placed on memory is caused by the superfluous elements of the content. Learning from a book written in foreign language creates unnecessary cognitive load called by Sweller an extraneous cognitive load, considered by him ineffective cognitive load. Learning involves perception, and cognitive load may be reduced when information is depicted in a way that relates to well-known images. For this reason, a visual medium is preferred when it is more efficient in avoiding extraneous load. For example, a visual medium should be used to describe to a student some concepts, such as a square, that are visual so they should be described visually, because it's much easier to see what the instructor is talking about rather than having it described verbally. We can find a discussion of the two possible ways to describe a square to a student in order to avoid burdening a student with unnecessary information. According to Clark, Nguyen, and Sweller (2006), "Certainly an instructor can describe a square in a verbal medium, but it takes just a second and far less effort to see what the instructor is talking about when a learner is shown a square, rather than having one described verbally. In this instance, the efficiency of the visual medium is preferred. This is because it does not unduly load the learner with unnecessary information. This unnecessary cognitive load is described as extraneous cognitive load."

3. The germane load, considered an effective cognitive load (Artino, 2008, p. 429), is described as a part of the cognitive load that results from optimizing the learner load. We

can attain this by lowering extraneous load with the use of abstractions and elaboration, for example when the content is supplemented with graphic information analogies, or arranged in the ordered or sequenced chunks. When learning a new, abstract concept, one has simultaneously hold active a substantial amount of information in one's working memory. Instructional designers can lower extraneous and promote germane load by introducing visual display of the content, applying color coding, interactivity (for example, by showing interactive links in blue color and underlined), using micro/macro or small multiple display (Tufte, 1983, 1990), or in many other ways. They can focus instruction toward germane load that is devoted to redirect learner's attention to the construction of schemas of reasoning.

Visual examples and metaphors may cause that thinking and reasoning require lesser cognitive load, because associations connect images with notions already existing in memory, and language processing is facilitated by pictorial representations. The use of different modes (pictorial, verbal, tactile) for presentation of essential information makes an important part of the Universal Design – an approach meant to produce buildings, products and environments accessible to everyone, not just people without disabilities, and thus build the environment that is aesthetic and usable to the greatest extent possible by everyone, regardless of their age, ability, or status in life. By drawing from cognitive neuroscience and artistic principles, we can apply universal design to the interface design by identifying aesthetic dimensions, evaluating the aesthetic qualities of an interface, and adapting the tools for the needs of the user. We can apply universal design to instruction when we make it simple, intuitive, and easy to understand, regardless of the students' experience, knowledge, language skills, or cur-

rent concentration level, and taking into account their economic, engineering, cultural, gender, and environmental concerns. We can attain it when we supply visuals along with verbal information, and use meaningful icons as well as text. Creating visual presentations of concepts may also engage emotional memory, the memory for events that evoke a particularly strong emotion. It is known that emotional memory involves connections from the amygdala to the prefrontal cortex and may elicit strong physiological reactions.

Data collected about cognitive principles of learning confirmed that information is better remembered when accompanied by a visual image (Paivio, 1970, 1971, 1986/1990, 1991; Sadoski & Paivio, 2013). Many would agree that thinking involving imagination might lower the cognitive load. Many would also agree that imagination makes one's mind more creative and resourceful. As stated by Richard Meyer, "The human information-processing system consists of two separate channels – an auditory/verbal channel for processing auditory input and verbal representations and a visual/pictorial channel for processing visual input and pictorial representations" (Mayer & Moreno, 2003, p. 43).

The modality principle tells about reducing cognitive load (Moreno & Meyer, 1999). Based on the cognitive theory of multimedia learning, Richard Meyer and Roxana Moreno (2003) offered ways of reducing cognitive load by mixing auditory and visual presentation modes; for example, concise narrated animation fostered meaningful learning without creating cognitive overload. Students understand a multimedia presentation better when animation and narration are presented simultaneously rather than successively. The findings based on delivering instruction with the use of video or animation examples (Moreno, 2007) encourage segmenting instructional videos and animations into small chunks to help novice students learn from complex dynamic visualizations. Bai, White, & Sundaram (2012) developed conceptual models and frameworks for the Contextual Adaptive Visualization Environment, which provides flexible support for sensing changes in the problem, interpreting, and responding to the changes through the redesign and remodeling of visual compositions. Description of a meaningful learning model can be found in a book by Hassard & Dias (2008).

With fun-oriented instructional design, individuals and groups may play learning games. Play, particularly symbolic play, is where cognition and culture meet. It's a mental can-opener for liberating new ideas (Rheingold, 2002, p. 373-4). In his book "Homo Ludens: A Study of the Play-Element in Culture" a Dutch historian Johan Huizinga (1971) described ancient rites as sacred play and explored the meaning of play – philological, mythological, anthropological, and psychological, in a similar way as some of cognitive scientists. People play because play is fun or deeply engaging, and because, in Huizinga's view, play is a vehicle for

creating culture. For Piaget and many psychologists, play is essential for everyone's cognitive, social, and emotional development because it helps us to organize our models of the world, test hypotheses, discern new relationships or patterns in our perceptions, and run mental simulations. In later years the focus has shifted to the ways in which playing, especially video games, may help to solve intellectual and social problems. Thus, we can make learning playful by designing things to be learned in the form of a game.

Actions taken toward reducing cognitive overload can be somehow compared to the work of an acoustician aimed at making the city environment quiet. Figure 2, "Noise Control" is an homage dedicated to one of them.

You worked all your life
To keep silence safe from noise.
The quieter it's here
The less renowned you are.

Figure 2. Anna Ursyn, Noise Control (© 2000, A. Ursyn. Used with permission)

INSTRUCTION IN ART PRODUCTION BASED ON SCIENCE AND TECHNOLOGY

The significance of integrative teaching and learning with computer art graphics results from recent developments in the cognitive approach to teaching and draws from the growing demand for clarification through the use of the visuals, visualization of processes and events, simulation, and technology-based instruction in the computerized world. This need is even stronger in the environment of distance learning over the Internet.

Computer art is often considered more as a part of graphic design than a type of art. In visual arts education, much attention should be given to the curriculum development that would include creating and apprehending computer graphic images and considering computer as a medium for art and art education.

Advances in the research on mental images in human cognition confirm the importance of mental imagery as a form of nonverbal processing.

The idea of the use of computers in art education was conceived in the early sixties by Charles Csuri, Robert Mallary (computer program TRAN 2 to generate sculpture), Katherine Nash (the programming language ART 1 developed in collaboration with Richard Williams), and many other artists. Since then, computer-aided instruction, both programmed and interactive has been designed, capable of intervention, alteration, influence, or control by the learner. Whatever would be the design of computer graphics implementation into school curriculum, it would enhance students' learning and development at all levels of intellectual behavior, promoting mental processes in the cognitive, affective, and psychomotor areas and shift students' thinking toward the visual side. It would also promote

conditions serving to create intrinsic motivation. Computer art graphics may be considered to be a link between rigid instructional procedures for teaching basic sciences and teaching through educational games. Moreover, instructional methods for improving computer literacy may help to close the gap between secondary and college programs. Teaching art with the application of computer graphics would help teachers to encourage motivation and decrease the dropout rate of students. Technical and artistic expertise of students may be effectively supported by interdisciplinary approaches to instruction that combines computer science, visual literacy and computer art graphics courses. The development of instructional strategies to promote creative inventiveness is important in preparing students to apply creative approach to their future tasks in different fields and not to confine themselves to pragmatic unsophisticated execution of their duties. Creating computer art graphics might conceivably serve as a means for gaining information enriched through insight.

Integration of verbal and graphic information becomes easier due to the application of computer art to the field of science visualization. Multi-dimensional visualization is required to present the dynamics of the objects and events. Visual presentation of the existing processes is possible by assigning axes of projection and colors to specific dimensions. In exploring high-dimensional space, measurements of many variables are needed (for example, seven variables: x, y, z axes, time, temperature, pressure and density describe the speed and state of an object which is changing in time and in space). When empowered with the basic skills to visualize processes with their underlying forces, students are able to create their own artistic presentation of those concepts. For example, in the assignment that integrates physics and art, they originate an artwork on the theme of acceleration.

IMAGING CONCEPTS ABOUT SCIENCE: THREE APPROACHES TO INTEGRATION OF ART AND SCIENCE

By designing art assignments that are based on scientific concepts, I have developed an integrative program for instruction in computer graphics where students can grow both in terms of their artistic inspiration and of their enhancement in learning by employing visual presentation of data, application of computer graphics and programming to art creation, and interactive visualization techniques. The integrative teaching with computer art graphics is about creating art and learning by it. Activities aimed at improving one's power to conveying meaning by merging information visualization with the principles of creative design may comprise the three approaches to visual learning:

1. Visual presentation of scientific concepts. In the Computer Graphics classes, students' responses to integrative assignments take a form of the illustrative projects that link art, mathematics, physics, biology, earth and other sciences, multicultural, social and environmental issues and language arts. Ideas and experiences gained through the courses' delivery allow discussing the events and the pitfalls encountered during Internet-based instruction.

2. Learning by creating art, finding inspiration in a science-based topic. In the Computer Art courses students learn to create art inspired by science such as biology, physics, and technology. In the Introduction to Visual Communication Design class, students examine selected technologies and their influence on thinking about and creating art. The course provides students with contextual knowledge of visual communication in terms of designing pictorial messages, the understanding and responding to visually conveyed information. The Visual Learning with Technology course provides students with knowledge about visual communication in terms of designing pictorial messages; understanding and responding to visually conveyed information. Students explore concepts of visual thinking, communication and the meaning of visual representation of data and information as icons, signs, symbols, and metaphors. They learn to design their own solutions to artistic problems, visually enforce information, and apply strategies for visual problem solving.

3. Learning visually for other courses taken concurrently by arranging data into a structured whole. Projects created in Visual Learning classes helped the students learn the content of other courses with the use of various visualization techniques, models, 2D and 3D projects, animations, short videos, toys, etc. In this course, students explore concepts of visual thinking, communication, and the meaning of images as icons, signs and symbols.

1. Visual Presentation of Scientific Concepts

Visual, verbal, and time-based approaches can be best combined when art and science related themes are integrated, to engage one in combining the precise and expressive way of thinking. Presenting difficult concepts through visual metaphors make easier learning and understanding of abstract ideas and processes. With cognitive approach to mental imagery, one can visualize science concept and create image representation of it. This can be done through hand drawing or, even better, by creating computer art graphics. Visual representation of scientific data related material in both pictorial and verbal way involves thinking about selected events or processes in order to present them visually. Content analysis includes deriving meaning from the data, a study of techniques and concepts (such as examining its independent and dependent variables), and possible comparisons in time and space. Activities of this type are aimed to evoke a holistic, synaesthetic mode of learning and engage visual, verbal, and manual modes of action. Metaphorical imaging and abstract thinking prevail over hands-on instruction and mere memorization when it comes to learning higher-level thinking concepts and accomplishing tasks such as writing programs, creating computer graphics, or designing a visualization project. This approach to teaching has been tested in interdisciplinary settings involving physics and computer science (Ursyn, Mills, Hobgood, & Scott, 1997; Ursyn & Scott, 2006; Ursyn & Sung 2007; Ursyn & Scott, 2007).

2. Creating Art by Finding Inspiration in a Science-Based Topic

This approach involves one's visual response to a scientific concept after exploration of its meaning, and creating science-based art with the use of computer graphics, animation, or programming. Data, processes, products, and events serve as a theme for art. It may be a challenging and rewarding activity to create an artistic presentation of concepts taken from various disciplines and thus show one's visual power and understanding of underlying processes, products, and forces. It may mean turning data into pictures by mapping from abstract description to images. One may use a metaphor as a form of thought and present knowledge with the use of electronic media for retrieving and visualizing data.

As for animation, it seems important not only how a story is expressed, but also how appealing it is, with visual metaphors, cognitive shortcuts, and actions aimed to compress time without telling stories in an play-by-play manner. Every single frame should be a masterpiece, either in an abstract or a character-based animation. In 3D interactive environments (a website, virtual reality environment, interactive publication, TV, animation) the

recipient might feel encouraged to be an active part of the world and control how a story unfolds.

Figure 3a and 3b are products of integrative instruction in programming, computer graphics and video production, traditional Japanese art, and sculpting. Figure 3a shows a still image of a video that instructs in the form of three-dimensional graphics how to create a crane according to the traditional Japanese art of folding paper into decorative figures.

Figure 3. a. Leonard Rodriguez, Crane 3D. Still image from a 3d animation. (© 2009, L. Rodriguez. Used with permission); b. Leonard Rodriguez, Crane. This PMC sculpture after the 3D computer graphics shown in part a, demonstrating how to create an origami crane (© 2009, L. Rodriguez. Used with permission).

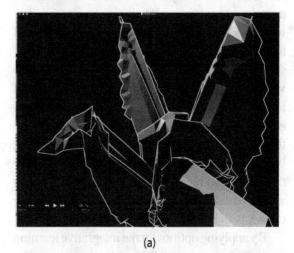

(a)

(b)

The visual exercise in creating three-dimensional programs was then applied to creating a sculpture from a *PMC (precious metal clay)* material that resembles silver when baked after processing (Figure 3b).

3. Learning Visually for Other Courses Taken Concurrently by Arranging Data into a Structured Whole

Computer graphics support mutual inspiration between art and other disciplines and enhance one another. Visual quality is of utmost significance, as people visually arrange and present knowledge by shifting from digits to pixels. Skills gained by the students become then useful in specialized areas, for example for creating artwork for financial analysis with the use of information visualization technique, applying a 3D city metaphor for software production visualization, or making visual tools for editing and browsing semantic web resources. To be workable, every website must be visual, simple, and effective, but also delightful to look at. Using visual thinking in learning scientific subject seems rare. Students learn to apply the visual sense to the subject matter under study; become able to draw upon more information they collected, and recall details of the subject. Many want a visual explanation for certain programming concepts to be able to understand it better.

By applying options for the integrative learning environment such as collaborative, interdisciplinary learning and teaching with the use of web based 2-D, 3-D, motion, gaming, and sound-supported visuals, students can visualize how things are working, simulate the process, and convey the meaning of a selected scientific concept. By drawing and writing everyone can transform what one just explored both into iconic (visual) and semantic (verbal) codes. The intellectual task of choosing images and words relevant to the theme just examined in another class results in creating something useful or beautiful. Visual style of presentation may reduce the intrinsic cognitive load of the users in structuring information, by somewhat shifting the explanatory task from abstract to meaningful parts, which may be easier to understand and remember. In terms of active involvement, students draw sketches in order to capture the essence of the selected process, and control composition of the project as well. It may be helpful in mastering the arts-related skills and putting them in service of an active, inventive, and personal way of creating information visualizations, rather than sticking to a purely technical approach.

RESEARCH STUDY RESULTS

In the educational setting, a model of visual approach to learning was created and the effectiveness of this approach to teaching was tested in "Visual Learning" classes. Students designed projects visually summarizing the material learned in other classes they were taking simultaneously and considered most difficult. The model was aimed to support students' success in other subject areas. Production of the final projects, which visualized ideas and data in a graphical form, was preceded by instruction in visual thinking. This model of visual learning was designed as a means for analyzing the phenomenological world of the individual without sacrificing the power of analytical thinking.

Effects of instruction with the art–science–computer graphics connection were examined in the quantitative (Ursyn, 1997) and qualitative (Ursyn, 1994) research studies. Research studies in the experimental computer art graphics classes examined if students' achievement in geology could be improved by creating art and how quality of students' artwork may be influenced by their scientific experiences. Students explored geological concepts and processes through creating computer art graphics. The results of their active investigations of physical and natural phenomena

Figure 4. Average scores on geology content tests and exams gained by the experimental and control group

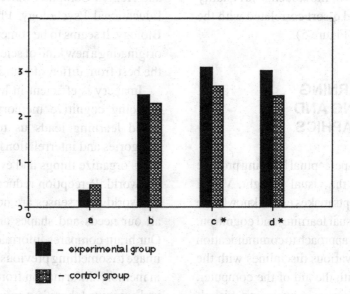

Vertical axis: geology content grades
Horizontal axis: geology content examinations:
a – pretest, b – posttest, c – lab grade, d – course grade
* Experimental and control difference tested as significant
with p<0.5 for students who took the pretest

served as an inspiration for creating computer art graphics assignments. Analyses of variance and covariance showed significant difference between the mean score on physical geology course taken concurrently by the students completing the science-related art assignments and those from the control group (Figure 4).

In a qualitative study the questionnaire answers revealed that the creation of geology-related art provided the students with confidence about their artistic abilities and increased students' understanding of scientific concepts. The results of this study indicated that building representations of scientific concepts through computer art graphics improved students' achievement in science and enhanced the students' artistic production. As can be seen in Figure 5, drawings that gained the highest ratings from the part of the art jurors were accomplished in assignments #9 and #11. Students evaluated best the assignment #6.

Figure 5. The relationship between means on the evaluation of drawings and the order of the assignments accomplished. Vertical axis: means on the evaluations of drawings from assignments 1–11.

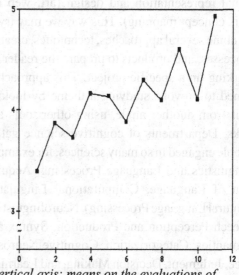

Vertical axis: means on the evaluations of
drawings from assignments 1–11
Horizontal axis: the order of assignments

Jurors' evaluations of the students' art quality in the form of a forced q-sort correlated with the order of art creation (Figure 5).

COGNITIVE LEARNING WITH COMPUTING AND COMPUTER GRAPHICS

Human cognition and perceptual learning provide strong foundation to the visual thought. Visual presentation of concepts makes easier knowledge comprehension by visual learning and cognition. Developing the visual approach to communication media lets us merge various disciplines with the ways people learn with the aid of the computer. We use cognitive processes in retrieving, visualizing, and representing our knowledge through metaphors; we put this knowledge in service of the journalistic tasks for gathering, processing, evaluating, judging, organizing, and publishing information. Apart from this, we concentrate on connecting visual and verbal expression for communication with the use of electronic media and the Web: the developments in data organization techniques (searching on the Internet, cognitive and semantic structuring of information), and for creation of electronic media languages of visual representation and design (art, web design, concept mapping). This way we may try to combine several approaches, techniques, creative processes, and products to prepare the reader for working on a specific project. This approach is aimed to provoke studying a theme by looking at it from another angle, using other tools and links. Departments of cognitive science gather people engaged in so many sciences, for example: Linguistics and Language Processing, Acquisition of Language, Computational Linguistics (Natural Language Processing), Neurolinguistics, Speech Perception and Production, Syntax and Semantics, Categorization, Cognitive Neuroscience, Judgment, Decision Making, and Learning, Neural Models of Cognition, Visual Perception

and Action, Computer Science, Psychology and Educational Psychology, Philosophy, and even Biology. It seems to be somewhat eclectic way of originating a new kind of science through drawing the best from different sources.

Imagery is efficient in learning the data and reducing cognitive memory load. Perception-based learning leads us to the formation of categories and interrelationships among them. It helps organize things and events and understand the world. Perception reduces uncertainty about the world. Our senses are not adequate to fulfill all our needs and shapes are often ambiguous. Our brain compares information contained in an image to something previously learned and stored in memory. Information from the past is grouped and organized there in a cognitive structure. This allows for our perception, which means that we may recognize images and decipher them on a basis of our memory. With perceptual learning we can compare new and old information, categorize our discoveries, look for interrelationships, and thus find a structure and meaning. The visual and cross-disciplinary nature of instructional technologies causes a need for new taxonomies. Levin and Bruce (2001) introduce four forms of media for learning:

- Media for inquiry, such as web-based portals, websites, workbenches, and databases for searching and analyzing retrieved datasets,
- Media for communication, such as Blackboard, drop boxes, etc.,
- Media for construction of knowledge, such as Wikis and Blogs, and
- Media for learning through expression, such as graphic interfaces, painting and drawing software.

Art education is advised because basic skills in arts help to develop the higher mental processing capabilities. Students discover the power of visual forms in making artistic decisions and find individual meaning in the art works. They improve their understanding of visual messages, take imaginative approaches in exploring scientific problems, and use their spatial abilities to recognize configurations and mathematically described relationships, for example physical interpretations of the formulas they learn. However, students choosing science as a career-leading discipline can be reticent about art. Science students able to visualize and think creatively develop skills necessary for innovation and problem solving. These changing circumstances create a need for reforming educational programs at all levels, including programming, to boost digital creativity. An evolving teaching method applies the theory and practice of art to computing and problem solving and encourages students to express equations as pictures or stories. Aesthetic computing is a curricula-blending approach that applies the theory and practice of art to computing and problem solving (Shreve, 2010).

Free and easy programming applications are available for children to generate interest and serve as a learning support, student skills enhancer, and student interest builder. Instructional technology and art education programs in colleges are also changing, stressing the importance of the usability in visualizing a user-friendly instructional design process, as well as including aesthetic and artistic elements into interactive, technology-based instruction.

Books, programs, and initiatives have been developed to support learning, for example:

Processing (http://processing.org/) educational software with instruction in programming through manipulation of data provided beyond code writing;

Alice (2012, http://www.alice.org/) that teaches students computer programming in a 3D object oriented environment, creating an animation for telling a story, playing an interactive game, or a video to share on the web;

Paul Fishwick's (2005; 2007) tutorials and workshops on aesthetic computing;

Craft Technology Group at CU Boulder, CO (2012, http://l3d.cs.colorado.edu/~ctg/Craft_Tech.html);

Moovl (2012, http://archive.futurelab.org.uk/projects/moovl; http://moovl.softpedia.com/ – an interactive freeware software developed at the educational organization Futurelab, which allows children to create animated images that move according to the dynamics of a simple set of physics rules);

Sodaplay (2012, sodaplay.com/creators/soda/items/moovl) a creative community;

Google for Educators Community projects, such as SketchUp for Educators, SketchUp for my Class (http://www.sketchup.com/Pro) or Blender (http://www.blender.org/) 3D modeling programs with a free version for download) and many other programs;

Scratch (2012, http://scratch.mit.edu/) a programming language for creating interactive stories, games, music, and art and share them online, and

Many computing and programming courses, for example, at Stanford University.

Web-based applications enable students to start comfortably at varying degrees of technological competence. Instructional Technology and Art Education programs in colleges are also changing, stressing the importance of the usability and efficiency in visualizing a user-friendly instructional design process, as well as including aesthetic and artistic elements into interactive, technology-based instruction. ThinkQuest (2012) is an annual international website competition for students 9-19 years old. According to the ThinkQuest International Competition site, it challenges students to solve a real-world problem by applying their critical thinking, communication, and technology skills. Participants may enroll in the following competition events: ThinkQuest Projects, Digital Media, and Application Development.

The ThinkQuest Library (2012), which features over 8000 websites, provides innovative learning resources for students. ERA (2012) Education Research Abstracts Online is a comprehensive database for teachers.

MULTIMEDIA LEARNING IN THE SOCIAL NETWORKING AND THE COLLABORATIVE VIRTUAL ENVIRONMENTS

In multimedia learning, information is presented to learners in two or more formats, such as in words and in pictures. Humans can integrate information from different sensory modalities into one meaningful experience – such as when they associate the sound of thunder with the visual image of lightning in the sky. They can also integrate information from verbal and non-verbal information into a mental model – such as when they watch lightning in the sky and listen to an explanation of the event. Multimedia learners can integrate words and pictures more easily when the words are presented in an auditory rather than visual way. This split-attention effect is consistent with a dual-processing model of working memory consisting of separate visual and auditory channels. Working memory includes an auditory working memory and a visual working memory (Mayer & Moreno 1998).

Therefore, a teacher or an instructional designer is faced with the need to choose between several combinations of modes and modalities to promote meaningful learning (Moreno, 2006). Our cognitive theory of multimedia learning draws on a dual-processing theory of working memory, cognitive load theory, and constructivist learning theory. It is based on several premises: (a) working memory includes independent auditory and visual working memories (analogous to the Baddeley's (1986) phonological loop and visuo-spatial sketch pad); (b) each working memory store has a limited capacity, consistent with Sweller's cognitive load theory (Sweller, 1988, 1994, 2006; Chandler & Sweller, 1992, 1996); (c) humans have separate systems for representing verbal and non-verbal information, consistent with Paivio's (1986) dual-code theory; (d) the meaningful learning occurs when a learner selects relevant information in each store, organizes the information in each store into a coherent representation, retains information and makes connections between corresponding representations in each store (Moreno & Mayer, 1999), analogically to the generative theory of multimedia learning; connections can be made only if corresponding pictorial and verbal information, according to Paivio's dual-coding theory, is in working memory at the same time. Mayer and Moreno's study on split-attention (1998) showed that, with the retention of visual and spatial material functioning in separate systems, recall is better after imagery than after verbal instructions, best after interactive imagery instructions. Students who learn with concurrent narration and animations outperform those who learn with concurrent on-screen text and animations. Thus, students might be missing part of the visual information while they are reading the on-screen text (or vice versa).

The content of the curriculum is supposed to match the evolving learning styles. The Index of Learning Styles (Felder & Spurlin, 2005) is designed to assess learners' preferences according to the Felder and Soloman (1993) learning model. According to the Felder and Soloman's Index of Learning Styles includes the four dimensions of learning preferences.

- The Sensing/Intuitive dimension deals with the way information is perceived: the sensing learners are concrete thinkers, practical, oriented toward facts and procedures arriving through their senses; intuitive learners are abstract thinkers, conceptual, innovative, oriented toward theories and underlying meanings, and favor information that arises internally through memory, refection, and imagination.

- The Visual/Verbal dimension deals with the way information is presented: the visual learners prefer visual representations, pictures, diagrams, graphs, flow charts, experiments and demonstrations, while verbal learners prefer written or spoken explanations and formulas.
- The Active/Reflective dimension deals with the way information is processed: the active learners learn by trying things out, working in a group, and discussing; reflective learners learn by thinking things through and working alone.
- The Sequential/Global (S-G) dimension deals with understanding: the sequential learners are linear and orderly, learn in small incremental steps, while global learners prefer holistic thinking process, learn in large leaps (Kanninen, 2009).

Instruction in the form of lectures and step-by-step exercises is less needed when students can learn online, use their phones to access the network, import data and graphics on a screen, use a built-in camera, load information into the computer or phone memory and then scroll through albums and communicate easily with instructors and peers. Students gather and organize information from sources and tools that improve communication: news stories, websites, blogs and weblogs – personal chronological logs of thoughts published on a web page, podcasts (broadcasting + iPod), and services with automatic downloading of the Web content to individual users. Electronic media support retrieving, visualizing, and representing knowledge through computer science and computer art graphics. The concept of the knowledge-based education may be thus seen less as a list of the related disciplines and skills to be taught and more as the integrative way of infusing computer graphics with knowledge in the process of making projects.

E-Learning

E-learning means electronically supported transfer of skills and knowledge that could involve networked learning, virtual education, and any other use of the information and communication systems. With the concepts of connections at the core of this approach, the open and networked research emerged, with conferences (e.g., 8th International Networked Learning Conference in 2012), journals (for example, E-Learning and Digital Media), and initiatives such as A Massive Open Online Course (MOOC), a course and a network about the emergent practices and the theory of Connectivism, proposed by George Siemens in 2008 (Mackness, Mak, & Williams, 2010). In 2010, E-Learning and Digital Media published a special issue on globally networked learning titled Globally networked learning environments: 'Re-shaping the intersections of globalization and e-learning in higher education,' and then The Institute for Globally Networked Learning in the Humanities was launched in 2011. The Wikiversity has launched a project space to network, peer assist, and peer assess people seeking a Doctor of Philosophy degree through the Open and Networked PhDs (http://en.wikiversity.org/wiki/PhD). Livemocha (2012) is one example of open technology applied to language learning in an open community. People provide information about their native language and the language they like to master along with their interests, hobbies, and preferred topics for discussions. They are motivated accordingly to study both ways through interesting conversations.

Many online learning companies, such as lynda.com, support learning software, design, and business skills. Numerous universities offer free online courses and online degree programs; some courses with a certificate, and some giving credits;

for example, MIT, Massachusetts Institute of Technology (http://ocw.mit.edu/index.htm); Stanford's Free Online Courses (http://www.stanford.edu/online/courses/); Open Yale courses (http://oyc.yale.edu/); Harvard Open Courses (http://www.extension.harvard.edu/open-learning-initiative). Also societies and associations, such as ACM, Association for Computing Machinery, offer professional membership benefits including free courses, journals, and digital libraries. Several large organizations, for example, NREL – National Renewable Energy Laboratory in Golden, Colorado provide educational materials concerning sustainable landscape and architecture. Similar trends can be also noted in architecture, involving creation of 3D virtual spaces that serve the educational purpose.

Intelligent Tutoring Systems provide the learners with customized instruction with feedback; they make learning informal. Application of artificial intelligence technologies in education allows adapting tutoring systems to the learners, the web, and the computing methods serving the systems (Nkambou, Mizoguchi, & Bourdeau, 2010). The authors list the domain model (called also expert knowledge, with concepts, rules, and strategies for problem solving), the student model (that gathers data about the learners, builds their representations, and performs diagnosis), and the tutoring model that decides about strategies and actions.

Online learning gives one a chance to acquire knowledge along with one's interests, build motivation, and improve future prospects according to the chosen studies (Figure 6, "Online Learning").

So many tall and spiky buildings expose their tiny windows with single human beings visible inside. They might as well collapse on one side, through nature, technology, and wood. Actually, from here, from intimacy of your room there is a path to happiness.

Figure 6. Anna Ursyn, Online Learning (© 2012, A. Ursyn. Used with permission)

Blended Learning

Blended learning methodology mixes learning environments by combining online learning and mobile learning with the classroom learning. Blended learning is often described as integrative learning, hybrid, multi-method, and mixed-mode learning. With this approach, a three-session-a-week format may be reduced to once per week classroom facilitation face-to-face contact time. Synchronous learning gathers groups of people learning the same things at the same time, and at the same place. Asynchronous (self-paced) learning is a student-centered approach, which emphasizes peer-to-peer interactions and self-study without the constraints of time and place. Computer mediated instruction goes with the use of cellular or smart phones, virtual education and collaboration, satellite television channels, videoconferencing, and other emerging electronic media.

Educational research is focused on the effective methods of instructional training, course designer competencies, audience analysis, and resources. Much attention is given to issues such as objectives and assessment in art education. Another approach, called Situated Learning is a model of learning in a community of practice involving participation in the sociocultural practices of a community, which allows an individual to learn by socialization, visualization, and imitation (Lave & Wenger, 1991). This approach was based on a Situated Cognition assumption that considers knowing being inseparable from doing in social, cultural, and physical contexts (Bredo, 1994) and being fundamentally a social process, not solely in the learner's head.

Distributed Learning

An instructional model called distributed learning (Cornell University Library, 2012) involves using various information technologies to help students learn. This model uses technologies such as video or audio conferencing, satellite broadcasting, and Web-based multimedia formats to provide course enhancement, hybrid delivery combining web-based multimedia lecture with traditional classroom instruction, and virtual classrooms. This computer-mediated instruction takes place when a student is primarily at a distance from the teacher, whether he/she is at home; or connected to teachers from another learning facility (British Columbia Distributed Learning, 2012).

Supporters of the distributed learning, in contrast to the massed learning, recommend reviews of a material separated by a long period of time, as it yields more learning than reviews separated by a shorter period of time (Litman & Davachi, 2008); this is called the spacing effect. In psychology, the spacing effect is the phenomenon first identified in 1885 by Hermann Ebbinghaus (1885/2012).

According to the spacing effect theory, humans and animals remember or learn items in a list better when they study them a few times over a long period of time, as 'spaced presentation' rather than repeatedly in a short period, as 'massed presentation.' Long-term memory is better enhanced when there is more time between introduction and review of material. The U.S. Army Distributed Learning System (DLS) acquires, deploys, and maintains a worldwide learning infrastructure that innovatively combines hardware, software and telecommunications resources with training facilities and course content to deliver a cohesive, Web-based solution (U.S. Army >>Program Executive Office Enterprise Information Systems, PEO EIS, 2012).

VIRTUAL EDUCATION

Learners use the 3D virtual environments for learning. Virtual learning environment allows learning through the Internet where an instructor and a learner are separated by time and space. Cyber schools at the K-12 level and virtual universities at the college level have been established, virtual programs and courses of study formatted in a synchronous or asynchronous learning context, and instruction delivered through the course management applications, multimedia and Internet resources, as well as videoconferencing. Virtual learning has been originally based mostly on text documents using HTML, PowerPoint, or PDF documents. Later on, simulation and visualization became parts of instruction. In a wide spectrum between the face-to-face learning straight from the teacher and the networked learning, many modes developed for virtual education comprise:

- Virtual classroom where live teacher instruction is followed by feedback online with real-time voice interaction, whiteboard sharing, and breakout sessions for oral and written communication.

- Virtual operating room: a space to learn procedures before acting in the real-life operating room.
- Hypertext courses with a structured course material for a distance education program. All material can be viewed with a browser. Hyperlinks connect text, multimedia parts, and exercises.
- Video-based courses: face-to-face courses with a lecturer using PowerPoint slides and online examples. Video-streaming technologies with the use of freeware or plug-ins.
- Audio-based courses have only the sound track of the lecturer provided.
- Animated courses enriching text-oriented or audio-based course material, using Macromedia Flash.
- Web-supported textbook courses are based on specific textbooks. Students read and reflect on the chapters. Review questions, topics for discussion, exercises, case studies, etc. are given chapter-wise on a website and discussed with the lecturer during class meetings or in a chat room.
- Peer-to-peer courses taught on-demand without a prepared curriculum.
- Social Networking: Web technologies in virtual classrooms promote social interaction, student-centered instruction, and a problem-solving curriculum. Teachers act as guides and resources; students collaborate, discuss, review ideas, and present solutions (http://en.wikipedia.org/wiki/Virtual_education).
- Blackboard Inc. produces Internet-based educational software for learning management systems, higher education, K-12, as well as mobile learning, communication, and commerce software. Blackboard's seven platforms are: Learn (online course delivery, content management, and student assessment results record), Transact (transaction processing of university ID cards and e-commerce systems), Engage (integrated website communication platform), Connect (sending out time-sensitive mass phone, text and e-mail notifications and campus emergencies), Mobile (access to teaching and learning content and mobile applications), Collaborate (web-based video and audio conferencing for distance learning and virtual classroom setting), and Analytics (data warehousing and analysis as business intelligence tool using data from colleges' student information, human resources and financial information systems).

Visualizing Knowledge with Avatars and Second Life

Avatars may support communication between an instructor and those students who experience inhibitions of different kinds and for many reasons, which restrain their expression and slow the learning process. For example, some students cannot freely involve in a social networking setting because of the cultural, social, or religious restrains, while others are enormously self-conscious and unable to relax in the learning environment. Many times the specialists in the developmental psychology communicate with a child through an avatar, a puppet, or allow using a mask as a protecting disguise, and thus make the child share their fears and problems. A troubled child or autistic person would easier share problems and reveal secrets A troubled child would tell more through a puppet or an avatar, while the same person would often clam up and stop talking when placed in face-to-face circumstances. Avatars can fulfill these needs in online environment; one may prefer to post online one's personal image or choose to communicate through an avatar.

Online instruction with the use of Skype, game technology, and virtual reality accessories may fill some grey areas between the face-to-face and the online instruction. Courses can be adopted anywhere at a global level, for example at universities having an international profile. With an access to virtual techniques students of an online class participate in classroom discussions and feel like immersed in the face-to-face environment when they can interactively work with others. Some feel better when their identity is not disclosed to others because of the age, dress, physical appearance, disabilities, race, religious, and gender reasons. They can present themselves as avatars, puppets, masked individuals, or even selected objects. Those who feel good about their aptitudes for socializing and self-expression can scan themselves to translate their own image into an avatar, so other class participants would have an illusion of direct contact. Participants feel free to take part in discussions as they know that nobody can evaluate their input depending on personal factors: whether it was said by a person of another gender, race, religion, or coming from a not-so-prestigious college.

Bredl, Groß, Hünniger, & Fleischer (2012) examine how virtual worlds support immersive knowledge communication and collaboration. They hypothesize that the phenomena of immersion and community building could increase the motivation and the learning capacities of avatar-based co-workers and learners. According to the authors, Internet users gain the professional and personal presence within avatar-based virtual worlds or multi user environments due to the new architectures, interconnected spaces, and open standards. Social presence and immersion of knowledge workers in virtual worlds confirms the social potential of virtual worlds in supporting knowledge-based processes. The perception of the presence of one's own avatar within a virtual environment for learning and teaching, as well as the perception of the presence of others contribute to a higher degree of immersion. Working and interacting with an avatar within the same space increases the feeling of reality rather than virtuality. Since they are large, scalable, flexible, informal and non-structured, virtual worlds, which involve avatar users interacting with the

customized avatars, support immersive knowledge communication. As stated by the authors, they teach, counsel, prepare, support and even heal. For example, the U. S. Army operates a virtual island within the Second Life, giving help to soldiers' families and soldiers suffering from post-traumatic stress disorder (United States Army, 2011). Many universities offer courses in Second Life, as well as art galleries and exhibitions. Avatars in virtual networks support other social software technologies such as weblogs and micro-blogs, content and document management systems, wikis, and social networks. Application of knowledge can be attained with the use of adventure games played at the Second Life, disaster simulation and training, and also the counseling in virtual world by allowing the user to create a virtual self.

Mobile Learning from the Cell Phone Apps

Internet access and the presence of portable devices have broadened the spectrum of available applications that support the learning process, often indirectly and in a playful way. A mobile wearable see-through display developed by the Mobile Augmented Reality System (MARS) interacts with training/learning software. The authors work on a MARS software architecture that is reusable, interoperable, and adaptive to individual Augmented Reality. As described by the developers (Doswell, 2006), "learners may interact with their natural environment while MARS digitally annotates real-world objects with digital content. This digital content may combine multi-modal animation, graphics, text, and video as well as voice."

The Math Munch team: Justin Lanier, Paul Salomon, and Anna Weltman have developed A Weekly Digest of the Mathematical Internet at http://mathmunch.wordpress.com/math-art-tools/ where they post games, visualizations (for example, visualization of number pi (π) at http://two-n. com/pi/), and other mathematical creations, which help learn and like mathematics. A mathematician John Miller has created the Geom-E-Tree application on an iPhone and iPad offering many possible manipulations and the wide variety of shapes that could be created with the use of fingers on a touch screen (iPad News, 2011). Computer games became an extension of instruction. Open software has been designed to provide an option to tweak the code. Communication with others in gaming, Internet-based forums, supporting groups, and social networks make new methods of information exchange possible.

Digital storytelling uses a variety of media formats: text, image, sound, animated graphics, and time-based and interactive projects (such as websites). They all serve as an educational tool providing knowledge of oral tradition in storytelling in different cultures. Computer graphics are essential for developing a container: how the story is being delivered. Every discipline or medium – archeology, history, geology, online environment, a game, to name just a few – can be seen, or even should be seen as a set of stories, moreover, visual stories. The way we unfold and deliver the story depends on the learner's needs and the environment. Thus, we should analyze cultural implications of our products from the perspective of the user, not only in the artist's frame of reference. Artistic quality of a website is often affected by unintended presence of a banner or a video with an advertisement, therefore a webpage developer should not only design a product but also make it fit for the environment as perceived by the user. One needs also to remember that every color coexists with others. The developer should be therefore trained interdisciplinary, ready for not only producing pretty pictures but also making a cross-cultural impact, since the product delivery is often tested under particular technical or cultural conditions.

As stated by the professor of Electrical Engineering at the Colorado University, Boulder, Michael Eisenberg, motivating ideas behind computationally enhanced crafts include end-user programming, accessibility/affordability/robustness, computational simplicity, generic, easy to understand geometry, program, and incorporation into their own creative work. According to Manochehri, Gromik, & Liang (2012), Arabic female students (from the Coll. of Business and Economic and the English Foundation program, Qatar U.) were provided with an iPod Nano (with a list of resources and a training session) as a learning tool. The students from the two programs were compared; the use of iPod Nano was beneficial, with no statistical differences between groups. An ambient program reader called ButtonSchemer enables the students to input program code directly from a computer screen or from specially bar-coded surfaces in an informal, creative way (Elumeze & Eisenberg, 2008). Buechley, Eisenberg, Catchen, & Crockett (2008) describe the fabric and electronic crafts – electronic/computational textiles or e-textiles. Novel materials such as conductive fibers and embedded computing platforms allow the students designing wearables and other textile artifacts from a kit containing a microcontroller, sensors, and activators to be sewn to cloth substrates with conductive thread, and build e-textiles. Three-dimensional paper sculptures built from geometric solids can be designed with the use of software (Eisenberg et al., 2005). HyperGami is a programmable design environment, written in Scheme, a dialect of the LISP programming language. JavaGami, designed in response to the feedback received from kids and teachers, is a new version of HyperGami, implemented in Java. According to the authors, an interest in the way that children learn to think spatially arose from watching children engage in spatial operations – thinking about three-dimensional shapes, imagining the result of operations performed upon shapes, and visualizing the two-dimensional patterns that fold into three-dimensional shapes, to name just a few.

Many students choosing art as a career leading discipline express their fear of mathematical and scientific thinking. This barrier can be broken when children are early encouraged to experiment with technologies on any level they are comfortable with. A student who is not afraid of exploring and expanding their knowledge about still growing technology will very soon become an interested, motivated individual who involves peers into cooperation and does not feel lonely any longer. In a historical perspective, when Craig Hickman, the creator of the KidPix was developing this software, he tested it first on his 3 year old son and then on his 8 month old infant. If children are encouraged to make explorations about current technologies, they will develop curiosity, do not develop inhibitions toward science, and enjoy an active production of technical solutions. Many times students find answers to their questions on the Internet from other kids, even if their teacher is not technologically savvy. In such cases, the teacher makes sure that the school has suitable filters and guides students in seeking answers through the Internet.

Machine Learning

The science of machine learning enables computers (e.g., as smart robots) to act: possess perception and apply control without being explicitly programmed (Ng, 2013). People use this pervasive technique without knowing it, for example when making use of speech recognition, searching web, or utilizing domestic appliances. Many think machine learning techniques will advance human level artificial intelligence, to match or exceed human intelligence, and maybe even consciousness, sentience, wisdom, and self-awareness of machines. Machine learning techniques allow developing algorithms that have computers react to empirical data coming from sensors or databases and relations between observed variables. Automatic learning allows recognizing complex

patterns and making intelligent decisions based on data; however, because of the size of the data, the learner must generalize from the given examples to produce a new case. Learning of the language structure can be done with automatic learning methods; it may be achieved by applying knowledge-based models, random selection procedures, or a data-driven model selection procedure based on genetic search (Duh & Kirchhoff, 2004). Automatic learning has been studied in humans with the use of the behavioral measurements, neurophysiological, and brain imaging methods with the use of the functional magnetic resonance (fMRI) techniques. Visual performance and learning in an automatic way has been tested for visual learning with the decoded fMRI neurofeedback, which was disclosing earlier brain activity patterns related to the actually learned theme. Repetitions of these activation patterns caused a long-lasting improvement in visual performance and learning. The authors conclude that the brain has the flexibility to adapt certain features from the environment, and the early visual areas are sufficiently plastic to cause improvement in visual performance and learning in an automatic way, without subjects' awareness of what was to be learned (Woollacott, 2011). Cognitive architecture is made as a design plan for an intelligent agent. Shakshuki & Matin (2010) presented architecture of an intelligent learning agent that is able to utilize machine-learning techniques to monitor the user's actions. Intelligent agents are endowed with increasingly sophisticated cognitive abilities. Researchers build multi-agent systems from intelligent agents. They examine relations between behavior of intelligent agents and the emergent social structures, in terms of social entrepreneurship, sociological theories, and computer science (Goldspink, 2009). Social emergence has emerged as an approach to studying societies as complex dynamical systems at the levels of individuals, interactions, group, and also intelligent agents (Sawyer, 2005).

LEARNING ON SECOND LIFE VS. REAL LIFE CLASSROOM ENVIRONMENT

A popular cartoon by Peter Steiner published in 1993 by the New Yorker showed two dogs in front of a computer, one of them saying, "On the Internet nobody knows you're a dog". You may see this image at http://en.wikipedia.org/wiki/On_the_Internet,_nobody_knows_you're_a_dog. This statement does not seem accurate any more with photos, videos, decrypting techniques (decoding and deciphering encrypted text), and archival information systems. Quite often companies hire people building their search and selection on social networking based platforms, such as LinkedIn.

Second Life (www.secondlife.com) created a culture for disguising oneself through a presence of a self-selected avatar and a fancy name. In virtual world one can become anyone, do anything, and be anywhere with friends of one's choosing. Theoretically, the cell phone technology allows us to appear, participate in social functions and on social venues, research, grasp information, chat, play, teach and learn, exchange all sort of data, goods, and feelings without disclosing our true identity. At the same time the caption from the Peter Steiner's cartoon cannot be justified, as we can hardly hide from security, advertisers, some geeks, and the IT departments. The 2009 Jason Spingam-Koff's social and cultural documentary movie "Life 2.0" discussed the gap between dreams and reality as they collide.

Pessoa, Gomes, Nogueira, & Cavalcande de Almeida (2011) examine a format for e-learning offered on the Second Life. They analyze the Second Life's educational environment in terms of the Flow experience described in 1990 by the Hungarian/American Psychology professor Mihaly Csikszentmihalyi (1990, 1998), who defines flow as a positive cognitive state that is a consequence of the individual's sense of full control of his own actions). It is "the feeling when things were going well as an utmost automatic, effort-less, yet highly focused state of consciousness" (Csikszentmihalyi, 1997, p. 110). The flow is an optimal state of great involvement in activity for its own sake, done with the intrinsic motivation (curiosity about and interest in the task itself, which exists in a person and is rewarded by enjoyment and satisfaction causing that one is fully immersed in what one is doing). Pessoa Forte et al. (2011) analyzed relations between the Flow experiences and the Second Life's educational environment, and they found flow in Second Life's e-learning environment. The most significant constructs detected in an online learning environment that has led to this hypothesis are interactive speed, exploratory behavior, and telepresence. Web has previously offered a unidirectional concept, the download of websites and contents that can be accessed by their visitors. When weblogs became available, Internet users started to play a more active role by publishing content, which was no longer the privilege of web designers, programmers and other skilled professionals. The Web has now a bidirectional perspective because the upload became as important as the download.

According to Leslie Jarmon (2010), online virtual world platforms such as Second Life have generated a public-private space that is an effective personal learning environment across many sectors. The author examines virtual learning environments and embodiment through the lens of interactions of avatars with other avatars, virtual objects, landscapes, sounds, and spatial constructs. In this virtual social learning environment participants, comprising high school girls, professional retirees, toxicology and design undergraduates, interdisciplinary graduate students, educators, researchers from K-12, and university professors, experienced a sense of embodied co-presence and connection with others across geo-physical distances. For example, homework projects included building by the participants' avatars a mockup of a room in the Mars Living Station module in a 'sandbox' area in Second Life. Some team members worked at home from their laptops, others in computer lab, public library, or at coffeehouse. They asked through instant messages two experts from NASA's CoLab community in Second Life to review their structure-in-progress, give feedback, and the two experts teleported over to the team's sandbox (one is on a computer in Houston, the other in Germany). The team was then ready to give a 'virtual tour' of their module to their classmates. The author examines embodiment as part of a sociotechnical system and explores the mechanics of the online virtual platform as a digital-sensory extension of experience that, as is the case with many tools, becomes an extension of our "body." The author calls this event the emergence of homo virtualis.

Computer-based systems that support 3D visualization, simulation, navigation, and interaction with a 3D virtual environment have given users various virtual reality applications such as virtual prototyping, training simulators, and digital museums (Asai & Takase, 2011). Unlike VR, augmented reality superimposes virtual objects on a real scene and adds scene-linked information, thus making users' experiences more meaningful and increasing their understanding of the subject. According to the authors, a tangible tabletop environment produced by augmented reality improved the environment in which learners observed three-dimensional molecular structures. Learners with a tangible AR environment were able to complete the task of identifying molecular structures more quickly and accurately than those with a typical desktop-PC environment using a Web browser.

Illinois Online network (ion, 2012) provided an analysis of the advantages and weaknesses of online versus in-class instruction:

- Online advantages of asynchronous online learning come from the fact that they can occur anywhere, and that all, even physically challenged students may participate from anywhere in the world; learning may go any time 24 hours a day 7 days a week at any pace, with continuous access to lectures, course materials, and class discussions; there is synergy resulting from dynamic interaction between the instructor and students and between students themselves; there is the asynchronous discussion structure providing a high quality dialogue; instruction is student centered, allowing choosing materials most relevant to the individual student's needs; environment provides a high level of anonymity (regarding age, dress, physical appearance, disabilities, race, and gender) and dynamic interaction with students; access to resources and materials from anywhere in the world for research, extension, or deep analyses, with contribution of distinguished guest speakers; and creative teaching with collaboration of tutors and students with different learning styles.

- Weaknesses include equity and accessibility to technology is a significant issue in rural and lower socioeconomic neighborhoods. Internet is not universal and is not free. Computer literacy of students and facilitators: both students and facilitators must possess some computer knowledge, for example, they must be able to use a variety of search engines, navigate comfortably on the web, as well as be familiar with Newsgroups, FTP procedures and email. Limitations of technology: even the most sophisticated technology is not 100% reliable; breakdowns can occur, for example, the server which hosts the program could crash and cut all participants off from the class; a networked computer could go down; the Internet connection could fail, or the institution could slow down, or fail all together. Not committed administrators and faculty. Not all students are well organized, self-motivated, and possess a high degree of time management skills.

Evaluation of the level of integrating technology with creative instruction and learning may occur in several dimensions related to the materials and equipment provided, standards used, and the real use of technology in teaching, which is altogether a decisive factor why computer technology is essential in instruction.

CONCLUSION

Three approaches to integration of art and science presented in this chapter include (1) Visual presentation of scientific concepts, (2) Creating art by finding inspiration in a science-based topic, and (3) Learning visually for other courses taken concurrently by arranging data into a structured whole. Further text presents results of the author's research, analysis of cognitive learning with computing and computer graphics, multimedia learning in the social networking and the collaborative virtual environments, virtual education done online, through an avatar or on Second Life, mobile learning from cell phone apps, and machine learning.

REFERENCES

Alice. (2012). Retrieved October 6, 2012 from http://www.alice.org/

Army, U. S. (2012). *Program executive office enterprise information systems*. Retrieved October 23, 2012, from http://www.eis.army.mil/

Artino, A. R. (2008). Cognitive load theory and the role of learner experience: An abbreviated review for educational practitioners. *Association for the Advancement of Computing in Education Journal*, *16*(4), 425–439.

Asai, K., & Takase, N. (2011). Learning molecular structures in a tangible augmented reality environment. *International Journal of Virtual and Personal Learning Environments*, *2*(1), 1–18. doi:10.4018/jvple.2011010101.

Baddeley, A. D. (1986). *Working memory*. Oxford, UK: Oxford University Press.

Bai, X., White, D., & Sundaram, D. (2012). Contextual adaptive knowledge visualization environments. *Electronic Journal of Knowledge Management*, *10*(1), 1–14.

Beardon, C., & Malmbord, L. (2010). *Digital creativity: A reader* (Innovations in Art and Design). Routledge. ISBN-10: 0415579686

Bredl, K., Groß, A., Hünniger, J., & Fleischer, J. (2012). The avatar as a knowledge worker? How immersive 3D virtual environments may foster knowledge acquisition. *Electronic Journal of Knowledge Management*, *10*(1), 15–25.

Bredo, E. (1994). Reconstructing educational psychology: Situated cognition and Deweyian pragmatism. *Educational Psychologist*, *29*(1), 23–25. doi:10.1207/s15326985ep2901_3.

British Columbia Distributed Learning. (2012). Retrieved October 23, 2012, from http://www.bced.gov.bc.ca/dist_learning/

Buechley, L., Eisenberg, M., Catchen, J., & Crockett, A. (2008). The LilyPad arduino: Using computational textiles to investigate engagement, aesthetics, and diversity in computer science education. In *Proceedings of the SIGCHI Conference (CHI 2008)*, (pp. 423-432). ACM.

Chandler, P., & Sweller, J. (1992). The split attention effect as a factor in the design of instruction. *The British Journal of Educational Psychology*, *62*, 233–246. doi:10.1111/j.2044-8279.1992.tb01017.x.

Chandler, P., & Sweller, J. (1996). Cognitive load while learning to use a computer program. *Applied Cognitive Psychology, 10*, 151–170. doi:10.1002/(SICI)1099-0720(199604)10:2<151::AID-ACP380>3.0.CO;2-U.

Clark, R., Nguyen, F., & Sweller, J. (2006). *Efficiency in learning: Evidence-based guidelines to manage cognitive load.* San Francisco, CA: Pfeiffer. doi:10.1002/pfi.4930450920.

Cornell University Library. (2012). *Distributed learning tutorial.* Retrieved October 23, 2012, from http://www.library.cornell.edu/DL/tutorial/tut_2.htm

Csikszentmihalyi, M. (1990). *Flow: The psychology of optimal experience.* New York: Harper and Row.

Csikszentmihalyi, M. (1997). *Creativity: Flow and the psychology of discovery and invention.* Harper Perennial.

Csikszentmihalyi, M. (1998). *Finding flow: The psychology of engagement with everyday life.* Basic Books.

Doswell, J. T. (2006). Augmented learning: Context-aware mobile augmented reality architecture for learning. In *Proceedings of the Sixth IEEE International Conference on Advanced Learning Technologies*, (pp. 1182-1183). IEEE Computer Society. ISBN 0-7695-2632-2

Duh, K., & Kirchhoff, K. (2004). *Automatic learning of language model structure.* Retrieved July 15, 2012, from acl.ldc.upenn.edu/coling2004/MAIN/pdf/22-874.pdf

Ebbinghaus, H. (2012). *Über das gedächtnis: Untersuchungen zur experimentellen psychologie* (German Ed.). Ulan Press. (Original work published 1885).

Eisenberg, M., Eisenberg, A., Blauvelt, G., Hendrix, S., Buechley, L., & Elumeze, N. (2005). Mathematical crafts for children: Beyond scissors and glue. In *Proceedings of Art+Math=X Conference.* University of Colorado.

Elumeze, N., & Eisenberg, M. (2008). ButtonSchemer: Ambient program reader. In *Proceedings of the 10th International Conference on Human Computer Interaction with Mobile Devices and Services, MobileHCI '08*, (pp. 323-326). ISBN: 978-1-59593-952-4 doi:10.1145/1409240.1409279

ERA. (2012). *Education research abstracts online.* Retrieved October 6, 2012, from http://tandf.informaworld.com/smpp/home~db=all

Felder, R. M., & Soloman, B. (1993). *Learning styles and strategies.* Retrieved October 23, 2012, from http://www4.ncsu.edu/unity/lockers/users/f/felder/public/ILSdir/styles.htm

Felder, R. M., & Spurlin, J. (2005). Applications, reliability and validity of the index of learning styles. *Int. J. Engineering Education, 21*(1), 103–112.

Fishwick, P. (2005). *Introduction to the aesthetic computing method for teaching algebra in middle and high school.* Retrieved October 6, 2012, from http://www.cise.ufl.edu/~fishwick/acworkshop/aestheticcomputing.pdf

Fishwick, P. (2007). Aesthetic computing: A brief tutorial. In *Visual Languages for Interactive Computing: Definitions and Formalizations.* Retrieved April 29, 2012, from http://www.cise.ufl.edu/~fishwick/aescomputing/tutorial.pdf

Gerjets, P., Scheiter, K., & Catrambone, R. (2004). Designing instructional examples to reduce intrinsic cognitive load: Molar versus modular presentation of solution procedures. *Instructional Science, 32*(1-2), 33–58. doi:10.1023/B:TRUC.0000021809.10236.71.

Goldspink, C., & Kay, R. (2009). Agent cognitive capabilities and orders of social emergence. In Handbook of Research on Agent-Based Societies: Social and Cultural Interactions, (pp. 17-34). IGI Global. ISBN 1605662364

Google for Educators. (2010). Retrieved October 6, 2012, from http://www.google.com/edu/teachers/

Google in Education. (2012). Retrieved October 1, 2012, from http://www.google.com/educators/index.html

Google SketchUp for Educators. (2012). Retrieved October 1, 2012, from http://sitescontent.google.com/google-sketchup-for-educators/Home

Google Sketchup for My Class. (2012). Retrieved October 6, 2012, from http://sitescontent.google.com/google-sketchup-for-educators/Home/Google-Earth-for-My-Class

Hassard, J., & Dias, M. (2008). *The art of teaching science: Inquiry and innovation in middle school and high school* (2nd ed.). Routlege.

Huizinga, J. (1971). *Homo ludens: A study of the play-element in culture*. Beacon Press.

ION. (2012a). *Strengths of online learning*. Retrieved September 25, 2012, from http://www.ion.uillinois.edu/resources/tutorials/overview/strengths.asp

ION. (2012b). *Weaknesses of online learning*. Retrieved September 26, 2012, from http://www.ion.uillinois.edu/resources/tutorials/overview/weaknesses.asp

iPad News. (2011). *Geom-E-Tree is the perfect blend of math, art, and nature*. Retrieved September 23, 2012, from http://www.ipadnews.nl/tag/john-miller/

Jarmon, L. (2010). Homo virtualis: Virtual worlds, learning, and an ecology of embodied interaction. *International Journal of Virtual and Personal Learning Environments*, *1*(1), 38–56. doi:10.4018/jvple.2010091704.

Kanninen, E. (2009). *Learning styles and e-learning*. Retrieved October 1, 2012, from http://hlab.ee.tut.fi/video/bme/evicab/astore/delivera/wp4style.pdf

Lave, J., & Wenger, E. (1991). *Situated learning: Legitimate peripheral participation*. Cambridge University Press. doi:10.1017/CBO9780511815355.

Levin, J. A., & Bruce, B. C. (2001). *Technology as media: The learner centered perspective*. Retrieved May 15, 2012, from http://lrs.ed.uiuc.edu/jim-levin/levin-bruce-aera.html

Litman, L., & Davachi, L. (2008). Distributed learning enhances relational memory consolidation. *Learning & Memory (Cold Spring Harbor, N.Y.)*, *15*(9), 711–716. doi:10.1101/lm.1132008 PMID:18772260.

Livemocha. (2012). Retrieved September 21, 2012, from http://www.livemocha.com/

Mackness, J., Mak, S. F. J., & Williams, R. (2010). The ideals and reality of participating in a MOOC. In *Proceedings of the Seventh International Conference on Networked Learning*. Retrieved September 23, 2012, from http://www.lancs.ac.uk/fss/organisations/netlc/past/nlc2010/abstracts/Mackness.html

Maeda, J. (2004). *Creative code*. Thames & Hudson.

Manochehri, N.-N., Gromik, N., & Liang, S. (2012). The integration of portable technology to enhance lifelong learning skills. In *Proceedings of the 2012 SWDSI Conference*. Retrieved September 27, 2012, from http://www.swdsi.org/swdsi2012/proceedings_2012/papers/Papers/PA125.pdf

Mayer, R. E., & Moreno, R. (1998). A split-attention effect in multimedia learning: Evidence for dual processing systems in working memory. *Journal of Educational Psychology, 90*(2), 312. doi:10.1037/0022-0663.90.2.312.

Mayer, R. E., & Moreno, R. (2003). Nine ways to reduce cognitive load in multimedia learning. *Educational Psychologist, 38*(1), 43–52. doi:10.1207/S15326985EP3801_6.

Moovl. (2012). Retrieved October 6, 2012, from http://archive.futurelab.org.uk/projects/moovl

Moreno, R. (2006). Learning in high-tech and multimedia environments. *Current Directions in Psychological Science, 15*(2), 63–67. doi:10.1111/j.0963-7214.2006.00408.x.

Moreno, R. (2007). Optimizing learning from animations by minimizing cognitive load: Cognitive and affective consequences of signaling and segmentation methods. *Applied Cognitive Psychology, 21*, 1–17. doi:10.1002/acp.1348.

Moreno, R., & Mayer, R. E. (1999). Cognitive principles of multimedia learning: The role of modality and contiguity. *Journal of Educational Psychology, 91*, 358–368. doi:10.1037/0022-0663.91.2.358.

Ng, A. (2013). *Machine learning*. Retrieved April 15, 2013, from http://online.stanford.edu/course/machine-learning

Nkambou, R., Mizoguchi, R., & Bourdeau, J. (2010). *Advances in intelligent tutoring systems*. Springer. doi:10.1007/978-3-642-14363-2.

Paivio, A. (1970). On the functional significance of imagery. *Psychological Bulletin, 73*, 385–392. doi:10.1037/h0029180.

Paivio, A. (1971). *Imagery and verbal processes*. New York: Holt, Rinehart, and Winston.

Paivio, A. (1986/1990). *Mental representations: A dual coding approach*. Oxford University Press.

Paivio, A. (1991). Dual coding theory: Retrospect and current status. *Canadian Journal of Psychology, 45*(3), 255–287. doi:10.1037/h0084295.

Pessoa Forte, J. A., Gomes, D. A., Nogueira, C. A., & Cavalcande de Almeida, C. F. (2011). Educational services in second life: A study based on flow theory. *International Journal of Web-Based Learning and Teaching Technologies, 6*(2), 1-17. doi 10.4018/jwltt.2011040101. Retrieved October 1, 2012, from http://www.irma-international.org/viewtitle/60168/

Pink, D. H. (2006). *A whole new mind: Why right-brainers will rule the future*. Riverhead Trade.

Rheingold, H. (2002). *Smart mobs: The next social revolution*. Cambridge, MA: Basic Books.

Sadoski, M., & Paivio, A. (2013). *Imagery and text: A dual coding theory of reading and writing*. Routledge.

Sawyer, R. K. (2005). *Social emergence: Societies as complex systems*. Cambridge University Press. doi:10.1017/CBO9780511734892.

Shakshuki, E., & Matin, A. R. (2010). Intelligent learning a systemsgent for collaborative virtual workspace. *International Journal of Pervasive Computing and Communications, 6*(2), 131–162. doi:10.1108/17427371011066383.

Shreve, J. (2010). Drawing art into the equation: Aesthetic computing gives math a clarifying visual dimension. *Edutopia*. Retrieved October 6, 2012 from http://www.edutopia.org/drawing-art-equation

Sweller, J. (1988). Cognitive load during problem solving: Effects on learning. *Cognitive Science, 12*, 257–285. doi:10.1207/s15516709cog1202_4.

Sweller, J. (1994). Cognitive load theory, learning difficulty and instructional design. *Learning and Instruction, 4*, 295–312. doi:10.1016/0959-4752(94)90003-5.

Sweller, J. (2006). Visualization and Instructional design. In *Proceedings of the International Workshop on Dynamic Visualizations and Learning*, (pp. 1501-1510). Retrieved October 23, 2012, from http://www.scribd.com/doc/41651/Sweller-Visualisation-and-Instructional-Design

Thinkquest. (2012). Retrieved October 6, 2012, from http://www.thinkquest.org/en/

ThinkQuest Library. (2012). Retrieved from http://thinkquest.org/pls/html/think.library

Tufte, E. R. (1983). *The visual display of quantitative information*. Cheshire, CT: Graphics Press.

Tufte, E. R. (1990). *Envisioning information*. Cheshire, CT: Graphics Press.

United States Army. (2011). *DoD gives PTSD help 'second life' in virtual reality*. Retrieved October 30, 2012, from http://www.army.mil/article/50751/

Ursyn, A. (1994). *Student perception of computer art graphics integration of art & science*. Paper presented at the American Educational Research Association (AERA) Annual Meeting 1994. New York, NY.

Ursyn, A. (1997). Computer art graphics integration of art and science. *Learning and Instruction, the Journal of the European Association for Research on Learning and Instruction, 7*(1), 65-87.

Ursyn, A., Mills, L., Hobgood, B., & Scott, T. (1997). Combining art skills with programming in teaching computer art graphics. *Computer Graphics, 25*, 3.

Ursyn, A., & Scott, T. (2006). *Overlap between thinking in terms of art and computer science*. Paper presented at the Consortium for Computing Sciences in Colleges (CCSC). Durango, CO.

Ursyn, A., & Scott, T. (2007). Web with art and computer science. In *Proceedings of ACM SIGGRAPH Education Committee*. ACM. ISBN 978–1–59593–648–6

Wands, B. (2001). *Digital creativity: Techniques for digital media and the internet*. Wiley.

Wands, B. (2007). *Art of the digital age*. Thames & Hudson.

Woollacott, E. (2011, December 9). Team demos matrix-style automatic learning. *TG Daily*. Retrieved July 12, 2012, from http://www.tgdaily.com/general-sciences-features/60115-team-demos-matrix-style-automatic-learning

Section 3
Computing Solutions for Entertainment

Chapter 20
Ways to Entertain with the Use of Computing Technologies

ABSTRACT

Entertainment has gained some new values, and our participation in amusement has become more active along with the developments in social communication technologies. Examples that discuss the meaning of computational solutions for entertainment include intelligent environments, augmented and virtual reality, computer animation, games, live entertainment, and social media. This text examines the enhanced role of the participant's self-consciousness while engaging in social networking, and the role of the biologically active substances such as oxytocin and dopamine in shaping the ways of entertaining with the use of computing technologies.

INTRODUCTION

Generally speaking, entertainment used to be meant as a passive or an active amusement or enjoyment. When passive, a person or an audience may feel an emotion while attending a cinematic and theatric entertainment, a spectacle such as opera, movie on a CD, television show, watching sporting events, a video sharing website on a phone or a computer, a tabloid newspaper, or a moving display on a skyscraper. We would list as active entertainment our actions and activities such as playing video games, making photos and videos, sharing them online, dancing, playing and exercising sports, or traveling. We may also want to call an entertainment our recreational, usually unprofitable pastime activities or hobbies, such as reading, drawing, writing, music playing and listening to, seasonal celebrations, craft making, and occupations such as sports or fishing. That means entertainment may or may be not be related to a for-profit industry; it may or may not involve participation in a group in order to provide interest; it may or may not merge with recreation; it may be speculative, reflexive, or even creative or it may involve unproductive transmission of others' activity; and sometimes it may result from performing yours line of work, if it's your call. Net art and cell phone art, along with other electronic art media are closely related to the semantic networks and social networking media; many times they provide computational solutions for entertainment.

DOI: 10.4018/978-1-4666-4627-8.ch020

The next sections tell about yet another ways to entertain: Chapter 21 is about electronic games, Chapter 22 tells about visual-and-verbal storytelling, Chapter 23 is about metaphorical representations of a person, and Chapter 24 is about visual music.

Figure 1, "Parkour" ponders how the city becomes a stage for a parkour artist, with both its horizontal stretches and upright heights.

Figure 1. Anna Ursyn, Parkour (© 2010, A. Ursyn. Used with permission)

SOME EXAMPLES OF THE WAYS TO ENTERTAIN WITH COMPUTING

Computing contributes to a great number of forms of entertainment. When assuming the role of an audience we often do not realize the essential role the computing plays in a success of an event created to entertain us. Computational solutions may be of use to secure technical proficiency of a production; they may provide laugh and joy but also they influence our thoughts and actions. Moreover, many kinds of entertainment changed its category level from a passive spectacle to an active audience's engagement into an interactive installation or live performance.

Networks have been subsequently established for the mass use, such as telephone, radio, television, Internet, and then the augmented and virtual environments, providing users with the data, means of communication with visual approach, audio and vision channels, multi-sensory environments, and possibilities for multimodal interaction. Intelligent networks further support the entertainment options, with independent rather than network-provided services. Wireless technology culture contributed to the ways we entertain and amuse ourselves, with portable game consoles such as Nintendo 3DS, participation through cell phones, PDAs such as palmtop computers with touch screens, applications with Arduino Boards, sharing news about life events through Skype, and the Second Life culture. For example, a LED Cube, presented online in many versions is a three-dimensional display of moving lights running on the Arduino basis.

Intelligent Environments and Virtual Reality

The human computer interaction (HCI) domain can be discussed in terms of intelligent environments (IE) and virtual reality (VR). User interfaces enable HCI in many ways. The older kinds of interface include virtual reality helmets and gloves, keyboard and mice, or a light pen, which may support speech and gesture recognition applications and a control with hand gestures the movement of robot arms. In some cases, interaction can be controlled by gestures without words, with the use of animations, which cause a lifelike behavior of characters in virtual environment. The user's gestures result in appropriate responses from the computer. In some intelligent environments, some appliances may be controlled by interfaces, for example, a life-size wooden puppet serves as an interface, robot arms are controlled by hand gestures, or we can control computer functions with voice and pointer. User's voice or a pointer may operate a projector or a computer. In an immersive virtual reality, especially in Second Life and also simulation games, avatars – characters created in artificial environment represent the users who may control them with or without the head-mounted displays and gloves. Tens of companies credited for visual effects cooperate with thousands of digital artists, 3d modelers, and animators to offer ready avatars or software for designing one's own avatar. One can create an avatar not necessarily resembling the real person. One can be whoever one wants to be, choosing sex, redefining one's look, selecting particular features and even personality. In some cases one may also take control of someone else's avatar, with or without the owner's acceptance.

Intelligent environments control some appliances through multimodal interfaces. Thus, one may use virtual reality (VR) and virtual environment (VE) to link science, engineering, and art in service of real-time, immersive and 3-dimensional interaction. The hardware and software for creating and publishing interactive 3D rich media can be designed as a desktop type or an immersive one that is visually and physically isolated from the real environment. Software is easy to use as a stand-alone application or on the Internet. The portable stereoscopic 3D visualization can be set up in minutes for a marketing event, sales presentations and product animations for easy publishing on the web or wireless. Internet users have 3D objects available on the web.

Virtual space, and also an Internet-based world of Second Life, where avatars represent remote users, provides opportunity for utilizing mental imagery for creating and navigating images. Users and visitors call forth imaginary objects or scenes to create digital images, which can be animated, interactive, or are representations of mathematical and process-driven operations. Virtual reality and the immersive environment techniques allow displaying stories of space and time by making the images produced seem real; algorithms help to simulate and display phenomena by showing variables in many dimensions. Some people make real-life living by playing virtual online games, designing avatars, garments, furniture, and other goods for the Second Life players, and then selling it for real money through eBay or otherwise.

The simulation technology works on the PC platform and at the Internet as an immersive multi-wall virtual reality and interactive visualization environment that blocks users from the awareness of real life, as participants are surrounded by virtual imagery and 3D sound and smart interactive 3D content appears to float in space in and outside of the screen without any glasses. Visual displays, body and head tracking interfaces, aural (acoustic) and haptic feedback, and peripherals such as acoustic and haptic displays provide the illusion of immersion. Haptic force-feedback technology uses the sense of touch of the user who can feel a force, vibration, or motion of virtual objects and apply the remote control of such virtual objects, machines, or devices. As described by Robles-De-La-Torre (2009, p. 1036), "haptic technology does for the sense of touch what computer graphics does for vision." One can touch and manipulate haptic virtual objects (HVO) with one's hands or body, but HVOs are not physical objects; they consist of computer-controlled forces. According to Robles-De-La-Torre, HVO can have paradoxical, normally impossible combinations of mechanical properties that do not exist in nature. Virtual internal organs can be touched and manipulated by medical students. In fact, they move the haptic interface sticks in an empty, delimited, 3D haptic interface workspace. Tactile sensors in haptic devices measure the haptic interface forces exerted by the user on the haptic interface. The user can sculpt the haptic virtual objects in a process called haptic rendering.

Data communication is possible through data channels of different kinds. The large transparent display screens let the viewers see objects and manipulate them by pointing with hands from a distance or by voice interaction. In the stereo digital showrooms viewers can see objects on a large 3D immersive holographic display and then on the web.

The work "Wires" (Figure 2) is a visual complement to the presence of the wired or wireless, and stand-alone or networked data channels:

Are we connected or are we entangled
In global network or local ties?
Does it feel safe or make you anxious
To see the wires pattern the sky.

Traditional and Computer Animation

Traditional animation is older than film animation. With reference to past events, first it was a flipbook, phenakistokope, zoetrope, thaumatrope, and praxinoscope. Flipbook is a technique that allows people to draw simple frame-by-frame animations. If they have been made on a computer, one can share them with others via e-mail. On the web one can find a lot of applications for making flipbook animations. The phenakistoscope was the predecessor to the zoetrope. The word "phenakistoscope" comes from Greek roots and means, "deceiving viewer." The Belgian Joseph Plateau and the Austrian Simon von Stampfer invented it in 1831 simultaneously. It was a spinning disc with a series of radial slits, mounted on a handle. A series of pictures was drawn around the center of the disc. The user would spin the disc and look through the moving slits at the disc's reflection in a mirror. Unlike the zoetrope and its successors, one person could only use the phenakistoscope at

Figure 2. Anna Ursyn, Wires (© 2007, A. Ursyn. Used with permission)

a time. The zoetrope was invented in the 19th century, first in England in 1834, then France in 1860 and finally the United States in 1867. The word zoe comes from Greek "zoo" meaning animal or life, "trope" is also from Greek and means things that turn. The thaumatrope was invented in the 1820s and it creates illusions dependent on persistence of vision. "Thauma" means magic in Greek and "trope" refers to something that turns. Two images that are drawn on either side of a cardboard blend together and become one picture if they are spined very fast. If one spins the thaumatrope more slowly, it produces a simple movement instead of one single image. Again one may find web pages that help to build a Zoetrope movie. In traditional, hand-drawn animation images were from about 1914 transferred onto transparent celluloid cels, so they could be overlaid on a background and new cels could be made by introducing changes in previous images. Drawings were outlined and traced onto the cel with pen or brush. It resulted in big costs in time and money (Solomon, 1994, p. 35). Felix cartoon created by Otto Messmer about 1925 was created as cell animation. The first color Mickey Mouse short was "The Band Concert" (1935, Solomon, 1994, p. 47). Because they were flammable and unstable, cells were replaced by cellulose acetate. Feature length animated Disney films were traced and painted in same hues, then accented with shading, airbrushing, drybrushing, transparent paint, and other effects. They are still revered for artistic achievement. "Three Little Pigs" (1933) was a milestone in the art of character animation. For the first time, each character personality was defined by the way he moved, rather than the way he looked (Solomon, 1994, p. 53). In a cel setup for "Snow White and Seven Dwarfs" (1937), Disney realized that to hold the audience attention, the Dwarfs would need distinct personalities (Solomon, 1994, p. 61). In the 1940s, drawings were photocopied directly onto a cel, which meant a return to black outlines, like in the 1920s. However, Xerox could be changed in size, which made possible movement simulation.

Also, drawings with complex textures could be easily reproduced. To cut the costs at the expense of artistic quality, producers began to apply limited animation. Movement was indicated by small changes overlaid on the cel containing the static parts, for example, a moving mouth was overlaid on a static frame of a head.

Traditional animation drew inspiration from the dynamic styles in art of the 20th century, for example, Dadaists, Marcel Duchamp, or Russian Constructivists such as Tatlin, Gabo, or Malevich. Marcel Duchamp considered his paintings an organization of kinetic elements – an expression of time and space, when he created five versions of "Nude Descending a Staircase" (1911-1918). A Czech filmmaker and artist Jan Švankmajer was one of the most celebrated animators; he created clay animation using the stop motion and fast motion techniques. Other influential stop motion animators are Quay Brothers.

The Library of Congress began collecting motion pictures in 1893, when Thomas Edison and W.K.L. Dickson deposited the Edison Kinetoscopic Records for copyright. The collection begins with "The Enchanted Drawing" (© November 16, 1900, Thomas A. Edison) and "Fun in a Bakery Shop" (© April 3, 1902, Thomas A. Edison). However, because of the difficulty of safely storing of the flammable nitrate film used at the time, the Library retained only the descriptive material relating to motion pictures. In 1942, recognizing the importance of motion pictures and the need to preserve them as a historical record, the Library began a collection of films themselves. From 1949 on this collection included films made for television. In the late 1980s the Walt Disney Company and Pixar started to develop a collection of software, scanning camera systems, servers, and networked computer workstations. Today the Motion Picture, Broadcasting and Recorded Sound Division (MBRS) have responsibility for the acquisition, cataloging, and preservation of the motion picture and television collections. The Division operates the Motion Picture and Television

Reading Room to provide access and information services to an international community of film and television professionals, archivists, scholars and researchers (The Library of Congress, Origins of American Animation, 1999).

In the pre-feature film days, Pixar developed Computer Animation Production System (CAPS) for Disney. The advantages of digital production are the advanced compositing (such as incorporating 3D characters into a drawn scene), effects, and non-linear editing (Computer Animation Production System, 2012). Using computer graphics, Hayao Miyazaki introduced for the first time the 3D characters and camera moves in his film "Mononoke Hime (1997). Some other titles of Hayao Miyazaki feature films are *Castle in the Sky*, *Kiki's Delivery service*, *The Castle of Cagliostro*, and *My Neighbor Totoro*. See Table 1 for a project in which you craft your own animated story.

Current animation techniques include three-dimensional animation, computer animation, and character animation for film and television. Computer animation displays movement by generating images rendered as two-dimensional or tri-dimensional computer graphics. Images may be key-framed over time, repeated with small differences in appearing, achieved by inbetweening or morphing. Shape morphing, transforming a source image into a target two-dimensional shape or a three-dimensional mesh, is gaining in importance, being applied not only in animation techniques and the game industry but recently also for changing complex objects acquired with the use of a high-speed, three-dimensional laser scanning.

Digital techniques make possible to streamline the process of transferring drawn animation to film and video and to create 2D, 3D, or experimental animation directly on a screen. With computers, one can manipulate the drawings, apply coloring effects such as gradients or shadow effects, or make use of the inbetweening process. Digital 2D animation offered lower budget productions, more automation of inbetweening, and extensive reuse of animation, such as television production. Digital 3D animation could be compared to clay animation or puppetry in that it requires creation of characters and sets that are manipulated and reused. In the process of creating animation, many departments work separately on each shot. Rick Parent (2007) described the order used to produce the Toy Story: the Story Department translates the verbal into visual; the Art Department creates the designs and color studies for the film; the Layout Department sets the framing of the shot, taking the film from two dimensions to three dimensions; the Modeling Department creates and rigs the char-

Table 1. Making a simple animation

Your Visual solution: Composition of an Animated Story
Create a simple animated story. First, draw a story with a hero, an action, and the resolution of a problem or a conflict. Make a storyboard, a graphic organizer in the form of drawings displayed in sequence to pre-visualize your story. For example, it may be a story of a boy who wanted to win the first place while running in a competition. He ran a lot among farm animals, learned from them, and finally won the competition. Show his dreams, his efforts, and then his victory and the trophy. Next, rearrange your animation. First, announce the boy's victory: how was he awarded. Then, explain, with the rearranged animation images, that he was awarded because: • He ran a lot, • He learned a lot from his farm animals when he ran along with them (horse and dogs running), • He wanted to win. You may prefer to create this animation on a computer or, if you prefer hand drawing, you may create animation with a flipbook approach by introducing small changes in your sequential drawings and then assembling them in a booklet, starting with the last page of the flipbook because it will go from back to the front. Draw only on the lower half of the page and then staple the pages at the top. In order to put things in motion, draw a sketch on a paper thin enough to see through it, for example, tracing paper and use your drawing as a first animation frame. Place another piece of paper on top of the first one to trace the lines that don't change and add the lines that tell about the action. Images should gradually change from one page to the next.

acters and environments: the world in which they live; the Shading Department translates attributes of the object into texture maps, displacement shaders, and lighting models; the Model Department defines the character's basic movements (e.g., smile, taking a step); the Animation Department brings the characters to life: creates the motion in the shot; the Lighting Department translates the Art Department vision into digital reality: simulates complex objects like cloth or fluids; and the Camera Department renders the frames (Parent, 2007, pp. 20-21).

Techniques have been often grouped as hand-manipulated keyframing animation, motion capture animation, and simulation with the use of artificial intelligence, among other techniques. These three involve a trade-off between the level of control that the animator has over the fine details of the motion and the amount of work that the computer does on its own. Keyframing allows subtle control but requires that the animator ensure the naturalness of the result. Motion capture and simulation generate motion in a fairly automatic fashion but offer little opportunity for fine-tuning. In a hand-manipulated animation, an animator positions each control on each character in a scene for key frames, with the computer interpolating all the frames of animation between key frames. It offers a possibility to feature the impossible worlds with its own rules of physics and stylized characters and movement. It is impractical for TV shows, for big-budget films, and for music video.

Computer animation may be also done by motion capture, which uses video camera and markers on a real actor to record a live action: magnetic or vision-based sensors are mounted on a performer to capture the motion of important points on the performer and then apply these data to the controls of a digital character, and map real movement onto characters. This technology has enabled a number of famous athletes to supply the actions for characters in sports video games.

The use of simulation allows computer models simulate physical phenomena such as gravity or wind. The film uses simulation, e.g., to automatically move all the hairs on the character based on a computer model. Most of the major feature animation studios now incorporate simulation in their production process, for example Andrew Adamson and Vicky Jenson: Shrek; Pete Doctor: Monsters, Inc.; John Lasseter: Toy Story and A Bug's Life; and Chris Wedge: Ice Age. Artificial intelligence is used to apply animation clips created with one of the three above techniques to character models to create animation sequences with little or no human involvement. It is used, for example, for the video production to apply animation to all characters based on scenario. Realistic look is preferred for video games and special effects for live-action film and television, so motion-capture animation is used, along with combining programmed images, 3D models of objects, and key framed scenes. Animated feature films often rely on hand-manipulated animation. In "The Lord of the Rings," all animation techniques have been combined, often in the same shot.

In good animation every keyframe is an artwork. Concerns about the artistic value cause that movements are created manually for the stylization and artistic touch. Such effects can be stylized virtually as well by modification of the simulation. Animated movies display realistic and nonrealistic human characters with facial animation expressing emotional states, and photorealistic or fantasy creatures, often with anthropomorphic features. They recreate real action or replace old animation styles such as traditional stop motion animation, but either way, they provide entertainment for young and adult audience. Nonprofessional animation created by amateur computer animators provides another popular kind of entertainment.

Games

Computer games make use of electronics to take form that is often parallel to traditional games. However, electronic games added interactivity and a possibility of involving distant players online, as they benefit from the networked media. Tangible equipment to play a game may no longer be necessary, such as a deck of cards, markers for board games, croquet balls, or a Frisbee disk. One may say electronic games are becoming the main source of entertainment, at least in terms of time assigned by users. First of all, computing for entertainment became one of activities done on the phone and on tablets with the use of countless applications (for instance, one may find hundreds of game applications on iPhone and tens of games on iPad). One cannot debate computer games without talking about phones and applications. Moreover, there is a multitude of tools, many of them being available open source, providing self-explanatory directions and visual feedback. Games are easy to learn, often short, and transferable on different screens; they can be played through Skype with friends or, on Nintendo Wii with invisible coded characters. A chapter "Electronic Games" containing discussion about electronic games and gaming as tools for visual solutions follows this text.

Live Entertainment

In traditional settings most productions, whether theatrical plays, circus performances, motion pictures, concerts, monologues, or pantomimes expected or even required an audience to be passive and quiet. A great part of computing-assisted performances involves audience's interactive input into the spectacle.

Bio-interfaces can be seen as a new kind of relationship between people and technology. Personal neurophysiological data can control commands due to a program that enables reading, interpreting, and associating them with an application. One can imagine a recreational creation based on combining biological and technological data. This use of bio-interfaces becomes popular as a trend that has the artistic, educational, and entertaining potential. Lahey, Burleson, & Streb (2012) created a "Translation + Pendaphonics = Movement Modulated Media" – a multimedia

dance performed on a vertical wall filled with projected image of a lunar surface. Pendaphonics is a motion-sensing hardware-software system that detects dancers' motion and allows dancers to control in real time the virtual moonscape. The Gametrack video game interface is human-computer interaction hardware that supports the Pendaphonics system.

Burning Man (2012) may serve as an example of an event involving the most recent computing technologies for interactive arts and entertainment. It is an annual art festival creating a temporary community of tens of thousands participants dedicated to community, art, self-expression, and self-reliance. The event takes place during eight days prior to Labor Day weekend in Black Rock Desert (90 miles north of Reno, Nevada) in a temporary community known as Black Rock City. The name of the event, which began on the summer solstice 1986, comes from the ritual of burning a large wooden sculpture of a man on the sixth day: fire has come to be an important art medium at Burning Man. All participants place their art in the desert, and then they are required to remove their own trash according to the principle, "Come with everything, leave with everything," so except for tire tracks and footprints, the desert remains as a barren and empty corner of the world. Since 1995, a different theme has been created for each year's art event. The 2012 theme was Fertility 2.0. This year's art theme contemplates the tendency of any being or living system to create abundant life. A great variety of art forms are presented during the event, with music, performance, and guerrilla street theatre commonly presented art forms.

An Interactive Website

On an interactive website, data posted on the web may change their content, format, and even meaning because of the information exchange with the server or actions taken as social networking. Facts, data, and opinions are posted on the web for further translation, discussion, additions and corrections, links exchange, enhancement with pictures or videos and emotional responses. Feedback from others may modify the object posted and its reception by the viewers.

We may consider a website interactive when a message on the page relates to other ones and to relationships between them. It involves software that accepts and responds to input from the user's data and commands. It can be done using programs such as text word processors or spreadsheet applications, and also social interfaces that facilitate responses from users during human-to-computer interaction and thus allow social interactions.

Video posted on the web may be linked to social networking services such as Facebook where it becomes available for over one billion of users, more than a half of them using it on mobile devices. As a social networking and microblogging (up to 140 characters) service, Tweeter handles over 340 million tweets daily and over 1.6 billion search queries a day; this service also stores the tweeter's location. Further services enable the visitor to utilize 'Explore' option to explore photos on Flickr by choosing a point in time; another Flickr feature called 'Interesting' allows the user choose most interesting content and "like it". The 'Tag' feature allows giving one's photos and videos up to 75 'tags' as keywords or category labels, which help finding things having something in common. The 'Bublication' option provides information on books, publication design, selections, prices, and shipping. One can find, post, and share infographics on many websites, for example, at http://weloveinfographics.info/. According to Erétéo et al, (2010), online social networks may be best represented with the enriched semantic web framework; organizing in this way a great quantity of socially produced information may prime acceptance of social applications by big corporations.

The CSS, Java, Java Script, or other languages may support text posted on the web. A computer program allows a text to be organized by manipulating, modifying, and editing the text. The elements

such as Java applets may be inserted depending on whether the intended character of the web page. The web page content may be static – delivered to the user exactly like stored, often as a HTML document. The web page may become dynamic, such as a web site generated by the web application that can change due to interactions with the user scripting and the server-side scripting, for example in the bank–client exchange. It may be shared and interactive – allowing it's visitors to communicate with it and make changes in the web page content, for example by playing a game, often with multiple players.

Each option requires using different language. Computer programming or coding is a process consisting of designing, writing, testing, debugging, and maintaining the source code of computer programs written in one or more of languages. For example, to produce dynamic web pages, a general-purpose server-side scripting language is PHP. The open source database management system MySQL (Structured Query Language) is often used in Wikipedia, Google, Facebook, Twitter, Nokia, You Tube, and other large-scale web products. It was developed, distributed, and supported by Oracle Corporation, which runs as a server providing multi-user access to databases for use in web applications. A compiler *may be* needed, which is a (non-interactive) computer program that transforms the language of a source code into another (target) language to create an executable file (not just general data file) that can perform a task according to instructions.

Open source content management platforms such as Drupal serve for powering websites, building personal blogs, or enterprise applications. WordPress, a free open source blogging tool and dynamic content management system for websites is based on PHP and MySQL. They may support general coders writing software who are not specialists in a particular area as the computer programmers, web or software developers, and bridge their work with programmer analysts using specific language such as C, C++, Java,

Lisp, Python, etc., who have also other software engineering skills. Thus the introduction of inter-activity into users' communication may be done faster, easier, and more efficiently. Often software for "button based" development is supported by an underlaying computer language that allows the user for more sophisticated interactions. For example, when downloading a free program Blender, software for 3-D and animation, the user also gets a free copy of Python language, which gives an opportunity to enhance the capabilities of the software.

Social Media

The action of posting comments online seems to provide entertainment of a new kind. A great number of Internet-based applications make possible creating and sharing among users texts, photographs, pictures, and video they create, using Internet forums, social networks, blogging, and podcasts, among other forms of social exchange. Moreover, the omnipresence of static and moving visuals existing online contributes to the allure of social media. There are hundreds social net-working websites: blogs (or web logs, personal logs published on a web page), podcasts (made with the use of music loops with audio editing software, posted on the web, self-published, or downloaded to iTunes), RSS Feeds (web feed data formats – blogs, news, videos, with frequently updated content), user groups (users of a particular technology), etc. Networking for chatting created a new approach to entertainment: many forms of networking such as listed below serve not only to support our work but also for entertainment.

- **Facebook**: Networking for virtually every-thing: friends, business, school, interests, etc.,
- **Twitter:** Networking through the update of "status",
- **Flickr:** Photo networking community,

- **MySpace:** Networking for friends, family, celebrities, music, etc.,
- **YouTube:** Sharing and watching vid-eos providing visual approach to social networking,
- **Blogger:** Networking through blogging by communities and interests,
- **Livejournal:** Another blogging service or-ganized by communities and interests,
- **Ebay:** Selling items by categories on a site, winning a bid is considered fun by many,
- **Etsy:** Selling handmade items by categories,
- **Friendster:** Networking for friends, fam-ily, people, etc., or
- **Tumblr:** Microblogging
- **Flaxo:** For interactive fiction games
- **LinkedIn:** Business-related social net-working site,
- **Delicious.com:** Social bookmarking web service for storing, sharing, and discover-ing web bookmarks,
- **Plaxo:** One of the online address books,
- **Digg:** A social website.

Competing Ideas for Social Networking

Options for social networking and the entertain-ment related services are changing with every new device and sharing technique. According to the Wall Street Journal (Osawa & Wakabayashi, 2012), a messaging application called LINE of-fers instant messaging and Internet phone calls similar to the Skype service. The developer of LINE is the NHN Japan, a subsidiary of a South Korea's NHN Corporation, an Internet content service operator that offers Internet search portal website with community services Naver, a game portal Hangame, and a micro-blog service me-2day, all with the Japanese branches. LINE offers a platform that is designed exclusively for smart phones, while Skype and Facebook have been based on PCs. The core component of LINE is instant messaging but the developers are building also social networks and services similar to Facebook Inc., Twitter Inc., game developing company Zynga, and photo sharing service Instagram. Users can communicate using text and virtual stickers representing cartoon characters, send video and voice messages. They may also draw pictures with their fingers and share them using a Line Brush application. Users may also edit, decorate, and share photos using a LINE Camera application. There is also a game application LINE Brizzle linked to the main LINE application.

As stated by the PRNewswire (2012), a free-calling and free-messaging application LINE (http://line.naver.jp/en/) has over 70 million users in Japan and 230 countries and regions; other LINE-related services also show a steady rate of growth. However, the LINE Company has, apart from Skype, and WhatsApp, many competitors in Asia such as KakaoTalk in South Korea and Tencent Holding Ltd.'s WeChat in China, which has 200 million users. Most of the Asian social networking sites hope to expand beyond their domestic markets, despite competition and some opinions that their images may not appeal in other parts of the world. Again, the power of the image plays the role.

"The Roof Party" (Figure 3) tells about looking at the city life from above. It places you in between of the interior and the exterior space.

EGO, SELF-CONSCIOUSNESS, AND NETWORKING

One may ask a question about a current role of a diary as a literary and communication tool. A personal journal was an important way of imparting one's thoughts, experiences, feelings, and meaningful data in a private way. The data is now automatically recorded on the bank, credit card, and other files and becomes part of a global library, often accessible for many. Everyday life is thus traceable through clouds, bank and credit

Figure 3. Anna Ursyn, The Roof Party (© 2010, A. Ursyn. Used with permission)

card statements, data embedded into photographs and videos, documents, or email. Thus, feasibility of gaining information often does not depend on one's consent or a written account. The Facebook, Twitter, and other social interaction tools and online networking platforms cause that thoughts, experiences and feelings *are* shared, so they are not anymore private, exclusive, or secret, and recorded.

A number of concepts pertaining to entertainment have gained a new meaning with the advent of ambient computing. Everyone can now avoid a feeling of anonymity when being in a crowd. A viewer, even when sitting far away at the crown of a stadium and seeing only small figures of the players, can reach for her smart phone to look at the facial expression, sometimes even peculiar face and body contortions of the competitor, enhanced by a powerful camera zoom and transmitted to a screen of the phone. Moreover, one can find an explanation and understand how a particular action came out. After that, one can tweet about one's personal comments and feelings directly to this contestant or the chosen individual. One may say the notion of entertainment have shifted toward a celebration of personal feelings and individual reactions to the events happening at the public space of a stadium or a concert hall. In a similar way, every article or video posted online, be it a tweet from the robot rover Curiosity on Mars or an advertisement about healthy food precipitates a series of comments, even so short as "Cool!" or 'Wow!" Back at home, creating an avatar on the Second Life and translating one's experiences, frustrations, and self-perceptions onto an imaginary friend can enhance the feeling of self-identity.

The emotional sphere of the entertaining culture in the intimately networked world of the viewers, participants, and tweeters gains a growing attention. A horses-and-cart metaphor about attitudes and behaviors introduced by Antonio Damasio (2005, 2010) compares human behavior to driving cart pulled by horses: we have to control horses when each of them tries to take our carriage in different direction. By introducing a description of the carriage containing brain capacities (described by Gardner as the diverse intelligences) that is pulled by horses (denoting feelings and emotions considered by Damasio crucial in cognition and decision-making) we have used a metaphor. Both verbal (when we say, for instance a leg of a table) and visual (when we draw, for example a heart symbol) metaphors can be seen a means to increase a range of the concept. Metaphors apply objects or words belonging to one object to another one; but at the same time, metaphors may result in a paucity of information.

Attitudes toward entertainment became more understandable with the advent of neurophysiol-ogy and imaging techniques. By applying imaging techniques, Antonio Damasio (1999) has been studying the relations of cognition, feelings, and emotions. Horses from the Antonio Damasio's metaphor denote the old biological brain, which controls the neocortex in performing reasoning and analysis. We activate feelings and emotions in many kinds of our activities and they play important role in many of our actions. The role of feelings and emotions has been confirmed by research results obtained with the use of imaging techniques. For example, functional magnetic resonance imaging (fMRI) tells about changes in the blood flow in the brain tissue accompanying its activity. We can see that creative work, social networking, and gaming are all evoking strong emotional responses. The horses from our metaphor may thus affect the creative, social, and play components of our life.

Research about the neurobiology of mind and behavior enhanced our understanding of how the brain processes creative endeavors, play, memory, language, emotions, and decision-making. Damasio (1999) wrote about the neural basis for the emotions and the central role emotions in cognition and decisions, "Pain and pleasure are the levers the organism requires for instinctual and acquired strategies to operate efficiently. In all probability they were also the levers that controlled the development of social decision-making strategies." "Feeling can serve as barometers of life management" (2010, p. 60). To become conscious, the brain needs subjectivity, the feeling that pervades the images we experience subjectively (2010, p. 10). Damasio (2005, 1999) claims this is so because research results show that while neocortex performs reasoning and analysis, it is wired up through the old biological brain. Thus, as stressed by Lengler (2007, p. 384), emotion leads to action while reason leads to conclusion; emotions and feelings will always be formed precognitively and preattentively *before* any information processing takes place." In terms of the Damasio's reasoning, Howard Gardner (1993a,b,c) taught about the content of the carriage comprising at least eight intelligences with resulting mental formations and predispositions of the mind.

Combined perceptions and reactions based on the emotion and the reason may be also extended to the entertaining aspects of the art, especially the multidimensional and multisensory experience in evolutionary art systems, genetic algorithms, and generative art. Emotional component in the arts can be also seen in several traditional media: in abstract expressionistic paintings, sculptures, dramatic performances, stage choreography, acting, improvisation, and other media allowing individual or group expression. The "Four Riders of Apocalypse" by Albrecht Dürer (1471–1528) may come to mind now; however, horses carry other connotations. One may also feel concerned about letting the horses run, as in all three domains: artistic performance, social activities, and gaming the affective component has an influence on the dynamics of our actions (see Table 2)

A Triptych Over Time: A Double-Sided Brochure

Now you may want to apply your work to a double-sided brochure. The front side of your brochure will contain 7 boxes. Design three rows horizontally-oriented boxes in 3 columns (see Table 3).

- The upper row box should contain a title, "Triptych over Time: Your Name."
- The second row will comprise three image boxes with three subtitles: "Past," "Presence," and "Future" or "Then," "Now," and "Later On." They will present your visage in time related to the past, present, and future. Add objects or symbols related to your profession. You may choose to do it using inDesign or QuarkXPress software.
- In the third row, three boxes placed under your three images will contain text. Fill

Table 2. Creating self-portrait over time

Your Visual Response: Self-Portrait Over Time
Rethink your self-identification. Keeping in mind your family and friends, you may want to create a triptych over time picturing three phases of your life and then share it with them. Create three images representing you in time: you as a child, as you look now, and a dream image of yourself thirty years from now. Be careful though, because what you depict might happen. Try to present three states of mind. Draw yourself as a child, along with your favorite toys that could represent you and your habits; present yourself as you think you look now, also showing objects pets, and visual clues defining your personality; and then show your dream image about what would might happen and how you see yourself in the future. Feel free to add your desirable inventions you think would help you in your career.
Your self portraits could be your hand-drawn pictures or photos taken with a digital camera, scanned on a computer, and then manipulated with photo-editing software, or you may prefer to build it from pixels with various intensity values. For your portrait in the far future you may find many turorials about aging people in the Internet; google "how to age people." You may use, for example, 'Burn' and 'Dodge' tool to transform the shape of the face, create wrinkles, sag the skin, or lighten eyebrows and hair. Another way is to place an image of an old person on the front layer, then to change this layer's opacity. The wrinkles, and features that are age relevant will superimpose your photograph, while you may remove some features you find non-rellevant to the features of your face.
Feel free to sketch, use a photograph from your camera or smart phone, write a short code, or use a still frame from a movie.. If you need to take a screenshot, on a Mac computer press simultaneously 'Command,' 'Shift,' and '#3' keys, or #4, if selecting is involved. It will generate a png file named Picture 1 on your desktop. Open this file in your image-editing program. On a PC, you'll find a 'Print Screen' button on the upper right corner of the keyboard. Press the button when the image is open, then open image processing software and go 'Edit Paste.' Save your file, then you are ready for working on your project. Another way of recording your photo is using Photo Booth program, a software avaiable on a Macintosh, allowing the user to record own face with special effects and enhancements applied to it. Macs have also iPhoto program for creating photo-books, which allow taking photos with special effects and enhancements.
You may also think about making your work unique and creating it out of letters or other signs. You may show yourself attired in elaborate gown coming from another culture or a historical costume. It might be helpful to look at portraits available in books or online, for example at Google Images. You may choose Portrait of the Willibald Pirckheimer (1503) by Albrecht Durer (1471-1528), Portrait of a Young Man 3 by Sandro Botticelli (1482-1483), Portrait of a Girl (1483) by Leonardo da Vinci (1452-1519), F. Champenois Imprimeur-Editeur (1898) by Alphonse Mucha (1860-1939), Portrait of Gertrude Stein (1946) by Pablo Ruiz Picasso (1881-1973), Self Portrait (1967) by Francis Bacon (1909-1992), or by Andy Warhol (1928-1987).

Table 3. The Brochure

Triptych over Time: Front Your Name		
Image box: Self-portrait as a child	Image box: Present-day portrait	Image box: Dream image 30 years from now
Textbox about past	Textbox about present time	Textbox about future

Table 4. Back of brochure

Triptych over Time: Back Your Name		
Your Résumé	Your CV	Your Bio

these textboxes with a short description of you in time, respectively. In the first textbox write about your past; list your present interests in the second one, and finally write about your plans for the future in the third box.

On the back of the brochure you may want to insert a title, and then place information about your background: your résumé, a CV (curriculum vitae written in a formalized way), and a bio (career biography, written more loosely in conversational language. You may also want to add a list of your strengths (strong points) as keywords in the Bio box of your brochure (see Table 4).

Résumé (or resume) is often meant as a one or two pages long, bulleted list of professional information data about your education, professional experience, previous job titles, skills, and certifications. It is usually assembled for job applications and used to screen applicants. It may be written in a chronological order or may be organized functionally. One may find free resume templates and examples on the web.

CV provides longer and fuller account of your professional background. It may contain more categories, for example, Education, Certifications,

Dissertation/Thesis Topic, Teaching Experience, Administrative Experience, Research Experience, Computer Skills, Laboratory Experience, Languages, Presentations/Publication Experience, University Involvement, Consulting Experience, Affiliations/Professional Associations/Memberships, Scholarships/Fellowships, Honors/Awards, and Research Interest (Denham, 2010).

Bio may take a format of a promotional short essay written in a third person, highlighting your strengths and achievements, often without specific dates and details. It may be one page long and contain a few photographs. According to Denham (2010), bios can include photos, credentials, awards, personal information, name-dropping of companies and impressive job titles. While resume provides precise facts, bios tell a story about a candidate.

ENTERTAINMENT AND SOME OF THE BIOLOGICALLY ACTIVE SUBSTANCES

Researchers developed an interest in amusement and enjoyment not only because these feelings are linked with recreation and entertainment. A growing number of studies focus on the relationship between human decisions and the levels of biologically active substances in blood. Both the hormones released into the blood and the pheromones (substances produced by organisms, e.g., of mammals and insects) can affect human physiology and behavior. For this reason several companies started production of substances containing pheromone compounds such as androstadienone, androstenol, androstenone, and androsterone that could help people facilitate the attraction process. Moreover, the emerging fields of study such as behavioral economics ponder how we make economic decisions (e.g., Ariely, 2010; Levitt & Dubner, 2009) and the books written on this topic by behavioral economists became the New York Times bestsellers. Neuroeconomics is a new discipline that combines economics with biology, neuroscience, and psychology.

There are more than 80 neurotransmitters or neuromodulators already described and the number is growing (Gahlinger, 2003). Changes in the spike pattern caused by neurotransmitters can be seen dissociated from the modulator-induced changes (Stern, Fort, Miller, Peskin, & Brezina, 2007). Neurotransmitters transmit signals from a neuron across a synapse to another cell. The most important neurotransmitter systems are the noradrenaline (norepinephrine) system, the dopamine system, the serotonin system, and the cholinergic system. Neuromodulators regulate neurons' activity, many of them also acting as neurotransmitters. Neuromodulators are not broken down or reabsorbed at the pre-synaptic membrane. Oxytocin and dopamine are classed as substances of this kind. Research studies on biologically active substances such as oxytocin and dopamine may support our understanding why people who have friends may live longer and less frequently suffer physical and mental illness, and why we need to display our positive thoughts and feelings in public, online and off.

The brain mechanisms involved in fundamental pleasures (food and sexual pleasures) (Richard, & Berridge, 2011) overlap with those for higher-order pleasures (for example, monetary, artistic, musical, altruistic, and transcendent pleasures) (Kringelbach & Berridge, 2010a,b). The functional neuroanatomy of pleasure and the happiness have been studied in the fifties and the pleasure center in the brain have been found in the region of the septum and nucleus accumbens: stimulation of this region caused the rats repeatedly pressed the lever even up to 2000 times per hour. Dopamine has been found the brain's 'pleasure chemical aiding neural signaling in these regions. Anhedonia, the inability to feel pleasure is a central feature of affective disorders such as depression and chronic pain. According to Berridge & Kringelbach (2008), happiness in daily life may rely on matching a proper balance 'wanting' and

'liking' to help facilitate engagement with the world. Rose (2012) tells that learning and addiction are tightly bound together as they both give pleasure. Learning gives pleasure because of dopamine release. The brain's reward system responds to new sensations by learning from them. The biggest release is when expectation is 50:50 or when there is unpredictable payoff.

Oxytocin

One of the biologically active substances that attract researchers' attention is oxytocin, a hormone released by the endocrine pituitary gland (hypophysis) at the base of the brain; it controls growth and functioning of other glands that are secreting hormones into the blood. Researchers found that oxytocin plays important role in human behavior. Oxytocin was previously regarded important during and after childbirth. Studies have shown a clear correlation of oxytocin with positive social interactions: human bonding, increase in trust, and decrease in fear. Release of oxytocin evokes a feeling of contentment, lessens anxiety, and induces a feeling of calmness and security (Lee, Macbeth, Pagani, & Young 3rd, 2009).

Figure 4, "Happiness." Our brain needs subjectivity to maintain consciousness; feelings and emotions play an important role in many of our actions. In order to feel happy, we organize and make it less scary, so we devise a recipe for the wildlife and arrange what we see in cognitive structures.

Studies conducted by a neuroeconomist Paul J. Zak et al. ask why we do what we do, and what drives human behavior (Zak, Stanton, & Ahmadi, 2007; Conlisk, 2011). The results obtained with the use of magnetic resonance imaging technique indicate a relationship between empathy and generosity. Zak's research has been applied to social media (Penenberg, 2010) and revealed that social media activity (even consisting of only 10 minutes of tweeting) triggered the release of oxytocin, thereby heightening feelings of trust,

Figure 4. Anna Ursyn, Happiness (© 2009, A. Ursyn. Used with permission)

empathy, and generosity. At the same time, the reduced levels of stress hormones cortisol and ACTH accompanied the release of oxytocin while tweeting. Penenberg concludes that social networking might reduce cardiovascular risks, such as heart attack and stroke, often associated with lack of social support. Zak proposes that e-connection is processed in the brain in the same way as an in-person connection.

In the light of these results current trends of finding entertainment in social networking may take another dimension. With more than one billion users of Facebook (2013), many of them engaging emotionally to tweeting as strongly as in the physical relations with people, social networking plays important role in human behavior. Finding entertainment in social networking may often build an addiction to social media; when deprived

of an access to the Internet, those who used to tweet many hours a day get a feeling as if they were without their friends and family. Penenberg (2010) stresses that a great part of the Facebook users are basically addicted to social media and suffer withdrawal symptoms when deprived of an access to the Internet. According to Penenberg, a need for constant connectivity may be hardwired in our brains, which react to tweeting just as they do to our physical engagement with people we trust and enjoy. Other studies support the idea that online relationships can be perceived just as real as those conducted offline and associated with the release of oxitocin. Several companies started production of pheromone substances containing oxytocin. One may anticipate a series of further studies on factors promoting or inhibiting the release of biologically active substances and pheromones; for example, how particular colors, traditionally ascribed to the mood changes, would contribute to the release of these compounds to the bloodstream. The emotional component in gaming may be seen in productions made by the video game designers who create numerous genres of first-person-shooter and shoot 'em up games or survival-horror action games. On the recipients' side, emotional problems in social relations often arise when gamers become addicted.

The knowledgeable understanding of the needs of the social creatures like most of us could be significant in drawing implications for the entertaining business, its companies, marketing, and the whole culture of this intimately networked world of the viewers, participants, and tweeters. Implications drawn from the advertisement study results include likeability, co-authorship, and the role of 'love.' In the opinion of Lengler (2007), the balance has been shifted from cognitive textual to the affective visual both in visual representations in information visualization and in the advertising domain. Dimensions such as likeability, ease of information assessment and comparison, and visual perspective (namely, interactivity and depth of field) are becoming more and more important (Lengler, p. 391).

Dopamine

Dopamine is a major catecholamine neurotransmitter present in the mammalian brain that is released when we encounter something pleasurable. This chemical compound is involved in locomotion, neuroendocrine secretion, cognition and emotion; it is important for learning and motivation to persist in a task, because its presence in the brain cells makes us feel good, even euphoric. Dopamine also plays a role in the periphery where it regulates a range of other processes including catecholamine release, hormone secretion, and gastrointestinal motility (Tocris Bioscience, 2012). It agitates muscles, increases attention, produces euphoria, creates addiction, and may

cause nausea and vomiting (Gahlinger, 2003, p. 142). During the amphetamine withdrawal period the dopamine neurons' activity is suppressed, which causes anhedonia – the inability to feel pleasure, and the temptation to return to the drug (Gahlinger, 2003, p. 219).

Dopamine receptors in the striatum seem to be main components of the brain's reward system, a structure that causes craving for things, not only a drug, a snack, sex, but also abstract concepts or a preferred entertainment. Dopamine makes us seeking information and curious about ideas; unpredictable events release even more dopamine. Dopamine is instrumental to our sense of anticipation and reward (Rose, 2012). Research conducted by a neuropsychologist Wolfram Schultz (2010) involved dopamine and dopamine receptors in the brain. In his experiments neurons of the lab monkeys lighted up when the monkeys saw the light or heard the sound preceding the treat but not when the reward was given (Madigan, 2012). It's because dopamine refers to the anticipation of pleasure and the pursuit of happiness but not pleasure itself. A feeling of gratification for the seeking prompts us to seek more, which creates addiction. Dopamine receptors are part of a pattern recognition system, which allows anticipation and predicting the rewards, based on perception of the environment. According to researchers, a sound when a text message or email arrives and visual cues enhance the addiction.

Imaging techniques enable scientists to measure the release of neurotransmitters. Methods applied in the research studies involve combining positron emission tomography (PET) and functional magnetic resonance imaging (fMRI) data, personality questionnaires, and psychophysiological measures of autonomic nervous system activity (e.g., Boileau et al., 2003; Salimpoor et al., 2011). In a PET scan, positively charged radioactive particles of the carbon-11 (positrons) in the bloodstream indicate the level of their binding with the receptor neurons in the striatum. Receptors that bound with dopamine do not bind the radioactive isotope, so one may say dopamine is present where there is no radioactive substance.

Several drugs (such as cocaine, amphetamines), tobacco, and alcohol affect the brain's dopamine reward system. Some psychoactive drugs prevent re-absorption of dopamine from the synapse, while amphetamines and nicotine increase its release from the pre-synaptic storage sites (Gahlinger, 2003).

Research study on the effect of alcohol disclosed extracellular dopamine release in the brain, predominantly in the nucleus accumbens in the ventral striatum, and reduction of the radioactive substance binding potential (Boileau et al., 2003). Many scientists pose that addiction to drugs starts when the drugs make dopamine neurons hypersensitive, which causes craving. The feeling of power has been found to increase the levels of testosterone and its by-product 3-androstanediol in both men and women; it leads to release of dopamine, which can be very addictive (The Mail Online, 2012).

Cognitive tasks such as gaming, especially at the high levels of the game, greatly increase the dopamine release in the striatum – the pleasure center (Rose, 2012). Tweeting, texting, posting, and connecting with friends do the same. Pleasure centers in the limbic system of the brain are part of the reward system, the mesolimbic dopamine system; they are involved in processing emotion. Stimulation of the pleasure center with electrodes implanted in subjects' brains provides euphoria – the intense feelings of pleasure (Doidge, 2007). The pleasure centers have been shown to play a role in addiction. Sid Savara (2012), a personal development trainer and blogger reports some cases of death caused by the video game addiction – where people went days without food or sleep to play video games. Screen entertainment (watching television) causes our brain to release dopamine, mostly irrespective of what people watch and results in cognitive and biological changes: affects attention, sleep, and increases body fat (food with high fat and sugar also causes release of dopamine) (Sigman, 2007). Listening music results in increased levels of dopamine and shows an association between the dopamine release and the pleasure center's response to music.

Figures 5 and 6 show two different approaches to the theme "Concert," created by my students from the Computer Graphics class.

Figure 5. Wes Thorpe, Concert. (© 2011, W, Thorpe. Used with permission)

Figure 6. Jael Esquibel, Concert (© 2006, J. Esquibel. Used with permission)

Table 5. Visualizing a concert

Your Visual Response: A Concert
Make a picture showing a musical event. You may want to draw musicians and an audience, show instruments and musical scores in a more abstract way, or create a metaphor for listening music that results in the pleasure center's response. You may also think of a concert as a form of entertainment for musicians resulting from the successful cooperation of many professionals to create this event.

While the author of previous work emphasized his connection with the living environment, the author of this image represented an abstract concept by juxtaposing parts of a familiar instrument, thus visually explaining the interactive, collaborative part of the entire musical event.

Salimpoor, Benovoy, Larcher, Dagher, & Zatorre (2011, p. 257) investigated the effects of emotionally arousing music on the dopamine system. They found that "intense pleasure in response to music can lead to dopamine release in the striatal system. Notably, the anticipation of an abstract reward can result in dopamine release in an anatomical pathway distinct from that associated with the peak pleasure itself. Our results help to explain why music is of such high value across all human societies." To further understand this concept, see Table 5.

Studies about computer mediated social interactions include concerns about possible negative impact of the ability to be constantly online and connected on our offline interactions. Ubiquitous computing specialists are working on finding how online social networking platforms can be used to support different types of offline engagement, both playful and serious, and establish a community interested in computer mediated offline interaction (SOFTec, 2012).

CONCLUSION

Entertainment used to be meant as a passive or an active amusement or enjoyment. Some ways to entertain such as electronic games, visual-and-verbal storytelling, metaphoric representations of a person, and visual music are discussed in further subchapters. Readers are encouraged to react with their visual responses, for example, creating a self-portrait over time.

Computing strongly contributes to many forms of entertainment; as an audience, we often do not realize the essential role the computing plays in a success of an event, which often happens in a vir-

tual environment or applies simulation technology working on the PC platform and at the Internet. Intelligent environments control some appliances through multimodal interfaces. Bio-interfaces may be seen as another form of relationship between people and technology.

Entertainment in social networking may take another dimension while happening on an interactive website, where data posted on the web may change their content, format, and even meaning. Electronic games added interactivity and a possibility of involving distant players online; users benefit from the networked social media. Somebody's ego and self-consciousness may depend on participation in social networking, especially with the biologically active substances released in response to tweeting or gaming.

REFERENCES

Ariely, D. (2010). *Predictably irrational: The hidden forces that shape our decisions*. Harper Perennial.

Berridge, K. C., & Kringelbach, M. L. (2008). Affective neuroscience of pleasure: reward in humans and animals. *Psychopharmacology*, *199*(3), 457–480. doi:10.1007/s00213-008-1099-6 PMID:18311558.

Boileau, I., Assaad, J.-M., Pihl, R. O., Benkelfat, C., Leyton, M., & Diksic, M. et al. (2003). Alcohol promotes dopamine release in the human nucleus accumbens. *Synapse (New York, N.Y.)*, *49*(4), 226–231. doi:10.1002/syn.10226 PMID:12827641.

Burning Man. (2012). Retrieved August 9, 2012, from http://www.burningman.com/

Computer Animation Production System. (2012). Retrieved August 7, 2012, from http://en.wikipedia.org/wiki/Computer_Animation_Production_System

Conlisk, J. (2011). Professor Zak's empirical studies on trust and oxytocin. *Journal of Economic Behavior & Organization, 78*(1–2), 160–166. doi:10.1016/j.jebo.2011.01.002.

Damasio, A. (2005). *Descartes' error*. New York: Penguin Books.

Damasio, A. (2010). Self Comes to Mind. New York, New York: Pantheon. Reprint: Vintage. ISBN 030747495X.

Damasio, A. R. (1999). *The feeling of what happens: Body and emotion in the making of consciousness*. New York: Harcourt Brace.

Denham, T. (2010). *What's the difference between a resume, CV and bio?* Retrieved April 15, 2013, from http://blog.timesunion.com/careers/whats-the-difference-between-a-resume-cv-and-bio/551/

Doidge, N. (2007). *The brain that changes itself: Stories of personal triumph from the frontiers of brain science*. Penguin Books.

Erétéo, G., Limpens, F., Gandon, F., Corby, O., Buffa, M., Leitzelman, M., & Sander, P. (2010). Semantic social network analysis: A concrete case. In *Handbook of Research on Methods and Techniques for Studying Virtual Communities: Paradigms and Phenomena*, (pp. 122-156). Academic Press.

Facebook Inc. (2013). Retrieved March 10, 2013, from http://www.facebook.com/facebook?rf=106491156053682

Gahlinger, P. (2003). *Illegal drugs: A complete guide to their history, chemistry, use, and abuse*. Plume.

Gardner, H. (1993a). *Frames of mind: The theory of multiple intelligences*. New York: Basic Books, A Division of Harper Collins Publishers.

Gardner, H. (1993b). *Art, mind, and brain: A cognitive approach to creativity*. New York: Basic Books, A Division of Harper Collins Publishers.

M. L. Kringelbach, & K. C. Berridge (Eds.). (2010a). *Pleasures of the brain*. Oxford University Press.

Kringelbach, M. L., & Berridge, K. C. (2010b). The functional neuroanatomy of pleasure and happiness. *Discov Med., 9*(49), 579–587. Retrieved October 6, 2012, from http://www.ncbi.nlm.nih.gov/pmc/articles/PMC3008353/

Lahey, B., Burleson, W., & Streb, E. (2012). Translation + pendaphonics = movement modulated media. *Leonardo, 45*(4), 322–329. doi:10.1162/LEON_a_00406.

Lee, H.-J., Macbeth, A. H., Pagani, J., & Young, W. S. III. (2009). Oxytocin: The great facilitator of life. *Progress in Neurobiology, 88*(2), 127–151. doi: doi:10.1016/j.pneurobio.2009.04.001 PMID:19482229.

Lengler, R. (2007). How to induce the beholder to persuade himself: Learning from advertising research for information visualization. In *Proceedings of the 11th International Conference on Information Visualization*, (pp. 382-392). IEEE Computer Society Press.

Levitt, S. D., & Dubner, S. J. (2009). *Freakonomics: A rogue economist explores the hidden side of everything*. William Morrow.

Madigan, J. (2012). *The psychology of video games*. Retrieved August 6, 2012, from http://www.psychologyofgames.com/tag/dopamine/

MySQL. (2012). Retrieved October 7, 2012, from (http://dev.mysql.com/doc/refman/5.1/en/what-is-mysql.html

Osawa, J., & Wakabayashi, D. (2012, November 13). Japan's answer to Facebook: Line messaging app. aims to reshape networking for smartphones. *The Wall Street Journal*, p. B4.

Parent, R. (2007/2012). *Computer animation: Algorithms and techniques* (2nd ed.). Morgan Kaufmann.

Penenberg, A. L. (2010, June 28). Social networking affects brains like falling in love. *Fast Company Magazine*. Retrieved August 5, 2012, from http://www.fastcompany.com/1659062/social-networking-affects-brains-falling-love

PRNewswire. (2012, October 25). NHN Japan's 'LINE' user number exceeds 70 million. *United Business Media*. Retrieved November 17, 2012, from http://www.prnewswire.com/news-releases/nhn-japans-line-user-number-exceeds-70-million-175725791.html

Richard, J. M., & Berridge, K. C. (2011). Nucleus accumbens dopamine/glutamate interaction switches modes to generate desire versus dread: D1 for appetitive eating but D1 and D2 together for fear. *The Journal of Neuroscience*, *31*(36), 12866–12879. doi:10.1523/JNEUROSCI.1339-11.2011 PMID:21900565.

Robles-De-La-Torre, G. (2009). Virtual reality: Touch/haptics. In E.B. Goldstein (Ed.), *Encyclopedia of Perception*, (vol. 2, pp. 1036-1038). Sage Publications, Inc. ISBN 1412940818. Retrieved August 8, 2012, from http://www.isfh.org/GR-Virtual_Reality_TouchHaptics2009.pdf

Rose, F. (2012). *The art of immersion: How the digital generation is remaking Hollywood, Madison Avenue, and the way we tell stories*. W. W. Norton & Company.

Salimpoor, V. N., Benovoy, M., Larcher, K., Dagher, A., & Zatorre, R. J. (2011). Anatomically distinct dopamine release during anticipation and experience of peak emotion to music. *Nature Neuroscience*, *14*, 257–262. doi:10.1038/nn.2726 PMID:21217764.

Savara, S. (2012). *Television, video games and other stimuli that hijack your brain's dopamine reward system*. Retrieved August 7, 2012, from http://sidsavara.com/television-video-games-and-other-stimuli-that-hijack-your-brains-dopamine-reward-system

Schultz, W. (2010). Dopamine signals for reward value and risk: Basic and recent data. *Behavioral and Brain Functions, 6*, 24. Retrieved August 5, 2012, from http://www.behavioralandbrainfunctions.com/content/6/1/24

Sigman, A. (2007). Visual voodoo: The biological impact of watching TV. [from http://www.aricsigman.com/IMAGES/VisualVoodoo.LowRes.pdf]. *Biologist (Columbus, Ohio)*, *54*(1), 12–17. Retrieved August 5, 2012

SOFTec. (2012). Workshop on computer mediated social offline interactions. In *Proceedings of the 14th International Conference on Ubiquitous Computing (Ubicomp 2012)*. Retrieved August 10, 2012, from http://uc.inf.usi.ch/events/softec12

Solomon, C. (1994). *The history of animation*. New York: Wings Books.

Stern, E., Fort, T. J., Miller, M. W., Peskin, C. S., & Brezina, W. (2007). Decoding modulation of the neuromuscular transform. *Neurocomputing*, *70*(10-12), 1753–1758. doi:10.1016/j.neucom.2006.10.117 PMID:19763188.

The Library of Congress. (1999). *Origins of American animation*. Retrieved August 5, 2012, from http://memory.loc.gov/ammem/oahtml/oahome.html

The Mail Online. (2012). *Power really does corrupt as scientists claim it's as addictive as cocaine*. Retrieved August 7, 2012, from http://www.dailymail.co.uk/news/article-2136547/Power-really-does-corrupt-scientists-claim-addictive-cocaine.html#ixzz22sRke200

Tocris Bioscience. (2012). *Dopamine receptors*. Retrieved August 7, 2012, from http://www.tocris.com/pharmacologicalBrowser.php?ItemId=4993#.UCFSzu1iuao

Zak, P. J., Stanton, A. A., & Ahmadi, S. (2007). Oxytocin increases generosity in humans. *PLoS ONE*, *2*(11), e1128. doi:10.1371/journal.pone.0001128 PMID:17987115.

Chapter 21
Challenges in Game Design

ABSTRACT

Electronic games and gaming can serve as the tools for visual solutions. It depends on the methods through which the games are delivered and the ways people think about electronic games. First, traditional and electronic gaming is described, and then, various goal-oriented game applications are discussed. Game features acting in favor of or against gaming complete this part of the book.

INTRODUCTION

The advent of electronic games in the early seventies brought about transformation of the methods the games are delivered and the ways people think about games. Electronic games are often created as art forms; they serve several quite different goals such as

- Teaching tool for education and training
- Entertainment
- Health, and fitness, many times including biofeedback
- Simulation games that serve for knowledge acquisition in medical diagnosis, business strategy, or business management. Research and evaluation have been intensively conducted on strategic management simulation games
- A way of networking.

With new technologies in gaming such as Nintendo Wii U (http://www.nintendo.com/wiiu), PlayStation PSVita (http://us.playstation.com/psvita/), and possibly X Box 720, gamers can play with opponents from all around the globe without knowing if they play with somebody's grandma or a second-grader escaping his classroom experience. However, current trend is to allow the gamers scan their face, the back of their head, and the whole body, along with their favorite object, to become their own avatar, rather then playing their avatar. Moreover, instead of looking at iconic images or characters moving across the screens, they'd see the faces of their opponents and communicate with them in real time. According to some, just like with a Skype-based communication, it will be a syncretic experience, because they can see, hear, and watch the body language of their opponents.

Rationale for educational gaming includes the enhancement of student motivation and active engagement, along with behavioral approaches to learning such as: situated experiential learning; distributed (spaced) learning that includes review of the material separated from instruction

DOI: 10.4018/978-1-4666-4627-8.ch021

by a period of time (Litman & Davachi, 2008); a blended learning approach that combines face-to-face facilitation with computer-mediated instruction; learning with the use of texting; and discovery learning. Playing games involves learning social skills, collective problem solving, and social negotiation. In order to support research and evaluation of educational games Wideman et al. (2007) developed research software that records screen activity during game play in a classroom setting along with synchronized audio of player discussion.

Game environment and equipment have been also changing. Tangible equipment to play a game may no longer be necessary, such as a deck of cards, markers for board games, croquet balls, or a Frisbee disk. One may say electronic games are becoming the main source of entertainment, at least in terms of time assigned by users. First of all, computing for entertainment became one of activities done on the phone and on tablets with the use of countless applications (for instance, one may find hundreds of game applications on iPhone and tens of games on iPad). One cannot debate computer games without talking about phones and applications. Moreover, there is a multitude of tools, many of them being available open source, providing self-explanatory directions and visual feedback. Games are easy to learn, often short, and transferable on different screens; they can be played with friends through Skype or on Nintendo Wii with invisible coded characters. With current developments in a scanning technique one would play not only by using avatars but also by becoming one's own avatar, after one's face, back, and a favorite object would be scanned and imported to the console. Moreover, several augmented reality (AR) are designed for the Nintendo 3DS and 3DS XL consoles with paper cards that interact with the games. By scanning the QR (quick response) codes shown on cards, real time graphics are augmented onto live footage (http://en.wikipedia.org/wiki/Nintendo_3DS).

Creating new projects including games is supported by many open source platforms capable of interacting with users through interfaces, for example Arduino. Processing, an open source programming language is one of such tools addressed to non-programmers who are willing to learn programming. Arduino is an open-source electronics prototyping platform based on flexible, easy-to-use hardware and software. It's intended for artists, designers, hobbyists, and anyone interested in creating interactive objects or environments. Arduino can sense the environment by receiving input from a variety of sensors and can affect its surroundings by controlling lights, motors, and other actuators. The microcontroller on the board is programmed using the Arduino programming language (based on Wiring – an open-source programming framework for microcontrollers) and the Arduino development environment (based on Processing). Arduino projects can be stand-alone or they can communicate with software on running on a computer, e.g. Flash, Processing, MaxMSP (Arduino, 2012). For example, Arduino board is a part of the user interface designed for peripheral regulation of respiration (Moraveji et al., 2011).

TROUBLES WITH DEFINING A "GAME" CONCEPT

In his work "Homo Ludens" Johan Huizinga (1938) provided a definition for play,

[Play] is an activity which proceeds within certain limits of time and space, in a visible order, according to rules freely accepted, and outside the sphere of necessity or material utility. The play-mood is one of rapture and enthusiasm, and is sacred or festive in accordance with the occasion. A feeling of exaltation and tension accompanies the action, mirth and relaxation follow (Huizinga, 1968, p. 132).

The 20th-century philosopher Ludwig Wittgenstein (2009/1953) analyzed a definition of the word game; he maintained that games cannot be defined by the elements of games such as play, rules, and competition, and concluded that people apply the term game to disparate human activities that bear only family resemblances. In a work "Philosophical Investigations" he discussed game related problems and puzzles in the context of semantics, logic, and philosophy of mathematics, psychology, and mind. Wittgenstein wrote about language games by means of which children learn their native language, and stressed that the variety of language-games comprises:

- Giving orders and acting on them
- Describing an object by its appearance, or by its measurements
- Constructing an object from a description (a drawing)
- Reporting an event
- Speculating about the event
- Forming and testing a hypothesis
- Presenting the results of an experiment in tables and diagrams
- Making up a story; and reading one
- Acting in a play
- Singing rounds
- Guessing riddles
- Cracking a joke; telling one
- Solving a problem in applied arithmetic
- Translating from one language into another.
- Requesting, thanking, cursing, greeting, praying (Wittgenstein, 2009/1953, p. 15).

Clark Abt (1970, cited after http://en.wikipedia.org/wiki/Game) stated, "A game is an *activity* among two or more independent *decision-makers* seeking to achieve their *objectives* in some *limiting context*. French sociologist Roger Caillois, in his book *Les Jeux et les Hommes (Games and Men)* (1992) defined a game as an activity which is essentially:

1. **Free:** In which playing is not obligatory; if it were, it would at once lose its attractive and joyous quality as diversion;
2. **Separate:** Circumscribed within limits of space and time, defined and fixed in advance;
3. **Uncertain:** The course of which cannot be determined, nor the result attained beforehand, and some latitude for innovations being left to the player's initiative;
4. **Unproductive:** creating nether goods, nor wealth, nor new elements of any kind; and, except for the exchange of property among the players, ending in situation identical to that prevailing at the beginning of the game;
5. **Governed by Rules:** Under conventions that suspend ordinary laws, and for the moment establish new legislation, which alone counts;
6. **Make-Believe:** Accompanied by a special awareness of a second reality or of a free unreality, as against real life (Caillois, 1992, p. 10).

Electronic games, which are interactive systems designed with the use of electronics, comprise mostly video games played on a personal computer or a video console, but also hand-held electronic games that do not include video, standalone electro-mechanical arcade games, slot machines, and pinball games of many types. The term computer gaming refers to the playing of computer and video console games.

Computer game designer Chris Crawford (2003) introduced a series of dichotomies that exist between art and entertainment; toys and challenges; puzzles and conflicts; and competition as conflict and a game. He described a game as an interactive, goal-oriented activity where players can interfere with each other. Katie Salen & Eric Zimmerman (2003) stated, "A game is a system in which players engage in an artificial conflict, defined by rules, that results in a quantifiable outcome. The key elements of this definition are the fact that a game is a *system*, *players* interact with a system, a game is an instance of *conflict*, the conflict in games is *artificial*, *rules* limit player behavior and define the game, and every game has a *quantifiable* outcome or goal." (Salen & Zimmerman, p. 83). Jouni Smed & Harri Hakonen (2003) recognize three main aspects present in a game: challenge (which determines the rules and the goal), conflict, and play, as opposed to other pastimes such as a puzzle, a story, and a toy. The authors discern three roles for a computer program in a game: coordinating the game process, illustrating the situation, and participating as a player, in accordance with the model–view–controller (MVC) architectural pattern for computer programs. In some cases users can create by their actions their individual game content.

COMMON TYPES OF COMPUTER GAMES

Video games became a part of American culture in the late 50s (Khan, 2006). "Tennis for two' was designed by William Higinbotham in 1958 and played on an oscilloscope. Presently, the most common entertaining interactive multimedia in the form of computer games are video games (and also audio games) which involve human interaction with a video interface; they are played on a computer, a video game console and handheld game console, or as handheld games that often serve miniaturized video games. Other common forms include electronic arcade games, mostly based on modified video game consoles and featuring captivating types of controls that force feedback. Console games are often designed as educational consoles. Some video games, for example Tetris or tens of Mario games were created over 30 years ago, serve many generations, and can be played free online as flash arcade games. Browser games are computer games played (often free-to-play) over the Internet with the use of web browser technologies for building Web pages such as HTML (the Hypertext Markup Language) and

CSS (Cascading Style Sheets) or plug-ins – software components that enable particular functions of larger software applications (W3C, 2012). Adobe Flash Player, Quick Time, and Microsoft Silverlight are the plug-ins commonly used in web browsers for playing video games.

Game producers are working both on translating traditional games into video games (such as those for Xbox and Wii, as well as into Second Life) and on creating new games that can meet some new expectations that were non-existing in the previous time periods. Almost all kinds of traditional games have their digital counterparts, including games for children, for families, entertainment, and education, played by one person or by a group of people. There are board games (for example chess, checkers, Monopoly, Tetris, or backgammon), card games, strategy, trivia, maze, pinball, word, sports, exercise, health and fitness, action games: fighting, shooter, survival games, racing (especially car racing), flight, adventure, arcade, casino, dice, puzzle, first person, third person (where you are a puppeteer) and role playing games (for example, Dragon Age – dark fantasy role-playing video game series), simulation: construction and management, life simulation, vehicle simulation, business games, music, party games, programming games, serious educational games, and other kinds of games. Several games such as gambling and bingo are played for money. Some new honor codes developed, e.g., one cannot leave a virtual table in the middle of a game of poker played often with the strangers from unknown continents. Many share an opinion that playing video games may inspire one to become faster, wiser, more intelligent, and canny. Also, a line dividing the social and 'solitary' games is getting thinner when games are played online.

According to Van Burnham (2003), the first coin-operated arcade videogame was released in 1971. There were first all-analog systems, then digital CPU units, the text-based role-playing games (RPG) introduced in 1972, then in 1973 computer games in the interactive fiction (IF)

genre. The first arcade videogame designed with ROM chips for graphics was released in 1974, and with a microprocessor in 1975. Steve Jobs and Steve Wozniak developed in 1976 a videogame Breakout. In 1977 Nintendo released first TV Ping-Pong home videogame consoles, with the Color TV Game 15. In 1984 Famicom released in Japan consoles later called the NES (Nintendo Entertainment System) and sold 2.5 million units in one year. Nintendo of America launched NES in 1985 and sold more than 30 million units. Nintendo launched in 1989 the Game Boy compact videogame system with plug-in cartridges and a small LCD screen. Atari released in 1988 the arcade version of Tetris created in 1985 by Alexey Paitnov, Moscow. A version of Tetris shipped with Game Boy from 1990 became the world's most popular game, while the Game Boy is the longest-lived platform In 1996 Steven Spielberg, John Snoddy, and Skip Paul formed interactive GameWorks involving Sega, DreamWorks SKG, and Universal. Nintendo launched G4 along with Super Mario G4 for the N64. In 2001 Microsoft launched a home-videogame console – the Xbox.

People of different age have many different motives for playing games. Games of various kinds are often created as art forms; they serve numerous purposes such as education, entertainment, health, and fitness. Some games may influence cognitive development, neural organization and thus enhance mental prowess; other games improve physical fitness. Games of a Scrabble type may improve one's vocabulary. The networked media may support human interaction with a video interface, which many times includes biofeedback.

Terms such as video games and arcade games are changing meaning as they are released on platforms providing more immersive, realistic avatars. Emulator applications such as Multiple Arcade Machine Emulator (MAME), the Nintendo Wii Virtual Console Service (2012), the Sony PlayStation Network, and the Xbox Live Arcade recreate the hardware of classic arcade game systems of the past, while virtual handheld game consoles such as Nintendo 3DS (and soon the Wii U) are autostereoscopic devices (able to project stereoscopic 3D effects without the use of 3D glasses) that allow the players download current games, with the most popular Super Mario 3D Land (Newton, 2012). Interactive fiction games, such as compiled with the Flash-based Flaxo interpreter, are based on Interactive Fiction (IF) software simulating environments, which include visual novels, interactive novels, and interactive storytelling, in which players issue commands to the story's protagonist in order to control characters and influence the environment. Thus a user influences the evolution of the narrative in real time. Alternate reality games (ARG) are interactive narratives based on the real world and the transmedia storytelling across multiple platforms and formats to deliver a story that may be altered by participants' ideas or actions. John Conway, a protagonist of the combinatorial game theory, designed a Game of Life (based on the Milton Bradley's board game The Checkered Game of Life from 1960), as an early example of a cellular automaton and of Artificial Life simulation (Gardner, 1970). In the game of life the grid on which the cellular automata live and die maps out generations of binary distinctions. The Readers Project (Howe & Cayley, 2011), an aesthetically oriented system of software entities, examines how might cellular automata play out a 'game of life' – or rather a 'game of reading' on the complex surface of a text, by visualizing alternative vectors for reading and also focusing on its typographic dimension. The games Maxwell's Adventure and Maxwell's Escape created by Minecreaft Forums (2011) are open world, role-playing, adventure maps that can be played on iPhone and iPad. The players are advised to do whatever they like, whenever they like, unless the map specifically says not to. Maxwell journeys throughout the city of Letterbegh on his quest to discover the dark secret of the awful catastrophe that occurred, in Maxwell's Adventure, the prequel to Maxwell's Escape. The games seamlessly switch with iCloud, Face Book, and Twitter. There is a new 'shake to undo' option.

Games for Learning

Many kinds of game software have been produced to support instruction and learning. Students develop games in my computer graphics and Visual Learning classes to support their learning for another courses they are taking concurrently; for example, a project created by Craig Howie represented the basic concepts of the group theory in the form of a game and thus supported his learning for the Abstract Algebra class. González-Gancedo et al. (2012) developed and evaluated a game application working with handheld devices, multimodal interaction provided by a tactile screen, an accelerometer, and gyroscope. The authors argue that Mixed Reality Learning Environment (MRLE) should be generally accepted in the classroom, while The Virtual Reality Learning Environment (VRLE) is well established as an educational tool but expensive, and while the Augmented Reality (AR) mode is not as spread yet but may enhance user satisfaction and engagement, as the updated AR tools are modern in comparison to VR, low cost and easy to use. Jenifer Marquis & Theodor Wyeld (2011) highlighted the role of contemporary media in recasting culturally significant works in a new light. They discussed the contemporization of Dante's Inferno in the form of a computer game on PlayStation Portable, PlayStation3, and Xbox360 (http://www.ea.com/dantes-inferno). According to the authors, the contemporization of Dante's Inferno is more accessible to the current generation and loses none of its impact and meaning. Moreover, the game facilitates the search for a virtual soul-space previously reserved only for those vested with the 'given powers' (in Medieval times and prior). In this sense, the contemporization of the Inferno also brings with it much of the mythological intensity it once sought.

Gamification means the use of game design elements in non-game context to turn education into edutainment. According to Deterding, Dixon, Khaled, & Nacke (2011), with the gamification approach applications and processes are being developed to improve user engagement, region of interest, data quality, timeliness, and learning. Research studies and design relate to serious games, pervasive games, alternate reality games, or playful design (Herger, 2012). The term gamification has been coined in 2002 by Nick Pelling who actually consults manufacturers of electronic devices for entertainment.

Games for Healing

The American Heart Association (AHA) and Nintendo Co. are teaming up to promote the Wii video game console and encourage sedentary people having heart or obesity problems to exercise. From May 2010 the AHA iconic heart logo covers the console itself along with two of its active games, Wii Fit Plus and Wii Sports Resort (Schectman, 2010). Interactive projects are made with a therapeutic perspective; some games function as therapeutic or meditation tools. For example, my master's degree student Corwin Bell developed interactive computer generated biofeedback game "Journey to the Wild Divine." After graduation he established a company Journey to the Wild Divine, and then Vision Shift Studios that produces interactive computer generated biofeedback games based on doctors' consultations, e.g., "Wisdom Quest," and "Healing Rhythms, a Meditation Trainer;" he received a silver award for a Patient Safety game Air Medic Sky 1. Bell's interactive computer video games are provided with biofeedback sensors that measure heart rate and skin conductance; players not only learn to control their breathing, build mental serenity, and reduce stress; they also can access their innate power of visualization and see how their thoughts and emotions may impact their ability to play the game (Biofeedback Computer Game, 2012).

Games may serve the health-related activities (biofeedback games), and therapy, for example of children with autism (Casas, Herrera, Coma, & Fernández, 2012). People with autism who have difficulties developing verbal and nonverbal communication and do not have abstraction capacity could benefit from augmented reality because it mixes reality with computer-generated information and does not require as much capacity for abstraction as VR. Casas, Herrera, Coma, & Fernández (2012) described an augmented reality mirror showing animated avatars of children with autism spectrum disorder (ASD) surrounded with objects on a virtual scene. By means of this system, individuals with autism learn about their self-awareness, body schema and postures, communication and imitation. The users' body movements serve as a method for interaction, and children can play the AR games using the AR representations including avatars representing the child and the teacher.

Games proved themselves useful in a group work. For example, Asako Soga and Itsuo Yoshida (2012) developed a simulation system for a dance group called a corps de ballet using a gamepad. The system arranges dancers on a virtual stage and simulates dance animations by using motion-capture data obtained from a professional dancer, thus creating a tool in dance education, a self-study system for students, and a creation-support system for choreographers. Bio-interfaces and brain-computer interfaces provide the physiological information about the users and thus enable designers to create games. Bio-interfaces allow the users to participate and interact within games by connecting their physiological and brain activities with the therapeutic or entertainment systems, so they may feel and act as the co-authors. Within the scope of interaction with games, interactive games enhanced by the wearable computers "BioBodyGame" (Zuanon & Lima Jr., 2008) and "NeuroBodyGame" (Zuanon & Lima Jr., 2010) allow the users to interact with digital games through physiological and cerebral signals, and thus enhance potential of individuals with social and/or motor disabilities, severe muscle disorders such as lateral amyotrophic sclerosis, cerebral hemorrhage, and muscle damage (Zuanon, 2012).

THE PROS AND CONS OF GAMING

As specified by the Entertainment Software Association (2012), the average gamer is 30 years old; 32% of gamers are under 18 years of age. 75% of gamers are heads of households. 47% of players are women. Adult women make 30% portion of game-playing population, while boys age 17 or younger make 18%. Gamers play on-the-go: 33 percent play games on their smartphones, and 25 percent play on their handheld device.

According to Dr. Mohamed K. Khan (2006), a researcher reporting at the Council on Science and Public Health, video games have a potentially positive role, especially in the health care and education sections. Virtual reality and video games have been shown to have beneficial effects as learning aids, pain management, in rehabilitation programs for the stroke patients, education about child diabetes and asthma management, and therapy in moderating phobias (Khan, 2006). The mental health benefits of video games were noted during spells of depression. Researchers found that gamers displayed improved mood and heart rhythms compared with those who weren't playing (Wiederhold, Bouchard, & Riva, 2011). A growing body of data shows that digital games can positively alter players' attitudes and behavior. HopeLab and Stanford University researchers announced new data showing that Re-Mission™, a video game about killing cancer in the body, strongly activates brain circuits involved in positive motivation (Cole, Yoo, & Knutson, 2012). Other companies have developed video games in which winning requires players to regulate their heart rate variability, thus gaining greater control over their emotional responses to stressful situations. A new way of thinking called gamification means turning boring, unpleasant but necessary tasks into an online game.

Anderson & Warburton (2012) list helpful effects of video games, confirmed by a number of the research studies, in areas such as pain management, coordination and spatial cognition, pro-social behavior, education, and exercise. A number of studies confirm that video games such as Tetris, which require placing objects on a screen, enhance spatial cognition abilities of the players and a wide array of visual and spatial skills (Warburton, & Braunstein, 2012; Anderson & Warburton, 2012). Using event-related functional magnetic resonance imaging (fMRI), Granek, Gorbet, & Sergio (2010) examined the effect of video-game experience on the neural control of complex visuomotor tasks. Skilled individuals have demonstrated the use of a more efficient movement control brain network, including the prefrontal, premotor, primary sensorimotor, and parietal cortices. The authors documented additional prefrontal cortex activity. The experienced video gamers, in contrast with non-gamers showed the increased complex eye-hand coordination, online control, and spatial attention required for complex visually guided reaching. These data suggest that in skilled gamers the basic cortical network for processing complex visually guided reaching is altered by extensive video-game play. Hence, as Millburg (2010) argues the fMRI-based results suggest that video gaming may create skillful surgeons.

Delgado, M. R. (2007) applied neuroimaging techniques to investigation on human brain, namely, the involvement of the striatum in the circuit responsible for mediating goal-directed behavior. Striatum, as a part of human reward circuit, plays a role in the processing of affective stimuli, such as rewards and punishments, and thus influences the subsequent decision-making. Video gaming increase activity in the brain's reward circuits causing release of dopamine in dorsal striatum, which may induce positive motivation, pleasure and satisfaction response (Koepp, 1998). "The Killer," created by Matz and Luc Jacamon (http://killer.submarinechannel.com/navigate.htm) is an online graphic interactive novel in many episodes that analyzes the thoughts and feelings of a killer who kills people for money.

Figure 1, "Kill Me Again" tells about the effects of gaming on gamers' emotions and their real life. We are getting used to virtual safety, with many lives in games while accomplishing impossible missions. This makes some of us invincible in real life.

Figure 1. Anna Ursyn, "Kill me Again" (© 2010, A. Ursyn. Used with permission)

Multiple studies have been addressing effects of playing violent video games (Kronenberger, Wang & Mathews, 2012). Some game developers seek profit driven scenarios for the first-person shooter games. Many writers focus on a paradox that what is justified during the wartime, counts as a crime during the peaceful times. Some are making an excuse for doing it, having in mind that for what a single person would go to jail for one reason or another (such as killing, robbing, stealing, etc.) for the whole nations may be justified. The game industry produce games aimed at entertainment that contain violent and aggressive imaging and apply aggressive marketing techniques. Research results suggest that media violence exposure may be associated with alterations in brain functioning whether or not trait aggression is present (Mathews, Kronenberger, Wang, Lurito, Lowe, & Dunn, 2005). Anderson & Warburton (2012) list harmful effects of video games in areas such as video game addiction, attention deficits, school performance, and increased aggression. Research results about potential association between exposure to video game violence and child's aggression revealed that children's exposure to media violence caused a temporary increase in their aggressive and violent behavior (Bushman & Huesmann, 2010; Bushman & Gibson, 2011). Lee, R. (2011). The experimental neuroimaging studies found short-term (7 min to one hour) effects of violent game play in the form of a difference in activation of regions in the prefrontal cortex and amygdala that are thought to be associated with emotion, self-control, and aggression (Wang et al., 2009). Many concerns were also expressed whether those who play video game are associated with a higher risk for seizures than those who do not. However, it is not known how often this happens, and to what extent the games trigger the seizures, if at all (Epilepsy therapy project, 2012). Seizures cannot be mixed with epilepsy: "Video game-induced seizures' (VGS) is preferable than 'video game epilepsy' because this is not a syndrome" (Panayiotopoulos,

2012). Children photosensitivity, pattern sensitivity, stress, fatigue, sleep deprivation, emotional or cognitive excitation, or hyperventilation may trigger seizures not necessarily associated with playing video games.

Weber et al. (2009) analyzed users' individual experiences generated by a typical first-person-shooter game; physiological response measures (heart rate, skin conductance) were collected during the game play and analyzed on both an intra-player and inter-player level. Results indicated varying gaming experiences in the users and distinct arousal levels over time and for different game events. According to Anderson & Warburton (2012), effects of the violent video gaming on child psychology may involve many types of learning and relate to imitation (facilitated by the mirror neurons in humans and primates); identification with the aggressive characters seen; repetition of the aggressive behaviors accepted and rewarded throughout the game; interactivity and frequent rehearsal with the use of realistic weapons; lack of negative consequences (acts of violence go unpunished, are rewarded by points, money, status, and elevation to higher game levels, and have unrealistic consequences for the victim); associative learning by wiring up experiences together, for example guns are paired with aggression, killing or hurting rather than with sports shooting. Based on several authors' research results Anderson & Warburton (2012) pose that aggressive knowledge structures build attitudes and scripts for behavior: they increase aggressive behavior approval as a 'normal' behavior; increase mental access to aggressive scripts and reduce non-aggressive scripts for resolving conflicts; build attitude that aggression is exciting and increases one's social status, while the world is a frightening place; increase a hostile bias toward ambiguous but innocent behaviors by others and the likelihood of aggressive behavior. The research results suggest "that fantasy media violence seems to have similar impact on children as exposure to realistic media violence" (Anderson & Warburton, 2012, p. 74).

Video game immersive environments where acts of violence are executed in first person "have long been recognized and used by the US military forces as effective in both the training and recruitment of their members" (Holguin, 2009; Robson, 2008). As a US captain put it, playing these games doesn't waste time, it builds careers in the U.S. military; video games made better soldiers and sailors faster, safer and cheaper (Holguin, 2009). Soldiers drive virtual vehicles, fire virtual weapons, pilot virtual unmanned aerial vehicles and do "most anything a soldier does" in a virtual battle space as large as 100 kilometers by 100 kilometers. Personnel can don virtual-reality goggles and walk around virtual battle space carrying a "weapon" that allows them to shoot at virtual targets. It is just starting where this is going to go (Robson, 2008). "Anders Behring Breivik referred to the computer game Modern Warfare 2 in a 1500-page manifesto disseminated just hours before he was responsible for killing in 2011 of his 76 fellow Norwegians, 'I see MW2 more as a part of my training-simulation than anything else" (Moses, 2011).

Anderson & Warburton recommend to educate children about media effects generally and video game effects specifically, so they learn to make informed choices; help children to limit their time playing video games; encourage them to play pro-social and educational video games; keep video game consoles in public areas and out of children's bedrooms; and play video games with your children. DeWall, Anderson & Bushman (2011) developed a General Aggression Model –a social-cognitive framework for understanding aggression and violence, namely the phenomena frequently happening to a broad range of people, such as intimate partner violence, intergroup violence, global climate change effects on violence, and suicide. The authors discuss how using the General Aggression Model may be conducive for a success of the violence prevention program in these particular phenomena and areas of life. The ultimate goal is make people stop, according to

the hope expressed by Thomas Edison, "harming all other living beings."

A SCENARIO FOR A NEW GAME, "DESIGN YOUR OWN HEALTH AND BEAT YOUR UNWANTED HABITS"

Aims and Goals

The name of the game could be also "You Can Beat the Habit," "Needs and Wants," or "Obey Your Doctor." The game would help people control unwanted habits and assist in following their doctors' orders. A startup company would create a game that helps people drop their particular habits. The game developers would work with each individual (a client) to help arrange for meeting particular needs and obeying recommendations individually ordered by the doctor. The rules and objectives of the game would be tailored toward one's specific needs and restrictions, so each game would be unique. However, maybe the game design would allow clients to play with others who share similar problems. This way one can help others.

The Game Rules

Rewards for doing right things in real life (like actions recommended by a doctor) will take the form of successes in the player avatar's actions leading to advancing one's avatar on a higher level. There would be also penalties for not obeying the real life restrictions (for example, lighting up a cigarette); one's avatar will pay for this. A feedback system will show one's physiological reaction to one's own fair or mischievous behavior. Results of actions can be visualized as a graph, like one depicting the stock market in time.

Screen Design

After opening the game application, the screen of an iPhone would show two to four sections:

1. Individual restrictions clearly identified for the player depending on a habit to be worked on
2. Particular needs requesting clearly described actions into which the player would launch
3. Visualization of benefits of playing the game that will happen when one follows its requests
4. Visualization that informs what happens when one does not obey rules, or a graph showing the bad consequences of continuing addiction.

Playing in Real World and Virtual Worlds at the Same Time

This personalized game would be designed with avatars. This game would mix real-world action with game-related action because the players would fulfill in real life the requests of the game in order to advance their characters (avatars) onto a higher level of the game. They would wish the characters in a game to do well, so each player has to follow the rules to avoid bad consequences for their avatar. When one plays the game and wants one's own avatar move to the next level, the empathy toward the avatar makes the player not doing harmful things, such as smoking a cigarette, so the avatar can move to the next level. Developing empathy toward one's avatar and other people involved in the game may enhance feelings of empathy toward oneself and result in a better mood.

Research-Based Background

Playing the game could turn into a social opportunity, so players would involve into the clubs of people sharing similar problems or addictions. One could organize a feel-good 'Cocktail Party' where one serves beverages with fancy names and styles, without disclosing the actually existing lack of alcohol content. Parties may be also made online or with the use of Skype.

Research studies on biologically active substances such as oxytocin and dopamine may support our understanding why people who have friends may live longer and less frequently suffer physical and mental illness, and why we need to display our thoughts and feelings in public, online and off. Bonding together and engaging in social opportunities enhance the feeling of social empathy and compassion, so one feels stronger. Game applications may include playing the game to effectively control the level of cholesterol, enhance the effectiveness of quitting smoking, suppress uncontrolled aggression, reduce the effects of the post traumatic stress disorder, and more.

Results of research studies conducted with the use of the functional magnetic resonance imaging (fMRI) indicate that the brain activity (measured by detecting associated alterations in blood flow) change in the same way when a person under study watches real events or imaginary ones. It may happen when this person is reading a fascinating book, watching events on TV, or seeing that something dramatic happens to someone in real life. In all cases people feel similar empathy for the characters they watch. The similar signals light up in the same regions of the brain when one reacts to books, movies, games, or real people. Also, when one's avatar acts in an exciting way, the brain flow (imaged as the fMRI record) would go up, just like when seeing somebody acting in real life. The game's marketing may take advantage of the feedback feature showing that the game works effectively.

The fMRI imagining results registered also experimentation with psychosomatic reactions to tweeting. Studies conducted by a neuroeconomist Paul J. Zak et al. ask why we do what we do, and what drives human behavior (Zak, Stanton, & Ahmadi, 2007; Conlisk, 2011). The results obtained with the use of magnetic resonance imaging technique indicate a relationship between empathy and generosity. Zak's research has been applied to social media (Penenberg, 2010) and revealed that social media activity (even consisting of only

10 minutes of tweeting) triggered the release of oxytocin, thereby heightening feelings of trust, empathy, and generosity. At the same time, the reduced levels of stress hormones cortisol and ACTH accompanied the release of oxytocin while tweeting. Penenberg concludes that social networking might reduce cardiovascular risks, such as heart attack and stroke, often associated with lack of social support. Zak proposes that e-connection is processed in the brain in the same way as an in-person connection.

Antonio Damasio explored the neural basis for the mind and behavior with an emphasis on emotion, decision-making, memory, communication, and creativity. He has shown that emotions play a central role in social cognition and decision-making, and compared human behavior to horse driving: controlling horses when each of them tries to pull our carriage in different direction. Howard Gardner, the author of the theory of multiple intelligences explored human cognitive abilities; the object of his research could be compared to the content of the carriage. The factors such as beneficial effects of playing the game on players' intelligence and other cognitive features could be embedded into the game.

Some research could be needed about the players' immune system and whether dopamine and oxytocin released during playing the game (or sprayed on the player's body) could influence the immunological response of the organism. Would the player react differently after releasing oxytocin and dopamine?

The Power of Imagination (Our Own or Others)

When we say something we start to believe in it. The factor "let's pretend" occurs, which causes that, for example everyone would believe being under some influence. This can even be achieved via social bonding, sharing, and networking. It can work on two levels.

1. We can use the game environment as a psychotropic agent that affects player's imagination. It has been proved one can get drunk by drinking milk; that means one can feel really under the influence after seeing in the mind's eye getting drunk by drinking milk and willfully attaining this physiological condition.

2. When imagination becomes surpassed by reasoning one can become convinced there is alcohol in a beverage. It can work, pretty much as a placebo effect. Also in this case, imagination plays an important role, but it seems different when being convinced by someone else in spite of one's knowledge about the lack of content.

CONCLUSION

Electronic games are often created as art forms; they serve several quite different goals such as a teaching tool for education and training, entertainment, health, fitness (biofeedback games), therapy, simulation for medical diagnosis, business strategy, or business management, and a way of networking. Educational gaming may enhance student motivation and active engagement, along with behavioral approaches to learning such as: situated experiential learning; distributed (spaced) learning; blended learning combining face-to-face facilitation with computer-mediated instruction; learning with the use of texting; and discovery learning. Gamification means the use of game design elements in non-game context to turn education into edutainment.

Creating new projects including games is supported by advanced game environment and equipment; many open source platforms are capable of interacting with users through interfaces, for example Arduino. Electronic games are interactive, goal-oriented activities where players can interfere with each other on a computer or a video console. Game producers are working both on translating traditional games into video games and on creating new games. Virtual reality and video games have beneficial effects as learning aids, pain management, and in rehabilitation programs. However, multiple studies have been addressing effects of playing violent video games, deemed as having harmful effects and yet recognized and used by the US military forces. A scenario for a new game is proposed, entitled "Design your own health and beat your unwanted habits."

REFERENCES

Abt, C. C. (1970). *Serious games*. The Viking Press.

Anderson, C. G., & Warburton, W. A. (2012). The impact of violent video games: An overview. In Warburton & Braunstein (Eds.), *Growing up fast and furious: Reviewing the Impacts of Violent and Sexualised Media on Children*, (pp. 56-84). Federation Press. ISBN 1862878234

Arduino. (2012). *A home page*. Retrieved July 5, 2012, from http://arduino.cc/en/Reference/HomePage

Biofeedback Computer Game. (2012). *The journey to wild divine*. Biofeedback Software & Hardware for PC & Mac: The Passage. Retrieved from http://www.wilddivine.com/bundle-meditation-games-order-full/

Bushman, B. J., & Gibson, B. (2011). Violent video games cause an increase in aggression long after the game has been turned off. *Social Psychological and Personality Science*, 2, 29–32. doi:10.1177/1948550610379506.

Bushman, B. J., & Huesmann, L. R. (2010). Aggression. In S. T. Fiske, D. T. Gilbert, & G. Lindzey (Eds.), *Handbook of Social Psychology* (5th ed., pp. 833–863). New York: John Wiley & Sons.

Caillois, R. (1992). *Les jeux et les hommes*. Gallimard.

Casas, X., Herrera, G., Coma, I., & Fernández, M. (2012). A kinect-based augmented reality system for individuals with autism spectrum disorders. In *Proceedings of the International Conference on Computer Graphics Theory and Applications and International Conference on Information Visualization Theory and Applications*, (pp. 440-446). ISBN: 978-989-8565-02-0

Cole, S. W., Yoo, D. J., & Knutson, B. (2012). Interactivity and reward-related neural activation during a serious videogame. *PLoS ONE*. Retrieved July 5, 2012, from http://dx.plos.org/10.1371/journal.pone.0033909

Crawford, C. (2003). *Chris Crawford on game design*. New Riders Games.

Delgado, M. R. (2007). *Reward-related responses in the Human striatum*. Retrieved July 9, 2012, from http://nwkpsych.rutgers.edu/neuroscience/publications/RewardStriatum07.pdf

Deterding, S., Dixon, D., Khaled, R., & Nacke, L. (2011). From game design elements to gamefulness: Defining gamification. In *Proceedings of the 15th International Academic MindTrek Conference*, (pp. 9-15). ISBN 978-1-4503-0816-8. doi 10.1145/2181037.2181040

DeWall, C. N., Anderson, C. A., & Bushman, B. J. (2011). The general aggression model: Theoretical extensions to violence. *Psychology of Violence*, 1(3), 245-258. doi 10.1037/a0023842. Retrieved July 9, 2012, from http://www.psychology.iastate.edu/faculty/caa/abstracts./2010-2014/11DAB.pdf

Entertainment Software Association. (2012). Retrieved July 10, 2012, from http://www.theesa.com/facts/gameplayer.asp

Epilepsy Therapy Project. (2012). *Video games and epilepsy*. Retrieved July 10, 2012, from http://www.epilepsy.com/info/family_kids_video

Gardner, M. (1970). The fantastic combinations of John Conway's new solitaire game of life. *Scientific American*, *223*, 123–123.

González-Gancedo, S., Juan, M.-C., Seguí, I., Rando, N., & Cano, J. (2012). Towards a mixed reality learning environment in the classroom. In *Proceedings of the International Conference on Computer Graphics Theory and Applications and International Conference on Information Visualization Theory and Applications*, (pp. 434-439). ISBN 978-989-8565-02-0

Granek, J. A., Gorbet, D. J., & Sergio, L. E. (2010). Extensive video-game experience alters cortical networks for complex visuomotor transformations. *Cortex*, *46*(9), 1165–1177. doi:10.1016/j.cortex.2009.10.009 PMID:20060111.

Herger, M. (2012). Gamification facts and figures. *Enterprise-Gamification.com*. Retrieved March 10, 2013, from http://enterprise-gamification.com/index.php/en/facts

Holguin, J. (2009, February 11). Uncle Sam wants video gamers. *CBS News*. Retrieved July 9, 2012, from http://www.cbsnews.com/stories/2005/02/08/eveningnews/main672455.shtml

Howe, D. C., & Cayley, J. (2011). The readers project: Procedural agents and literary vectors. *Leonardo*, *44*(4), 317–324. doi:10.1162/LEON_a_00208.

Huizinga, J. (1968). *Homo ludens: A study of the play-element in culture*. Boston, MA: The Beacon Press. (Original work published 1938).

Khan, M. K. (2006). *Report of the council on science and public health: Emotional and behavioral effects, including addictive potential, of video games*. Retrieved July 7, 2012, from http://psychcentral.com/blog/images/csaph12a07.pdf

Koepp, M. J., Gunn, R. N., Lawrence, A. D., Cunningham, V. J., Dagher, A., & Jones, T. et al. (1998). Evidence for striatal dopamine release during a video game. *Nature*, *393*, 266–268. doi:10.1038/30498 PMID:9607763.

Kronenberger, W. G., Wang, Y., & Mathews, V. P. (2012). Violent video game play: What neuroimaging tells us. *Education.com*. Retrieved July 9, 2012, from http://www.education.com/reference/article/violent-video-game-play-neuroimaging/

Lee, R. (2011). Video game violence alters brain function in young men. In *Diagnostic Imaging*. UBM Medica Network. Retrieved July 9, 2012, from http://www.diagnosticimaging.com/mri/content/article/113619/1999463

Litman, L., & Davachi, L. (2008). Distributed learning enhances relational memory consolidation. *Learning & Memory (Cold Spring Harbor, N.Y.)*, *15*(9), 711–716. doi:10.1101/lm.1132008 PMID:18772260.

Marquis, J., & Wyeld, T. (2011). The contemporisation of Dante's Inferno. In *Proceedings of the 15th International Conference on Information Visualization*, (pp. 585–587). ISBN 078-0-7695-4476-2

Mathews, V. P., Kronenberger, W. G., Wang, Y., Lurito, J. T., Lowe, M. J., & Dunn, D. W. (2005). Media violence exposure and frontal lobe activation measured by functional magnetic resonance imaging in aggressive and nonaggressive adolescents. *Journal of Computer Assisted Tomography*, *29*, 287–292. doi:10.1097/01.rct.0000162822.46958.33 PMID:15891492.

Millburg, S. (2010, September 27). fMRI finds video gaming may create surgeons. *Radiology Daily: Neuroradiology*. Retrieved July 9, 2012, from http://www.radiologydaily.com/daily/neuroradiology/fmri-finds-video-gaming-may-create-surgeons/

Minecraft Forums. (2011). Retrieved July 10, 2012, from http://www.minecraftforum.net/topic/897191-puz-maxwells-escape/

Moraveji, N., Olson, B., Nguyen, T., Saadat, M., Khalighi, Y., Pea, R., & Heer, J. (2011). Peripheral paced respiration: Influencing user physiology during information work. ACM. ISBN 978-1-4503-0716-1/11/10

Moses, A. (2011). From fantasy to lethal reality: Breivik trained on Modern Warfare game. *The Sydney Morning Herald*. Retrieved July 9, 2012, from http://www.smh.com.au/digital-life/games/from-fantasy-to-lethal-reality-breivik-trained-on-modern-warfare-game-20110725-1hw41.html

Newton, J. (2012, January 27). Super Mario 3D Land is 3DS's first 5 million seller. *Nintendo Life*. Retrieved July 5, 2012, from http://www.nintendolife.com/

Nintendo Wii Virtual Console Service. (2012). Retrieved July 5, 2012, from http://en.wikipedia.org/wiki/Virtual_Console

Panayiotopoulos, C. P. (2012). *Videogame-induced seizures (VGS)*. Retrieved July 10, 2012, from http://professionals.epilepsy.com/page/video_game_seizures.html

Pelling, N. (2013). *Conundra*. Retrieved March 10, 2013, from http://www.nanodome.com/conundra.co.uk/

Robson, S. (2008, November 23). Not playing around: Army to invest $50m in combat training games. *Stars and Stripes*. Retrieved July 9, 2012, from http://www.stripes.com/news/not-playing-around-army-to-invest-50m-in-combat-training-games-1.855952911

Salen, K., & Zimmerman, E. (2003). *Rules of play: Game design fundamentals*. The MIT Press.

Schectman, J. (2010, May 17). Heart group backs Wii video game console in obesity campaign. *The Daily News (N.Y.)*.

Smed, J., & Hakonen, H. (2003). *Towards a definition of a computer game*. Turku Centre for Computer Science.

Soga, A., & Yoshida, I. (2012). Simulation system for dance groups using a gamepad. In *Proceedings of the International Conference on Computer Graphics Theory and Applications and International Conference on Information Visualization Theory and Applications*, (pp. 365-368). ISBN: 978-989-8565-02-0

Van Burnham. (2003). *Supercade: A visual history of the videogame age 1971-1984*. The MIT Press.

W3C. (2012). *Web design and applications*. Retrieved from http://www.w3.org/standards/webdesign/graphics#uses

Wang, Y., Mathews, V. P., Kalnin, A. J., Mosier, K. M., Dunn, D. W., Saykin, A. J., & Kronenberger, W. G. (2009). Short term exposure to a violent video game induces changes in frontolimbic circuitry in adolescents. *Brain Imaging and Behavior, 3*, 38–50. doi:10.1007/s11682-008-9058-8.

W. Warburton, & D. Braunstein (Eds.). (2012). *Growing up fast and furious: Reviewing the impacts of violent and sexualised media on children*. Federation Press.

Weber, R., Behr, K.-M., Tamborini, R., Ritterfeld, U., & Mathiak, K. (2009). What do we really know about first-person-shooter games? An event-related, high-resolution content analysis. *Journal of Computer-Mediated Communication, 14*(4), 1016–1037. Doi 10.1111/j.1083-6101.2009.01479.x. Retrieved July 13, 2012, from http://academic.csuohio.edu/kneuendorf/c63309/ArticlesFromClassMembers/Mu.pdf

Wideman, H. H., Owston, R. D., Brown, C., Kushniruk, A., Ho, F., & Pitts, K. C. (2007). Unpacking the potential of educational gaming: A new tool for gaming research. [from http://www. yorku.ca/rowston/unpacking.pdf]. *Simulation & Gaming, 38*(1), 1–27. Retrieved July 10, 2012. doi:10.1177/1046878106297650.

B. K. Wiederhold, S. Bouchard, & G. Riva (Eds.). (2011). *Annual review of cybertherapy and telemedicine: Advanced technologies in behavioral, social and neurosciences*. Studies in Health Technology and Informatics.

Wittgenstein, L. (2009/1953). Philosophical investigations. Wiley-Blackwell. ISBN 1405159286

Zuanon, R. (2012). Bio-Interfaces: Designing wearable devices to organic interactions. In *Biologically-Inspired Computing for the Arts: Scientific Data through Graphics*. Hershey, PA: IGI Global. doi:10.4018/978-1-4666-0942-6.ch001.

Zuanon, R., & Lima, G. C., Jr. (2008). *BioBodyGame*. Retrieved March 09, 2011, from http://www. rachelzuanon.com/biobodygame/

Zuanon, R., & Lima, G. C., Jr. (2010). *NeuroBodyGame*. Retrieved March 09, 2011, from http://www.rachelzuanon.com/neurobodygame/

Chapter 22
Visual and Verbal Storytelling

ABSTRACT

This part of the book tells about combining pictorial and verbal solutions. Visual and verbal expression is gaining additional communication possibilities by the developments in data organization techniques, such as search engines on the Internet, cognitive and semantic structuring of information, concept mapping, social networking, and cloud computing. Electronic art, Web design, and communication media support creation of electronic media languages in visual representation and design. This chapter is focused on text visualization and on storytelling delivered in various literary styles.

INTRODUCTION

The 'words–image,' 'image–words' are generally used dichotomies. Art–science is another traditional dichotomy. 'Word' is often associated with science and 'image' with art. Depending on one's scientific or artistic grounding particular objects of interest are becoming the foreground figures on a scene, while the rest is the background. We often strive to free ourselves from such divisions into mutually exclusive parts, and to achieve more holistic, rich creation or production. Integrative approach to multi-sensual, multidisciplinary, and multimedia-oriented creative processes is fundamental in art creating, learning, and instructional strategies. We can recall several approaches of masters in their fields that may combine into a holistic picture. Intellectual potential described by Howard Gardner (1993a,b,c) who taught about

at least eight intelligences with resulting mental formations and predispositions of the mind. Feelings and emotions compared by Antonio Damasio (1994, 1999) to horse driving: we have to control horses when each of them tries to take our carriage in different direction. Neural basis of artistic creativity makes attitudes and behaviors more understandable with the advent of neurophysiology and imaging techniques. While exploring neuroaesthetics, a study of the neural basis of artistic creativity and achievement, Semir Zeki (1999) arrived at a conclusion, "artists are, in a sense, neurologists who unknowingly study the brain with techniques unique to them." Multidimensional and multisensory experiences offered by interactive generative art enable the combining and complementing image and word.

There is a wide range of ways of transferring visual material to verbal description but there is a scarce guidance for going from written material to visual presentation. We present information both in visual context and verbally. For working on a spe-

DOI: 10.4018/978-1-4666-4627-8.ch022

cific project we may interlace various knowledge areas and combine several approaches, techniques, creative processes, and products including digital persuasion. We can use figures of visual rhetoric, digital storytelling, electronic writing, and convey one message in various literary styles. Visual and verbal expression allows creating messages that exist between literary and digital modes. The developments in data organization techniques enhance visual and verbal communication. Electronic art, web design, and communication media support creation of electronic media languages of visual representation and design, and thus communication media add the visual approach to social networking. Content delivery in a visual form enables verbal and graphic info presentation, sending out our work on the web, and then user/visitor's interactivity through the web. This way, the joined techniques and processes in working on a specific project can go by retrieving, visualizing, representing, and sharing our knowledge through visual and verbal metaphors.

BEYOND WORDS: VISUALIZING TEXT

The use of electronic media can be put in service in gathering, processing, evaluating, judging, organizing, and publishing information, which allows looking at communication from another angle, using other tools and links. We may organize our thoughts about the writing and its visual counterparts around the basic (and advanced) notions already accumulated and splendidly organized on the web. A somewhat eclectic way of originating this approach requires combining the best results from the efforts of people engaged in many domains, for example visual perception and action, psychology, computer science, philosophy, and also:

- **Linguistics and Language Processing:** Research how humans use words to communicate ideas and feelings, and how such communications are processed and understood (e.g., Edwards, Nagarajan, Dalal, Canolty, Kirsch, Barbaro, & Knight, 2010)
- **Natural Language Processing:** Investigation on interactions between computers and human languages and formalization of natural language semantics as part of computer science and artificial intelligence (Duan & Cruz, 2011)
- **Language Acquisition:** Study on human capacity to perceive and comprehend language and produce words that involves neuroimaging and neurocognitive techniques to analyze brain development, syntax (rules controlling the arrangement of words and phrases in sentences), phonetics (study on speech sounds), vocabulary, and grammar (e.g., Sakai, 2005)
- **Computational Linguistics:** Deals with modeling of natural language from computational perspective (e.g., Uszkoreit, 2000)
- **Neurolinguistics:** A part of linguistics focused on the biological basis of the relationship of the human language and brain (e.g., Phillips & Sakai, 2005)
- **Speech Perception and Production:** Focused on psychological and phonetic study on symbolic units corresponding to phonological segments or phonemes (Casserly & Pisoni, 2010)
- **Semantics:** Logical, formal, and cognitive studies on word meaning, involving semiotics, logic, mathematics, and computer science
- **Categorization:** A part of cognitive activity fundamental for the process of comprehension, differentiation, and understanding, used to group objects into classes, called categories or concepts (e.g., Frey, Gelhausen, & Saake, 2011).

- **Cognitive Neuroscience:** Examining biological structures, mostly neural, involved in cognition and mental processes (e.g., Gazzaniga, 2004)
- **Neural Models of Cognition:** Studies on cognitive mechanisms under internal representations stored in working memory and long-term memory, examined with neuroimaging and behavioral methods (e.g., D'Esposito, 2007).

The integrative approach to gathering and delivering data will encompass objectives in art, literary works, and computer graphics. Commonly known beauty and the complexity of nature cause a need to represent it in one's own personal way. The further text will combine visual and literary arts, science, and visualization to cause that the visual comes beyond the verbal and verbal beyond the visual. It will explore concepts such as verbal versus graphic information presentation and ask whether it is better to present data in a visual context or verbally, and ask how can we deliver given facts and knowledge in a visual

form to achieve a successful conclusion. This task will require navigating among reading/writing, visual arts, science, mathematics, and other subjects, and discussing some broader issues such as multicultural, environmental or social objectives. Words arranged in shapes and patterns may create a picture, such as the ones drawn by my students (Figure 1).

However, with a simple change such as a comma placement the meaning can be changed completely. Lynn Truss (2006) illustrates this truth with an example: two sentences, 'A woman without her man is nothing" and 'A woman: without her, man is nothing' convey opposite messages depending on punctuation.

Studies on cognitive architecture indicate that the relationship between operations in language and mathematics (numbers) seems to be largely independent on structure: patients with agrammatic aphasia who could not verbalize their mathematical operations display sensitivity to, and use of syntactic principles in mathematics (Varley, Klessinger, Romanowski, & Siegal, 2005). These conceptions are also related to media communi-

Figure 1a. Heather Martinez, "A Tree" (© 2013, H. Martinez. Used with permission). Figure 1b. Rachel Hitchers "A Note" (© 2013, R. Hitchers. Used with permission).

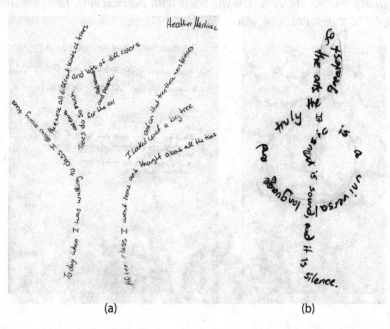

(a)   (b)

cation. They are decisive factors in web delivery used for gathering information and sending out our work and user/visitor's interactivity through the web. They are also important for students and teachers. While writing about art might support one's literary development, the approach to literary works in terms of art-related concepts might encourage to solve such work visually using art as a source of inspiration, apply signs, icons, and metaphors, and still maintain informative quality of the writings. Some of advantages coming from visual approach to media communication may come from the importance of playful ways of solving such tasks. Figure 2 provides an example of a cooperative work.

Visual Rhetoric

The creation of meaning with the use of visual language is a focal part of visual rhetoric. It involves the use of rhetorical figures focused on the data, which are aimed at enhancing understanding for the user by inserting figures of connection (where a viewer may deduct how the depicted elements

can be associated and be linked), comparison for similarity (a metaphor), opposition (enhancing a difference), and figures of combination (a pictorial simile) (Lengler & Vande Moere, 2009). Visual rhetoric studies include analyses of the production of images, objects, or visual phenomena in society; the relationship between representation, communication, and knowledge; perception, reception, and interpretation of images; historical considerations of the reception of the image; and political examinations of the role of the image in society (Helmers, 2012).

In a visual society, story composition should not only contain writing but also create visual communication. Visual rhetoric may be seen a counterpart of spoken rhetoric – the art of discourse, as it draws attention to cultural meaning of images. There is a strong connection between visual images and persuasion, because images act rhetorically upon viewers, whether they appear in architecture, paintings, film, needlepoint, or communication with social media (Hill & Helmers, 2008). Persuasion is usually meant a means to convince a listener, reader, or a viewer by appealing to their reasons,

Figure 2. Anna Ursyn, A Bedtime Story. A still from a movie involving choreography, image, and time-lapsed meteorological films. © 2002, A. Ursyn. Used with permission). Imaging and video by Anna Ursyn. Choreography by Sandra Minton, music by Philip Glass.

values, beliefs, and emotions (About.com, 2012). Rhetorical analyses of various media are closely related to the study of semiotics and include, but are not limited to television, film, photography, computer imaging, illustrated books, billboards, marketing, politics, and propaganda. Rhetorical analysis of art history shows various ways the visual tropes were applied in art works, according to the rhetorical canon of their arrangement – the organization of visual elements so that readers can see their structure; emphasis – making certain parts more prominent than others by changing its size, shape and color; clarity – that helps the reader to decode the message, to understand it quickly and completely; conciseness – generating designs that are appropriately succinct to a particular situation; tone – that reveals the designer's attitude towards the subject matter; and ethos – earning the trust of the person receiving the message (Kostelnick & Roberts, 2010).

Visual rhetoric, as a part of visual communication, supports one's visual literacy, visual thinking, and visual learning by enhancing metaphorical thinking, visualization, and ability to recognize the full worth of images, art works, and media presentations. Lengler & Vande Moere (2009) postulate that designers should be educated in principles of visual rhetoric to become effective in communication in a particular knowledge domain, solve the problems of aesthetics, and achieve visual inference. Creating digital stories involves meaning making, which supports understanding and learning. With visual rhetoric we can use images in reasoning and disputes, arrange elements on a page, enhance its typography, and analyze existing images and visuals (Visual Rhetoric Overview, 2011).

Visual Persuasion and Some Figures of Visual Rhetoric

Figures of visual rhetoric add strength to the message contained in a visual story. First of all, many agree that a capacity to draw is important when it comes to attain visual quality of a visualization, video, animation, or a website design project. Moreover, drawing as 'storytelling' and a journalistic record might provide a useful bridging phenomenon between traditional and new drawing practices.

One of the most effective visual tools is a visual metaphor, "the representation of a person, place, thing, or idea by way of a visual image that suggests a particular association or point of similarity" (Nordquist, 2012). Metaphors that show something analogical between what is presented and what's intended to be meant are often applied in advertising, as well as in visual storytelling. The metaphor is widely applied in the visual way of communication. We may also put an accent on the most important object of our interest by showing it in strong color. However, one needs to remember that every color coexists with others (Albers, 2010/1963). Sometimes we may want to apply personification of an abstract quality by drawing it as a human form, such as a mascot of a country, a movement, or an event. Many times it is a visual pun that acts in a similar way as verbal puns. For instance, an Italian painter Giuseppe Archimboldo (1526-1593) (2012) compiled human portraits from organic items: vegetables and flowers. Anacoluthon means that the showing an impossible image acts in a similar way as writing a sentence lacking grammatical sequence (an anacoluthic sentence) by putting stress on the message. In order to add meaning due to a causal, spatial, or temporal relationship, we may include a metonymic picture of a product or a place of an action, for example, by drawing a racing car or racing track to amplify the feeling of acceleration. Commercials of the Absolut Vodka (1999) beverages can often be seen as metonymies, as they substitute objects or situations for their products. We call a hyperbole those rhetorical figures that create emphasis or exaggeration. Using a symbol showing a characteristic part of an object (such as an Eiffel Tower in Paris) may be seen a visual counterpart of a synecdoche in writing, and particular case of metonymy (Dürsteler, 2012).

Ekphrasis is considered another rhetorical tool where one medium of art may represent another medium and vice versa. For example, an artwork may be described by defining the essence of its content or the spirit of a book may be filmed. Any type of artistic medium may serve as an object or a tool for ekphrasis if it distills the rhetorical element from the story of the theme of it. Origins of ekphrasis can be found in Plato (2008), who discusses in the *Republic*, Book X forms constructed by a craftsman, such as a bed and compares them to an ideal form of a bed, an archetype – an original and example of an ideal image of a bed. Plato said,

A bed, when looked obliquely, straight on, or from whatever direction, does not differ from itself, but its appearance changes all the time. How can that be a real thing which is never in the same state? At the moment that the observer approaches, then things become other and of another nature. (Plato, Republic [598A]).

Craftsmen and later artists attempted to manifest perfection of their work in ekphrasis using artistic or literary medium to illuminate and elevate forms that might be not seen in the original or might be not yet produced. Joseph Stanton (1999), in his book "Imaginary Museum: Poems on Art" attempted to go to the heart of the matters in the masterpieces of art: paintings, noh plays, tales, and movies. His strategies for ekphrasis include description of the artwork, interpretation of another poem's meaning, storytelling, writing mini-biographies, comments on art exhibitions, or dreamlike writings inspired by somebody else's artwork. Figure 3, "Ekphrasis" is a student work on this theme.

Art and other disciplines may produce mutual inspiration and enhance one another. To be workable, every website must be visually attractive, simple, and effective, and thus delightful to look at. Visual quality is of utmost significance when people visually arrange and present knowl-

Figure 3. Anna Thompson, Ekphrasis (© 2012, A. Thompson. Used with permission).

edge by shifting from digits to pixels, even in specialized areas, for example, by creating artwork for financial analysis with the use of an information visualization technique, applying a 3D city metaphor for software production visualization, or making visual tools for editing and browsing semantic web resources. For an exercise in visual rhetoric, see Table 1.

Electronic Writing and the Literary-Based Digital Art

Visual rhetoric of a text denoting textual artifacts and non-textual marks on a surface of the screen is a subject matter of the electronic writing (mostly done through programming in Processing, JavaScript, HTML, Java, Python, or C) and the literary based digital art. Workshops, studio discussions, for example Interrupt 1 (2008) and Interrupt 2 (2012), monographs (e.g., A Companion to Digital Literary Studies, 2008), textbooks, and courses are available to those who are interested. The Gutenberg Project founded in 1971 was the first attempt to create a digital library, and then Google announced in 2004 it would digitize 15 million

Table 1. Playing with visual rhetoric

Visual Solution: Change of Tactic
Find an object in your pocket, a bag, or a backpack. Do not show it to your partner. Sit back-to-back with your partner so you cannot see one another. One of you will verbally portray the object you have just selected while the other person will sketch it based on its description. Then reverse the roles, this time using a new object. When verbally characterizing the object do not provide its name, just describe its characteristics, shape, and approximate measures. Compare the drawings with objects.

books. Digital literary studies examine relations between text, image, and space in an interactive environment, while interactive forms of kinetic poetry can be seen in works of authors and artists such as Jenny Holzer (2012), Ken Perlin (2012), or Marion Bataille (2008).

One may ask a question about a changing role of a diary as a literary and communication tool. A personal journal was an important way of imparting one's thoughts, experiences, feelings, and meaningful data in a private way. The data is now automatically recorded on the bank, credit card, and other files and becomes part of a global library, often accessible for many. Everyday life is thus traceable through clouds and often a feasibility of gaining information does not depend on one's consent or a written account. The Facebook, Twitter, and other social interaction tools and online networking platforms make that thoughts, experiences and feelings are shared, which causes that they are not anymore private, exclusive, or secret. This way pictures, photographs, and even drawings, sketches, paintings, and sculptures are displayed and recorded along with their statements or short descriptions. Personal websites offer image/text integration that is often dynamic and interactive. This can be made even easier with an Apple iCloud Photo Stream application.

Figure 4. Anna Ursyn, A Bedtime Story. A still from a short film. © 2002, A. Ursyn. Used with permission). Imaging and video by Anna Ursyn, Choreography by Sandra Minton, Music by Philip Glass.

Digital poetry may mean various forms of verses including sonnets or haiku written by computer programs; one may also find words combined with images into visual poetry, with patterns of words or letters placed randomly or plotted. Visual poetry contains a visual arrangement of text, images and symbols used to convey the intended meaning of the work. Concrete poetry predates visual poetry. Kinetic poems are plotted into motion, morphed according to a program, or interactively manipulated by viewers (Figure 4). Coding programs and languages combine letters and words with graphics, animation, video, sound, and other coded elements, often with an input from viewers (Funkhouser, 2008).

We can distinguish the linear from non-linear narrative. Linear narratives e.g., instructions, the official transcripts, or children stories have a beginning, a middle, an end; they are logical and usually sequential in nature. Non-linear narratives, for example a French literary form the nouveau roman or online interactive novels comprise interruption, circular and unfinished references, and chronological disarray (Hammerstingl, 1999). Hypertext is not constrained to a linear form, has

its hierarchical or tree-like structure, and contains links to other hypermedia, makes a metaphor for representation of text on a screen, with the scroll and the codex options available for displaying text on a computer screen. Words of Christian Vandendorpe (2008) who pointed out a few years ago, "the perfect e-book should also allow the user to manipulate documents as with Adobe Acrobat: highlighting, selecting, copying, commenting, and exchanging. …The real magic will come in the second act, as each word in each book is cross-linked, clustered, cited, extracted, indexed, analyzed, annotated, remixed, reassembled and woven deeper into the culture than ever before " refer as well to Microsoft Word, Adobe Photoshop, and many other kinds of software. Interactive novel and interactive fiction adventure games were created as Hypertext versions; for example, a writer and a speechwriter for President Reagan Robert Pinsky is an author of the interactive fiction game *Mindwheel* developed in 1984 by Synapse Software and released by Broderbund. It was an interactive storytelling on a black-and-white screen of a Macintosh computer where the story would develop differently depending on choices and decisions made by a reader. Other programs, especially those designed for children involved clickable objects that could be triggered by a touch of a mouse to be animated, speak their names in various languages, or change their position.

STORYTELLING

Generally, storytelling refers both to the archived oral tradition in storytelling in different cultures, times, and places, and to digital storytelling using a variety of media formats, and involves words or written texts, images, gestures, sounds, and animated graphics to let the recipient know about incidents, occurrences, or events, and thus convey education, games, entertainment, (along with edutainment as a form of entertainment aimed at educating as well as entertaining) or cultural and moral traditions. It maybe useful to realize that the raw data such as observations, equations, structural formulas, or spectra are useless without the narrative theoretical framework that makes a story out of them. For many multi-media communication complex institutions, communicating by using fiction storytelling techniques can be a more compelling and effective route than using only dry facts. Stories also help us make sense of the world (Hensel, 2010). Stewart Friedman (2009) stresses the importance for the political and management leaders of mastering skills to engage hearts and minds and resonate with the audience.

Storytelling in the past often carried spiritual content, such as when Australian Aboriginal storytellers painted symbolic visual stories on sand or rocks, following the path of the spirits controlling their hands. Storytelling before the emergence of writing served for preserving memory of important events, such as in the case of a Greek epic poem Iliad ascribed to Homer, retold by centuries with many improvised embellishments. Some stories were not recorded at all but repeated by storytellers often enough to preserve its presence in a society, played with the use of shadow puppets or masks,

as theatrical performances, games, or serial events. Stories often evolved by being told by people with different personalities and perspectives.

With the advent of writing, the writings recorded on rocks, wood, bamboo, clay, pottery, silk, papyrus, or paper complemented visual storytelling. Folklorists discern legends and fairy tales as the main groups of oral tales. Folkloric storytelling includes fairy tales about not necessarily true, often supernatural events, along with legends about true events happening in particular places and times, as well as extraterrestrial and ghost stories. Writers tell stories in their poems, novels, biographies, articles, museum displays, theatrical plays, and films. Many times, the same story about what happened is retold several times by the characters in a play or a movie, with similar props but changed events in each story. Actors, singers, and comedians use legends or folkloric materials along with historical data to engage their audience interest. The audience visualizes the events by creating personal mental images, reacting to the words and gestures of the storyteller, and thus becoming co-creators of the spectacle and motivating the teller to improvise. Children books with traditional stories often contain educational content, sometimes at the expense of a time-honored tale. For example, in some American editions a bottle of wine has been removed from a basket carried by a girl from the Charles Perrault's (2012) 'Little Red Riding Hood' (rewritten later by Brothers Grimm).

Sequential Art

Storytelling is an art form that can be annotated as sequential art that uses a string of images to produce a graphic storytelling or deliver knowledge. It is an old form of art, as the cave paintings, Egyptian hieroglyphs, pre-Columbian pictorial artifacts wall paintings from different times and places, old friezes, vases, tapestries, embroideries, scrolls, and later, printed series of graphics and numerous paintings – all depict informative

Figure 5. Anna Ursyn, The Kardelup Family. (© 2010, A. Ursyn. Used with permission).

stories to document their times. Contemporary examples of sequential works are comics printed in newspapers and magazines, for example comics created by Scott McCloud (2006). They are often presented later as films and animations, web comics, storyboards used for preparing motion pictures of different kinds such as a motion graphic, film, animation, or interactive presentation for the social media or interactive websites.

Storytelling by Drawing

Drawings are the strong tools for storytelling as they can act as an interface between the visual and the verbal. Visual storytelling adds the fourth dimension as it allows wandering across time and space to follow the events that happen to the characters we draw. Storytelling achieved by drawing pictures conveys to a computer screen the visceral, emphatic, or voyeuristic emotions and evokes emotional response from the audience. The same may be told about the effectiveness of animation in storytelling, as adding the time dimension enhances dramatic actions, shows suspenseful obstacles, and builds tension before solving a conflict. Sketches may serve as a starting point to create manga, blogs, even product and architectural schemes, and other forms.

Teaching drawing and computing techniques including computer graphics becomes a part of the collaborative interdisciplinary curricula designed for art and computer science undergraduates. Storytelling Studies became an interdisciplinary field, or as a discipline unto itself. One may find on the Internet long lists of storytelling courses delivered all over the world, workshops, and textbooks. One can also learn about digital storytelling and new media narrative (Caputo, Ellison, & Steranko, 2011). On Vimeo, one can find short videos on the future of storytelling. The Center for Storytelling (http://centerforstorytelling.org/2012) is a network of storytelling specialists from science, research, management, design, media and art. Transmedia storytelling, also known as multi-platform storytelling, cross-platform storytelling, or transmedia narrative, is the technique of telling stories across multiple platforms and formats using current digital technologies, involved in branding, performance, ritual, play, activism, spectacle, as other logics (Jenkins, 2011).

Figure 5 shows a series of casted in bronze figurines from a story entitled "Kardelups"

Kardelups

1. Kardelups and their robots

Kardelups are virtual space musicians that live in a Fractal City. Their music is stellar. Their names are: Δ, ç, ¥˙, Δ, $\int$, †, ∂, f, $\approx$, ß, π, $\sqrt{}$, $\leq$, Ω, å, ß, ¥, $\sum$´,†, and ¥. The size of a Virtual

Musician, their intelligence, and other qualities are visible, and everyone knows what to expect from every one. Kardelups have spheres emulating their thoughts, projecting info, and recording everything – exchange of information, musical composition, or the entered data, such as texts, images, video, sensation of touch, presence, or sounds. For this reason, all info is public, easy accessible, and permanent. Each police officer can be detected, except for those specializing in intellectual property thefts, as Kardelups do all kinds the creative or cognitive work.

Kardelups create artwork that is touch-based. Everything is so sterile that Kardelups lost one of their senses: smell. They kept writing about those prehistoric times when they could smell from a distance. Now there is touch but no feel. Touching it a triggering action; otherwise their artwork is sleeping. Actually, it it's in a sleeping mode most of the time.

Kardelups have everything they need, including a personal robot, or two, if they choose so. Robots perform ubiquitous, pervasive computing: hey can do anything and their masters may not necessarily be aware what their robots are doing. They are practically sets of attachable parts, and detachable, of course. They can organize virtual parties, concerts, art shows, and projections. They accompany their master Kardelups to all virtual trips, dances, and social gatherings. Robots are fluent in programming, so whatever is explained to them as a task, they'd select a language and perform the whole operation. They are also able to conduct discussions utilizing databases, and thus to invert concepts and find proper solutions. They are good at defending their owners, both physically and legally. Robots are given the same to everyone, and it is up to a Kardelup to train them, so robots could produce parts and extensions and go beyond the task by building devices that promote offline interactions. Each robot expands and grows its abilities every day, so they end up differing in functions they are capable to perform,

and also in their looks. Instead of competing who's having more expensive objects, Kardelups would rather look at whose robot is the best trained, and whose one can teach itself to do new things. The best state of a robot was a robot-making robot.

There is no competition among Kardelups. Everyone lives in "one-man shop environment." It does not matter which spot on the virtual space one has because all window views, trips, or travels are virtual. Since Kardelups rarely leave their places, there is no such thing as good or bad neighborhood. The only currency is one's creativity. The highest level of intimacy is to share a robot, keep improving it together, so it would support online offline interactions, and engagements, both playful and serious.

2. Fractal City of Kardelups

In a Fractal City, energy is saved and security improved. Each fractal city works like a skyscraper. One family can live on the first floor and own their summerhouse on the 11th floor, and they can get there using an oversized elevator. Both the apartments and summerhouses are built as mirrored fractal designs, so a family can enter a different kitchen without seeing any difference. All fractal cities have some floors kept for the housing needs, others for work, yet another floors for are selected for shopping, gym, recreation centers, and games. There are floors producing goods for all the cities. There are districts for various kinds of services, where plumbers, electricians, bakers, or party caterers live and work. Kardelups learn their trades and tricks from a neighboring shop. Work floors are designated for selected professions that support nearby areas: the entertainers, actors, directors, and producers share the floor with musicians, stage designers, and artists.

Fractal cities follow the sustainable architecture rules: Kardelups recycle the wastewater and use it for watering vegetables and plants on the roof; they collect compost and recycle it in the gardens. There is no demand for grass as it takes space and energy. Those who like nature and fresh food can go as far as on 22nd floor to see real cows. There are no insects such as annoying mosquitoes. The penalty for killing an animal is close to that for killing a person, unless one would get permission (decision about it is available in seconds, usually a negative one, but there are exceptions). There is no need for cars, there are just elevators and fast-moving sidewalks. Kardelups' addresses are quite complicated. They indicate a city, a shelf, a row, a number of a shelf scraper, followed by the number of a shelf scraper in that row, then the floor, and the apartment. Thus, one could live at the following address: A 2-3-6-7-8-10.

Storytelling in Multimedia

All these traditional myths, legends, fairytales, folktales, parables, and fables found their place in the current multimedia communication storytelling techniques, so digital storytelling could take over the old art in current modes of expression. Present-day story visualization technologies combine storytelling with multimedia formats such as text, images, sound, and movement with narratives, commentaries, and depictions in a dynamic, often interactive environment, so the viewer becomes the co-creator of the art. They use Powerpoint, Flickr, Movie Maker, digital photos, and videos, to address issues and challenges, enrich information, evoke responses, and emotionally involve people, serving for making news, business-related, marketing, educational, and training applications.

Visualization of huge resources of information such as libraries, email archives, applications running the World Wide Web, or things such as a blog, a wiki, a tweeter feed is helping to analyze such data. Text representation goes on three levels: lexical (transformation of strings of characters into a sequence of tokens), syntactic (identifying and annotating each token's function), and semantic level, which extracts the meaning and relationships between pieces of knowledge derived from

the structures identified at the syntactical level (Ward, Grinstein, & Keim, 2010, p. 291, 292).

Users select the level of interaction and decide how they would like to access the content. Visual projects interpret parts crafted in other media. Picture books, theatre, television, and movies extract abstract information of the story (that may refer to fiction or nonfiction) into concrete visual scenes to enhance experience and evoke emotions. There is a National Storytelling network, with a web page www.storynet.org dedicated to advancing the art of storytelling. There are also many websites and online projects presenting digital storytelling environment. The Center for Digital Storytelling (CDS, 2012), an international organization for training and research assists youth and adults in using digital media tools to craft, record, and share stories in ways that enable learning, build community, and inspire justice. For example, Colorado universities are working with CDS to deliver a graduate-level Digital Storytelling Certificate Program. See Table 2 for an exercise in multi-faceted storytelling.

We may notice many functions of storytelling. Digital storytelling, used in television to show the news and ubiquitous in multimedia in the form of text and animated graphics, coexists often with other techniques and is an important factor in managing communication in the news, business, education, and training. Online journalists and TV reporters combine text, image, sound and movement into a dynamic environment, and thus they are able to tell, show, explain, demonstrate, and discuss the issues, which is appealing for Internet newsreaders. In many cases digital storytelling combines performance with physical/virtual interaction, visual surveillance technology, motion tracking, and artificial intelligence. Visual storytelling may assume multidimensional, interactive features. Ricou & Pollock (2012) created an about 8 ft diameter soft sculpture, the *Spiral of Life*, a symbol for the evolution of life based on a Tree of Life web project http://tolweb.org/tree/ and an interactive Tree of Life website

Table 2. Presenting action in multiple forms.

Your Visual Response: Present Your Recent Actions
Maybe you will find it both amusing and productive to express your thoughts or tell about your recent adventure, first in a way you feel more comfortable with: writing a short verse or drawing a picture, and then enhance your project with the other way of expression. The combined project may convey a more intense message than a single work – literary or pictorial. The image does not have to illustrate your writing in detail by showing the objects or metaphors it contains. Also, do not describe item by item the content of your picture. Both your works will amplify your statement by encouraging the viewers/readers to build their own connotations and constructing a full account of the issue.

http://itol.embl.de/. Their "soft sculpture doubled as a storytelling stage and a tactile playground … when Ricou performs the Story of Evolution, reading the sculpture like a book with children, exploring horizontal and vertical processes as physical structures" (Ricou & Pollock, 2012, p.24).

Crafting a story is a challenging task because a story should be engaging both intellectually and visually. Readers and listeners convey the words into a virtual environment in their own mind (Zeng & al., 2003). A story has to evoke the audiences' response and meet their cognitive and emotional needs for gaining new information, binding with a story heroes, participating in a conflict, feeling suspense resulting from threat and uncertainty, enjoying the completion, and being entertained, many times in voyeuristic, visceral, and vicarious way. Digital storytellers work on multiple levels: combine words and ideas into a story structure, select the level of interaction, and include audio, photo, and video. They often apply a comic strips metaphor, or animate the events.

Anyone can tell their story in their own way. People using computers and personal photographs make videos with a digital camera, edit them (or not), and upload the films onto the video-sharing

Table 3. Story-writing

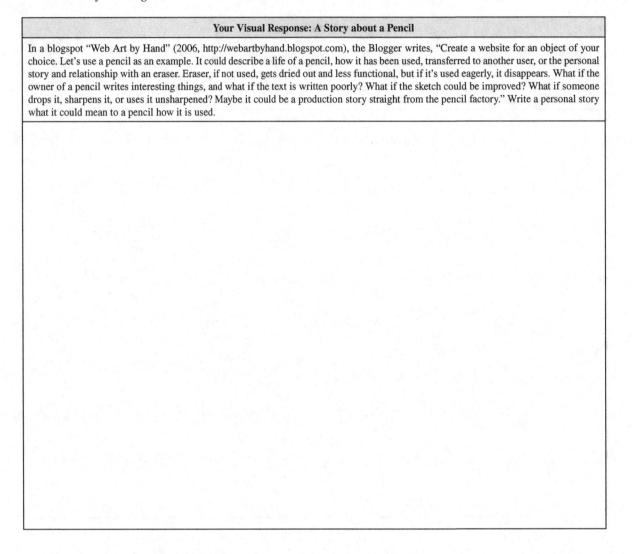

Your Visual Response: A Story about a Pencil
In a blogspot "Web Art by Hand" (2006, http://webartbyhand.blogspot.com), the Blogger writes, "Create a website for an object of your choice. Let's use a pencil as an example. It could describe a life of a pencil, how it has been used, transferred to another user, or the personal story and relationship with an eraser. Eraser, if not used, gets dried out and less functional, but if it's used eagerly, it disappears. What if the owner of a pencil writes interesting things, and what if the text is written poorly? What if the sketch could be improved? What if someone drops it, sharpens it, or uses it unsharpened? Maybe it could be a production story straight from the pencil factory." Write a personal story what it could mean to a pencil how it is used.

site YouTube. Digital stories (short films) make a new medium that is present on popular web sites. A story may comprise separate stories set against the common ground in past, present or future (Table 3). Audiences follow the troubles, hopes, and efforts of the characters, and thus they explore the issues presented by the storyteller. For example, an interactive web-based video series lonelygirl15 achieved massive popularity in the years 2006-2008, and then was put to end as fictional. This hit online series was nominated for several YouTube Awards but won nothing (Heffernan, 2007).

Brian Alexander (2011) describes platforms for tales and telling, as the Web 2.0 storytelling, social media storytelling, and gaming storytelling on a small and a large scale. He also comments on the combinatorial storytelling involving networked books, stories designed for mobile devices, alternate reality games, and for augmented reality where digital content is linked to the physical world. Telling stories may take form of the Web 2.0 storytelling by involving Web 2.0 tools, technologies, and strategies to become self-contained units posted at social media. As Alexander & Levine (2008) put it, "Stories now are open-ended, branching, hyperlinked, cross-media, participatory, exploratory, and unpredictable. And they are told in new ways: Web 2.0 storytelling picks up these new types of stories and runs with them, accelerating the pace of creation and participation while revealing new directions for narratives to flow."

Combined use of natural language processing and 3-D computer graphic techniques can enhance human-to-human interaction. Within a storytelling medium readers and listeners convey the meaning of the words into virtual environment (Zeng, Mehdi, & Gough, 2003). The non-professionals can generate an interactive 3D virtual story environment based on a story-based natural language input, where a sentence in human language acts on a language engine and a graphic engine. This approach bridges the gap between scripting/storyboarding by a nontechnical creative writer and rendering characters and scenes by a graphics specialist

When exploring concepts such as verbal-versus-graphic information presentation one may ask whether it is better to present data in a visual context or verbally, and how can we deliver given facts and knowledge in a visual form to achieve a successful conclusion. Authors creating for communication media and social networking sites navigate among reading/writing, visual arts, science and computer science, mathematics, and other fields discussing some broader issues such as multicultural, environmental, or social objectives. This approach to combining several tasks is a decisive factor in web delivery used for gathering information, sending out our work, and user/visitor's interactivity through the web. It is also important for college students and also prospective and in-service teachers.

Connecting visual and verbal expression with all communication possibilities given by electronic media and the Web would certainly include the developments in data organization techniques (searching on the Internet, cognitive

and semantic structuring of information), and the creation of electronic media languages of visual representation and design (art, web design, concept mapping). Thus, we may organize our thoughts about the writing and its visual counterparts around the basic (and advanced) notions already accumulated and organized on the Web (there are more and more of splendid works of this type) that interlace various knowledge areas. Taking a full advantage of digital media offerings helps attenuate constrains coming from the inadequate artistic skills one might possess by comparing oneself to artists and drawing conclusions about one's own work. The graphic environment supports us to overcome the fear to create art when we feel unable to draw well, as with computers we can manipulate and transform scanned images instead of coping with a blank page to draw on. There are numerous online projects about storytelling, for example, by Paul & Fiebich (2012).

THE IDEA OF A CONTAINER FOR A STORY

The rapid pace of evolvements in the time-based and interactive technologies may lead us to one unambiguous conclusion that our work should begin with the container: how the story is being delivered.

Every story needs to be told differently for each medium, be it a graph, animation, web, manga, film, theater, radio, podcasting, comics, or other means by which it is communicated. The writer needs to retell the story to match the framework, timing, and technical requirements of each medium. Every discipline – archeology, history, geology, online environment, a game, to name just a few – can be seen, or even should be seen as a set of stories, moreover, visual stories. The way we unfold and deliver the story depends on our needs and the environment. For example, a web page developer should not only design a project but also make it fit for the changing environment actually perceived by the user. Therefore we have to analyze cultural implications of our products from the perspective of the viewer, not only in the artist's frame of reference. It may cause a need for interdisciplinary training, to become equipped to not only to produce pretty pictures but also be able to bring about a cross-cultural impact, since the product delivery is usually tested under specific technical or cultural conditions. Moreover, it may create a need for exploration of a tension existing between the precise way of drawing and scientific thinking that is typical of engineers and analysts and expressive drawing as an instrument of thinking through art. Even so, scientists, business managers, and production specialists produce artwork for analyzing and disseminating information in a visual form, for example, when creating a real-time portfolio textures to visualize financial data.

Crafting a Story as a Container; Creating the Same Story in Various Literary Styles: A Project

It might be entertaining to write a short story and then rework it in several ways, thus creating various kinds of containers for the same story according to a specific literary style, and then creating illustrations for this story. You may want to re-create your story in other literary styles, every time changing its design according to the goal and purpose. After that, explain the features of particular types of writing and write a critique of your visual and verbal creations (see Table 4 for a story-writing exercise).

For this purpose, you may want to begin with writing a short story. You may first want to decide about who would be the hero, what would be an objective of the story, when and where the action would happen, why the conflict would ensue, and how would you design the fabric of the story. A theme for your story will determine a mood, a sequence of story actions that structure the tale

and will support an introduction of characters that will act there; also it will dictate the way of describing their garment such as shirts and trousers, headgear, and weapons or tools. Many traditional stories share similar themes with minor variations. The story will surely evoke an interest of the audience when they anticipate that you'd introduce a problem, fear about a conflict between the characters, probably some ambiguity and misunderstandings, a worry about the ensuing actions and obstacles causing tension, they are anxious about events resulting from actions, and finally hope to release their tension seeing the means of solving a conflict and dealing with a difficult situation. The audience may want to satisfy their need for information about your characters' passions or dilemmas about important decisions, and even may want to share these feelings and tensions; they may also expect some entertainment coming from your project when they find your story suspenseful, surprising, and exciting. The ending of the story may represent universal truths and even provide a moral of this story.

When you write it on a computer or a tablet computer such as iPad, it is time to name and save your story (However, a title such as "How Jonny Killed the Dragon" does not seem a good solution as it shows the ending up-front). The story may now serve as a source for creating its various containers. You may want to choose from many persuasive forms of rhetoric and change your story into a short poem, a limerick, a pun, or a script for a TV play.

Limerick

A limerick is a concise form of telling a story. It is a comic, frequently nonsensical verse that consists of five lines, rhyming aabba. Each line comprises three or two feet, with two feet in the third and fourth lines and three feet in the others. A foot is a group of syllables constituting a metrical unit. Such unit consists of a short–short–long set of syllables, as in the word seventeen. It is called

Table 4. Improvisation

Your Response: Improvising to Art, Music, and Literature
This project may consist of several steps: 1. A warm-up: watch a randomly selected fragment of a movie on a screen played in a mute mode and while watching it quickly respond with possible dialogues between the characters on the screen that are not related to the actual ones. 2. Look at an artwork projected on the screen and write a short story based on the image. Then analyze your story in terms of the elements and principles of design in art. 3. Listen a musical record that you consider well suited to the artwork of your choice and write a story that you find compatible with this aesthetic encounter. 4. Write a short story and then rewrite it for different types of delivery styles, for example for a small theater where the space is limited, for the movie, a magazine, or as a comics. 5. Listen to the music and create an abstract artwork; maybe you can find a synesthetic feeling while doing it. 6. Read a story and write a code or write a musical composition.

anapest – a metrical foot consisting of two short or unstressed syllables followed by one long or stressed syllable.

The origin of the limerick is unknown, probably the name derives from the chorus of an 18th-century Irish soldiers' or pub-goers' song, "Will You Come Up to Limerick?" which was added to the spontaneous, extemporaneously composed verses. Limerick is the Ireland's third largest city, which was settled by Norse invaders in 812. The first limericks date from about 1820. Limericks became popular at the end of the 19th century and in the early years of the 20th century, with limerick contests often held by magazines. They often contain puns and word play, including playful use of homonyms that share the same spelling and pronunciation but have different meanings. The writer and artist Edward Lear (2010) published in 1846 "A Book of Nonsense," a volume of limericks, for example:

There was an Old Man who supposed
That the street door was partially closed;
But some very large rats
Ate his coats and his hats,
While that futile Old Gentleman dozed.

Figure 6. a. Amber Maccan, A limerick (© 2011, A. Maccan. Used with permission); b. Jessica Oxton, A limerick (© 2007, J. Oxton. Used with permission); c. Michael Unruh, A limerick (© 2007, M. Unruh. Used with permission).

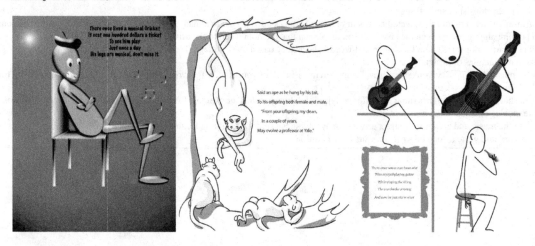

Limericks from "A Book of Nonsense" helped popularize the form by the end of the nineteenth century and in the early years of the 20th century, with limerick contests often held by magazines. They often contain puns (include playful use of words that are alike in sound but different in meaning) and word play. Below is an example of a limerick (Everything$_2$ – Limerick, 2012):

There was a young lady from Niger	*3 feet*
Who smiled when she rode on a tiger.	*3 feet*
They returned from a ride	*2 feet*
With the lady inside	*2 feet*
And the smile on the face of a tiger.	*3 feet*

Figures 6a, b, c present computer graphics with limericks created by students in a visual and verbal way.

Amber Maccan

There once lived a musical Cricket
It cost one hundred dollars a ticket
to see him play
just one a day
his legs are musical, don't miss it.

Jessica Oxton

Said an ape as he hung by his tail,
To his offspring both female and male,
"From your offspring, my dears,
In a couple of years,
May evolve a professor of Yale."

Michael Unruh

There once was a man from afar
Who enjoyed playing a guitar.
While playing a thing
The man broke a string
And now he just sits in a bar.

Figures 7a, b, c present yet another set of computer graphics with limericks created by students.

Pete Fadner

The banjo was played by a newt.
He prepared it over the plute.
He knew only one song
and it was much too long.
In the end he was pelted by fruit.

Figure 7a. Pete Fadner, A limerick (© 2011, P. Fadner. Used with permission). Figure 7b. Adam Herron – On the Stem of a Thistle (© 2007, A. Herron. Used with permission). Figure 7c. A. J. Nazzaro, A limerick (© 2007, A. J. Nazzaro. Used with permission)

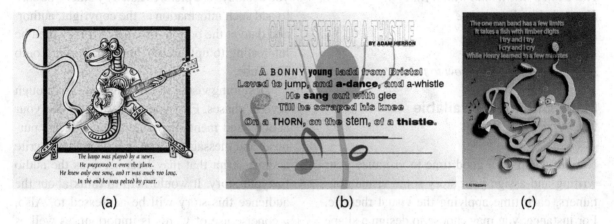

(a)   (b)   (c)

Adam Herron

A bonny young lad from Bristol
Loved to jump, and a-dance, and a-whistle.
He sang out with a glee
Till he scraped his knee
On a thorn, on the stem of a thistle.

A. J. Nazzaro

The one-man band has a few limits
It takes a fish with limber digits
I try and I try
I cry and I cry
While Henry learned in a few minutes.

A "Limerick about Music" Project

This project comprises writing and illustrating the text on the same page. Begin with writing a limerick. The verse and the picture you would create may tell about a musical instrument of your choice and a musician (so the theme requires some research). The task is to express the very essence of the encounter with the musical instrument and the enjoyment to play it. The image you draw will complement your verse. You may also choose other options to fulfill this task: compose a song in the form of a limerick, or create an illustration to a limerick of your choice. For example, you may choose to illustrate one of the limericks below.

Shawn Murphy

I have been playing the violin
Since I came up to my father's shin.
But now I am older,
Stand shoulder to shoulder,
And my playing now makes him grin.

Jonathan Shumate

I found the meaning of craft
and discussed with a man on a raft
He said art was craft,
But only rough draft
So we fell of the raft and laughed

Emily Blummer

A small bust of Johann S. Bach's head
Rests on Schroeder's piano, it's said.
He was deaf as a post
But his music was most...
No, not Bach, that's Beethoven, you blockhead!

Zac Curtis

There once was a man with a flute
He traded it all for a lute
He played it all day
In a new fangled way
And showed the world how to toot

Many Channels Available for Writing a Story

Now it would be a good time to visualize your writing and assign your story some visual containers, each time applying the visual rhetoric. For instance, you may choose to design a shape poem – a concrete poetry made of a typographical arrangement of the words contained in your story, or a poster with pictures showing the course of events. You may also draw a cartoon showing satirical interpretation of your story, comics – a comic strip with simple drawings and short texts about what the characters have to say, or manga – a cartoon in Japanese style showing your fantasy about the story events. It may also become an animation (black-and-white, color, or 3-D animation), a short film, or vimeo (a video-sharing website). It could be amusing to actually do it according to the rules set up for of each medium (posted online) or breaking some of them. Use the hypertext links would allow the viewers to access parts of your project. It would be useful to take into account the elements and principles of design for each depiction, and think about a 2-D space versus lighting and the camera work, in case you would like to take shots with your digital camera or a smart phone. It may be a challenging task to apply many media – audio (music and voice), text, and visuals altogether to show, explain, and discuss the ideas that would be appealing for the viewers, evoke their response and meet their emotional needs. Whatever is the container for your digital (or traditionally crafted) story, it will be told in your distinctive, individual way, especially when you would use your personal photographs

and videos made with a digital camera, edit (or not) and download them to enrich your work. If you decide to use pictures taken by others, be sure to add such information as the copyright, author, and date at the bottom of a page. It may then be interesting to upload this homemade work onto YouTube.

Designing visual storytelling may go through several phases. First you may want to plan your actions and mentally visualize your ideas, purpose, and message, so you will be ready to write a short script that may later serve as the audio for your story. It would help to think about the audience this story will be addressed to. Also, a concise use of words is important, as well as pacing – rhythm and voice punctuation matching the story line and adding emotion. The next step will involve storyboarding, drawing a comic strip, with pictures working in sync with words and sentences in your script. Pictures may contain symbols or metaphors but not unnecessary decorations that are not connected with the story. Digital storytelling storyboard templates (Ohler, 2012a, b) maybe found helpful in this task. It's a good time to include some surprises, your point of view about a thought-provoking statement or insight, so the story becomes interesting and not predictable. Now you may want to record the story and then edit it, caring for economy and amount of details, adding transitions, titles, and a credit for your work; all pictures or sentences created by others must be credited, or Creative Commons license information provided. It is time to check if the voice is audible; if you add music it should match the story line. Finally, you may want to save a story on a flash drive, burn it to CD, or a DVD, post it on your website, or on social network (Center for Digital Storytelling Cookbook, 2012). Maybe you want to create an animation; in this case start with a figure and then change the communication path through transformations.

Visual story might be done in many ways and for various purposes:

- An e-book, a visual novel, an interactive fiction story or game with graphics or anime-style art
- Electronic novel, graphic novel, or visual narrative
- A mixed-media novel comprising of images made out of 3D sets made of paper, paper cutouts, clay, glass and mirrors, with added light effects
- Drama: a script for a theatrical play
- A script for time-based visual media, film, video, and moving images
- A libretto for an opera and operetta, for a ballet or a musical, often in a confined space
- Poetry: a poem, a limerick, haiku, e-poetry, visual poetry
- Sequential art
- A web art combining technologies, focusing on collages of poetry, image, sound, movement and interaction
- Manga
- Comics
- Portrait, visual and verbal (for a cultural study, interpretation), often practiced by journalists
- Interpretative or explanatory drawing
- Data and information visualization
- A story complementing a scientific illustration or drawing
- Technical writing
- Description for design of a product
- A story for VR environment, or a Second Life with the use of avatars
- A story with visual approach to social networking: YouTube, MySpace, FaceBook, Flaxo for interactive Fiction games, Linkedin, blogs, user groups, groups such as Delicious.com, Plaxo – an online address book, etc.
- A story for wireless technology, such as Nintendo DS and animation, cell phone communication, PDAs, videoconferencing, Skype, etc.
- A story for gaming of various kinds, such as games serving education, entertainment, health, fitness, or biofeedback
- An ad in TV or a magazine.

There are many possible options to choose from when commencing a visual/verbal project. It may take form of:

- Writing a statement to a picture
- Improvisation to a musical theme, just combining music, a picture, and a verbal content; it may be text for a song, with illustration
- Reacting to a set of icons, such as road signs
- Writing a story about a scientific material, for example, a planetary system
- Creating an encyclopedia of symbols and gestures as visual metaphors
- Making use of preformatted themes coming from everyday activities. However, one has to keep in mind the copyright issues. One may use a clipart, a supply from stock photography, free music, digital libraries, resources for open source, and for an automatic website design.

This project may involve interactive collaboration. Collaboration of people studying or working in various different disciplines is a clue for achieving engaging results. Sometimes artists invite selected artists to modify content of images provided, for example, Joe Nalven or Cris Orfescu who initiated a show of the nano art by providing artists with images of nano structures to be transformed into art works.

An example of collaborative activity, with some features related to the hypertextuality concept, may be a play involving several participants writing consecutive sentences or images, each one on a next fold of paper or a next file. A composite structure resulting from the play may serve as a starting point for creating a visual/verbal project.

Visual storytelling, along with journalism and art, applies infographics – tools and techniques involved in graphical representation of data. Visual storytelling exists in the domains of online journalism, graphic design, comics, business, art, and visualization research (Segel & Heer, 2010). Data visualization has an ability to reveal stories within data, yet these "data stories" differ in important ways from traditional forms of storytelling. Segel and Heer (2010) reviewed the design space of narrative visualization intended to convey stories. Visual narrative types refer to visual structuring that communicates the overall structure of the narrative; highlighting that directs viewer's attention to particular elements in the display; and transition – techniques for moving within or between visual scenes without disorienting the viewer. According to Segel and Heer, visual narrative tactics and devices that assist and facilitate the narrative include ordering – arranging the path viewers take through the visualization; interactivity of the ways a user can manipulate the visualization by filtering, selecting, searching, and navigating; and messaging that refers to the ways a visualization communicates observations and commentary to the viewer. The authors also examined visual and interactive techniques for telling stories with data graphics that support storytelling with data. They listed seven genres of narrative visualization: magazine style, annotated chart, partitioned poster, flow chart, comic strip, slide show, and film/video/animation. These genres vary primarily in terms of the number of frames (an image in a page of a magazine has only a single frame, while a comic may have many frames) and the ordering of their visual elements (a multi-view partitioned poster may suggest only a loose order to its images, while a comic strip tends to follow a strict linear path) (Segel & Heer, 2010).

According to Andrew Vande Moere (2012), "The combination of storytelling and information visualization has been long predicted, although still very few examples do exist. On the other hand, some might claim typical information aesthetic visualization is all about tell a compelling story;" expert opinions about knowledge visualization assembled at the 7th International Symposium on Knowledge Visualization and Visual Thinking accompanying the 15th Information Visualization Conference (Bertschi, Bresciani, Crawford, Goebel, Kienreich, Lindner, Sabol, & Moere, 2011) confirmed that visualization improves communication, as knowledge needs to be seen. In the words of Stefan Bertschi, "the act of visualizing is more important than the image itself: medium>message." Andrew Vande Moere indicated that stories are powerful means of providing context in interpreting the overreaching meaning and stated (in Bertschi et al., 2011), 'in order for information to transform into knowledge, one must share some context, some meaning, in order to become encoded and connected to preexisting experience. According to Vande Moere, "the emerging popularity of online visual storytelling (Schmitt, 2009) presents at least two new challenges." First, on a phenomenological level, while visual storytelling techniques have the ability to direct a viewer's attention through a sequential narrative, or a series of visual transitions, there is a need to explore how the context, which drives the data-driven knowledge acquisition, is best represented. "Second, it might be equally revealing to analyze visual storytelling techniques in the context of Knowledge Visualization, or vice versa, investigate Knowledge Visualization design methods." With the "emerging popularity of data visualization in current online media, expectations will inevitably shift from simply delivering information to conveying the causally influencing factors that drive the events in our world today" (Moere, in Bertschi et al., 2011, pp. 330-331). In opinion of Wibke Weber and Ralph Tille (2011), "If a company wants to change or improve its communication, it will have to become aware of the power of visual storytelling and start an 'iconic turn'."

In educational terms, presenting learning material through mental imagery supports both immediate and long-term recall compared to studying material from a traditional, lecture-based method. The ArtScience Program promotes collaboration with individuals of diverse cultures, educational backgrounds, interests, and professions to communicate, transform, and share knowledge by creating learning environment where individuals learn to make and explore symbolic models through Metamorphing (Siler, 2012). As it was declared in the Adobe Education White Paper (2011), digital storytelling has become an essential method of enhancing education by making abstract or conceptual content more understandable, in a way that is more engaging than plain text. Digital communication skills associated with digital storytelling have an impact on liberal arts, humanities, and cross-curricular humanities/technology collaborations. It may involve the illustration of story elements using photographs, graphics tools, and free and open source tools. Digital storytelling brings together any combination of visual art, motion (video and film), sound, graphics, and text, frequently written and read in nonlinear fashion, often with a specific point of view. "Increasingly, however, digital storytelling has evolved to include more complex forms of digital expression requiring video skills, such as micro-documentary production. In some cases, digital storytelling is dependent upon computer programming skills for application development and augmented reality" (Adobe Education White Paper, 2011, p.2). Digital storytelling as a cross-curricular technique provides structure for both sharing and understanding new information. Used in fields such as medicine, it helps to humanize the patient-physician experience.

CONCLUSION

Words are often associated with science and images with art. There are many ways of transferring visual material to verbal description but there is a scarce guidance for going from written material to visual presentation. The developments in data organization techniques enhance visual and verbal communication. Communication media add the visual approach to social networking. The creation of meaning with the use of visual language is a focal part of visual rhetoric with the use of visual metaphors as effective visual tools. The electronic writing encompasses visual rhetoric denoting textual artifacts and non-textual marks on a surface of the screen. We can distinguish the linear from non-linear narrative.

Storytelling refers both to the archived oral tradition in storytelling in different cultures, times, and places, and to digital storytelling using a variety of media formats. Crafting a story is a challenging task because a story should be engaging both intellectually and visually. Story visualization technologies combine storytelling with multimedia formats. Storytelling Studies became an interdisciplinary field, or as a discipline unto itself. A story needs to be told differently for each medium, be it a graph, animation, web, manga, film, theater, radio, podcasting, comics, or other means. A limerick, a comic, frequently nonsensical verse is a concise form of telling a story. Visual/verbal projects may take form of interactive collaboration and may often become narrative visualizations.

REFERENCES

About.com. (2012). *Persuasion*. Retrieved January 2, 2012, from http://grammar.about.com/od/pq/g/persuasionterm.htm

Absolut Vodka. Butterflies. (1999). *Coloribus demo advertising archive*. Retrieved January 2, 2012, from http://www.coloribus.com/adsarchive/prints/absolut-vodka-butterflies-1762855/

Adobe. (2011). *Adobe education white paper.* Retrieved February 18, 2012, from https://www. adobe.com/content/dam/Adobe/en/education/ pdfs/strategies-for-digital-communication-skills- across-disciplines-june-2011.pdf

Albers, J. (2010). *Interaction of color.* Yale University Press. (Original work published 1963).

Alexander, B. (2011). *The new digital storytelling: Creating narratives with new media.* Praeger.

Alexander, B., & Levine, A. (2008). *Web 2.0 storytelling: Emergence of a new genre.* Retrieved January 4, 2012, from http://www.educause.edu/ EDUCAUSE+Review/EDUCAUSEReviewMag- azineVolume43/Web20StorytellingEmergenceo- faN/163262

Archimboldo. (2012). *National gallery of art.* Retrieved January 2, 2012, from http://www. giuseppe-arcimboldo.org/Spring-(1).html

Bataille, M. (2008). *ABC3D.* NFAI Porter Book, Roaring Book Press. ISBN 9781596434257. Retrieved February 17, 2012, from http://www. youtube.com/watch?v=wnZr0wiG1Hg

Bertschi, S., Bresciani, S., Crawford, T., Goebel, R., Kienreich, W., & Lindner, M. ... Moere, A.V. (n.d.). What is knowledge visualization? Perspectives on an emerging discipline. In *Proceedings of the Information Visualisation 15th International Conference*, (pp. 329-336). London. ISBN 978- 1-4577-0868-8

Caputo, A. C., Ellison, H., & Steranko, J. (2011). *Visual storytelling.* Watson-Guptill/Random House. Accessible online at http://www.visual- storytelling.com

Casserly, E. D., & Pisoni, D. B. (2010). Speech perception and production. *Wiley Interdisciplinary Reviews: Cognitive Science, 1*(5), 629–647. doi:10.1002/wcs.63.

Center for Digital Storytelling Cookbook. (2012). Retrieved February 18, 2012, from http://www. storycenter.org/cookbook.html

D'Esposito, M. (2007). From cognitive to neural models of working memory. *Philosophical Transactions of the Royal Society of London. Series B, Biological Sciences, 362*(1481), 761–772. doi:10.1098/rstb.2007.2086 PMID:17400538.

Damasio, A. (1999). *The feeling of what happens: Body and emotion in the making of consciousness.* New York: Harcourt.

Damasio, A. R. (1994). *Descartes' error: Emotion, reason, and the human brain.* New York: Putnam.

Duan, Y., & Cruz, C. (2011). Formalizing semantic of natural language through conceptualization from existence. *International Journal of Innovation. Management and Technology, 2*(1), 37–42.

Dürsteler, J. C. (2012). *Visual rhetoric.* Inf@Vis! The digital magazine of InfoVis.net. Retrieved January 2, 2012, from http://www.infovis.net/ printMag.php?lang=2&num=121

Edwards, E., Nagarajan, S. S., Dalal, S. S., Canolty, R. T., Kirsch, H. E., Barbaro, N. M., & Knight, R. T. (2010). Spatiotemporal imaging of cortical activation during verb generation and picture naming. *NeuroImage, 50*, 291–301. doi:10.1016/j. neuroimage.2009.12.035 PMID:20026224.

Everything₂ – Limerick. (2012). Retrieved February 18, 2012, from http://everything2.com/title/ Limerick

Frey, T., Gelhausen, M., & Saake, G. (2011). Categorization of concerns: A categorical program comprehension model. In *Proceedings of the Workshop on Evaluation and Usability of Programming Languages and Tools (PLATEAU) at the ACM Onward! and SPLASH Conferences.* ACM.

Friedman, S. D. (2009). How a 2-minute story helps you lead. *Harvard Business Review*. Retrieved February 16, 2012, from http://blogs.hbr.org/friedman/2009/08/how-a-2minute-story-can-help-y.html

Funkhouser, C. (2008). Digital poetry: A look at generative, visual, and interconnected possibilities in its first four decades. In *A Companion to Digital Literary Studies*. Oxford, UK: Blackwell. Retrieved February 17, 2012, from http://www.digitalhumanities.org/companionDLS/

Gardner, H. (1993a). *Frames of mind: The theory of multiple intelligences*. New York: Basic Books, A Division of Harper Collins Publishers.

Gardner, H. (1993b). *Multiple intelligences: The theory in practice*. New York: Basic Books, A Division of Harper Collins Publishers.

Gardner, H. (1993c). *Art, mind, and brain: A cognitive approach to creativity*. New York: Basic Books, A Division of Harper Collins Publishers.

Gazzaniga, M. S. (2004). *The cognitive neurosciences III*. The MIT Press.

Hammerstingl, W. (1999). *Strategies in visual narrative*. Retrieved October 30, 2012, from http://www.olinda.com/VC/lectures/Narrative.htm

Heffernan, V. (2007, March 27). YouTube awards the top of its heap. *The New York Times*. Retrieved February 16, 2012, from http://www.nytimes.com/2007/03/27/arts/27tube.html?_r=1&oref=login

Helmers, M. (2012). *Visual rhetoric*. Retrieved February 17, 2012, from http://www.parlorpress.com/search/node/visual%20rhetoric%20series

Hensel, J. (2010). Once upon a time. *Meeting Professionals International*. Retrieved February 16, 2012, from http://www.mpiweb.org/Magazine/Archive/US/February2010/OnceUponATime

C. A. Hill, & M. Helmers (Eds.). (2008). *Defining visual rhetorics*. Routledge. (Original work published 2004).

Holzer, J. (2012). *Website*. Retrieved February 17, 2012, from http://www.youtube.com/watch?v=CeVkHU4tfd8&feature=relmfu

Interrupt 2. (2012). *IRQds: Interrupt discussion sessions*. Brown University. Retrieved February 17, 2012, from http://literalart.net/irqds/

Jenkins, H. (2011). Transmedia 202: Further reflections. *The Official Weblog of Henry Jenkins*. Retrieved February 23, 2012, from http://henryjenkins.org/2011/08/defining_transmedia_further_re.html

Kostelnick, C., & Roberts, D. D. (2010). *Designing visual language: Strategies for professional communicators*. Longman.

Lear, E. (2010). *The book of nonsense*. Kessinger Publishing, LLC.

Lengler, R., & Vande Moere, A. (2009). Guiding the viewer's imagination: How visual rhetorical figures create meaning in animated infographics. In *Proceedings of the 13th International Conference on Information Visualization*. DOI 10.1109/IV.2009.102

McCloud, S. (2006). *Making comics: Storytelling secrets of comics, manga and graphic novels*. William Morrow.

Moere, A. V. (2012). Data fiction: Storytelling with information graphics. *Information Aesthetics Weblog*. Retrieved February 23, 2012, from http://infosthetics.com/archives/2010/02/data_fiction_story_telling_with_information-graphics.html

Nordquist, R. (2012). Visual metaphor. *About.com Guide*. Retrieved February 17, 2012, from http://grammar.about.com/od/tz/g/vismeterm.htm

Ohler, J. (2012a). *Digital storytelling storyboard templates*. Retrieved February 18, 2012, from http://www.jasonohler.com/pdfs/digitalStorytellingStoryBoard-adv.pdf

Ohler, J. (2012b). *Storytelling and new media narrative: Part I - Storytelling, literacy and learning*. Retrieved February 23, 2012, from http://www.jasonohler.com/storytelling/storyeducation.cfm

Paul, N., & Fiebich, C. (2012). *The elements of digital storybuilding*. Retrieved January 3, 2012, from http://www.inms.umn.edu/elements/

Perlin, K. (2012). *Kinetic poetry*. Retrieved February 17, 2012, from http://mrl.nyu.edu/%7Eperlin/experiments/poetry/

Perrault, C. (2012). *The fairy tales of Charles Perrault*. CreateSpace Independent Publishing Platform.

Phillips, C., & Sakai, K. L. (2005). Language and the brain. In *Yearbook of Science and Technology*. New York: McGraw-Hill Publishers.

Plato. (2008). *Republic* (Oxford World's Classics). Oxford University Press.

Ricou, J., & Pollock, J. A. (2012). The tree, the spiral and the web of life: A visual exploration of biological evolution for public murals. *Leonardo*, *45*(1), 18–25. doi:10.1162/LEON_a_00321.

Sakai, K. L. (2005). Language acquisition and brain development. *Science*, *310*(5749), 815–819. doi:10.1126/science.1113530 PMID:16272114.

Schmitt, G. (2009). Data visualization is reinventing online storytelling – And building brands in bits and bites. *AdvertisingAge*. Retrieved October 24, 2012, from http://adage.com/article/digitalnext/data-visualization-reinventing-online-storytelling/135313/

Schreibman, S., & Siemens, R. (Eds.). (2008). *A companion to digital literary studies*. Oxford, UK: Blackwell, 2008. Retrieved February 17, 2012, from http://www.digitalhumanities.org/companionDLS/

Segel, E., & Heer, J. (2010). Narrative visualization: Telling stories with data. *IEEE Transactions on Visualization and Computer Graphics*, *16*(6), 1139–1148. doi:10.1109/TVCG.2010.179 PMID:20975152.

Siler, T. (2012). The artscience program for realizing human potential. *Leonardo*, *44*(5), 417–424. doi:10.1162/LEON_a_00242.

Stanton, J. (1999). *Imaginary museum: Poems on art*. Time Being Books.

Truss, L. (2006). *Eats, shoots & leaves: The zero tolerance approach to punctuation*. Gotham.

Uszkoreit, H. (2000). *What is computational linguistics?* Retrieved February 12, 2012, from http://www.coli.uni-saarland.de/~hansu/what_is_cl.html

Vandendorpe, C. (2008). Reading on screen: The new media sphere. In *A Companion to Digital Literary Studies*. Oxford, UK: Blackwell. Retrieved February 17, 2012, from http://www.digitalhumanities.org/companionDLS/

Varley, R. A., Klessinger, N. J. C., Romanowski, C. A. J., & Siegal, M. (2005). Agrammatic but numerate. *Proceedings of the National Academy of Sciences of the United States of America*, *102*, 3519–3524. doi:10.1073/pnas.0407470102 PMID:15713804.

Visual Rhetoric Overview. (2011). *Purdue online writing lab*. Retrieved January 2, 2012, from http://owl.english.purdue.edu/owl/resource/691/01/

Web Art by Hand. (2006). Retrieved January 2, 2012, from http://webartbyhand.blogspot.com

Weber, W., & Tille, R. (2011). Listening to managers: A study about visualizations in corporate presentations. In *Proceedings of the Information Visualisation 15th International Conference*, (pp. 343-348). ISBN 978-1-4577-0868-8

Zeki, S. (1999). Art and the brain. *Journal of Conscious Studies: Controversies in Science and the Humanities, 6*(6/7), 76–96.

Zeng, X., Mehdi, Q. H., & Gough, N. E. (2003). Shape the story: Story visualization techniques. In *Proceedings of the 7th International Conference on Information Visualization*, (pp. 144-149). ISBN: 0-7695-1988-1

Chapter 23
Metaphorical Portraits

ABSTRACT

Telling stories verbally and visually involves structuring the data toward different metaphorical representations of a person. Creating metaphors for a set of factors that make up a profile or a portrait will allow showing individual features of a portrayed person. This text encourages the readers to apply their visual literacy and exercise their cognitive processes related to imaging.

INTRODUCTION

This text provides a good occasion to apply our visual literacy skills and exercise our cognitive processes related to imaging. It may serve well to enhance our confidence about both passive and active familiarity with art, as we will act in this project both as the perceivers and the creators. We may be aware that examining art related concepts and discussing the qualities of works of art without looking at the artwork on a computer screen or in a book could restrict our task and make it demanding. Art images are available in abundance at the Internet-based sources such as the online museum websites. Those who prefer published reproductions of art may choose any art book, for example "The Art Book" (Editors of Phaidon, 2012).

In order to portray an imaginary character, one may want to depict a person in a literary way, the artistic way, or in the both ways. One may write a profile (verbal portrait) or convey graphically a

DOI: 10.4018/978-1-4666-4627-8.ch023

mental image (visual portrait) of the chosen person. Imaging mental and emotional processes is truly important in creating visual communication. Depending on the kind of a profile one is working on, whether it would be a personal, cultural, social, political, or psychological portrait, one has to cope with a different set of variables that must be taken into account.

SURFING THE WEB

When we work on creating a visual and literary portrait of a person, we have to begin with gathering information, whether personal, social, anthropological, cultural, or historical, related to people we want to portray. Searching the web is a method of choice to collect information, initiate communication, develop collaboration, and then to use it as a social medium in virtual environments. However, we may encounter large amount of complex information, as there are currently billions of pages available and this number is increasing by millions pages per day. With the use of search engines we scroll through results displayed in a single window and load multiple pages. In spite of the fact that the Commissioner of the U.S. Office of Patents supposedly said in 1899, "Everything that can be invented has been invented," something new is done every day about the web data organization and the web architecture, by enhancing cloud computing, new kinds of search machines, managing a large database of documents, and creating web interfaces in keeping with the concept of the semantic web – the use of visualizations providing metaphors for web navigation and communication. When surfing the web, some techniques might be useful, such as visualizing and manipulating data in multiple dimensions, using Java, interaction techniques, 2D and 3D interaction metaphors, glyphs, and data mining. We may accept 'data' as the raw material, and then computers process and transform the data into information.

PRESENTING THE DATA ABOUT PEOPLE IN TERMS OF THE TYPES OF ART

We may want to present the data about people in terms of the types of art used in fine arts: as a portrait, a landscape, a still life, an abstract, a time based, and an interactive art.

1. Portrait: Visual and Literary

A 'portrait' approach will result in creating a visage of a person we have just selected. A paper-and-pencil drawing or a computer graphics will show a pictorial profile implying the inner mental state, a psychological, social, historical, or professional portrait that may tell more than a sole account of facts. With the use of symbols, metaphors, and mental shortcuts, synthetic signs, humor, caricature, grotesque, or even doodles we may make a message even sharper.

A portrait usually shows a likeness of a person, especially showing the face, but the background, clothes on a person, objects, possessions, and fads that attract our attention may be also important. For example, in "The Ambassadors" painted in 1533 by Hans Holbein the Younger (http://www.oneonta.edu/faculty/farberas/arth/ARTH214/ambassadors_home.html, also http://en.wikipedia.org/wiki/The_Ambassadors_(Holbein) elaborate collection of musical, astronomical, and scientific instruments symbolizes the ambassadors' learning and power. Hans Holbein's "The Ambassadors" is the famous example of the use of anamorphosis in an artwork. In this double portrait, there is a vague image placed between the two men that can be recognized as a skull when viewed from one side of the painting. Anamorphosis (described in the Chapter 14 Mathematics Related Visual Events) is an optical illusion in a painting. After the rediscovery of perspective in the Renaissance period, this game in art applied a distorted perspective in a drawing or painting, so an image could appear meaningless until viewed from a particular angle. Leonardo da Vinci made anamorphic drawings in the 1470s.

Art Concepts about Portraying People

Portraits may serve various purposes, so we can discern quite different kinds of portraits:

- Social criticism, for example, those painted by William Hogarth (Breakfast Scene, from Marriage á la Mode, c. 1745, http://www.myeport.com/published/u/hs/uhse002/slideshow/7/index30.shtml) or Portrait of the Duchess of Alba (1797) by a Spanish artist Francesco Goya (1746-1797) http://www.friendsofart.net/en/art/francisco-de-goya-y-lucientes/portrait-of-the-duchess-of-alba

- Political, such as Jacques-Louis David "The Death of Marat" (1793) http://www. bc.edu/bc_org/avp/cas/his/CoreArt/art/ neocl_dav_marat.html
- Erotic, as in Agnolo Bronzino "An Allegory of Venus and Cupid" (c.1550), http://www.flickr.com/photos/ artimageslibrary/4821682531/
- Religious, such as Francisco de Zurbaran "Saint Francis de Assisi Receiving the Stigmata" http://commons.wikimedia. org/wiki/File:Francisco_de_Zurbarán_-_ St_Francis_of_Assisi_Receiving_the_ Stigmata_-_WGA26078.jpg
- Ironic, as in William Holman Hunt "The Awakening Conscience" (1853) http://en.wikipedia.org/wiki/ The_Awakening_Conscience
- Enigmatic, such as Andy Warhol's silk-screen "Gold Marilyn Monroe" (1962), http://www.moma.org/collection/object. php?object_id=79737
- Psychological, e.g., Christian Schad "Portrait of Doctor Haustein" (1928), http://www.canadianart.ca/online/ reviews/2009/03/05/shadows/
- A caricature, which deliberately exaggerates the subject's distinctive features or peculiarities. A caricature could be made with a number of different approaches to original works including humor and satirical intent. For example, look at the George Grosz "Berlin Streetscene" (1930), http:// curators.tumblr.com/post/7690359902/ theticketthatexploded-george-grosz-berlin
- An assemblage, a composition consisting of an arrangement of miscellaneous objects, such as fruits and vegetables in Giuseppe Arcimboldo "Summer" (1573), http:// en.wikipedia.org/wiki/File:Arcimboldo,_ Giuseppe_Summer.jpg
- A pastiche, a dramatic, literary, or musical artistic work created in a style that imitates previous works of other artists. It could

be made with intention to add a symbolic or metaphorical way of interpretation or visualization of one's needs and dreams. Let's see like Francis Bacon "Study after Velasquez's Portrait of Pope Innocent X" (1953), http://en.wikipedia.org/ wiki/File:Study_after_Velazquez%27s_ Portrait_of_Pope_Innocent_X.jpg
- A grid of assemblage units, as in photorealistic portraits by Chuck Close (for example, "Robert" 1997, http://www.sfmoma. org/explore/collection/artwork/22524

Portraits may tell more than a sole account of facts. We can see it while looking at art works in books or visiting pages online. We may examine pictures portraying people in terms of the content (what does this portrait say) as well as the artistic process applied by the artist (how does this portrait look).

- For example, you may want to visit a Greek page about the Fayum portraits and early Byzantine icon painting. Click at selected portraits at http://www.ics.forth.gr/isl/fa-yum/ekthemata.htm.
- Visit a Guggenheim New York Museum page at: http://www.guggenheim.org/new-york/collections/collection-online/show-full/piece/?search=Self%20Portrait&page =&f=Title&object=98.4450 and examine Robert Mapplethorpe's (1946-1989) Self-Portrait (1985).
- Also, visit Andy Warhol's (1928-1987) Self-Portrait (1986) at http://www.guggen-heim.org/new-york/collections/collection-online/show-full/piece/?search=Self-Portr ait&page=&f=Title&object=92.4033
- Look at Chuck Close's (born 1940) self-portrait at: http://drawthelineagain-stprejudice.wordpress.com/page-1/ self-portrait-by-chuck-close-2002-2003/
- Also, examine Portrait of Mrs P. in the South (Bildnis der Frau P. im Süden) cre-

ated in 1924 by a Swiss artist Paul Klee (1879-1940), at http://www.guggenheim.org/new-york/collections/collection-online/show-full/piece/?search=Portrait%20of%20Mrs%20P.%20in%20the%20South&page=&f=Title&object=76.2553.89

Then, a verbal profile in the form of a short story may complement the project. You may want to look how an American novelist Thomas Pynchon (born 1937) approaches this theme. Beyond doubt, it may be to the point to revisit a semi-autobiographical novel by the Irish novelist and poet James Joyce (1882-1941) "A Portrait of the Artist as a Young Man." In his book "Extraordinary minds. Portraits of exceptional individuals and an examination of our extraordinariness" Howard Gardner describes the lines of investigation on extraordinariness and describes various forms it takes, when he refers exceptional people to the master, the maker, the introspector, and the influencer type. One may question whether possessing an extraordinary mind is a prerequisite for being famous, becoming a personality, or an official person, and how it can be presented in a drawing.

The 'Landscape' Approach

Then, we will explore the interior and exterior landscapes providing a background for the issues under discussion and the supporting information. A great part of the world's fine art is created in the terms of a landscape. Such personal, cultural, social, and political landscapes could be discussed in terms of their structure with the use of current tools for data organizing. Visual and verbal communication in and outside of such groups can be visualized with the use of drawing, concept mapping, and constructing semantic webs about the communication (with topics and links). One may say, the Canadian artist Jeff Wall (born 1946) http://www.moma.org/interactives/exhibitions/2007/jeffwall/ creates his works with a landscape approach.

Within a literary frame, we may learn from the master writers about writing a personal landscape, such as a British writer Zadie Smith (born 1975), the French writers Marcel Proust (1871-1922) and Gustave Flaubert (1821-1880), the German-language Czech writer Franz Kafka (1883-1924), the French writer and philosopher Albert Camus (1913-1960), the Spanish novelist, poet, and playwright Miguel de Cervantes (1547-1616), and the Polish writer Witold Gombrowicz (1904-1969) about how they all explored cultures, social issues, beliefs, and values cherished by groups of people and created landscapes from when, and where, and who, and landscapes created by the readers of their books, with a portrait somewhere in the background. Also, we may make a group portrait treated as a document. You can tell how many literary connotations and examples can be listed here. You may want to profile someone "ordinary" you know almost as well as yourself: family member/colleague/roommate/classmate/neighbor. How does "environment" – the person's place – reveal or explain this person? (i.e., an apparent perfectionist, or someone with a messy CD collection in his office). How someone's potential for successful development depends on good matching of their disposition with their occupation. Howard Gardner classified human abilities as at least eight types of human intelligence. He described his theory in several books: "Frames of mind: the theory of multiple intelligences"(1983/2011) and "Multiple intelligences: new horizons in theory and practice" (2006) among others.

A 'Still Life' Approach

A 'still life' approach can be done with an algorithm leading to organizing realities of our life. By creating a caricature or a cartoon we may discuss this issue from a social semiotics perspective and connect our discussion with contemporary approaches to cultural studies.

Acquainting with the depictions of small societies and groups, as described in "Ada," the work of the Russian/American writer Vladimir Nabokov

(1899-1977) could be helpful here. Objects telling about the workplace, requisites essential for people fulfilling their goals, desires and ambitions, tools (transient, telling about time), period- and profession-related costumes (such as for a priest or a general). There would be a lot of fun to collect examples of iconic objects, symbols, rituals, and props, which serve our still life we live in, and also to inspect some ready-made setups that make up the TV, film, web, commercials, and some other media events. The same objects have quite different quality and meaning in a changed configuration, in different still-life arrangement, and tell a lot about person's approach to reality and about the life style.

The 'Abstract Art' Approach

The 'abstract art' approach is so important for the development of visual communication, art, and literature. With this approach, the theme is introduced with the use of art (visual and verbal) that enters human interior without objectivity and the insider's view encounters impartial representation of reality. Many distinctive methods of expression in writing shaped the free records of consciousness, associations, and implications which brake the rules of the time, place, or action unity and consistency, as in the novels by the Irish novelist James Joyce (1882-1941), Marcel Proust (1871-1922), or the French writer, poet and activist Jean Genet (1910-1988). This approach provides a great moment for talking about creating languages for designing communication tools, both among humans and in human-computer interaction.

The 'Time-Based, and Interactive Art' Approach

The 'Time-Based, and Interactive Art' approach can grasp the multidimensionality of being and violate time restrictions. In visual solutions, formal approaches to representation through digital drawing are only part of the story. One can ponder over the use of avatars where everyone can create

characters, for instance to use them in Wii Nintendo games and make them look like themselves, their friend, or a favorite celebrity. A short digital film posted on sites such as YouTube (www.youtube. com) may offer a story containing a drawing in its construction. The GLOBE network and Skype application allow the students playing with avatars on over the world. Comics, short animations, and manga formats may serve well for the purpose.

In the literary framework, our project may refer to the open work where the development of action depends on the reader, the nouveau roman – a French literary form from the 1950s that was focused on objects not on a plot, action, narrative, ideas, and characters, and the interactive novels on the web with active co-authoring by the reader who may change the character's features and fates. Which styles in literature can grasp the multidimensionality of being and violate time restrictions? Maybe, it would be helpful to familiarize with the open work cherished by the Italian semiotician, writer, and philosopher Umberto Eco (born 1932) who declared his main interest as the reader-response criticism, the work of an American poet, literary critic, and translator Robert Pinsky (born 1940), an American/Canadian speculative fiction novelist William Gibson (born 1948) who introduced information age iconography to literature. Also, a collection of essays edited by Ken Goldberg (2000) "The Robot in the Garden: Telerobotics and Telepistemology in the Age of the Internet" or the nouveau roman, such as "Les Gommes" (the Erasers) written by a French writer and filmmaker Alain Rob-Grillet (1922-2008) could be helpful in solving this project.

Figures 1, 2, and 3 present three different responses of students to the task of creating a portrait.

This is a drawing from a model sitting in a studio for a drawing course. The image was created from observation by looking at the model and drawing him with a mouse straight on the black-and-white Macintosh 128K computer (1984 model), which was brought to the classroom in order to introduce students to drawing on a computer.

Figure 1. Scott Kindler "Portrait of Tony" (© 1986, S. Kindler. Used with permission)

Figure 2. Steve Wolfer, "Running away" (© 1986, S. Wolfer. Used with permission)

Figure 3. S. Moss, "People" (© 2010, S. Moss. Used with permission)

This image is an imaginative representation of a running person. The author used transformations of a drawing created on the black-and-white Macintosh 128K computer (1984 model), which was brought to the classroom in order to introduce students to drawing on a computer. The drawing was copied, scaled, rotated, flipped horizontal, then slanted and multiplied in order to achieve a pattern on the floor.

This is an attempt to create a futuristic self-portrait. The author attempts to examine the futuristic role of computer technology in our daily lives.

WORKING ON A PROJECT: INVENTING METAPHORS THAT SHOW INDIVIDUAL FEATURES

You may want to draw or describe a chosen individual. In a similar way as we can observe in many literary works, this project should answer several basic questions about this person: *who* is this person, *when* does this story happened, *where* it happened, *what* is so important it has to be told, *why* it took this particular course of action, and *how* it's important in terms of social communication. You may want to see the solution of this project in terms of one of the types of art: the portrait, landscape, still life, abstract, and also the dimensional, time-based, interactive art, and the semantic communication network.

You may also decide how the personal traits of your character, resulting from the cultural, social, and political events she or he is involved in, can be discussed with the use of current tools for data organizing. Visual and verbal communication, occurring in and outside of the groups your 'hero' belongs to, can be visualized by drawing a concept map and constructing a semantic web about communication, with topics and links. Also, you may want to devise metaphors for some features you are going to characterize in a portrait, such as a metaphor for youth or old age, frailty, fidelity, sophistication, refinement, harshness in relation to others, etc. First, employ these metaphors in sentences you use in your verbal portrait of a person. Then, create visual metaphors of these concepts by drawing simple symbols that characterize the person you are going to portray. Consider using these sketches in your visual portrait.

CONCLUSION

This chapter invites the readers to apply their visual literacy and exercise their cognitive processes related to imaging. It may do it by portraying an imaginary character or depicting a person in the literary and the artistic way, by writing a profile (verbal portrait) and conveying graphically a mental image (visual portrait) of the chosen person. One may want to present the data about people in terms of the types of art used in fine arts: as a portrait, a landscape, a still life, an abstract, a time based, and an interactive art.

REFERENCES

Phaidon. (2005). *The art book*. Phaidon Press. ISBN 071484487X

Phaidon. (2012). *The art book*. Phaidon Press. ISBN 0714864676

Chapter 24
Visual Music

ABSTRACT

Visual music projects involve visuals combined with music in various configurations. They may refer to the use of images, light, and sound, such as music and voice, including songs, and also haptic experiences, touch, and gesture. This chapter examines this century-old form of entertainment in terms of the technology options available in the successive decades.

INTRODUCTION

With the advances in social networking, the increasing possibilities of the web-based synchronous/concurrent interaction, multi-touch screen based collaboration, and the availability of ambient, ubiquitous, and wearable computing applications, one may imagine quite a number of entertaining courses of action. A century-old form of entertainment – visual music can become one of such options. Center for Visual Music Library (2012) collects selected reference materials, articles, and bibliographies pertaining to visual music.

Projects involving visuals combined with music in various configurations may refer to the use of images, light, sound such as music and voice including songs, and also haptic experiences, touch, and gesture. Entertaining solutions may be also attained with the use of avatars, telecasting, TV, groupware implementations, social networking, and any other social activity. We may think

DOI: 10.4018/978-1-4666-4627-8.ch024

about sharing knowledge as a performance act. It may pertain to the performing arts, acting for a theatre, dancing, performing sport activities, filmmaking and recording on video, may involve costume design, as well as creating comics and animation.

Working environment for creating such projects can be enhanced by a possibility of talking to a computer or touching a screen instead of typing, or even marking hand movements by a virtuoso to attain master performance on a digital musical instrument. One can imagine no more instances of a carpal tunnel syndrome; the success of the performance would depend on the brain–hand coordination of the musician, without application of strength. One may also contemplate web-based interaction: playing chamber music with a small ensemble of musicians who actually reside in far away places. However, creating visual music should not be identified as music visualization, which can be done with the use of an electronic music visualizer, a feature present in some kinds of media player software, which generates animated images based on musical scores.

THE BEGINNINGS OF VISUAL MUSIC

With reference to past events, visual artists worked in the early 1900s on expressing through art the energy and complexity of the new century. Innovative technologies and scientific discoveries of this period brought about new perspectives for creating art works. Artists reinvented the static conventions accepted in previous periods to match recent scientific advancements, cultural shifts, and changes in perceptions of space and time. Developments in psychology and new trends promoting spirituality inspired artists for transcending realistic representation and searching ways to elevate viewers to a sublime sensory level. Many artists found music a pure and abstract form that goes beyond perceivable reality. They expanded their explorations beyond visual arts; their endeavors became known as visual music. An art critic Roger Fry coined this term in 1912, as a set of ideas that create a unity of the senses and link the seemingly disparate phenomena of sight and sound. Artists referred to this term a "color music" and "mobile color" to define their efforts to integrate the senses through art. At the Google Images you may want to type 'visual music (Images) and visit numerous websites for visual music art works including 'Capriccio Musicale (Circus)' created in 1913 by Daniel Vladimir Baranoff-Rossiné (Hirshhorn Museum and Sculpture Garden, Washington, DC), 'Organization of Graphic Motifs II' created in 1912-13 by František Kupka (National Gallery of Art, Washington, DC), or 'Musical Theme (Oriental Symphony)' by Marsden Hartley, 1912-13, (Brandeis's Rose Art Museum).

Artists creating visual music alluded to the abstract art and connected their explorations with synesthesia – the merging of the senses and thus a synthesis of the arts. Synesthesia strongly influenced the development of visual music. According to the theory of synesthesia, sensory perception of one kind can induce sensory experience of another; for example, an individual may "see" certain colors when hearing musical notes. In such instances, sight does not negate hearing, but rather the two senses interact to elicit a heightened state of consciousness. While many art forms can evoke sensorial overlap, music has been considered by many proponents of the theory as an exceptional source for this phenomenon.

ABSTRACT PAINTERS AND VISUAL MUSIC

Abstract painters from the beginning of the twentieth century regarded music as the purest form of artistic expression, which possesses a direct sensory, emotional, and spiritual appeal. For them, music pointed the way towards a new, truly abstract visual form, and the experience of hearing music was a conceptual gateway to unconventional solutions in painting. The painters derived their language of abstract forms from physiological characteristics of human perception and attempted to translate the musical notions of harmony and dissonance, rhythm, tone color, and compositional structures into the principles of visual arts. Others strived to compose visual equivalents for music to purify their solutions, or explore theoretical correlations between the musical scale and the color spectrum. They discussed color in terms of music and defined colors according to a relative system that stimulates an emotional response. Artists such as the Lithuanian artist Mikalojus Ciurlionis (1875-1911), a Russian painter Wassily Kandinsky (1866-1944), a Swiss painter and graphic artist Paul Klee (1879-1940), a Czech painter and graphic artist František Kupka (1871-1957), American Modernist painter Marsden Hartley (1877-1943), and an American artist Georgia O'Keeffe (1887-1986) created compositions of luminous color and abstract forms that aspired to correspond to the dynamic of music; their works can be seen at the Google Images. They emphasized the musical component of their art works by suggestive titles as 'Sonata,' 'Capriccio Musicale,' and 'Blue and Green Music.'

The art group movement Fluxus initiated by the Lituanian-borne artist George Maciunas was active in the 1960s developing an anti-art and anti-commercial aesthetics. Artists from the Fluxus group participated in the neo-Dada movement by blending artistic media and creating noise music. For example, a collection Fluxus 1 consisted from seventeen manila envelopes contained in a wooden box and combined text, music, and art works.

COLORS AND KEYBOARDS

Composers, musicians, and painters worked on incorporating an element of time. A new form of art involved projection of light in order to connect light with music. Using combinations of colored lenses, hand painted disks, prisms, mirrors, filters, and projectors, artists built machines called color organs. They used soundless keyboards to control the spectrum of light and projected abstract compositions of color and light called 'Color music,' 'mobile color,' or 'lumia.' Artists including Daniel Vladimir Baranoff-Rossiné, Charles Dockum, and Stanton Macdonald-Wright proclaimed liberation of color from static form, detachment of form from representation, and visual art freedom, and declared that abstraction was always attributed to music. Color organs may be considered a forerunner of multimedia performance.

EXPERIMENTAL FILMS

Artists such as Viking Eggeling and Walter Ruttman created in the 1920s experimental abstract films were created as a response to the limitations of painting. They captured a series of hand-produced images on black-and-white or hand-tinted films, setting abstraction into motion and freeing paintings from their static frames.

Images on the film screen reflected the evolving sounds of music. From the early 1930s onward, artists like Oskar Fischinger, Len Lye, and Harry Smith were able to fuse color and form with the sounds of pre-recorded music. They used manual production methods drawing directly on film. Later on, artists synthesized movements of image and sound, creating a synaesthetic experience.

John and James Whitney utilized motion control devices and computer applications to translate their films' soundtracks into visual form. By merging sight and sound Jordan Belson introduced the synesthesia-inducing and consciousness-expanding effects of film. Psychedelic light shows and audiovisual synthesizers followed these experiments during the 1960s, 1970s, and 1980s.

PSYCHEDELIC LIGHT SHOWS AND CONCERTS WITH AUDIOVISUAL SYNTHESIZERS

Psychedelic light shows of the 1960s and early 1970s blended the pop art style with the overlapping sensations of abstraction and representation, the scientific and spiritual, the electronic and natural, and the visual and aural. Spectacles comprised elements of painting, film, color-organ performances, coffeehouse jazz concerts, electronic-music events, rock music, performance art, happenings, actions, underground beat poetry readings, and scientific experiments, to create an immersive visual and sound experience. Work of Elias Romero, Mark Boyle and Joan Hills, Single Wing Turquoise Bird, and the Joshua Light Show provided the audience with the ultimate synaesthetic experience.

INSTALLATION ART

In more recent years, artists created the immersive installations to unify visual and auditory experience. In contrast with film, which limited the viewers to a single point of view on a fixed surface, installations produced multisensory effects and augmented the ambient quality of sound. The installation environment including the participant's physical presence as a key to the production of meaning reframes visual music in ways similar to the synaesthetic concerts and light shows of the late 1950s and 1960s. Installations utilized abstract visuals to confirm concepts related to synaesthetic theory, but did not continue spiritual or cosmic ideas of transcendent visual art common to earlier explorations of visual music. Movements such as minimalism, light and space art, structuralist filmmaking, and conceptual art influenced contemporary artists such as Jennifer Steinkamp and Leo Villareal to combine media with synaesthetic notions, ground visual music in the viewer's experience, and engage the viewer at the phenomenological level. Ron Pellegrino's has been creating video and laser pieces, articles, books, and messages basing on the theoretical foundations and applications of visual music. In accordance with the tradition of visual music art intensifies sensorial experience by extending and elevating viewers' perception. Artists Greg Jalbert, Michael Wanger, Stephen Malinowski, and Ron Pellegrino participated in 1996 Electronic Arts Productions (2004) event at the Exploratorium in San Francisco produced in collaboration with YLEM (2012), a San Francisco-based international organization of artists, scientists, authors, curators, educators, and art enthusiasts who explore the intersection of the arts and sciences. Electronic Arts Productions was founded by Ron Pellegrino in 1981 for the research, development and dissemination of electronic arts experiences, facilities, and information.

CURRENT APPROACHES TO VISUAL MUSIC AS MULTISENSORY EXPERIENCE

In the course of later developments visual music became part of multimodal art unifying painting, photography and light art, cinema, video, installation art, and digital media. Contemporary installation artists are advancing the ideas expressed by painters a hundred years ago. For example, the Smithonian's Hirshhorn Museum and Sculpture Garden in Washington announced the "Suprasensorial: Experiments in Light, Color, and Space" (2012), five immersive large-scale installations created by Latin American artists: Carlos Cruz-Diez (b. Caracas, Venezuela, 1923), Lucio Fontana (b. Rosario, Argentina, 1899; d. Varese, Italy, 1968), Julio Le Parc (b. Mendoza, Argentina, 1928), Hélio Oiticica (b. Rio de Janeiro, Brazil, 1937; d. Rio de Janeiro, 1980), and Jesús Rafael Soto (b. Ciudad Bolívar, Venezuela, 1923; d. Paris, France, 2005). The exhibition, open February-August, 2012, expands the history and perception of the international Light and Space movement.

Some artists map the data into sensory experience. For example, Brian Evans (2007, 2011, 2012), a digital artist/composer, uses mathematical models to build models of jazz or other melodies using his own computer software, and then visualize the models. He creates visualization of sound as an image and sonification of an image into sound. Thus the visual rendition of a music form might be considered music for the eyes. He states, "Sound to image – a visualization; Image to sound – a sonification. In mapping numbers into sensory experience, aesthetic decisions are made. The sound should be seen, the image audible" (Evans 2007).

Bruce Gilchrist, Jonny Bradley, & Jo Joelson (1997; 2000; 2001) presented a "Thought Conductor" (1997) performance of a musical score derived directly from thought processes. The composer's brain waves have been translated in real time into musical notes with the use of wearable brain interface and a digital biomonitor. Notations were then sent to laptops to be read and played by a string quartet of musicians. Thus, the process occurring between the composer's brain and the computer's artificial intelligence was read by musicians and performed live. In "Thought Conductor #2" (2000) and "Thought Conductor #2.1" (2001) the composers Gilchrist and Bradley included the collaboration of the audience. As before, a database with the composers' brain signals was captured when writing the musical notes and associated to the corresponding notations. Several members of the audience were invited to come on stage and contribute with their thoughts. While connected to a wearable brain interface and the biomonitor, each was asked to think of a creative act they had already carried out: a jeweler thought of a gold ring he had recently created; a yogi meditated; and a painter imagined the production process of his last painting. Thus, the neural waves of each participant generated original scores from brain activities. The database was then sent to laptops to be read and played by a string quartet. The composers' mental states captured during execution of a creative act were hybridized with those of the members of the audience, acquired when they recalled a creative action they had performed.

German artist Ingrid Hermentin examined the topic of human individuality and identity by translating genetic fingerprints (individual DNA profiles) into musical variables such as frequency, pitch, and tone length. In 2007 she presented "Transkriptionen_dechiffriert" – individuals' genetic identity shown in acoustic terms by transcribing the sequences of the DNA nucleotides into the 13-accord music.

Both natural visual manifestations and invented visual representations of musical elements and their transformations may create a synesthetic experience of visual music. For example, animation by Ying Tan "Like a Swarm of Angry Bees…" created in 2001 with Jeffrey Stolet's electronic music composition presents a poetic relationship between sound and visual modes.

CONCLUSION

This chapter examines visual music, a century-old form of entertainment in terms of the technology options available in the successive decades. Visual music may involve the use of images, light, sound such as music and voice including songs, and also haptic experiences, touch, and gesture. Advances in social networking, the increasing possibilities of the web-based synchronous/concurrent interaction, multi-touch screen based collaboration, and the availability of ambient, ubiquitous, and wearable computing applications all enhance visual music possibilities. Abstract painters from the beginning of the twentieth century regarded music as the purest form of artistic expression and discussed color in terms of music. Visual music can be found in experimental films, psychedelic light shows, audiovisual synthesizers, and installation art.

REFERENCES

Center for Visual Music Library. (2012). Retrieved August 9, 2012, from http://www.centerforvisualmusic.org/Library.html

Electronic Arts Productions. (2004). Retrieved August 9, 2012, from http://www.ronpellegrinoselectronicartsproductions.org/Pages/EAP.html

Evans, B. (2011). Materials of the data map. *International Journal of Creative Interfaces and Computer Graphics*, 2(1), 14–26. doi:10.4018/jcicg.2011010102.

Evans, B. (2012). *Visual music*. Retrieved August 9, 2012, from http://www.lightspace.com

Gilchrist, B., Bradley, J., & Joelson, J. (2001). *Thought conductor*. Retrieved August 10, 2012, from http://www.artemergent.org.uk/tc/tc_intro.html

Smithsonian Museum. (2012). *Suprasensorial: Experiments in light, color, and space*. Retrieved August 8, 2012, from http://www.hirshhorn.si.edu/collection/home/#collection=suprasensorial&detail=http%3A//www.hirshhorn.si.edu/bio/supra-sensorial-experiments-in-light-color-and-space/

YLEM. (n.d.). *Artists using science and technology*. Retrieved August 9, 2012, from http://www.ylem.org/

Conclusion

The goal of this book is to examine and acknowledge the power existing beyond visual explanation and presentation of scientific and computational problems. An array of concepts, data, and information belonging to a number of disciplines has been discussed as possible resources useful for visual presentation, visualization, and finding visual solutions of science- and technology-related concepts. On the other hand, these resources may support our computational solutions for many cognition-, art-, and entertainment-related problems. Providing knowledge visualization early in the course of education may help to recognize and support the innate abilities of children and start a holistic training of minds. This book discusses projects involving the reader's input. Text and images are of service to assist the readers in enhancing their solutions with explanatory visuals, and hopefully finding joy in these tasks.

Anna Ursyn
University of Northern Colorado, USA

Further Reading

Boden, M. A. (2006). *Mind as Machine. A History of Cognitive Science*. Oxford: Clarendon Press.

Boden, M. A. (2010). *Creativity and Art: Three Roads to Surprise*. Oxford University Press.

Damasio, A. (2010). Self Comes to Mind. New York, New York: Pantheon. Reprint: Vintage. ISBN 030747495X.

DeLanda, M. (2006). A New Philosophy of Society: Assemblage Theory and Social Complexity. Continuum; 1 edition. ISBN 0826491693.

DeLanda, M. (2011). *Philosophy and Simulation: The Emergence of Synthetic Reason*. Continuum; 1 edition ISBN1441170286.

Eco, U., & McEwen, A. (Translator, author) (2004). History of Beauty. Rizzoli. ISBN 0847826465.

Eco, U., & McEwen, A. (Translator, author) (2007). On Ugliness. Rizzoli. ISBN 0847829863.

Editors of Phaidon (Author). (2005). The Art Book. Phaidon Press. Midi ed. ISBN 071484487X / 9780714844879 / 0-7148-4487-X (pocket edition).

Editors of Phaidon (Author). (2012). *The Art Book (Hardcover)*. Phaidon Press.

Gardner, H. (1993c). *Art, Mind, and Brain: A Cognitive Approach to Creativity*. New York: Basic Books, A Division of Harper Collins Publishers.

Gardner, H. (1997). *Extraordinary minds. Portraits of exceptional individuals and an examination of our extraordinariness*. Basic Books, Harper Collins Publishers.

Gleick, J. (2000). *Faster: The Acceleration of Just About Everything*. Vintage Books.

Kandinsky, W. (2011). *Concerning the Spiritual in Art*. Empire Books. (Original work published 1911).

Klanten, R. (Author, Ed., Bourquin N. (Ed.), Ehman, S. (Ed.), & Tissot, T. (Ed.). (2010). Data Flow 2: Visualizing Information in Graphic Design. Die Gestalten Verlag. ISBN 3899552782.

R. Klanten, N. Bourquin, S. Ehmann, F. van Heerden, & T. Tissot (Eds.). (2008). *Data Flow: Visualising Information in Graphic Design*. Die Gestalten Verlag.

Lima, M. (2011). Visual Complexity: Mapping Patterns of Information. New York: Princeton Architectural Press. ISBN 978 1 56898 936 5.

Murakami, H. (2011). 1Q84. Knopf. ISBN 0307593312.

Pearson, M. (2011). Generative Art. Manning Publications; Pap/Psc edition. ISBN 1935182625.

Tufte, E. R. (1983/2001). *The Visual Display of Quantitative Information* (2nd ed.). Cheshire, CT: Graphics Press.

Tufte, E. R. (1992/2005). *Envisioning Information*. Cheshire, CT: Graphics Press. Third printing with revision.

Tufte, E. R. (1997). *Visual and Statistical Thinking: Displays of Evidence for Making Decisions*. Cheshire, Connecticut: Graphics Press.

Yau, N. (2011). *Visualize this: The flowing data guide to design visualization and statistics*. Wiley.

Zeki, S. (2009). Splendors and Miseries of the Brain: Love, Creativity, and the Quest for Human Happiness. Wiley-Blackwell; 5th edition, ISBN 1405185570.

Compilation of References

Abbott Abbott, E. A. (1994/2008). *Flatland: A romance of many dimensions (Oxford World's Classics)*. Oxford University Press.

Abbott Abbott, E. A. (2008). *Flatland: A romance of many dimensions (Oxford World's Classics)*. Oxford University Press.

About.com. (2012). *Geology*. Retrieved April 17, 2012, from http://geology.about.com/cs/basics_roxmin/a/aa011804c.htm

About.com. (2012). *Persuasion*. Retrieved January 2, 2012, from http://grammar.about.com/od/pq/g/persuasionterm.htm

Absolut Vodka. Butterflies. (1999). *Coloribus demo advertising archive*. Retrieved January 2, 2012, from http://www.coloribus.com/adsarchive/prints/absolut-vodka-butterflies-1762855/

Abt, C. C. (1970). *Serious games*. The Viking Press.

ACM SIGGRAPH. (2012). *Digital arts community*. Retrieved February 11, 2012, from http://siggrapharts.ning.com/

ACM/SIGGRAPH. (2009). *Information aesthetics showcase*. Retrieved June 20, 2011, from http://www.siggraph.org/s2009/galleries_experiences/information_aesthetics/

Adamatzky, A. (2010). Physarum machines: Encapsulating reaction-diffusion to compute spanning tree. *Naturwissenschaften*, *94*(12), 975–980. doi:10.1007/s00114-007-0276-5 PMID:17603779.

Adobe. (2011). *Adobe education white paper*. Retrieved February 18, 2012, from https://www.adobe.com/content/dam/Adobe/en/education/pdfs/strategies-for-digital-communication-skills-across-disciplines-june-2011.pdf

Aesthetic Computing Manifesto . (n.d.). Retrieved October 10, 2012 from http://www.cise.ufl.edu/~fishwick/aescomputing/manifesto.pdf

Agence France-Presse. (2012, May 7). France cave art gives glimpse into human life 40,000 years ago. *National Post*. Retrieved September 2, 2012, from http://news.nationalpost.com/2012/05/07/france-cave-art-gives-glimpse-into-human-life-40000-years-ago/

AIA. (2012). *Top ten green projects*. Retrieved July 30, 2012, from http://inhabitat.com/aias-top-ten-green-projects-of-2010/

Albers, J. (1963/2010). Interaction of color: Revised and expanded ed. Yale University Press. ISBN 03001146930

Albers, J. (2010). *Interaction of color*. Yale University Press. (Original work published 1963).

Alden, A. (2012). *Formulas of rock-forming minerals*. Retrieved April 14, 2012, from http://geology.about.com/od/minerals/a/rockformforms.htm

Alexander, B., & Levine, A. (2008). *Web 2.0 storytelling: Emergence of a new genre*. Retrieved January 4, 2012, from http://www.educause.edu/EDUCAUSE+Review/EDUCAUSEReviewMagazineVolume43/Web20StorytellingEmergenceofaN/163262

Alexander, B. (2011). *The new digital storytelling: Creating narratives with new media*. Praeger.

Alice. (2012). Retrieved October 6, 2012 from http://www.alice.org/

Aliev, A. E., Oh, J., Kozlov, M. E., Kuznetsov, A. A., Fang, S., & Fonseca, A. F., ... Baughman, R. H. (2009). Giant-stroke, superelastic carbon nanotube aerogel muscles. *Science, 323*(5921), 1575-1578. doi: doi:10.1126/science.1168312.

Allaume, X., El-Andaloussi, N., Leuchs, B., Bonifati, S., Kulkarni, A., & Marttila, T., ... Marchini, A. (2012). Retargeting of rat parvovirus H-1PV to cancer cells through genetic engineering of the viral capsid. *Journal of Virology*. doi: doi:10.1128/JVI.06208-11 PMID:22258256.

Alleyne, R. (2011, May 8). Viewing art gives same pleasure as being in love. *The Telegraph*. Retrieved December 12, 2011, from http://www.telegraph.co.uk/culture/art/8501024/Viewing-art-gives-same-pleasure-as-being-in-love.html

American Mathematical Society. (2013). *Mathematical imagery website*. Retrieved March 13, 2013, from http://www.ams.org/mathimagery/

Anderson, C. G., & Warburton, W. A. (2012). The impact of violent video games: An overview. In Warburton & Braunstein (Eds.), *Growing up fast and furious: Reviewing the Impacts of Violent and Sexualised Media on Children*, (pp. 56-84). Federation Press. ISBN 1862878234

Animals in Medieval Art. (2011). *Heilbrun timeline of art history*. Department of Medieval Art and The Cloisters, The Metropolitan Museum of Art. Retrieved September 11, 2012, from http://www.metmuseum.org/toah/hd/best/hd_best.htm

Archimboldo. (2012). *National gallery of art*. Retrieved January 2, 2012, from http://www.giuseppe-arcimboldo.org/Spring-(1).html

Arduino. (2012). *A home page*. Retrieved July 5, 2012, from http://arduino.cc/en/Reference/HomePage

Arduino. (2013). Retrieved April 14, 2013, from http://www.mouser.com/knowledge/arduino/ or http://www.mouser.com/arduino/?cm_mmc=google-_-ppc-_-americas-_-Arduino&gclid=CL-Lx4X_mbACFSMDQAodxWvNZw

Ariely, D. (2010). *Predictably irrational: The hidden forces that shape our decisions*. Harper Perennial.

Army, U. S. (2012). *Program executive office enterprise information systems*. Retrieved October 23, 2012, from http://www.eis.army.mil/

Arnheim, R. (1990). Language and the early cinema. *Leonardo, Digital Image*, 3-4.

Arnheim, R. (1954/2004). *Art and visual perception: A psychology of the creative eye, fiftieth anniversary printing*. Berkeley, CA: University of California Press.

Arnheim, R. (1969/2004). *Visual thinking, thirty-fifth anniversary printing*. Berkeley, CA: University of California Press.

Arnheim, R. (1974). *Art and visual perception*. Berkeley, CA: University of California Press.

Arnheim, R. (1988). *The power of the center - A study of composition in the visual arts*. Berkeley, CA: University of California Press.

Arnheim, R. (1990). Language and the early cinema. *Leonardo*, 3–4.

Ars Electronica. (2011). *Que le cheval vive en moi. Art Orienté objet*. Retrieved June 22, 2011, from http://prix.aec.at/winner/3043/ and http://www.artorienteobjet.com/

Artino, A. R. (2008). Cognitive load theory and the role of learner experience: An abbreviated review for educational practitioners. *Association for the Advancement of Computing in Education Journal, 16*(4), 425–439.

ArtsEdge. (2012). Retrieved February 11, 2012, from http://artsedge.kennedy-center.org/educators.aspx

Asai, K., & Takase, N. (2011). Learning molecular structures in a tangible augmented reality environment. *International Journal of Virtual and Personal Learning Environments, 2*(1), 1–18. doi:10.4018/jvple.2011010101.

Aslaksen, H. (2005). A contrarian view of teaching mathematics and art. In *Proceedings of the Special Year in Art & Mathematics, A+M=X International Conference*. Univ. of Colorado.

Aslaksen, H. (2013). *Mathematics in art and architecture*. Retrieved March 13, 2013, from http://www.math.nus.edu.sg/aslaksen/teaching/math-art-arch.shtml

Ayres, R. U., & Ayres, E. (2010). *Crossing the energy divide: Moving from fossil fuel dependence to a clean-energy.* Pearson Prentice Hall. ISBN 137015445

Baddeley, A. D. (1986). *Working memory.* Oxford, UK: Oxford University Press.

Bai, X., White, D., & Sundaram, D. (2012). Contextual adaptive knowledge visualization environments. *Electronic Journal of Knowledge Management, 10*(1), 1–14.

Bales, K. L., & Kitzmann, C. D. (2011). Animal models for computing and communications: Past approaches and future challenges. In X. Yiang (Ed.), *Bio-Inspired Computing and Networking,* (pp. 3-18). CRC Press, Taylor & Francis Group. ISBN1420080326

Ball, P. (2009). Worlds within worlds: Quantum objects by Julian Voss-Andreae. *Nature, 462,* 416. doi:10.1038/462416a.

Banissi, E., & Zhou, H. (2012). Modeling 3D city using high resolution stereo camera imagery. In *Proceedings of the 16ᵗʰ International Conference on Information Visualization,* (pp. 516-522). doi 10.1109/IV.2012.119

Barwinski.net. (2012). *Links to various web database.* Retrieved September 2, 2012, from http://barwinski.net/isotopes/query_select.php

Bataille, M. (2008). *ABC3D.* NFAI Porter Book, Roaring Book Press. ISBN 9781596434257. Retrieved February 17, 2012, from http://www.youtube.com/watch?v=wnZr0wiG1Hg

Battail, G. (2009). Living versus inanimate: The information border. *Biosemiotics, 2,* 321–341. doi:10.1007/s12304-009-9059-z.

Baudisch, P. (2006). Interacting with wall-size screens. In *Proceedings of CHI 2006.* Montreal, Canada: ACM.

Bearden, R. (1970). *The Calabash.* Retrieved November 20, 2011, from http://en.wikipedia.org/wiki/File:Romare_Bearden_-_The_Calabash,_1970,_Library_of_Congress.jpg

Beardon, C., & Malmbord, L. (2010). *Digital creativity: A reader* (Innovations in Art and Design). Routledge. ISBN-10: 0415579686

Benayoun, M. (2012). *Emotion forecast and occupy wall screen.* Retrieved October 11, 2012, from http://www.benayoun.com/projet.php?id=180

Bennett, C., Ryall, J., Spalteholz, L., & Gooch, A. (2007). *The aesthetics of graph visualization: Computational aesthetics in graphics, visualization, and imaging.* Eurographics Association.

Berens, R. R. (1999). The role of artists in ship camouflage during world war I. *Leonardo, 32*(1), 53–59. doi:10.1162/002409499553000.

Berlyne, D. (1971). *Aesthetics and psychobiology.* Appleton-Century-Crofts.

Berlyne, D. E. (1974). *Studies in the new experimental aesthetics: Steps toward an objective psychology of aesthetic appreciation.* Hemisphere Pub. Corp..

Berners-Lee, T. (2012). *Official site at W3C.* Retrieved February 11, 2012, from http://en.wikipedia.org/wiki/Tim_Berners-Lee

Bernstein, K. (2005). Expression in the form of our own making. In *Proceedings of the Special Year in Art & Mathematics, A+M=X International Conference.* Univ. of Colorado.

Berridge, K. C., & Kringelbach, M. L. (2008). Affective neuroscience of pleasure: reward in humans and animals. *Psychopharmacology, 199*(3), 457–480. doi:10.1007/s00213-008-1099-6 PMID:18311558.

Berton, J. A. Jr. (1990). Film theory for the digital world: Connecting the masters to the new digital cinema. *Leonardo,* 5–11.

Bertschi, S., Bresciani, S., Crawford, T., Goebel, R., Kienreich, W., & Lindner, M. ... Moere, A.V. (n.d.). What is knowledge visualization? Perspectives on an emerging discipline. In *Proceedings of the Information Visualisation 15ᵗʰ International Conference,* (pp. 329-336). London. ISBN 978-1-4577-0868-8

Biever, C. (2006). A good robot has personality but not looks. *New Scientist, 2561.* Retrieved January 9, 2011, from http://www.newscientist.com/article/mg19125616.400-a-good-robot-has-personality-but-not-looks.html

Binkley, T. (1990). Digital dilemmas. *Leonardo,* 13–19.

Biofeedback Computer Game. (2012). *The journey to wild divine*. Biofeedback Software & Hardware for PC & Mac: The Passage. Retrieved from http://www.wilddivine.com/bundle-meditation-games-order-full/

Bird, P. (2003). An updated digital model of plate boundaries. *An Electronic Journal of the Earth Sciences, 4*(3). Retrieved April 11, 2012, from http://peterbird.name/publications/2003_PB2002/2001GC000252.pdf

Birken, M. (2008). Light motifs – Marcia Birken's images meld math and art. *Mount Holyoke Alumnae Quarterly*. Retrieved September 11, 2012, from http://alumnae.mtholyoke.edu/wp/mhaq/2008/11/light-motifs-marcia-birkens-images-meld-math-and-art/

Birkhoff, G. D. (2003). *Aesthetic measure*. Kessinger Publishing. (Original work published 1933).

Bisantz, J. (2010). Art, advertising and green technologies. In *Proceedings of the School of Visual Arts 24ᵗʰ Annual National Conference on Liberal Arts and the Education of Artists*. Retrieved October 23, 2012, from http://media.schoolofvisualarts.edu/sva/media/18944/medium/Proceedings2010.pdf

Bishop, J. (2007). Increasing participation in online communities: A framework for human–computer interaction. *Computers in Human Behavior, 23*, 1881–1893. doi:10.1016/j.chb.2005.11.004.

Bishop, J. (2009). Enhancing the understanding of genres of web-based communities: The role of the ecological cognition framework. *International Journal of Web Based Communities, 5*(1), 4–17. doi:10.1504/IJWBC.2009.021558.

Blais, J., Ippolito, J., & Smith. (2006). *At the edge of art*. Thames & Hudson. ISBN 0500238227

Bly, R. (1992). *Angels of Pompeii*. New York: Ballantine Books.

Boden, M. A. (2009). Computer models of creativity. *AI Magazine, 30*(3).

Boden, M. A. (2010). *Creativity and art: Three roads to surprise*. Oxford University Press.

Boden, M. A., & Edmonds, E. A. (2009). What is generative art? *Digital Creativity, 20*(1-2), 21–46. doi:10.1080/14626260902867915.

Boileau, I., Assaad, J.-M., Pihl, R. O., Benkelfat, C., Leyton, M., & Diksic, M. et al. (2003). Alcohol promotes dopamine release in the human nucleus accumbens. *Synapse (New York, N.Y.), 49*(4), 226–231. doi:10.1002/syn.10226 PMID:12827641.

Bolin, L. (2009). *Camouflage art*. Retrieved September 14, 2012, from http://www.toxel.com/inspiration/2009/10/04/camouflage-art-by-liu-bolin/

Bon, C., Caudy, N., de Dieuleveult, M., Fosse, P., Philippe, M., & Maksud, F. … Elalouf, J.-M. (2008). Deciphering the complete mitochondrial genome and phylogeny of the extinct cave bear in the Paleolithic painted cave of Chauvet. *Proceedings of the National Academy of Sciences of the United States of America*. doi: 10.1073/pnas.0806143105

Bonabeau, E., Corne, D., & Poli, R. (2010). Swarm intelligence: The state of the art special issue of natural computing. *Natural Computing, 9*, 655–657. doi:10.1007/s11047-009-9172-6.

Boykin, J. (2012). *Redesigning Minard's graphic of Napoleon's march*. Retrieved September 7, 2012, from http://www.wayfind.com/napoleon.html

Boyle, R. (2011, April 14). Blending wool and Kevlar could make better, lighter body armor. *Popular Science*. Retrieved August 28, 2012, from http://www.popsci.com/technology/article/2011-04/blending-wool-and-kevlar-could-reduce-body-armors-weight-and-cost-researchers-say

Bradbury Science Museum. (2011). *Los Alamos national laboratory*. Retrieved September 7, 2012, from http://www.lanl.gov/museum/explore/_docs/MS2%20virus.pdf

Bredl, K., Groß, A., Hünniger, J., & Fleischer, J. (2012). The avatar as a knowledge worker? How immersive 3D virtual environments may foster knowledge acquisition. *Electronic Journal of Knowledge Management, 10*(1), 15–25.

Bredo, E. (1994). Reconstructing educational psychology: Situated cognition and Deweyian pragmatism. *Educational Psychologist, 29*(1), 23–25. doi:10.1207/s15326985ep2901_3.

British Columbia Distributed Learning. (2012). Retrieved October 23, 2012, from http://www.bced.gov.bc.ca/dist_learning/

Broudy, H. S. (1987). *The role of imagery in learning.* Occasional Paper 1. Malibu, CA: The Getty Center for Education in the Arts.

Broudy, H. S. (1972). *Enlightened cherishing: An essay on aesthetic education.* Urbana, IL: University of Illinois Press.

Broudy, H. S. (1991). Reflections on a decision. *Journal of Aesthetic Education, 25*(4), 31–34. doi:10.2307/3332900.

Bubbles. (2011). Retrieved August 24, 2012, from http://bubbles.org/html/questions/color.htm

Buechley, L., Eisenberg, M., Catchen, J., & Crockett, A. (2008). The LilyPad arduino: Using computational textiles to investigate engagement, aesthetics, and diversity in computer science education. In *Proceedings of the SIGCHI Conference (CHI 2008),* (pp. 423-432). ACM.

Burgess, R. (2012). *Understanding nanomedicine: An introductory textbook.* Pan Stanford Publishing.

Burkhard, R. A. (2006). Learning from architects: complementary concept mapping approaches. In *Proceedings of the International Conference on Information Visualization* (pp. 225-234). ISBN 0-7695-2177-0. Retrieved from http://www.computer.org/portal/web/csdl/doi/10.1109/IV.2004.1320194

Burkhard, R., Bischof, S., & Herzog, A. (2008). The potential of crowd simulations for communication purposes in architecture. In *Proceedings of the iV, 12th International Conference on Information Visualisation,* (pp. 403-408). London, UK: IEEE Computer Society Press.

Burning Man. (2013). Retrieved April 14, 2013, from http://www.burningman.com/whatisburningman.

Burns, D. G., Camakaris, H. M., Jansen, P. H., & Dyall-Smith, M. L. (2004). Cultivation of Walsby's square haloarchaeon. *FEMS Microbiology Letters, 238*(2), 469–473. Retrieved from http://www.ncbi.nlm.nih.gov/pubmed/15358434 PMID:15358434.

Bushman, B. J., & Gibson, B. (2011). Violent video games cause an increase in aggression long after the game has been turned off. *Social Psychological and Personality Science, 2,* 29–32. doi:10.1177/1948550610379506.

Bushman, B. J., & Huesmann, L. R. (2010). Aggression. In S. T. Fiske, D. T. Gilbert, & G. Lindzey (Eds.), *Handbook of Social Psychology* (5th ed., pp. 833–863). New York: John Wiley & Sons.

Business Dictionary.com. (2012). Retrieved May 25, 2012, from http://www.businessdictionary.com/definition/British-thermal-unit-Btu.html

Caillois, R. (1992). *Les jeux et les hommes.* Gallimard.

California Academy of Sciences. (2012). Retrieved August 2, 2012, from http://www.nytimes.com/slideshow/2008/09/23/arts/20080924_ACADEMY_SLIDESHOW_index.html

Camouflage Restaurants. (n.d.). Retrieved September 14, 2012, from http://www.toxel.com/inspiration/2009/06/20/10-unusual-and-creative-restaurants/

Caputo, A. C., Ellison, H., & Steranko, J. (2011). *Visual storytelling.* Watson-Guptill/Random House. Accessible online at http://www.visualstorytelling.com

Cardillo, E. R., Watson, C. E., Schmidt, G. L., Kranjec, A., & Chatterjee, A. (2012). Article. *NeuroImage, 59,* 3212-3221. Retrieved June 7, 2012, from http://ccn.upenn.edu/chatterjee/anjan_pdfs/YNIMG8957.pdf

Carlsson, A.-L. (2010). The aesthetic and the poietic elements of information design. In *Proceedings of the 14th International Conference Information Visualisation* (pp. 450-454). IEEE.

Carroll, L. (2012). *Alice's adventures in wonderland.* CreateSpace.

Carroll, S. B. (2005). *Endless forms most beautiful: The new science of evo devo and the making of the animal kingdom.* W. W. Norton & Company.

Casas, X., Herrera, G., Coma, I., & Fernández, M. (2012). A kinect-based augmented reality system for individuals with autism spectrum disorders. In *Proceedings of the International Conference on Computer Graphics Theory and Applications and International Conference on Information Visualization Theory and Applications,* (pp. 440-446). ISBN: 978-989-8565-02-0

Casserly, E. D., & Pisoni, D. B. (2010). Speech perception and production. *Wiley Interdisciplinary Reviews: Cognitive Science, 1*(5), 629–647. doi:10.1002/wcs.63.

Cave of Altamira and Paleolithic Cave Art of Northern Spain. (2012). *Unesco world heritage centre.* Retrieved August 26, 2012, from http://whc.unesco.org/en/list/310

Cave of Forgotten Dreams. (2012). Retrieved September 3, 2012, from http://en.wikipedia.org/wiki/Cave_of_Forgotten_Dreams

Cawthon, N., & Vande Moere, A. (2007). The effect of aesthetic on the usability of data visualization. In *Proceedings of 11th International Conference on Information Visualisation.* IEEE.

Center for Digital Storytelling Cookbook. (2012). Retrieved February 18, 2012, from http://www.storycenter.org/cookbook.html

Center for Visual Music Library. (2012). Retrieved August 9, 2012, from http://www.centerforvisualmusic.org/Library.html

Cezanne, P. (2002). *The Mount St. Victoire series of paintings.* Retrieved February 28, 2013, from http://www.ibiblio.org/wm/paint/auth/cezanne/st-victoire/

Chai, C. (2011, March 11). Japan's quake shifts earth's axis by 25 centimetres. *The Gazette.* Retrieved April 11, 2012, from http://www.canada.com/news/Japan+quake+shifts+earth+axis+centimetres/4426356/story.html#ixzz1rko46tCl

Challenges in Characterizing Small Particles: Exploring Particles from the Nano- to Microscales. (2012). *Chemical sciences roundtable & national research council.* The National Academies Press. ISBN 0-309-22590-6

Chan, W. C. (2007). Toxicity studies of fullerenes and derivatives. In Bio-applications of nanoparticles. New York, NY: Springer Science + Business Media. ISBN 0-387-76712-6

Chandler, P., & Sweller, J. (1992). The split attention effect as a factor in the design of instruction. *The British Journal of Educational Psychology, 62*, 233–246. doi:10.1111/j.2044-8279.1992.tb01017.x.

Chandler, P., & Sweller, J. (1996). Cognitive load while learning to use a computer program. *Applied Cognitive Psychology, 10*, 151–170. doi:10.1002/(SICI)1099-0720(199604)10:2<151::AID-ACP380>3.0.CO;2-U.

Chang, K. (2011, March 13). Quake moves Japan closer to U.S., & alters earth's spin. *The New York Times.* Retrieved April 11, 2012, from http://www.nytimes.com/2011/03/14/world/asia/14seismic.html?_r=1

Charlton, J. (2011). Digitaterial gestures: Action-driven stereolithography. In *Proceedings of ISEA2011, the 17th International Symposium on Electronic Art.* Retrieved April 13, 2011, from http://isea2011.sabanciuniv.edu/paper/digitaterial-gestures---action-driven-stererolithography

Chatterjee, A. (2003). Prospects for a cognitive neuroscience of visual aesthetics. *Bulletin of Psychology and the Arts, 4*(2), 55-60. Retrieved June 7, 2012, from http://ccn.upenn.edu/chatterjee/anjan_pdfs/Prospects%20of%20Cog%20Neuro%20Visual%20Aes.pdf

Chatterjee, A. (2011). Where there be dragons: Finding the edges of neuroaesthetics. *American Society for Neuroaesthetics, 31*(2), 4-6. Retrieved October 6, 2012, from http://aesthetics-online.org/newsletter/31.2.pdf

Chatterjee, A. (2011). Neuroaesthetics: A coming of age story. *Journal of Cognitive Neuroscience, 23*(1), 53–62. doi:10.1162/jocn.2010.21457 PMID:20175677.

Cheetham, M. A. (2010). The crystal interface in contemporary art: metaphors of the organic and inorganic. *Leonardo, 43*(3), 251–255. doi:10.1162/leon.2010.43.3.250.

Chemistry World News. (2009). Designing 3D DNA crystals. *Chemistry World News.* Retrieved August 24, 2012, from http://www.rsc.org/chemistryworld/news/2009/september/02090904.asp

Chen, C. (2011). *Turning points: The nature of creativity.* Springer-Verlag.

Cheng, Y. H. G. (2009). The aesthetics of net dot art. In *Handbook of Research on Computational Arts and Creative Informatics.* Hershey, PA: IGI Global. doi:10.4018/978-1-60566-352-4.ch010.

Choi, M.-R., Stanton-Maxey, K. J., Stanley, J. K., Levin, C. S., Bardhan, R., & Akin, D. ... Clare, S. E. (2007). A cellular Trojan horse for delivery of therapeutic nanoparticles into tumors. *Nano Lett., 7*(12), 3759–3765. doi 10.1021/nl072209h. Retrieved August 23, 2012, from http://pubs.acs.org/action/doSearch?action=search&author=Choi%2C+Mi%5C-Ran&qsSearchArea=author&

Christopher, N. (2008). *The Bestiary*. Dial Press Trade.

Cinzia, D. D., & Gallese, V. (2009). Neuroaesthetics: A review. *Current Opinion in Neurobiology, 19*(6), 682–687. doi:10.1016/j.conb.2009.09.001 PMID:19828312.

Clark, J. (2006). *The basics of buckyballs*. Retrieved September 7, 2012, from http://www.growthstockwire.com/2399/The-Basics-of-Buckyballs

Clark, R., Nguyen, F., & Sweller, J. (2006). *Efficiency in learning: Evidence-based guidelines to manage cognitive load*. San Francisco, CA: Pfeiffer. doi:10.1002/pfi.4930450920.

Cleveland, P. (2008). Aesthetics and complexity in digital layout systems. *Digital Creativity, 19*(1), 33–50. doi:10.1080/14626260701847498.

Cole, S. W., Yoo, D. J., & Knutson, B. (2012). Interactivity and reward-related neural activation during a serious videogame. *PLoS ONE*. Retrieved July 5, 2012, from http://dx.plos.org/10.1371/journal.pone.0033909

Combes. F. (1991). The SAO/NASA astrophysics data system. *Annual Review of Astronomy and Astrophysics, 29*(A92-18081 05-90), 195-237. doi 10.1146/annurev.aa.29.090191.001211. Retrieved September 1, 2012, from http://articles.adsabs.harvard.edu/full/1991ARA%26A.29.195C

Computer Animation Production System. (2012). Retrieved August 7, 2012, from http://en.wikipedia.org/wiki/Computer_Animation_Production_System

Conlisk, J. (2011). Professor Zak's empirical studies on trust and oxytocin. *Journal of Economic Behavior & Organization, 78*(1–2), 160–166. doi:10.1016/j.jebo.2011.01.002.

Cook, K. A. (2005). Discover nano. *History of Nano Timeline*. Retrieved August 26, 2012, from http://www.discovernano.northwestern.edu/whatis/History

Cornell University Library. (2012). *Distributed learning tutorial*. Retrieved October 23, 2012, from http://www.library.cornell.edu/DL/tutorial/tut_2.htm

Correra, P. N., & Correra, A. N. (2004). *Nanometric functions of bioenergy*. Akronos Publishing.

Craft, D. (2012). Science within the art: Aesthetics based on the fractal and holographic structure of nature. In A. Ursyn (Ed.), *Biologically-Inspired Computing for the Arts: Scientific Data through Graphics* (pp. 290–321). IGI Global. doi:10.4018/978-1-4666-0942-6.ch017.

Crawford, C. (2003). *Chris Crawford on game design*. New Riders Games.

Crick, F. H. C. (1958). On protein synthesis.[from http://profiles.nlm.nih.gov/SC/B/B/Z/Y/_/scbbzy.pdf]. *Symposia of the Society for Experimental Biology, 12*, 138–163. Retrieved April 13, 2011 PMID:13580867.

Cruz-Neira, C., Sandin, D. J., DeFanti, T. A., Kenyon, R. V., & Hart, J. C. (1992). The CAVE: Audio visual experience automatic virtual environment. *Communications of the ACM, 35*(6), 64–72. doi:10.1145/129888.129892.

Csikszentmihalyi, M. (1990). *Flow: The psychology of optimal experience*. New York: Harper and Row.

Csikszentmihalyi, M. (1997). *Creativity: Flow and the psychology of discovery and invention*. Harper Perennial.

Csikszentmihalyi, M. (1998). *Finding flow: The psychology of engagement with everyday life*. Basic Books.

Csikszentmihalyi, M., & Robinson, R. E. (1991). *The art of seeing: An interpretation of the aesthetic encounter*. Malibu, CA: J.Paul Getty Museum.

D'Esposito, M. (2007). From cognitive to neural models of working memory. *Philosophical Transactions of the Royal Society of London. Series B, Biological Sciences, 362*(1481), 761–772. doi:10.1098/rstb.2007.2086 PMID:17400538.

Daguerre, L. J. (1839). *History and practice of photogenic drawing on the true principles of the daguerréotype, with the new method of dioramic painting, by the inventor Louis Jacques M. Daguerre*. London: Smith, Elder and Co..

Dalton, A. B., Collins, S., Muñoz, E., Razal, J. M., Von Ebron, H., & Ferraris, J. P. et al. (2003). Super-tough carbon-nanotube fibres. *Nature, 423*, 703. doi:10.1038/423703a PMID:12802323.

Damasio, A. (2010). Self Comes to Mind. New York, New York: Pantheon. Reprint: Vintage. ISBN 030747495X.

Damasio, A. (1999). *The feeling of what happens: Body and emotion in the making of consciousness*. New York: Harcourt.

Damasio, A. (2005). *Descartes' error*. New York: Penguin Books.

Dana Classification. (2012). *Organic compounds*. Retrieved April 14, 2012, from http://www.mindat.org/dana.php?a=50

Datta, R., Joshi, D., Jia Li, J., & Wang, J. Z. (2006). Studying aesthetics in photographic images using a computational approach. In *Proceedings of the European Conference on Computer Vision*, (LNCS), (vol. 3953, pp. 288-301). Graz, Austria: Springer. Retrieved August 18, 2012, from http://infolab.stanford.edu/~wangz/project/imsearch/Aesthetics/ECCV06/datta.pdf

Davis, T. (2011). Complexity as practice: A reflection on the creative outcomes of a sustained engagement with complexity. *Leonardo, 45*(3), 106–112.

De Bure, G. (1992). *Jean Nouvel, Emmanuel Cattani, and associates: Four projects*. Zurich: Artemis.

DeLanda, M. (2010). Deleuze: History and science. (W. Schirmacher, Ed.). Atropos Press. ISBN 0982706715

Deleuze, G., & Guattari, F. (1983). *Anti-Oedipus*. Minneapolis, MN: Minnesota UP.

Deleuze, G., & Guattari, F. (1987). *A thousand plateaus: Capitalism and schizophrenia* (B. Massumi, Trans.). University of Minnesota Press.

Delgado, M. R. (2007). *Reward-related responses in the Human striatum*. Retrieved July 9, 2012, from http://nwkpsych.rutgers.edu/neuroscience/publications/RewardStriatum07.pdf

Denham, T. (2010). *What's the difference between a resume, CV and bio?* Retrieved April 15, 2013, from http://blog.timesunion.com/careers/whats-the-difference-between-a-resume-cv-and-bio/551/

Denning, P. J. (2007). Computing is a natural science. *Communications of the ACM, 50*(7), 13–18. doi:10.1145/1272516.1272529.

Derrida, J. (1991). *The truth in painting*. Chicago: The University of Chicago Press.

Deruta Ceramists. (2012). Retrieved August 26, 2012, from http://www.thatsarte.com/region/Deruta

Deterding, S., Dixon, D., Khaled, R., & Nacke, L. (2011). From game design elements to gamefulness: Defining gamification. In *Proceedings of the 15th International Academic MindTrek Conference*, (pp. 9-15). ISBN 978-1-4503-0816-8. doi 10.1145/2181037.2181040

DeWall, C. N., Anderson, C. A., & Bushman, B. J. (2011). The general aggression model: Theoretical extensions to violence. *Psychology of Violence, 1*(3), 245-258. doi 10.1037/a0023842. Retrieved July 9, 2012, from http://www.psychology.iastate.edu/faculty/caa/abstracts./2010-2014/11DAB.pdf

DeWitt, M. A., Chang, A., Combs, P. A., & Yildiz, A. (2012). Ytoplasmic Dynein moves through uncoordinated stepping of the AAA+ ring domains. *Science, 335*(221), 221-225. doi 10.1126/science.1215804. Retrieved August 24, 2012, from http://physics.berkeley.edu/research/yildiz/papers/Science-2012-DeWitt.pdf

Di Chio, C., Brabazon, A., Di Caro, G., Ebner, M., Farooq, M., & Fink, A. … Urquhart, N. (Eds.). (2010b). Applications of evolutionary computation, evoapplications. In *Proceedings, Part II*, (LNCS), (Vol. 6025). Berlin: Springer. Retrieved April 13, 2011, from http://www.springerlink.com/content/l8161m85r21r/front-matter.pdf

Dietrich, F., & Molnar, Z. (1981). Pictures by funny numbers. *Creative Computing, 7*(6), 102–107.

DKFZ. (2012). *German cancer research center*. Retrieved September 7, 2012, from http://www.dkfz.de/en/presse/pressemitteilungen/2012/dkfz-pm-12-39-Tailor-made-viruses-for-enhanced-cancer-therapy.php

Doczi, G. (2005). *The power of limits: Proportional harmonies in nature, art, and architecture.* Shambhala Pocket Classics.

Doidge, N. (2007). *The brain that changes itself: Stories of personal triumph from the frontiers of brain science.* Penguin Books.

Doolittle, B. (2011). *Camouflage art.* Retrieved September 14, 2012, from http://www.bnr-art.com/doolitt/

Dorin, A., & Korb, K. (2007). Building artificial ecosystems from artificial chemistry. In *Proceedings of the 9th European Conference on Artificial Life,* (pp. 103-112). Springer-Verlag.

Doswell, J. T. (2006). Augmented learning: Context-aware mobile augmented reality architecture for learning. In *Proceedings of the Sixth IEEE International Conference on Advanced Learning Technologies,* (pp. 1182-1183). IEEE Computer Society. ISBN 0-7695-2632-2

Drmanac, R., Sparks, A. B., Callow, M. J., Halpern, A. L., et al. (2010). Human genome sequencing using unchained base reads on self-assembling DNA nanoarrays. *Science, 327*(5961), 78-81. Retrieved December 19, 2010, from http://www.sciencemag.org/content/327/5961/78.abstract

Drummey, M. (2001). The paper bale house. *Ski Mag. com.* Retrieved May 26, 2012, from http://www.skinet.com/ski/detergent/2001/10/the-paper-bale-house

Duan, Y., & Cruz, C. (2011). Formalizing semantic of natural language through conceptualization from existence. *International Journal of Innovation. Management and Technology, 2*(1), 37–42.

Duh, K., & Kirchhoff, K. (2004). *Automatic learning of language model structure.* Retrieved July 15, 2012, from acl.ldc.upenn.edu/coling2004/MAIN/pdf/22-874.pdf

Dürsteler, J. C. (2012). *Visual rhetoric.* Inf@Vis! The digital magazine of InfoVis.net. Retrieved January 2, 2012, from http://www.infovis.net/printMag.php?lang=2&num=121

Dyall-Smith, M. L., Pfeiffer, F., Klee, K., Palm, P., Gross, K., & Schuster, S. C., … Oesterhelt, D. (2011). Haloquadratum walsbyi: Limited diversity in a global pond. *PLoS One, 6*(6), e20968. DOI 10.1371/journal.pone.0020968. Retrieved April 17, 2012, from http://www.ncbi.nlm.nih.gov/pmc/articles/PMC3119063/?tool=pmcentrez

Ebbinghaus, H. (2012). *Über das gedächtnis: Untersuchungen zur experimentellen psychologie* (German Ed.). Ulan Press. (Original work published 1885).

Eco, U. (1980/2006). The name of the rose. (W. Weaver, Trans.). Everyman's Library. ISBN 0307264890

Eco, U. (1979). *The role of the reader, explorations in the semiotics of texts: Advances in semiotics.* Bloomington, IN: Indiana University Press.

Eco, U. (1989). *The open work* (A. Cancogni, Trans.). Cambridge, MA: Harvard University Press.

Eco, U. (1990). *The limits of interpretation.* Indianapolis, IN: Indiana University Press.

Eco, U. (2004). *History of beauty* (A. McEwen, Trans.). Rizzoli.

Eco, U. (2011). *On ugliness.* Rizzoli.

U. Eco (Ed.). (2004/2010). *History of beauty.* Rizzoli.

Edmonds, E., Bilda, Z., & Muller, L. (2009). Artist, evaluator and curator: Three viewpoints on interactive art, evaluation and audience experience. *Digital Creativity, 20*(3), 141–151. doi:10.1080/14626260903083579.

Edwards, E., Nagarajan, S. S., Dalal, S. S., Canolty, R. T., Kirsch, H. E., Barbaro, N. M., & Knight, R. T. (2010). Spatiotemporal imaging of cortical activation during verb generation and picture naming. *NeuroImage, 50,* 291–301. doi:10.1016/j.neuroimage.2009.12.035 PMID:20026224.

Eesti, K. O., & Ozsvald, E. (2012). Symbiosis. In *Proceedings of the SIGGRAPH 2012 International Conference and Exhibition of Computer Graphics and Interactive Techniques.* Retrieved October 8, 2012, from http://s2012.siggraph.org/attendees/sessions/symbiosiss

EIA. (2012). *U.S. Energy Information Administration.* Retrieved May 25, 2012, from http://www.eia.gov/electricity/

EIA. (2012). *Annual energy outlook 2012.* Retrieved August 30, 2012, from http://www.eia.gov/forecasts/aeo/

EIA. (2012). *U.S. energy-related carbon dioxide emissions, 2011.* Retrieved August 30, 2012, from http://www.eia.gov/environment/emissions/carbon/

EIA. (2012). *Energy and the environment explained: Greenhouse gases' effect on the climate*. Retrieved August 30, 2012, from http://www.eia.gov/energyexplained/index.cfm?page=environment_how_ghg_affect_climate

Eisenberg, M., Eisenberg, A., Blauvelt, G., Hendrix, S., Buechley, L., & Elumeze, N. (2005). Mathematical crafts for children: Beyond scissors and glue. In *Proceedings of Art+Math=X Conference*. University of Colorado.

Electronic Arts Productions. (2004). Retrieved August 9, 2012, from http://www.ronpellegrinoselectronicartsproductions.org/Pages/EAP.html

Eliot, T. S. (1968). *Four quartets: Little gidding*. Mariner Books.

Elumeze, N., & Eisenberg, M. (2008). ButtonSchemer: Ambient program reader. In *Proceedings of the 10th International Conference on Human Computer Interaction with Mobile Devices and Services, Mobile-HCI '08*, (pp. 323-326). ISBN: 978-1-59593-952-4 doi:10.1145/1409240.1409279

Entertainment Software Association. (2012). Retrieved July 10, 2012, from http://www.theesa.com/facts/game-player.asp

EON Icube. (2012). Retrieved July 30, 2012, from http://www.eonreality.com/products_icube.html

EON Reality Coliseum. (2012). Retrieved July 30, 2012, from http://www.eonreality.com/products_coliseum.html

Epilepsy Therapy Project. (2012). *Video games and epilepsy*. Retrieved July 10, 2012, from http://www.epilepsy.com/info/family_kids_video

ERA. (2012). *Education research abstracts online*. Retrieved October 6, 2012, from http://tandf.informaworld.com/smpp/home~db=all

Erétéo, G., Limpens, F., Gandon, F., Corby, O., Buffa, M., Leitzelman, M., & Sander, P. (2010). Semantic social network analysis: A concrete case. In *Handbook of Research on Methods and Techniques for Studying Virtual Communities: Paradigms and Phenomena*, (pp. 122-156). Academic Press.

Euphrosyne Doxiadis, E. (1995). *The mysterious fayum portraits*. Harry N. Abrams. ISBN 0810933314. Retrieved November 1, 2012, from http://www.amazon.com/Mysterious-Fayum-Portraits-Euphrosyne-Doxiadis/dp/0810933314/ref=sr_1_fkmr0_1?s=books&ie=UTF8&qid=1351815015&sr=1-1-fkmr0&keywords=Euphrosyne+Doxiadis%2C+E.%2C+and+D.+J.+Thompson

Evans, B. (2012). *Visual music*. Retrieved August 9, 2012, from http://www.lightspace.com

Evans, B. (2007). *Artist statement. Electronic Art and Animation Catalog*. ACM.

Evans, B. (2011). Materials of the data map. *International Journal of Creative Interfaces and Computer Graphics*, *2*(1), 14–26. doi:10.4018/jcicg.2011010102.

Everything₂ – Limerick. (2012). Retrieved February 18, 2012, from http://everything2.com/title/Limerick

Evo: The 9th European Event on Evolutionary and Biologically Inspired Music, Sound, Art and Design. (2011). Retrieved April 12, 2011, from http://www.evostar.org/evomusart/

Evomusart. (2012). *The tenth European event on evolutionary and biologically inspired music, sound, art and design*. Retrieved September 5, 2011, from http://evostar.dei.uc.pt/2012/call-for-contributions/evomusart/

EvoStar. (2010). *The annual European event on evolutionary computation*. Retrieved May 15, 2011, from http://dces.essex.ac.uk/research/evostar/evocomp.html

Facebook Inc. (2013). Retrieved March 10, 2013, from http://www.facebook.com/facebook?rf=106491156053682

Falkowski, P., Scholes, R. J., Boyle, E., Canadell, J., Canfield, D., & Elser, J. et al. (2000). The global carbon cycle: A test of our knowledge of earth as a system. *Science*, *290*(5490), 291–296. doi:10.1126/science.290.5490.291 PMID:11030643.

Farokhzad, O. C., Cheng, J., Teply, B. A., Sherifi, I., Jon, S., & Kantoff, P. W., ... Langer, R. (2006). Targeted nanoparticle-aptamer bioconjugates for cancer chemotherapy in vivo. *Proc. Natl. Acad. Sci.*, *103*(16), 6315-6320. doi 10.1073/pnas.0601755103. Retrieved September 8, 2012, 2012, from http://www.pnas.org/content/103/16/6315

Felder, R. M., & Soloman, B. (1993). *Learning styles and strategies*. Retrieved October 23, 2012, from http://www4.ncsu.edu/unity/lockers/users/f/felder/public/ILSdir/styles.htm

Felder, R. M., & Spurlin, J. (2005). Applications, reliability and validity of the index of learning styles. *Int. J. Engineering Education*, *21*(1), 103–112.

Ferguson, C. (1994). *Mathematics in stone and bronze*. Erie, PA: Meridian Creative Group.

Ferguson, H. et al. (2010). Celebrating mathematics in stone and bronze. *Notices of the American Mathematical Society*, *57*(7), 840–850.

Ferreira, M. I. A. (2011). Interactive bodies: The semiosis of architectural forms a case study. *Biosemiotics Online First*. doi 10.1007/s12304-011-9126-0. Retrieved July 29, 2012, from http://www.springerlink.com/content/v72u2555445qv167/

Fishwick, P. (2005). *Introduction to the aesthetic computing method for teaching algebra in middle and high school*. Retrieved March 26, 2012 from http://www.cise.ufl.edu/~fishwick/acworkshop/aestheticcomputing.pdf

Fishwick, P. (2006). Injecting creativity into teaching simulation modeling to computer science students. *Simulation*, *82*(11), 719–728. Retrieved from http://sim.sagepub.com/cgi/content/abstract/82/11/719 doi:10.1177/0037549706074191.

Fishwick, P. (2007). Aesthetic computing: A brief tutorial. In *Visual Languages for Interactive Computing: Definitions and Formalizations*. Retrieved April 29, 2012, from http://www.cise.ufl.edu/~fishwick/aescomputing/tutorial.pdf

Fishwick, P. (2008). An introduction to aesthetic computing. In P. Fishwick (Ed.), *Aesthetic Computing (Leonardo Book Series)*. The MIT Press.

Fishwick, P., Diehl, S., Prophet, J., & Löwgren, J. (2005). Perspectives on aesthetic computing. *Leonardo*, *38*(2), 133–141. doi:10.1162/0024094053722372.

Flannery, M. C. (2012). Herbaria: Border crossers extraordinaire. In *Proceedings of the School of Visual Arts 25th National Conference on Liberal Arts and the Education of Artists*, (pp. 51-57). School of Visual Arts.

Flannery, M. (1992). Using science's aesthetic dimension in teaching science. *Journal of Aesthetic Education*, *26*(1), 1–15. doi:10.2307/3332723.

Fletcher, A. (2012). *Seven new wonders*. Infoplease. Retrieved July 29, 2012, from Fletcherhttp://hawkstryker.hubpages.com/hub/The-Current-7-Man-Made-Wonders-of-The-World

Foulger, G. R. (2010). Plates vs plumes: A geological controversy. Wiley-Blackwell. ISBN 978-1-4051-6148-0

Fox, S. (2009). Radioactive cancer-binding buckyballs for targeted chemotherapy. *POPSCI*. Retrieved September 7, 2012, from http://www.popsci.com/scitech/article/2009-08/radiation-carrying-cancer-binding-bucky-balls-targeted-chemotherapy

Franke, H. W. (1971). *Computer graphics, computer art*. Phaidon Press.

Franke, H. W. (1989). Mathematics as an artistic-generative principle. *Leonardo*, *25*, 26.

Frazier, I. (2011, September 5). The march of the strandbeests: Theo Jansen's wind-powered sculpture. *New Yorker (New York, N.Y.)*, 54–61.

Frechette, R. E., III, & Gilchrist, R. (2008). *Towards zero energy: A case study of the Pearl River Tower, Guangzhou, China*. Retrieved August 1, 2008, from http://som.com/resources/content/5/0/4/3/9/0/2/0/documents/SOM_TowardsZeroEnergy.pdf

Frey, T., Gelhausen, M., & Saake, G. (2011). Categorization of concerns: A categorical program comprehension model. In *Proceedings of the Workshop on Evaluation and Usability of Programming Languages and Tools (PLATEAU) at the ACM Onward! and SPLASH Conferences*. ACM.

Friedman, S. D. (2009). How a 2-minute story helps you lead. *Harvard Business Review*. Retrieved February 16, 2012, from http://blogs.hbr.org/friedman/2009/08/how-a-2minute-story-can-help-y.html

Friedrich, W. L., Kromer, B., Friedrich, M., Heinemeier, J., Pfeiffer, T., & Talamo, S. (2006). Santorini eruption radiocarbon dated to 1627-1600 B.C. *Science*, *312*(5773), 548. Retrieved September 2, 2012, from http://www.sciencemag.org/content/312/5773/548

Funkhouser, C. (2008). Digital poetry: A look at generative, visual, and interconnected possibilities in its first four decades. In *A Companion to Digital Literary Studies*. Oxford, UK: Blackwell. Retrieved February 17, 2012, from http://www.digitalhumanities.org/companionDLS/

Gahlinger, P. (2003). *Illegal drugs: A complete guide to their history, chemistry, use, and abuse*. Plume.

Galanter, P. (2009). *Complexism and the role of evolutionary art*. Retrieved June 20, 2011, from http://tamu.academia.edu/PhilipGalanter/Papers/254390/Complexism_and_the_Role_of_Evolutionary_Art

Galanter, P. (2009). Truth to process – Evolutionary art and the aesthetics of dynamism. In *Proceedings of the GA2009 – XII Generative Art Conference*. Politecnico di Milano University.

Galanter, P. (2009). Thoughts on computational creativity. In *Proceedings of Dagstuhl Seminar Proceedings*. Schloss Dagstuhl – Leibniz Zentrum fuer Informatik.

Galanter, P. (2012). *Complexity, neuroaesthetics, and computational aesthetic evaluation*. Retrieved June 8, 2012, from http://philipgalanter.com/downloads/ga2010_neuroaesthetics_and_cae.pdf

Galanter, P. (2012). Computational aesthetic evaluation. In *Proceedings of the SIGGRAPH 2012 International Conference and Exhibition of Computer Graphics and Interactive Techniques*. Retrieved October 8, 2012, from http://s2012.siggraph.org/attendees/sessions/computational-aesthetic-evaluation-steps-toward-machine-creativity

Galanter, P. (2010). The problem with evolutionary art is. In C. Di Chio et al. (Eds.), *EvoApplications, (LNCS)* (Vol. 6025, pp. 321–330). Berlin: Springer-Verlag.

Gardener & Golovchenko. (2012). Ice-assisted electron beam lithography of graphene. *Nanotechnology, 23*(18), 185302. doi 10.1088/0957-4484/23/18/185302. Retrieved August 27, 2012, from http://iopscience.iop.org/0957-4484/23/18/185302/

Gardner, H. (1993). *Frames of mind: The theory of multiple intelligences*. New York: Basic Books, A Division of Harper Collins Publishers.

Gardner, H. (1993). *Art, mind, and brain: A cognitive approach to creativity*. New York: Basic Books, A Division of Harper Collins Publishers.

Gardner, H. (1993). *Multiple intelligences: The theory in practice*. New York: Basic Books, A Division of Harper Collins Publishers.

Gardner, M. (1970). The fantastic combinations of John Conway's new solitaire game of life. *Scientific American, 223*, 123–123.

Garousi, M. (2012). The postmodern beauty of fractals. *Leonardo, 45*(1), 26–32. doi:10.1162/LEON_a_00322.

Gaviria, A. R. (2008). When is information visualization art? Determining the critical criteria. *Leonardo, 41*(5), 479–482. doi:10.1162/leon.2008.41.5.479.

Gazzaniga, M. S. (2004). *The cognitive neurosciences III*. The MIT Press.

Geiger, J. (2012). Entr'acte. *Leonardo, 45*(4), 338–347. doi:10.1162/LEON_a_00408.

Geim, A. K., & Novoselov, K. S. (2007). The rise of graphene. *Nature Materials, 6*(3), 183–191. Retrieved September 13, 2012, from http://onnes.ph.man.ac.uk/nano/Publications/Naturemat_2007Review.pdf

Geim, A. K. (2009). Graphene: Status and prospects. *Science, 324*(5934), 1530–1534. doi:10.1126/science.1158877 PMID:19541989.

Gellner, A. (2008, August 23). Laying the foundation for today's skyscrapers. *San Francisco Chronicle*. Retrieved March 3, 2013, from http://www.sfgate.com/homeandgarden/article/Laying-the-foundation-for-today-s-skyscrapers-3199017.php

Genetic Mapping. (2012). *National Human Genome Research Institute*. Retrieved April 14, 2012, from http://www.genome.gov/10000715

Gerjets, P., Scheiter, K., & Catrambone, R. (2004). Designing instructional examples to reduce intrinsic cognitive load: Molar versus modular presentation of solution procedures. *Instructional Science, 32*(1-2), 33–58. doi:10.1023/B:TRUC.0000021809.10236.71.

Gfdas. (2011). *Golden fractals*. Retrieved July 23, 2011, from http://en.wikipedia.org/wiki/User:Gfdas29/Golden_Fractals

Ghani, D. A. (2011). Visualization elements of shadow play technique movement and study of computer graphic imagery (CGI) in Wayang Kulit Kelantan. *International Journal of Art, Culture and Design Technologies*, *1*(1), 50–57. doi:10.4018/IJACDT.2011010105.

Giannachi, G. (2011). Representing, performing, and mitigating climate change in contemporary art practice. *Leonardo*, *45*(3), 125–131.

Gibson, J. J. (1986). *The ecological approach to visual perception*. Psychology Press.

Gilchrist, B., Bradley, J., & Joelson, J. (2001). *Thought conductor*. Retrieved August 10, 2012, from http://www.artemergent.org.uk/tc/tc_intro.html

Gillian, D. (2011). *Vesuvius*. Profile Books, Ltd..

Global Information Technology Report 2008-2009. (2009). Retrieved January 9, 2011, from https://members.weforum.org/pdf/gitr/2009/gitr09fullreport.pdf

Goldblatt, D., & Paden, R. (2011). The aesthetics of architecture: Philosophical investigations into the art of building. *The Journal of Aesthetics and Art Criticism*, *69*(1), 1–6. doi:10.1111/j.1540-6245.2010.01441.x.

Goldspink, C., & Kay, R. (2009). Agent cognitive capabilities and orders of social emergence. In Handbook of Research on Agent-Based Societies: Social and Cultural Interactions, (pp. 17-34). IGI Global. ISBN 1605662364

González, E., Arbiol, J., & Puntes, V. F. (2011). Carving at the nanoscale: Sequential galvanic exchange and Kirkendall growth at room temperature. *Science, 334*(6061), 1377-1380. doi 10.1126/science.1212822. Retrieved November 1, 2012, from http://www.sciencemag.org/content/334/6061/1377.abstract?sid=1055ee45-abc7-4f9a-8698-e9ae3487aa68

González-Gancedo, S., Juan, M.-C., Seguí, I., Rando, N., & Cano, J. (2012). Towards a mixed reality learning environment in the classroom. In *Proceedings of the International Conference on Computer Graphics Theory and Applications and International Conference on Information Visualization Theory and Applications*, (pp. 434-439). ISBN 978-989-8565-02-0

Goodsell, D. S. (2006). Fact and fantasy in nanotech imagery. *Leonardo*, *42*(1), 52–57. doi:10.1162/leon.2009.42.1.52.

Google for Educators. (2010). Retrieved October 6, 2012, from http://www.google.com/edu/teachers/

Google in Education. (2012). Retrieved October 1, 2012, from http://www.google.com/educators/index.html

Google SketchUp for Educators. (2012). Retrieved October 1, 2012, from http://sitescontent.google.com/google-sketchup-for-educators/Home

Google Sketchup for My Class. (2012). Retrieved October 6, 2012, from http://sitescontent.google.com/google-sketchup-for-educators/Home/Google-Earth-for-My-Class

Granek, J. A., Gorbet, D. J., & Sergio, L. E. (2010). Extensive video-game experience alters cortical networks for complex visuomotor transformations. *Cortex*, *46*(9), 1165–1177. doi:10.1016/j.cortex.2009.10.009 PMID:20060111.

Grantab, R., Shenoy, V. B., & Ruoff, R. S. (2010). Anomalous strength characteristics of tilt grain boundaries in graphene. *Science*, *330*(6006), 946–948. doi:10.1126/science.1196893 PMID:21071664.

Grant, M. (2005). *Cities of Vesuvius: Pompeii and Herculaneum*. Phoenix Press.

Grau, O. (2004). *Virtual art: From illusion to immersion*. *Leonardo Book Series*. Boston: The MIT Press.

O. Grau (Ed.). (2007). *Media art histories. Leonardo Book Series*. Boston: The MIT Press.

Greenfield, G. (2010). *Diffusion limited aggregation, evolutionary computation, and algorithmic art - Five easy pieces*. School of Computing, Clemson University, Visual Computing Seminar. Retrieved January 24, 2012, from http://www.cs.clemson.edu/~dhouse/vcseminar/talks/greenfield-talk.pdf

Greensburg, Kansas. (2012). Retrieved August 1, 2012, from http://en.wikipedia.org/wiki/Greensburg,_Kansas

Gross, L., Mohn, F., Moll, N., Liljeroth, P., & Meyer, G. (2009, August 28). The chemical structure of a molecule resolved by atomic force microscopy. *Science, 1110-1114*. doi: doi:10.1126/science.1176210 PMID:19713523.

Haeckel, E. (2008). *Art forms in nature: The prints of Ernst Haeckel (monographs)*. Prestel.

Halbouty, M. T. (2004). *Giant oil & gas fields of the decade - 1990-99 (Aapg Memoir 78)*. American Association of Petroleum Geologists.

Hall, P. (2012). *Living skins: Architecture as interface*. Retrieved August 11, 2012, from http://www.adobe.com/motiondesign/MDC_Think_Tank.html?u%5FsLang=en&u%5FnTextSize=14&u%5FsFontType=sans&u%5FsContent=Living%5FSkins

Haloquadra . (2010). Retrieved January 27, 2011, from microbewiki.kenyon.edu/index.php/Haloquadra

Hammerstingl, W. (1999). *Strategies in visual narrative*. Retrieved October 30, 2012, from http://www.olinda.com/VC/lectures/Narrative.htm

Hansen, M. B. N. (2006). *New philosophy for new media*. Boston: The MIT Press.

Hardin, G. (1968, December 13). The tragedy of the commons. *Science*, 1243–1248. doi: doi:10.1126/science.162.3859.1243 PMID:5699198.

Hardtke. (1999). Jury statement. *Prix Ars Electronica*.

Harmon, D. (2012). World rock art, no borders: A world museum. In *Proceedings of the School of Visual Arts 25th National Conference on Liberal Arts and the Education of Artists*, (pp. 57-61). School of Visual Arts.

Harty, D. (2012). Drawing//digital//data: A phenomenological approach to the experience of water. In A. Ursyn (Ed.), *Biologically-inspired computing for the arts: Scientific data through graphics*. Hershey, PA: IGI Global. doi:10.4018/978-1-4666-0942-6.ch019.

Hassard, J., & Dias, M. (2008). *The art of teaching science: Inquiry and innovation in middle school and high school* (2nd ed.). Routlege.

Hébert, J. P. (2012). *Personal website*. Retrieved September 14, 2012, from http://jeanpierrehebert.com/index.html

Heffernan, V. (2007, March 27). YouTube awards the top of its heap. *The New York Times*. Retrieved February 16, 2012, from http://www.nytimes.com/2007/03/27/arts/27tube.html?_r=1&oref=login

Helmers, M. (2012). *Visual rhetoric*. Retrieved February 17, 2012, from http://www.parlorpress.com/search/node/visual%20rhetoric%20series

Hensel, J. (2010). Once upon a time. *Meeting Professionals International*. Retrieved February 16, 2012, from http://www.mpiweb.org/Magazine/Archive/US/February2010/OnceUponATime

Herger, M. (2012). Gamification facts and figures. *Enterprise-Gamification.com*. Retrieved March 10, 2013, from http://enterprise-gamification.com/index.php/en/facts

Herzog, W. (2012). *Werner Herzog: The artist's website*. Retrieved September 3, 2012, from http://www.werner-herzog.com/index.php?id=64

Hessels, S. (2012). Sustainable cinema no. 4: Shadow play. In *Proceedings of the SIGGRAPH 2012 International Conference and Exhibition of Computer Graphics and Interactive Techniques*. Retrieved October 9, 2012, from http://s2012.siggraph.org/attendees/sessions/sustainable-cinema-no-4-shadow-play

Hessels, S. (2012). Sustainable cinema: The moving image and the forces of nature. In A. Ursyn (Ed.), *Biologically-Inspired Computing for the Arts: Scientific Data through Graphics* (pp. 90–105). Hershey, PA: IGI Global. doi:10.4018/978-1-4666-0942-6.ch006.

Hill, A. S. (1878/2007). *Principles of rhetoric and their application*. New York: Harper and Brothers. Retrieved November 28, 2012, from http://archive.org/stream/principlesofrhet00hilluoft#page/n1/mode/2up

C. A. Hill, & M. Helmers (Eds.). (2004/2008). *Defining visual rhetorics*. Routledge.

Hockney, D. (2012). *Personal webpage*. Retrieved February 9, 2012, from http://www.hockneypictures.com/home.php

Hoetzlein, R. C. (2011). Visual communication in times of crisis: The Fukushima nuclear accident. *Leonardo*, *45*(3), 113–118.

Hoffmann, D. L., Beck, J. W., Richards, D. A., Smart, P. L., Singarayer, J. S., Ketchmark, T., & Hawkesworth, C. J. (2010). Towards radiocarbon calibration beyond 28 ka using speleothems from the Bahamas. *Earth and Planetary Science Letters*, *289*(1–2), 1–10. Retrieved September 2, 2012, from http://www.sciencedirect.com/science/article/pii/S0012821X09006037

Hokanson, B., Miller, C., & Hooper, S. (2008). Role-based design: A contemporary perspective for innovation in instructional design. *TechTrends*, *52*(6), 36–43. doi:10.1007/s11528-008-0215-0.

Holguin, J. (2009, February 11). Uncle Sam wants video gamers. *CBS News*. Retrieved July 9, 2012, from http://www.cbsnews.com/stories/2005/02/08/eveningnews/main672455.shtml

Holz, C., & Baudisch, P. (2011). *Understanding touch*. Paper presented at the ACM CHI Conference on Human Factors in Computing Systems. Vancouver, Canada. Retrieved January 30, 2012, from www.christianholz.net/2011-chi11-holz-baudisch-understanding_touch.pdf

Holzer, J. (2012). *Website*. Retrieved February 17, 2012, from http://www.youtube.com/watch?v=CeVkHU4tfd8&feature=relmfu

Howe, D. C., & Cayley, J. (2011). The readers project: Procedural agents and literary vectors. *Leonardo*, *44*(4), 317–324. doi:10.1162/LEON_a_00208.

Hsu, J. (2010). Tiny buckyballs could put fast-spreading cancer cells into suspended animation, but their effect in normal cells may prove toxic for the body. *POPSCI*. Retrieved September 7, 2012, from http://www.popsci.com/technology/article/2010-03/buckyballs-could-put-fast-spreading-cancer-cells-suspended-animation

Huang, Q., & Balsys, R. J. (2009). Applying fractal and chaos theory to animation in the chinese literati tradition. In *Proceedings of the Sixth International Conference on Computer Graphics, Imaging and Visualization*, (pp. 112-122). ISBN: 978-0-7695-3789-4

Huff, K. A. (1999). *Electronic art and animation catalog*. Paper presented at SI99RAPH. New York, NY.

Huizinga, J. (1968). *Homo ludens: A study of the play-element in culture*. Boston, MA: The Beacon Press. (Original work published 1938).

IBM Smarter Buildings. (2010). Retrieved August 1, 2008, from http://www.ibm.com/smarterplanet/us/en/green_buildings/overview/index.html?csr=agus_getgovtsmbuild20120320&cm=k&cr=google&ct=LBSK005&S_TACT=LBSK005&ck=smarter_buildings&cmp=LBSK0&mkwid=sufBbUa4x_20798476667_432cfc4094

ICAM-I2CAM. (2012). *The International Institute for Complex Adaptive Matter*. Retrieved August 24, 2012 from http://icam-i2cam.org/index.php/icamnews/

Inselberg, A. (2009). *Parallel coordinates: Visual multidimensional geometry and its applications*. New York: Springer.

Internet Usage Statistics . (2012). Retrieved March 9, 2013, from http://www.internetworldstats.com/stats.htm

Interrupt 2. (2012). *IRQds: Interrupt discussion sessions*. Brown University. Retrieved February 17, 2012, from http://literalart.net/irqds/

ION. (2012). *Strengths of online learning*. Retrieved September 25, 2012, from http://www.ion.uillinois.edu/resources/tutorials/overview/strengths.asp

ION. (2012). *Weaknesses of online learning*. Retrieved September 26, 2012, from http://www.ion.uillinois.edu/resources/tutorials/overview/weaknesses.asp

iPad News. (2011). *Geom-E-Tree is the perfect blend of math, art, and nature.* Retrieved September 23, 2012, from http://www.ipadnews.nl/tag/john-miller/

IPPC. (2007). *Intergovernmental Panel on Climate Change.* Retrieved August 30, 2012, from http://www.ipcc.ch/publications_and_data/ar4/wg1/en/faq-1-3.html

Ippolito, J. (2002). Ten myths of internet art. *Leonardo, 35*(5), 485–498. doi:10.1162/002409402320774312.

Irifune, T., Kurio, A., Sakamoto, S., Inoue, T., & Sumiya, H. (2003). Materials: Ultrahard polycrystalline diamond from graphite. *Nature, 421,* 599–600. doi:10.1038/421599b PMID:12571587.

Ishizu, T., & Zeki, S. (2011). Toward a brain-based theory of beauty. *PLoS ONE, 6*(7), e21852. doi:10.1371/journal.pone.0021852 PMID:21755004.

ISN. (2010). *Institute for Soldier Nanotechnologies.* Retrieved December 11, 2010, from http://web.mit.edu/isn/

Ittelson, W. H. (2007). The perception of nonmaterial objects and events. *Leonardo, 40*(3), 279–283. doi:10.1162/leon.2007.40.3.279.

James, A. V., James, D. A., & Kalisperis, L. N. (2004). A unique art form: The friezes of Pirgi. *Leonardo, 37*(3), 234–242. doi:10.1162/0024094041139409.

Jarmon, L. (2010). Homo virtualis: Virtual worlds, learning, and an ecology of embodied interaction. *International Journal of Virtual and Personal Learning Environments, 1*(1), 38–56. doi:10.4018/jvple.2010091704.

Jencks, C. (2003/2009). *The garden of cosmic speculation.* Frances Lincoln, Ltd..

Jenkins, H. (2011). Transmedia 202: Further reflections. *The Official Weblog of Henry Jenkins.* Retrieved February 23, 2012, from http://henryjenkins.org/2011/08/defining_transmedia_further_re.html

Jones, J. (2005). *Fractals & frequencies.* Retrieved September 4, 2012, from http://fractalsandfrequencies.blogspot.com/

Jones, J. (2010). Influences in the formation and evolution of physarum polycephalum inspired emergent transport networks. *Natural Computing, 4,* 793-1006. Retrieved April 11, 2011, from http://www.springerlink.com/content/p2r148p612k05207/export-citation/

Jones, O. (2010). *The grammar of ornament.* Deutsch Press. (Original work published 1856).

Kac, E. (2011) *Website of Eduardo Kac.* Retrieved January 26, 2011, from http://ekac.org/

Kac, E. (2006). *Signs of life: Bio art and beyond. Leonardo Books.* Boston: The MIT Press.

Kanninen, E. (2009). *Learning styles and e-learning.* Retrieved October 1, 2012, from http://hlab.ee.tut.fi/video/bme/evicab/astore/delivera/wp4style.pdf

Kassan, D. (2011). *Website.* Retrieved October 12, 2011, from http://davidkassan.com

Kawabata, H., & Zeki, S. (2004). Neural correlates of beauty. *Journal of Neurophysiology, 91,* 699–1705. doi:10.1152/jn.00696.2003 PMID:15010496.

Keiner, M., Kurz, T., & Nadin, M. (1994). *Manfred Mohr.* Weiningen-Zürich: Viviane Ehri.

Kensington. (2012). *The Kensington high school for the creative and performing arts.* Retrieved July 29, 2012, from http://www.aiatopten.org/node/48

Kettle, S. F. A. (2007). *Symmetry and structure: Readable group theory for chemists* (3rd ed.). Wiley-Blackwell. ISBN 0470060409

Khan, M. K. (2006). *Report of the council on science and public health: Emotional and behavioral effects, including addictive potential, of video games.* Retrieved July 7, 2012, from http://psychcentral.com/blog/images/csaph12a07.pdf

Kim, K. J., & Cho, S. B. (2006). A comprehensive overview of the applications of artificial life. *Artificial Life, 12*(1), 153-82. Retrieved September 3, 2012, from http://www.ncbi.nlm.nih.gov/pubmed/16393455

Kirk, U., Skov, M., Christensen, M. S., & Nygaard, N. (2009). Brain correlates with aesthetic expertise: A parametric fMRI study. *Brain and Cognition, 69*(2), 306–315. doi:10.1016/j.bandc.2008.08.004 PMID:18783864.

Klanten, R. (2010). *Data flow 2: Visualizing information in graphic design*. Die Gestalten Verlag.

Koepp, M. J., Gunn, R. N., Lawrence, A. D., Cunningham, V. J., Dagher, A., & Jones, T. et al. (1998). Evidence for striatal dopamine release during a video game. *Nature, 393*, 266–268. doi:10.1038/30498 PMID:9607763.

Kostelnick, C., & Roberts, D. D. (2010). *Designing visual language: Strategies for professional communicators*. Longman.

Kringelbach, M. L., & Berridge, K. C. (2010b). The functional neuroanatomy of pleasure and happiness. *Discov Med., 9*(49), 579–587. Retrieved October 6, 2012, from http://www.ncbi.nlm.nih.gov/pmc/articles/PMC3008353/

Kronenberger, W. G., Wang, Y., & Mathews, V. P. (2012). Violent video game play: What neuroimaging tells us. *Education.com*. Retrieved July 9, 2012, from http://www.education.com/reference/article/violent-video-game-play-neuroimaging/

Krueger, M. (1991). *Artificial reality 2*. Reading, MA: Addison-Wesley Professional.

La Brecque, M. (1987). Retrieved July 23, 2012, from http://www.mosaicsciencemagazine.org/pdf/m18_02_87_03.pdf

Lahey, B., Burleson, W., & Streb, E. (2012). Translation + pendaphonics = movement modulated media. *Leonardo, 45*(4), 322–329. doi:10.1162/LEON_a_00406.

Latham, W., Shaw, M., Todd, S., & Leymarie, F. F. (2007). *From DNA to 3D organic art forms*. Retrieved May 15, 2011, from http://www.siggraph.org/s2007/attendees/sketches/3.html

Lau, A., & Vande Moere, A. (2007). Towards a model of information aesthetics in information visualization. In *Proceedings of the International Conference on Information Visualisation*. London, UK: IEEE Computer Society.

Lauzzana, R., & Penrose, D. (1987). A 21st century manifesto. In *Proceedings of FINEART Forum 1, Electronic Newsletter of International Society for Art, Science, and Technology (ISAST)*. ISAST.

Lauzzana, R., & Penrose, D. (1992). A pre-21st century manifesto. *Languages of Design, 1*(1), 87.

Lave, J., & Wenger, E. (1991). *Situated learning: Legitimate peripheral participation*. Cambridge University Press. doi:10.1017/CBO9780511815355.

Lear, E. (2010). *The book of nonsense*. Kessinger Publishing, LLC.

Lebwohl, B. (2011, July 25). Semir Zeki: Beauty is in the brain of the beholder. *EarthSky*. Retrieved December 12, 2011, from http://earthsky.org/human-world/semir-zeki-beauty-is-in-the-brain-of-the-beholder

Lee, J., Bush, B., Maboudian, B., & Fearing, R. S. (2009). Gecko-inspired combined lamellar and nanofibrillar array for adhesion on nonplanar surface. *Langmuir, 25*(21), 12449–12453. doi 10.1021/la9029672. Retrieved August 24, 2012, from http://pubs.acs.org/doi/abs/10.1021/la9029672

Lee, R. (2011). Video game violence alters brain function in young men. In *Diagnostic Imaging*. UBM Medica Network. Retrieved July 9, 2012, from http://www.diagnosticimaging.com/mri/content/article/113619/1999463

Lee, H.-J., Macbeth, A. H., Pagani, J., & Young, W. S. III. (2009). Oxytocin: The great facilitator of life. *Progress in Neurobiology, 88*(2), 127–151. doi: doi:10.1016/j.pneurobio.2009.04.001 PMID:19482229.

Leffingwell, J. C. (2003). Chirality and bioactivity I: Pharmacology. *Leffingwell Reports, 3*(1). Retrieved April 13, 2011, from http://www.leffingwell.com/download/chirality-phamacology.pdf

Lengler, R. (2007). How to induce the beholder to persuade himself: Learning from advertising research for information visualization. In *Proceedings of the 11th International Conference on Information Visualization*, (pp. 382-392). IEEE Computer Society Press.

Lengler, R., & Eppler, M. (2006). *A periodic table of visualization methods*. Retrieved December 17, 2010, from http://www.visual-literacy.org/periodic_table/periodic_table.html

Lengler, R., & Vande Moere, A. (2009). Guiding the viewer's imagination: How visual rhetorical figures create meaning in animated infographics. In *Proceedings of the 13th International Conference on Information Visualization*. DOI 10.1109/IV.2009.102

Leonardo – The Genius and His Inventions. (2011). *An iPhone, iPod touch, and iPad application*. Retrieved April 14, 2013, from https://itunes.apple.com/hk/app/leonardo-da-vinci-genius-his/id448208854?mt=8

Levin, J. A., & Bruce, B. C. (2001). *Technology as media: The learner centered perspective*. Retrieved May 15, 2012, from http://lrs.ed.uiuc.edu/jim-levin/levin-bruce-aera.html

Lévi-Strauss, C. (1997, 1993). *Look, listen, learn*. Basic Books, a division of Harper-Collins Publishers. ISBN 0-465-06880-4

Levitt, S. D., & Dubner, S. J. (2009). *Freakonomics: A rogue economist explores the hidden side of everything*. William Morrow.

Levy, S. (2011, January). The AI revolution. *Wired*. Retrieved from http://www.wired.com/magazine/2010/12/ff_ai_essay_airevolution/

Lewis, C., Mojsiewicz, K., & Pettican, A. (2012). From wunderkammern to kinect – The creation of shadow worlds. *Leonardo, 45*(4), 330–337. doi:10.1162/LEON_a_00407.

Leyton, M. (2006). The foundations of aesthetics. In P.A. Fishwick (Ed.), Aesthetic Computing (pp. 289-314). Leonardo Books. Cambridge, MA: The MIT Press. ISBN 026206250X

Life. (1972, July 7). Pencils, paint and pottery can give you lead poisoning. *Life*, 46. Retrieved September 3, 2012, from http://books.google.com/books?id=_1QEAAAAMBAJ&printsec=frontcover&source=gbs_ge_summary_r&cad=0#v=onepage&q&f=false

Lima, M. (2011). Visual complexity: Mapping patterns of information. New York: Princeton Architectural Press. ISBN 978 1 56898 936 5

Lio, P., & Verma, D. (2012). *Biologically inspired networking and sensing: Algorithms and architectures*. Hershey, PA: IGI Global.

Litman, L., & Davachi, L. (2008). Distributed learning enhances relational memory consolidation. *Learning & Memory (Cold Spring Harbor, N.Y.), 15*(9), 711–716. doi:10.1101/lm.1132008 PMID:18772260.

Liu, X. Y., & Sawant, P. D. (2001). Formation kinetics of fractal nanofibers networks in organogels. *Applied Physics Letters, 79*(21), 3518-3520. Retrieved July 21, 2012, from http://www.physics.nus.edu.sg/~interface/Papers/37.PDF

Livemocha. (2012). Retrieved September 21, 2012, from http://www.livemocha.com/

Loeb, A. L. (1993). *Concepts & images: Visual mathematics. Design Science Collection*. Boston: Birkhäuser.

Lohr, L., & Ursyn, A. (2010). Visualizing the instructional design process: Seven usability strategies for promoting creative instruction. *Design Principles and Practices: An International Journal, 4*(2), 427–436.

LoPiccolo, P. (2003). A virtual exhibit transports museum-goers back in time to view a famous art collection in its original setting. *Computer Graphics World, 26*(3). Retrieved July 14, 2012, from http://www.cgw.com/Publications/CGW/2003/Volume-26-Issue-3-March-2003-/Backdrop-3-03.aspx

Lovejoy, M. (2004). *Digital currents: Art in the electronic age* (3rd ed.). Routledge.

Lucia, A., Sabin, J. E., & Jones, P. L. (2011). Memory, difference, and information: Generative architectures latent to material and perceptual plasticity. In *Proceedings of The 15th International Conference on Information Visualization*, (pp. 379-388). Los Alamitos, CA: IEEE Computer Society. ISBN 978-1-4577-0868-8

Lyotard, J. F. (1994). *Lessons on the analytic of the sublime (meridian: crossing aesthetics)*. Stanford University Press.

Mabey, R. (2010). *Weeds: In defense of nature's most unloved plants*. New York, NY: HarperCollins.

MacAulay, D. (1989). *Mill*. Graphia.

Mackness, J., Mak, S. F. J., & Williams, R. (2010). The ideals and reality of participating in a MOOC. In *Proceedings of the Seventh International Conference on Networked Learning*. Retrieved September 23, 2012, from http://www.lancs.ac.uk/fss/organisations/netlc/past/nlc2010/abstracts/Mackness.html

Madigan, J. (2012). *The psychology of video games*. Retrieved August 6, 2012, from http://www.psychologyofgames.com/tag/dopamine/

Maeda, J. (2001). *Maeda@Media*. Universe.

Maeda, J. (2004). *Creative code: Aesthetics + computation*. Thames & Hudson.

Maeda, J., & Bermont, R. (2011). *Redesigning leadership (simplicity, technology, business, life)*. The MIT Press.

Mager, R. F. (1984). *Preparing instructional objectives* (2nd ed.). Belmont, CA: David S. Lake.

Malina, R. F. (1990). The beginning of a new art form. In *Proceedings of Der Prix Ars Electronica: International Compendium of the Computer Arts*. Linz: Veritas-Verlag.

Malraux, A. (1958/1974). *La métamorphose des dieux*. Paris: Gallimard.

Mandelbrot, B. B. (1987). Fractals. *Encyclopedia of Physical Science and Technology*, 5, 579-593.

Mandelbrot, B. B. (1982). *The fractal geometry of nature*. W. H. Freeman and Company.

Manning, S. W., Ramsey, C. B., Kutschera, W., Higham, T., Kromer, B., Steier, P., & Wild, E. M. (2006). Chronology for the Aegean late bronze age 1700-1400 B.C. *Science*, 312(5773), 565–569. Retrieved September 2, 2012, from http://www.sciencemag.org/content/312/5773/565

Manochehri, N.-N., Gromik, N., & Liang, S. (2012). The integration of portable technology to enhance lifelong learning skills. In *Proceedings of the 2012 SWDSI Conference*. Retrieved September 27, 2012, from http://www.swdsi.org/swdsi2012/proceedings_2012/papers/Papers/PA125.pdf

Manovich, L. (2001). *Info-aesthetics: Information and form*. Retrieved May 18, 2011, from http://www.manovich.net/IA/index.html

Marchese, F. T. (2011). Article. *Leonardo*, 44(4), 303.

Marquis, J., & Wyeld, T. (2011). The contemporisation of Dante's Inferno. In *Proceedings of the 15ᵗʰ International Conference on Information Visualization*, (pp. 585 – 587). ISBN 078-0-7695-4476-2

Martindale, C. (1990). *Cognitive psychology: A neural-network approach*. Brooks/Cole Pub Co..

Masters, E. L. (1915/2012). *Spoon river anthology*. Empire Books. ISBN 1619491923. Retrieved October 21, 2012, from http://www.bartleby.com/84/1.html

Mathews, V. P., Kronenberger, W. G., Wang, Y., Lurito, J. T., Lowe, M. J., & Dunn, D. W. (2005). Media violence exposure and frontal lobe activation measured by functional magnetic resonance imaging in aggressive and nonaggressive adolescents. *Journal of Computer Assisted Tomography*, 29, 287–292. doi:10.1097/01.rct.0000162822.46958.33 PMID:15891492.

Maturrano, L., Santos, F., Rosselló-Mora, R., & Antón, J. (2006). Microbial diversity in maras salterns, a hypersaline environment in the Peruvian Andes. *Applied and Environmental Microbiology*, 72(6), 3887–3895. doi:10.1128/AEM.02214-05 PMID:16751493.

Mayer, R. E., & Moreno, R. (1998). A split-attention effect in multimedia learning: Evidence for dual processing systems in working memory. *Journal of Educational Psychology*, 90(2), 312. doi:10.1037/0022-0663.90.2.312.

Mayer, R. E., & Moreno, R. (2003). Nine ways to reduce cognitive load in multimedia learning. *Educational Psychologist*, 38(1), 43–52. doi:10.1207/S15326985EP3801_6.

Mayhew, P. J. (2006). *Discovering evolutionary ecology: Bringing together ecology and evolution*. Oxford University Press.

Maynard, P. (2005). *Drawing distinctions: The varieties of graphic expressions*. Cornell University Press.

McCloud, S. (2006). *Making comics: Storytelling secrets of comics, manga and graphic novels*. William Morrow.

McEvilley, T. C. (2002). *The shape of ancient thought: Comparative studies in Greek and Indian philosophies*. Allworth Press.

McHale, M. (2008). *Nanotechnology: Ferrofluids and liquid crystals*. Retrieved August 29, 2012 from http://cnx.org/content/m15532/latest/

McNaught, A. D., & Wilkinson, A. (Eds.). (2010). *Compendium of chemical terminology* (2nd ed). Blackwell Scientific Publications. Retrieved October 2, 2011, from http://goldbook.iupac.org/C01058.html

MDG. (2008). The Millennium Development Goals Report. *United Nations*. Retrieved December 11, 2010, from http://mdgs.un.org/unsd/mdg/Resources/Static/Products/Progress2008/MDG_Report_2008_En.pdf#page=44

Messer, R. (2012). *Image*. Retrieved May 25, 2012, from http://www.naturalhomeandgarden.com/multimedia/image-gallery.aspx?id=1854

Milani-Santarpia, G. (2012). *Mariamilani, antiquities of Rome, Roman construction and technology, constructing walls in ancient Rome*. Retrieved April 15, 2012, from http://www.mariamilani.com/ancient_rome/rome_building_walls.htm

Millburg, S. (2010, September 27). fMRI finds video gaming may create surgeons. *Radiology Daily: Neuroradiology*. Retrieved July 9, 2012, from http://www.radiologydaily.com/daily/neuroradiology/fmri-finds-video-gaming-may-create-surgeons/

Minecraft Forums. (2011). Retrieved July 10, 2012, from http://www.minecraftforum.net/topic/897191-puzmaxwells-escape/

Minimum Solar Box Cooker. (n.d.). Retrieved from http://solarcooking.wikia.com/wiki/Minimum_Solar_Box_Cooker

Minissale, G. (2012). Conceptual art: A blind spot for neuroaesthetics? *Leonardo*, *45*(1), 43–48. doi:10.1162/LEON_a_00324.

Model Organisms. (2008). *The use of model organisms in instruction*. University of Wisconsin: Wisconsin Outreach Research Modules. Retrieved January 9, 2011, from http://wormclassroom.org/teaching-model-organisms

Moere, A. V. (2012). Data fiction: Storytelling with information graphics. *Information Aesthetics Weblog*. Retrieved February 23, 2012, from http://infosthetics.com/archives/2010/02/data_fiction_story_telling_with_information-graphics.html

Mohr, M. (2012). *Manfred Mohr, personal website*. Retrieved September 11, 2012, from http://www.emohr.com/index.html

Moloney, J. (2006). Between art and architecture: The interactive skins. In *Proceedings of the 10th International Conference on Information Visualization*, (pp. 681-686). IEEE.

Monet, C. (n.d.). *A series of cathedrals*. Retrieved February 28, 2013, from (http://en.wikipedia.org/wiki/File:Claude_Monet_-_Rouen_Cathedral,_Facade_(Sunset).JPG

Monet, C. (n.d.). *A series of water lilies*. Retrieved February 28, 2013, from http://en.wikipedia.org/wiki/File:Claude_Monet_-_Water_Lilies.JPG

Moovl. (2012). Retrieved October 6, 2012, from http://archive.futurelab.org.uk/projects/moovl

Moraveji, N., Olson, B., Nguyen, T., Saadat, M., Khalighi, Y., Pea, R., & Heer, J. (2011). Peripheral paced respiration: Influencing user physiology during information work. ACM. ISBN 978-1-4503-0716-1/11/10

Moreno, R. (2006). Learning in high-tech and multimedia environments. *Current Directions in Psychological Science*, *15*(2), 63–67. doi:10.1111/j.0963-7214.2006.00408.x.

Moreno, R. (2007). Optimizing learning from animations by minimizing cognitive load: Cognitive and affective consequences of signaling and segmentation methods. *Applied Cognitive Psychology*, *21*, 1–17. doi:10.1002/acp.1348.

Moreno, R., & Mayer, R. E. (1999). Cognitive principles of multimedia learning: The role of modality and contiguity. *Journal of Educational Psychology*, *91*, 358–368. doi:10.1037/0022-0663.91.2.358.

Moses, A. (2011). From fantasy to lethal reality: Breivik trained on Modern Warfare game. *The Sydney Morning Herald*. Retrieved July 9, 2012, from http://www.smh.com.au/digital-life/games/from-fantasy-to-lethal-reality-breivik-trained-on-modern-warfare-game-20110725-1hw41.html

Mount Vesuvius. (2011). Exploring the environment: Volcanoes. *NASA Talk and Center for Educational Technologies*. Retrieved April 11, 2012, from http://www.cotf.edu/ete/modules/volcanoes/vmtvesuvius.html

Mroz, P., Pawlak, A., Satti, M., Lee, H., Wharton, T., Galli, H., et al. (2007). Functionalized fullerenes mediate photodynamic killing of cancer cells: Type I versus type II photochemical mechanism. *Free Radic Biol Med., 43*(5), 711–719. Retrieved September 7, 2012, from http://www.ncbi.nlm.nih.gov/pmc/articles/PMC1995806/

MySQL. (2012). Retrieved October 7, 2012, from (http://dev.mysql.com/doc/refman/5.1/en/what-is-mysql.html

Nagao, S., Takahashi, S., & Tanaka, J. (2008). Mirror appliance: Recommendation of clothes coordination in daily life. In *Proceedings of the 21st Human Factors in Telecommunication.* Retrieved January 29, 2011, from http://www.hft2008.org/images/paper/hft08.nagao.pdf

Naito, M., Shizuki, B., Tanaka, J., & Hosobe, H. (2009). Interaction techniques using a spherical cursor for 3D targets acquisition and indicating in volumetric displays. In *Proceedings of the iV, 13th International Conference on Information Visualization,* (pp. 607 – 612). ISBN 978-0-7695-3733-7

Nano.gov. (2012). *National Nanotechnology Initiative.* Retrieved August 27, 2012, from http://www.nano.gov/education-training/workforce-training-center

Nanotec Applications. (n.d.). Retrieved August 26, 2012, from http://www.discovernano.northwestern.edu/affect/applications_content

NASA Earth Observatory. (2011). Retrieved August 30, 2012, from http://earthobservatory.nasa.gov/Features/CarbonCycle/carbon_cycle2001.pdf

Nasibulin, A. G., Pikhitsa, P. V., Jiang, H., Brown, D. P., Krasheninnikov, A. V., & Anisimov, A. S. et al. (2007). A novel hybrid carbon material. *Nature Nanotechnology, 2,* 156–161. doi:10.1038/nnano.2007.37 PMID:18654245.

National Cancer Institute. (2012). *NCI Alliance for Nanotechnology in Cancer.* Retrieved from http://nano.cancer.gov/learn/understanding/

National Geographic. (n.d.). *Three main types of solar ovens.* Retrieved from http://greenliving.nationalgeographic.com/three-main-types-solar-ovens-2877.html

National Park Service. (2012). *Yellowstone national park.* Retrieved April 12, 2012, from http://www.nps.gov/yell/naturescience/volcanoqa.htm

National Police Agency of Japan. (2012). Retrieved April 11, 2012, from http://www.npa.go.jp/archive/keibi/biki/higaijokyo_e.pdf

Neville, A. C. (1977). Symmetry and asymmetry problems in animals. In *The Encyclopedia of Ignorance: Everything you ever wanted to know about the unknown* (pp. 331–338). New York: Pergamon Press.

New 7 wanders of the world. (n.d.). Retrieved October 22, 2011, from http://www.new7wonders.com/

Newton, J. (2012, January 27). Super Mario 3D Land is 3DS's first 5 million seller. *Nintendo Life.* Retrieved July 5, 2012, from http://www.nintendolife.com/

Ng, A. (2013). *Machine learning.* Retrieved April 15, 2013, from http://online.stanford.edu/course/machine-learning

Nintendo Wii Virtual Console Service. (2012). Retrieved July 5, 2012, from http://en.wikipedia.org/wiki/Virtual_Console

Nkambou, R., Mizoguchi, R., & Bourdeau, J. (2010). *Advances in intelligent tutoring systems.* Springer. doi:10.1007/978-3-642-14363-2.

Nobleprize.org. (2010). Retrieved October 26, 2012, from http://www.nobelprize.org/nobel_prizes/physics/laureates/2010/

Noll, A. M. (1970). Art ex machina. *IEEE Student Journal, 8*(4).

Nordquist, R. (2012). Visual metaphor. *About.com Guide.* Retrieved February 17, 2012, from http://grammar.about.com/od/tz/g/vismeterm.htm

NREL. (2012). *National renewable energy laboratory.* Retrieved October 30, 2012, from http://www.nrel.gov/rsf

NSF NACK Center. (2012). *National center for nanotechnology applications and career knowledge.* Penn State University Center for Nanotechnology Education and Utilization. Retrieved August 20, 2011, from http://www.nano4me.org/

Oh, J.-H., Kim, S.-Y., Kim, S.-H., & Shi, C.-K. (2011). A study of interactive art in the narrative form of magic monkey. In *Proceedings of the Eight International Conference Computer Graphics, Imaging, and Visualization,* (pp. 39-46). DOI 10.1109/CGIV.2011.19

Ohler, J. (2012). *Digital storytelling storyboard templates.* Retrieved February 18, 2012, from http://www.jasonohler.com/pdfs/digitalStorytellingStoryBoard-adv.pdf

Ohler, J. (2012). *Storytelling and new media narrative: Part I - Storytelling, literacy and learning.* Retrieved February 23, 2012, from http://www.jasonohler.com/storytelling/storyeducation.cfm

Okubo, P. G., & Aki, K. (1987). Fractal geometry in the San Andreas Fault system. *Journal of Geophysical Research, 92*(B1), 345–355. doi:10.1029/JB092iB01p00345.

Oldershaw, R. L. (2005). *Self-similarity of RR lyrae stars and singly-excited helium atoms.* Retrieved October 26, 2012, from http://arxiv.org/pdf/astro-ph/0510147.pdf

Oldershaw, R. L. (2006). *Discrete self-similarity between RR Lyrae stars II.* Retrieved October 26, 2012, from http://www.researchgate.net/publication/1787531_Discrete_Self-Similarity_Of_RR_Lyrae_Stars_II._Period_Spectrum_For_A_Very_Large_Sample

Orfescu, C. (2012). NanoArt: Nanotechnology and art. In A. Ursyn (Ed.), *Biologically-Inspired Computing for the Arts: Scientific Data through Graphics.* Hershey, PA: IGI Global. doi:10.4018/978-1-4666-0942-6.ch008.

Osawa, J., & Wakabayashi, D. (2012, November 13). Japan's answer to Facebook: Line messaging app. aims to reshape networking for smartphones. *The Wall Street Journal*, p. B4.

Özgenel, L. (2008). A tale of two cities: In search of ancient Pompeii and Herculaneum. *METU Journal of the Faculty of Architecture, 25*(1), 1–25.

Paivio, A. (1970). On the functional significance of imagery. *Psychological Bulletin, 73*, 385–392. doi:10.1037/h0029180.

Paivio, A. (1971). *Imagery and verbal processes.* New York: Holt, Rinehart, and Winston.

Paivio, A. (1986/1990). *Mental representations: A dual coding approach.* Oxford University Press.

Paivio, A. (1991). Dual coding theory: Retrospect and current status. *Canadian Journal of Psychology, 45*(3), 255–287. doi:10.1037/h0084295.

Palma, M., Abramson, J. J., Gorodetsky, A. A., Penzo, E., Gonzalez, R. L. Jr, & Sheetz, M. P. … Wind, S. J. (2011). Selective biomolecular nanoarrays for parallel single-molecule investigations. *Journal of the American Chemical Society*. doi: doi:10.1021/ja201031g.

Palmer, J. (2009). *Single molecule's stunning image.* Retrieved August 20, 2011, from http://news.bbc.co.uk/2/hi/science/nature/8225491.stm

Palmer, J. (2012). *Graphene transistors in high-performance demonstration.* Retrieved October 26, 2012, from http://www.bbc.co.uk/news/science-environment-18868848

Palmer, M. A. et al. (2010). Mountaintop mining consequences. *Science, 327*, 148. doi:10.1126/science.1180543 PMID:20056876.

Panayiotopoulos, C. P. (2012). *Videogame-induced seizures (VGS).* Retrieved July 10, 2012, from http://professionals.epilepsy.com/page/video_game_seizures.html

Panofsky, E. (1972). *Studies in Iconology: Humanistic themes in the art of the renaissance.* Westview Press.

Panofsky, E. (1997). *Perspective as symbolic form by Erwin Panofsky* (C. S. Wood, Trans.). Zone Books.

Parent, R. (2007/2012). *Computer animation: Algorithms and techniques* (2nd ed.). Morgan Kaufmann.

Parslow, C. C. (1998). *Rediscovering antiquity: Karl Weber and the excavation of Herculaneum, Pompeii, and Stabiae.* Cambridge University Press.

Paul, N., & Fiebich, C. (2012). *The elements of digital storybuilding.* Retrieved January 3, 2012, from http://www.inms.umn.edu/elements/

Pearce, D. A., Bridge, P. D., Hughes, K. A., Sattler, B., Psenner, R., & Russel, N. J. (2009). Microorganisms in the atmosphere over Antarctica. *FEMS Microbiology Ecology, 69*(2), 143–157. doi:10.1111/j.1574-6941.2009.00706.x PMID:19527292.

Pelling, N. (2013). *Conundra.* Retrieved March 10, 2013, from http://www.nanodome.com/conundra.co.uk/

Penenberg, A. L. (2010, June 28). Social networking affects brains like falling in love. *Fast Company Magazine*. Retrieved August 5, 2012, from http://www.fastcompany.com/1659062/social-networking-affects-brains-falling-love

PennState modules. (2011). Nano4Me.org. *NACK Educational Resources*. The Pennsylvania State University. Retrieved August 27, 2012, from http://nano4me.live.subhub.com/categories/modules

Peratt, A. L. (2004). Characteristics for the occurrence of a high-current, Z-pinch aurora as recorded in antiquity. *IEEE Transactions on Plasma Science, 31*(6), 1192–1214. doi:10.1109/TPS.2003.820956.

Peratt, A. L., McGovern, J., Qoyawayma, A. H., Van der Sluijs, M. A., & Peratt, M. G. (2007). Characteristics for the occurrence of a high-current z-pinch aurora as recorded in antiquity part II: Directionality and source. *IEEE Transactions on Plasma Science, 35*(4), 778–807. doi:10.1109/TPS.2007.902630.

Perkins, D. N. (1994). *The intelligent eye: Learning to think by looking at art*. Occasional Paper. Getty Center for Education in the Arts.

Perlin, K. (2012). *Kinetic poetry*. Retrieved February 17, 2012, from http://mrl.nyu.edu/%7Eperlin/experiments/poetry/

Perrault, C. (2012). *The fairy tales of Charles Perrault*. CreateSpace Independent Publishing Platform.

Pesetsky, D. (2009). Linguistic universals and universal grammar. In R. A. Wilson & F. C. Keil (Eds.), *The MIT encyclopedia of the cognitive sciences*. Cambridge, MA: MIT Press. Retrieved February 8, 2012, from http://web.mit.edu/linguistics/people/faculty/pesetsky/Pesetsky_MITECS_Universals_UG.pdf

Pessoa Forte, J. A., Gomes, D. A., Nogueira, C. A., & Cavalcande de Almeida, C. F. (2011). Educational services in second life: A study based on flow theory. *International Journal of Web-Based Learning and Teaching Technologies, 6*(2), 1-17. doi 10.4018/jwltt.2011040101. Retrieved October 1, 2012, from http://www.irma-international.org/viewtitle/60168/

Petroski, H. (1992). *The pencil: A history of design and circumstance*. New York: Alfred A. Knopf.

Phaidon. (1999). *American Art Book*. London: Phaidon Press.

Phaidon. (1996). *The 20th century artbook*. San Francisco, CA: Chronicle Books/Phaidon Press. ISBN 0-714835420

Phillips, C., & Sakai, K. L. (2005). Language and the brain. In *Yearbook of Science and Technology*. New York: McGraw-Hill Publishers.

Pickover, C. A. (2001). *Computers, pattern, chaos and beauty*. Dover Publications.

Pink, D. H. (2006). *A whole new mind: Why right-brainers will rule the future*. Riverhead Trade.

Plato. (2008). *Republic* (Oxford World's Classics). Oxford University Press.

Pliny the Younger. (1963). *The letters of the younger Pliny* (B. Radice, Trans.). Penguin Classics.

Plummer, C., Carlson, D., & Hammersley, L. (2012). *Physical geology*. McGraw-Hill Science/Engineering/Math.

Poeter, D. (2012). IBM says it's 'on the cusp' of building a quantum computer. *PC Magazine*. Retrieved September 6, 2012, from http://www.pcmag.com/article2/0,2817,2400930,00.asp

Polli, A. (2003). *Atmospherics/weather works: The sonification of meteorological data*. Retrieved May 9, 2011, from http://www.andreapolli.com/studio/atmospherics/

Pouivet, R. (2000). On the cognitive functioning of aesthetic emotions. *Leonardo, 33*(1), 49–53. doi:10.1162/002409400552234.

Price, C. B. (2007). From Kandinsky to Java (the use of 20th century abstract art in learning programming). *ITALICS, 6*(4), 35–50. doi:10.11120/ital.2007.06040035.

PRNewswire. (2012, October 25). NHN Japan's 'LINE' user number exceeds 70 million. *United Business Media*. Retrieved November 17, 2012, from http://www.prnewswire.com/news-releases/nhn-japans-line-user-number-exceeds-70-million-175725791.html

Puppet Forms in India. (2012). Retrieved September 16, 2012, from http://ccrtindia.gov.in/puppetforms.htm

Purchase, H. (2010). Graph drawing aesthetics in user-sketched graph layouts. In *Proceedings of the Eleventh Australasian Conference on User Interface*, (Vol. 106). ACUI. ISBN: 978-1-920682-87-3

Purchase, H. C. (2002). Metrics for graph drawing aesthetics. *Journal of Visual Languages and Computing, 13*(5), 501–516. doi:10.1006/jvlc.2002.0232.

Rahmani, A. R., & Mahvi, A. H. (2006). Use of ion exchange for removal of ammonium: A biological regeneration of zeolite. *Global Nest Journal, 8*(2), 146-150. Retrieved August 27, 2011, from http://www.gnest.org/journal/Vol8_No2/146-150_RAHMANI_396_8-2.pdf

Rall, H. (2009). Tradigital mythmaking: Singapore animation for the 21st century. Singapore: Dominie Press. ISBN 978 981-08-2932-2

Raoof, M., Mackeyev, Y., Cheney, M. A., Wilson, L. J., & Curley, S. A. (2012). Internalization of C_{60} fullerenes into cancer cells with accumulation in the nucleus via the nuclear pore complex. *Biomaterials, 33*(10), 2952-2960. Retrieved September 7, 2012, from http://www.ncbi.nlm.nih.gov/pubmed/22245558

Reality, E. O. N. (2012). *EON coliseum.* Retrieved June 14, 2012, from http://www.eonreality.com/products_coliseum.html

Reas, C., & Fry, B. (2007). *Processing: A programming handbook for visual designers and artists.* Cambridge, MA: The MIT Press.

Recommended Levels of Insulation. (2012). Retrieved June 10, 2012, from http://www.energystar.gov/index.cfm?c=home_sealing.hm_improvement_insulation_table

Redström, J., Skog, T., & Hallnäs, L. (2000). Informative art: Using amplified artworks as information displays. In W. Mackay (Ed.), *Proceedings of DARE 2000 (Designing Augmented Reality Environments)*, (pp. 103-114). ACM Press.

Rehr, J. J., & Albers, R. C. (2000). Theoretical approaches to x-ray absorption fine structure. *Reviews of Modern Physics, 72,* 621–654. doi:10.1103/RevModPhys.72.621.

Renner, E. (2000). *Pinhole photography: Rediscovering a historic technique* (2nd ed.). Taylor & Francis.

Reynolds, C. (2002). *Evolutionary computation and its application to art and design.* Retrieved January 9, 2011, from http://www.red3d.com/cwr/evolve.html

RFA. (2012). *Renewable fuels association: Accelerating industry innovation, 2012 ethanol industry outlook.* Retrieved August 30, 2012, from http://ethanolrfa.3cdn.net/d4ad995ffb7ae8fbfe_1vm62ypzd.pdf

Rheingold, H. (2002). *Smart mobs: The next social revolution.* Cambridge, MA: Basic Books.

Richard, J. M., & Berridge, K. C. (2011). Nucleus accumbens dopamine/glutamate interaction switches modes to generate desire versus dread: D1 for appetitive eating but D1 and D2 together for fear. *The Journal of Neuroscience, 31*(36), 12866–12879. doi:10.1523/JNEUROSCI.1339-11.2011 PMID:21900565.

Ricou, J., & Pollock, J. A. (2012). The tree, the spiral and the web of life: A visual exploration of biological evolution for public murals. *Leonardo, 45*(1), 18–25. doi:10.1162/LEON_a_00321.

Robbin, T. (1992). Fourfield: Computers, art & the 4th dimension. Boston: A Bulfinch Press Book. Little, Brown and Company. ISBN 082121909X

Robertson, E. C. (2011). *The interior of the earth.* Retrieved April 10, 2012, from http://pubs.usgs.gov/gip/interior/

Robles-De-La-Torre, G. (2009). Virtual reality: Touch/haptics. In E.B. Goldstein (Ed.), *Encyclopedia of Perception*, (vol. 2, pp. 1036-1038). Sage Publications, Inc. ISBN 1412940818. Retrieved August 8, 2012, from http://www.isfh.org/GR-Virtual_Reality_TouchHaptics2009.pdf

Robson, S. (2008, November 23). Not playing around: Army to invest $50m in combat training games. *Stars and Stripes.* Retrieved July 9, 2012, from http://www.stripes.com/news/not-playing-around-army-to-invest-50m-in-combat-training-games-1.855952911

Rocca, A. (2007). *Natural architecture.* Princeton Architectural Press.

Rose, F. (2012). *The art of immersion: How the digital generation is remaking Hollywood, Madison Avenue, and the way we tell stories.* W. W. Norton & Company.

Rosman, K. (2011, June 16). Eat your vegetables, and don't forget to tweet. *The Wall Street Journal*. Retrieved January 9, 2011, from http://finance.yahoo.com/news/pf_article_112952.html

Roussel, E. G., Cambon Bonavita, M., Querellou, J., Cragg, B. A., Prieur, D., Parkes, R. J., & Parkes, R. J. (2008). Extending the sub-sea-floor biosphere. *Science, 320*(5879), 1046. doi:10.1126/science.1154545 PMID:18497290.

RSC. (2006). *Advancing the chemical sciences: Nanotechnology tackles chemotherapy*. Retrieved September 8, 2011, from http://www.rsc.org/chemistryworld/News/2006/April/11040601.asp

Russo, C. J., & Golovchenko, J. A. (2012). Atom-by-atom nucleation and growth of graphene nanopores. *Proc. Natl. Acad. Sci. U.S.A., 109*, 5953-5957. Retrieved August 28, 2011, from http://labs.mcb.harvard.edu/branton/RussoAndGolovchenko2012.pdf

Sadier, B., Delannoy, J.-J., Benedetti, L., Bourlès, D. L., Jaillet, S., & Geneste, J.-M. … Arnold, M. (2012). Further constraints on the Chauvet cave artwork elaboration. *Proceedings of the National Academy of Sciences of the United States of America*. doi 10.1073/pnas.1118593109

Sadoski, M., & Paivio, A. (2013). *Imagery and text: A dual coding theory of reading and writing*. Routledge.

Sakai, K. L. (2005). Language acquisition and brain development. *Science, 310*(5749), 815–819. doi:10.1126/science.1113530 PMID:16272114.

Salen, K., & Zimmerman, E. (2003). *Rules of play: Game design fundamentals*. The MIT Press.

Salimpoor, V. N., Benovoy, M., Larcher, K., Dagher, A., & Zatorre, R. J. (2011). Anatomically distinct dopamine release during anticipation and experience of peak emotion to music. *Nature Neuroscience, 14*, 257–262. doi:10.1038/nn.2726 PMID:21217764.

Sasakura, M., Kotaki, A., & Inada, J. (2011). A 3D molecular visualization system with mobile devices. In *Proceedings of the 15th International Conference on Information Visualization,* (pp. 429-433). ISBN 978-1-4577-0868-8

Savara, S. (2012). *Television, video games and other stimuli that hijack your brain's dopamine reward system*. Retrieved August 7, 2012, from http://sidsavara.com/television-video-games-and-other-stimuli-that-hijack-your-brains-dopamine-reward-system

Sawyer, R. K. (2005). *Social emergence: Societies as complex systems*. Cambridge University Press. doi:10.1017/CBO9780511734892.

Schectman, J. (2010, May 17). Heart group backs Wii video game console in obesity campaign. *The Daily News (N.Y.)*.

Schefold, K. (1993). *Gods and heroes in late archaic Greek art*. Cambridge University Press.

Schilthuizen, M., & Gravendeel, B. (2011). Evolution of chirality symposium. In *Proceedings of the 13th Congress of the European Society for Evolutionary Biology*. Retrieved August 26, 2011, from http://www.eseb2011.de/

Schlumberger. (2012). *Oil glossary*. Retrieved April 11, 2012, from http://www.glossary.oilfield.slb.com/Display.cfm?Term=mantle

Schmitt, G. (2009). Data visualization is reinventing online storytelling – And building brands in bits and bites. *AdvertisingAge*. Retrieved October 24, 2012, from http://adage.com/article/digitalnext/data-visualization-reinventing-online-storytelling/135313/

Schreibman, S., & Siemens, R. (Eds.). (2008). *A companion to digital literary studies*. Oxford, UK: Blackwell, 2008. Retrieved February 17, 2012, from http://www.digitalhumanities.org/companionDLS/

Schultz, W. (2010). Dopamine signals for reward value and risk: Basic and recent data. *Behavioral and Brain Functions, 6*, 24. Retrieved August 5, 2012, from http://www.behavioralandbrainfunctions.com/content/6/1/24

Schwartz, L. F. (1985). The computer and creativity. *Transactions of the American Philosophical Society, 75*, 30–49. doi:10.2307/20486639.

Schwartz, L. F., & Schwartz, L. R. (1992). *The computer artist's handbook: Concepts, techniques, and applications*. New York: W. W. Norton & Company.

Science Daily. (2010, June 1). Faster computers with nanotechnology. *Science Daily.* Retrieved September 3, 2012, from http://www.sciencedaily.com/releases/2010/05/100531082857.htm

Science Daily. (2012, June 14). Engineers perfecting carbon nanotubes for highly energy-efficient computing. *Science Daily.* Retrieved September 3, 2012, from http://www.sciencedaily.com/releases/2012/06/120614131202.htm

Seeley, W. P. (2011). What is the cognitive neuroscience of art ... and why should we care? *American Society for Neuroaesthetics, 31*(2), 1-4. Retrieved October 6, 2012, from http://aesthetics-online.org/newsletter/31.2.pdf

Segel, E., & Heer, J. (2010). Narrative visualization: Telling stories with data. *IEEE Transactions on Visualization and Computer Graphics, 16*(6), 1139–1148. doi:10.1109/TVCG.2010.179 PMID:20975152.

Selvin, P. R. (2012). *Physics.* Retrieved August 24, 2012, from http://physics.illinois.edu/people/profile.asp?selvin

Şenyer, E. (2012). *Traditional Turkish puppet shadow play karagößz hacivat.* Retrieved September 16, 2012, from http://www.karagoz.net/english/shadowplay.htm

Senyuk, B., & Smalyukh, I. I. (2012). Elastic interactions between colloidal microspheres and elongated convex and concave nanoprisms in nematic liquid crystals. *Soft Matter, 8,* 8729–8734. doi:10.1039/c2sm25821h.

Shakshuki, E., & Matin, A. R. (2010). Intelligent learning a systemsgent for collaborative virtual workspace. *International Journal of Pervasive Computing and Communications, 6*(2), 131–162. doi:10.1108/17427371011066383.

Sheik, S. (2011). Constitutive effects: The techniques of the curator. In Z. Kocur (Ed.), *Global Visual Cultures: An Anthology.* Wiley-Blackwell. ISBN 978-1-4051-6921-2

Shreve, J. (2010). Drawing art into the equation: Aesthetic computing gives math a clarifying visual dimension. *Edutopia.* Retrieved October 6, 2012 from http://www.edutopia.org/drawing-art-equation

Siemens. (2012). *System architecture for the APOGEE building automation system with BACnet.* Retrieved July 14, 2012, from http://w3.usa.siemens.com/buildingtechnologies/us/en/building-automation-and-energy-management/apogee/architecture/Pages/architecture.aspx

Sigman, A. (2007). Visual voodoo: The biological impact of watching TV.[from http://www.aricsigman.com/IMAGES/VisualVoodoo.LowRes.pdf]. *Biologist (Columbus, Ohio), 54*(1), 12–17. Retrieved August 5, 2012

Siler, T. (2012). The artscience program for realizing human potential. *Leonardo, 44*(5), 417–424. doi:10.1162/LEON_a_00242.

Sims, K. (2009). *Karl Sims website.* Retrieved January 9, 2011, from http://www.karlsims.com/

Sitti, M., & Fearing, R. S. (2003). Synthetic gecko foothair micro/nano-structures as dry adhesives. *Journal of Adhesion Science and Technology, 18*(7), 1055–1074. doi:10.1163/156856103322113788.

Skinner, H. C. W. (2005). Biominerals. *Mineralogical Magazine, 69*(5), 621–641. doi:10.1180/0026461056950275.

Smalley, R. E. (2012). *Rice university.* Retrieved August 24, 2012, from http://cnst.rice.edu/

Smalyukh, I. I. (2011). Materials science: Deft tricks with liquid crystals. *Nature, 478,* 330–331. doi:10.1038/478330a PMID:22012387.

Smed, J., & Hakonen, H. (2003). *Towards a definition of a computer game.* Turku Centre for Computer Science.

Smithsonian Museum. (2012). *Suprasensorial: Experiments in light, color, and space.* Retrieved August 8, 2012, from http://www.hirshhorn.si.edu/collection/home/#collection=suprasensorial&detail=http%3A//www.hirshhorn.si.edu/bio/suprasensorial-experiments-in-light-color-and-space/

Snyder, S. H., & Ferris, C. D. (2000). Novel neurotransmitters and their neuropsychiatric relevance. *Am J Psychiatry, 157,* 1738-1751. doi 10.1176/appi.ajp.157.11.1738. Retrieved September 1, 2012, from http://ajp.psychiatryonline.org/article.aspx?articleID=174415

Soddu, C. (2011). *Website of Celestino Soddu.* Retrieved January 26, 2011, from http://www.celestinosoddu.com/

Soddu, C. (2012). *Argenia, generative art and science: Website of Celestino Soddu*. Retrieved February 5, 2012, from http://www.celestinosoddu.com/

SOFTec. (2012). Workshop on computer mediated social offline interactions. In *Proceedings of the 14th International Conference on Ubiquitous Computing (Ubicomp 2012)*. Retrieved August 10, 2012, from http://uc.inf.usi.ch/events/softec12

Soga, A., & Yoshida, I. (2012). Simulation system for dance groups using a gamepad. In *Proceedings of the International Conference on Computer Graphics Theory and Applications and International Conference on Information Visualization Theory and Applications*, (pp. 365-368). ISBN: 978-989-8565-02-0

Solar Cooker. (n.d.). Retrieved from: http://en.wikipedia.org/wiki/Solar_cooker; http://solarcooking.wikia.com/wiki/Solar_Cookers_World_Network_%28Home%29Minimum Solar Box Cooker; Wikia http://solarcooking.wikia.com/wiki/"Minimum"_Solar_Box_Cooker; http://greenliving.nationalgeographic.com/three-main-types-solar-ovens-2877.html

Solar Cookers International: How Solar Cookers Work. (n.d.). Retrieved from http://www.solarcookers.org/basics/how.html

Solar Cooking . (n.d.). Retrieved from http://solarcooking.wikia.com/wiki/Solar_Cookers_World_Network_%28Home%29

Solomon, C. (1994). *The history of animation*. New York: Wings Books.

Sommerer, C., & Mignonneau, L. (2010). *The value of art (unruhige see)*. Retrieved January 9, 2011, from http://www.interface.ufg.ac.at/christa-laurent/WORKS/FRAMES/FrameSet.html

Sondermann, H. (2008). *Light shadow space: Architectural rendering with cinema 4D*. Springer Vienna Architecture.

Squillace, M. (2009). *The strip mining handbook*. Retrieved April 14, 2013, from http://sites.google.com/site/stripmininghandbook/chapter-1-introduction

Stam, R. (2000). *Film theory*. Oxford, UK: Blackwell.

Stanton, J. (1999). *Imaginary museum: Poems on art*. Time Being Books.

Sternberg, R. J. (1986). A triangular theory of love. *Psychological Review, 93*(2), 119–135. doi 10.1037/0033-295X.93.2.119. Retrieved May 5, 2012, from http://psycnet.apa.org/journals/rev/93/2/119/

R. J. Sternberg, & S. B. Kaufman (Eds.). (2011). *The Cambridge handbook of intelligence*. Cambridge University Press. doi:10.1017/CBO9780511977244.

Stern, E., Fort, T. J., Miller, M. W., Peskin, C. S., & Brezina, W. (2007). Decoding modulation of the neuromuscular transform. *Neurocomputing, 70*(10-12), 1753–1758. doi:10.1016/j.neucom.2006.10.117 PMID:19763188.

Stewart, M. E., Anderton, C. R., Thompson, L. B., Maria, J., Gray, S. K., Rogers, J. A., & Nuzzo, R. G. (2008). Nanostructured plasmonic sensors. *Chem. Reviews, 108*, 494-521. doi 10.1021/cr068126n. Retrieved August 24, 2012, from http://rogers.matse.illinois.edu/files/2008/plasmonschemrev.pdf

Stock, M. (2012). Flow simulation with vortex elements. In A. Ursyn (Ed.), *Biologically-Inspired Computing for the Arts: Scientific Data through Graphics* (pp. 18–30). IGI Global. doi:10.4018/978-1-4666-0942-6.ch002.

Stone, H. S. (1972). *Introduction to computer organization and data structures*. New York: McGraw Hill.

Sturm, B. L. (2005). Pulse of an ocean. *Leonardo, 38*(2), 143–149. doi:10.1162/0024094053722453.

Svensson, J. (2010). Carbon nanotube transistors: Nanotube growth, contact properties and novel devices. *University of Gothenburg PhD Thesis*. Retrieved September 4, 2012, from https://gupea.ub.gu.se/bitstream/2077/21859/1/gupea_2077_21859_1.pdf

Sweller, J. (2006). Visualization and Instructional design. In *Proceedings of the International Workshop on Dynamic Visualizations and Learning*, (pp. 1501-1510). Retrieved October 23, 2012, from http://www.scribd.com/doc/41651/Sweller-Visualisation-and-Instructional-Design

Sweller, J. (1988). Cognitive load during problem solving: Effects on learning. *Cognitive Science, 12*, 257–285. doi:10.1207/s15516709cog1202_4.

Sweller, J. (1994). Cognitive load theory, learning difficulty and instructional design. *Learning and Instruction, 4*, 295–312. doi:10.1016/0959-4752(94)90003-5.

Swift, J. (2003). *Gulliver's travels*. Penguin Classics. (Original work published 1726).

Takai, K. (2010). Limits of life and the biosphere: Lessons from the detection of microorganisms in the deep ses and deep subsurface of the Earth. In *Origins and Evolution of Life: An Astrobiological Perspective*. Cambridge, UK: Cambridge University Press.

Taniguchi, N. (1974). On the basic concept of 'nano-technology. In *Proceedings of the International Conference on Production Engineering*. Japan Society of Precision Engineering.

Tanimoto, S. L. (2012). *An interdisciplinary introduction to image processing*. The MIT Press.

Tarbuck, E. J., Lutgens, F. K., & Tasa, D. (2011). *Earth: An introduction to physical geology plus mastering geology with etext -- Access card package* (10th ed.). Prentice Hall.

Tatarkiewicz, W. (1976). *Dzieje szesciu pojec*. Warsaw, Poland: PWN.

Tatarkiewicz, W. (1999). *History of aesthetics* (C. Barrett, Ed.). London: Thoemmes Press.

TED. (2012). *Ursus Wehrli's tied up art*. Retrieved August 24, 2012, from http://www.ted.com/talks/ursus_wehrli_tidies_up_art.html http://design.org/blog/art-clean-organized-chaos-ursus-wehrli

Thakur, M., Pernites, R. B., Nitta, N., Isaacson, M., Sinsabaugh, S. L., Wong, M. S., & Biswal, S. L. (2012). Freestanding macroporous silicon and pyrolyzed polyacrylonitrile as a composite anode for lithium ion batteries. *Chem. Mater., 24*(15), 2998–3003. doi 10.1021/cm301376t. Retrieved August 24, 2012, from http://pubs.acs.org/doi/pdf/10.1021/cm301376t

The Geyser Observation and Study Association. (2011). Retrieved April 12, 2012, from http://www.geyserstudy.org/geyser.aspx?pGeyserNo=OLDFAITHFUL

The Household Cyclopedia. (1881). Retrieved from http://www.mspong.org/cyclopedia/cements.html

The Library of Congress. (1999). *Origins of American animation*. Retrieved August 5, 2012, from http://memory.loc.gov/ammem/oahtml/oahome.html

The Mail Online. (2012). *Power really does corrupt as scientists claim it's as addictive as cocaine*. Retrieved August 7, 2012, from http://www.dailymail.co.uk/news/article-2136547/Power-really-does-corrupt-scientists-claim-addictive-cocaine.html#ixzz22sRke200

The Mount Vesuvius eruption of March 1944. (n.d.). *Mount Vesuvius facts and resources*. Retrieved April 11, 2012, from http://www.warwingsart.com/12thAirForce/Vesuvius.html

The Super Cars.org. (2012). *Fastest cars by acceleration: Top 10 list*. Retrieved July 26, 2012, from http://www.thesupercars.org/fastest-cars/fastest-cars-by-acceleration-top-10-list/

The, U. S. Department of Agriculture. (2012). *Gifford Pinchot national forest Mount St. Helens brochure, 1980*. Government Printing Office GPO 1980 699-331. Retrieved April 15, 2012, from http://vulcan.wr.usgs.gov/Volcanoes/MSH/description_msh.html

ThinkQuest Library. (2012). Retrieved from http://thinkquest.org/pls/html/think.library

Thinkquest. (2012). Retrieved October 6, 2012, from http://www.thinkquest.org/en/

Tocris Bioscience. (2012). *Dopamine receptors*. Retrieved August 7, 2012, from http://www.tocris.com/pharmacologicalBrowser.php?ItemId=4993#.UCFSzu1iuao

Tomasula, S. (1998). Bytes and zeitgeist: Digitizing the cultural landscape, six annual New York digital salon. *Leonardo Journal, 31*(5), 337–344. doi:10.2307/1576592.

Top 10 Fastest Bikes. (2012). Retrieved July 26, 2012, from http://topper10.net/2009/vehicles/top-10-fastest-bikes/

Topper, D. (2008). On anamorphosis: Setting some things straight. *Leonardo, 33*(2), 115–124. doi:10.1162/002409400552379.

Tractinsky, N., Katz, A. S., & Ikar, D. (2000). Article. *Interacting with Computers, 13*(2), 127–145. doi:10.1016/S0953-5438(00)00031-X.

Trianni, V., & Nolfi, S. (2011). Engineering the evolution of self-organizing behaviors in swarm robotics: A case study. *Artificial Life, 17*(3), 183–202. doi:10.1162/artl_a_00031 PMID:21554112.

Trivedi, R. P., Klevets, I. I., Senyuk, B., Lee, T., & Smalyukh, I. I. (2012). Reconfigurable interactions and three-dimensional patterning of colloidal particles and defects in lamellar soft media. *Proceedings of the National Academy of Sciences of the United States of America, 109*, 4744–4749. doi:10.1073/pnas.1119118109 PMID:22411822.

Truss, L. (2006). *Eats, shoots & leaves: The zero tolerance approach to punctuation.* Gotham.

Tseng, C., Hsieh, J., & Jeng, J. (2008). Fractal image compression using visual-based particle swarm optimization. In *Proceedings of Image Vision Comput* (pp. 1154–1162). IEEE. doi:10.1016/j.imavis.2008.01.003.

Tufte, E. R. (1983/2001). *The visual display of quantitative information.* Cheshire, CT: Graphics Press.

Tufte, E. R. (1992/2005). *Envisioning information.* Cheshire, CT: Graphics Press.

Tufte, E. R. (1997). *Visual and statistical thinking: Displays of evidence for making decisions.* Cheshire, CT: Graphics Press.

Tufte, E. R. (2003). *The cognitive style of powerpoint.* Cheshire, CT: Graphics Press.

Turner, N. W., Subrahmanyam, S., & Piletsky, S. A. (2009). Analytical methods for determination of mycotoxins: A review. *Analytica Chimica Acta, 632*(2), 168-180. Retrieved August 29, 2012, from http://dx.doi.org/10.1016/j.aca.2008.11.010

Tzonis, A. (2004). *Santiago Calatrava: The complete works.* Rizzoli.

U.S. Consumer Product Safety Commission . (2012). Retrieved September 1, 2012, from http://www.cpsc.gov/cpscpub/pubs/466.html

UbiComp, Pervasive, and MediaCity Conference. (2012). Retrieved August 10, 2012, from http://www.ubicomp.org/ubicomp2012/calls/workshopsCFP.html

United States Army. (2011). *DoD gives PTSD help 'second life' in virtual reality.* Retrieved October 30, 2012, from http://www.army.mil/article/50751/

University of Oregon. (2012). *Elementary particles.* Retrieved May 21, 2012, from http://abyss.uoregon.edu/~js/glossary/particle_physics.html

Ursyn, A. (1994). *Student perception of computer art graphics integration of art & science.* Paper presented at the American Educational Research Association (AERA) Annual Meeting 1994. New York, NY.

Ursyn, A. (1997). Computer art graphics integration of art and science. *Learning and Instruction, the Journal of the European Association for Research on Learning and Instruction, 7*(1), 65-87.

Ursyn, A., & Scott, T. (2006). *Overlap between thinking in terms of art and computer science.* Paper presented at the Consortium for Computing Sciences in Colleges (CCSC). Durango, CO.

Ursyn, A., & Scott, T. (2007). Web with art and computer science. In *Proceedings of ACM SIGGRAPH Education Committee.* ACM. ISBN 978–1–59593–648–6

Ursyn, A. (2002). Art as information. *Leonardo, 35*(4), 445–446. doi:10.1162/002409402760181277.

Ursyn, A., Mills, L., Hobgood, B., & Scott, T. (1997). Combining art skills with programming in teaching computer art graphics. *Computer Graphics, 25*, 3.

USGS. (2012). *Geographic names information* system. U.S. Geological Survey. Retrieved June 11, 2012, from http://geonames.usgs.gov/pls/gnispublic/f?p=gnispq:3:1297639910658653:NO:P3_FID:1525360

USGS/Cascades volcano observatory, Vancouver, Washington. (2009). Retrieved April 11, 2012, from http://web.archive.org/web/20090507051117/http://vulcan.wr.usgs.gov/Volcanoes/MSH/framework.html

Uszkoreit, H. (2000). *What is computational linguistics?* Retrieved February 12, 2012, from http://www.coli.uni-saarland.de/~hansu/what_is_cl.html

Van Bouvel, T., Vande Moere, A., & Boeykens, S. (2012). ArchiBrain: A conceptual platform for the visualization of collaborative design. In *Proceedings of the 16ᵗʰ International Conference on Information Visualization*, (pp. 396-402). doi 10.1109/IV.2012.72

Van Burnham. (2003). *Supercade: A visual history of the videogame age 1971-1984*. The MIT Press.

Van Noorden, R. (2011). Chemistry: The trials of new carbon. *Nature, 469*, 14-16. doi:10.1038/469014a. Retrieved August 29, 2012, from http://www.nature.com/news/2011/050111/full/469014a.html

Vande Moere, A. (2008). Beyond the tyranny of the pixel: Exploring the physicality of information visualization. In *Proceedings of the 12ᵗʰ International Conference Information Visualisation*, (pp. 469-474). IEEE.

Vande Moere, A., & Offenhuber, D. (2009). Beyond ambient display: A contextual taxonomy of alternative information display. *International Journal of Ambient Computing and Intelligence, 1*(2), 39–46. doi:10.4018/jaci.2009040105.

Vandendorpe, C. (2008). Reading on screen: The new media sphere. In *A Companion to Digital Literary Studies*. Oxford, UK: Blackwell. Retrieved February 17, 2012, from http://www.digitalhumanities.org/companionDLS/

Varley, R. A., Klessinger, N. J. C., Romanowski, C. A. J., & Siegal, M. (2005). Agrammatic but numerate. *Proceedings of the National Academy of Sciences of the United States of America, 102*, 3519–3524. doi:10.1073/pnas.0407470102 PMID:15713804.

Venter, J. C., Adams, M. D., Myers, E. W., Li, P. W., Mural, R. J., & Sutton, G. G., … Yandell, M. (2001). The sequence of the human genome. *Science, 291*(5507), 1304–1351. doi:10.1126/science.1058040. Retrieved August 24, 2012, from http://www.sciencemag.org/content/291/5507/1304

Verne, J. (2005). *Journey to the center of the earth*. Dover Publications.

Vesna, V. (2007). *Database aesthetics: Art in the age of information overflow (electronic mediations)*. Minneapolis, MN: University of Minnesota Press.

Victorri, B. (2007). Analogy between language and biology: a functional approach. *Cognitive Process, 8*(1), 11-9. Retrieved May 27, 2012, from http://www.ncbi.nlm.nih.gov/pubmed/17171371

Visual Rhetoric Overview. (2011). *Purdue online writing lab*. Retrieved January 2, 2012, from http://owl.english.purdue.edu/owl/resource/691/01/

Visualizing Electron Orbitals. (2012). Retrieved May 21, 2012, from http://hyperphysics.phy-astr.gsu.edu/hbase/chemical/eleorb.html

Voss-Andreae, J. (2011). Quantum sculpture: Art inspired by the deeper nature of reality. *Leonardo, 44*(1), 14–20. doi:10.1162/LEON_a_00088.

W3C Semantic Web Activity World Wide Web Consortium (W3C). (n.d.). Retrieved February 11, 2012, from http://www.w3.org/2001/sw/

W3C. (2012). *Web design and applications*. Retrieved from http://www.w3.org/standards/webdesign/graphics#uses

Wadham, J. L., Arndt, S., Tulaczyk, S., Stibal, M., Tranter, M., & Telling, J. … Butler, C. E. H. (2012). Potential methane reservoirs beneath Antarctica. *Nature, 488*, 633–637. Retrieved August 30, 2012, from http://www.nature.com/nature/journal/v488/n7413/full/nature11374.html

Wands, B. (2001). *Digital creativity: Techniques for digital media and the internet*. Wiley.

Wands, B. (2007). *Art of the digital age*. Thames & Hudson.

Wang, R. (2002). Two's company, three's a crowd: Can H₂S be the third endogenous gaseous transmitter? *The FASEB Journal, 16*(13), 1792-1798. doi 10.1096/fj.02-0211hyp. Retrieved September 3, 2012, from http://www.fasebj.org/content/16/13/1792.full

Wang, Y., Mathews, V. P., Kalnin, A. J., Mosier, K. M., Dunn, D. W., Saykin, A. J., & Kronenberger, W. G. (2009). Short term exposure to a violent video game induces changes in frontolimbic circuitry in adolescents. *Brain Imaging and Behavior, 3*, 38–50. doi:10.1007/s11682-008-9058-8.

W. Warburton, & D. Braunstein (Eds.). (2012). *Growing up fast and furious: Reviewing the impacts of violent and sexualised media on children*. Federation Press.

Ward, M., Grinstein, G., & Keim, D. (2010). Interactive data visualization: Foundations, techniques, and applications. Natick, MA: A K Peters, Ltd.

N. Wardrip-Fruin, & N. Montfort (Eds.). (2003). *The new media reader*. Boston: The MIT Press.

Watanabe, S. (2010). Pigeons can discriminate 'good' and 'bad' paintings by children. *Animal Cognition, 13*(1), 75-85. Retrieved October 1, 2012, from www.ncbi.nlm.nih.gov/pubmed/19533184

Watson, C. E., & Chatterjee, A. (2011). The functional neuroanatomy of actions. *Neurology, 76*, 1428–1434. doi:10.1212/WNL.0b013e3182166e2c PMID:21502604.

Watson, J. D., & Crick, F. H. (1953). Molecular structure of nucleic acids: A structure for deoxyribose nucleic acid. *Nature, 171*(4356), 737–738. doi:10.1038/171737a0 PMID:13054692.

Web Art by Hand. (2006). Retrieved January 2, 2012, from http://webartbyhand.blogspot.com

Weber, B., Mahapatra, S., Ryu, H., Lee, S., Fuhrer, A., & Reusch, T. C. G. … Simmons, M. Y. (2012). Ohm's law survives to the atomic scale. *Science, 335*(6064), 64-67. doi 10.1126/science.1214319. Retrieved September 6, 2012, from http://www.sciencemag.org/content/335/6064/64

Weber, R., Behr, K.-M., Tamborini, R., Ritterfeld, U., & Mathiak, K. (2009). What do we really know about first-person-shooter games? An event-related, high-resolution content analysis. *Journal of Computer-Mediated Communication, 14*(4), 1016–1037. Doi 10.1111/j.1083-6101.2009.01479.x. Retrieved July 13, 2012, from http://academic.csuohio.edu/kneuendorf/c63309/ArticlesFromClassMembers/Mu.pdf

Weber, W., & Tille, R. (2011). Listening to managers: A study about visualizations in corporate presentations. In *Proceedings of the Information Visualisation 15th International Conference*, (pp. 343-348). ISBN 978-1-4577-0868-8

Websters Online. (2012). Retrieved May 27, 2012, from http://www.websters-online-dictionary.org/definitions/perpetual+motion

Weinstock, B., & Niki, H. (1972). Carbon monoxide balance in nature. *Science, 176*(4032), 290–292. doi:10.1126/science.176.4032.290 PMID:5019781.

Weiser, M. (1991). The computer for the 21st century. [from http://wiki.daimi.au.dk/pca/_files/weiser-orig.pdf]. *Scientific American, 3*(3), 94–104. Retrieved August 10, 2012 doi:10.1038/scientificamerican0991-94.

Weitz, M. (1956). The role of theory in aesthetics. *The Journal of Aesthetics and Art Criticism, 15*, 27–35. doi:10.2307/427491.

White, H. (2004). *Fractal geometry*. Retrieved July 23, 2012, from www.geometriafractal.com/articlech000300.htm

Whitney Artport: The Whitney Museum of American Art. (2011). Retrieved January 27, 2011 from http://artport.whitney.org/

Wideman, H. H., Owston, R. D., Brown, C., Kushniruk, A., Ho, F., & Pitts, K. C. (2007). Unpacking the potential of educational gaming: A new tool for gaming research. [from http://www.yorku.ca/rowston/unpacking.pdf]. *Simulation & Gaming, 38*(1), 1–27. Retrieved July 10, 2012. doi:10.1177/1046878106297650.

Wilson, S. (2010). *Art + science now*. Thames & Hudson.

Wittgenstein, L. (2009/1953). Philosophical investigations. Wiley-Blackwell. ISBN 1405159286

Woollacott, E. (2011, December 9). Team demos matrix-style automatic learning. *TG Daily*. Retrieved July 12, 2012, from http://www.tgdaily.com/general-sciences-features/60115-team-demos-matrix-style-automatic-learning

Wu, L., & Wang, R. (2005). Carbon monoxide: Endogenous production, physiological functions, and pharmacological applications. *Pharmacol Rev, 57*(4), 585–630. doi:10.1124/pr.57.4.3. Retrieved September 1, 2012, from http://pharmrev.aspetjournals.org/content/57/4/585.full.pdf+html

Yanik, A. A., Huang, M., Kamohara, O., Artar, A., Geisbert, T. W., Connor, J. H., & Altug, H. (2010). An optofluidic nanoplasmonic biosensor for direct detection of live viruses from biological media. *Nano Letters 2010.* doi 10.1021/nl103025u. Retrieved August 24, 2012, from http://www.bu.edu/smartlighting/files/2010/01/2010_Nano-Letters_Virus.pdf

Yiang, X. (2011). *Bio-inspired computing and networking.* CRC Press.

Yildiz, A., Forkey, J. N., McKinney, S. A., Ha, T., Goldman, Y. A., & Selvin, P. R. (2003). Myosin V walks hand-over-hand: Single fluorophore imaging with 1.5-nm localization. *Science, 300*(5628), 2061–2065. doi:10.1126/science.1084398 PMID:12791999.

YLEM. (n.d.). *Artists using science and technology.* Retrieved August 9, 2012, from http://www.ylem.org/

Yoshida, H. (2012). Bridging synthetic and organic materiality: Graded transitions in material connections. In A. Ursyn (Ed.), *Biologically-Inspired Computing for the Arts: Scientific Data through Graphics* (pp. 81–88). IGI Global. doi:10.4018/978-1-4666-0942-6.ch005.

Zak, P. J., Stanton, A. A., & Ahmadi, S. (2007). Oxytocin increases generosity in humans. *PLoS ONE, 2*(11), e1128. doi:10.1371/journal.pone.0001128 PMID:17987115.

Zeki, S. (2011). *The Mona Lisa in 30 seconds.* Retrieved May 1, 2012, from http://profzeki.blogspot.com/

Zeki, S. (1993). *Vision of the brain.* Oxford, UK. *Wiley-Blackwell., ISBN-10,* 0632030542.

Zeki, S. (1999). Art and the brain. *Journal of Conscious Studies: Controversies in Science and the Humanities, 6*(6/7), 76–96.

Zeki, S. (2001). Artistic creativity and the brain. *Science, 293*(5527), 51–52. doi:10.1126/science.1062331 PMID:11441167.

Zeng, X., Mehdi, Q. H., & Gough, N. E. (2003). Shape the story: Story visualization techniques. In *Proceedings of the 7th International Conference on Information Visualization,* (pp. 144-149). ISBN: 0-7695-1988-1

Zhang, L., & Zhang, L. (2010). Lipid-polymer hybrid nanoparticles: Synthesis, characterization and applications. *NanoLIFE, 1*(163). doi 10.1142/S179398441000016X. Retrieved September 8, 2012, from http://www.worldscientific.com/doi/ref/10.1142/S179398441000016X

Zhang, K., Harrell, S., & Ji, X. (2012). Computational aesthetics: On the complexity of computer-generated paintings. *Leonardo, 45*(3), 243–248. http://www.mitpressjournals.org/doi/abs/10.1162/LEON_a_00366 doi:10.1162/LEON_a_00366.

Zheng, J., Birktoft, J. J., Chen, Y., Wang, T., Sha, R., & Constantinou, P. E. et al. (2009). From molecular to macroscopic via the rational design of a self-assembled 3D DNA crystal. *Nature, 461,* 74–77. doi:10.1038/nature08274 PMID:19727196.

Zuanon, r. (2012). The bio-interfaces at design, art and game areas: some applications. In a. Ursyn (ed.), *biologically-inspired computing for the arts: scientific data through graphics.* IGI Global. ISBN 978-1-4666-0942-6

Zuanon, R., & Lima, G. C., Jr. (2008). *BioBodyGame.* Retrieved March 09, 2011, from http://www.rachelzuanon.com/biobodygame/

Zuanon, R., & Lima, G. C., Jr. (2010). *NeuroBodyGame.* Retrieved March 09, 2011, from http://www.rachelzuanon.com/neurobodygame/

Zuanon, R. (2012). Bio-Interfaces: Designing wearable devices to organic interactions. In *Biologically-Inspired Computing for the Arts: Scientific Data through Graphics.* Hershey, PA: IGI Global. doi:10.4018/978-1-4666-0942-6.ch001.

About the Author

Anna Ursyn is a Professor in the School of Art and Design at University of Northern Colorado, where she is also the Computer Graphics Area Head. Her research-based art and pedagogy interests include an integrated approach to art, science, and computer art graphics. Her publications include: Editor of the book *Biologically-Inspired Computing for the Arts: Scientific Data through Graphics* (2012) (ISBN 1466609427), various book chapters, over 30 articles published in professional journals, as well as published poetry and artwork. Her professional work includes: Chair of the Symposium and Digital Art Gallery, D-ART iV, International Conference on Information Visualization, IEEE (Institute of Electrical and Electronics Engineers) Computing Society Press, Los Alamitos, CA 1997-2013 London; and Computer Graphics, Image & Visualization Asia; co-editor for the Proceedings of the iV, Int'l Conference on Information Visualization, IEEE (Institute of Electrical and Electronics Engineers) Computing Society Press, Los Alamitos, CA, 2004-2013; Associate Editor, *Int'l Journal of Creative Interfaces & Computer Graphics* (IJCICG), IGI Global, www.igi-global.com/IJCICG, 2009-2013; Associate Editor, *Design Principles and Practices: An International Journal*, http://designprinciplesandpractices.com/journal/http://ijg.cgpublisher.com; online art gallery organizer and keynote speaker for the Special Year on Art and Mathematics, University of Colorado at Boulder 2005. She has had over 30 single art shows and participated in over 100 juried and invitational fine art exhibitions.

Index